Fodor's

ESSENTIAL
HAWAII

Welcome to Hawaii

Hawaii overflows with natural beauty. Piercing the surface of the Pacific from the ocean floor, the Hawaiian Islands are garlanded with soft sand beaches and dramatic volcanic cliffs. Long days of sunshine and fairly mild year-round temperatures make this an all-season destination, and the Islands' offerings—from urban Honolulu on Oahu to the luxury resorts of Maui to the natural wonders of Kauai and the Big Island—appeal to all kinds of visitors. As you plan your trip to Hawaii, please confirm that places are still open and let us know when we need to make updates by writing to us at editors@fodors.com.

TOP REASONS TO GO

★ **Beaches:** Every island claims its share of postcard-perfect strands.

★ **Resorts:** Spas, pools, lavish gardens, and golf courses make relaxing easy.

★ **Pearl Harbor:** This historic memorial site on Oahu is not to be missed.

★ **Napali Coast:** Kauai's jagged emerald-green coast makes an unforgettable excursion.

★ **Whale-watching:** In winter humpback whales swim right off Maui's shores.

★ **Volcanoes National Park:** On the Big Island you can explore the world's most active volcano.

Contents

MAPS

Fodor's Features

Chapter 1

EXPERIENCE HAWAII

37 ULTIMATE EXPERIENCES

Hawaii offers terrific experiences that should be on every traveler's list. Here are Fodor's top picks for a memorable trip.

1 Oahu's North Shore

Spend a day on the North Shore. Start off in Kaneohe and drive up Kamehameha Highway all the way to Haleiwa, stopping along the way at fruit stands, shrimp trucks, beaches, world-famous surfing spots (don't miss Waimea Bay), and scenic overlooks. *(Ch. 3)*

2 Kona Coffee Plantation Tours

Local coffee farmers love to share their passion with the public, and most offer free tours. Kona coffee estate farms stretch from Holualoa to South Kona. *(Ch. 5)*

3 Horseback Riding

Saddle up and get ready to ride the ranges, cliffs, and trails of the Big Island on horseback. It's one of the best ways to take in the island's beautiful scenery. *(Ch. 5)*

4 Mountain Tubing

A century ago, Lihue Plantation dug waterways to irrigate its fields. Now you can take a tubing tour via the waterways for a glimpse of Kauai's hidden interior. *(Ch. 6)*

5 Deep-Sea Fishing

The deep Pacific waters surrounding Kauai are teeming with fish. Charters, which depart from Lihue or Port Allen, visit the best spots and provide all the gear. *(Ch. 6)*

6 Small-Town Maui Charm

Discovered by hippies in the '70s, Paia continues to be a hip and happening place with galleries, eateries, antique stores, and, of course, surf shops. *(Ch. 4)*

7 Snorkeling in Hanauma Bay

This nature preserve nestled in a volcanic crater with a vibrant reef is a phenomenal, family-friendly place to see colorful fish and other sea life. Advance reservations are now required. *(Ch. 3)*

8 Hawaii Volcanoes National Park

Witness the primal birth of living land from two eruption sites flowing from the Big Island's Kilauea Volcano, currently the world's most active volcano. *(Ch. 5)*

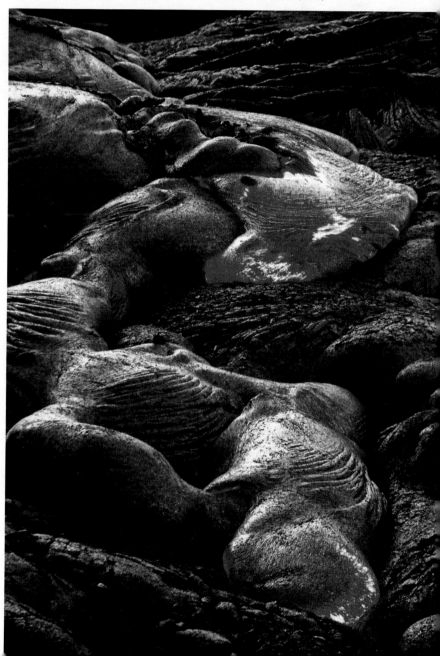

9 Whale-Watching

Humpback whales hang out in the Auau Channel off Maui every winter; boats leaving from Lahaina can be in the midst of these gentle giants within 15 minutes. *(Ch. 4)*

10 Surfing

On Oahu, Waikiki's many surf schools make it popular with beginners. Less-crowded White Plains has better novice conditions as well as lots of surf amenities. *(Ch. 3)*

11 Attending a Luau

Guests are treated to Hawaiian-style storytelling, complete with hula dancing, traditional knife dancing, and fire poi ball throwing at traditional luaus. *(Ch. 3–8)*

12 Shave Ice on Oahu

Matsumoto's on the North Shore may be the most well-known, but many (including former president Barack Obama) prefer Island Snow in Kailua. *(Ch. 3)*

13 Golfing at Duffer's Paradise

Maui is heaven for any golfer. Here you'll find perfectly stunning weather, gorgeous views, and fantastic course layouts for any skill level. *(Ch. 4)*

14 Beaches

The Big Island's most beautiful beaches, including Anaehoomalu Bay, Hapuna Beach, and Kaunaoa Beach, flank the Kohala Coast. *(Ch. 5)*

15 Sacred Heiaus

Remains of sacred structures of the Kauai kingdom are found in Wailua along Route 580 between the mouth of the Wailua River and Mt. Waialeale. *(Ch. 6)*

16 Waimea Canyon

A vast canyon on Kauai's West Side, this geologic wonder measures a mile wide, more than 14 miles long and 3,600 feet deep. *(Ch. 6)*

17 Pro Surfers at Waimea Bay

During winter, when waves can crest past 20 feet, Waimea Bay is one of the best places in the world to watch the pros catch the big ones. *(Ch. 3)*

18 Pearl Harbor

You can't go to Oahu and skip a visit to Pearl Harbor National Memorial, which preserves the USS *Arizona* and other World War II sites. *(Ch. 3)*

19 The Big Island Lava Tubes

Thurston Lava Tube in Hawaii Volcanoes National Park is convenient; Kula Kai Caverns and Kilauea Caverns of Fire are fascinating but require expert guides. *(Ch. 5)*

20 Diving at the Cathedrals of Lanai

These lava tubes comprise one of Maui's primo diving spots (technically off Lanai) boasting a variety of multicolored fish, eels, turtles, dolphins, and octopi. *(Ch. 8)*

21 The Waipio Valley

This lush, waterfall-laden valley—surrounded by sheer, fluted 2,000-foot cliffs—was once a favorite retreat for Hawaiian royalty. *(Ch. 5)*

22 Plate Lunches

Everyone should try this bargain-priced Hawaii lunch tradition: an entrée with white rice and a scoop of macaroni salad. It's an island favorite. *(Ch. 3)*

23 Iolani Palace

The only royal residence in the United States gives you an introduction to Hawaii's monarchy era, which ended with the overthrow of Queen Liliuokalani in 1893. *(Ch. 3)*

24 Sunrises in Haleakala National Park

Haleakala National Park's Puuulaula Overlook is Maui's highest point and the best place to see the sunrise. On a clear day, you can see Molokai, Lanai, and Hawaii Island. *(Ch. 4)*

25 Kauai's Poipu Beach

Popular with tourists and locals, Poipu Beach has calm waters ideal for snorkeling, and you might just spot an endangered Hawaiian monk seal. *(Ch. 6)*

26 Hula Shows

For a more traditional, less touristy introduction to hula and Hawaiian music, go to the free hula show that's held several nights a week on Kuhio Beach. *(Ch. 3)*

27 Molokini Crater

Tropical fish thrive at Molokini Crater, a partially submerged crater about 3 miles off Maui's southern coast that serves as a fortress against the waves. *(Ch. 4)*

28 The Road to Hana

One of the world's most famous drives, this dangerous road has more than 600 curves and crosses some 50 gulch-straddling bridges in 52 coastline miles. *(Ch. 4)*

29 Helicopter Vistas

Kauai's interior is best seen via helicopter. Tours give access to breathtaking scenery like Napali Coast and Waimea Canyon. *(Ch. 6)*

30 Kayaking the Wailua River

Only Kauai has navigable rivers. Kayaking up the Wailua River leads you into a mystical realm of lush rain forests, velvety green mountains, and secret, crystal-clear waterfalls. *(Ch. 6)*

31 Waikiki

The best way to enjoy Waikiki's famed tourist strip is by foot: skip the traffic, burn off some mai tai calories, and catch the sights you might otherwise miss. *(Ch. 3)*

32 Green Sand Beaches

It's worth the effort to drive to the end of South Point Road in Kau and hike about three miles to stunning, olivine Papakolea Beach. Take lots of water. *(Ch. 5)*

33 Lahaina

Once an active hub for whaling, pineapple, and sugar, Lahaina is a busy town with restaurants, shops, and galleries. *(Ch. 4)*

34 Haleakala National Park's Bamboo Forest

The park's 4-mile round-trip Pipiwai Trail, which many consider the island's best hike, is a dramatic realm of plunging waterfalls, archaic ferns, and an immense bamboo forest. *(Ch. 4)*

35 Napali Coast Sunset Sails

Kauai sunsets are sublime, and perhaps the best way to experience that magical hour of the day is by boat, facing the stunning Napali Coast. *(Ch. 6)*

36 Stargazing at Maunakea

The sunset and stargazing at Maunakea's summit are both outstanding. The visitor center at 9,200 feet (as high as most rental cars are allowed to go) is open daily. *(Ch. 5)*

37 Iao Valley

Central Maui's iconic, green-mantled natural spire rises 1,200 feet above a verdant valley; go early in the day before clouds obscure the views. *(Ch. 4)*

WHAT'S WHERE

1 **Oahu.** Honolulu and Waikiki are here—and it's a great big luau. The island has hot restaurants and lively nightlife as well as gorgeous white-sand beaches, knife-edged mountain ranges, and cultural sites, including Pearl Harbor.

2 **Maui.** The phrase "Maui no ka oi" means Maui is the best, the most, the tops. There's good reason for the superlatives. It's got a little of everything, perfect for families with divergent interests.

3 **Big Island of Hawaii.** It has two faces, watched over by snowcapped Maunakea and steaming Mauna Loa. The Kona side has parched, lava-strewn lowlands, and eastern Hilo is characterized by lush flower farms, waterfalls, and fresh lava forming daily.

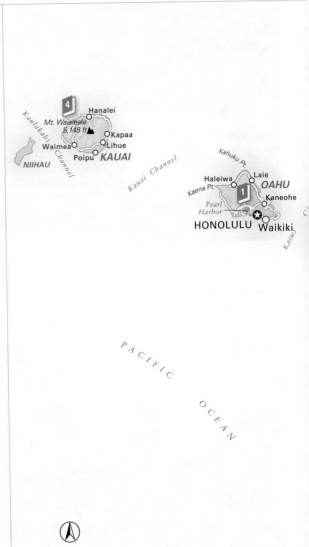

4 Kauai. This is the "Garden Island," and it's where you'll find the lush, green, folding sea cliffs of Napali Coast; the colorful and awesome Waimea Canyon; and more beaches per mile of coastline than any other Hawaiian island.

5 Molokai. It's the least changed, most laid-back of the Islands. Come here to ride a mule down a cliff to Kalaupapa Peninsula; to experience the Kamakou Preserve, a 2,774-acre wildlife refuge; and for plenty of peace and quiet.

6 Lanai. For years, there was nothing here except for pineapples and red-dirt roads. In 2012, Oracle billionaire Larry Ellison purchased 98% of the island, and it still attracts the well-heeled in search of privacy, with two upscale resorts, archery and shooting, four-wheel-drive excursions, and superb scuba diving.

Hawaii Today

Hawaiian culture and tradition have experienced a renaissance over the last few decades. There's been a real effort to revive traditions and to respect history as the Islands go through major changes. New resort developments often have a Hawaiian cultural expert on staff to ensure cultural sensitivity and to educate newcomers. Nonetheless, development itself remains the biggest issue for all Islanders, with land prices still skyrocketing, putting popular areas out of reach for locals. Traffic is becoming a problem on roads that were not designed to accommodate all the drivers (particularly on Oahu and Maui), and the Islands' limited natural resources are being seriously tapped while 90% of Hawaii's food and energy are still imported despite government efforts to increase sustainability.

SUSTAINABILITY

Although sustainability is an effective buzzword and an authentic direction for the Islands' dining establishments, the reality is that 90% of Hawaii's food and energy is imported. However, solar power is making a major inroad in power production: on some sunny days, for a few hours, the Kauai electric grid is 100% powered by alternative energy sources. In fact, Kauai leads the state in alternative energy solutions, including hydro.

Most of the agricultural land in Hawaii was used for mono-cropping of pineapple or sugarcane, both of which have all but vanished. Pioneer Mill in Lahaina conducted its last sugar harvest in 1999, and Hawaiian Commercial & Sugar Co. in Central Maui followed suit in 2016. When Maui Pineapple Co. halted production in 2009, a group of former employees started Maui Gold Pineapple Co., cultivating fields on the lower slopes of Haleakala to supply the fresh fruit market with its sweeter, less acidic pineapple variety.

The loss of large-scale agriculture is slowly opening the door to more diversified farming, including coffee, fruit orchards, livestock grazing, and biofuels.

Oahu has begun educating its communities on the importance of keeping beaches and oceans clean and ensuring that marine life and reefs remain healthy. You won't find plastic straws in your cocktails on Oahu, where plastic shopping bags are also prohibited (so pack reusable bags, if needed). Further, all sunblock sold here must be reef-safe, the result of a January 2021 mandate, and the city of Honolulu has committed to create a carbon-neutral economy, using renewable energy, a green infrastructure, and sustainable waste management.

Hawaii Tourism's newly introduced Malama Hawaii program (⊕ *www.gohawaii.com/malama*) encourages travelers to be mindful while experiencing the Islands—by visiting with *kokua* (care) and *kuleana* (responsibility); by finding ways to *malama* (give back) to the land through volunteer programs; and by buying local to support the many great family-run shops and restaurants. A number of hotels are even offering special "Malama" packages.

TOURISM AND THE ECONOMY

Tourism is by far the state's most important industry. In 2019, the arrival of 10.4 million visitors to the state surpassed a long-expected milestone. According to the Hawaii Tourism Authority, there were, on average, more than 250,000 visitors in the Islands on any given day, spending about $17.8 billion in 2019 alone, up 1% from 2018. The worldwide COVID pandemic stopped Hawaii tourism in its tracks for at least a year, a mixed blessing. Residents could enjoy uncrowded beaches and roads, but the state suffered economically from the effects of layoffs, lockdowns, and closures. Mask requirements and testing/vaccination protocols prior to arrival combined to make Hawaii one of the safest places to visit during most of 2020–2021. But the economy may take several more years to fully recover.

Attuned to local attitudes and visitor demand for more authentic experiences, the tourism industry has adopted more ecoconscious practices. Many residents feel development shouldn't happen without regard for impacts on neighboring communities and the natural environment.

The belief that an industry based on the Hawaiians' *aloha* (welcome, love and fellowship) should protect, promote, and empower local culture and provide more entrepreneurial opportunities for local people have become more critical of tourism businesses. More companies are incorporating Hawaiiana programs and traditional cultural values in their policies and practices, and aim not only to provide a commercially viable tour but also to ensure that visitors leave feeling connected to their host.

The concept of *kuleana,* a word denoting both privilege and responsibility, is a traditional value. Having the privilege to live in such a sublime place comes with the responsibility to protect it.

SOVEREIGNTY

Political sovereignty issues continue to divide Native Hawaiians, who have formed diverse organizations, each operating with separate agendas and lacking one collectively defined goal. Ranging from achieving complete independence to solidifying a nation within a nation, existing sovereignty models remain fractured and their future unresolved. However, the sovereignty movement began gaining new traction in 2019

as Hawaiians formed a protest site at the base of Mauna Kea to prevent the building of the Thirty Meter Telescope at the summit of the mountain, a place considered sacred by many. The camp of the "protectors" (their preferred name) includes daily protocol that includes hula, chanting, and prayers, as well as free health care, meals, and a university. Ripple effects from this protector movement have been seen across the Islands, particularly on Oahu, and a new political party has formed to address issues of particular interest to Native Hawaiians.

The Native Hawaiian Government Reorganization Act of 2009, introduced by the late Senator Daniel Akaka, would have granted Native Hawaiians federal recognition similar to Native American status. Despite 12 years of lobbying, the "Akaka Bill" never mustered enough votes to pass.

RISE OF HAWAIIAN PRIDE

After the overthrow of the monarchy in 1893, a process of Americanization began. Traditions were duly silenced in the name of citizenship. Teaching the Hawaiian language was banned from schools, and children were distanced from their local customs.

But Hawaiians are resilient people, and with the rise of the civil rights movement they began to reflect on their own national identity, bringing an astonishing renaissance of the Hawaiian culture to fruition.

The people rediscovered language, hula, chanting, and even the traditional Polynesian art of canoe building and wayfinding (navigation by the stars without use of instruments). This cultural resurrection is now firmly established in today's Hawaiian culture, with a palpable pride that exudes from Hawaiians young and old.

What to Eat and Drink in Hawaii

SHAVE ICE

Shave ice is simple in its composition—fluffy ice drizzled in Technicolor syrups. Shave ice traces its roots to Hawaii's plantation past. Japanese laborers would use the machetes from their field work to finely shave ice from large frozen blocks and then pour fruit juice over it.

MUSUBI

Musubi are Hawaii's answer to the perfect snack. Portable, handheld, and salty, *musubi* are a great go-to any time of day. The local comfort food is a slice of fried Spam encased in packed white rice and snugly wrapped with nori, or dried seaweed. Available everywhere, *musubi* are usually just a few dollars.

MAI TAI

When people think of a Hawaiian cocktail, the colorful mai tai often comes to mind. It's the unofficial drink to imbibe at a luau and refreshingly tropical. This potent concoction has a rum base and is traditionally made with orange curaçao, orgeat, fresh-squeezed lime juice, and simple syrup.

HAWAIIAN PLATE

The Hawaiian plate comprises the delicious, traditional foods of Hawaii, all on one heaping plate. You can find these combo meals anywhere, from roadside lunch wagons to five-star restaurants. Get yours with the melt-in-your-mouth shredded kalua pig, pork, or chicken *laulau* (cooked in ti leaves) with *lomi* salmon (diced salmon with tomatoes and onions) on the side and the coconut-milk *haupia* for dessert. Most Hawaiian plates come with the requisite two scoops of white rice. Don't forget to try *poi*, or pounded and cooked taro.

POKE

In Hawaiian, *poke* is a verb that means to slice and cut into pieces. It perfectly describes the technique Hawaiians have used for centuries to prepare poke the dish. The cubed raw fish, most commonly *ahi* (yellowfin tuna), is traditionally tossed with Hawaiian sea salt, *limu kohu* (red seaweed), or *inamona* (crushed kukui nuts). Today, countless varieties of this must-try dish are served in all kinds of restaurants across the Islands. Poke shacks offer no-frills, made-to-order poke.

SAIMIN

This only-in-Hawaii noodle dish is the culinary innovation of Hawaii plantation workers in the late 1800s who created a new comfort food with ingredients and traditions from their home countries.

Poke

MANAPUA

When *kamaaina*, or Hawaii residents, are invited to a potluck, business meeting, or even an impromptu party, you'll inevitably see a box filled with *manapua*. Inside these airy white buns are pockets of sweet *char siu* pork. Head to cities and towns around the Islands, and you'll find restaurants with manapua on their menus, as well as manapua takeout places serving a variety of fillings. There's sweet potato, curry chicken, *lap cheong* (or Chinese sausage)—and even sweet flavors, such as custard and *ube*, a purple yam popular in Filipino desserts.

MALASADA

Malasadas are a beloved treat in Hawaii. The Portuguese pastries are about the size of a baseball and are airy, deep-fried, and dusted with sugar. They are best enjoyed hot and filled with custard; fillings are a Hawaiian variation on the original.

LOCO MOCO

The traditional version of one of Hawaii's classic comfort-food dishes consists of white rice topped with a hamburger patty and fried eggs and generously blanketed in rich, brown gravy. Cafe 100 in Hilo on the Big Island is renowned as the home of the *loco moco*, but you'll find this popular staple everywhere. It can be eaten any time of day.

KONA COFFEE

In Kona, on the Big Island, coffee reigns supreme. There are roughly 600 coffee farms dotting the west side of the island, each producing flavorful (and quite expensive) coffee grown in the rich, volcanic soil. Kona coffee is typically hand-harvested from August through December.

What to Buy in Hawaii

MACADAMIA NUT CANDY
Macadamia nuts are native to Australia, but the gumball-sized nut remains an important crop in Hawaii. It was first introduced in the late 1880s as a windbreak for sugarcane crops. Today, mac nuts are a popular local snack and are especially good baked in cookies or other desserts.

LEI
As a visitor to Hawaii, you may well receive a lei, either a shell, kukui nut, or fragrant flower variety, as a welcome to the Islands. *Kamaaina* (Hawaii residents) mark special occasions by gifting lei.

ALOHA WEAR
Aloha wear in Hawaii has come a long way from the polyester fabrics with too-bright, kitschy patterns (although those still exist). Local designers have been creating dressy, modern aloha attire with softer prints that evoke Island botanicals, heritage, and traditional patterns. Hawaii residents don aloha wear for everything from work to weddings.

LAUHALA
The hala tree is most known for its long, thin leaves and the masterful crafts that are created from them. Lauhala weavers make baskets, hats, mats, jewelry, and more, using intricate traditional patterns and techniques.

JEWELRY
Island-inspired jewelry comes in many styles. Tahitian pearl pendants and earrings are a local favorite, as are delicate, inexpensive shell pieces. The most coveted are Hawaiian heirloom bracelets in gold or silver with one's name enameled in Old English script.

HAWAIIAN COFFEE

Reminisce about your Hawaii getaway each time you brew a cup of aromatic, full-bodied coffee, whether it's from Kona or Kauai. All the main islands grow distinctive coffee. Stores and cafés sell bags of varying sizes, and in some places you can buy direct from a farmer.

HAWAIIAN SEA SALT

A long tradition of harvesting salt beds by hand continues today on all the Islands. The salt comes in various colors, including inky black and brick red—the result of the salt reacting and mixing with activated charcoal and *alaea* (volcanic clay). It is renowned by chefs around the state.

HAWAIIAN HONEY

With its temperate climate and bountiful foliage, Hawaii is ideal for honeybees. The Islands' unique ecosystem contributes to honeys with robust flavors and textures, including elixirs extracted from the blossoms of the macadamia nut tree, the lehua flower, and the invasive Christmasberry shrub.

UKULELE

In Hawaiian, *ukulele* means "the jumping flea." The small instrument made its way to the Islands in the 1880s via Portuguese immigrants who brought with them the four-string, guitar-like *machete de braga*. It is famous as a solo instrument today, with virtuoso artists like Jake Shimabukuro and Taimane Gardner popularizing the ukulele's versatile sound.

KOA WOOD

If you're looking for an heirloom keepsake from the Islands, consider a koa wood product. Grown only in Hawaii, the valuable koa is some of the world's rarest and hardest wood. Hawaiians traditionally made surfboards and canoes from these trees, which today grow only in upland forests.

Flora and Fauna in Hawaii

KUKUI

The *kukui*, or candlenut, is Hawaii's state tree, and Hawaiians have had many uses for it. Oil was extracted from its nuts and burned as a light source and also rubbed on fishing nets to preserve them. The juice from the husk's fruit was used as a dye. The small kukui blossoms and nuts also have medicinal purposes.

PLUMERIA

Also known as frangipani, this fragrant flower is named after Charles Plumier, the noted French botanist who discovered it in Central America in the late 1600s. Plumeria come in shades of white, yellow, pink, red, and orange. The hearty, plentiful blossoms are frequently used in lei.

HUMPBACK WHALES

Each year, North Pacific humpback whales make the long journey to Hawaii from Alaska. With its warm, protected waters, Hawaii provides the ideal place for the marine mammals to mate and to birth, and to nurse their young. They arrive between November and May, and their presence is an anticipated event. You can see them up close during whale-watching boat tours.

GARDENIA

The gardenia is a favorite for lei makers because of its sweet smell. The plant is native to tropical regions throughout China and Africa, but there are also endemic gardenias in Hawaii. The nanu gardenia is found only in the Islands and has petite white blossoms.

HONU

The *honu*, or Hawaiian green sea turtle, is a magical sight. The graceful reptile is an endangered and protected species in Hawaii. It's easier to encounter *honu* during a snorkeling or scuba-diving excursion, but they occasionally can be spotted basking on beaches.

MONK SEAL

Known as the *ilio holo i ka uaua*, meaning "dog that runs in rough water," monk seals are endemic to Hawaii and critically endangered. The majority of these mammals, which can grow to more than seven feet long, live in the remote, uninhabited Northwestern Hawaiian Islands.

TROPICAL FISH

Approximately 25% of the fish species in the Islands are endemic. Snorkeling in Hawaii is a unique, fun opportunity to see colorful fish found nowhere else on Earth. Interestingly, Hawaii's state fish, the *humuhumunukunukuapuaa*, or reef trigger, is not endemic to the state.

NENE GOOSE

Pronounced *nay-nay*, the endemic nene goose (Hawaii's state bird) is one of the world's rarest. A descendant of the Canada goose, it has been bred back from the edge of extinction and reintroduced into the wild. Use caution driving in national and state parks, which they frequent.

HIBISCUS

In 1923, the Territory of Hawaii passed a law designating hibiscus as Hawaii's official flower. While there are more than 30 introduced species of the large, colorful flowers throughout the Islands, there are five endemic types. The endemic hibiscus has yellow blossoms and is known in Hawaiian as *mao hau hele*, which means the "traveling green tree."

PIKAKE

These small, delicate blossoms are known for their hypnotic, sweet scent. The jasmine flower was introduced from India and was a favorite of Princess Kaiulani. *Pikake*, which is the Hawaiian word for the blossom as well as for a peacock—another favorite of the princess—is the subject of many *mele*, or Hawaiian songs.

Choosing Your Island

You've decided to go to Hawaii, but should you stay put and relax on one island or try sampling more than one? If all you have is a week, it is probably best to stick to just one island. You traveled all this way, why spend your precious vacation time at car-rental counters, hotel check-in desks, and airports? But, with seven or more nights, a little island-hopping is a great way to experience the diversity of sights and experiences that are packed into this small state. Here are some of our favorite island-pairing itineraries for every type of trip.

FAMILY TRAVEL: OAHU AND MAUI

If you're traveling with children, Oahu and Maui have the most options.

Why Oahu: Oahu is by far the most kid-friendly island. For sea life, visit the Waikiki Aquarium and Sea Life Park or let the little ones get up close and personal with fish at Hanauma Bay. At Pearl Harbor, you can visit an aircraft carrier or, if the kids are at least four, a World War II submarine. Then there's the Honolulu Zoo and a slippery slide–filled water park, not to mention some very family-friendly and safe beaches. *Plan to spend 4 nights.*

Why Maui: Whales! Though you can see whales from any island between November and April, there's no better place than Maui. If your visit doesn't fall during peak whale-watching season, visit the Hawaiian Islands Humpback Whale National Marine Sanctuary or the Maui Ocean Center (to get an up-close look at some of Hawaii's smaller sea creatures). Away from the water, there's the Sugar Cane Train. *Plan to spend at least 3 nights.*

ROMANCE: MAUI AND KAUAI

If you're getting away for seclusion, romantic walks along the beach, and the pampering at world-class spas, consider Maui and Kauai.

Why Maui: You'll find waterfalls, salt-and-pepper sand beaches, and incredible views as you follow the twisting turning Road to Hana. The luxury resorts in Wailea or Kaanapali provide lots of fine dining and spa treatment options. And for those who want to start their day early, there's the drive up to Haleakala to see the sun rise—or for couples who prefer to sleep in, there's the arguably even more spectacular sunset from the summit. *Plan to spend 4 nights.*

Why Kauai: The North Shore communities of Hanalei and Princeville provide the opportunity to get away and indulge in some spectacular beaches, hiking, and helicopter rides. At Princeville, you can experience views straight out of *South Pacific* as well as excellent dining and spas while a drive to Kee Beach at the end of the road provides options for pulling over and grabbing a beach, all for just the two of you. *Plan to spend at least 3 nights.*

GOLF, SHOPPING, AND LUXURY: MAUI AND THE BIG ISLAND

For luxurious travel, great shopping, restaurants, and accommodations you can't beat Maui and the Big Island.

Why Maui: The resorts at Wailea and Kaanapali have endless options for dining, shopping, and spa treatments. And, the golf on Maui can't be beat with Kapalua, the Dunes at Maui Lani, and Makena Resort topping the list of spectacular courses. *Plan to spend 4 nights.*

Why the Big Island: In addition to having incredible natural scenery, the Big Island offers world-class resorts and golfing along the Kohala Coast. The Mauna Kea and Hapuna golf courses rank among the top in state while the courses at Mauna Lani Resort and Waikoloa Village allow the unusual experience of playing in and around lava flows. Gourmet dining and spa treatments are readily available at the top resorts, and you'll find shopping opportunities at King's Shops at Waikoloa Village as well as within many of the resorts themselves. Or, travel to Hawi or Waimea (Kamuela) for authentic island boutiques. *Plan to spend at least 3 nights.*

NATURAL BEAUTY AND PRISTINE BEACHES: THE BIG ISLAND AND KAUAI

Really want to get away and experience nature at its most primal? The Big Island is the place to start, followed by a trip to Kauai.

Why the Big Island: Home to 11 different climate zones, the Big Island is large enough to contain all the other Hawaiian Islands. There are countless options for those who want to get off the beaten track and get their hands (and feet) dirty—or sandy as the case may be. See lava flowing or steam rising from Kilauea. Visit beaches in your choice of gold, white, green, or black sand. Snorkel or dive just offshore from an ancient Hawaiian settlement. Or, hike through rain forests to hidden waterfalls. The choices are endless on this island. *Plan to spend at least 4 nights.*

Why Kauai: The Napali Coast is the main draw for those seeking secluded beaches and incredible scenery. If you're interested in hiking to otherwise inaccessible beaches along sheer sea cliffs, this is as good as it gets. Or, head up to Waimea Canyon to see the "Grand Canyon of the Pacific." Want waterfalls? Opaekaa Falls outside Lihue is one of the state's most breathtaking. And there's no better place for bird-watching than Kilauea Point National Wildlife Refuge. *Plan to spend at least 3 nights.*

VOLCANIC VIEWS: THE BIG ISLAND AND MAUI

For those coming to Hawaii for the volcanoes, there are really only two options: the Big Island and Maui.

Why the Big Island: Start by flying into Hilo and head straight to Hawaii Volcanoes National Park and Kilauea Volcano. Plan to spend at least two days at Kilauea—you'll need time to really explore the caldera, drive to the end of Chain of Craters Road, and have some time for hiking in and around this active volcano. While eruptions are unpredictable (and more rare these days), helicopter companies can get you views of otherwise inaccessible lava flows. You can also make a visit up to the summit of Maunakea with a tour company. From here you'll see views not only of the observatories (Maunakea is one of the best places in the world for astronomy), but also Kilauea and Haleakala volcanoes, which loom in the distance. *Plan to spend at least 4 nights.*

Why Maui: Though all the islands in Hawaii were built from the same hot spot in Earth's crust, the only other island to have had volcanic activity in recorded history is Maui, at Haleakala. The House of the Sun (as Haleakala is known) has great hiking and camping opportunities. *Plan to spend 3 nights.*

Kids and Families

With dozens of adventures, discoveries, and fun-filled beach days, Hawaii is a blast with kids. Even better, the things to do here do not appeal only to small fry. The entire family, parents included, will enjoy surfing, discovering a waterfall in the rain forest, and snorkeling with sea turtles. And there are plenty of organized activities for kids that will free parents' time for a few romantic beach strolls.

CHOOSING A PLACE TO STAY

Condos: Condo and vacation rentals are a fantastic value for families vacationing in Hawaii. You can cook your own food, which is cheaper than eating out and sometimes easier (especially if you have a finicky eater in your group), and you'll get twice the space of a hotel room for about a quarter of the price. If you decide to go the condo route, be sure to ask about the size of the complex's pool (some try to pawn a tiny soaking tub off as a pool) and whether barbecues are available.

Resorts: All the big resorts make kids' programs a priority, and it shows. When you are booking your room, ask about "kids eat free" deals and the number of kids' pools at the resort. Also check out the size of the groups in the children's programs, and find out whether the cost of the programs includes lunch, equipment, and activities.

OCEAN ACTIVITIES

Hawaii is all about getting your kids outside—away from TV and video games. And who could resist the turquoise water; the promise of spotting dolphins or whales; and the fun of bodyboarding, snorkeling, or surfing?

On the beach: Most people like being in the water, but toddlers and school-age kids are often completely captivated by Hawaii's beaches. The swimming pool at your condo or hotel is always an option, but don't be afraid to hit the beach with a little one in tow. There are several in Hawaii that are nearly as safe as a pool—completely protected bays with pleasant white-sand beaches. As always, use your judgment, and heed all posted signs and lifeguard warnings.

On the waves: Surf lessons are a great idea for older kids, especially if Mom and Dad want a little quiet time. Beginner lessons are always on safe and easy waves and last anywhere from two to four hours.

The underwater world: If your kids are ready to try snorkeling, Hawaii is a great place to introduce them to the underwater world. Even without the mask and snorkel, they'll be able to see colorful fish darting this way and that, and they may also spot turtles and dolphins at many of the island beaches.

LAND ACTIVITIES

In addition to beach experiences, Hawaii has rain forests, botanical gardens, aquariums (Oahu and Maui), and even petting zoos and hands-on children's museums that will keep your kids entertained and out of the sun for a day.

AFTER DARK

At night, younger kids get a kick out of luau, and many of the shows incorporate young audience members, adding to the fun. The older kids might find it all a bit lame, but there are a handful of new shows in the Islands that are more modern, incorporating acrobatics, lively music, and fire dancers. If you're planning on hitting a luau with a teen in tow, we highly recommend going the modern route.

Weddings and Honeymoons

Hawaii is one of the country's foremost honeymoon destinations. Romance is in the air here, and the white, sandy beaches, turquoise water, swaying palm trees, balmy tropical breezes, and brilliant sunshine put people in the mood for love. So it goes without saying that Hawaii has also become a popular wedding destination, especially as new resorts and hotels entice visitors and with same-sex marriage legal. Once the knot is tied, why not stay for the honeymoon?

THE BIG DAY

Choosing the perfect place: You really have two choices to make: the ceremony location and where to hold a reception. For the former, Hawaii boasts stunning beaches, sea-hugging bluffs, gardens, private residences, resort lawns, and, of course, places of worship. As for the reception, there are these same choices, as well as restaurants and even a luau. If you decide to go outdoors, make sure to have a backup plan for inclement weather. If you're taking the plunge on a public beach, a state permit is required.

Finding a wedding planner: If you're planning to invite more than an officiant and your loved one to your ceremony, consider a Hawaii-based wedding planner who can help select a location, design the floral scheme, and recommend a photographer. They can also plan the menu and choose a restaurant, caterer, or resort, and suggest Hawaiian traditions to incorporate into your vows. If it's a resort wedding, most have on-site wedding coordinators; however, there are many independent planners around Kauai who specialize in certain types of ceremonies—by locale, size, religious affiliation, and so on. Share your budget. Get a proposal—in writing. Request a detailed list of the exact services they'll provide. If possible, meet the planner in person.

Getting your license: There's no waiting period in Hawaii, no residency or citizenship requirements, and no required blood test or shots. You can apply and pay the fee online; however, both partners must appear together in person before a marriage-license agent to receive the marriage license (the permit to get married) at the State Department of Health, The Wine Shop in Koloa, or an independent agent. You'll need proof of age—the legal age to marry is 18. Upon approval, a marriage license is immediately issued and costs $60. After the ceremony, your officiant will mail the marriage certificate to the state. Approximately four months later, you will receive a copy in the mail. The person performing your wedding must be licensed by the Hawaii Department of Health, even if he or she is a licensed officiant. Be sure to ask.

Wedding attire: In Hawaii, anything goes, from long, formal dresses with trains to bikinis. For men, a pair of solid-color slacks with a nice aloha shirt is appropriate. If you're getting hitched on the beach, why not go barefoot?

Local customs: The most obvious traditional Hawaiian wedding custom is the lei exchange, in which the bride and groom take turns placing a lei around the neck of the other—with a kiss. Bridal lei are usually floral, whereas the groom's is typically made of twisted ti or *maile,* a green leafy garland. Brides often also wear a *lei poo,* a circular floral headpiece.

THE HONEYMOON

Do you want champagne and strawberries delivered to your room? A breathtaking swimming pool? A five-star restaurant? Then a resort is the way to go. A small inn is also good if you're on a tight budget or don't plan to spend much time in your room. The lodging choices are almost as plentiful as the beaches here.

The History of Hawaii

Hawaiian history is long and complex; a brief survey can put into context the ongoing renaissance of native arts and culture.

THE POLYNESIANS

Long before both the Vikings and Christopher Columbus, Polynesian seafarers set out to explore the vast stretches of the open ocean in double-hulled canoes. They didn't just flail around and land here by accident; they understood the deep nuances of celestial navigation and were masters of the craft. From western Polynesia, they traveled back and forth between Samoa, Fiji, Tahiti, the Marquesas, and the Society Isles, settling on the outer reaches of the Pacific, Hawaii, and Easter Island, as early as AD 300. The golden era of Polynesian voyaging peaked around AD 1200, after which the distant Hawaiian Islands were left to develop their own unique cultural practices and subsistence in relative isolation.

The Islands' symbiotic society was deeply intertwined with religion, mythology, science, and artistry. Ruled by an *alii*, or chief, each settlement was nestled in an *ahupuaa*, a pie-shaped land division from the uplands, through the valleys, and down to the shores. Everyone contributed, whether it was by building canoes, catching fish, making tools, or farming land, thereby developing a sustainable society.

A UNITED KINGDOM

When the British explorer Captain James Cook arrived in Kealakekua Bay on the Big Island in 1778, he was greeted by the Hawaiians as a person of important stature. With guns and ammunition purchased from subsequent foreign trading ships, the Big Island chief, Kamehameha the Great, gained a significant advantage over the other *alii* (chiefs). He united Hawaii into one kingdom in 1810,

bringing an end to the frequent interisland battles that dominated Hawaiian life.

Tragically, the new kingdom was beset with troubles. Native religion was abandoned, and *kapu* (laws and regulations) were eventually abolished. The European explorers brought diseases with them, and within a few decades the Native Hawaiian population was decimated.

New laws regarding land ownership and religious practices eroded the underpinnings of pre-contact Hawaii. Each successor to the Hawaiian throne sacrificed more control over the Island kingdom. As Westerners permeated Hawaiian culture, so did social unrest.

MODERN HAWAII

In 1893, the last Hawaiian monarch, Queen Liliuokalani, was overthrown by a group of American and European businesspeople and government officials, aided by an armed militia. This led to the creation of the Republic of Hawaii, and it became a U.S. territory for the next 60 years. The loss of Hawaiian sovereignty and the conditions of annexation have haunted the Hawaiian people since the monarchy was deposed.

Pearl Harbor in Oahu was attacked in 1941, which engaged the United States immediately into World War II. Tourism, from its beginnings in the early 1900s, flourished after the war and naturally inspired rapid real estate development in Waikiki and then elsewhere. In 1959, Hawaii officially became the 50th state.

In the late 1960s and 1970s, the Native Hawaiian community began to celebrate a return to its roots with the revival of traditional hula as a cultural practice, the journeys of the voyaging canoes, and a resurgence of Hawaiian music and language. This movement, called the Hawaiian Renaissance, has influenced life in the Islands ever since.

HAWAIIAN CULTURAL TRADITIONS HULA, LEI, AND LUAU

HULA: MORE THAN A FOLK DANCE

Hula has been called "the heartbeat of the Hawaiian people" and also "the world's best-known, most misunderstood dance." Both are true. Hula isn't just dance. It is storytelling.

Chanter Edith McKinzie calls it "an extension of a piece of poetry." In its adornments, implements, and customs, hula integrates every important Hawaiian cultural practice: poetry, history, genealogy, craft, plant cultivation, martial arts, religion, protocol. So when 19th-century Christian missionaries sought to eradicate a practice they considered depraved, they threatened more than just a folk dance.

With public performance outlawed and private hula practice discouraged, hula went underground for a generation. The fragile verbal link by which culture was transmitted from teacher to student hung by a thread. Even increasing literacy did not help because hula's practitioners were a secretive and protected circle.

As if that weren't bad enough, vaudeville, Broadway, and Hollywood got hold of the hula, giving it the glitz treatment in an unbroken line from "Oh, How She Could Wicky Wacky Woo" to "Rock-A-Hula Baby." Hula became shorthand for paradise: fragrant flowers, lazy hours. Ironically, this development assured that hundreds of Hawaiians could make a living performing and teaching hula. Many danced 'auana (modern form) in performance; but taught kahiko (traditional), quietly, at home or in hula schools.

Today, decades after the cultural revival known as the Hawaiian Renaissance, language immersion programs have assured a new generation of proficient chanters, songwriters, and translators. Visitors can see more—and more authentic—traditional hula now than at any other time in the last 200 years.

Like the culture of which it is the beating heart, hula has survived.

Lei poo. Head lei. In *kahiko,* greenery only. In auana, flowers.

Face emotes appropriate expression. Dancer should not be a smiling automaton.

Shoulders remain relaxed and still, never hunched, even with arms raised. No bouncing.

Eyes always follow leading hand.

Lei. Hula is rarely performed without a shoulder lei.

Arms and hands remain loose, relaxed, below shoulder level—except as required by interpretive movements.

Traditional hula skirt is loose fabric, smocked and gathered at the waist.

Hip is canted over weight-bearing foot.

Knees are always slightly bent, accentuating hip sway.

Kupee. Ankle bracelet of flowers, shells, or foliage.

In *kahiko,* feet are flat. In *auana,* they may be more arched, but not tiptoes or bouncing.

BASIC MOTIONS

Speak or sing

Moon or sun

Grass shack or house

Mountains or heights

Love or caress

At backyard parties, hula is performed in bare feet and street clothes, but in performance, adornments play a key role, as do rhythm-keeping implements such as the *pahu* drum and the *ipu* (gourd).

In hula *kahiko* (traditional style), the usual dress is multiple layers of stiff fabric (often with a pellom lining, which most closely resembles *kapa*, the paperlike bark cloth of the Hawaiians). These wrap tightly around the bosom but flare below the waist to form a skirt. In pre-contact times, dancers wore only kapa skirts. Men traditionally wear loincloths.

Monarchy-period hula is performed in voluminous muumuu or high-necked muslin blouses and gathered skirts. Men wear white or gingham shirts and black pants.

In hula *auana* (modern), dress for women can range from grass skirts and strapless tops to contemporary tea-length dresses. Men generally wear aloha shirts, but sometimes grass skirts over pants or even everyday gear.

SURPRISING HULA FACTS

■ Grass skirts are not traditional; workers from Kiribati (the Gilbert Islands) brought this custom to Hawaii.

■ In olden-day Hawaii, *mele* (songs) for hula were composed for every occasion—name songs for babies, dirges for funerals, welcome songs for visitors, celebrations of favorite pursuits.

■ Hula *mai* is a traditional hula form in praise of a noble's genitals; the power of the *alii* (royalty) to procreate gave mana (spiritual power) to the entire culture.

■ Hula students in old Hawaii adhered to high standards: scrupulous cleanliness, no sex, daily cleansing rituals, certain food prohibitions, and no contact with the dead. They were fined if they broke the rules.

WHERE TO WATCH

If you're interested in "the real thing," there are annual hula festivals on each island. Check the individual island visitors' bureaus websites at ⊕ *www.gohawaii.com*.

If you can't make it to a festival, there are plenty of other hula shows—at most resorts, many lounges, and even at certain shopping centers. Ask your hotel concierge for performance information.

ALL ABOUT LEI

Lei brighten every occasion in Hawaii, from birthdays to bar mitzvahs to baptisms. Creative artisans weave nature's bounty—flowers, ferns, vines, and seeds—into gorgeous creations that convey an array of heartfelt messages: "Welcome," "Congratulations," "Good luck," "Farewell," "Thank you," "I love you." When it's difficult to find the right words, a lei expresses exactly the right sentiment.

WHERE TO BUY THE BEST LEI

Most airports in Hawaii have lei stands where you can buy a fragrant garland upon arrival. Every florist shop in the Islands sells lei; you can also treat yourself to a lei while shopping for provisions at any supermarket or box store. And you'll always find lei sellers at crafts fairs and outdoor festivals.

LEI ETIQUETTE

■ To wear a closed lei, drape it over your shoulders, half in front and half in back. Open lei are worn around the neck, with the ends draped over the front in equal lengths.

■ Pikake, ginger, and other sweet, delicate blossoms are "feminine" lei. Men opt for cigar, crown flower, and ti leaf lei, which are sturdier and don't emit as much fragrance.

■ Lei are always presented with a kiss, a custom that supposedly dates back to World War II when a hula dancer fancied an officer at a U.S.O. show. Taking a dare from members of her troupe, she took off her lei, placed it around his neck, and kissed him on the cheek.

■ You shouldn't wear a lei before you give it to someone else. Hawaiians believe the lei absorbs your mana (spirit); if you give your lei away, you'll be giving away part of your essence.

ORCHID

Growing wild on every continent except Antarctica, orchids—which range in color from yellow to green to purple—comprise the largest family of plants in the world. There are more than 20,000 species of orchids, but only three are native to Hawaii—and they are very rare. The pretty lavender vanda you see hanging by the dozens at local lei stands has probably been imported from Thailand.

MAILE

Maile, an endemic twining vine with a heady aroma, is sacred to Laka, goddess of the hula. In ancient times, dancers wore maile and decorated hula altars with it to honor Laka. Today, "open" maile lei usually are given to men. Instead of ribbon, interwoven lengths of maile are used at dedications of new businesses. The maile is untied, never snipped, for doing so would symbolically "cut" the company's success.

ILIMA

Designated by Hawaii's Territorial Legislature in 1923 as the official flower of the island of Oahu, the golden ilima is so delicate it lasts for just a day. Five to seven hundred blossoms are needed to make one garland. Queen Emma, wife of King Kamehameha IV, preferred ilima over all other lei, which may have led to the incorrect belief that they were reserved only for royalty.

PLUMERIA

This ubiquitous flower is named after Charles Plumier, the noted French botanist who discovered it in Central America in the late 1600s. Plumeria ranks among the most popular lei in Hawaii because it's fragrant, hardy, plentiful, inexpensive, and requires very little care. Although yellow is the most common color, you'll also find plumeria lei in shades of pink, red, orange, and "rainbow" blends.

PIKAKE

Favored for its fragile beauty and sweet scent, pikake was introduced from India. In lieu of pearls, many brides in Hawaii adorn themselves with long, multiple strands of white pikake. Princess Kaiulani enjoyed showing guests her beloved pikake and peacocks at Ainahau, her Waikiki home. Interestingly, pikake is the Hawaiian word for both the bird and the blossom.

KUKUI

The kukui (candlenut) is Hawaii's state tree. Early Hawaiians strung kukui nuts (which are quite oily) together and burned them for light; mixed burned nuts with oil to make an indelible dye; and mashed roasted nuts to consume as a laxative. Kukui nut lei may not have been made until after Western contact, when the Hawaiians saw black beads from Europe and wanted to imitate them.

LUAU: A TASTE OF HAWAII

The best place to sample Hawaiian food is at a backyard luau. Aunts and uncles are cooking, the pig is from a cousin's farm, and the fish is from a brother's boat.

But even locals have to angle for invitations to those rare occasions. So your choice is most likely between a commercial luau and a Hawaiian restaurant.

Some commercial luau are less authentic; they offer little of the traditional diet and are more about umbrella drinks, spectacle, and fun.

For greater culinary authenticity, folksy experiences, and rock-bottom prices, visit a Hawaiian restaurant (most are in anonymous storefronts in residential neighborhoods). Expect rough edges and some effort negotiating the menu.

In either case, much of what is known today as Hawaiian food would be as foreign to a 16th-century Hawaiian as risotto or chow mien. The pre-contact diet was simple and healthy—mainly raw and steamed seafood and vegetables. Early Hawaiians used earth ovens and heated stones to cook seafood, taro, sweet potatoes, and breadfruit and seasoned their food with sea salt and ground kukui nuts. Seaweed, fern shoots, sweet potato vines, coconut, banana, sugarcane, and select greens and roots rounded out the diet.

Successive waves of immigrants added their favorites to the ti leaf–lined table. So it is that foods as disparate as salt salmon and chicken long rice are now Hawaiian— even though there is no salmon in Hawaiian waters and long rice (cellophane noodles) is Chinese.

AT THE LUAU: KALUA PORK

The heart of any luau is the *imu*, the earth oven in which a whole pig is roasted. The preparation of an imu is an arduous affair for most families, who tackle it only once a year or so, for a baby's first birthday or at Thanksgiving, when many Islanders prefer to imu their turkeys. Commercial luau operations have it down to a science, however.

THE ART OF THE STONE

The key to a proper imu is the *pohaku*, the stones. Imu cook by means of long, slow, moist heat released by special stones that can withstand a hot fire without exploding. Many Hawaiian families treasure their imu stones, keeping them in a pile in the backyard and passing them on through generations.

PIT COOKING

The imu makers first dig a pit about the size of a refrigerator, then lay down *kiawe* (mesquite) wood and stones, and build a white-hot fire that is allowed to burn itself out. The ashes are raked away, and the hot stones covered with banana and ti leaves. Well-wrapped in ti or banana leaves and a net of chicken wire, the pig is lowered onto the leaf-covered stones. *Laulau* (leaf-wrapped bundles of meats, fish, and taro leaves) may also be placed inside. Leaves—ti, banana, even ginger—cover the pig followed by wet burlap sacks (to create steam). The whole is topped with a canvas tarp and left to steam for the better part of a day.

OPENING THE IMU

This is the moment everyone waits for: The imu is unwrapped like a giant present and the imu keepers gingerly wrestle out the steaming pig. When it's unwrapped, the meat falls moist and smoky-flavored from the bone, looking just like Southern-style pulled pork, but without the barbecue sauce.

WHICH LUAU?

Most resort hotels have luau on their grounds that include hula, music, and, of course, lots of food and drink. Each island also has at least one "authentic" luau. For lists of the best luau on each island, visit the Hawaii Visitors and Convention Bureau website at ⊕ *www. gohawaii.com*.

MEA AI ONO: GOOD THINGS TO EAT.

LAULAU
Steamed meats, fish, and taro leaf in ti-leaf bundles: fork-tender, a medley of flavors; the taro resembles spinach.

Laulau

LOMI LOMI SALMON
Salt salmon in a piquant salad or relish with onions and tomatoes.

POI
Poi, a paste made of pounded taro root, may be an acquired taste, but it's a must-try during your visit.

Consider: The Hawaiian Adam is descended from *kalo* (taro). Young taro plants are called "keiki" (children). Poi is the first food after mother's milk for many Islanders. *Ai*, the word for food, is synonymous with poi in many contexts.

Lomi lomi salmon

Not only that, locals love it. "There is no meat that doesn't taste good with poi," the old Hawaiians said.

But you have to know how to eat it: with something rich or powerfully flavored. "It is salt that makes the poi go in," is another adage. When you're served poi, try it with a mouthful of smoky kalua pork or salty *lomi lomi* salmon. Its slightly sour blandness cleanses the palate. And if you don't like it, smile and say something polite. (And slide that bowl over to a local.)

Poi

E HELE MAI AI! COME AND EAT!

Local-style Hawaiian restaurants tend to be inconveniently located in well-worn storefronts with little or no parking, outfitted with battered tables and clattering Melmac dishes, but they personify aloha, invariably run by local families who welcome tourists who take the trouble to find them.

Many are cash-only operations and combination plates, known as "plate lunch," are a standard feature: one or two entrées, two scoops of steamed rice, one scoop of macaroni salad, and—if the place is really old-style—a tiny portion of coarse Hawaiian salt and some raw onions for relish.

Most serve some foods that aren't, strictly speaking, Hawaiian, but are beloved of *kamaaina* (locals), such as salt meat with watercress (preserved meat in a tasty broth), or *akubone* (skipjack tuna fried in a tangy vinegar sauce).

What to Read and Watch

HAWAIIAN MYTHOLOGY BY MARTHA BECKWITH

This exhaustive work of ethnology and folklore was researched and collected by Martha Beckwith over decades and published when she was 69. *Hawaiian Mythology* is a comprehensive look at the Hawaiian ancestral deities and their importance throughout history.

HAWAII'S STORY BY HAWAII'S QUEEN, BY LILIUOKALANI

This poignant book by Queen Liliuokalani chronicles the 1893 overthrow of the Hawaiian monarchy and her plea for her people. It's an essential read to understand the political undercurrent and the push for sovereignty that exists in the Islands more than 125 years later.

LETTERS FROM HAWAII BY MARK TWAIN

In 1866, when Samuel Clemens was 31, he sailed from California and spent four months in Hawaii. He eventually mailed 25 letters to the *Sacramento Union* newspaper about his experiences. Along the way, Twain sheds some cultural biases as he visits Kilauea Volcano, meets with Hawaii's newly formed legislators, and examines the sugar trade.

SHOAL OF TIME: A HISTORY OF THE HAWAIIAN ISLANDS BY GAVAN DAWS

Perhaps the most popular book by this best-selling Honolulu author is *Shoal of Time*. Published in 1974, the account of modern Hawaiian history details the colonization of Hawaii and everything that was lost in the process.

MOLOKAI BY ALAN BRENNERT

The writer's debut novel, set in the 1890s, follows a Hawaiian woman who contracts leprosy as a child and is sent to the remote, quarantined community of Kalaupapa on the island of Molokai,

where she then lives. The Southern California–based author was inspired to write the book during his visits to Hawaii.

HAWAII SAYS "ALOHA" BY DON BLANDING

First published in 1928, this volume of enchanting, rhyming verse about Hawaii evokes the rich details about the Islands that mesmerized the author in the 1920s and for the rest of his life. Blanding also illustrated this and many other books and was later named Hawaii's poet laureate.

THE DESCENDANTS

Based on the book by local author Kaui Hart Hemmings, the film adaptation starring George Clooney and directed by Alexander Payne was filmed on Oahu and Kauai. It spotlights a contemporary, upper-class family in Hawaii as they deal with family grief and landholdings in flux.

BLUE HAWAII

The 1961 musical features the hip-shaking songs and moves of Elvis Presley, who plays tour guide Chadwick Gates. Elvis famously sings "Ke Kali Nei Au," or "The Hawaiian Wedding Song," at the iconic and now-shuttered Coco Palms Resort on Kauai. (The resort has remained closed since 1992 following Hurricane Iniki.)

MOANA

The release of *Moana* in 2016 was celebrated by many in Hawaii and the Pacific for showcasing Polynesian culture. The now-beloved animated movie, which tells the story of the demigod Maui, features the voice talents of Aulii Cravalho and Dwayne Johnson. In 2018, *Moana* was re-recorded and distributed in Olelo Hawaii, or the Hawaiian language, with Cravalho reprising her role. It marked the first time a Disney movie was available in Hawaiian.

Chapter 2

TRAVEL SMART

2

Updated by Karen Anderson,
Tiffany Hill, Syndi Texeira,
and Mary F. Williamson

★ **CAPITAL:**
Honolulu

POPULATION:
1,412,687

LANGUAGE:
Hawaiian and English

$ **CURRENCY:**
USD

AREA CODE:
808

⚠ **EMERGENCIES:**
911

DRIVING:
On the right

⚡ **ELECTRICITY:**
200v/50 cycles; electrical
plugs have two round prongs

🕐 **TIME:**
Six hours behind New York

🌐 **WEB RESOURCES:**
www.gohawaii.org
www.hvcb.org

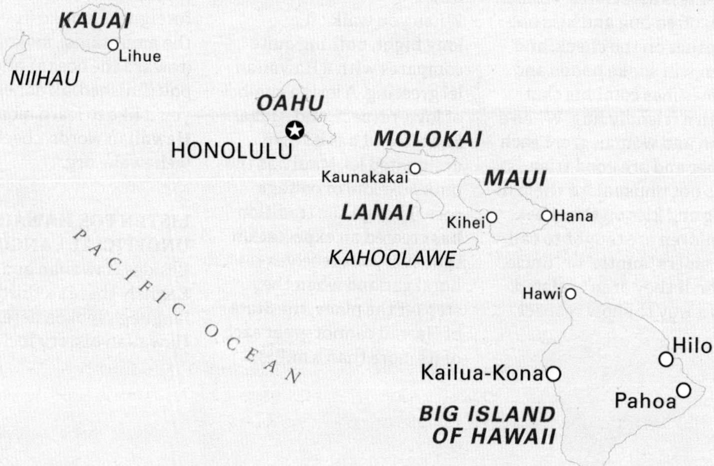

KAUAI
Lihue
NIIHAU

OAHU
HONOLULU
MOLOKAI
Kaunakakai
MAUI
LANAI
Kihei
Hana
KAHOOLAWE

PACIFIC OCEAN

Hawi

Hilo
Kailua-Kona
Pahoa
BIG ISLAND
OF HAWAII

Know Before You Go

Do they really hand you a lei when you arrive? What are some common Hawaiian phrases? How can you help protect the coral? Traveling to Hawaii is an easy adventure, but we've got tips to make your trip seamless and more meaningful. Below are all the answers to FAQs about Hawaii.

DON'T CALL IT "THE STATES"

Hawaii was admitted to the Union in 1959, so residents can be somewhat sensitive when visitors refer to their hometowns as "back in the States." Instead, refer to the contiguous 48 states as "the continent." You won't appear to be such a *malihini* (newcomer) when you do.

WELCOME ISLAND-STYLE GREETINGS

Hawaii is a friendly place, which is reflected in the day-to-day encounters with friends, family, and even business associates. Women will often hug and kiss one another on the cheek, and men will shake hands and sometimes combine that with a friendly hug. When a man and woman greet each other and are good friends, it is not unusual for them to hug and kiss on the cheek. Children are taught to call all elders "auntie" or "uncle," even if they aren't related; it's a way to show respect.

LOOK, BUT DON'T TOUCH

Help protect Hawaii's wildlife by loving it from a distance. Stay at least 10 feet away from turtles on land and in the water, and 50 feet from monk seals, wherever you encounter them. Though they may not look it, corals are alive and fragile; harming them also harms the habitat for reef fish and other marine life. Avoid touching or stepping on coral, and take extra care when entering and exiting the water.

ENJOY A FRESH FLOWER LEI

When you walk off a long flight, nothing quite compares with a Hawaiian lei greeting. A lei is a symbol of love, respect, and Aloha. Each Island has its own designated lei, Maui has the pink *Lokelani* or cottage rose. Though the tradition has created an expectation that everyone receives this floral garland when they step off the plane, the State of Hawaii cannot greet each of its more than 8 million annual visitors. If you've booked a vacation with a wholesaler or tour company, a lei greeting might be included in your package. If not, it's easy to arrange a lei greeting before you arrive at Kahului Airport with Ali'i Greeting Service (☎ 808/877–7088; ⊕ aliigreetingservice.com). An orchid lei is considered standard and costs about $29 per person. You can tuck a single flower behind your ear; a flower behind the left ear means you are in a relationship or unavailable, while the right ear indicates you are looking for love.

APPRECIATE THE HAWAIIAN LANGUAGE

Hawaiian and English are both official state languages, the latter being more prominent. However, making an effort to learn some Hawaiian words can be rewarding. Hawaiian words you are most likely to encounter during your visit to the Islands are *aloha* (hello and good-bye), *mahalo* (thank you), *keiki* (child), *haole* (Caucasian or foreigner), *mauka* (toward the mountains), *makai* (toward the ocean), and *pau* (finished, all done). If you'd like to learn more Hawaiian words, check out wehewehe.org.

LISTEN FOR HAWAII'S UNOFFICIAL LANGUAGE

Besides Hawaiian and English, there's a third language spoken here. Hawaiian history includes waves of immigrants, each bringing their native language. To communicate, they developed a dialect known as Hawaiian Pidgin English, or "Pidgin" for short. In 2015, the U.S. Census added Hawaiian Pidgin to the list of official languages in Hawaii. If you listen closely, you will know what is said by the inflections and body language. For an informative and sometimes hilarious view of Pidgin, check out *Pidgin to da Max* by Douglas Simonson and *Fax to da Max* by Jerry Hopkins. Both are available at most local bookstores in the Hawaiiana sections and various stores. While it's nice to appreciate this unique language, it's not wise to emulate it, as it can be considered disrespectful.

BE MINDFUL OF LOCAL CUSTOMS

If you're invited to the home of friends living in Hawaii (an ultimate compliment), bring an *omiyage* (small gift) and take off your shoes when you enter their house. Try to participate in a cultural festival during your stay in the Islands; there is no better way to get a glimpse of Hawaii's mosaic of cultures and traditions.

INSECTS AND PESTS

It's the tropics, so don't be surprised if you encounter an extra-large flying cockroach at night or the occasional mosquito buzzing around you during the day. Pack insect repellent and anti-itch spray. A rare but emerging disease in Hawaii, rat lungworm disease, can be contracted by accidental consumption of a slug or slug residue hidden in lettuce or other types of vulnerable produce. Never eat fruit that you pick up off the ground. Think twice about eating locally grown lettuce unless it was grown hydroponically.

CHECK THE WEATHER

Of all the islands in the Hawaiian Islands chain, the Big Island is the most diverse in terms of weather. The variety of elevations and the vast expanse of differing topography produce weather patterns that can vary from one town to the next on any given day. Take, for example, the seaside enclave of Puako near Kawaihae in South Kohala. It can get searing hot and windy one moment, while just a 15-minute drive up the highway in Waimea, it could be chilly "sweater weather." Some areas of the Big Island are incredibly rainy, like the entire town of Hilo; other areas stay relatively arid, such as the resort zones in South Kohala. At the higher elevations, such as in Volcano, it can get downright bone-chilling, with temperatures dropping into the low 40s on some nights. Pack accordingly and bring layers.

On Maui, it seems there's a natural wonder around every corner. But don't be caught off guard by the pretty vistas—the environment can change in an instant, and with little or no warning. Strong ocean currents, flash flooding, and rockslides are a real threat, especially during extreme weather events. If you're hiking somewhere like Haleakala National Park, you'll want to check the wind, rain, and snow conditions, as all three elements are common. The County of Maui offers safety tips for visitors (⊕ co.maui.hi.us/oceansafety), and it's a good idea to familiarize yourself with local conditions before heading out on any adventure.

Kauai's environment can change in an instant, and with little or no warning. Strong ocean currents, flash floods, and rockslides are a real threat, especially during extreme weather events. If you're hiking, consult wind and rain conditions and predictions. Hurricane season runs from June to November.

Getting Here and Around

Air

Flying time to Oahu or Maui is about 10 hours from New York, 8 hours from Chicago, and 5 hours from Los Angeles.

All the major airline carriers serving Hawaii fly direct to Honolulu; some also offer nonstops to Maui, Kauai, and the Big Island, though most flights to the latter two come from the West Coast only. Honolulu International Airport, although open-air and seemingly more casual than most major airports, can be very busy. Allow extra travel time during busy mornings and afternoons.

Plants and plant products are subject to regulation by the Department of Agriculture, both on entering and leaving Hawaii. Upon leaving, you must have your bags x-rayed and tagged at the airport's agricultural inspection station before proceeding to check-in. Pineapples and coconuts with the packer's agricultural inspection stamp pass freely; papayas and certain other fruits must be treated, inspected, and stamped. But most other fruits are banned for export to the U.S. mainland. Flowers pass except for citrus-related flowers, fruits, or parts; jade vine; and mauna loa. Also banned are insects, snails, soil, cotton, cacti, sugarcane, and all berry plants.

Bringing your dog or cat with you is a tricky process and not something to be done lightly. Hawaii is a rabies-free state and requires animals to pass strict quarantine rules, which you can find online at Most airlines do not allow pets to travel in the cabin on flights to Hawaii (though Alaska Airlines and Hawaiian Airlines are notable exceptions). If specific pre- and post-arrival requirements are met, most animals qualify for a five-day-or-less quarantine.

AIRPORTS

All of Hawaii's major islands have their own airports, but Honolulu's International Airport (officially known as Daniel K. Inouye International Airport) is the main stopover for most domestic and international flights. From Honolulu, there are flights to the Neighbor Islands almost every half-hour from early morning until evening. In addition, some carriers offer nonstop service directly from the mainland to Maui, Kauai, and the Big Island on a limited basis.

BIG ISLAND OF HAWAII

Those flying to the Big Island regularly land at one of two fields. Ellison Onizuka Kona International Airport at Keahole, on the west side, serves Kailua-Kona, Keauhou, the Kohala Coast, North Kohala, Waimea, and points south. Hilo International Airport is more appropriate for those planning visits based on the east side of the island. Waimea-Kohala Airport, called Kamuela Airport by residents, is used primarily for private flights between islands but offers daily flights via Mokulele Airlines. Check with your hotel to see if it runs an airport shuttle. If you're not renting a car, you can choose from multiple taxi companies serving the Hilo Airport. The approximate taxi rate is $3 for the initial ⅛th mile, plus $3 for each additional mile, with surcharges for waiting time (40¢ per minute) and baggage ($1 per bag) for up to six people. The local Hele-On county bus also services the Hilo airport. At the Kona airport, taxis are available. SpeediShuttle also offers transportation between the airport and hotels, resorts, and condominium complexes from Waimea to Keauhou. Uber and Lyft have designated pickup areas at the Kona and Hilo airports.

OAHU

The Daniel K. Inouye International Airport (HNL) is roughly 20 minutes (9 miles) west of Waikiki (60 minutes during rush hour) and is served by most of the major domestic and international carriers. To travel to other islands from Honolulu, you can depart from either the interisland terminal or the commuter terminal, located in two separate structures adjacent to the main overseas terminal building. A free Wiki-Wiki shuttle bus operates between terminals.

KAUAI

On Kauai, visitors fly into Lihue Airport (LIH), on the East Side of the island. Some major hotels provide airport shuttles to and from Lihue Airport. In addition, travelers who've booked a tour with Kauai Island Tours, Roberts Hawaii, IMI Tours, or Polynesian Adventure Tours will be picked up at the airport. Speed-iShuttle offers transportation between the airport and hotels, resorts, and time-share complexes on the island. Another option is to hire a taxi or limousine. Cabs are available curbside at baggage claim. Cab fares to locations around the island are estimated as follows: Poipu $35–$42, Wailua–Waipouli $18–$20, Lihue–Kukui Grove $10-$15, Princeville–Haena $75–$95. Kauai Luxury Transportation & Tours offers service to Lihue Airport. Uber and Lyft are somewhat recent arrivals on the island. You can expect to pay around $75–$80 for a ride from the airport to Princeville (approximately 30 miles).

MAUI

Kahului Airport handles major airlines and interisland flights; it's the only airport on Maui with direct service from the mainland. Kapalua–West Maui Airport is served by Hawaiian and Mokulele airlines. If you're staying in West Maui and flying in from another island, you can avoid the hour drive from the Kahului Airport by flying into Kapalua–West Maui Airport. Hana Airport in East Maui is small; Mokulele Airlines offers daily flights between Kahului and Hana.

If you're not renting a car, you'll need to take a taxi, rideshare, or SpeediShuttle if your hotel is along its route. Maui Airport Taxi & Shuttle serves the Kahului Airport. Cab fares for up to five passengers to locations around the island are estimated as follows: Kaanapali $79, Kahului $15, Kapalua $99, Kihei $45, Lahaina $69, Maalaea $35, Makena $59, Wailea $49, and Wailuku $20. It will cost more, but the shuttles can accommodate up to 12 passengers. SpeediShuttle offers transportation between the Kahului Airport and hotels, resorts, and condominium complexes throughout Maui. There is an online reservation and fare-quote system for information and bookings. You can expect to pay around $78 per couple to Kaanapali and $55 to Wailea.

MOLOKAI AND LANAI

Molokai's Hoolehua Airport and Lanai Airport are small and centrally located. Both rural airports handle a limited number of flights per day. There's a small airfield at Kalaupapa on Molokai and required visitor permits are available via tour companies listed on the National Park Service website ⊕ nps.gov. Visitors coming from the U.S. mainland to these islands must first stop on Oahu or Maui and change to an interisland flight. Lanai Airport has a federal agricultural inspection station, so guests departing to the mainland can check luggage directly.

Getting Here and Around

Bicycle

Biki Bikeshare Hawaii (⊕ *gobiki.org*) has 1,300 aqua, cruiser-style bicycles at 130 solar-powered stations in the Waikiki and Honolulu corridor. You can unlock a bike from a station using your credit card, without having to sign up for the member pass. A one-way fare costs $4.50 for 30 minutes. There's also a multistop pass for $30, which gets you 300 minutes of riding time. ■TIP➔ **There is a $50 security hold placed on your card when you check out a bike.**

Bus

BIG ISLAND OF HAWAII

Although public transportation isn't very practical for the average vacationer, depending on where you're staying, you can take advantage of the affordable Hawaii County Mass Transit Agency's Hele-On Bus, which travels several routes throughout the island. Mostly serving local commuters, the Hele-On Bus costs $2 per person (students and senior citizens pay $1). Just wait at a scheduled stop for the next bus. A one-way journey between Hilo and Kona takes about four hours. There's regular service in and around downtown Hilo, Kailua-Kona, Waimea, North and South Kohala, Honokaa, and Pahoa. Nevertheless, some routes are served only once a day, so if you are planning on using the bus, study up carefully before assuming the bus serves your area.

Visitors staying in Hilo can take advantage of the Transit Agency's Shared Ride Taxi program, which provides door-to-door transportation in the area. A one-way fare is $2, and a book of 15 coupons can be purchased for $30. Visitors to

Kona can also take advantage of free trolleys operated by local shopping centers.

KAUAI

On Kauai, the County Transportation Agency operates the Kauai Bus, which provides service between Hanalei and Kekaha. It also provides limited service to the airport and to Koloa and Poipu. The fare is $2 for adults, and frequent-rider passes are available. The new North Shore Shuttle now operates to Kee Beach from either Waipa or Princeville, depending on road construction. Updates about fares, routes, and a hop-on, hop-off option are posted at ⊕ *gohaena.com*. The website ⊕ *getaroundkauai.com* has information about resources for sustainable transportation choices.

MAUI

Maui Bus, operated by the tour company Roberts Hawaii, offers 12 routes in and between various Central, South, and West Maui communities. You can travel in and around Wailuku, Kahului, Lahaina, Kaanapali, Kapalua, Kihei, Wailea, Maalaea, the North Shore (Paia), and Upcountry (including Kula, Pukalani, Makawao, Haliimaile, and Haiku). The Upcountry and Haiku Islander routes include a stop at Kahului Airport. All routes cost $2 per boarding; children five and under ride free.

OAHU

Getting around by bus is convenient and affordable on Oahu, particularly in the most heavily touristed areas of Waikiki. Options include Honolulu's municipal transit system, affectionately known as TheBus; the Waikiki Trolleys, brass-trimmed, open-air, hop-on-hop-off vehicles that look like trolleys or large double-decker buses; and brightly painted private buses, some of them free, that shuttle you to such commercial attractions as dinner cruises, shopping centers, and the like.

TheBus is one of the best bargains on Oahu. You can use it to travel around the island or just down Kalakaua Avenue for $2.75. Buses stop in Waikiki every 10–15 minutes to take passengers to nearby shopping areas. Although free transfers have been discontinued, you can purchase a one-day pass for $5.50. Just ask the driver when boarding. Exact change is required, and dollar bills are accepted. Monthly passes cost $70.

The company's website has timetables, route maps, and real-time bus tracking, or you can download the free DaBus2 app for your smartphone. You can call to speak with a representative for route advice, or you can find privately published booklets at most drugstores and other convenience outlets.

The Waikiki Trolley has three lines—each beginning and ending in Waikiki—and dozens of stops that allow you to plan your own itinerary. A one-day pass costs $25 ($5 for the Pink Line) for a single line and $45 for all lines. Four-day ($65) and seven-day ($75) all-line passes are also available.

The Ocean/Diamond Head Tour (Blue Line) stops at the Duke Kahanamoku statue; along Diamond Head and Kahala; the Halona Blow Hole; Sea Life Park; and Koko Marina. As its name suggests, the Ala Moana Shopping Tour (Pink Line) goes to the Ala Moana Center, a sprawling outdoor mall. The City Arts District Tour (Red Line) travels between Waikiki, Chinatown, and Kakaako and includes stops at the Honolulu Museum of Art, the capitol, Iolani Palace, Punchbowl Crater, and Ala Moana.

Car

BIG ISLAND

It's essential to rent a car when visiting the Big Island. As the name suggests, it's a very big island, and it takes a while to get from one destination to another.

Fortunately, when you circle the island by car, you are treated to miles and miles of wondrous vistas of every possible description. In addition to using standard compass directions such as east and west, Hawaii residents often refer to places as being either *mauka* (toward the mountains) or *makai* (toward the ocean).

It's difficult to get lost along the main roads of the Big Island. Although their names may challenge the visitor's tongue, most roads are well marked; in rural areas look for mile marker numbers. Free publications containing basic road maps are given out at car rental agencies, but if you are doing a lot of driving, invest about $4 in the standard Big Island map available at local retailers. GPS might be unreliable in remote areas.

Driving the roads on the Big Island can be dangerous, as there's no margin for error to avoid a head-on collision. Distracted drivers are all too common. Most roads and main highways are two lanes with no shoulders; if there is a shoulder to access, it might be riddled with rocks, debris, and potholes. Speeding and illegal passing are frequent occurrences along winding, remote roads. In addition, most roads are not well lit at night. Fatalities can happen at a moment's notice, whether on the main highway from the airport to the resorts, the Saddle Road, the upper road from Waimea to Hawi, or on the Hawaii Belt Road that wraps around the island. During Ironman week, cyclists pose additional potential hazards on all

Getting Here and Around

roads in West Hawaii. Use extreme caution when driving on the Big Island, and of course, do not drive after drinking.

For those who want to travel from the west side to the east side, or vice versa, the rerouted and repaved Saddle Road, known as the Daniel K. Inouye Highway, is a nice shortcut across the middle of the island. This is especially convenient if you are staying on the west side of the island and wish to visit the east side. Hazardous conditions such as fog and speeding are common.

KAUAI

The independent way to experience all of Kauai's stunning beauty is to get in a car and explore. The 15-mile stretch of Napali Coast, with its breathtaking, verdant-green sheer cliffs, is the only outer part of the island that's not accessible by car. Otherwise, one main road can get you from Barking Sands Beach on the West Side to Haena on the North Shore.

While driving on Kauai, you will come across several one-lane bridges. If you are the first to approach a bridge, the car on the other side will wait while you cross. If a car on the other side is closer to the bridge, then you should wait while the driver crosses. If you're enjoying the island's dramatic views, pull over to the shoulder so you don't block traffic.

MAUI

Should you plan to do any sightseeing on Maui, it's best to rent a car. Even if all you want to do is relax at your resort, you may want to hop in the car to check out one of the Island's popular restaurants. Many of Maui's roads are two lanes, so allow plenty of time to your next destination. Check the local traffic reports and google maps for delays. During morning and afternoon rush hours, traffic can be awful. Morning (6:30–9:30 am) and afternoon (3:30–6:30 pm) rush-hour traffic around Kahului, Paia, Kihei, and Lahaina can cause significant delays, so use caution. When returning your rental car, give yourself about 3½ to 4 hours before your transpacific flight departure time due to traffic and long airport security lines. Remember to drive with Aloha. On Molokai and Lanai, four-wheel-drive vehicles are recommended for exploring off the beaten path. Many of the roads are poorly paved or unpaved.

OAHU

Thanks to public transit, you don't need a car in Waikiki. Elsewhere on the island, though, a car can be invaluable. Avoid the obvious tourist cars—candy-color convertibles, for example—and never leave anything valuable inside, even if you've locked the vehicle. A GPS (either on your smartphone or a separate device) will help guide you through Oahu's sometimes-confusing streets. Reserve in advance to ensure availability (rentals can book up, especially during holidays and summer breaks) and to get the best rates. Also, be prepared to pay for parking; most hotels in Honolulu (and many outside of Honolulu) charge for parking. Except for one area around Kaena Point, major highways follow Oahu's shoreline and traverse the island at two points. Rush-hour traffic (6:30–9:30 am and 3 or 3:30–6 pm) can be frustrating around Honolulu and the outlying areas. Winter swells also bring heavy traffic to the North Shore, as people hoping to catch the surfing action clog the two-lane Kamehameha Highway. Parking along many streets is curtailed during these times, and tow-away zones are strictly enforced. Read curbside signs before leaving your vehicle, even at a meter.

GASOLINE

National chains like 76, 7-Eleven, and Shell are ubiquitous, and accept all major credit cards right at the pump or inside the station. Gasoline is generally more expensive than on the mainland United States (other than in California). Neighbor Islands have higher gasoline prices than Oahu.

In rural areas, it's not unusual for gas stations to close early. If you see that your tank is getting low, don't take any chances; fill up at the nearest station.

ROAD CONDITIONS

It's difficult to get lost in most of Hawaii. Although their names may challenge a visitor's tongue, roads and streets are well marked; just watch out for the many one-way streets in Waikiki. Keep an eye open for the Hawaii Visitors and Convention Bureau's red-caped King Kamehameha signs, which mark attractions and scenic spots. Free publications containing high-quality road maps can be found on all islands. And, of course, a GPS or your passenger's smartphone are great options for finding your way around, too.

Asking for directions will almost always produce a helpful explanation from the locals, but you should be prepared for a Hawaiian term or two. Instead of using compass directions, remember that Hawaii residents refer to places as being either *mauka* (toward the mountains) or *makai* (toward the ocean).

Many of Hawaii's roads are two-lane highways with limited shoulders—and yes, even in paradise, there is traffic, especially during the morning and afternoon rush hour. In Hawaii, turning right on a red light is legal, except where noted. Hawaii has a strict seat-belt law that applies to both drivers and passengers.

The fine for not wearing a seat belt is $102. Mobile phone use is strictly limited to talking on a hands-free mobile device, and only for those over 18. Many police officers drive their own cars while on duty, strapping the warning lights to the roof. Because of the color, locals call them "blue lights."

Use caution during heavy downpours, especially if you see signs warning of falling rocks. If you're enjoying views from the road or need to study a map, pull over to the side. Remember the aloha spirit when you are driving: allow other cars to merge; don't honk (it's considered extremely rude in the Islands); leave a comfortable distance between your car and the car ahead of you; use your headlights, especially during sunrise and sunset; and use your turn signals.

ROADSIDE EMERGENCIES

If you have an accident or car trouble, call the roadside assistance number on your rental car contract or AAA Help. If you find that your car has been broken into or stolen, report it immediately to your rental car company and they can assist you. Call 911 for any emergency.

RULES OF THE ROAD

Be sure to buckle up, as Hawaii has a strictly enforced mandatory seat-belt law for front- and backseat passengers. Children under four must be in a car seat (available from car-rental agencies), and children ages four to seven must be seated in a booster seat or child safety seat with restraint such as a lap and shoulder belt. Hawaii also prohibits texting or talking on the phone (unless you are over 18 and using a hands-free device) while driving. The highway speed limit is usually 55 mph. In-town traffic travels 25–40 mph. Jaywalking is not uncommon, so watch for pedestrians, especially in congested

Getting Here and Around

areas such as Waikiki and downtown Honolulu. Unauthorized use of a parking space reserved for persons with disabilities can net you a $250–$500 fine.

Hawaii's drivers are generally courteous, and you rarely hear a horn. People will slow down and let you into traffic with a wave of the hand. A friendly wave back is customary. If a driver sticks a hand out the window in a fist with the thumb and pinky sticking straight out, this is a good thing: it's the *shaka*, the Hawaiian symbol for "hang loose," and is often used to say "thanks."

CAR RENTALS

If you plan to do lots of sightseeing, it's best to rent a car. Even if all you want to do is relax at your resort, you may want to hop in the car to check out a popular restaurant. All the big national rental car agencies have locations throughout Hawaii. There also are several local rental car companies so be sure to compare prices before you book. While in the Islands, you can rent anything from an econobox to a Ferrari. On the Big Island, Lanai, and Molokai, four-wheel-drive vehicles are recommended for exploring off the beaten path. It's wise to make reservations far in advance and make sure that a confirmed reservation guarantees you a car, especially if visiting during peak seasons or for major conventions or sporting events.

Rates begin at about $30 to $40 a day for an economy car with air-conditioning, automatic transmission, and unlimited mileage, depending on your pickup location. This does not include the airport concession fee, general excise tax, rental vehicle surcharge, or vehicle license fee. When you reserve a car, ask about cancellation penalties and drop-off charges should you plan to pick up the car in one location and return it to another.

In Hawaii you must be 21 years of age to rent a car, and you must have a valid driver's license and a major credit card. Those under 25 will pay a daily surcharge of $10 to $30. Your unexpired mainland driver's license is valid for rental for up to 90 days. Request car seats and extras such as GPS when you make your reservation. Car seats and boosters range from about $10 to $15 per day.

Essentials

Dining

Whether you're looking for a dinner for two in a romantic oceanfront dining room or a family get-together in a hole-in-the-wall serving traditional Hawaiian fare like *kalua* (cooked in an underground oven) pig, you'll find it throughout the Islands. When it comes to eating, Hawaii has something for every taste bud and every budget. With chefs using locally grown fruits and vegetables, vegetarians often have many exciting choices for their meals. And because Hawaii is a popular destination for families, restaurants almost always have a children's menu. When making a reservation at your hotel's dining room, ask about free or reduced-price meals for children.

MEALS AND MEALTIMES

Breakfast is usually served from 6 or 7 am to 9:30 or 10 am.

Lunch typically runs from 11:30 am to around 1:30 or 2 pm and will include salads, sandwiches, and lighter fare. The "plate lunch," a favorite of many locals, usually consists of an Asian protein—like shoyu chicken, seared ahi or teriyaki beef—served with two scoops of white rice and a scoop of macaroni or potato salad.

Dinner is usually served from 5 to 9 pm and, depending on the restaurant, can be a simple or lavish affair. Stick to the chefs' specials if you can, because they usually represent the best of the season. *Poke* (marinated raw tuna) is a local specialty and can often be found on *pupu* (appetizer) menus.

Meals in resort areas are pricey and only sometimes excellent. The restaurants we include are the best in each price category. Unless otherwise noted, the restaurants listed are open daily for lunch and dinner.

RESERVATIONS

Regardless of where you are, it's a good idea to make a reservation if you can. In some places, it's expected. We only mention reservations specifically when they are essential or when they are not accepted. For popular restaurants, book as far ahead as you can (often a month or more), and reconfirm as soon as you arrive. Large parties should always call ahead to check the reservations policy.

WINE, BEER, AND SPIRITS

Hawaii has a new generation of micro-breweries, including on-site microbreweries at many restaurants. The drinking age in Hawaii is 21 years of age, and a photo ID must be presented to purchase alcoholic beverages. Bars are open until 2 am; venues with a cabaret license can stay open until 4 am. No matter what you might see in the local parks, drinking alcohol in public parks or on the beaches is illegal. It's also illegal to have open containers of alcohol in motor vehicles.

⊕ Health

In addition to being the Aloha State, Hawaii is known as the Health State. The life expectancy here is 83 years, the longest in the nation. Balmy weather makes it easy to remain active year-round, and the low-stress aloha attitude certainly contributes to general well-being. When you are visiting the Islands, however, there are a few health issues to keep in mind.

The Hawaii State Department of Health recommends that you drink 16 ounces of water per hour to avoid dehydration when hiking or spending time in the sun. Use zinc-based sunblock, wear UV-reflective sunglasses, and protect your head with a visor or hat for shade. If you're not acclimated to warm, humid

Essentials

weather, allow time for rest stops and refreshments. When visiting freshwater streams, be aware of the tropical disease leptospirosis, which is spread by animal urine and carried into streams and mud. Symptoms include fever, headache, nausea, and red eyes. If left untreated, it can cause liver and kidney failure, respiratory failure, internal bleeding, and even death. To avoid this, don't swim or wade in freshwater streams or ponds if you have open sores and don't drink from any freshwater streams or ponds. Wash all locally grown leafy vegetables thoroughly to protect yourself against rat lungworm disease, which is rare but extremely serious. The Islands have their share of bugs and insects that enjoy the tropical climate as much as visitors do. Most are harmless but annoying. When planning to spend time outdoors in hiking areas, wear long-sleeve shirts and pants and use mosquito repellent. In very damp or rocky places, you may encounter the dreaded local centipede. Blue or brown in color, centipedes can grow as long as eight inches. If surprised, they might sting, which can be painful and last for days. If you are stung by a centipede, wash the site of your bite thoroughly to prevent infection. When camping, shake out your sleeping bag before climbing in, and check your shoes in the morning, as centipedes like warm, moist places. If planning on hiking or traveling in remote areas, always carry a first-aid kit and appropriate medications for sting reactions.

When visiting freshwater streams, be aware of the tropical disease leptospirosis, which is spread by animal urine and carried into streams and mud. Symptoms include fever, headache, nausea, and red eyes; they may not appear immediately. If left untreated, it can cause

liver and kidney damage, respiratory failure, internal bleeding, and even death. To avoid this, don't swim or wade in freshwater streams or ponds if you have open sores, and don't drink from any freshwater streams or ponds, especially after heavy rains. On the Islands, fog is a rare occurrence, but there often can be "vog," an airborne haze of gases released from volcanic vents on Hawaii Island. During certain weather conditions such as "Kona Winds," the vog can settle over the Islands and wreak havoc with respiratory conditions, especially asthma or emphysema. If susceptible, stay indoors and get emergency assistance if needed.

COVID-19

Although COVID-19 brought travel to a virtual standstill for most of 2020 and 2021, vaccinations have made travel possible and safe again. Remaining requirements and restrictions—including those for unvaccinated travelers—can, however, vary from one place (or even business) to the next.

 Hours

Even people in paradise have to work. Generally, local business hours are weekdays 8–5. Banks are usually open Monday–Thursday 8:30–4 and until 6 on Friday. Some banks have Saturday morning hours.

Many self-serve gas stations stay open around the clock, with full-service stations usually open from around 7 am until 9 pm. The larger U.S. post offices are open weekdays 8:30 am–4:30 pm and Saturday 8:30–noon. Check operating hours for smaller post offices.

Most museums generally open their doors between 9 am and 10 am and stay open until 5 pm Tuesday–Saturday. Many museums operate with afternoon hours only on Sunday and close on Monday. Visitor-attraction hours vary throughout the state, but most sights are open daily, with the exception of major holidays such as Christmas. Check local publications upon arrival for attraction hours and schedules if visiting over holiday periods. The local dailies carry a listing of local cultural events for those time periods.

Stores in resort areas sometimes open as early as 8, with shopping-center opening hours varying from 9:30 to 10 on weekdays and Saturday, a bit later on Sunday. Bigger malls stay open until 9 weekdays and Saturday and close at 5 on Sunday. Boutiques in resort areas may stay open to catch after-dinner shoppers.

🛏 Lodging

Hawaii truly offers something for everyone. Are you looking for a luxurious oceanfront resort loaded with amenities, an intimate two-room bed and breakfast tucked away in a lush rain forest, a house with a pool and incredible views for your extended family, a condominium just steps from the 18th hole, or even a campsite at a national park? You can find all these and more throughout the Islands.

Most hotels and other lodgings require you to give your credit card details before they will confirm your reservation. Get confirmation in writing and have a copy of it handy when you check in. Be sure you understand the hotel's cancellation policy. Some places allow you to cancel without any kind of penalty—even if you prepaid to secure a discounted rate—if you cancel at least 24 hours in advance.

Others require you to cancel a week in advance or penalize you the cost of one night. Small inns and bed and breakfasts are most likely to require you to cancel far in advance. Most hotels allow children under a certain age to stay in their parents' room at no extra charge, but others charge for them as adults; find out the cutoff age for discounts.

Hotel reviews have been shortened. For full information, visit www.Fodors.com.

BED-AND-BREAKFASTS

For many travelers, nothing compares to the personal service and guest interaction offered at bed and breakfasts. There are hundreds of them throughout the Islands; many even invite their guests to enjoy complimentary wine tastings and activities such as lei making and basket weaving. Each island's website also features a listing of member B&Bs that are individually owned.

CONDOMINIUM AND HOUSE RENTALS

Vacation rentals are perfect for couples, families, and friends traveling together who like the convenience of staying at a home away from home. Properties managed by individual owners can be found on online vacation-rental listing directories such as HomeAway, Vacation Rentals By Owners (VRBO), and Airbnb, as well as on the visitors bureau website for each island. There also are several Islands-based management companies with vacation rentals.

Compare companies, as some offer Internet specials and free night stays when booking. Policies vary, but most require a minimum stay, usually greater during peak travel seasons.

Essentials

💼 Packing

Hawaii is casual: sandals, bathing suits, and comfortable, informal clothing are the norm. Year-round, clothing of cotton or rayon proves very comfortable. Beach-going women love to wear the *pareu,* or sarong. Men will look right at home in T-shirts and board shorts.

One of the most important things to pack is sunscreen. Some traditional sunscreens are harming coral reefs; state-wide legislation now bans the sale of sunscreens that contain oxybenzone and octinoxate. So if you do want to use reef-safe sunscreen, buy products that are zinc-based or reef approved. Even better? Buy a long-sleeved rash guard, available at all major retailers. That way, you have no gunky lotions or harmful chemicals to deal with while out enjoying the reefs. Hats and sunglasses offer important sun protection, too. Both are easy to find in island shops if you don't bring them with you. All major hotels in Hawaii (and most small ones) provide beach towels.

Only a few upscale restaurants require a jacket for dinner. The aloha shirt is accepted dress in Hawaii for business and most social occasions. Shorts are acceptable daytime attire, along with a T-shirt or polo shirt. There's no need to buy expensive sandals on the mainland—here you can get flip-flops (called "slippers" by locals) for under $5. Golfers should remember that many courses have dress codes requiring a collared shirt; call courses for details. If you're not prepared, you can buy appropriate clothing at resort pro shops. If you're visiting in winter, bring a sweater or light- to medium-weight jacket. A polar fleece pullover is ideal and makes a great impromptu pillow.

If your vacation plans include Hilo or Maui's northern coast, you'll want to pack a compact umbrella and a light poncho. And if you'll be visiting Hawaii Volcanoes National Park or Haleakala National Par, make sure you pack appropriately, as weather ranges from hot and dry along the shores to chilly, foggy, and rainy at the summits. Sturdy boots are recommended if you'll be hiking or camping in either park.

➕ Safety

Hawaii is generally a safe tourist destination, but it's still wise to stick to the same commonsense safety precautions you would normally follow in your own hometown. Hotel and visitor-center staff can provide information should you decide to head out on your own to more remote areas. Because many of the models and colors are obvious, rental cars are magnets for break-ins, so don't leave any valuables in them, not even in a locked trunk. Thieves watch areas such as beach parking lots, and can pop your hood and be gone in 60 seconds. Avoid poorly lighted areas, beach parks, and isolated areas after dark as a precaution. When hiking, stay on marked trails, no matter how alluring the temptation might be to stray; changing weather conditions can cause landscapes to become muddy and slippery, so staying on marked trails lessens the possibility of a fall or getting lost. This is especially true on the wetter, windward side. Heed warnings about dangerous currents in rivers and swimming holes. Ocean safety is of the utmost importance when visiting any island destination. Visitors often get into trouble because the beach looks benign and they can't wait to get in the water, so they throw caution to the wind and jump in. Avoid swimming if the conditions seem rough or dangerous. Most beaches on the Big Island do not have lifeguards. Unfortunately, most of the drowning deaths that occur in Hawaii are visitors. Winter brings higher, more dangerous surf, so please exercise caution. Don't swim alone; follow the international signage posted at beaches, which alerts swimmers to strong currents, man-of-war or box jellyfish, sharp coral, high surf, sharks, and dangerous shore breaks. At coastal lookouts along cliff tops, heed the signs indicating that waves can climb over the ledges. If there are lifeguards, ask about current conditions, and if the red flags are up, or if a high surf advisory has been issued by the National Weather Service indicating swimming and surfing are risky, don't go in. Waters that look calm on the surface can harbor strong currents and undertows, and sometimes people who were "just wading" have been dragged out to sea and never seen again. When in doubt, don't go out!

Women traveling alone are generally safe in Hawaii, but always follow the same safety precautions you would use in any major destination. When booking hotels, request rooms closest to the elevator, and always keep your hotel room door and balcony doors locked. Stay away from isolated areas after dark. If you stay out late at a bar, use caution when exiting and returning to your car or lodging; most establishments will be glad to give you an escort to your car.

Taxes

Hawaii does not have a state sales tax, but individual islands do. Businesses on the Big Island collect a 4.7120% general excise tax on all purchases including food and services, Kauai County and Maui has a 4.5% sales tax on all purchases including food, and 4.7% will be tacked onto goods and services you purchase on Oahu. The state sales tax plus the hotel room tax (13.25%) add approximately 18% to your hotel bill. A $5-per-day road tax is assessed on each rental car ($3 with Hawaii driver's license).

Tipping

As this is a major vacation destination and many of the people who work in the service industry rely on tips to supplement their wages, tipping is not only common, but expected. Consider a tip of 18% to 20% for excellent restaurant service, even at casual eateries. It's customary to tip all service folk at hotels and resorts, from valets to housekeepers. Keeping a stash of "singles" in your wallet or handbag makes this easy.

Hawaiian Vocabulary

Although an understanding of Hawaiian is by no means required on a trip to the Aloha State, a *malihini*, or newcomer, will find plenty of opportunities to pick up a few of the local words and phrases. Traditional names and expressions are widely used in the Islands. You're likely to read or hear at least a few words each day of your stay.

Simplifying the learning process is the fact that the Hawaiian language contains only seven consonants—*H, K, L, M, N, P, W,* and the silent *'okina,* or glottal stop, written '—plus one or more of the five vowels. All syllables, and therefore all words, end in a vowel. Each vowel, with the exception of a few diphthongized double vowels, such as *au* (pronounced "ow") or *ai* (pronounced "eye"), is pronounced separately. Thus *'Iolani* is four syllables (ee-oh-la-nee), not three (yo-la-nee). Although some Hawaiian words have only vowels, most also contain some consonants, but consonants are never doubled.

Pronunciation is simple. Pronounce *A* "ah" as in *father; E* "ay" as in *weigh; I* "ee" as in *marine; O* "oh" as in *no; U* "oo" as in *true.*

Consonants mirror their English equivalents, with the exception of *W.* When the letter begins any syllable other than the first one in a word, it is usually pronounced as a *V. 'Awa,* the Polynesian drink, is pronounced "ava," *'ewa* is pronounced "eva."

Almost all long Hawaiian words are combinations of shorter words; they are not difficult to pronounce if you segment them. *Kalaniana'ole,* the highway running east from Honolulu, is easily understood as *Kalani ana 'ole.* Apply the standard pronunciation rules—the stress falls on the next-to-last syllable of most two- or three-syllable Hawaiian words—and Kalaniana'ole Highway is as easy to say as Main Street.

Now about that fish. Try *humu-humu nuku-nuku āpu a'a.*

The other unusual element in Hawaiian language is the *kahakō,* or macron, written as a short line (ˉ) placed over a vowel. Like the accent (´) in Spanish, the kahakō puts emphasis on a syllable that would normally not be stressed. The most familiar example is probably *Waikīkī.* With no macrons, the stress would fall on the middle syllable; with only one macron, on the last syllable, the stress would fall on the first and last syllables. Some words become plural with the addition of a macron, often on a syllable that would have been stressed anyway. No Hawaiian word becomes plural with the addition of an *S,* since that letter does not exist in the language.

Note that Hawaiian diacritical marks are not printed in this guide.

PIDGIN
You may hear Pidgin English, the unofficial language of Hawaii. It is a Creole language, with its own grammar, evolved from the mixture of English, Hawaiian, Japanese, Portuguese, and other languages spoken in 19th-century Hawaii, and it is heard everywhere.

GLOSSARY
What follows is a glossary of some of the most commonly used Hawaiian words. Hawaiian residents appreciate visitors who at least try to pick up the local language.

'a'ā: rough, crumbling lava, contrasting with *pāhoehoe,* which is smooth.

'ae: yes.

aikane: friend.

āina: land.

akamai: smart, clever, possessing savoir faire.

akua: god.

ala: a road, path, or trail.

ali'i: a Hawaiian chief, a member of the chiefly class.

aloha: love, affection, kindness; also a salutation meaning both greetings and farewell.

'ānuenue: rainbow.

'a'ole: no.

'apōpō: tomorrow.

'auwai: a ditch.

auwē: alas, woe is me!

'ehu: a red-haired Hawaiian.

'ewa: in the direction of 'Ewa plantation, west of Honolulu.

hala: the pandanus tree, whose leaves (*lau hala*) are used to make baskets and plaited mats.

hālau: school.

hale: a house.

hale pule: church, house of worship.

hana: to work.

haole: foreigner. Since the first foreigners were Caucasian, *haole* now means a Caucasian person.

hapa: a part, sometimes a half; often used as a short form of *hapa haole*, to mean a person who is part-Caucasian.

hau'oli: to rejoice. *Hau'oli Makahiki Hou* means Happy New Year. *Hau'oli lā hānau* means Happy Birthday.

heiau: an outdoor stone platform; an ancient Hawaiian place of worship.

he mea iki or **he mea 'ole:** you're welcome.

holo: to run.

holoholo: to go for a walk, ride, or sail.

holokū: a long Hawaiian dress, somewhat fitted, with a yoke and a train. It was worn at court, and at least one local translates the word as "expensive muumuu."

holomū: a post–World War II cross between a *holokū* and a mu'umu'u, less fitted than the former but less voluminous than the latter, and having no train.

honi: to kiss; a kiss. A phrase that some tourists may find useful, quoted from a popular hula, is *Honi Ka'ua Wikiwiki:* Kiss me quick!

honu: turtle.

ho'omalimali: flattery, a deceptive "line," bunk, baloney, hooey.

huhū: angry.

hui: a group, club, or assembly. A church may refer to its congregation as a *hui* and a social club may be called a *hui*.

hukilau: a seine; a communal fishing party in which everyone helps to drive the fish into a huge net, pull it in, and divide the catch.

hula: the dance of Hawaii.

iki: little.

ipo: sweetheart. Commonly seen as "ku'uipo," or "my sweetheart."

ka: the. This is the definite article for most singular words; for plural nouns, the definite article is usually *nā*. Since there is no *S* in Hawaiian, the article may be your only clue that a noun is plural.

Hawaiian Vocabulary

kahuna: a priest, doctor, or other trained person of old Hawaii, endowed with special professional skills that often included prophecy or other supernatural powers.

kai: the sea, saltwater.

kalo: the taro plant from whose root *poi* (paste) is made.

kamā'aina: literally, a child of the soil; it refers to people who were born in the Islands or have lived there for a long time.

kanaka: originally a man or humanity, it is now used to denote a male Hawaiian or part-Hawaiian, but is occasionally taken as a slur when used by non-Hawaiians. *Kanaka maoli* is used by some Native Hawaiian rights activists to embrace part-Hawaiians as well.

kāne: a man, a husband. If you see this word (or *kane*) on a door, it's the men's room.

kapa: also called by its Tahitian name, *tapa,* a cloth made of beaten bark and usually dyed and stamped with a repeat design.

kapakahi: crooked, cockeyed, uneven. You've got your hat on *kapakahi.*

kapu: keep out, prohibited. This is the Hawaiian version of the more widely known Tongan word *tabu* (taboo).

kēia lā: today.

keiki: a child; *keikikāne* is a boy, *keikiwahine* a girl.

kōkua: to help, assist. Often seen in signs like "Please *kōkua* and throw away your trash."

kona: the leeward side of the Islands, the direction (south) from which the *kona* wind and *kona* rain come.

kula: upland.

kuleana: a homestead or small plot of ground on which a family has been installed for some generations without necessarily owning it. By extension, *kuleana* is used to denote any area or department in which one has a special interest or prerogative. You'll hear it used this way: "If you want to hire a surfboard, see Moki; that's his *kuleana.*"

kupuna: grandparent; elder.

lā: sun.

lamalama: to fish with a torch.

lānai: a porch, a balcony, an outdoor living room.

lani: heaven, the sky.

lauhala: the leaf of the *hala,* or pandanus tree, widely used in handicrafts.

lei: a garland of flowers.

lōlō: feeble-minded, crazy.

luna: a plantation overseer or foreman.

mahalo: thank you.

mahina: moon.

makai: toward the ocean.

mālama: to take care of, preserve, protect

malihini: a newcomer to the Islands.

mana: the spiritual power that the Hawaiians believe inhabits all things and creatures.

manō: shark.

manuahi: free, gratis.

mauka: toward the mountains.

mauna: mountain.

mele: a Hawaiian song or chant, often of epic proportions.

Mele Kalikimaka: Merry Christmas (a transliteration from the English phrase).

Menehune: a Hawaiian pixie. The Menehune were a legendary race of little people who accomplished prodigious work, such as building fishponds and temples in the course of a single night.

moana: the ocean.

mu'umu'u: the voluminous dress in which the missionaries enveloped Hawaiian women. Culturally sensitive locals have embraced the Hawaiian spelling but often shorten the spoken word to "mu'u." Most English dictionaries include the spelling "muumuu."

nani: beautiful.

nui: big.

'ohana: family.

'ono: delicious.

pāhoehoe: smooth, unbroken, satiny lava.

palapala: document, printed matter.

pali: a cliff, precipice.

pānini: prickly pear cactus.

paniolo: a Hawaiian cowboy, a rough transliteration of *español*, the language of the Islands' earliest cowboys.

pau: finished, done.

pilikia: trouble. The Hawaiian word is much more widely used here than its English equivalent.

pū: large conch shell used to trumpet the start of luau and other special events.

puka: a hole.

pule: prayer, blessing. Often performed before a meal or event.

pupule: crazy, like the celebrated Princess Pupule. This word has replaced its English equivalent in local usage.

pu'u: volcanic cinder cone.

tūtū: grandmother

waha: mouth.

wahine: a female, a woman, a wife, and a sign on the ladies' room door; the plural form is *wāhine*.

wai: freshwater, as opposed to saltwater, which is *kai*.

wailele: waterfall.

wikiwiki: to hurry, hurry up (since this is a reduplication of *wiki*, quick, neither *W* is pronounced as a *V*).

2

Travel Smart HAWAIIAN VOCABULARY

Great Itineraries

Best of the Big Island in a Week

Experiencing the best of the Big Island requires some drive time, plus some downtime.

DAY 1: HISTORIC KAILUA VILLAGE

Start your first day in Kailua-Kona with a stroll around Historic Kailua Village. Eat breakfast or brunch at one of the ocean-front restaurants along Alii Drive. Stroll the seaside village's many gift stores, art galleries, and apparel boutiques. Historic landmarks include royal **Hulihee Palace** and the oldest Christian church in Hawaii, **Mokuaikaua Church.** In the afternoon, take a ride on the **Atlantis Submarine,** or take a sunset dinner sail with **Body Glove Cruises.**

Logistics: The village is walkable. There are paid and free lots behind the stores on the *mauka* (mountain) side of Alii Drive.

DAY 2: BEST KOHALA BEACHES

Head north to the beautiful sand beaches of the Kohala Coast. Check out **Anaehoomalu Bay** in Waikoloa Beach Resort. Not only can you rent beach amenities including kayaks or stand-up paddleboards, you'll also be near Queens' MarketPlace with its restaurants and shops. For lunch, try **Lava Lava Beach Club,** right on the beach at Anaehoomalu Bay. Head north to Kawaihae and visit **Puukohola Heiau National Historic Site,** where King Kamehameha I oversaw the building of a great temple. On the way back, make a stop at **Hapuna Beach State Recreation Area.**

Logistics: Parking is easy at Waikoloa Beach Resort. Distance and time traveled: 35 miles one-way, 40 minutes one-way, starting in Kailua-Kona. Car, via Queen Kaahumanu Highway.

Tips

- Book manta ray or kayaking tours in advance, as they are popular.

- Plan your time at Hawaii Volcanoes National Park carefully so you can see what you want.

DAY 3: KEALAKEKUA BAY

In South Kona, **Kealakekua Bay State Historical Park** attracts visitors to this marine conservation district frequented by spinner dolphins. The **Captain James Cook Monument,** a white obelisk on a wharf across the bay at Kaawaloa Flats, marks near where the navigator was slain in 1779. Guided kayak tours are available, and snorkeling is excellent. In the afternoon, visit **St. Benedict Painted Church** plus **Puuhonua O Honaunau National Historical Park.** On your way back north, stop at **Greenwell Farms** in Kealakekua for a Kona coffee farm tour.

Logistics: Take the lower bypass road from Keauhou or the upper road from Kailua-Kona, and head down Napoopoo Road to the end. Distance and time traveled: 44 miles round-trip, 35 minutes one-way, starting in Kailua-Kona. Car, via Highway 11.

DAY 4: HAWAII VOLCANOES NATIONAL PARK

It's a long drive from Kona to **Hawaii Volcanoes National Park,** so leave early to get to the park by 11 am. Begin at the **Kilauea Visitor Center,** where you can review maps, buy trail-guide booklets, or talk to the rangers. Stroll along a boardwalk to the **sulfur banks** and **steam vents.** Along the way, stop at **Volcano Art Center** to view fantastic local art. Drive to the Steaming Bluffs and walk to an overlook with views of Halemaumau Crater and

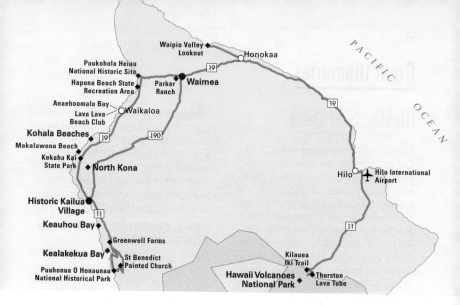

Kilauea Caldera. Then drive down Chain of Craters Road to visit **Thurston Lava Tube** and the adjacent **Kilauea Iki Trail.** Afterward, stop by **Volcano House** and eat lunch or dinner at **The Rim.**

Logistics: The park is open 24/7, but entrance fees are charged during normal visiting hours. Distance from Kailua-Kona one-way: 90 miles. Time traveled one-way: 2½ hours.

DAY 5: WAIMEA AND UPCOUNTRY

At the foothills of Maunakea, this small upcountry town is home to **Parker Ranch,** one of the country's largest privately owned cattle ranches. You can book several activities in town, including horseback riding and tours of two historic homes. Waimea has great restaurants, including **Merriman's** and **Big Island Brewhaus.** Not far from Waimea, **Waipio Valley** is a beautiful destination best explored by horseback or guided tour. The nearby town of **Honokaa** still feels like a slice of the old sugar plantation days.

Logistics: Waimea can be reached via the upper road (Highway 190) from Kailua-Kona, or up Kawaihae Drive from the lower road near the Kohala Coast resorts. Distance from Kailua-Kona: 39 miles one-way.

DAY 6: KEAUHOU BAY

Keauhou is just south of Kailua-Kona on Alii Drive. Here you'll find lots of recreational activities, including tennis, golf, and stand-up paddleboarding. **Keauhou Shopping Center** has movie theaters, restaurants, and cafés. Some of the island's most popular activities are the nighttime manta ray tours with operators who depart nightly from Keauhou Harbor.

Logistics: You'll need your car to drive around the area. Distance from Kailua-Kona: 5 miles one-way on Alii Drive. Time traveled one-way: 10 minutes.

DAY 7: NORTH KONA

Two of the best beaches near Kailua-Kona take some time to get to. **Kekaha Kai State Park,** also known as **Mahaiula,** is accessed down a long gravel road that winds through a lava field on the way to a wonderful white-sand beach. About a 20-minute walk south across a lava field from Kekaha Kai State Park, **Makalawena Beach** is a gem and worth the hike. If you go to Makalawena, pack water, a shade umbrella, food, and sunscreen. End your trip with a great dinner in town or at a resort.

Logistics: On Wednesday, the park is closed. Distance from Kailua-Kona: 17 miles one-way.

Great Itineraries

Highlights of Oahu

From *mauka* (mountains) to *makai* (sea), Oahu is probably the Hawaiian island most likely to please all types of travelers—whether you're an outdoorsy type, a beach bum, a foodie, or a family—and a week should give you enough time to see the highlights. You can either use the bus or take taxis or rideshares while you're in Honolulu, but rent a car to get out on the island and get a true feel for all things Oahu.

DAY 1: WAIKIKI

Given the time difference between Hawaii and the rest of the United States, you'll probably be jet-lagged. Grab coffee and head for a beach: Waikiki, Sans Souci, or Fort DeRussy. You'll see locals on their morning jogs at Kapiolani Park and catching waves at their favorite shore break.

Once caffeinated, hit Kalakaua Avenue on foot, the best way to shop and sight-see. Got kiddos in tow? Try the Waikiki Aquarium or the Honolulu Zoo. Get some refreshments with tea at the Moana Surfrider, the oldest hotel in Waikiki, or mai tais and *pupu* (hors d'oeuvres) at Duke's Waikiki (a better deal at lunch). In the afternoon, take a surf lesson in the beginner-friendly waves of Waikiki. Finish your day with a seaside dinner.

DAY 2: PEARL HARBOR

Give yourself a whole day for Pearl Harbor. Note that only the USS *Arizona* and the visitor center, which are operated by the National Park Service, are free; the other sights are operated by private entities and charge admission. Also, you must reserve tickets for the USS *Arizona* Memorial online in advance (for a small fee).

After your ferry ride out to the memorial, you can also explore the USS *Bowfin* submarine or take a shuttle to Ford Island and visit the restored USS *Missouri* battleship (the "Mighty Mo") and the Pearl Harbor Aviation Museum. Return to Waikiki for some late-afternoon beach time and a good dinner.

DAY 3: DOWNTOWN HONOLULU AND CHINATOWN

Cab or bus it to downtown Honolulu for a guided tour of the royal residence, Iolani Palace, where you'll get an excellent overview of Hawaii's monarchical era, from the early 1800s through its overthrow in 1893. For more historical highlights, walk between Honolulu Hale (Hawaiian for "house"), Kawaiahao Church, the Hawaiian Mission Houses Historic Site and Archives, the Hawaii State Capitol, Washington Place, the King Kamehameha I statue, and Aliiolani Hale. Several companies offer guided walks of the area.

Continue walking the ½ mile through Honolulu's business district into Chinatown for lunch at one of its eclectic eateries. Browse the shops, art galleries, and cultural sites, like Mauna Kea Marketplace, Chinatown Cultural Plaza, the Izumo Taishakyo Mission, and Kuan Yin Temple.

DAY 4: DIAMOND HEAD AND KAIMUKI

Today you will go the opposite direction from downtown. Tours of Shangri La, the opulent former waterfront home of heiress Doris Duke, with its Islamic art and architecture, book up well in advance, but it's well worth the effort to make an online reservation for a small surcharge. Shuttles to the Kahala home-turned-museum start and end at the Honolulu Museum of Art.

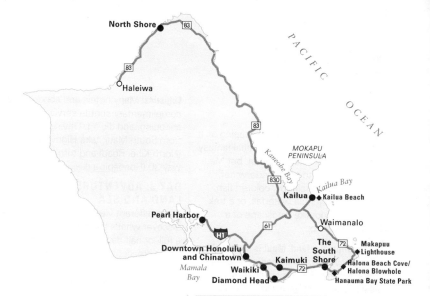

After your tour, grab a to-go lunch from Diamond Head Market & Grill, and enjoy it at the picnic tables at Diamond Head State Monument. Then hike the park's relatively easy 1½-hour, 1.6-mile trail up and down this dormant volcano. Finish the day with dinner in the foodie neighborhood of Kaimuki.

DAY 5: KAILUA AND THE SOUTH SHORE

Head to Windward Oahu for a stop in Kailua, a swim at its quintessential beach, and lunch at Kalapawai Cafe & Deli. Next, drive along the southeastern shore via Waimanalo, and choose your afternoon adventure: 1) do the easy, stroller-friendly hike at Makapuu Point Lighthouse, with great whale-watching views in winter and spring; 2) snorkel at Hanauma Bay State Park, the pristine preserve where you'll have more space to swim with the fish after the morning-to-midday rush; or 3) stop at the Halona Blowhole lookout and the *From Here to Eternity* Halona Beach Cove nearby.

DAY 6: THE NORTH SHORE

The beaches here are home to some of the world's most famous surf breaks. Each winter, surfers from around the globe converge to catch barreling waves

Tips

■ If this is your first visit, stay in Waikiki, which has most of the island's hotels.

■ You don't need a car in Honolulu, but you'll need one to explore farther afield.

■ Don't forget your hat, sunscreen, and good walking shoes any day you head out.

■ Be sure to reserve your free USS *Arizona* Memorial tickets online in advance ($1 charge).

■ Check ahead on any COVID-19 requirements that might be in place at the time of your visit.

of 15 feet or higher. Haleiwa is filled with surf shops, boutiques, and restaurants. Grab lunch from Haleiwa Joe's Seafood Grill or Uncle Bo's Pupu Bar & Grill. Enjoying a frozen treat at Matsumoto's Shave Ice is a sweet way to end the day.

Great Itineraries

Maui in 1 Week

Lounging beside the pool or napping on a sandy beach may fulfill your initial fantasy of a tropical Hawaiian vacation, but Maui has much more to offer: underwater encounters with rainbow-colored fish, an icy dip in a jungle waterfall, or a trek across the moonlike landscape of a dormant volcano.

⚠ **As a tropical island, Maui is susceptible to dangerous surf, flash flooding, and other natural hazards. Always check road, ocean, and wilderness advisories before venturing out.**

DAY 1: GETTING SETTLED
On your way out of Kahului Airport, stop at Costco, Target, or Walmart to pick up beach gear, sunscreen, food, and drink.

Once ensconced at your hotel or condo, unwind from your long flight by exploring the grounds, dozing by the pool, or splashing in the ocean—isn't it why you came to Maui?

Logistics: Road signs will point you to the two main resort areas: Highway 311 (Maui Veterans Highway) to 31 (Piilani), south to Kihei and Wailea, and Highway 380 (Kuihelani) to 30 (Honoapiilani) west to Lahaina and Kapalua.

DAY 2: SURF, SAND AND ... FORE!
Head to the nearest beach for snorkeling, swimming, sunbathing, or surfing in the gentle waves of Cove Park in Kihei or Launiupoko in West Maui. If golf's more your game, hit the tournament-quality golf links in the resort areas. You can find more affordable rates at the scenic Waiehu, Waikapu, and Maui Lani courses in Central Maui. Spend the evening (when it's cooler) visiting Lahaina town, filled with shops, restaurants, and art galleries.

Logistics: Many hotels and condos offer complimentary shuttle service to golfing, shopping, and dining. Driving to Lahaina from South Maui, take Highway 310 (North Kihei Road) and turn left on Highway 30 (Honoapiilani).

DAY 3: ADVENTURE ON LAND AND SEA
Get a different view of the island—and discover what's beneath the surface—on a full- or half-day boat excursion to Molokini, a crescent-shaped islet that sits 3 miles off South Maui, or snorkeling, scuba diving, or dolphin- and whale-watching trip. If you prefer dry land, head to Maui Tropical Plantation in Waikapu, which offers tram tours and a country store; it's also the home base for Flyin Hawaiian Zipline and Maui Zipline's introductory course. Plan to be back early enough for a sunset luau at your resort or at Old Lahaina Luau.

Logistics: Boat tours leave from Maalaea Harbor in South Maui and Lahaina Harbor in West Maui. To get to the Maui Tropical Plantation from West Maui, follow Highway 30 (Honoapiilani) south to Waikapu; from South Maui, take Highway 310 (North Kihei Road) and turn right onto Highway 30.

DAY 4: HALEAKALA AND UPCOUNTRY
At the 10,000-foot summit of this dormant volcano, sunrise is so popular that the National Park Service now requires reservations (make yours as early as possible, up to 60 days in advance of your visit). To avoid the crowd, consider planning your day in reverse. Start with some terrific bodysurfing at Baldwin Beach Park on the North Shore, followed by lunch in the former plantation town of Paa, home to charming boutiques and cafés. Once Upcountry, tour Surfing

Goat Dairy, Ali'i Kula Lavender, or Mau-iWine, before heading to the Haleakala summit in the afternoon when the park is uncrowded. It's not sunrise, but the spectacular sunset vista encompasses at least three islands and the broad expanse separating Maui's two mountains.

Logistics: To reach Haleakala from South Maui, take Highway 311 (Maui Veterans Highway) out of Kihei to connect with Highway 36 (Hana) and then Highway 37 (Haleakala). From West Maui, follow Highway 30 (Honoapiilani) to 380 (Kuihelani), connecting to Highway 36.

DAY 5: THE ROAD TO HANA

Today's the day to tackle the 600 curves of the Road to Hana (Highway 36/360). There aren't a lot of dining options in Hana, but many hotels offer picnic baskets for the road, or fill your cooler and gas tank in Paia, the last chance for provisions. Pause to stretch your legs at the Keanae Arboretum, picturesque Keanae Landing, or any of the roadside waterfalls. Approaching Hana town, turn into Waianapanapa State Park, with its rugged lava outcroppings, black-sand beach, trails, and caves with freshwater pools. There isn't much reason to stop in Hana town, except for lunch at the food trucks if you didn't bring your own, so continue on to the Kipahulu District of Haleakala National Park, site of the Pools of Oheo (nicknamed Seven Sacred Pools) and 400-foot Waimoku Falls. (Check for updates on closures due to flash flooding and landslides.) Don't leave Kipahulu without visiting the gravesite of famed aviator Charles Lindbergh, who is buried at 19th-century Palapala Hoomau Congregational Church.

Logistics: Follow directions to Haleakala, but stay on Highway 36/360 (Hana).

DAY 6: BACK TO THE BEACH

A full day is needed to recover from a trek to Hana, so take it easy with a visit to the Maui Ocean Center, where you'll be mesmerized by the sharks, rays, and tuna circling the 750,000-gallon open-ocean tank. Then spend the rest of the day relaxing in the water or at the spa with lunch beside the pool.

Logistics: From South Maui, take Highway 31 (Piilani) to 310 (North Kihei Road), then head a short distance left on Highway 30 (Honoapiilani). From West Maui, head south on Highway 30 to Maalaea/Maui Ocean Center.

DAY 7: CENTRAL MAUI

Squeeze in a final session at the beach or pool before checking out of your hotel and heading to Central Maui to be closer to the airport. If you like history, Hale Hoikeike at the Bailey House features the Island's largest collection of Hawaiian artifacts. Just five minutes up the road is Iao Valley State Park and one of the most photographed landmarks in Hawaii: Iao Needle. Eat like a local with lunch or an early dinner at Umi Maui, Miko's Cuisine, Ichiban Okazuya, or A Saigon Cafe in Wailuku or 808 on Main, Cafe O'Lei at the Dunes, or Tin Roof in Kahului. If there's still time, visit Kanaha Beach Park by Kahului Airport to watch world-class wind- and kitesurfers or shop for gifts and souvenirs at the many malls.

Logistics: From South Maui, take Highway 311 (Maui Veterans Highway) all the way to 32 (Kaahumanu) in Kahului, then turn left toward Wailuku; from West Maui, Highway 30 (Honoapiilani) leads right into Wailuku town. Kahului Airport is a 10-minute drive from here.

Great Itineraries

The Best of Kauai in 8 Days

Kauai is small, but its major byways generally circumnavigate the island with no through-roads, so it can take more time than you expect to get around. Taking a boat ride along Napali Coast, hiking the Kalalau Trail, kayaking the Wailua River, marveling at a waterfall, watching whales at Kilauea Lighthouse, shopping for gifts at Koloa Town shops—there's so much to see and do. Rather than trying to check everything off your list in one fell swoop, choose your favorites and devote a full day to the experiences, allowing time to relax.

DAY 1: SETTLE IN ON THE EAST SIDE

The East Side of the island is a convenient area to make a home base. Stay here, and you'll have the easiest access to most of the island's top attractions. Fresh off a long flight, you'll likely want to relax by the pool at your hotel/condo or walk the coastal path at **Kealia Beach Park,** just north of funky Kapaa Town. The far end near the rock jetty is for safe swimming and easy bodysurfing. There are plenty of welcoming, casual dining options around Kapaa, or try **Hukilau Lanai** for a fantastic first meal.

Logistics: Wailua/Kapaa traffic can be a nightmare, so avoid rush and midday times. It's 10 miles from the airport to Kapaa, but drive times can vary from 15 to 35 minutes. Kealia Beach is three minutes north of Kapaa and has plenty of parking.

DAY 2: TAKE IT ALL IN

For an incredible, and literal, overview of Kauai's beaches, forests, canyons, waterfalls, and ocean, take a morning helicopter trip out of Lihue with **Blue Hawaiian Helicopters** or **Jack Harter Helicopters**. These are expensive trips, but the images of the rolling verdant carpet far below will linger long in your memory. A rainy-day way to get a good island overview is with a visit to the **Kauai Museum.** Afternoon is free for beach time or laid-back shopping in Kapaa Town. An alternative is to have lunch in Lihue and lounge on **Kalapaki Beach.**

Logistics: Kalapaki Bay is five minutes south of Lihue.

DAY 3: EAST SIDE OFFERINGS

Check out the Kapaa/Wailua area, which has a little something for everyone. Rent a bike at **Kauai Cycle** and this time coast along Ke Ala Hele Makalae, enjoying the coastal path's ocean views and invigorating fresh air. Or take a moderate, 2-mile (one-way) hike on the **Sleeping Giant Trail** for panoramic vistas of the entire East Side. Then get back on the main road for a short drive up to **Opaekaa Falls,** one of the Wailua River's mightiest displays, and nearby temple ruins.

Logistics: From mid-Kapaa to the starting point of the Sleeping Giant Trail is 3 miles; just avoid rush hours.

DAY 4: SOUTH SHORE SIGHTS

Start with a hike on the **Mahaulepu Heritage Trail** near Poipu for wondrous ocean-side views of pristine beaches and craggy ledges. A quick dip at **Poipu Beach Park** will refresh your limbs after your hike. Grab lunch in Poipu or Koloa, then drive down Lawai Road to **Spouting Horn,** Kauai's version of Old Faithful. Across the road is the **National Tropical Botanical Garden,** where you can tour beautiful grounds of exotic flora and learn about biodiversity in Hawaii and the Pacific.

Logistics: The Mahaulepu Trail is about 10 minutes from Koloa Town. From there to Spouting Horn is about another 10-minute drive.

DAY 5: AT SEA ON NAPALI COAST

Choose your preferred watercraft (Zodiac for adventure rafting or catamaran for pleasure cruising) and depart from the boat harbor in Eleele for an unforgettable journey along the breathtakingly scenic Napali Coast. Most trips are about four hours and usually include a light snack; some include drinks. Don't schedule anything too demanding afterward, as you'll likely be pleasantly tired, and you'll want to savor the memories of the sights you just beheld. If you wish, though, just a mile from Eleele is Hanapepe, an artsy, historic small town that's great for a stroll and some browsing in locally owned shops and galleries; don't miss the Swinging Bridge.

Logistics: Eleele is about 16 miles west of Lihue Airport.

DAY 6: EXPLORE NATURAL WONDERS

In the mountains of Kokee on the West Side, you'll enjoy the splendor of the mountains, the ocean, the sunlight, and the crisper air. Stop along the way at the scenic overlooks of **Waimea Canyon** and be dazzled by the interplay of light and shadow as the sun moves across this spectacular landscape. Take a break at Kanaloahuluhulu Meadow to have lunch at **Kokee Lodge** and check out the **Kokee Natural History Museum** next door (a big trail map is on the porch). Continue another 5 miles or so to the postcard-worthy **Kalalau Lookout.**

Logistics: Drive up from Waimea Town and come down on the Kekaha side, which is less steep and best for sunset watching. It's about 30 minutes straight up to the meadow, but scenic stops stretch it out.

DAY 7: NORTH SHORE PLAYGROUND

The North Shore's plentiful sights and activities include swimming, surfing, golf, tennis, botanical gardens, hiking, and horseback riding. Visit **Limahuli Garden & Preserve** in Haena, which features an ancient Hawaiian layout of a typical self-sufficient community, or **Na Aina Kai Botanical Gardens & Sculpture Park**, with its artistic side and working-farm focus. At **Kilauea Lighthouse,** behold the cliffs, exotic birds, and magnificent coastal view. Spend the rest of your day at **Hanalei Bay** swimming, taking a surf lesson, or just strolling the 2-mile crescent-shape beach.

Logistics: Limahuli is about a 15-minute ride west of Hanalei/Waipa by car or on the shuttle.

DAY 8: HIKE PART OF THE KALALAU TRAIL

Now experience Napali Coast from land. The moderate trek to Hanakapiai Beach offers incredible views peering straight down over the sea, a visit to a dramatic beach (don't swim), and a hike up a stream to a 300-foot waterfall. You won't be taking the arduous 11-mile journey (one-way) of the entire coastal Kalalau Trail, so take your time and enjoy Kauai's scenery. Be sure to secure a permit if you plan to hike beyond Hanakapiai or camp.

Logistics: Well ahead of your trip, check ⊕ gohaena.com for the latest reservation information for accessing the park and trailhead. It's a roller-coaster 2 miles to Hanakapiai Beach; allow an hour one-way. The hike up the valley is also 2 miles—but plan on 90 minutes each way. Factor in time to return, wear sturdy shoes, stay hydrated, and only do this hike if you're fit.

Contacts

Air

AIRPORT INFORMA-TION Ellison Onizuka Kona International Airport at Keahole **(KOA)**. ✉ *73-200 Kupipi St., Kailua-Kona* ☎ *808/327–9520* ⊕ *hawaii. gov/koa.* **Daniel K. Inouye International Airport.** (*HNL*). ✉ *300 Rodgers Blvd., Airport Area* ☎ *808/836–6411* ⊕ *airports.hawaii.gov/hnl.* **Hilo International Airport (ITO)**. ✉ *2450 Kekuanaoa St., Hilo* ☎ *808/961–9300* ⊕ *hawaii.gov/ito.* **Hana Airport (HNM)**. ✉ *700 Alalele Rd., Hana* ☎ *808/872– 3830* ⊕ *airports.hawaii. gov/hnm.* **Kahului Airport (OGG)**. ✉ *1 Keolani Place, Kahului* ☎ *808/872–3830* ⊕ *airports.hawaii.gov/ogg.* **Kapalua–West Maui Airport (JHM)**. ✉ *4050 HI-30, 4050 Honoapiilani Hwy, Lahaina* ☎ *808/665–6108* ⊕ *airports.hawaii.gov/ jhm.* **Lanai Airport (LNY)**. ✉ *Lanai Ave., Lanai City* ☎ *808/565–7942* ⊕ *airports.hawaii.gov/lny.* **Lihue Airport (LIH)**. ✉ *Lihue* ☎ *808/274–3800* ⊕ *www. hidot.hawaii.gov/airports.* **Molokai Airport (MKK)**. ✉ *3980 Airport Loop, Hoolehua* ☎ *808/567– 9660* ⊕ *airports.hawaii. gov/mkk.* **Waimea-Kohala Airport (MUE)**. ✉ *Waimea-Kohala Airport Rd., Waimea (Hawaii County)* ☎ *808/887–8126* ⊕ *hawaii.gov/mue.*

MAINLAND AIRLINE CONTACTS Alaska Airlines. ☎ *800/252–7522* ⊕ *www. alaskaair.com.* **American Airlines.** ☎ *800/433–7300* ⊕ *www.aa.com.* **Delta Airlines.** ☎ *800/221–1212 for U.S. reservations, 800/241–4141 for international reservations* ⊕ *www.delta.com.* **Hawaiian Airlines.** ☎ *800/367– 5320* ⊕ *www.hawaiia-nairlines.com.* **Southwest.** ☎ *800/435–9792* ⊕ *www. southwest.com.* **United Airlines.** ☎ *800/864–8331 for U.S. reservations* ⊕ *www.united.com.*

INTERISLAND AIRLINE CONTACTS Hawaiian Airlines. ☎ *800/367–5320* ⊕ *www.hawaiianairlines. com.* **Mokulele Airlines.** ☎ *866/260–7070* ⊕ *www. mokuleleairlines.com.*

🚌 Bus

Hele-On Bus. ✉ *Kailua-Kona* ☎ *808/961–8744* ⊕ *www. heleonbus.org.* **Kauai Bus.** ✉ *Lihue* ☎ *808/246–8110* ⊕ *www.kauai.gov/ transportation.* **Maui Bus.** ✉ *2145 Kaohu St., Suite 102, Wailuku* ☎ *808/871– 4838* ⊕ *mauicounty.gov/ bus.*

TROLLEY CONTACTS Waikiki Trolley. ✉ *Honolulu* ☎ *808/465–5543* ⊕ *wai-kikitrolley.com.*

📍 Visitor Information

Hawaii Beach Safety. ⊕ *hawaiibeachsafety.com.* **Hawaii Department of Land and Natural Resources.** ⊕ *dlnr.hawaii.gov.* **Hawaii Tourism Authority.** ⊕ *www. gohawaii.com.* **Island of Hawaii Visitors Bureau.** ✉ *68-1330 Mauna Lani Dr., Puako ✣ In Shops at Mauna Lani* ☎ *808/885– 1655* ⊕ *www.gohawaii. com/islands/hawaii-big-island.* **Kauai Visitors Bureau.** ✉ *4334 Rice St., #101, Lihue* ☎ *808/245–3971* ⊕ *www.gohawaii.com/ kauai.* **Maui Visitors Bureau.** ✉ *427 Ala Makani Street, Kahului* ⊕ *gohawaii.com/ islands/maui.* **Oahu Visitors Bureau** ⊕ *www.gohawaii. com/islands/oahu.*

Chapter 3

OAHU

Updated by Powell Berger,
Marla Cimini, Cheryl Crabtree,
and Anna Weaver

⊙ Sights	🍴 Restaurants	🛏 Hotels	🛍 Shopping	🍸 Nightlife
★★★★★	★★★★★	★★★★★	★★★★★	★★★★★

WELCOME TO OAHU

TOP REASONS TO GO

★ **Pearl Harbor:** This historic memorial in Honolulu is a sobering, don't-miss sight.

★ **Waikiki:** Busy but beautiful, with a perfect beach for first-time surfers.

★ **Great food:** Simple plate lunches, fresh sushi, creative Hawaii regional cuisine.

★ **Polynesian Cultural Center:** The famous luau provides insight into island culture.

★ **Nightlife:** From upscale jazz bars to local hangouts, Honolulu comes alive after dark.

★ **North Shore:** Shave ice, big waves, pro surfers, and a slower pace add appeal here.

1 Honolulu. The vibrant capital city is home to the nation's only royal palace. It also encompasses Waikiki—dressed in lights at the base of Diamond Head—and Pearl Harbor.

2 West (Leeward) and Central Oahu. This rugged western side of the island has become a "second city" of suburban homes, golf courses, and resorts surrounding lagoons in the Ko Olina area. Although the interstate cuts through the region, fertile Central Oahu is an integral part of Hawaii's rich cultural history.

3 North Shore. Best known for its miles of first-rate surf breaks and green sea turtle sightings, the North Shore is home to the legendary laid-back surf town of Haleiwa. This plantation area also has farms, restaurants, and hiking trails.

4 Windward (East) Oahu. The sleepy neighborhoods at the base of the majestic Koolau Mountains offer a respite from the bustling city. In the southeastern corner of Oahu, Honolulu's main bedroom communities crawl up the steep valleys that flow into Maunalua Bay.

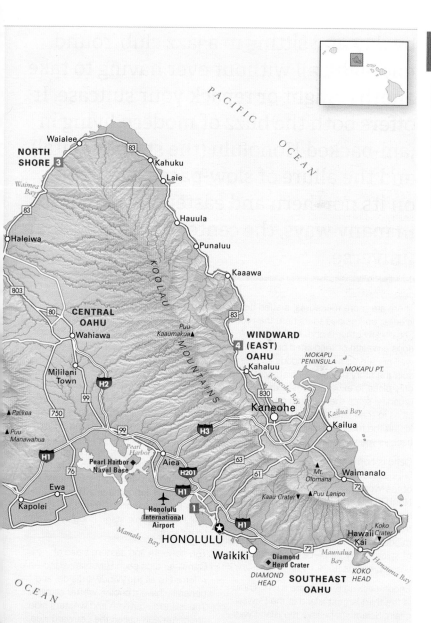

PACIFIC OCEAN

Waialee

NORTH SHORE 3

83

Kahuku

Laie

Waimea Bay

83

Hauula

Haleiwa

Punaluu

803

Kaaawa

80

KOOLAU

CENTRAL OAHU

83

Wahiawa

Puu Kaaumakua▲

WINDWARD (EAST) OAHU 4

MOKAPU PENINSULA

MOKAPU PT.

Kahaluu

Mililani Town

H2

MOUNTAINS

830

99

Kaneohe Bay

Kaneohe

Kailua Bay

▲Palikea

750

99

H3

Kailua

▲Puu Manawahua

H1

Pearl Harbor

Pearl Harbor Naval Base◆

Aiea

63

Mt. Olomana▲

Waimanalo

61

Ewa

76

H201

H1

Kaau Crater▼

▲Puu Lanipo

72

Kapolei

✈

1

Honolulu International Airport

H1

Koko Crater▼

Mamala Bay

HONOLULU

Hawaii Kai

Waikiki

72

◆ **Diamond Head Crater**

Maunalua Bay

KOKO HEAD

Hanauma Bay

OCEAN

DIAMOND HEAD

SOUTHEAST OAHU

Oahu is one-stop Hawaii—all the allure of the Islands in a plate-lunch mix that has you kayaking around offshore islets by day and sitting in a jazz club 'round midnight, all without ever having to take another flight or repack your suitcase. It offers both the buzz of modern living in jam-packed Honolulu (the state's capital) and the allure of slow-paced island life on its northern and eastern shores. It is, in many ways, the center of the Hawaiian universe.

There are more museums, staffed historic sites, and guided tours here than you'll find on any other island. And only here does a wealth of renovated buildings and well-preserved neighborhoods so clearly spin the story of Hawaii's history. It's the only place to experience Islands-style urbanity, since there are no other true cities in the state. And yet you can get as lost in the rural landscape and be as laid-back as you wish.

Oahu is home to Waikiki, the most famous Hawaiian beach, as well as some of the world's most famous surf on the North Shore and Hawaii's best known historical site—Pearl Harbor. If it's isolation, peace, and quiet you want, Oahu might not be for you, but if you'd like a bit of spice with your piece of paradise, this island provides it.

Encompassing 597 square miles, Oahu is the third-largest island in the Hawaiian chain. Scientists believe the island was formed about 4 million years ago by three shield volcanoes: Waianae, Koolau, and the recently discovered Kaena. Recognized in mid-2014, Kaena is the oldest of the three and has long since been submerged 62 miles from Kaena Point on Oahu's northwestern side. Waianae created the mountain range on the western side of the island, whereas Koolau shapes the eastern side. Central Oahu is an elevated plateau bordered by the two mountain ranges, with Pearl Harbor to the south. Several of Oahu's most famous natural landmarks, including Diamond Head and Hanauma Bay, are tuff rings and cinder cones formed during a renewed volcanic stage (roughly 1 million years ago).

The northern and eastern sides of Oahu—and on each Hawaiian island—are referred to as the Windward side, and generally have a cooler, wetter climate. The island's southern and western sides are commonly called the Leeward side, and are typically warmer and more arid. The island's official flower, the little orange *ilima,* grows predominantly in the east, but lei throughout the island incorporate *ilima.* Numerous tropical fish call the reef at Hanauma Bay home, migrating humpback whales can be spotted off the coast past Waikiki and Diamond Head from December through April, spinner dolphins pop in and out of the island's bays, and the 15 islets off Oahu's eastern coast provide refuge for endangered seabirds.

Oahu is the most visited Hawaiian island because early tourism to Hawaii started here. It's also the most inhabited island today—69% of the state's population lives on Oahu—due to job opportunities and the island's military bases. Although Kilauea Volcano on Hawaii was a tourist attraction in the late 1800s, it was the building of the Moana Hotel on Waikiki Beach in 1901 and subsequent advertising of Hawaii to wealthy San Franciscans that really fueled tourism in the Islands. Oahu was drawing tens of thousands of guests yearly when, on December 7, 1941, Japanese Zeros appeared at dawn to bomb Pearl Harbor. Though tourism understandably dipped during the war (Waikiki Beach was fenced with barbed wire), the subsequent memorial only seemed to attract more visitors, and Oahu remains hugely popular with tourists to this day.

Planning

Beaches

Tropical sun mixed with cooling trade winds and pristine waters make Oahu's shores a literal heaven on Earth. But contrary to many assumptions, the island is not one big beach. There are miles and miles of coastline without a grain of sand, so you need to know where

you're going to fully enjoy the Hawaiian experience.

Much of the island's southern and eastern coast is protected by inner reefs. The reefs provide still coastline water but not much as far as sand is concerned. However, where there are beaches on the south and east shores, they are mind-blowing. In West Oahu and on the North Shore you can find the wide expanses of sand you would expect for enjoying the sunset. Sandy bottoms and protective reefs make the water an adventure in the winter months. Most visitors assume the seasons don't change a bit in the Islands, and they would be mostly right—except for the waves, which are big on the South Shore in summer and placid in winter. It's exactly the opposite on the north side, where winter storms bring in huge waves, but the ocean becomes glass-like come May and June.

Getting Here and Around

AIR

The Daniel K. Inouye International Airport (HNL)—also known as Honolulu International Airport—is roughly 20 minutes (9 miles) west of Waikiki (60 minutes during rush hour) and is served by most of the major domestic and international carriers. To travel to other islands from Honolulu, you can depart from either the interisland terminal or the commuter terminal, located in two separate structures adjacent to the main overseas terminal building. A free Wiki-Wiki shuttle bus operates between terminals.

BUS

Getting around by bus is convenient and affordable on Oahu, particularly in the most heavily touristed areas of Waikiki. Options include Honolulu's municipal transit system, affectionately known as TheBus; the Waikiki Trolleys, brass-trimmed, open-air, hop-on-hop-off vehicles that look like trolleys or large double-decker buses; and brightly painted private buses, some of them free, that shuttle you to such commercial attractions as dinner cruises, shopping centers, and the like.

TheBus is one of the best bargains on Oahu. You can use it to travel around the island or just down Kalakaua Avenue for $2.75. Buses stop in Waikiki every 10–15 minutes to take passengers to nearby shopping areas. Although free transfers have been discontinued, you can purchase a one-day pass for $5.50. Just ask the driver when boarding. Exact change is required, and dollar bills are accepted. Monthly passes cost $70.

The company's website has timetables, route maps, and real-time bus tracking, or you can download the free DaBus2 app for your smartphone. You can call to speak with a representative for route advice, or you can find privately published booklets at most drugstores and other convenience outlets.

The Waikiki Trolley has three lines—each beginning and ending in Waikiki—and dozens of stops that allow you to plan your own itinerary. A one-day pass costs $25 ($5 for the Pink Line) for a single line and $45 for all lines. Four-day ($65) and seven-day ($75) all-line passes are also available.

The Ocean/Diamond Head Tour (Blue Line) stops at the Duke Kahanamoku statue; along Diamond Head and Kahala; the Halona Blow Hole; Sea Life Park; and Koko Marina. As its name suggests, the Ala Moana Shopping Tour (Pink Line) goes to the Ala Moana Center, a sprawling outdoor mall. The City Arts District Tour (Red Line) travels between Waikiki, Chinatown, and Kakaako and includes stops at the Honolulu Museum of Art, the capitol, Iolani Palace, Punchbowl Crater, and Ala Moana.

CAR

Thanks to public transit, you don't need a car in Waikiki. Elsewhere on the island, though, a car can be invaluable. Avoid the obvious tourist cars—candy-color convertibles, for example—and never leave anything valuable inside, even if you've locked the vehicle. A GPS (either on your smartphone or a separate device) will help guide you through Oahu's sometimes-confusing streets.

Reserve in advance to ensure availability (rentals can book up, especially during holidays and summer breaks) and to get the best rates. Also, be prepared to pay for parking; most hotels in Honolulu (and many outside of Honolulu) charge for parking.

Except for one area around Kaena Point, major highways follow Oahu's shoreline and traverse the island at two points. Rush-hour traffic (6:30–9:30 am and 3 or 3:30–6 pm) can be frustrating around Honolulu and the outlying areas. Winter swells also bring heavy traffic to the North Shore, as people hoping to catch the surfing action clog the two-lane Kamehameha Highway. Parking along many streets is curtailed during these times, and tow-away zones are strictly enforced. Read curbside signs before leaving your vehicle, even at a meter.

Asking for directions will almost always produce a helpful explanation from the locals, but you should be prepared for a Hawaiian term or two. Instead of using compass directions, remember that Hawaii residents refer to places as being either *mauka* (toward the mountains) or *makai* (toward the ocean).

Other directions depend on your location. In Honolulu, for example, people say to "go Diamond Head," which means toward that famous landmark, or to "go *ewa*," meaning in the opposite direction. A shop on the *mauka*–Diamond Head corner of a street is on the mountain side of the street on the corner closest

Driving Times

Waikiki to Ko Olina	1 hour
Waikiki to Haleiwa	45 minutes
Waikiki to Hawaii Kai	25 minutes
Waikiki to Kailua	30 minutes
Waikiki to downtown Honolulu	10 minutes
Waikiki to airport	25 minutes
Kaneohe to Turtle Bay	1 hour
Hawaii Kai to Kailua	25 minutes
Haleiwa to Turtle Bay	20 minutes

3

Oahu PLANNING

to Diamond Head. It all makes perfect sense once you get the lay of the land.

Here are some average driving times—without traffic—that will help you plan your excursions.

RIDE-SHARING

Both Uber and Lyft operate on Oahu, including in designated locations at the airport. Although you may still want to rent a car while you're on island—especially if you're staying in or visiting the North Shore or towns on the east side of Oahu—ride-shares are good for quick trips and evenings out when you want to avoid parking or you want to imbibe.

Restaurants

Oahu has undergone a renaissance at both ends of the dining spectrum. Consider budgeting for a meal in at least one pricey restaurant, where chefs such as Roy Yamaguchi, Ed Kenney, Chris Kajioka, or others you've seen on the Food Network and Travel Channel put a sophisticated spin on local foods and flavors. Dishes that take cues from Japan, China, Korea, the Philippines, the United States, and Europe are often filtered through an Island sensibility. Take advantage of the location and order the superb local

fish—mahimahi, *opakapaka* (Hawaiian pink snapper), ono, and opah.

Spend the rest of your food dollars where budget-conscious locals do: in plate-lunch places and small ethnic eateries, at lunch wagons, or at window-in-the-wall delis. Snack on a *musubi* (a handheld rice ball wrapped with seaweed and topped with Spam), slurp shave ice with red-bean paste, or order Filipino pork adobo with rice and macaroni salad.

In Waikiki, you can find everything from upscale dining rooms with a view to Japanese noodle shops. By going just a few miles in any direction, you can save money and eat like a local. On Kaimuki's Waialae Avenue, for example, you'll find a coffee shop, a Chinese bakery, an Italian bistro, a dim-sum restaurant, elevated Hawaiian food, Mexican food, and a Hawaii regional-cuisine standout (3660 on the Rise)—all in three blocks and 10 minutes from Waikiki.

Chinatown, 15 minutes in the other direction and easily reached by the Waikiki Trolley, is another dining (and shopping) treasure, not only for Chinese but also for Vietnamese, Filipino, Burmese, and Mexican food. There's even a chic little tea shop. Kakaako, the developing urban area between Waikiki and Chinatown, also offers a mix of local eateries, upscale restaurants, and ethnic takeout.

Although restaurants are fewer outside Honolulu and Waikiki, they tend to be filled with locals and are cheaper and more casual. Thanks to its popular Kailua and Lanikai Beaches, Windward Oahu's dining scene features everything from plate lunches to creative regional offerings. Kapolei, once dominated by Mainland chains and fast-food joints, is now another area with a variety of quality eateries.

Restaurant and hotel reviews have been shortened. For more information, visit Fodors.com. Restaurant prices are for a main course at dinner. Hotel prices are for two people in a standard double room in high season. Condo price categories reflect studio and one-bedroom rates. Prices exclude 13.96% tax.

What It Costs in U.S. Dollars			
$	$$	$$$	$$$$
RESTAURANTS			
Under $17	$17–$26	$27–$35	Over $35
HOTELS			
Under $180	$180–$260	$261–$340	Over $340

Hotels

If you like the action and choices of big cities, consider Waikiki, a 24-hour playground with everything from surf to karaoke bars. For an escape from urban life, look to the island's leeward or windward sides or to the North Shore, where the surf culture creates a laid-back atmosphere.

Most of Oahu's major hotels and resorts are in busy Waikiki, where you don't need a car to reach key sights and amenities as public transportation can get you around town as well as around the island. You'll find places to stay along the entire stretches of both Kalakaua and Kuhio Avenues, with smaller and quieter hotels and condos at the eastern end of Waikiki and more business-centric accommodations on the western edge, near the Hawaii Convention Center, Ala Moana Center, and downtown.

Leeward Oahu, in the Ko Olina resort area, is about 20 minutes from Honolulu International Airport (40 minutes from Waikiki) and has great golf courses and quiet beaches that make for a relaxing getaway. Note, though, that you'll need a car to explore, and all the resorts in this area charge hefty parking fees.

Other low-key options are on Windward Oahu—home to Turtle Bay, one of the island's premier resorts—or the North Shore. Both have quaint eateries and coffee shops, local boutiques, and some of the island's best beaches.

Nightlife

Oahu is the best of all the Islands for nightlife. The island's few clubs are in Waikiki, but there are bars just about everywhere. On weeknights, it's likely that you'll find the working crowd, still in their business-casual attire, downing chilled beers even before the sun goes down. Though you might call it happy hour, the locals call it *pau hana,* which translates to "done with work." Those who don't have to wake up early in the morning should change into a fresh outfit and start the evening closer to 10 pm.

On the weekends, it's typical to have dinner at a restaurant before hitting the bars at around 9:30. Some barhoppers start as early as 7, but even they usually don't patronize more than two establishments a night because getting from one Oahu nightspot to the next often requires transportation. Happily, cab services are plentiful, and the rideshares Uber and Lyft give Honolulu a San Francisco feel.

The drinking age is 21 on Oahu and throughout Hawaii. Many bars will admit younger people but will not serve them alcohol. By law, all establishments that serve alcoholic beverages must close by 2 am. The only exceptions are a handful in Waikiki with a cabaret license, which can stay open until 4 am. Remember that some establishments may require proof of vaccination before entering.

■TIP→ **Some places have a cover charge of $5–$10, but with many establishments, arriving early means you don't have to pay.**

Where to Stay on Oahu

Neighborhood	Local Vibe	Pros	Cons
Honolulu	Lodging options are limited in downtown Honolulu, but if you want an urban feel, look no farther.	Access to a wide selection of art galleries, boutiques, and restaurants, as well as Chinatown.	No beaches within walking distance. If you're looking to get away from it all, this is not the place.
Waikiki	Lodgings abound in Waikiki, from youth hostels to five-star accommodations. The area is always abuzz with activity, and anything you desire is within walking distance.	You can surf in front of the hotels, wander miles of beach, and explore restaurants and bars.	This is tourist central. Prices are high, and you are not going to get the true Hawaii experience.
Windward Oahu	More in tune with the local experience, this is where you'll find many privately listed (e.g., on Airbnb or VRBO) places and enjoy the lush side of Oahu.	From beautiful vistas to green jungles, this side really captures the tropical paradise most people envision when dreaming of a Hawaii vacation.	The lushness comes at a price—it rains a lot on this side. Also, luxury is not the specialty here; if you want pampering, stay elsewhere.
The North Shore	This is true country living, with one luxurious resort exception. It's bustling in the winter (when the surf is up) and slower-paced in the summer.	Amazing surf and long stretches of sand truly epitomize the beach culture in Hawaii. Historic Haleiwa has enough stores to keep shopaholics busy.	There is no middle ground for accommodations; you're either in backpacker cabanas or $300-a-night suites. There is also zero nightlife, and traffic can be heavy during winter months.
West (Leeward) Oahu	This is the resort side of the rock; there isn't much outside these resorts but plenty on the grounds to keep you occupied for a week.	Ko Olina's lagoons offer the most kid-friendly swimming on the island, and the golf courses are magnificent. Rare is the rainy day out here.	You are isolated from the rest of Oahu, with fewer shopping options or jungle hikes.

3

Oahu PLANNING

Performing Arts

Oahu has a thriving arts and culture scene, especially in the summer. Check local newspapers, such as the *Honolulu Star-Advertiser* or *MidWeek,* for the latest events. Websites like ⊕ *gohawaii.com* also have listings.

Shopping

Savvy shoppers hunt for luxury goods at high-end malls *and* scout tiny boutiques and galleries for items created by local artists and artisans. Honolulu's Chinatown and Kakaako neighborhoods, Kailua on the windward side, and Haleiwa on the North Shore often have the most original merchandise. Some small stores carry imported clothes and gifts—a reminder that, on this island halfway between Asia and the United States, shopping is a multicultural experience.

Tours

Guided tours are convenient; you don't have to worry about finding a parking spot or getting admission tickets. Most of the tour guides have taken special classes in Hawaiian history and lore, and many are certified by the state of Hawaii. On the other hand, you won't have the freedom to proceed at your own pace, nor will you have the ability to take a detour trip if something else catches your attention.

BUS AND VAN TOURS

Polynesian Adventure

BUS TOURS | This company leads tours of Pearl Harbor and other Oahu sights and also offers a circle-island tour by motor coach, van, or minicoach. ⊠ *Honolulu* ☎ *888/206–4531* ⊕ *polyad.com* ⊠ *From $62.*

THEME TOURS

Discover Hawaii Tours

SPECIAL-INTEREST TOURS | In addition to circle-island and other Oahu-based itineraries on motor coaches and minicoaches, this company can also get you from Waikiki to the lava flows of the Big Island or to Maui's Hana Highway and back in one day. ⊠ *Honolulu* ☎ *808/824–3995* ⊕ *discoverhawaiitours.com* ⊠ *From $50.*

E Noa Tours

SPECIAL-INTEREST TOURS | This outfitter's certified tour guides conduct circle-island and Pearl Harbor tours, with pickups from Ko Olina and Waikiki. E Noa also owns Waikiki Trolley. ⊠ *Honolulu* ☎ *808/591–2561* ⊕ *enoa.com* ⊠ *From $60.*

Visitor Information

CONTACTS Hawaii Tourism Authority. ☎ *800/464–2924 for brochures* ⊕ *www. gohawaii.com.* **Oahu Visitors Bureau.** ☎ *800/464–2924* ⊕ *www.gohawaii.com/ islands/oahu.*

Honolulu

As the seat of government, a center of commerce and shipping, and an entertainment and recreation mecca, Honolulu plays many (sometimes conflicting) roles that make it a dynamic, ever-evolving urban delight. Hipsters and scholars, sightseers and foodies, nature lovers and culture vultures can all find their bliss in Hawaii's only true metropolis.

Once there was the broad bay of Mamala and the narrow inlet of Kou, fronting a dusty plain occupied by a few thatched houses and the great Pakaka *heiau* (shrine). Nosing into the narrow passage in 1794, British sea captain William Brown named the port Fair Haven. Later, Hawaiians would call it Honolulu, or "sheltered bay," and it gained further importance in 1804, when King Kamehameha I built a stately compound near the harbor here after reluctantly abandoning his Big Island home to better protect Hawaiian interests.

As shipping traffic increased, the settlement grew into a Western-style town of streets and buildings, tightly clustered around the single freshwater source, Nuuanu Stream. Not until piped water became available in the early 1900s did Honolulu spread across the greening plain, becoming both a city and a county. Two hundred years later, the entire island is, in a sense, Honolulu, which has no official boundaries, extending across flatlands, from Pearl Harbor to Waikiki, and high into the hills.

The main areas of Waikiki, Pearl Harbor, downtown, and Chinatown have the lion's share of the sights, but greater Honolulu's residential neighborhoods also have a lot to offer, including folksy restaurants and takeout places favored by locals. Visits to these areas also afford glimpses of classic Hawaiian homes, from the breezy, double-wing bungalows, with their swooping, Thai-style rooflines, to the tiny, green-and-white, plantation-era houses, with their corrugated tin roofs and window-flanked central doors and porches.

Also common are "Grandma-style" gardens and *ohana* houses, with smaller backyard homes or apartments allowing extended families to live together. In these districts, carports rarely shelter cars but instead serve as rec rooms—beneath the roof, parties are held and neighbors sit to "talk story," and atop it, gallon jars of pickled lemons ferment in the sun.

Waikiki and Diamond Head

Approximately 3 miles east of downtown Honolulu, Waikiki is Oahu's primary resort area. A mix of historic and modern hotels and condos front the sunny 2-mile stretch of beach, and many have clear views of Diamond Head. The area is home to much of the island's dining, nightlife, and shopping—from posh boutiques to hole-in-the-wall eateries to craft booths at Duke's Marketplace.

Waikiki was once a favorite retreat for Hawaiian royalty. In 1901, the Moana Hotel debuted, introducing Waikiki as an international travel destination. The region's fame continued to grow when Duke Kahanamoku helped popularize the sport of surfing, offering lessons to visitors at Waikiki. You can see Duke immortalized in a bronze statue, with a surfboard, on Kuhio Beach.

Today there is a decidedly "urban resort" vibe here. Streets are clean, gardens are manicured, and the sand feels softer than at beaches farther down the coast. At first glance, there isn't much of a local culture—it's mainly tourist crowds—but if you explore the neighborhood, you can still find the relaxed surf-y vibe and friendly "aloha spirit" that has drawn people here for more than a century.

Diamond Head Crater is perhaps Hawaii's most recognizable natural landmark. It got its name from sailors who thought they had found precious gems on its slopes; these later proved to be calcite crystals, a much more common mineral. Hawaiians saw a resemblance in the sharp angle of the crater's seaward slope to the oddly shaped head of the ahi fish and so called it Leahi, though later they Hawaiianized the English name to Kaimana Hila. It is commemorated in a widely known hula—*A ike i ka nani o Kaimana Hila, Kaimana Hila, kau mai i luna* ("We saw the beauty of Diamond Head, Diamond Head set high above").

Sprawling Kapiolani Park lies in the shadow of Diamond Head, which is just beyond the easternmost limits of Waikiki. King David Kalakaua established the park in 1877, naming it after his queen and dedicating it "to the use and enjoyment of the people." In this 500-acre expanse, you can go for a stroll, play all sorts of field sports, enjoy a picnic, see wild animals and tropical fish at the Honolulu Zoo and the Waikiki Aquarium, or hear live music at the Waikiki Shell or the Kapiolani Park Bandstand.

GETTING HERE AND AROUND

Bounded by the Ala Wai Canal on the north and west, the beach on the south, and the Honolulu Zoo to the east, Waikiki is compact and easy to walk around. TheBus runs multiple routes here from the airport and downtown Honolulu. By car, finding Waikiki from H1 can be tricky; look for the Punahou exit for the west end of Waikiki and the King Street exit for the eastern end.

For those with a Costco card, the cheapest gas on the island is at the three Costco stations. The one in Honolulu is on Arakawa Street, between Dillingham Boulevard and Nimitz Highway; the one in Waipio is at 94-1231 Ka Uka Boulevard; and the one in Kapolei is at 4589 Kapolei Parkway.

 Sights

★ Diamond Head State Monument

STATE/PROVINCIAL PARK | FAMILY | Panoramas from this 760-foot extinct volcanic peak, once used as a military fortification, extend from Waikiki and Honolulu in one direction and out to Koko Head in the other, with surfers and windsurfers scattered like confetti on the cresting waves below. The 360-degree perspective is a great orientation for first-time visitors. On a clear day, look east past Koko Head to glimpse the outlines of the islands of Maui and Molokai.

To enter the park from Waikiki, take Kalakaua Avenue east, turn left at Monsarrat Avenue, head a mile up the hill, and look for a sign on the right. Drive through the tunnel to the inside of the crater. The ¾-mile trail to the top begins at the parking lot. Be aware that the hike

up to the crater has numerous stairs to climb; if you aren't in the habit of getting occasional exercise, this might not be for you. At the top, you'll find a somewhat awkward scramble through a tunnel and bunker out into the open air, but the view is worth it.

As you walk, note the color of the vegetation: if the mountain is brown, Honolulu has been without significant rain for a while, but if the trees and undergrowth glow green, you'll know it's the wet season (winter) without looking at a calendar. Winter is when rare Hawaiian marsh plants revive on the floor of the crater. Wear a hat and take bottled water with you to stay hydrated under the tropical sun as there are no water stations (or any shade) along the hike. Keep an eye on your watch if you're here at day's end: the gates close promptly at 6 pm. ■ TIP➜ **To beat the heat and the crowds, rise early and make the hike before 8 am.** ⊠ *Diamond Head Rd. at 18th Ave., Diamond Head* ☎ *808/587–0300* ⊕ *dlnr.hawaii.gov/dsp/parks/oahu/diamond-head-state-monument* ⬚ *$5 per person (non-Hawaii resident), $25 per non-commercial vehicle (cash only).*

Honolulu Zoo

ZOO | FAMILY | The world definitely has bigger and better (and newer) zoos, but this 42-acre facility features well-paved, walkable trails amid a lush garden with tropical flowers. To get a glimpse of the endangered nene, the Hawaii state bird, check out the zoo's Kipuka Nene Sanctuary. Other highlights include a Japanese Giant Salamander habitat and an ectotherm complex, which houses a Burmese python, elongated tortoises, and a giant African snail. Though many animals prefer to remain invisible—particularly the big cats—the monkeys and elephants appear to enjoy being seen and are a hoot to watch. It's best to get to the zoo right when it opens because the animals are livelier in the cool of the

Despite the steep climb, Diamond Head, an extinct volcanic crater on the eastern edge of Waikiki, is one of Honolulu's most popular hiking destinations.

morning. Children adore the petting zoo, where they can make friends with a llama or stand in the middle of a koi pond.

There's an exceptionally good gift shop. On weekends, the Art on the Zoo Fence, on Monsarrat Avenue on the Diamond Head side outside the zoo, has affordable artwork by local contemporary artists. Metered parking is available all along the *makai* (ocean) side of the park and in the lot next to the zoo—but it can fill up early. TheBus makes stops here along the way to and from Ala Moana Center and Sea Life Park (Routes 8 and 22). ⊠ *151 Kapahulu Ave., Waikiki* ☏ *808/971–7171* ⊕ *www.honoluluzoo.org* ☑ *$19.*

Kapiolani Park Bandstand

PERFORMANCE VENUE | **FAMILY** | The Victorian-style Kapiolani Park Bandstand, which was built in the late 1890s, is the park's stage for community entertainment and concerts. Founded by King Kamehameha III in 1836, the Royal Hawaiian Band is the nation's only city-sponsored band and performs free concerts at the bandstand as well as at Iolani Palace and the center stage at Ala Moana Center. Visit the band's website for concert dates (⊕ *www.rhb-music.com*), and check event-listing websites and the *Honolulu Star-Advertiser*—Oahu's local newspaper—for information on other coming bandstand attractions. ⊠ *2805 Monsarrat Ave., Waikiki* ☏ *808/922–5331.*

Waikiki Aquarium

AQUARIUM | **FAMILY** | This small yet fun attraction harbors more than 3,500 organisms and 500 species of Hawaiian and South Pacific marine life, including an endangered Hawaiian monk seal and a zebra shark. The Living Reef exhibit showcases diverse corals and fascinating reef environments found along Hawaii's shorelines. Check out exhibits on the Northwestern Hawaiian Islands (which explains the formation of the island chain) and Ocean Drifters (about various types of jellyfish). A 60-foot exhibit houses sea horses, sea dragons, and pipefish.

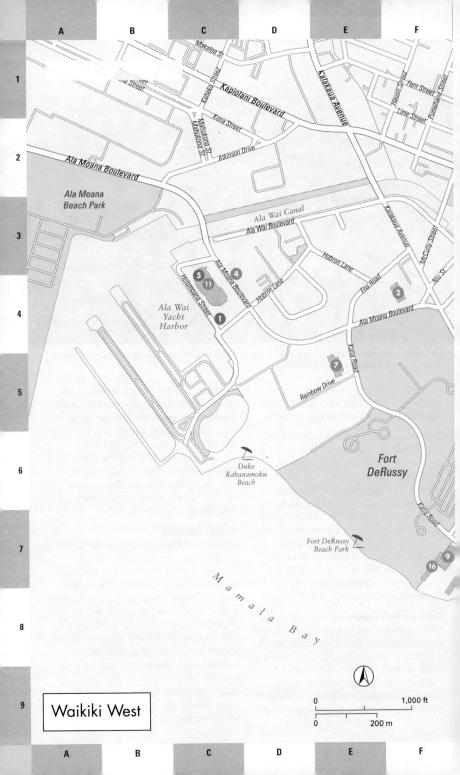

Restaurants ▼

Hotels ▼

KEY

🔴 *Restaurants*

🔴 *Hotels*

A free self-guided mobile audio tour is available via your own smartphone. The aquarium offers activities of interest to adults and children alike, with a focus on the importance of being eco-friendly and keeping our oceans clean. ⊠ *2777 Kalakaua Ave., Waikiki* ☎ *808/923–9741* ⊕ *www.waikikiaquarium.org* ⊒ *$12.*

☺ Beaches

In 2021, the 2-mile Waikiki Beach—which runs from Hilton Hawaiian Village on one end to Kapiolani Park and Diamond Head on the other—underwent a major sand-replenishment project that added more than 20,000 cubic yards to the shoreline. Although it's one contiguous strand, it's as varied as the people who inhabit the Islands. Whether you want to kick back and watch the action from the shade or you want to get out in or on the water, you can find whatever you need here.

If you're staying outside the area and driving to it, park at either end of the beach and walk in. Metered parking is plentiful and affordable ($1 per hour) to the west, at Ala Wai Harbor, and to the east, at Kapiolani Park and the Honolulu Zoo. Resorts also have parking, but the hourly rates are high.

Duke's Beach
BEACH | FAMILY | Named for Hawaii's famous Olympic swimming champion and waterman, Duke Kahanamoku, this hard-packed beach fronting the Hilton Hawaiian Village Waikiki Beach Resort is great for families. It's the only stretch of Waikiki with shade trees on the sand, and its waters are very calm thanks to a rock wall that creates a semiprotected cove. The ocean clarity here is not as good as elsewhere, but this is a small price to pay for peace of mind about youngsters. **Amenities:** food and drink; parking (fee); showers; toilets. **Best for:** sunset; swimming; walking. ⊠ *2005 Kalia Rd., Waikiki.*

★ Fort DeRussy Beach Park
BEACH | FAMILY | A wide, soft, ultra-white shore with gently lapping waves makes this fine beach a family favorite for running-jumping-frolicking fun. Other bonuses include the shaded, grassy grilling area, the sand volleyball courts, and the many aquatic rental options. The beach fronts the Hale Koa Hotel as well as Fort DeRussy. **Amenities:** food and drink; lifeguards; showers; toilets; water sports. **Best for:** swimming; walking. ⊠ *2161 Kalia Rd., Waikiki.*

Kahaloa and Ulukou Beaches
BEACH | The "it" spots for the bikini crowd—and just about everyone else—have most of the catamaran charters that sail out to Diamond Head, as well as surf-board and outrigger canoe rentals that make it easy to take advantage of the Canoes surf break. Chair and umbrella rentals are available, and great music and outdoor dancing beckon at the lively Duke's restaurant, where shirt and shoes not only aren't required, they're discouraged. The Royal Hawaiian Hotel and the Moana Surfrider are both also here. **Amenities:** food and drink; lifeguards; parking (fee); showers; toilets; water sports. **Best for:** partiers; surfing. ⊠ *2259 Kalakaua Ave., Waikiki.*

Kuhio Beach Park
BEACH | FAMILY | Featuring a bronze statue of Duke Kahanamoku, the father of modern-day surfing, this lively beach is bordered by a landscaped walkway with a few benches and some shade. It's great for strolls and people-watching any time of day. Check out the Kuhio Beach hula mound Tuesday, Thursday, and Saturday at 6:30 (at 6, Nov.–Jan.) for free hula and Hawaiian-music performances and a sunset torch-lighting ceremony. Surf lessons for beginners are available from the beach center every half hour. **Amenities:** food and drink; lifeguards; showers; toilets; water sports. **Best for:** surfing; walking. ⊠ *2461 Kalakaua Ave.,*

Waikiki ⊕ Go past Moana Surfrider Hotel to Kapahulu Ave. pier.

Queen's Surf Beach

BEACH | FAMILY | Once the site of Queen Liliuokalani's beach house, this strand near the Waikiki Aquarium draws locals and tourists of all ages—and it seems as if someone is always playing a steel drum. Banyan trees offer shade, the bronze *Surfer on a Wave* sculpture by artist Robert Pashby honors surfing, volleyball nets welcome pros and amateurs alike, and waters that are part of an aquatic reserve provide superb snorkeling opportunities. The beach is also near what is considered the area's premier bodyboarding spot: the break called The Wall. **Amenities:** lifeguards; showers; toilets. **Best for:** swimming; walking. ⊠ *2598 Kalakaua Ave., Waikiki ⊕ Across from entrance to Honolulu Zoo.*

Kaimana (Sans Souci) Beach

BEACH | FAMILY | Across from the zoo, at the eastern end of Waikiki along what is known as the Gold Coast, this small rectangle of sand is a local-favorite sunning spot for beach lovers of all ages. Although it's usually quieter than the stretches of beach in the heart of town, it's also close to the conveniences of Waikiki. Children can splash safely in its shallow waters, which are protected (for now) by the walls of the historic natatorium, a long-closed, Olympic-size, saltwater swimming arena. Serious swimmers and triathletes also train in the channel beyond the reef here. The Kaimana Beach Hotel and popular Hau Tree lanai restaurant are next door. **Amenities:** lifeguards; parking (fee); showers; toilets. **Best for:** swimming; walking. ⊠ *2776 Kalakaua Ave., Waikiki ⊕ Across from Kapiolani Park, between New Otani Kaimana Beach Hotel and Waikiki War Memorial Natatorium.*

🍴 Restaurants

Waikiki has become a great destination for food lovers, with a new generation of innovative chefs and a renewed focus on using local ingredients, indigenous produce, and farm- and ocean-to-table cuisine. Although there are a number of familiar "chain" restaurants and traditional steak houses here, you can also find some solid choices for a variety of meals at all price points—from upscale dining rooms with a view to budget-friendly Japanese noodle shops.

Beachhouse at the Moana

$$$$ | MODERN HAWAIIAN | At this elegant, indoor-outdoor restaurant in Waikiki's oldest hotel, try for a table on the veranda, which overlooks the courtyard and a majestic banyan tree. Although it's open all day—and even serves afternoon tea—the Beachhouse is an especially delightful spot for a sunset dinner, when menu options range from crab cakes and paella to pork chops and steaks. **Known for:** gourmet dinners and afternoon tea; romantic setting; oceanfront dining. $ *Average main: $44* ⊠ *Moana Surfrider Hotel, 2365 Kalakaua Ave., Waikiki* ☎ *808/921–4600* ⊕ *www.beachhouse-waikiki.com.*

★ Bogart's Café

$$ | AMERICAN | Well established as a local favorite, this unassuming restaurant is situated in a strip mall near Diamond Head and away from the bustle of Waikiki. It's a great spot to grab a bagel or açai bowl in the morning or to linger over a post-sunset dinner—perhaps enjoying seared scallops with cauliflower puree, a pork chop with braised fennel, or one of the pasta dishes, including the chef's signature *cacio e pepe* featuring cheese imported from Italy's Dolomites region. **Known for:** sophisticated dinner menu; some outdoor seating; a neighborhood staple and local favorite for all-day dining. $ *Average main: $22* ⊠ *3045 Monsarrat*

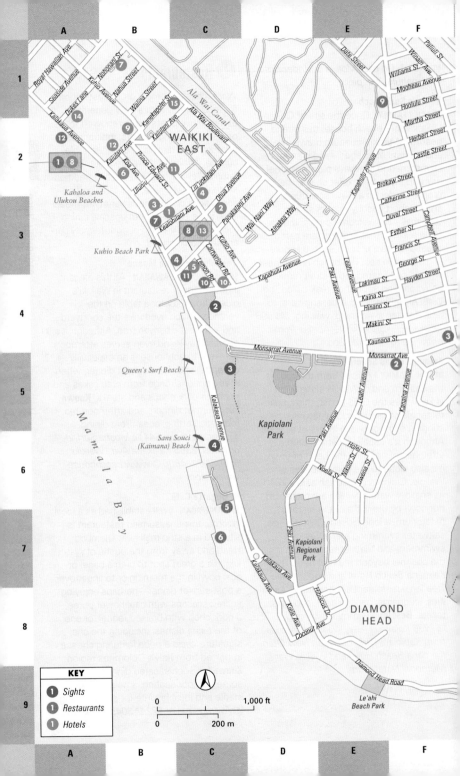

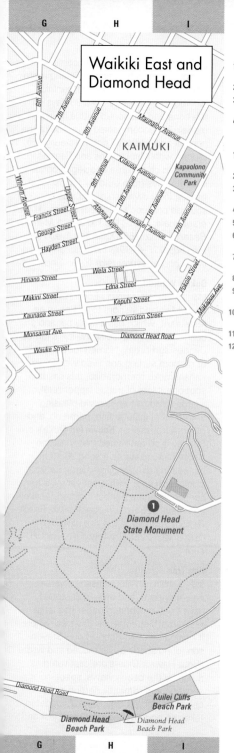

Waikiki East and Diamond Head

KAIMUKI

Diamond Head
State Monument

Kuilei Cliffs
Beach Park

Diamond Head
Beach Park

Diamond Head
Beach Park

Sights ▼

1 Diamond Head
  State Monument.........**I7**
2 Honolulu Zoo.............**C4**
3 Kapiolani Park
  Bandstand................**C5**
4 Waikiki Aquarium........**C6**

Restaurants ▼

1 Beachhouse at the
  Moana **A2**
2 Bogart's Café.............**F5**
3 Diamond Head
  Market & Grill............**F4**
4 d.k Steakhouse...........**C3**
5 Hau Tree **C7**
6 Michel's at the
  Colony Surf...............**C7**
7 Morimoto Asia
  Waikiki **B3**
8 Queensbreak.............**C3**
9 Side Street Inn
  Kapahulu.................**E1**
10 Teddy's
  Bigger Burgers..........**C4**
11 Tiki's Grill and Bar........**C4**
12 Waikiki Food Hall **A2**

Hotels ▼

1 Alohilani Resort
  Waikiki Beach...........**B3**
2 Aston at the
  Waikiki Banyan **C3**
3 Aston Waikiki
  Beach Tower............**B3**
4 Hilton Waikiki Beach....**C2**
5 Hotel Renew..............**C3**
6 Hyatt Regency Waikiki
  Beach Resort & Spa....**B2**
7 Ilima Hotel **B1**
8 Moana Surfrider,
  A Westin Resort & Spa,
  Waikiki Beach...........**A2**
9 Ohana Waikiki East
  by Outrigger.............**B2**
10 Queen Kapiolani
  Hotel.....................**C4**
11 Royal Grove Waikiki....**B2**
12 Sheraton Princess
  Kaiulani **B2**
13 Waikiki Beach Marriott
  Resort & Spa.............**C3**
14 Waikiki Beachcomber
  By Outrigger.............**A1**
15 Waikiki Sand
  Villa Hotel................**C1**

Ave., Waikiki ☎ *808/739–0999* 🌐 *www.bogartscafe.com.*

★ Chart House Waikiki

$$$$ | **AMERICAN** | Enjoy sunset views over the yacht harbor, live music, and signature "Guy-Tai" cocktails at this Waikiki landmark opened in 1969 by surfing legend Joey Cabell. The extensive menu maintains the midcentury notion of fine dining, with oysters Rockefeller, shrimp cocktail, and steaks (including a bison tenderloin from Ted Turner's ranch) alongside poke, macadamia-nut-crusted mahimahi, and the fan-favorite "Joey's ahi mignon." Early birds can take advantage of the "surf break" menu, and there's also a very popular weekend brunch (book in advance). **Known for:** old-time steak house atmosphere with live music and strong cocktails; generations of regulars; sought-after tables on the lanai (book well in advance). [$] *Average main: $48* ✉ *1765 Ala Moana Blvd., Waikiki* ☎ *808/941–6669* 🌐 *charthousewaikiki.com* 🕓 *No lunch.*

Diamond Head Market & Grill

$ | **AMERICAN** | **FAMILY** | Just five minutes from Waikiki's hotels is chef Kelvin Ro's one-stop food shop—indispensable if you have accommodations with a kitchen or want a quick grab-and-go meal. Join surfers, beachgoers, and Diamond Head hikers at the takeout window to order gourmet sandwiches and plates, such as hand-shaped burgers, portobello mushroom sandwiches, Korean *kalbi* ribs, and grilled ahi with wasabi-ginger sauce, rice, and salad. Selections include sandwiches, bento boxes, and salads. **Known for:** picnic fare for the beach; well-priced grab-and-go dinners; excellent desserts and scones. [$] *Average main: $14* ✉ *3158 Monsarrat Ave., Diamond Head* ☎ *808/732–0077* 🌐 *www.diamondheadmarket.com.*

d.k Steakhouse

$$$$ | **STEAKHOUSE** | D. K. Kodama serves steaks that are free from hormones, antibiotics, and steroids and come straight from Oahu's first dry-aging room. Consider trying the 22-ounce *paniolo* (cowboy) rib eye—dry-aged 30 days on the bone and seasoned with a house-made rub—accompanied by a side of the popular and addictive potatoes au gratin, topped with Maui onions and Parmesan. **Known for:** gluten-free and vegan options; sunset views from outdoor tables; local flavors, local ownership, and locally sourced produce and select meats. [$] *Average main: $55* ✉ *Waikiki Beach Marriott Resort & Spa, 2552 Kalakaua Ave., Waikiki* ☎ *808/931–6280* 🌐 *dkrestaurants.com/index.php/restaurants/dk* 🕓 *No lunch.*

Duke's Waikiki

$$$ | **AMERICAN** | **FAMILY** | Locals often bring Mainland visitors to this open-air restaurant, which has a lively bar and a beachfront setting facing Waikiki's famed Canoes surf break. Named for the father of modern surfing and filled with Duke Kahanamoku memorabilia, this casual spot offers lots of pupus (appetizers), a large salad bar, and crowd-pleasing entrées that include fish, prime rib, and *huli huli* (rotisserie). **Known for:** Duke's on Sunday is so renowned that musician Henry Kapono wrote a song about it; bar seating usually offers faster service; iconic local spot with great views, a fun bar scene, and a perfect location. [$] *Average main: $28* ✉ *Outrigger Waikiki Beach Resort, 2335 Kalakaua Ave., Waikiki* ☎ *808/922–2268* 🌐 *www.dukeswaikiki.com.*

Hau Tree

$$$ | **AMERICAN** | Countless anniversaries, birthdays, and other milestones have been celebrated under this lanai restaurant's spectacular *hau* tree, where it's said that even Robert Louis Stevenson found shade as he mused and wrote about Hawaii. Diners are captivated as much by the beach views, spectacular sunsets, and romantic setting as by celebrated chef Chris Kajioka's updated takes on eggs Benedict at breakfast and

tuna tartar, scallops, or Kurobuta pork chops later in the day. **Known for:** spectacular views of the beach by day and the moonlit water by night; an updated menu and attentive service; the romantic beach dining spot folks dream about. [$] *Average main: $29* ✉ *The New Otani Kaimana Beach Hotel, 2863 Kalakaua Ave., Waikiki* ☎ *808/921–7066* 🌐 *www.kaimana.com.*

★ Island Vintage Wine Bar

$$ | **WINE BAR** | Tucked away on the second floor of the Royal Hawaiian Center, this stylish, sleek, and cozy spot has a selection of more than 40 international wines by the glass—all served via a high-tech vending machine that uses prepaid cards. The food menu is limited, but a few favorites include oversize Wagyu burgers, poke bites with nori chips, and cheese and charcuterie plates. **Known for:** a subdued happy hour; massive Wagyu burgers; vending-machine wines by the glass. [$] *Average main: $25* ✉ *Royal Hawaiian Center, 2301 Kalakaua Ave., Bldg. C, Level 2, Waikiki* ☎ *808/799–9463* 🌐 *www.islandvintagewinebar.com.*

La Mer

$$$$ | **FRENCH** | With spectacular Diamond Head views and an elegant, art deco–tinged interior, La Mer is a romantic, second-floor restaurant, where windows open to the breezes and the sounds of the ocean and Halekulani Hotel's nightly hula show. Three-, four-, or seven-course dinners might feature *kampachi* (amberjack) ceviche with ginger caviar fennel, roasted John Dory with artichokes *barigoule* (braised in white-wine broth), or tomahawk steak (rib eye) with vegetables. **Known for:** impressive wine list and a sommelier to match; classy bar with cocktail and small-bite pairings; it doesn't get more romantic than this. [$] *Average main: $160* ✉ *Halekulani Hotel, 2199 Kalia Rd., Waikiki* ☎ *808/923–2311* 🌐 *www.halekulani.com/dining/la-mer* 🕒 *No lunch* 👔 *Long-sleeved, collared (or aloha) shirts required for men.*

Pupu 🍴

Entertaining Hawaii-style means having a lot of *pupu*—the local term for appetizers or hors d'oeuvres—which are often served during *pau hana*, the Islands-style happy hour when locals wind down from the workday and enjoy a couple of drinks. Popular pupu include sushi, tempura, teriyaki chicken or beef skewers, barbecued meat, and the favorite: *poke* (pronounced "po-keh"), or raw fish, seasoned with seaweed, shoyu, and other flavorings.

Michel's at the Colony Surf

$$$$ | **FRENCH** | This romantic restaurant on Waikiki's tranquil Gold Coast features beachside sunset views and traditional French fare. It opened in 1962, and the surroundings reflect this, with lots of wood and stone, bow-tied servers preparing lobster bisque and steak tartare table-side, and a charm that's beloved by old-time locals but sometimes lost on younger diners. **Known for:** classic French cuisine with some local twists; a pricey experience and a retro vibe; the sound of the surf and live music most nights. [$] *Average main: $65* ✉ *Colony Surf, 2895 Kalakaua Ave., Waikiki* ☎ *808/923–6552* 🌐 *www.michelshawaii.com* 🕒 *No lunch.*

Morimoto Asia Waikiki

$$$$ | **JAPANESE FUSION** | Iron Chef Masaharu Morimoto serves classics and new fusion favorites at his second-floor restaurant—a sleek space with a lanai, a gorgeous bar, and a dining room designed for entertaining clients or celebrating with friends. Enjoy some Morimoto specialties, including *ishiyaki buri bop* (yellowtail seared tableside with pickled daikon, royal fern, and egg yolk) or spicy black pepper steak, as well as dim

sum, sushi, and creative specialty rolls. **Known for:** casual elegance in a lovely spot; Asian-fusion menu with enough classics to draw loyalists; attentive service and great food. $ *Average main: $41* ✉ *Alohilani Resort, 2490 Kalakaua Ave., Waikiki* ☎ *808/922–0022* ⊕ *morimotoasiawaikiki.com.*

100 Sails Restaurant and Bar

$$$$ | ECLECTIC | FAMILY | The spacious, airy 100 Sails continues the everything-you-can-imagine buffet tradition (with crab legs and prime rib, of course), along with plenty of à la carte small bites, an emphasis on locally sourced ingredients, and a commitment to knock-out presentation. And then there are the views—night after night, the sunsets over the harbor deliver stunning shows of color. **Known for:** views and sunsets to rival those anywhere else in Waikiki; high-quality food and a huge selection; international buffet for every meal. $ *Average main: $60* ✉ *Hawaii Prince Hotel Waikiki, 100 Holomoana St., Waikiki* ☎ *808/944–4494* ⊕ *www.100sails.com.*

★ Orchids

$$$$ | SEAFOOD | Perched along the seawall at historic Gray's Beach, in the luxe Halekulani resort, Orchids is a locus of power breakfasters, ladies who lunch, and those celebrating special occasions at Sunday brunch or dinner. The louvered walls are open to the breezes, sprays of orchids add color, the contemporary international dishes are perfectly prepared, and the wine list is intriguing. **Known for:** lovely ocean views and live music at sunset; a menu with something for just about everyone; island breezes, ocean sounds, and stellar service and food. $ *Average main: $42* ✉ *Halekulani Hotel, 2199 Kalia Rd., Waikiki* ☎ *808/923–2311* ⊕ *www.halekulani.com/dining/orchids-restaurant* 🏛 *Collared shirts required for men.*

Queensbreak

$$$ | AMERICAN | FAMILY | Across from popular Kuhio Beach, and three floors up from busy Waikiki on the pool deck at the Waikiki Beach Marriott Resort & Spa, this laid-back, multilevel, terrace restaurant is a great place to grab a casual bite (fish tacos, poke, Caesar salad, burgers) and a beer, a glass of wine, or a tropical cocktail. In addition to ocean views, you can enjoy happy hour specials and live music. **Known for:** casual favorites on the menu; live music in the evening; outdoor dining. $ *Average main: $35* ✉ *Waikiki Beach Marriott Resort & Spa, 2552 Kalakaua Ave., Waikiki* ☎ *808/922–6611* ⊕ *www.queensbreak.com.*

Side Street Inn Kapahulu

$$ | ECLECTIC | FAMILY | The original Hopaka Street pub is famous as the place where celebrity chefs gather after hours; this second Kapahulu Avenue location is also popular and closer to Waikiki. Local-style bar food—salty panfried pork chops with a plastic tub of ketchup, *lup cheong* fried rice, and passion fruit–glazed ribs—is served in huge, shareable portions. **Known for:** popular local spot with a crowd of regulars; sports-bar feel with lots of fried food; portions that can seemingly feed you for a week. $ *Average main: $25* ✉ *614 Kapahulu Ave., Waikiki* ☎ *808/739–3939* ⊕ *www.sidestreetinn.com* ��� *No lunch.*

Teddy's Bigger Burgers

$ | BURGER | Modeled after 1950s diners, this casual spot serves classic, tender, messy burgers—including the Hawaiian teriyaki burger with grilled pineapple and the Kailua with Swiss cheese, mushrooms, and grilled onions—along with turkey and veggie burgers, salads, and chicken breast and fish sandwiches. The fries are crispy, and the shakes rich and sweet. **Known for:** diner-style service, with food to go; local chain for dependable quick lunches across the island; messy burgers, great fries, and

Waikiki and Honolulu, looking west to Diamond Head, as seen from above

rich milkshakes. [$] *Average main: $12* ✉ *Waikiki Grand Hotel, 134 Kapahulu Ave., Waikiki* ☎ *808/926–3444* 🌐 *www.teddysbb.com.*

★ Tiki's Grill and Bar

$$$ | **MODERN HAWAIIAN** | Tiki's is the kind of fun place people come to Waikiki for: a retro–South Pacific spot with a back-of-the-bar faux volcano, open-air lounge with live local music, indoor-outdoor dining, and a fantastic view of the beach across the street. Chef Ronnie Nasuti turns out beautifully composed plates and puts fresh twists on the super-familiar—like spicy "volcano" chicken wings, watermelon and feta salad, or Thai-style shrimp puttanesca. **Known for:** Pacific Rim menu inspired by a noted Islands chef; can get pricey, but a fun experience worthy of a hana hou (encore); surprisingly good food in a made-for-TV setting. [$] *Average main: $32* ✉ *Aston Waikiki Beach Hotel, 2570 Kalakaua Ave., Waikiki* ☎ *808/923–8454* 🌐 *www.tikisgrill.com.*

★ Waikiki Food Hall

$ | **HAWAIIAN** | **FAMILY** | At this bright, lively, upscale food court on the third floor of the Royal Hawaiian Center, you can feast on local and Japanese options ranging from massive, juicy burgers to spicy shrimp tacos to exquisite smoothies topped with colorful, edible designs—all emphasizing the use of fresh, local ingredients. Vendors here include Five Star Shrimp, Milk, JTRRD, Meatally Boys, POTAMA (Pork Tamago Onigiri), Honolulu Burger Co., Surfer's Cafe, and Tap Bar. **Known for:** variety of vendors offering upscale options that you can mix and match; lots of seating; new and modern. [$] *Average main: $14* ✉ *Royal Hawaiian Center, 2201 Kalakaua Ave., Bldg. C, 3rd fl., Waikiki* ✥ *Above the Cheesecake Factory* ☎ *808/922–2299 for Royal Hawaiian Center* 🌐 *www.waikikifoodhall.com.*

Hotels

A stay in Waikiki puts you in the heart of the action, and though parking can be difficult and pricey, you really don't need a car as there's ready access to the beach, restaurants, activities, and affordable public transportation. To be slightly removed from the main scene, however, opt for accommodations on the *ewa* (western) end of Waikiki.

The hotel selection ranges from super-luxe resorts to small, no-frills places where surfers and beachgoers hang out in the lobby. Room sizes, styles, and configurations can vary tremendously even in the same hotel, so ask questions to ensure that you get an ocean view, say, or have other requirements met. Also inquire about extras: for instance, some hotels—even if they aren't right on the sand—provide their guests with sunblock, towels, chairs, and other beach accessories.

★ Alohilani Resort Waikiki Beach

$$$ | HOTEL | FAMILY | The centerpiece of this modern, stylish high-rise, across the street from the beach in the center of Waikiki, is the lobby's mesmerizing aquarium, filled with nearly 300,000 gallons of seawater and colorful marine life. **Pros:** new and modern, with several on-site restaurants; cutting-edge fitness facilities and spa; excellent guest lounge. **Cons:** large hotel that can feel impersonal; you must cross the street for the beach; resort fee is $48 per day. $ *Rooms from: $275* ⊠ *2490 Kalakaua Ave., Waikiki* ☎ *808/922–1233* ⊕ *www.alohilaniresort. com* ⌐ *839 rooms* ⦿ *No Meals.*

Aston at the Waikiki Banyan

$$ | RESORT | FAMILY | Families and active travelers love the convenience and action of this hotel, often referred to as "the Banyan," just a block from Waikiki Beach, the aquarium, the zoo, and bustling Kalakaua Avenue. **Pros:** many suites have great views as well as kitchens; fabulous and massive recreation deck for the entire family; shuttle service around Waikiki. **Cons:** resort fee is $25 per day; sharing hotel with residents; suites are individually owned so conditions can vary greatly. $ *Rooms from: $200* ⊠ *201 Ohua Ave., Waikiki* ☎ *808/922–0555, 877/997–6667 toll-free for reservations* ⊕ *www.astonwaikikibanyan.com* ⌐ *876 suites* ⦿ *No Meals.*

Aston Waikiki Beach Tower

$$$$ | RESORT | FAMILY | Here, in the center of Waikiki, you get the elegance of a luxury all-suites condominium combined with the intimacy and service of a boutique hotel. **Pros:** roomy suites with quality amenities; great private lanai and views; a recreation deck with something for everyone. **Cons:** you must cross a busy street to the beach; space, amenities, and location don't come cheap; resort fee is $35 per day. $ *Rooms from: $699* ⊠ *2470 Kalakaua Ave., Waikiki* ☎ *808/926–6400, 855/776–1766 toll-free* ⊕ *www.astonwaikikibeachtower.com* ⌐ *140 suites* ⦿ *No Meals.*

The Breakers Hotel

$ | HOTEL | With a homey atmosphere and a vintage vibe, this small, low-rise complex—two blocks from the beach and close to the Waikiki Beach Walk entertainment, dining, and retail complex—transports its guests back to 1960s-era Hawaii. **Pros:** intimate atmosphere with fabulous poolside courtyard; great location; a throwback to a different era. **Cons:** parking is extremely limited (but free); showers only; a bit worn down and dated. $ *Rooms from: $170* ⊠ *250 Beach Walk, Waikiki* ☎ *808/923–3181, 800/923–7174 toll-free* ⊕ *www.breakers-hawaii. com* ⌐ *63 rooms* ⦿ *No Meals.*

DoubleTree by Hilton Alana – Waikiki Beach

$$ | HOTEL | A convenient location—a 10-minute walk from the Hawaii Convention Center—a professional staff, pleasant public spaces, and a 24-hour business center and small gym draw a global clientele to this reliable chain

hotel. **Pros:** walkable to the beach and Ala Moana mall; walk-in glass showers with oversize rain showerheads; heated outdoor pool and 24-hour fitness center. **Cons:** little local flavor; resort fee is $30 per day; a 10-minute walk to the beach. Ⓢ *Rooms from: $230* ✉ *1956 Ala Moana Blvd., Waikiki* ☎ *808/941–7275* ⊕ *www. hilton.com/en/hotels/hnlkadt-double-tree-alana-waikiki-beach* ⇱ *317 rooms* ⦿ *No Meals.*

Embassy Suites by Hilton Waikiki Beach Walk

$$$ | **RESORT** | **FAMILY** | In a place where space is at a premium, this resort in the heart of Waikiki's Beach Walk dining and shopping area offers families and other groups spacious, one- and two-bedroom suites stylishly decorated in relaxing earth tones with splashes of color. **Pros:** no resort fee; spacious and modern rooms; free hot breakfast and happy hour reception daily. **Cons:** lobby feels more like a business hotel; property can seem busy and noisy; no direct beach access. Ⓢ *Rooms from: $319* ✉ *201 Beachwalk St., Waikiki* ☎ *800/362–2779 toll-free, 808/921–2345 direct to hotel* ⊕ *www. embassysuiteswaikiki.com* ⇱ *369 suites* ⦿ *Free Breakfast.*

The Equus

$ | **HOTEL** | **FAMILY** | On the *ewa* (western) end of Waikiki, a block from both the Ala Moana Center and Ala Moana Beach Park, this modern, family-owned, boutique hotel has a Hawaiian country theme that pays tribute to Hawaii's polo-playing history. **Pros:** casual and fun atmosphere; attentive staff; nicely furnished rooms. **Cons:** must cross a major road to reach the beach; resort fee is $25 a day; busy, hectic area. Ⓢ *Rooms from: $160* ✉ *1696 Ala Moana Blvd., Waikiki* ☎ *808/949–0061* ⊕ *www.equushotel.com* ⇱ *67 rooms* ⦿ *No Meals.*

★ Halekulani

$$$$ | **RESORT** | Its name translates to the "house befitting heaven," and this beach-front haven does, indeed, seem like a slice of heaven thanks to impeccable service and spacious guest rooms that are artfully appointed with marble and wood, neutral color schemes, modern furniture, updated technology, and bathrooms that have oversize soaking tubs as well as showers. **Pros:** heavenly interior and exterior spaces; award-winning spa and wonderful bars and restaurants; no resort fee. **Cons:** narrow beachfront with little room for sunbathing; lofty room rates; might feel a bit formal for Waikiki. Ⓢ *Rooms from: $500* ✉ *2199 Kalia Rd., Waikiki* ☎ *808/923–2311 direct to hotel, 800/367–2343 reservations toll-free* ⊕ *www.halekulani.com* ⇱ *453 rooms* ⦿ *No Meals.*

★ Halepuna Waikiki by Halekulani

$$$$ | **HOTEL** | This high-rise boutique property offers the same outstanding service and attention to detail as its elegant sister hotel, the Halekulani, but without the beachfront location and higher prices. **Pros:** fresh, modern, and well appointed; great access to Waikiki Beach and Beach Walk shopping and dining; no resort fee. **Cons:** rooms can be small; swimming pool can get busy; no direct beach access. Ⓢ *Rooms from: $366* ✉ *2233 Helumoa Rd., Waikiki* ☎ *808/921–7272 direct to hotel, 800/422–0450 reservations toll-free* ⊕ *www.halepuna.com* ⇱ *297 rooms* ⦿ *No Meals.*

Hilton Hawaiian Village Waikiki Beach Resort

$$$ | **RESORT** | **FAMILY** | Location, location, location: this five-tower mega-resort sprawls over 22 acres on Waikiki's widest stretch of beach, with the greenery of neighboring Fort DeRussy creating a buffer zone between it and central Waikiki's high-rise lineup. **Pros:** activities and amenities can keep you and the kids busy for weeks; stellar spa and fitness center; a large variety of room options. **Cons:** resort fee is $50 per day; parking is expensive ($49 per day for self-parking); size of property can be overwhelming. Ⓢ *Rooms from: $325* ✉ *2005 Kalia Rd.,*

Waikiki ☎ 808/949–4321, 800/774–1500 toll-free ⊕ www.hiltonhawaiianvillage. com ⬩ 4499 rooms ⦿❘ No Meals.

Hilton Waikiki Beach

$$ | HOTEL | On the Diamond Head end of Waikiki and two blocks from Kuhio Beach, this 37-story high-rise is great for travelers who want to be near the action but not right in it. **Pros:** central location; every room has a lanai; pleasant, comfortable public spaces. **Cons:** $45 a day (valet only parking); older property that shows some wear; resort fee is $30 per day. $ *Rooms from: $225 ⊠ 2500 Kuhio Ave., Waikiki ☎ 808/922–0811 direct to hotel, 888/370–0980 toll-free ⊕ www. hiltonwaikikibeach.com ⬩ 609 rooms ⦿❘ No Meals.*

Hotel Renew

$ | HOTEL | Just a block from Waikiki Beach, this stylish boutique hotel focuses on wellness and renewal, making it a calm alternative to the big, bustling resorts that dominate the area. **Pros:** free beach supplies, including towels, chairs, umbrellas, and snorkel gear; personalized, upscale service; close to zoo, aquarium, and beach. **Cons:** daily amenity fee of $25; rooms do not have lanai; no pool. $ *Rooms from: $165 ⊠ 129 Paoakalani Ave., Waikiki ☎ 808/687–7700, 877/997–6667 toll-free ⊕ www.hotelrenew.com ⬩ 72 rooms ⦿❘ No Meals.*

Hyatt Regency Waikiki Beach Resort & Spa

$$$ | RESORT | FAMILY | There's no other resort between the ocean and this high-rise hotel, which is across the street from Kuhio Beach and features a lively, atrium-style lobby with three levels of shopping (including a farmers' market on Tuesday and Thursday afternoons), a two-story waterfall, gardens, and free live evening entertainment. **Pros:** on-site spa and many shopping and dining options; spacious rooms with soaring windows and lanai; beach chairs and towels for guests. **Cons:** on-site pool is quite small; resort fee is $45 per day; in a very busy and crowded part of Waikiki. $ *Rooms*

Condo Comforts

The local **Foodland** grocery-store chain has two locations near Waikiki, one in Market City in Kaimuki (⊠ 2939 Harding Ave. ☎ 808/734–6303) and the other in the Ala Moana Center (⊠ 1450 Ala Moana Blvd. ☎ 808/949–5044).

The popular ABC convenience stores have many locations. In addition to beach supplies, apparel, and just about everything else, some also sell foodstuffs, made-to-order meals, and alcoholic beverages.

from: $300 ⊠ 2424 Kalakaua Ave., Waikiki ☎ 808/923–1234 direct to hotel, 800/633–7313 toll-free for reservations ⊕ www.hyattregencywaikiki.com ⬩ 1230 rooms ⦿❘ No Meals.

Ilima Hotel

$ | HOTEL | FAMILY | Tucked away on a residential side street near Waikiki's Ala Wai Canal, this locally owned, 17-story, condo-style hotel is a throwback to old Waikiki, offering large units that are ideal for families. **Pros:** free parking (first-come, first-served); spacious rooms with separate bedrooms and kitchens; friendly and helpful service. **Cons:** resort fee is $29 per day; no ocean views; furnishings are dated (though renovations are planned). $ *Rooms from: $160 ⊠ 445 Nohonani St., Waikiki ☎ 808/923–1877, 800/801–9366 ⊕ www.ilima.com ⬩ 98 units ⦿❘ No Meals.*

Luana Waikiki Hotel & Suites

$$ | HOTEL | FAMILY | If you like Hawaiiana and appreciate a bit of kitsch, this welcoming hotel with both rooms and condo units is a great option. **Pros:** free yoga and folding bicycles; sundeck with pool and barbecue grills; on-site coin-operated laundry facilities. **Cons:** resort fee is $25 per day; pool is small; no direct beach access. [$] *Rooms from: $225* ✉ *2045 Kalakaua Ave., Waikiki* ☎ *808/955–6000 direct to hotel, 855/747–0755 toll-free* 🌐 *www.aquaaston.com/hotels/luana-waikiki-hotel-and-suites* 🛏 *225 units* 🍴 *No Meals.*

Moana Surfrider, A Westin Resort & Spa, Waikiki Beach
$$$$ | RESORT | Waikiki's oldest hotel is still a wedding and honeymoon favorite, with a sweeping main staircase and Victorian furnishings in its historic (and expensive) Moana Wing and more contemporary rooms in its 1950s-era Diamond Head Tower and refurbished Surfrider Tower, where oceanfront suites have two separate lanai—one for sunrise and another for sunset. **Pros:** elegant, historic property; lovely beach bar that often features live music; can't beat the location. **Cons:** resort fee is $42 per day; expensive parking ($35 per day for self-parking across the street); you'll likely dodge bridal parties in the lobby. [$] *Rooms from: $479* ✉ *2365 Kalakaua Ave., Waikiki* ☎ *808/922–3111, 866/716–8112 toll-free* 🌐 *www.moana-surfrider.com* 🛏 *791 rooms* 🍴 *No Meals.*

Ohana Waikiki East by Outrigger
$$ | HOTEL | FAMILY | If you want to be in central Waikiki and don't want to pay beachfront lodging prices, consider the Ohana Waikiki East, which is a mere two blocks from the beach and within walking distance of shopping, restaurants, and nightlife. **Pros:** reasonable rates close to the beach; in the middle of the Waikiki action; spacious accommodations. **Cons:** an older property with signs of wear and tear; resort fee is $25 per day and parking fee is $35 per night; very basic public spaces. [$] *Rooms from: $259* ✉ *150 Kaiulani Ave., Waikiki* ☎ *808/922–5353 direct to hotel, 866/956–4262 toll-free* 🌐 *www.outrigger.com/hotels-resorts/hawaii/oahu/ohana-waikiki-east-by-outrigger* 🛏 *441 rooms* 🍴 *No Meals.*

Looking for a Private Beach?

Oahu's oldest hotels—the Royal Hawaiian Hotel and Moana Surfrider—are also the only hotels in Waikiki with property lines that extend into the sand. They have created private roped-off beach areas with lounge chairs and umbrellas that can be accessed only by hotel guests for a fee. The areas are adjacent to the hotel properties at the top of the beach and usually require reservations during the busy season.

Outrigger Reef Waikiki Beach Resort
$$$ | HOTEL | FAMILY | A prime location and aloha spirit keep guests returning to the Outrigger Reef, where rooms were renovated and the beach was widened in 2021, with 23 new rooms, a beachfront restaurant, and a luxury guest lounge added in 2022. **Pros:** on the beach; direct access to Waikiki Beach Walk; attentive staff. **Cons:** views from nonoceanfront rooms are uninspiring; resort fee is $40 per day; pool is not beachfront. [$] *Rooms from: $319* ✉ *2169 Kalia Rd., Waikiki* ☎ *808/923–3111 direct to hotel, 866/956–4262 toll-free, 800/688–7444* 🌐 *www.outriggerreef-onthebeach.com* 🛏 *669 rooms* 🍴 *No Meals.*

Outrigger Waikiki Beach Resort
$$$$ | RESORT | FAMILY | Outrigger's star property sits on one of the finest sections of Waikiki Beach, a location that—along with an array of cultural and dining options and great live-music and bar scenes—make it a favorite. **Pros:** the best beach bar in Waikiki; on-site activities and amenities (including a spa) abound; excellent lounge that's worth splurging on an upgrade to access. **Cons:** resort fee is $40 per day; rooms are dated; a busy property (often used as

a pedestrian throughway to the beach). [$] *Rooms from: $450* ✉ *2335 Kalakaua Ave., Waikiki* ☎ *808/923–0711, 808/956–4262, 800/442–7304 toll-free* 🌐 *www.outriggerwaikikihotel.com* 🛏 *525 rooms* 🍴 *No Meals.*

Prince Waikiki

$$$$ | **HOTEL** | The sleek, modern Prince—which looks to Asia both in its high-style decor and such pampering touches as the traditional *oshiburi* (chilled hand towel) for refreshment upon check-in—has luxury oceanfront rooms and suites overlooking the Ala Wai Boat Harbor at Waikiki's *ewa* (western) edge. **Pros:** fantastic views from all rooms; no resort fee; parking included. **Cons:** no beach access; rooms don't have lanai; busy property. [$] *Rooms from: $400* ✉ *100 Holomoana St., Waikiki* ☎ *888/977–4623 toll-free for reservations, 808/956–1111 direct to hotel* 🌐 *www.princewaikiki.com* 🛏 *563 rooms* 🍴 *No Meals.*

Queen Kapiolani Hotel

$$$ | **HOTEL** | With a contemporary look combined with a retro nod to the 1970s, the Queen Kapiolani Hotel is a short walk from the beach and is known for its stunning, unobstructed views of Diamond Head—a fabulous backdrop for its expansive pool deck. **Pros:** incredible Diamond Head views; beach gear available at valet desk; large collection of museum-quality art. **Cons:** bathrooms are small and a bit dated; noise from pool bar can be bothersome; resort fee is $40 per day. [$] *Rooms from: $280* ✉ *150 Kapahulu Ave., Waikiki* ☎ *808/650–7841* 🌐 *www.queenkapiolani.com* 🛏 *315 rooms* 🍴 *No Meals.*

Royal Grove Waikiki

$ | **HOTEL** | This pink, six-story hotel feels like a throwback to the days of boarding houses—when rooms were outfitted for function, not style, and served with simple hospitality at a price that didn't break the bank. **Pros:** very economical Waikiki option; no resort fee; a bit of local flavor. **Cons:** rooms and property are very dated; no on-site parking and minimum stays during busy seasons; no air-conditioning in some rooms. [$] *Rooms from: $150* ✉ *151 Uluniu Ave., Waikiki* ☎ *808/923–7691* 🌐 *www.royalgrovehotel.com* 🛏 *87 rooms* 🍴 *No Meals.*

★ The Royal Hawaiian, a Luxury Collection Resort, Waikiki

$$$$ | **RESORT** | There's nothing like the iconic "Pink Palace of the Pacific," which is on 14 acres of prime Waikiki Beach and which has held fast to the luxury and grandeur that first defined it in the 1930s, when it became a favorite of the rich and famous. **Pros:** can't beat it for history; mai tais and sunsets are amazing; luxury in a prime location. **Cons:** high-traffic driveway entrance in center of Waikiki; very small swimming pool; resort fee is $42 per day. [$] *Rooms from: $525* ✉ *2259 Kalakaua Ave., Waikiki* ☎ *808/923–7311, 866/716–8110 toll-free* 🌐 *www.royal-hawaiian.com* 🛏 *528 rooms* 🍴 *No Meals.*

Sheraton Princess Kaiulani

$$ | **HOTEL** | **FAMILY** | The Princess Kaiulani sits across the street from the regal Moana Surfrider, without some of the more elaborate amenities (such as a spa or a kid's club), but with rates that are considerably kinder to the wallet. **Pros:** in the heart of everything in Waikiki, with the beach right across the street; beach service with chairs, towels, fruit, and water available; great value for the location. **Cons:** self parking is $42 per night; resort fee is $37 per day; lobby area can feel like Grand Central Station. [$] *Rooms from: $259* ✉ *120 Kaiulani Ave., Waikiki* ☎ *808/922–5811, 866/716–8109 toll-free* 🌐 *www.princess-kaiulani.com* 🛏 *1040 rooms* 🍴 *No Meals.*

★ Sheraton Waikiki

$$$$ | **HOTEL** | **FAMILY** | Towering over its neighbors along the beachfront, this big, busy hotel offers stunning views from most of its modern rooms, which have been updated in neutral shades with

Hotel Cultural Programs

In 2022, the state launched its Malama Hawaii program, which encourages visitors to learn about and care for the land and to seek authentic Island experiences. As part of this program, some hotels are offering special packages and voluntourism opportunities. Be sure to ask about them when booking.

In addition to lei-making and hula-dancing lessons, you can learn how to strum a ukulele, listen to Grammy Award–winning Hawaiian musicians, watch a revered master *kumu* (teacher) share the art of ancient hula and chant, chat with a marine biologist about Hawaii's endangered species, learn about the island's sustainability efforts, or get a lesson in the Hawaiian language or in the art of canoe making.

splashes of color. **Pros:** fresh, modern guest rooms; variety of on-site activities and dining options; swimming pools often ranked among the Islands' best. **Cons:** resort fee is $42 per day; room sizes and views vary; busy atmosphere clashes with laid-back Hawaiian style. $ *Rooms from: $455* ⊠ *2255 Kalakaua Ave., Waikiki* ☎ *808/922–4422, 866/716–8109 toll-free for reservations* ⊕ *www.sheraton-waikiki.com* ➲ *1636 rooms* ❖ *No Meals.*

Shoreline Hotel Waikiki

$$$$ | **HOTEL** | Situated on bustling Seaside Avenue, this 14-story, 1970s-era property has been transformed into an urban-chic boutique hotel with both island and retro touches that playfully blend 20th-century style with modern necessities. **Pros:** great location in the middle of Waikiki; resort fee waived if you book direct; hipster decor a refreshing break from old-style Hawaiiana. **Cons:** rooms are inconsistently sized and equipped; pool is accessed via two flights of stairs; if splashy colors aren't your thing, skip it. $ *Rooms from: $359* ⊠ *342 Seaside Ave., Waikiki* ☎ *808/931–2444, 855/931–2444 toll-free* ⊕ *www.shorelinehotelwaikiki.com* ➲ *135 rooms* ❖ *No Meals.*

Surfjack Hotel & Swim Club

$$$ | **HOTEL** | A surfing vibe and authentic, whimsical Hawaiian touches throughout (the lobby, for instance, evokes the living room of the interior designer's grandmother) set this hip boutique property apart from other modernized midcentury digs. **Pros:** hipster, urban-chic vibe that works; retro, locally designed decor; Ed Kenney restaurant on-site. **Cons:** far from the beach; rooms can be inconsistent; resort fee is $25 per day. $ *Rooms from: $300* ⊠ *412 Lewers St., Waikiki* ☎ *808/923–8882* ⊕ *www.surfjack.com* ➲ *112 rooms* ❖ *No Meals.*

Waikiki Beach Marriott Resort & Spa

$$$$ | **RESORT** | **FAMILY** | Set on 5 acres across from Kuhio Beach and close to Kapiolani Park, the Honolulu Zoo, and the Waikiki Aquarium, this flagship Marriott offers daily activities for children and adults and has an expansive pool deck with ocean views, several pools, plenty of cabanas and lounge chairs, and the Queensbreak restaurant. **Pros:** massive pool deck; lots of airy, tropical public spaces; central location in Waikiki. **Cons:** self-parking is $45 per day; resort fee is $37 per day; large impersonal hotel, requires lots of walking. $ *Rooms from: $350* ⊠ *2552 Kalakaua Ave., Waikiki*

☎ 808/922–6611, 800/367–5370 toll-free 🌐 www.marriottwaikiki.com 🛏 1310 rooms 🍴 No Meals.

Waikiki Beachcomber by Outrigger
$$ | HOTEL | FAMILY | Almost directly across from the Royal Hawaiian Center and next to International Market Place, the Beachcomber is a well-situated high-rise hotel for families as well as those looking for a boutique feel in the heart of the action. **Pros:** great beach views from some rooms; renovated and stylish; lovely pool area. **Cons:** not beachfront; resort fee is $35 per day; very busy area in the thick of Waikiki action. *[$] Rooms from: $260 ✉ 2300 Kalakaua Ave., Waikiki ☎ 808/922–4646, 877/418–0711 🌐 www.waikikibeachcomber.com 🛏 496 rooms 🍴 No Meals.*

Waikiki Sand Villa Hotel
$ | HOTEL | FAMILY | This family-run property offers economical rates and proximity to the beach, restaurants, and shops—all just three blocks away. **Pros:** recently refreshed rooms; pool and foot spa great for lounging; no resort fee. **Cons:** 10-minute walk to the beach; street noise from Ala Wai can get loud; noise from the bar might annoy some. *[$] Rooms from: $165 ✉ 2375 Ala Wai Blvd., Waikiki ☎ 808/922–4744, 800/247–1903 toll-free 🌐 www.waikikisandvillahotel.com 🛏 214 rooms 🍴 No Meals.*

Waikiki Shore
$$ | HOTEL | FAMILY | Nestled between Fort DeRussy Beach Park and the Outrigger Reef Resort, the only condo hotel directly on Waikiki Beach is beloved by some for its spaciousness and by others for its quieter, western-end location. **Pros:** right on the beach; great views from spacious private lanai; units available in different sizes. **Cons:** extra cleaning fee can be hefty; two management companies rent here, so ask questions when booking; some units are dated and amenities in them vary. *[$] Rooms from: $230 ✉ 2161 Kalia Rd., Waikiki ☎ 808/952–4500 Castle reservations, 808/922–3871 Outrigger reservations local, 800/688–7444 Outrigger reservations toll-free 🌐 www.castleresorts.com 🛏 168 suites 🍴 No Meals.*

Nightlife

★ Duke's Waikiki
BARS | Making the most of its spot on Waikiki Beach, Duke's is a bustling destination featuring live music everyday. This laid-back bar-and-grill's surf theme pays homage to Duke Kahanamoku, who popularized the sport in the early 1900s. Contemporary Hawaiian musicians like Henry Kapono and the Maunalua group have performed here, as have nationally known musicians like Jimmy Buffett. It's not unusual for surfers to leave their boards outside to step in for a casual drink after a long day on the waves. The cocktail menu is filled with Island-style drinks: try a sunset sour or coconut mojito while watching the Waikiki waves. *✉ Outrigger Waikiki, 2335 Kalakaua Ave., Suite 116, Waikiki ☎ 808/922–2268 🌐 www.dukeswaikiki.com.*

Hideout
BARS | Located at the Laylow Hotel, one of Waikiki's newer properties, this mini-oasis has a firepit, tiki torches, comfy couches, and palm trees swaying overhead. Although there's a full food menu, it's best to come here for expertly mixed cocktails or mocktails and some pupu—perhaps the poke tacos or the pork belly Brussels sprouts. A daily happy hour from 4:30 to 6:30 pm makes things easier on the wallet. *✉ Laylow Hotel, 2299 Kuhio Ave., Waikiki ☎ 808/628–3060 🌐 www.hideoutwaikiki.com.*

Hula's Bar and Lei Stand
DANCE CLUBS | Hawaii's oldest and best-known gay-friendly nightspot offers panoramic views of Diamond Head by day and high-energy club music by night. Check out the all-day happy hour, which starts at 10 am. There's an abundance of drink specials on weekends and discounted

pitchers of beer and cocktails on Sunday. Food options include nachos, tacos, pork sliders, and more. Celebrity patrons have included Elton John, Adam Lambert, and Dolly Parton. ⊠ *Waikiki Grand Hotel, 134 Kapahulu Ave., 2nd fl., Waikiki* ☎ *808/923–0669* ⊕ *www.hulas.com.*

★ Lewers Lounge

BARS | Set back from the main entrance of the Halekulani hotel and decked out with dramatic drapes and cozy ban-quettes, Lewers Lounge is a great place for cocktails, both classic and contem-porary. Standouts include Chocolate Dreams (made with Van Gogh Dutch Chocolate Vodka) and the Lost Passion (tequila, Cointreau, and fresh juices topped with champagne). Enjoy your libation with great nightly live jazz and tempting desserts, such as the hotel's famous coconut cake. ⊠ *Halekulani Hotel, 2199 Kalia Rd., Waikiki* ☎ *808/923–2311* ⊕ *www.halekulani.com/dining/lewers-lounge.*

Lulu's Waikiki

BARS | Even if you're not a surfer, you'll love this place's retro vibe and unob-structed second-floor view of Waikiki Beach. The open-air setting, casual dining menu, and tropical drinks are all you need to help you settle into your vacation. The venue transforms from a nice spot for breakfast, lunch, or dinner (happy hour is 3 to 5 pm) into a bustling, high-energy club with live music lasting into the wee hours. ⊠ *Park Shore Waikiki Hotel, 2586 Kalakaua Ave., Waikiki* ☎ *808/926–5222* ⊕ *www.luluswaikiki.com.*

★ Mai Tai Bar at the Royal Hawaiian

BARS | The bartenders here sure know how to mix up a killer mai tai. This is, after all, *the* establishment that first made the famous drink in the Islands. The pink umbrella–shaded tables at the outdoor bar are front-row seating for sunsets and also have an unobstructed view of Diamond Head. It's an ideal spot to soak in the island vibes just steps from the sand. Contemporary Hawaiian

Mai Tais

Hard to believe, but the cocktail known all over the world as the mai tai has been around for more than 50 years. Although the recipe has changed slightly over time, the original formula, created by bar owner Victor J. "Trader Vic" Bergeron, included 2 ounces of 17-year-old J. Wray & Nephew rum over shaved ice, ½ ounce of DeKuyper orange curaçao, ¼ ounce of Trader Vic's rock-candy syrup, ½ ounce of orgeat syrup, and the juice of one fresh lime. Done the right way, this tropical drink still lives up to the name "mai tai!," meaning "out of this world!"

musicians hold jam sessions on stage nightly, and small bites are also available. ⊠ *Royal Hawaiian Hotel, 2259 Kalakaua Ave., Waikiki* ☎ *808/923–7311* ⊕ *www.royal-hawaiian.com/dining-overview/mai-tai-bar.*

★ Maui Brewing Co.

BARS | The craft beers produced by this Lahaina-based company are Island favorites, and a visit to this brewpub adjacent to the Beachcomber hotel's lobby means you don't have to island hop to sample its offerings at the source. Ask about limited-release drafts to imbibe the brand's hidden gems, or order a flight of freshly brewed beers. Maui Brewing strives to source local ingredi-ents for its beer and its food, and the menu here includes a poke bowl made with locally caught tuna, a kale salad that incorporates Waianae-based Naked Cow Dairy feta, and a Brewmaster pizza featuring Honolulu-based Kukui sausage. ⊠ *Waikiki Beachcomber by Outrigger, 2300 Kalakaua Ave., 2nd fl., Waikiki* ☎ *808/843–2739* ⊕ *www.mbcrestau-rants.com/waikiki.*

RumFire

BARS | Locals and visitors head here for the convivial atmosphere, the trendy decor, and the million-dollar view of Waikiki Beach and Diamond Head. Come early to get a seat for happy hour (3–5 pm daily). If you're feeling peckish, there's a menu of tasty, Asian-influenced small plates. RumFire also features original cocktails, signature shots, and daily live music. On Friday and Saturday nights, the bar gets even livelier once local DJs start spinning. ⊠ *Sheraton Waikiki, 2255 Kalakaua Ave., Waikiki* ☎ *808/922–4422* ⊕ *www.rumfirewaikiki.com.*

Sky Waikiki Raw & Bar

LIVE MUSIC | This bar 19 stories above the city offers nearly 360-degree bird's-eye views of Diamond Head, the Waikiki beaches, and the classic coral Royal Hawaiian hotel. It's also one of the best spots to take in a Waikiki sunset. Be sure to order the popular SkyTai cocktail as you enjoy the views. There are also happy hour drink specials daily and a limited menu featuring fresh seafood. The indoor club, where resident DJs spin on Friday and Saturday nights, exudes contemporary-L.A. chic. ⊠ *Waikiki Trade Center, 2270 Kalakaua Ave., Waikiki* ☎ *808/979–7590* ⊕ *www.skywaikiki.com.*

🆕 Performing Arts

DINNER CRUISES AND SHOWS

Magic of Polynesia

MAGIC | **FAMILY** | Hawaii's top illusionist, John Hirokawa, displays mystifying sleight of hand in this highly entertaining show, which incorporates contemporary hula and Islands music into its acts. It's held in the Waikiki Beachcomber by Outrigger's showroom, and reservations are required for dinner (nightly at 5:45) and the show (at 7). Menu choices range from ginger-sesame–glazed chicken to a deluxe steak-and-lobster combo. Walk-ins are permitted if you just want the entertainment. The box office is open daily from noon to 9 pm. ⊠ *Waikiki Beachcomber by Outrigger, 2300 Kalakaua Ave., Waikiki* ☎ *808/971–4321* ⊕ *www.waikikibeachcomber.com/things-to-do/the-magic-of-polynesia-show.*

LUAU

Royal Hawaiian Luau: Aha'aina

FOLK/TRADITIONAL DANCE | **FAMILY** | With a beachfront location in the middle of Waikiki, the Royal Hawaiian's Aha'aina luau is an exceptional, upscale event with hula, fire dancing, live music, Hawaiian-inspired and luau-favorite dishes, and more. Options range from "standard dinner and show" to "premium dinner and show." The three-hour event is held two nights a week (Monday and Thursday); be sure to reserve in advance during the high season. ⊠ *The Royal Hawaiian, a Luxury Collection Resort, 2259 Kalakaua Ave., Waikiki* ☎ *808/921–4600* ⊕ *www.royal-hawaiianluau.com* 🎫 *From $200.*

Waikiki Starlight Luau

FOLK/TRADITIONAL DANCE | **FAMILY** | This Waikiki luau is done spectacularly on the rooftop of Hilton Hawaiian Village. There isn't an *imu* ceremony, but the live entertainment is top-notch, and the views are unparalleled. Prices vary depending on your age and where you want to sit. The event also includes dinner with traditional specialties, games, and cultural activities, such as hula lessons and conch blowing. It's held Sunday–Thursday at 5 pm. ⊠ *Hilton Hawaiian Village, 2005 Kalia Rd., Waikiki* ☎ *808/941–5828* ⊕ *www.hiltonhawaiianvillage.com.*

MUSIC

★ Blue Note Hawaii

MUSIC | Music lovers adore this intimate venue, which draws local and national acts throughout the year. Acoustics are fantastic, and seating is at tables, all with excellent views. The atmosphere is sophisticated, and the food here is excellent, too, with small and large plates offered. It's worthwhile to find out who's performing while you're in town so you can purchase tickets in advance, since

Inexpensive Local Souvenirs

Hawaii can be an expensive place. If you're shopping for souvenirs or gifts, consider the following relatively affordable items, which are sold all over the island.

Locally published, Hawaii-themed books for children and adults can be found at places like **Na Mea Hawaii/ Native Books** in Ward Village/China-town and **BookEnds** in Kailua.

Just when you thought peanut butter couldn't get any better, someone added coconut to it and made it even more delicious. The coconut peanut butter from **North Shore Goodies** makes a great gift.

If you are a fan of plate lunches, **Rainbow Drive-In** has T-shirts with regular orders—"All rice," "Gravy all over," "Boneless"—printed on them. They come packed in an emblematic plate-lunch box.

Relive your memories of tea on the veranda by purchasing Island Essence Tea at **Moana Surfrider**.

Harvested from a salt farm on Molokai, **Hawaii Traditional Gourmet Sea Salts** come in a variety of flavors, including black lava, red alaea clay, and classic. They're colored to match their flavor, so they are beautiful as well as tasty.

Foodland makes insulated cooler bags that are decorated with uniquely local designs that go beyond tropical flowers and coconuts. Look for the pidgin or poke designs. The Hawaii-themed reuseable totes at **Whole Foods** are also very popular.

Made with all-natural, island ingredients, like kukui-nut oil and local flowers and herbs, even seaweed, indigenous bar soap is available online or in stores like **Blue Hawaii Lifestyle.**

the more popular acts sell out quickly. This 300-seat room is centrally located (at the Outrigger resort), so you can grab a drink at Duke's before or after the show. ⊠ *Outrigger Waikiki Beach Resort, 2335 Kalakaua Ave., Waikiki* ☎ *808/777–4890* ⊕ *www.bluenotehawaii. com* ⊠ *From $35.*

◔ Shopping

Waikiki's hotels and malls or other shopping centers all have notable shops, and the abundance of name-brand and specialty items will be energizing or overwhelming, depending on your sensibilities.

Clothing, jewelry, and handbags from Europe's top designers sit next to Hawaii's ABC Store, a chain of convenience stores that sells groceries as well as souvenirs. Now more than ever, it's possible to find interesting, locally produced items and independent stores in Waikiki, but you must be willing to search beyond the expensive purses and the tacky wooden tikis to find innovation and quality.

Larger shopping centers (including the Royal Hawaiian Center) may offer some type of parking validation with purchase, so be sure to check or ask in advance.

CLOTHING
Newt at the Royal

HATS & GLOVES | Newt is known for high-quality, handwoven Panama hats and tropical sportswear for men and women. ⊠ *The Royal Hawaiian Hotel, 2259 Kalakaua Ave., Waikiki* ☎ *808/923– 4332* ⊕ *www.newtattheroyal.com.*

Waikiki Beachboy Store

SWIMWEAR | FAMILY | Tucked away in the Royal Hawaiian's lobby, this tiny shop is a great place to pick up a memento of your surf lesson. It's filled with a variety of high-quality Waikiki Beach Services gear, including the best-selling logo rash guards and T-shirts of the type worn by their beachboys and surf instructors. There's also a selection of locally designed bathing suits from Pualani Hawaii, swimwear from the Colombian brand Maaji, accessories, sunscreen, and original artwork. ⊠ *Royal Hawaiian Resort, 2259 Kalakaua Ave., Shop 9, Waikiki* ☎ *808/922–2223* ⊕ *www.waikikibeachservices.com/waikiki-beach-boy-store.*

FOOD

★ Honolulu Cookie Company

FOOD | To really impress those back home, pick up a box of locally baked, gourmet cookies. Choose from dozens of delicious flavors of premium shortbread delights with a wide variety of sizes, all designed for travel. In addition to the location in the Royal Hawaiian Center, there are a number of these stores in Waikiki, so you probably won't be able to avoid them—even if you try. ⊠ *Royal Hawaiian Center, 2233 Kalakaua Ave., Waikiki* ☎ *808/931–8937* ⊕ *www.honolulucookie.com.*

GIFTS

★ Aloha Collection

HANDBAGS | Located in the Moana Surfrider hotel, the flagship store of this innovative company is filled with colorful, lightweight, "splash-proof" bags of all sizes, shapes, and styles—from tiny zippered travel pouches to eye-catching beach bags to oversize totes. The company continually offers new patterns and styles, so bag lovers will always find a unique beach- and/or travel-friendly option. ⊠ *Moana Surfrider, 2369 Kalakaua Ave., Diamond Head Wing Shop #1, Waikiki* ⊕ *aloha-collection.com.*

Buying Flowers and Fruit

You can bring home fresh pineapple, papaya, or coconut to share with friends and family. Orchids will also brighten your home and remind you of your trip to the Islands. By law, all fresh fruit and plant products must be inspected by the Department of Agriculture before export. Ask at the shop about agricultural rules so a surprise confiscation doesn't spoil your departure. Shipping to your home usually is best.

★ House of Mana Up

SOUVENIRS | Mana Up is a groundbreaking organization that promotes Hawaii-based entrepreneurs and shares their unique products with consumers. Its large retail store in the Royal Hawaiian Center not only showcases innovative, locally made items but also shares the stories of the makers behind them. It's fun to browse for gourmet chocolate, edible coffee bars, art, sustainable food wrappers, surf-inspired clothing, extra-comfy flip-flops (called slippers in Hawaii), children's books, and much more. All the profits are used to support these small businesses. ⊠ *Royal Hawaiian Center, 2201 Kalakaua Ave., Space A108 (1st fl.), Waikiki* ☎ *808/425–4028* ⊕ *www.manauphawaii.com.*

★ Keep it Simple

GENERAL STORE | Founded by local entrepreneurs Jillian Corn and Hunter Long (who is also a professional skateboarder), Keep it Simple strives to promote a healthier planet by selling high-quality, natural, organic, and/or vegan items with minimal (or zero) packaging. Look for unique beauty and bath products and accessories, as well as items for the kitchen and elsewhere in the home.

✉ *Waikiki Beach Walk, 240 Lewers St., Waikiki* ☎ *808/744–3115* ⊕ *www.keepit-simplezerowaste.com.*

JEWELRY
Philip Rickard
JEWELRY & WATCHES | This famed jeweler creates heirloom-quality Hawaiian pieces in platinum and different shades of gold that feature traditional scrolling patterns, enameled names, and inlays. Items from the outfit's Wedding Collection are often sought by celebrities. ✉ *International Market Place, 2330 Kalakaua Ave., Level 1, Banyan Court, #105, Waikiki* ☎ *808/924–7972* ⊕ *www.philiprickard. com.*

SHOPPING CENTERS
★ Royal Hawaiian Center
MALL | This three-block-long center has more than 110 establishments, including an Apple Store and ABC Store, as well as local gems, such as Oiwi Ocean Gear, Mana Up, Fighting Eel, Honolulu Cookie Company, Koi Honolulu, Hawaiian Island Arts, Island Soap & Candleworks, and Royal Hawaiian Quilts. In addition to a number of restaurants, you can dine at the Waikiki Food Hall. Complimentary cultural classes, a theater, and nightly outdoor entertainment round out the offerings. Note for drivers: the center offers free parking for three hours with validation at shops and restaurants. ✉ *2201 Kalakaua Ave., Waikiki* ☎ *808/922–0588* ⊕ *www.royalhawaiian-center.com.*

2100 Kalakaua
MALL | The ultimate destination for designer shopping in Hawaii is this elegant town house–style center, where shops include Chanel, Coach, Tiffany & Co., Yves Saint Laurent, Bottega Veneta, Gucci, Hugo Boss, Miu Miu, and Moncler. ✉ *2100 Kalakaua Ave., Waikiki* ☎ *808/922–2246* ⊕ *www.luxuryrow.com.*

Waikiki Beach Walk
MALL | This open-air mall at the west end of Kalakaua Avenue and next to the Royal Hawaiian Center contains 70 locally owned stores and restaurants. Get reasonably priced, fashionable resort wear at Mahina, find unique pieces by local artists at Under the Koa Tree, or buy local delicacies from the Poke Bar. Of course, you can pick up T-shirts, bathing suits, and casual beach attire here, too. The mall also features free local entertainment on its outdoor fountain stage at least once a week. ✉ *226 Lewers St., Waikiki* ☎ *808/931–3591* ⊕ *www. waikikibeachwalk.com.*

Pearl Harbor

On December 7, 1941, the Japanese bombed Pearl Harbor. It was the catalyst for the United States' entrance into World War II. On that fateful day, more than 2,000 people died, and a dozen ships were sunk. Here, at what is still a key Pacific naval base, the attack is remembered every day by thousands of visitors. In recent years, the memorial has also been the site of reconciliation ceremonies involving Pearl Harbor veterans from both sides. There are five distinct sights in Pearl Harbor, but only two are part of the Pearl Harbor National Memorial, with the others privately operated. Make reservations for the national park portion.

◉ Sights

Battleship *Missouri* Memorial
MILITARY SIGHT | **FAMILY** | Together with the *Arizona* Memorial, the USS *Missouri's* presence in Pearl Harbor perfectly frames America's World War II experience, which began December 7, 1941, and ended on the "Mighty Mo's" starboard deck with the signing of the Terms of Surrender. To begin your visit on the fully restored vessel, pick up tickets online or at the Pearl Harbor Visitor Center. Then board a shuttle bus for the eight-minute ride to Ford Island and the teak decks and towering superstructure of the last American battleship ever built. Join a guided tour to

learn more about the *Missouri*'s long and dramatic history. The Heart of the *Missouri* tour (an additional $25) provides an up-close look at the battleship's engineering spaces, accessing its engine rooms, gun turret, damage control station, and aft battery plot room.

The *Missouri* is 887 feet long and 209 feet tall, with nine 116-ton guns capable of firing up to 23 miles. Absorb these numbers during the tour, then stop to take advantage of the view from the decks. Near the entrance is a gift shop, as well as a lunch wagon and shave ice stand that serve hamburgers, hot dogs, pizza, and other treats. ✉ *Ford Island, 63 Cowpens St., Pearl Harbor* ⟴ *You cannot drive directly to the USS Missouri; you must take a shuttle bus from Pearl Harbor Visitor Center* ☏ *808/455–1600* ⊕ *ussmissouri.org* ✉ *From $34.99* ⊘ *Closed Sun.–Tues.*

Pearl Harbor Aviation Museum

HISTORY MUSEUM | FAMILY | Opened on December 7, 2006, this tribute to aviation in the Pacific battlefield of World War II is on Ford Island in Hangars 37 and 79, actual seaplane hangars that survived the Pearl Harbor attack. The museum consists of a theater where a short film on Pearl Harbor is shown, an education center, a restoration shop, a gift store, and a restaurant. Exhibits—many of which are interactive and feature sound effects—include an authentic Japanese Zero and various other vintage aircraft that help to narrate such great battles as the Doolittle Raid on Japan, Midway, and Guadalcanal. The actual Stearman N2S-3 that President George H. W. Bush flew is housed in Hangar 79.

Ride in Fighter Ace 360 Flight Simulators, and take a docent-led tour for additional fees. Purchase tickets online, at the Pearl Harbor Visitor Center, or at the museum itself after you get off the shuttle bus that departs for the museum and the USS *Missouri* from the visitor center. ✉ *Ford Island, 319 Lexington Blvd., Pearl Harbor* ⟴ *Access is only via the shuttle bus to Ford Island from the Pearl Harbor Visitor Center* ☏ *808/441–1000* ⊕ *pearlharboraviationmuseum.org* ✉ *$25.99.*

★ Pearl Harbor Visitor Center

VISITOR CENTER | The gateway to the Pearl Harbor National Memorial and the starting point for visitors to this historic site has interpretive exhibits in two separate galleries (*Road to War* and *Attack*) that feature photographs and personal memorabilia from World War II veterans. There are also other exhibits, a bookstore, and a Remembrance Circle, where you can learn about the people who lost their lives on December 7, 1941. Survivors are sometimes on hand to give their personal accounts and answer questions. The visitor center is also where you start your tour of the USS *Arizona* Memorial if you have reserved the requisite timed-entry ticket (⊕ *www.recreation.gov;* $1 reservation fee). ✉ *Pearl Harbor National Memorial, 1 Arizona Memorial Pl., Pearl Harbor* ☏ *808/954–8759, 866/332–1941 toll-free* ⊕ *nps.gov/perl* ✉ *Free (timed-entry ticket fee $1).*

★ USS *Arizona* Memorial

NATIONAL PARK | FAMILY | Lined up tight in a row of seven battleships off Ford Island, the USS *Arizona* took a direct hit on December 7, 1941, exploded, and rests still on the shallow bottom where she settled. You must reserve tickets (⊕ *www.recreation.gov*) ahead of time to ensure access to the memorial; same-day, first-come, first-served tickets are no longer offered. As spaces are limited and tend to fill up, reserve as far ahead as possible; you can do so up to two months in advance. When your tour starts, you watch a short documentary film, then board the ferry to the memorial.

The swooping, stark-white structure, which straddles the wreck of the USS *Arizona,* was designed by Honolulu

Continued on page 119

USS *West Virginia* (BB48), 7 December 1941

PEARL HARBOR

December 7, 1941. Every American then alive recalls exactly what they were doing when the news broke that the Japanese had bombed Pearl Harbor, the catalyst that brought the United States into World War II.

Although it was clear by late 1941 that war with Japan was inevitable, no one in authority seemed to have expected the attack to come in just this way, at just this time. So when the Japanese bombers swept through a gap in Oahu's Koolau Mountains in the hazy light of morning, they found the bulk of America's Pacific fleet right where they hoped it would be: docked like giant stepping stones across the calm waters of the bay named for the pearl oysters that once prospered there. More than 2,000 people died that day, including 49 civilians. A dozen ships were sunk.

And on the nearby air bases, virtually every American military aircraft was destroyed or damaged. The attack was a stunning success, but it lit a fire under America, which went to war with "Remember Pearl Harbor" as its battle cry. Here, in what is still a key Pacific naval base, the attack is remembered every day by thousands of visitors, including many curious Japanese, who for years heard little World War II history in their own country. In recent years, the memorial has been the site of reconciliation ceremonies involving Pearl Harbor veterans from both sides.

GETTING AROUND

Pearl Harbor is both a working military base and the most-visited Oahu attraction. Five distinct destinations share a parking lot and are linked by footpath, shuttle, and ferry.

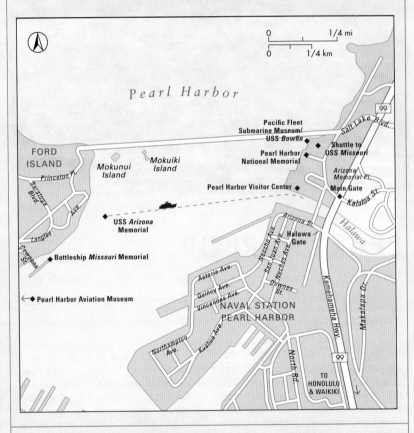

The visitor center is accessible from the parking lot. The USS *Arizona* Memorial itself is in the middle of the harbor; get tickets for the ferry ride online ahead of time. The Pacific Fleet Submarine Museum/USS *Bowfin* are also reachable from the parking lot. The USS *Missouri* is docked at Ford Island, a restricted area of the naval base. Vehicular access is prohibited. To get there, take a shuttle bus from the station near the *Bowfin*.

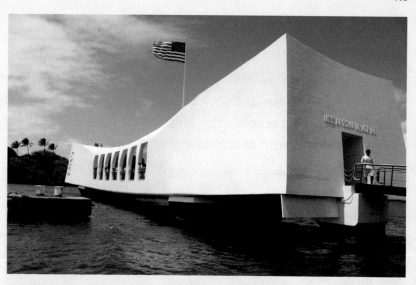

ARIZONA MEMORIAL

Snugged up tight in a row of seven battleships off Ford Island, the USS *Arizona* took a direct hit that December morning, exploded, and rests still on the shallow bottom where she settled.

The swooping, stark-white memorial, which straddles the wreck of the USS *Arizona*, was designed to represent both the depths of the low-spririted, early days of the war, and the uplift of victory.

A visit here begins at the Pearl Harbor Visitor Center, which recently underwent a $58 million renovation. High definition projectors and interactive exhibits were installed, and the building was modernized. From the visitor center, a ferry takes you to the memorial itself, and shuttles access the USS *Oklahoma*.

A somber, contemplative mood descends upon visitors during the ferry ride to the *Arizona*; this is a place where 1,177 crewmen lost their lives. Gaze at the names of the dead carved into the wall of white marble. Scatter flowers (but no lei—the string is bad for the fish). Salute the flag. Remember Pearl Harbor.

☎ *808/422–3399*
⊕ *www.nps.gov/perl*

USS *MISSOURI* (BB63)

BATTLESHIP *MISSOURI* MEMORIAL

Together with the *Arizona* Memorial, the *Missouri's* presence in Pearl Harbor perfectly bookends America's WWII experience, which began December 7, 1941, and ended on the "Mighty Mo's" starboard deck with the signing of the Terms of Surrender.

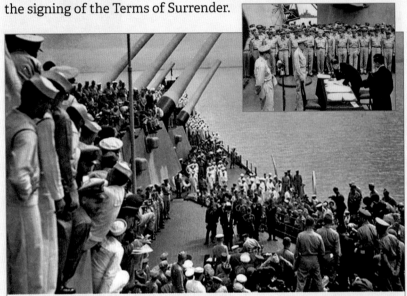

Surrender of Japan, USS *Missouri*, 2 September 1945

In the parking area behind the Pacific Fleet Submarine Museum, board a shuttle for an eight-minute ride to Ford Island and the teak decks and towering superstructure of the *Missouri*. The largest battleship ever built, the *Missouri* famously hosted the final act of WWII, the signing of the Terms of Surrender. The commission that governs this floating museum has surrounded it with WWII-style buildings, among them a lunch wagon, a shaved ice stand, and a souvenir shop.

■TIP➔ Definitely hook up with a tour guide (no additional charge) or audio tour—these add a great deal to the experience.

The *Missouri* is all about numbers: 209 feet tall, six 239,000-pound guns, capable of firing up to 23 miles away. Absorb these during the tour, then stop to take advantage of the view from the decks. The Mo is a work in progress, with only a handful of her hundreds of spaces open to view.

☎ *808/455-1600* or *877/644-4896*
⊕ *www.ussmissouri.org*

USS *BOWFIN* (SS287)

PACIFIC FLEET SUBMARINE MUSEUM & PARK

Launched one year to the day after the Pearl Harbor attack, the USS *Bowfin* reportedly sank 44 enemy ships during WWII and now serves as the centerpiece of a museum honoring all submariners.

Although the *Bowfin* no less than the *Arizona* Memorial commemorates the lost, the mood here is lighter. Perhaps it's the childlike scale of the boat, a metal tube just 16 feet in diameter, packed with ladders, hatches, and other obstacles, like the naval version of a jungle gym. Perhaps it's the World War II-era music that plays in the covered patio. Or it might be the museum's touching displays—the penciled sailor's journal, the Vargas girlie posters. Aboard the boat nicknamed "Pearl Harbor Avenger," compartments are fitted out as though "Sparky" was away from the radio room just for a moment, and "Cooky" might be right back to his pots and pans. The museum includes many artifacts to spark family conversations, among them a vintage dive suit that looks too big for Shaquille O'Neal.

A caution: The *Bowfin* could be hazardous for very young children; no one under four allowed.

☎ *808/423–1341*
⊕ *www.bowfin.org*

PEARL HARBOR AVIATION MUSEUM

This museum opened on December 7, 2006, as as a tribute to aviation in the Pacific. Located on Ford Island in Hangars 37 and 79, actual seaplane hangars that survived the Pearl Harbor attack, the museum is made up of a theater where a short film on Pearl Harbor kicks off the tour, an education center, a shop, and a restaurant. Exhibits—many of which are interactive and involve sound effects—include an authentic Japanese Zero in a diorama setting, vintage aircraft, and the chance to play the role of a World War II pilot using one of six flight simulators. Various aircrafts are employed to narrate the great battles: the Doolittle Raid on Japan, the Battle of Midway, Guadalcanal, and so on. The actual Stearman N2S-3 in which President George H. W. Bush soloed is housed in Hangar 79.

☎ *808/441–1000*
⊕ *www.pearlharboraviationmuseum.org*

PLAN YOUR PEARL HARBOR DAY LIKE A MILITARY CAMPAIGN

DIRECTIONS

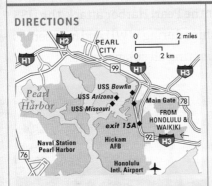

Take H–1 west from Waikiki to Exit 15A and follow signs. Or take TheBus route 20 or 47 from Waikiki. Beware high-priced private shuttles. It's a 30-minute drive from Waikiki.

WHAT TO BRING

You must present a valid, government-issued, photo ID.

It's best to travel light. No bags (even small purses) are allowed, so plan to carry cameras and stash cell phones and other items in pockets or to check bags at the visitor center ($5). Lines for this can be long, so allow plenty of time, particularly if you have timed-entry memorial tickets.

All you really need, though, are comfortable walking shoes, a light jacket, sunglasses, and sunscreen. One final note: Leave nothing in your car; theft is a problem despite security patrols.

HOURS

Visitor center hours are 7 am to 5 pm daily. Most attractions don't open till 8 am, and some close at 4. Note, too, that last entry is often an hour before closing.

TICKETS

Arizona: Free. $7.99 for museum audio tours; $1 per-person ticket reservation fee.

Aviation: $25.99 adults, $14.99 children; from $10.70 for flight simulator.

Missouri: $34.99 adults, $17.49 children.

Bowfin: $21.99 adults, $12.99 children. Children under 4 may go into the museum but not aboard the *Bowfin*.

Passport to Pearl Harbor: 1-day access to all ships and exhibits; $89.99 adults (ages 13+), $44.95 children, $1 per-person reservation fee (buy at ⊕ *recreation.gov*).

KIDS

This might be the day to enroll younger kids in the hotel children's program. Preschoolers chafe at long waits, and attractions involve some hazards for toddlers. Older kids enjoy the *Bowfin* and *Missouri*, especially.

MAKING THE MOST OF YOUR TIME

You could see the highlights in half a day, but it would be rushed, so plan on a full day.

Timed tickets for the USS *Arizona* Memorial can be reserved up to two months in advance. Same-day, first-come, first-served tickets are no longer sold.

SUGGESTED READING

Pearl Harbor and the USS Arizona Memorial, by Richard Wisniewski. 76-page magazine-size quick history.

Bowfin, by Edwin P. Hoyt. Dramatic story of undersea adventure.

The Last Battleship, by Scott C. S. Stone. Story of the Mighty Mo.

architect Alfred Preis to represent both the depths of the low-spirited, early days of the war and the uplift of victory. A somber, contemplative mood descends upon visitors during the ferry ride; this is a place where 1,777 people died. Gaze at the names of the dead carved into the wall of white marble. Look at oil on the water's surface, still slowly escaping from the sunken ship. Scatter flowers (but no lei—the string is bad for the fish). Salute the flag. Remember Pearl Harbor. ⊠ *Pearl Harbor National Memorial, Pearl Harbor* ☎ *808/422–3399* ⊕ *nps.gov/perl* ✆ *Free (advanced reservation timed-entry tickets $1); audio tours and other features cost extra.*

Pacific Fleet Submarine Museum

MILITARY SIGHT | FAMILY | A new and expanded Pacific Fleet Submarine Museum opened in 2021 after a $20 million renovation. Its centerpiece is the USS *Bowfin,* which launched one year to the day after the Pearl Harbor attack and which claimed to have sunk 44 enemy ships during World War II. Like the *Arizona* Memorial, the so-called Pearl Harbor Avenger commemorates the lost, but the mood here is lighter. Perhaps it's the childlike scale of the boat, a metal tube just 16 feet in diameter and packed with ladders, hatches, and other obstacles, like the naval version of a jungle gym.

Compartments aboard the vessel are fitted out as though "Sparky" is away from the radio room just for a moment and "Cooky" might be back to his pots and pans any minute. Among the intriguing artifacts is a vintage dive suit known as JAKE that looks too big for Shaquille O'Neal and is now in the gift shop window. A guided audio tour is included with admission to this privately operated museum. A snack bar is also on-site.

For safety reasons, children under four are not allowed aboard the submarine, though they can visit the museum. You can also purchase shuttle tickets to

access the USS *Oklahoma* Memorial at the *Bowfin*'s ticket counter, though you'll probably want to include that stop with a visit to the USS *Missouri* or the Pearl Harbor Aviation Museum, both of which are on Ford Island along with the sunken *Oklahoma* submarine. ⊠ *11 Arizona Memorial Pl., Pearl Harbor* ☎ *808/423–1341* ⊕ *www.bowfin.org* ✆ *$21.99* ✆ *Tickets available in advance or on arrival.*

Downtown

Throughout downtown, which is about 6 miles east of Honolulu International Airport, the city's past and present are delightfully intertwined, as evidenced by the architecture. Postmodern glass-and-steel office buildings look down on the Aloha Tower, built in 1926 and, until the early 1960s, the tallest structure in Honolulu.

You'll also find history in the cut-stone, turn-of-the-20th-century storefronts on Merchant Street; the gracious, white-columned, American-Georgian manor that was the home of the Islands' last queen; the jewel-box palace occupied by the monarchy before it was overthrown; the Spanish-inspired stucco and tile-roofed Territorial Era government buildings; and the 21st-century glass pyramid of the First Hawaiian Bank Building.

GETTING HERE AND AROUND

To reach downtown Honolulu from Waikiki by car, take Ala Moana Boulevard to Alakea Street, and turn right; three blocks up on the right, between South King and Hotel Streets, there's a municipal parking lot in Alii Place. There are also public lots in buildings along Alakea, Smith, Beretania, and Bethel Streets (Chinatown Gateway on Bethel Street is a good choice). The best parking downtown, however, is metered street parking along Punchbowl Street—when you can find it.

Shangri La

The marriage of heiress Doris Duke to a much older man when she was 23 didn't last. But their around-the-world honeymoon did leave her with two lasting loves: Islamic art and architecture, which she first encountered on that journey; and Hawaii, where the honeymooners made an extended stay while Doris learned to surf and befriended Islanders unimpressed by her wealth.

Today, visitors to her beloved Oahu home—where she spent most winters—can share both loves by touring her estate. The sought-after tours are coordinated by and begin at the Honolulu Museum of Art in downtown Honolulu. A short van ride then takes small groups to the house itself, on the far side of Diamond Head.

Another option is to take the highly popular and convenient TheBus to the Aloha Tower Marketplace, or you can take a trolley from Waikiki.

◉ Sights

★ Honolulu Museum of Art

ART MUSEUM | Originally built around the collection of a Honolulu matron who donated much of her estate to the museum, the Honolulu Academy of Arts is housed in a maze of courtyards, cloistered walkways, and quiet, low-ceiling spaces. There's an impressive permanent collection that includes the third-largest assembly of Hiroshige's ukiyo-e Japanese prints in the country (donated by author James Michener); Italian Renaissance paintings; and American and European art by Monet, van Gogh, and Whistler, among many others. The newer Luce Pavilion complex, nicely incorporated into the more traditional architecture of the museum, has a traveling-exhibit gallery, a Hawaiian gallery, an excellent café, and a gift shop. The Doris Duke Theatre screens art films. This is also the jumping-off point for tours of Doris Duke's striking estate, which is now the Shangri La Museum of Islamic Art, Culture, and Design. If you wish to visit, you should reserve tickets well in advance. ⊠ *900 S. Beretania St., Downtown*

☎ *808/532–8700* ⊕ *honolulumuseum.org* 🎟 *$20* ⊗ *Closed Mon.–Wed.*

★ Iolani Palace

CASTLE/PALACE | America's only official royal residence, on the site of an earlier palace, was completed in 1882. It contains the thrones of King Kalakaua and his successor (and sister) Queen Liliuokalani. Bucking the stereotype of simple island life, the palace had electric lights even before the White House. Downstairs galleries showcase the royal jewelry, as well as a kitchen and offices that have been restored to the glory of the monarchy. The palace gift shop and ticket office are now in what was formerly the Iolani Barracks, built to house the Royal Guard. The palace has self-guided audio tours and guided tours. ■ TIP→ **Guided tours are only available in the mornings, and it's best to make reservations a few days in advance.** ⊠ *364 S. King St., Downtown* ☎ *808/522–0822* ⊕ *www.iolanipalace. org* 🎟 *$30 guided tour, $25 audio tour* ⊗ *Closed Sun. (except for monthly Kamaaina Sun.).*

Kamehameha I Statue

PUBLIC ART | Honoring the Big Island chieftain who united all the warring Hawaiian Islands into one kingdom at the turn of the 18th century, this statue, which stands with one arm outstretched in welcome, is one of two cast in Paris

Take a guided tour of Iolani Palace, America's only royal residence, built in 1882.

by American sculptor T. R. Gould. The original statue, lost at sea and replaced by this one, was eventually salvaged and is now in Kapaau, on the Big Island, near the king's birthplace. Each year on the king's birthday (June 11), the more famous copy is draped in fresh lei that reach lengths of 18 feet and longer. A parade proceeds past the statue, and Hawaiian civic clubs, women in hats and impressive long *holoku* dresses, and men in sashes and cummerbunds honor the leader, whose name means "The One Set Apart." ✉ *417 S. King St., outside Aliiolani Hale, Downtown* ⊕ *www.goha-waii.com/islands/oahu/regions/honolulu/king-kamehameha-statue.*

Kawaiahao Church
CHURCH | Fancifully called Hawaii's Westminster Abbey, this historic house of worship witnessed the coronations, weddings, and funerals of generations of Hawaiian royalty. Each of the building's 14,000 coral blocks was quarried from reefs offshore at depths of more than 20 feet and transported to this site. Interior woodwork was created from the forests of the Koolau Mountains. The upper gallery displays paintings of the royal families. The graves of missionaries and of King Lunalilo are adjacent. Services in English, with songs and prayers in Hawaiian, are held each Sunday. An all-Hawaiian service is held at 5 pm on the second and fourth Sunday of the month (Kawaiahao's affiliation is United Church of Christ). Although there are no guided tours, you can look around the church at no cost. ✉ *957 Punchbowl St., at King St., Downtown* ☎ *808/469–3000* ⊕ *kawaiahao.org* ✉ *Free.*

🍴 Restaurants

Honolulu Museum of Art Café
$$ | AMERICAN | The Honolulu Museum of Art's cool courtyards and galleries filled with works by masters from Monet to Hokusai are well worth a visit, and, afterward, so is this popular lunch restaurant. The open-air café is flanked by a burbling water feature and 8-foot-tall ceramic "dumplings" by artist Jun Kaneko—a

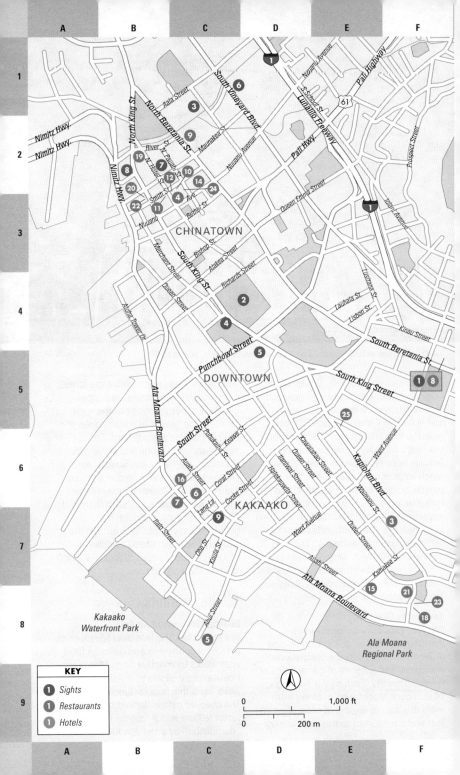

Downtown, Chinatown, Kakaako, and Ala Moana

G   H   I

Punchbowl Crater

Aliiolani Street

Prospect Street

Spencer Street

Thurston Avenue

Lunalilo Street

Victoria St.

Pensacola Street

Piikoi Street

Liholiho Street

Kewalo Street

Lunalilo Freeway

Matlock Avenue

Kinau Street

South Beretania Street

Young Street

South King Street

Pensacola Street

Piikoi Street

Alder Street

Birch Street

Elm St.

Rycroft Street

Liona St.

Ahana St.

Kalakaua St.

Kamaile St.

Keeaumoku Street

Kanunu St.

Amana St.

Makaloa St.

Kapiolani Boulevard

Kona Street

Piikoi Street

Kaheka Street

ALA MOANA

Ala Moana Boulevard

Ala Moana Regional Park

Kona St.

Atkinson Drive

Ala Wai Canal
Ala Wai Boulevard

G   H   I

Sights ▼

1 Honolulu Museum of Art **F5**
2 Iolani Palace **D4**
3 Izumo Taishakyo Mission of Hawaii **C1**
4 Kamehameha I Statue **C4**
5 Kawaiahao Church **D5**
6 Kuan Yin Temple **C1**
7 Maunakea Marketplace **B2**
8 Oahu Market **B2**
9 POW! WOW! Hawaiian Murals **C7**

Restaurants ▼

1 Akasaka **I8**
2 Bac Nam **G6**
3 Chef Chai **F7**
4 Fête **C3**
5 53 By The Sea **C8**
6 Hank's Haute Dogs **C6**
7 Highway Inn Kakaako **C6**
8 Honolulu Museum of Art Café **F5**
9 Legend Seafood Restaurant **C2**
10 Little Village Noodle House **C2**
11 Livestock Tavern **B3**
12 Lucky Belly **C2**
13 Mariposa **H8**
14 Mei Sum Dim Sum **C2**
15 Merriman's Honolulu **E8**
16 Moku Kitchen **C6**
17 MW Restaurant **I8**
18 Panya **F8**
19 Pho To Chau Restaurant **B2**
20 The Pig and the Lady **B3**
21 Scratch Kitchen **F8**
22 Senia **B3**
23 Tangō Contemporary Cafe **F8**
24 Terry's Place **C2**
25 Yanagi Sushi **E5**

Hotels ▼

1 Ala Moana Hotel **I8**

tranquil setting in which to eat your salad or sandwich, shaded by a 75-year-old monkeypod tree. **Known for:** limited but beautifully prepared menu of soups, salads, sandwiches, and mains; nice spot for Sunday brunch; piadina pesto-caprese flatbread sandwich. $ *Average main: $18* ✉ *Honolulu Museum of Art, 900 S. Beretania St., Downtown* ☎ *808/532–8734* ⊕ *honolulumuseum.org/cafe* ✆ *Closed Mon.–Wed. No dinner.*

Yanagi Sushi

$$$ | **JAPANESE** | One of relatively few restaurants to serve a complete menu until 2 am (until 10 pm on Sunday) offers not only sushi and sashimi around a small bar, but also *teishoku* (combination menus), tempura, stews, and cook-it-yourself shabu-shabu. The fish can be depended on for freshness and variety. **Known for:** baked crabmeat volcano roll, spicy shrimp tempura roll, live abalone sashimi; local favorite; late-night happy hour. $ *Average main: $28* ✉ *762 Kapiolani Blvd., Downtown* ☎ *808/597–1525* ⊕ *www.yanagisushi-hawaii.com.*

 ## Nightlife

★ Bar Leather Apron

BARS | This intimate, James Beard Award–nominated cocktail spot, oddly situated in the mezzanine of an office building, seats only six at the bar along with a few other tables. So you'll want to make reservations to enjoy bespoke cocktails that utilize only the finest liquors and ingredients. Owners Tom Park and Justin Park (no relation) have cultivated a reputation for their E Hoo Pau Mai Tai made with a five-year-old, raisin-infused El Dorado rum and another 12-year-old El Dorado rum, as well as coconut water syrup, spiced orgeat, ohia blossom honey, lime, vanilla, and absinthe—all served with a kiawe wood–smoke presentation. ✉ *Topa Financial Center, 745 Fort St., Mezzanine Level, Suite 127A, Downtown* ☎ *808/524–0808* ⊕ *www.barleatherapron.com* ✆ *Closed Sun. and Mon.*

Murphy's Bar & Grill

PUBS | On the edge of Chinatown and the financial district, this bar has served drinks to such locals and visitors as King Kalakaua and Robert Louis Stevenson since the late 1800s. The kind of Irish pub you would find in Boston, Murphy's offers a break from all the tropical, fruit-garnished drinks found in Waikiki, and it's definitely the place to be on St. Patrick's Day. Friendly bartenders and waitstaff serve Guinness on tap, pub food favorites, and Irish specialties like corned beef and cabbage and shepherd's pie. If you time it right, you can try their incredible house-made pies, which are served only on Friday and quickly sell out. ✉ *2 Merchant St., Downtown* ☎ *808/531–0422* ⊕ *www.murphyshawaii.com.*

Performing Arts

DINNER CRUISES AND SHOWS
Atlantis Cruises

CONCERTS | The sleekly high-tech *Majestic,* designed to sail smoothly in rough waters, powers farther along Waikiki's coastline than its competitors. Enjoy seasonal whale-watching trips between January and March during the day or year-round sunset cocktail and dinner cruises aboard the 400-passenger boat. (Atlantis is also known for its submarine tours off Waikiki.) The boat's dining room is elegantly laid out, and the standard Hawaiian buffet fare perfectly accompanies the tropical cocktails, Champagne, beer, or guava juice. Most passengers are honeymooners and those celebrating anniversaries and birthdays—or even the occasional proposal—and this, plus the Hawaiian music, makes the atmosphere festive. For the best view of Waikiki and the sunset, head to the top deck. ✉ *1 Aloha Tower Rd., Pier 6, Downtown* ☎ *808/973–9800, 800/381–0237* ⊕ *majestichawaii.com* ✆ *From $65.*

Chinatown

Chinatown's original business district was made up of dry-goods and produce merchants, tailors and dressmakers, barbers and herbalists. The meat, fish, and produce stalls remain, but the mix is heavier now on gift and curio stores, lei stands, jewelry shops, and bakeries, with a smattering of noodle makers and travel agents and dozens of restaurants.

The name "Chinatown" here has always been a misnomer. Though three-quarters of Oahu's Chinese lived closely packed in these 25 acres in the late 1800s, even then the neighborhood was half Japanese. Today you hear Vietnamese and Tagalog as often as Mandarin and Cantonese, and there are voices of Japan, Singapore, Malaysia, Korea, Thailand, Samoa, and the Marshall Islands, as well.

Perhaps a more accurate name is the one used by early Chinese: *Wah Fau* (Chinese port), signifying a landing and jumping-off place. As soon as they finished their plantation contracts, Chinese laborers hurried into the city to start businesses here. It's a launching point for today's immigrants, too: Southeast Asian shops almost outnumber Chinese establishments; stalls carry Filipino specialties like winged beans and goat meat; and you'll find Japanese, Cambodian, Laotian, Thai, and Korean cuisine and goods for sale.

In the half century after the first Chinese laborers arrived in Hawaii in 1852, Chinatown was a link to home for the all-male cadre of workers who planned to return to China rich and respected. Merchants not only sold supplies, they held mail, loaned money, wrote letters, translated documents, sent remittances to families, served meals, offered rough bunkhouse accommodations, and were the center for news, gossip, and socializing.

Although much happened to Chinatown in the 20th century—beginning in January 1900, when almost the entire neighborhood was burned to the ground to halt the spread of bubonic plague—it remains a bustling, crowded, noisy, and odiferous place bent primarily on buying and selling and sublimely oblivious to its status as a National Historic District or encroaching gentrification.

GETTING HERE AND AROUND

Chinatown occupies 15 blocks immediately north of downtown Honolulu—it's flat, compact, and very walkable. Street parking can be hard to find depending on the time and day of the week. There are many paid municipal and private parking lots with varying rates.

 ## Sights

Izumo Taishakyo Mission of Hawaii

RELIGIOUS BUILDING | From Chinatown Cultural Plaza, cross a stone bridge to the Izumo Taishakyo Mission of Hawaii to visit the shrine established in 1906. It honors Okuninushi-no-Mikoto, a *kami* (god) who is believed in Shinto tradition to bring good fortune if properly courted (and thanked afterward). ⊠ *215 N. Kukui St., Chinatown* ✢ *At the canal* ☏ *808/538–7778* ⊕ *izumotaishahawaii. com.*

Kuan Yin Temple

TEMPLE | A couple of blocks *mauka* (toward the mountains) from Chinatown is the oldest Buddhist temple in the Islands. Mistakenly called a goddess by some, Kuan Yin, also known as Kannon, is a bodhisattva—one who chose to remain on Earth doing good even after achieving enlightenment. Transformed from a male into a female figure centuries ago, she is credited with being particularly sympathetic to women. You will see representations of her all over the Islands: holding a lotus flower (beauty from the mud of human frailty), as at the temple; pouring out a pitcher of oil (like mercy flowing); or as a sort of Madonna with a child. Visitors are permitted but should be mindful that this is a practicing place of worship. ✉ *170 N. Vineyard Blvd., Chinatown ✥ Park at Foster Botanical Gardens.*

Maunakea Marketplace
MARKET | FAMILY | On the corner of Maunakea and Hotel Streets is this busy plaza surrounded by shops and an air-conditioned indoor market and food court where you can buy fresh seafood and seasonal local produce or chow down on banana *lumpia* (spring rolls) and fruit smoothies or bubble tea (juices and flavored teas with tapioca balls inside). It gets packed during Chinese Lunar New Year. ✉ *1120 Maunakea St., Chinatown* 🌐 *geyserholdings.com/maunakea.*

Oahu Market
MARKET | FAMILY | In this tenant-owned market founded in 1904, you'll find a taste of old-style Chinatown, where you might spot a whole butchered pig, head intact, on display, and where glassy-eyed fish of every size and hue lie forlornly on ice. Bizarre magenta dragonfruit, ready-to-eat *char siu* (Cantonese barbecued pork) and pork belly, and bins brimming with produce add to the color. You'll find some of the cheapest Oahu prices on fruits and vegetables in this and other Chinatown markets. ✉ *N. King St., Chinatown ✥ At Kekaulike St.*

🍴 Restaurants

Fête
$$ | AMERICAN | At lunch, regulars pack into this tiny, brick-walled space for the burgers and specials; at dinner, they come for the pasta and locally sourced seafood dishes or the to-die-for twice-fried Kauai chicken with grits and collard greens. Here, you'll probably get cozy with the table next to you as wait staffers glide between tables with full trays and great attitudes. **Known for:** great pau hana (happy hour) menu; craft cocktails and extensive drink menu; Brooklyn-meets-Hawaii menu. [$] *Average main: $25* ✉ *2 N. Hotel St., Chinatown* ☎ *808/369–1390* 🌐 *fetehawaii.com* 🕘 *Closed Sun.*

Legend Seafood Restaurant
$ | CHINESE | At this large Chinatown institution, the dim sum cart ladies stop at your table and show you their Hong Kong–style fare. If you come for breakfast dim sum, arrive before 9 am, especially on weekends, if you want to hear yourself think. **Known for:** dim sum, reasonably priced by the dish; easy parking in the cultural plaza parking lot; still-warm custard tarts. [$] *Average main: $13* ✉ *Chinese Cultural Plaza, 100 N. Beretania St., Suite 108, Chinatown ✥ In the Chinatown Cultural Plaza* ☎ *808/532–1868* 🌐 *www.legendseafoodhonolulu.com.*

★ **Little Village Noodle House**
$$ | CHINESE | Unassuming and budget-friendly, Little Village is so popular with locals that it expanded to the space next door. Considered some of the best Chinese food on Oahu, the extensive Pan-Asian menu is filled with crowd-pleasers like honey-walnut shrimp and crispy orange chicken. **TIP→ Two hours of free parking are available in the lot immediately to the right of the restaurant (if you can nab a space).** **Known for:** fun interior design with village decor; BYOB; something for everyone on the menu. [$] *Average main: $18* ✉ *1113 Smith St., Chinatown* ☎ *808/545–3008* 🌐 *littlevillagehawaii.com* 🕘 *Closed Tues. No lunch Mon., Wed., and Thurs.*

Livestock Tavern
$$ | MODERN AMERICAN | Livestock Tavern scores big with its seasonal offerings of comfort foods and craft cocktails and its cowboy-minimalist decor. Although meat, including some of the best burgers in town, commands the menu, offerings like *burrata*, creative salads, sandwiches, and fish round out the possibilities. **Known for:** go-to lunch spot; fresh-cut fries; lively bar scene. [$] *Average main: $20* ✉ *49 N. Hotel St., Chinatown* ☎ *808/537–2577* 🌐 *livestocktavern.com.*

Lucky Belly

$$ | **ASIAN** | A hip local crowd sips cocktails and slurps huge bowls of noodles with a modern twist at this popular fusion ramen bar known for its savory broth and its trendy small plates, such as pork belly buns and oxtail dumplings. The service here is unpretentious and attentive if you eat in, but you can also order your food to go, and late-night hours make it a great stop after shows at the Hawaii Theatre or when dinner elsewhere didn't quite do the trick. **Known for:** small but unique cocktail menu; "Belly Bowl" with smoked bacon, sausage, and pork belly; steaming hot pot dishes. [$] *Average main: $17* ✉ *50 N. Hotel St., Chinatown* ☎ *808/531–1888* 🌐 *luckybellyhi.com* 🕒 *Closed Sun. No lunch.*

Mei Sum Dim Sum

$ | **CHINESE** | In contrast to the sprawling, noisy halls where dim sum is generally served, Mei Sum is compact, shiny, and bright—it's also favored by locals who work in the area. Be ready to guess and point at the color photos of dim sum favorites or the items on the carts as they come by, or ask fellow diners for suggestions. **Known for:** house special garlic rice; dim sum made fresh daily; deep-fried garlic eggplant. [$] *Average main: $11* ✉ *1170 Nuuanu Ave., Suite 102, Chinatown* ✣ *Next to post office* ☎ *808/531–3268* 🌐 *www.meisumdimsum.com.*

Pho To Chau Restaurant

$ | **VIETNAMESE** | Those people lined up on River Street know where to go for bowls of steaming pho (Vietnamese beef noodle soup) with all the best trimmings. This hole-in-the-wall storefront was the go-to pho spot long before hipsters and foodies found Chinatown. **Known for:** old-school, 1970s decor; large pho can be easily shared; no-frills service and sometimes a wait for food once seated. [$] *Average main: $10* ✉ *1007 River St., Chinatown* ☎ *808/533–4549* 💳 *No credit cards* 🕒 *No dinner* ☞ *Cash only.*

★ **The Pig and the Lady**

$$ | **ASIAN** | Chef Andrew Le's casual noodle house attracts downtown office workers by day and becomes a creative contemporary restaurant at night, pulling in serious chowhounds. Drawing on both his Vietnamese heritage and multicultural island flavors, the talented, playful Le is a wizard with spice and acid, turning out dishes of layered flavor. **Known for:** house-made soft-serve custards and sorbets, including unexpected flavors; Hanoi-style egg coffee; banh mi sandwiches at lunch and pho all day. [$] *Average main: $20* ✉ *83 N. King St., Chinatown* ☎ *808/585–8255* 🌐 *thepigandthelady.com* 🕒 *Closed Sun. and Mon.*

★ **Senia**

$$$ | **MODERN AMERICAN** | Every item on the modern American menu at this small, sophisticated, James Beard Award nominee is carefully concocted and artfully plated. You can order à la carte or indulge in the pricey tasting menu at the Chef's Counter; dessert is a must thanks to pastry chef Mimi Mendoza's delectable works of art. **Known for:** sophisticated cocktails and an encyclopedic wine menu; Senia cookie made with peanut butter, toffee, and Valrhona chocolate; charred cabbage that looks like a mossy rock but mesmerizes the tastebuds. [$] *Average main: $30* ✉ *75 N. King St., Chinatown* ✣ *Between The Pig & The Lady and Smith & Kings* ☎ *808/200–5412* 🌐 *restaurantsenia.com* 🕒 *Closed Sun. and Mon. No lunch.*

Terry's Place

$$ | **BISTRO** | This country-style European bistro is in a quiet courtyard next to its sister wine shop. Owner Terry Kakazu brings her wine expertise to the menu of classic, elevated comfort food. **Known for:** extensive wine list; great place for groups and celebrations; small plates to share. [$] *Average main: $25* ✉ *31 N. Pauahi St., Chinatown* ☎ *808/533–4277* 🌐 *terrys.place* 🕒 *Closed Sun. and Mon. No lunch.*

Nightlife

Encore Saloon

BARS | Although this bar serves good Mexican-inspired food (try the pork carnitas burrito), it's best known for its impressive drinks menu featuring more than 50 varieties of tequila and mezcal. You can also get wine and canned beer. ✉ *10 N. Hotel St., Chinatown* ☎ *808/367–1656* ⊕ *www.encoresaloon. com* ⊗ *Closed Sun.*

J. Dolan's

BARS | The drinks and rotating beers on tap at this Irish, *Cheers*-like bar are reasonably priced by Honolulu standards, and its menu of New York–style pizzas, both classic and inventive, is a crowd-pleaser, too. ✉ *1147 Bethel St., Chinatown* ☎ *808/537–4992* ⊕ *jdolans. com.*

The Manifest

BARS | With exposed red brick, big skylights, and rotating exhibitions of work by local photographers and painters, The Manifest has an artist's loft feel to it. It's a café by day and a cocktail bar and night club by night, so it serves a good cup of joe as well as quality cocktails. ✉ *32 N. Hotel St., Chinatown* ⊕ *www.manifesthawaii.com* ⊗ *Closed Sun.*

The Tchin Tchin! Bar

BARS | This chill bar gets its name from the Chinese expression "qing, qing" (which means "please please"), often used as a toast; soldiers returning from the Chinese Opium Wars introduced it in France and throughout Europe. With an extensive wine menu—by the glass and the bottle—plus a selection of single malt bourbon, whiskey, and scotch, it's an ideal spot for a drink or tapas-style food. The bar's rooftop lanai is the best place to sit, romantically lit with string lights and featuring a large living wall flourishing with ferns. ✉ *39 N. Hotel St., Chinatown* ☎ *808/528–1888* ⊕ *thetchintchinbar.com* ⊗ *Closed Sun. and Mon.*

Shopping

Pauahi Street

OTHER SPECIALTY STORE | Along Pauahi Street, between the cross streets of Smith and Bethel, are several hip and trendy stores, coffee shops, and restaurants. Roberta Oaks sells modern aloha wear for men, women, and children. There's also a location of Fighting Eel, with its fashionable local clothing and accessories. BAS Bookshop has a well-curated selection of art and design books from around the world, along with pottery, clothes, and other small items. A branch of Morning Glass Coffee shares an open hallway with the music-centric EP Bar. Native Books at Arts & Letters, Valia Honolulu, Ginger13, and The ARTS at Marks Garage are among the other offerings in this area. ✉ *Pauahi Street, Chinatown.*

Kakaako

This 600-acre section of Honolulu between the Ala Moana Center and downtown is in the process of a redevelopment plan that began in 2012. It's definitely a neighborhood in transition, with everything from ramshackle mechanic shops to the University of Hawaii's medical school.

Its old warehouses and mom-and-pop storefronts are gradually being replaced by luxury condos, trendy restaurants, local boutiques, and big-box retailers like T. J. Maxx. New happenings, such as the Honolulu Night Market pop-up shopping event, are also taking root.

Sights

POW! WOW! Hawaii Murals

PUBLIC ART | The POW! WOW! Worldwide art collective was founded in Hawaii in 2010 and has spread to nearly 20 cities around the world. Its most visible Oahu endeavor is a multiblock area where

You won't soon forget the eye-popping murals the Pow! Wow! collective has painted on the buildings in the redeveloping Kakaako neighborhood.

colorful, eclectic, and innovative murals are painted on once-derelict looking warehouses and other buildings. Every year around Valentine's Day, artists from all over come to refresh existing murals and add new ones. The event wraps up with a big food, art, and entertainment festival centered at the SALT at Our Kakaako complex, but you can grab a bite and take in the unique street art here at any time of the year. ⊠ *Kakaako* ✛ *Murals are centered on Cooke, Auahi, and Pohukaina Sts.* ☏ *808/223–7462* ⊕ *www. powwowworldwide.com/murals/hawaii.*

🍴 Restaurants

53 by the Sea

$$$$ | **CONTEMPORARY** | Housed in a McVilla aimed at attracting a Japanese wedding clientele, this restaurant serves contemporary Continental food that focuses primarily on beautifully plated, well-prepared standards—albeit with a million-dollar view of Honolulu. Perched at the water's edge, with famed surf break Point Panic offshore, 53 by the Sea uses its setting to great advantage—the crescent-shape dining room faces the sea, so even if you're not at a table nestled against the floor-to-ceiling windows, you have a fine view. **Known for:** free valet parking; on-site wedding chapel in case the mood strikes; odd villa decor that somehow works. $ *Average main: $50* ⊠ *53 Ahui St., Kakaako* ☏ *808/536–5353* ⊕ *53bythesea.com.*

Hank's Haute Dogs

$ | **HOT DOG** | **FAMILY** | Owner Hank Adaniya's idea of a hot dog involves things like a duck and foie gras sausage with truffle mustard and stone fruit compote. Originally a true hole-in-the-wall, the gentrified Hank's is still a tiny spot where you can go classic with the Chicago Dog, made with the traditional fixings (including neon-green relish), or gourmet with the butter-seared lobster sausage topped with garlic-relish aioli. **Known for:** fries, truffle fries, and onion rings to die for; part of Kakaako's SALT area; 11 varieties of dogs daily, plus another 5 or so daily specials. $ *Average main: $9* ⊠ *324 Coral*

St., Kakaako ☎ 808/532–1265 🌐 www.hankshautedogs.com ☞ Remember to get parking validated.

Highway Inn Kakaako

$ | **MODERN HAWAIIAN** | **FAMILY** | Highway Inn serves what it does best: local favorites like Kalbi ribs, *kalua* (roasted in an underground oven) pork sliders, beef stew, and old-fashioned hamburger steaks. This is also a great spot to try poi (the pudding-like dish made of pounded taro). **Known for:** relatively close to the cruise terminal; signature combo plates; Kakaako location is in SALT complex. *[$] Average main: $16 ✉ 680 Ala Moana Blvd., Kakaako ☎ 808/954–4955 🌐 www.myhighwayinn.com.*

Merriman's Honolulu

$$$ | **BISTRO** | This is fine dining without the fussiness, where cordial, well-trained servers present your "Bag O' Biscuits" or smoking oysters on the half shelf with equal aplomb and know all the details of each menu item. The large Hawaiian-French bistro has floor-to-ceiling windows and native wood accents throughout, and chef-owner Peter Merriman focuses on farm-to-table food, using Oahu-sourced ingredients as much as possible. **Known for:** tableside poke; Waialua chocolate purse (a take on molten lava cake); lobster potpie. *[$] Average main: $35 ✉ 1108 Auahi St., Suite 170, Kakaako ☎ 808/215–0022 🌐 merrimanshawaii.com.*

Moku Kitchen

$$ | **HAWAIIAN** | **FAMILY** | In the hip SALT complex, Moku appeals to both foodies and families with authentic farm-to-table cuisine and a laid-back, urban setting. It's one of legendary chef Peter Merriman's restaurants and focuses on upcountry farm fare cooked in the on-site rotisserie; pizzas, salads, and sandwiches; and craft cocktails. **Known for:** impressive list of craft cocktails, wine, and beer, including the signature monkeypod mai tai; live music; happy hour. *[$] Average main: $20 ✉ SALT at Our Kakaako, 660 Ala Moana Blvd., Kakaako ☎ 808/591–6658 🌐 www.mokukitchen.com.*

Tangö Contemporary Cafe

$$ | **ECLECTIC** | On the ground floor of a glass-sheathed condominium, Tangö's spare contemporary setting stays humming through breakfast, lunch, and dinner. Finnish chef Göran Streng honors his heritage a bit with unfussy dishes such as gravlax with crispy skin, but the menu is, by and large, "general bistro," running from bouillabaisse to herb-crusted rack of lamb, with some Asian nods. **Known for:** loco moco (unlike any you'll have elsewhere); attentive staff; Hamakua mushroom risotto. *[$] Average main: $25 ✉ Hokua Bldg., 1288 Ala Moana Blvd., Kakaako ☎ 808/593–7288 🌐 tangocafehawaii.com ⏲ No dinner Sun.*

🍸 Nightlife

Aloha Beer

BREWPUBS | At this cool brewpub, you order everything at the counter and then grab a seat in either the industrial indoor taproom or the casual outdoor area. The HI Brau Room upstairs, which has its own speakeasy-style entrance, is definitely worth checking out for unique cocktails, too. With 12 beers on draft, including the Hop Lei IPA, Waimanalo Farmhouse, Froot Loops, and Portlock Porter, you can find something to your taste. If you're hungry, there's also pretty good food—snacking boards, hearty sandwiches, small plates, and steak frites. *✉ 700 Queen St., Kakaako ☎ 808/544–1605 🌐 www.alohabeer.com.*

★ Bevy Bar

BARS | Tucked at the end of a row of new boutiques, Bevy is urban, modern, and furnished with upcycled materials (its benches are upholstered in denim jeans, and its tabletops feature flattened wine boxes). Locals in the know come for artisan cocktails created by owner and master mixologist Christian Self, who deftly concocts libations with obscure ingredients and complex flavors. Look for live music on some nights. ✉ *675 Auahi St., Kakaako* ☎ *808/594–7445* 🌐 *bevyhawaii.com* 🕒 *Closed Mon.*

★ Waikiki Brewing Company

BREWPUBS | This company not only brews its own quality craft beer but also serves delicious food. This is its second location—the original is in Waikiki at 1945 Kalakaua Avenue—and it always offers nine beers on tap, including the Skinny Jeans IPA and the Hana Hou Hefe, to which orange peel and strawberry puree are added before fermentation. You can also buy six-packs at the bar to go. Here, the chef smokes meat in house using local kiawe wood, resulting in tender and flavorful beef brisket, pulled pork, chicken, and bratwurst. Accompanying barbecue sauces are made with Waikiki Brewing beer. ✉ *831 Queen St., Kakaako* ☎ *808/591–0387* 🌐 *waikikibrewing.com.*

Shopping

Anne Namba Designs

MIXED CLOTHING | This designer combines the beauty of classic kimonos with contemporary styles to make unique pieces for career and evening. In addition to women's apparel, she designs a men's line. ✉ *324 Kamani St., Kakaako* ☎ *808/589–1135* 🌐 *www.annenamba.com.*

Ala Moana

Ala Moana abuts Waikiki to the east (stopping at the Ala Wai Canal) and King Street to the north. Kakaako, Kewalo Basin Harbor, and the Blaisdell Center complex roughly mark its western edge. Probably its most notable attraction is the sprawling Ala Moana Center, jam-packed with almost any store you could wish for.

Beaches

Honolulu proper only has one beach: Ala Moana. Popular with locals, it hosts everything from Dragon Boat competitions to the Lantern Floating Ceremony.

★ Ala Moana Regional Park (*Ala Moana Beach Park*)

BEACH | **FAMILY** | A protective reef makes Ala Moana essentially a ½-mile-wide saltwater swimming pool. Very smooth sand and no waves create a haven for families and stand-up paddleboarders. After Waikiki, this is the most popular beach among visitors, and the free parking area can fill up quickly on sunny weekends. On the Waikiki side is a peninsula called Magic Island, with shady trees and paved sidewalks ideal for jogging. Ala Moana Regional Park also has playing fields, tennis courts, and a couple of small ponds for sailing toy boats. The beach is for everyone, but only in the daytime; after dark, it's a high-crime area, with many unhoused people. **Amenities:** food and drink; lifeguards; parking (free); showers; toilets. **Best for:** swimming; walking. ✉ *1201 Ala Moana Blvd., Ala Moana* 🌐 *www.honolulu.gov/parks.*

Restaurants

Akasaka

$$ | **JAPANESE** | Step inside this tiny sushi bar, tucked amid the strip clubs behind the Ala Moana Hotel, and you'll swear you're in an out-of-the-way Edo neighborhood. Don't be deterred by its dodgy neighbors or its reputation for inconsistent service—this is where locals come when they want the real deal, and you'll be greeted with a cheerful *"Iraishaimase!"* (Welcome!) before sitting at a diminutive table or perching at the small sushi bar. **Known for:** spicy tuna roll; no pretense, nothing fancy; popular local spot for late-night food. [$] *Average main: $21* ✉ *1646 B Kona St., Suite B, Ala Moana* ☎ *808/942–4466* 🌐 *www.akasakahawaii.com* 🕒 *No lunch on Sun.*

Bac Nam

$ | **VIETNAMESE** | Tam and Kimmy Huynh's menu ranges far beyond the usual pho and *bun* (cold noodle dishes) found at many Vietnamese restaurants. This welcoming, no-frills, hole-in-the-wall spot, which locals swear by, features lamb curry, tapioca dumplings, head-on tamarind shrimp, and other dishes that hail from both North and South Vietnam. **Known for:** limited free parking behind the restaurant; excellent crabmeat curry soup; spring and summer rolls. [$] *Average main: $12* ✉ *1117 S. King St., Ala Moana* ☎ *808/597–8201* 🕒 *Closed Sun.*

Chef Chai

$$$ | **FUSION** | This contemporary dining room in a condo building across from the Blaisdell Center is the go-to spot before and after plays or concerts. The creative starters and seafood and meat entrées on the eclectic, global-fusion menu are healthier than the norm as they don't rely on butter or cream, with dishes like lobster bisque thickened instead with squash puree. **Known for:** ahi tartare with avocado mousse in miniwaffle cones; excellent desserts; early-bird and prix-fixe menu options that will leave you stuffed. [$] *Average main: $30* ✉ *Pacifica Honolulu, 1009 Kapiolani Blvd., Ala Moana* ☎ *808/585–0011* 🌐 *chefchai.com* 🕒 *Closed Mon. and Tues.*

Mariposa

$$$ | **HAWAIIAN** | Yes, the popovers and the wee cups of bouillon are available at lunch, but in every other regard, the menu at this Neiman Marcus restaurant departs from the classic model, incorporating a clear sense of Pacific place. The breezy, open-air veranda, with a view of Ala Moana Regional Park, the twirling ceiling fans, and the life-size hula-girl murals say "Hawaii." It's still a spot for ladies who lunch, but it also welcomes a more casual crowd. **Known for:** corn chowder; lovely Hawaii-style interiors; extensive cocktail menu. [$] *Average main: $35* ✉ *Neiman Marcus, Ala Moana Center, 1450 Ala Moana Blvd., Ala Moana* ☎ *808/951–3420* 🌐 *neimanmarcushawaii.com/Restaurants/Mariposa.htm.*

★ MW Restaurant

$$$ | **HAWAIIAN** | The "M" and "W" team of husband-and-wife chefs Michelle Karr-Ueko and Wade Ueko combine their collective experience (20 years alongside chef Alan Wong, a side step to the famed French Laundry, and some serious kitchen time at comfort food icon Zippy's) to create a uniquely local menu with a decidedly upscale twist. Michelle's flair for sweets has resulted in a dessert menu as long as the main one, including tropical fruit creamsicle brûlée, an MW candy bar, and the frozen *lilikoi* (Hawaiian passion fruit) soufflé. **Known for:** nice craft cocktails; excellent fish dishes; scrumptious desserts (save room). [$] *Average main: $35* ✉ *888 Kapiolani Blvd., Suite 201, Ala Moana* ☎ *808/955–6505* 🌐 *www.mwrestaurant.com.*

Panya

$$ | **ECLECTIC** | Run by Hong Kong–born sisters Alice and Annie Yeung, this easy-breezy café is known for its pastries, desserts, and happy hours but also offers crowd-pleasing, contemporary fare, both American (salads, sandwiches, pastas) and Asian (Thai-style steak salad, Japanese-style fried chicken, Singaporean seafood *laksa*). Dine inside for the air-conditioning and disco vibe, or choose a spot on the covered lanai. **Known for:** eclectic and extensive menu; Japanese cheesecake; French-style pastries and cakes. [$] *Average main: $18* ✉ *1288 Ala Moana Blvd., Kakaako* ☎ *808/946–6388* 🌐 *www.panyabistro.com* 🕒 *Closed Mon.*

Scratch Kitchen

$$ | **MODERN AMERICAN** | Tucked into the chic South Shore Market in Kakaako's Ward Village, Scratch Kitchen has hipster decor, an open kitchen, and creative comfort food. It's popular for breakfast and brunch and has both small plates and generous entrées on its dinner menu. **Known for:** spicy (and good) chicken and

waffles; large portions; milk 'n' cereal pancakes. [$] *Average main: $18* ✉ *South Shore Market at Ward Village, 1170 Auahi St., Kakaako* ✥ *Enter on side of building, along Queen St.* ☎ *808/589–1669* 🌐 *www.scratch-hawaii.com.*

Hotels

Ala Moana Hotel

$$$ | **HOTEL** | A decent value in a pricey hotel market, location is the hallmark of this property, which is connected to Oahu's largest mall, the Ala Moana Center, by a pedestrian ramp and is just a 10-minute walk from Waikiki, a two-minute stroll from Ala Moana Beach Park, and a block from the convention center. **Pros:** great value (and no resort fee); refreshed pool deck, lobby, and a new Starbucks; very convenient location. **Cons:** smaller and older rooms in Kona Tower; expensive parking; outside the heartbeat of Waikiki. [$] *Rooms from: $269* ✉ *410 Atkinson Dr., Ala Moana* ☎ *808/955–4811, 866/488–1396* 🌐 *www.alamoanahotelhonolulu.com* 🛏 *1100 rooms* 🍴 *No Meals.*

Nightlife

Mai Tai's

BARS | After a long day of shopping at the Ala Moana Center, the fourth-floor Mai Tai's is the perfect spot to relax. What you will find is live entertainment and happy hour specials for both food and drink. What you won't find is a cover charge or a dress code. To avoid waiting in line, arrive before 9 pm. ✉ *Ala Moana Center, 1450 Ala Moana Blvd., Ala Moana* 🌐 *instagram.com/maitaisalamoana.*

Shopping

BOOKS

★ Na Mea Hawaii

BOOKS | In addition to Island-style clothing for adults and children, Hawaiian cultural items, and unusual artwork, such as Niihau-shell necklaces, this boutique's book selection covers Hawaiian history and language and includes children's books set in the Islands. Na Mea also has classes on Hawaiian language, culture, and history. ✉ *Ward Village, 1200 Ala Moana Blvd., Suite 270, Ala Moana* ☎ *808/596–8885* 🌐 *www.nameahawaii.com.*

CLOTHING

Reyn Spooner

MIXED CLOTHING | This is a good place to buy the aloha-print fashions residents wear. Look for the limited-edition Christmas shirt, a collector's item manufactured each holiday season. Reyn Spooner has seven locations statewide and offers styles for men and children and, sometimes, limited-edition women's wear. ✉ *Ala Moana Shopping Center, 1450 Ala Moana Blvd., Shop 2247, Ala Moana* ☎ *808/949–5929* 🌐 *www.reynspooner.com.*

CRAFTS

Na Hoku

JEWELRY & WATCHES | If you look at the wrists of *kamaaina* (local) women, you might see Hawaiian heirloom bracelets fashioned in either gold or silver and engraved in a number of Islands-inspired designs. Na Hoku sells these and other traditional Hawaiian jewelry along with an array of modern Island-influenced designs that capture the heart of the Hawaiian lifestyle in all its elegant diversity. There are a number of Na Hoku locations on Oahu, as well as on the other Islands and the Mainland. ✉ *Ala Moana Center, 1450 Ala Moana Blvd., Shop 2006, Ala Moana* ☎ *808/946–2100* 🌐 *www.nahoku.com.*

FOOD

Longs Drugs

FOOD | Try Longs at the Ala Moana Center (or one of its many other outposts) to stock up on chocolate-covered macadamia nuts, candies, cookies, Islands tea, and 100% Kona coffee—at reasonable prices—to carry home. ✉ *Ala Moana*

Shopping Center, 1450 Ala Moana Blvd., 2nd level, Ala Moana ☎ *808/941–4010* ⊕ *longs.staradvertiser.com.*

GIFTS
Blue Hawaii Lifestyle

SOUVENIRS | The Ala Moana store carries a large selection of locally made products, including soaps, honey, tea, salt, chocolates, art, and CDs. Every item is carefully selected from various Hawaiian companies, artisans, and farms—from the salt fields of Molokai to the lavender farms of Maui to the single-estate chocolate of Oahu's North Shore. An in-store café serves healthy smoothies, panini, tea, and espresso. ⊠ *Ala Moana Shopping Center, 1450 Ala Moana Blvd., Shop 2312, Ala Moana* ☎ *808/949–0808* ⊕ *www.bluehawaiilifestyle.com.*

SHOPPING CENTERS
Ala Moana Shopping Center

MALL | FAMILY | The world's largest open-air shopping mall is a five-minute bus ride from Waikiki. More than 350 stores and 160 dining options (including multiple food courts) make up this 50-acre complex, which is a unique mix of national and international chains as well as smaller, locally owned shops and eateries—and everything in between. The newer Lanai @ Ala Moana Center is worth stopping at for a range of casual dining options in one spot. More than 30 luxury boutiques in residence include Gucci, Louis Vuitton, and Christian Dior. All of Hawaii's major department stores are here, including the state's only Neiman Marcus and Nordstrom, plus Macy's, Target, and Bloomingdale's. ⊠ *1450 Ala Moana Blvd., Ala Moana* ☎ *808/955–9517* ⊕ *www.alamoanacenter.com.*

Ward Village

SHOPPING CENTER | FAMILY | Heading west from Waikiki toward downtown Honolulu, you'll run into a section of town with five distinct shopping-complex areas; there are more than 135 specialty shops and 40 eateries here. The Ward Entertainment Center features

16 movie screens, including a state-of-the-art, 3-D, big-screen auditorium, and all theaters have reclining chairs and access to an extended food menu and alcoholic beverages for those of age. The South Shore Market is a contemporary collection of local shops and restaurants, plus T. J. Maxx and Nordstrom Rack. For distinctive Hawaiian gifts, such as locally made muumuus, koa-wood products, and Niihau shell necklaces, visit Martin & MacArthur and Na Mea Hawaii. Over at the Ward Gateway Center, the Ohana Hale Marketplace is worth a stop to visit 140 local small businesses, including food stalls, apparel and accessories shops, and gift and craft stands. You can hop on TheBus or take a trolley from Waikiki. There's also free parking around the entire Ward Village, though sometimes you have to circle for awhile to find a spot. Valet parking is also available. ⊠ *1050-1200 Ala Moana Blvd., Ala Moana* ☎ *808/591–8411* ⊕ *www.wardvillage. com/shopping.*

Makiki Heights

Makiki is home to the more unassuming neighborhood where former president Barack Obama grew up. Highlights include the exclusive Punahou School he attended and the notable Central Union Church, as well as the Tantalus area overlook.

🍴 Restaurants

Honolulu Burger Company

$ | BURGER | FAMILY | Owner Ken Takahashi retired as a nightclub impresario on the Big Island to become a real-life burger king. This modest spot is the home of the locavore burger, made with range-fed beef, Manoa lettuce, tomatoes, and a wide range of toppings, all island-grown—and you can taste the difference. **Known for:** Blue Hawaii Burger with blue cheese and bacon; a presence at local farmers' markets or elsewhere

The Bishop Museum is Hawaii's state historical museum and the repository for the royal artifacts of the last surviving direct descendant of King Kamehameha the Great.

in its own food truck; Miso Kutie Burger topped with red miso glaze and Japanese cucumber slices. $ *Average main: $13* ✉ *1295 S. Beretania St., Makiki Heights* ☎ *808/626–5202* ⊕ *honoluluburgerco. com* ⊘ *Closed Mon.*

Kalihi-Liliha-Kapalama

North of downtown Honolulu, just off H1, is the tightly packed neighborhood of Kalihi. It's home to large industrial pockets but also the stellar Bishop Museum and great local eateries, like Mitsu-Ken.

Liliha-Kapalama (that latter is sometimes referred to as just "Palama") is the sliver of land that runs from ocean to mountain (known as an *ahupuaa* in Hawaiian). It's presided over by famed Kamehameha Schools, which from its hillside perch looks down on a warren of modest homes and shops.

◉ Sights

★ Bishop Museum

SCIENCE MUSEUM | FAMILY | Founded in 1889 by Charles R. Bishop as a memorial to his wife, Princess Bernice Pauahi Bishop, the museum began as a repository for the royal possessions of this last direct descendant of King Kamehameha the Great. Today, it's the state's designated history and culture museum. Its five exhibit halls contain almost 25 million items that tell the history of the Hawaiian Islands and their Pacific neighbors.

Gain understanding of the entire region in the Pacific Hall, and learn about the culture of the Islands through state-of-the-art and often-interactive displays in the Hawaiian Hall. Spectacular artifacts—lustrous feather capes, bone fishhooks, the skeleton of a giant sperm whale, photography and crafts displays, and a well-preserved grass house—are displayed inside a three-story, 19th-century, Victorian-style gallery. The building alone,

The Punchbowl, yet another extinct volcanic crater, is home to the National Memorial Cemetery of the Pacific, the largest military cemetery in Hawaii.

with its huge turrets and immense stone walls, is worth seeing.

In the 16,500-square-foot science adventure wing, it's hard to miss the three-story simulated volcano where regular "lava melts" take place to the delight of younger (and young at heart) visitors. Also check out the planetarium, daily tours, *lauhala*-weaving and science demonstrations, special exhibits, the Shop Pacifica, and the Bishop Museum Café, which serves *ono* (delicious) Hawaiian food by local restaurant Highway Inn. ⊠ *1525 Bernice St., Kalihi* ☏ *808/847–3511* ⊕ *www.bishopmuseum.org* ⊠ *$25 (parking $5)*.

Nuuanu

Immediately *mauka* of Kalihi, off the Pali Highway, are a renowned resting place and a carefully preserved home where royal families retreated during the doldrums of summer. Nuuanu Pali was the sight of a famous battle that was key to King Kamehameha I's success in uniting all the Hawaiian Islands under his rule and becoming the Islands' first monarch. Nuuanu Valley is known for its lush, quiet beauty and has several notable cemeteries, churches, and embassies.

◉ Sights

National Memorial Cemetery of the Pacific
CEMETERY | Nestled in the bowl of Puowaina, or Punchbowl Crater, this 112-acre cemetery is the final resting place for more than 50,000 U.S. war veterans and family members and is a solemn reminder of their sacrifice. Among those buried here is Ernie Pyle, the famed World War II correspondent who was killed by a Japanese sniper on Ie Shima, an island off the northwest coast of Okinawa. Intricate stone maps provide a visual military-history lesson. Puowaina, formed 75,000–100,000 years ago during a period of secondary volcanic activity,

translates as "Hill of Sacrifice." Historians believe this site once served as an altar where ancient Hawaiians offered sacrifices to their gods. **■TIP→ The entrance to the cemetery has unfettered views of Waikiki and Honolulu—perhaps the finest on Oahu.** ✉ *2177 Puowaina Dr., Nuuanu* ☎ *808/532–3720* 🌐 *www.cem.va.gov/cems/nchp/nmcp.asp* 🎟 *Free.*

Queen Emma Summer Palace

HISTORIC HOME | Queen Emma, King Kamehameha IV's wife, used this small but stately New England–style home in Nuuanu Valley as a retreat from the rigors of court life in hot and dusty Honolulu during the mid- to late 1800s. Guided tours highlight the residence's royal history and its eclectic mix of European, Victorian, and Hawaiian furnishings, most of which are original to the home. There are excellent examples of feather-covered kahilis, *umeke* (bowls), and koa-wood furniture. Visitors also learn how Queen Emma established what is today the largest private hospital in Hawaii, opened a school for girls, and ran as a widow for the throne, losing to King Kalakaua. A short drive away, you can visit the Royal Mausoleum State Monument, where she, her husband, and their son, Albert, who died at age four, are buried beside many other Hawaiian royals. Guided tours are offered Tuesday through Saturday by appointment. ✉ *2913 Pali Hwy., Nuuanu* ☎ *808/595–3167* 🌐 *www.daughtersofhawaii.org* 🎟 *$14* 🕓 *Closed Sun. and Mon.*

Moiliili

Packed into the neighborhood of Moiliili, about 3 miles from Waikiki, are flower and lei shops, restaurants, and little stores selling Hawaiian and Asian goodies. Most places of interest are along King Street, between Isenberg Street and Waialae Avenue.

🍴 Restaurants

Chiang Mai Thai Cuisine

$$ | THAI | Long beloved for its northern Thai classics, such as spicy curries and stir-fries and sticky rice in woven-grass baskets, made using family recipes, Chiang Mai is a short cab ride from Waikiki. Some dishes, like the signature barbecue Cornish game hen with lemongrass and spices, show how acculturation can create interesting pairings. **Known for:** limited parking in a small lot in back; local business-lunch favorite; spring rolls and Chiang Mai wings. [$] *Average main: $25* ✉ *2239 S. King St., Moiliili* ☎ *808/941–1151* 🌐 *www.chiangmairestaurant.com* 🕓 *No lunch weekends.*

Fukuya Delicatessen

$ | JAPANESE | Get a taste of local Japanese culture at this family operation on the main thoroughfare in Moiliili, a mile or so *mauka* (toward the mountains) out of Waikiki. Open since 1939, the delicatessen offers take-out breakfasts and lunches, Japanese snacks, noodle dishes, and confections—and it's a local favorite for catering, from parties to funeral gatherings. **Known for:** mochi tray, offering samples of everything; kid-friendly menu; nori-wrapped chicken. [$] *Average main: $8* ✉ *2710 S. King St., Moiliili* ☎ *808/946–2073* 🌐 *fukuyadeli.com* 🕓 *Closed Mon. and Tues. No dinner.*

Imanas Tei

$$$ | JAPANESE | *Nihonjin* (Japanese nationals) and locals flock to this tucked-away, bamboo-ceilinged restaurant for its tasteful, simple decor and equally tasteful—and perfect—sushi, sashimi, *nabe* (hot pots prepared at the table), and grilled dishes. You assemble your meal dish by dish, and the cost can add up if you aren't careful. **Known for:** long waits; traditional izakaya experience; simple food that some feel is better than in Japan. [$] *Average main: $30* ✉ *2626 S. King St., Moiliili* ☎ *808/941–2626* 🌐 *imanastei.com* 🕓 *Closed Sun. No lunch.*

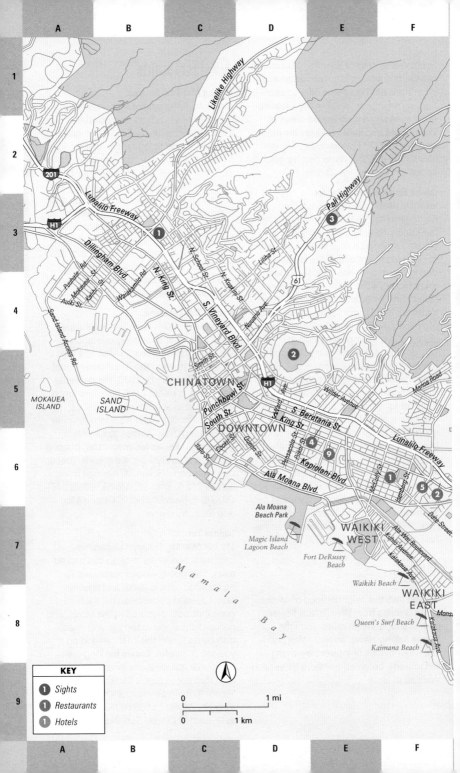

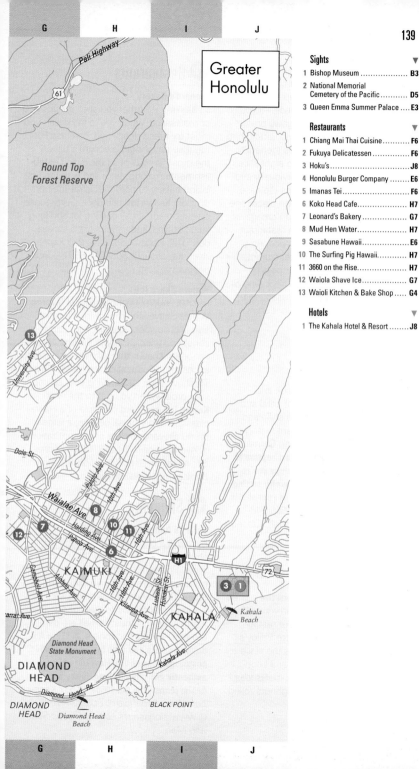

Greater Honolulu

Sasabune Hawaii
$$$$ | **JAPANESE** | Try to get a coveted seat at the counter, and prepare for an unforgettable sushi experience—if you behave, as chef Seiji Kumagawa prefers that diners eat *omakase*-style, letting him send out his favorite courses (generally two pieces of sushi or six to eight slices of sashimi), each priced individually and each served with instructions ("please, no *shoyu* on this one" or "one piece, one bite"). People who've defied Kumagawa have been kicked out of the restaurant midmeal. **Known for:** fast service; no phone calls allowed in the restaurant; one of Honolulu's top sushi spots. [$] *Average main: $150* ✉ *1417 S. King St., Moiliili* ☎ *808/947–3800* 🌐 *sasabuneh.com* 🕒 *Closed Sun. and Mon. Lunch is takeout only.*

Shopping

Maui Divers Design Center
JEWELRY & WATCHES | For a look into the harvesting and design of coral and black pearl jewelry, visit this shop and take a free tour at its adjacent factory near the Ala Moana Shopping Center. ■ **TIP→ Avoid the "Pick a Pearl" option at their other kiosk locations unless you're prepared to be upsold on a jewelry setting or two for the pearls "found" in your shells.** ✉ *1520 Liona St., Moiliili* ☎ *808/946–2929* 🌐 *www.mauidivers.com* 🕒 *Closed Sat. and Sun.*

Kapahulu

Walk just a few minutes from the eastern end of Waikiki, and you'll find yourself in this very local main drag of restaurants, bars, and shops, where Bailey's Antiques and Aloha Shirts is the place for rare, wearable collectibles, and Leonard's Bakery is the place for *malasadas* (Portuguese deep-fried doughnuts rolled in sugar).

🍴 Restaurants

Leonard's Bakery
$ | **BAKERY** | Whether you spell it *malasada* or *malassada,* when you're in Hawaii, you must try these deep-fried, holeless Portuguese doughnuts. Leonard's Bakery is the most famous of all the island establishments making them and was the first island bakery to commercialize their production. **Known for:** pão doce (Portuguese sweet bread); small parking lot and long lines; original and various filled malasadas. [$] *Average main: $2* ✉ *933 Kaphalulu Ave., Kapahulu* ☎ *808/737–5591* 🌐 *leonardshawaii.com.*

Waiola Shave Ice
$ | **CAFÉ** | **FAMILY** | Longtime local favorite Waiola Shave Ice, known for its supersoft and powdery shave ice (or snow cone) and wide variety of flavors, became nationally known through regular appearances on the reboot of the *Hawaii Five-0* TV show. It's a fast-moving line, so know your order when you get to the window. **Known for:** excellent example of a Hawaii classic; slightly brusk service; a large menu allowing for lots of customization. [$] *Average main: $4* ✉ *3113 Mokihana St., Kapahulu* ☎ *808/949–2269* 🌐 *facebook.com/WaiolaShaveIce.*

Shopping

Bailey's Antiques & Aloha Shirts
ANTIQUES & COLLECTIBLES | Vintage aloha shirts are the specialty at this kitschy store. Prices range from $3.99 to several hundred dollars for the 15,000 shirts in stock. Thousands of them are used; others are creations by top designers. The tight space and musty smell are part of the thrift-shop atmosphere. ■ **TIP→ Antiques hunters can also buy old-fashioned postcards, glassware, Hawaiian LPs, authentic military clothing, funky hats, and denim jeans from the 1950s.** ✉ *517 Kapahulu Ave., Kapahulu* ☎ *808/734–7628* 🌐 *www.alohashirts.com* 🕒 *Closed Sun. and Mon.*

Kaimuki

Ten minutes beyond Kapahulu, this commercial thoroughfare runs through a neighborhood that, despite ongoing development, still has a good number of cool old Craftsman bungalows. Kaimuki has also become a food mecca, rivaled only by Chinatown, with perhaps Oahu's most diverse concentration of eateries. If you want to discover the island's culinary trends, this is the place to do it.

🍴 Restaurants

★ Koko Head Cafe

$ | **MODERN HAWAIIAN** | When Lee Anne Wong, best known as a competitor on the first season of Bravo's *Top Chef,* moved to the Islands, foodies waited with bated breath for this, her first restaurant. It's a lively yet laid-back café, where she took the concept of breakfast and flipped it, creating innovative dishes like Elvis's Revenge, a peanut butter and banana tempura sandwich with candied bacon, and her signature dumplings, which change daily. **Known for:** creative cocktail menu; crazy busy weekends; cornflake french toast. $ *Average main: $15* ⊠ *1145c 12th Ave., Kaimuki* ☎ *808/732–8920* ⊕ *kokoheadcafe.com* ☾ *No dinner.*

Mud Hen Water

$$ | **HAWAIIAN** | The name of this restaurant is the English translation of *waialae* (meaning a gathering spot around a watering hole). Renowned chef Ed Kenney explores modern interpretations of the Hawaiian foods he remembers from his childhood with an ever-changing locavore menu. **Known for:** beet poke; sorbetto and gelato; small plates and snacks. $ *Average main: $17* ⊠ *3452 Waialae Ave., Kaimuki* ☎ *808/737–6000* ⊕ *www.mudhenwater.com* ☾ *Closed Mon. Brunch Sun. only.*

The Surfing Pig Hawaii

$$$ | **BARBECUE** | This fancier sibling of the island's four Kono's barbecue spots focuses on Americana-tinged-with-Hawaiian food and drink served in a small, lofted eatery with a surfer-industrial vibe. Heaping portions of juicy smoked and grilled meats are the specialty, but the menu also has several great fish appetizers and entrées. **Known for:** pork, beef, and porchetta slider trio; a strong neighborhood brunch option; old-fashioned with bacon-infused bourbon, bacon garnish, and "smoking" cloche presentation. $ *Average main: $30* ⊠ *3605 Waialae Ave., Kaimuki* ☎ *808/744–1992* ⊕ *thesurfingpighawaii.com.*

3660 on the Rise

$$$$ | **MODERN HAWAIIAN** | Named for its address on Honolulu's premier Waialae Avenue, this restaurant brought fresh dining to Kaimuki when it opened in 1992, inspiring a neighborhood dining renaissance. Loyalists swear by the steaks, the crab cakes, and the signature dish, ahi *katsu* wrapped in *nori* (seaweed) and deep-fried, with a wasabi-ginger butter sauce. **Known for:** good desserts; somewhat dated interior; special-occasion restaurant. $ *Average main: $40* ⊠ *3660 Waialae Ave., Kaimuki* ☎ *808/737–1177* ⊕ *3660ontherise.com* ☾ *Closed Mon. No lunch.*

Manoa

Manoa is probably best known as the home of the University of Hawaii's main campus. The surrounding area is chock-full of interesting coffee shops, restaurants, and stores supported by the collegiate and professorial crowd. History and beauty linger around verdant Manoa Valley at places like the Manoa Chinese Cemetery, Manoa Falls, and Lyon Arboretum. Manoa Valley Theatre puts on topnotch community productions year-round.

Restaurants

★ Waioli Kitchen & Bake Shop

$ | AMERICAN | Dating from 1922, this historic café surrounded by the verdant Manoa Valley landscape is part of the Hawaii Salvation Army headquarters and has been independently operated by Ross and Stefanie Anderson since late 2018. A short menu of simple, delicious breakfast and lunch items are ordered at the counter and delivered to your chosen table, either inside the cozy, multiroom bungalow or on the covered lanai. **Known for:** assorted house-made pastries, scones, muffins, breads, jams, and jellies; honey and salt produced on the property and a burgeoning garden; braised short rib loco moco. $ *Average main: $10* ✉ *Salvation Army Headquarters, 2950 Manoa Rd., Manoa* ☎ *808/744–1619* ⊕ *waiolikitchen.com* ⊗ *Closed Mon. and Tues. No dinner.*

Kahala

Oahu's wealthiest neighborhood has streets lined with multimillion-dollar homes. Lanes at intervals along tree-lined Kahala Avenue provide public access to Kahala's quiet, narrow coastal beaches offering views of Koko Head. Kahala Mall includes restaurants, a movie theater, and a Whole Foods grocery store. Kahala is also the home of the private Waialae Country Club, where the golf course hosts the Sony Open PGA tournament in January.

Restaurants

Hoku's

$$$$ | ASIAN FUSION | Everything about Hoku's speaks of quality and sophistication: the wall of windows with their beach views, the avant-garde cutlery and dinnerware, the solicitous staff, and the carefully constructed Euro-Pacific cuisine. The tasting menus frequently change, focusing even more on seasonal cuisine made with fresh, local ingredients (including herbs from the hotel's on-site herb garden). **Known for:** panoramic views from every table; setting and service that can outshine the food; relaxed elegance in the grande dame of Hawaii's social scene. $ *Average main: $110* ✉ *The Kahala Hotel & Resort, 5000 Kahala Ave., Kahala* ☎ *808/739–8760* ⊕ *www. hokuskahala.com* ⊗ *No lunch. Tasting or set menus only.*

Hotels

★ The Kahala Hotel & Resort

$$$$ | RESORT | FAMILY | Hidden away in the upscale residential neighborhood of Kahala (on the other side of Diamond Head from Waikiki), this elegant ocean-front hotel with top-notch service, one of Hawaii's very first luxury resorts, has hosted celebrities, princesses, the Dalai Lama, and nearly every president since Lyndon Johnson. **Pros:** away from hectic Waikiki; top-notch Hoku's restaurant; heavenly spa. **Cons:** in a residential neighborhood, so not much to do within walking distance of hotel; small pool; far from Waikiki. $ *Rooms from: $495* ✉ *5000 Kahala Ave., Kahala* ☎ *808/739–8888, 800/367–2525 toll-free* ⊕ *www.kahalaresort.com* ⤳ *338 rooms* ⫶⊙⫶ *No Meals.*

Shopping

Kahala Mall

MALL | FAMILY | This indoor mall has more than 100 stores and restaurants, with a mix of national retailers and not-to-be-missed, homegrown boutiques, clothing stores, and galleries. You can also browse local foods and products at Whole Foods. For post-shopping entertainment, see what's playing at the Kahala Theatres, where you'll also find a full kitchen and bar. ✉ *4211 Waialae Ave., Kahala* ☎ *808/732–7736* ⊕ *www.kahalamall-center.com.*

West (Leeward) and Central Oahu

The rugged Waianae Range of mountains bisects the leeward side of the island from the central plateau. The queen of the range, Mount Kaala, is the highest peak on Oahu (4,003 feet) and dominates the landscape on all sides when clouds fail to obscure its majesty. The mountains shield the western slopes from trade winds and heavy rain that falls to the north and east. The western side thus appears drier, and its beaches are known for their pristine white sands and crystal clear waters that are excellent for snorkeling and diving. This geography (combined with flows from the western slopes of the parallel eastern Koolau Range) also results in abundant water flows to the fertile central valley plains—where much of Oahu's delectable bounty originates. The region's eastern portion edges Pearl Harbor and includes the Aloha Stadium, Hawaii's Plantation Village, the Wet 'n' Wild Hawaii water park, and Waikele Premium Outlets near Waipio. Kapolei, Oahu's burgeoning "second city," lies due west of Pearl Harbor. It is a planned community, where, for years, the government has been trying to attract enough jobs to lighten inbound traffic to downtown Honolulu. A major mall and community center, Ka Makana Alii, opened here in 2017 to serve an expected influx of shoppers in the ensuing decades. Ko Olina—a lively, privately owned community centered on a golf course, several major resorts, and four man-made lagoons—occupies the island's southwestern tip. Some locals avoid Leeward and Central Oahu because of traffic that tends to bottleneck at the intersection of the H1, H2, and H3 freeways. But those who time their travels to avoid the traffic find great rewards throughout the region, especially the chance to explore the gorgeous and remote west coast beaches, including the far-flung Hawaiian communities of Nanakuli and Waianae and the end of the road at Keawaula, aka Yokohama Bay. A visit to Ko Hana Distillers and a walk through the Dole Plantation's 3-acre maze (the world's largest) near Wahiawa are well worth including in any Central Oahu excursion itinerary.

GETTING HERE AND AROUND

It's relatively easy to get to West Oahu, which begins at folksy Waipahu and continues past Makakilo and Kapolei on H1 and Highway 93, Farrington Highway. It takes about a half hour to reach Ko Olina from Waikiki, but rush hour traffic can create delays.

A couple of cautions as you head to the leeward side: Highway 93 is a narrow, winding, two-lane road, notorious for accidents. There's an abrupt transition from an expansive freeway to a two-lane highway at Kapolei, and by the time you reach Nanakuli, it's a country road, so *slow down*. Also be aware of congestion between Ko Olina and Waianae during commuter hours.

Kapolei

22 miles west of downtown Honolulu.

The planned community of Kapolei, where, for years, the government has been trying to attract enough jobs to lighten inbound traffic to downtown Honolulu, is often called Oahu's "second city." It occupies much of 1800s business mogul James Campbell's 41,000-acre Ewa plain estate, which once cultivated vast tracts of sugarcane and pineapple.

The first phases broke ground starting in the 1980s. Today, it is a thriving community with government centers, industrial parks, big-box malls, businesses small and large, and the West Oahu campus of the University of Hawaii. The Ko Olina complex to the west is officially part of the district and has a Kapolei zip code.

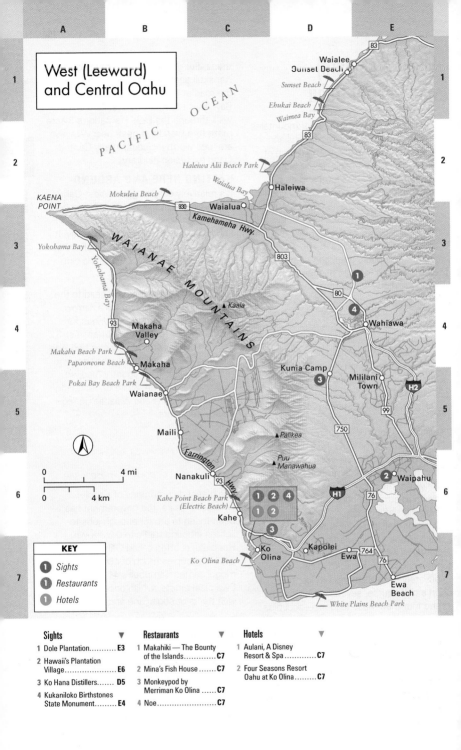

West (Leeward) and Central Oahu

PACIFIC OCEAN

Waialee
Sunset Beach
Sunset Beach
Ehukai Beach
Waimea Bay

83

83

Haleiwa Alii Beach Park
Mokuleia Beach
Waialua Bay
Haleiwa

KAENA POINT

930
Waialua
Kamehameha Hwy.

Yokohama Bay
803

WAIANAE MOUNTAINS

Yokohama Bay

▲ *Kaala*

80

1

4

Wahiawa

93
Makaha Valley

Makaha Beach Park
Papaoneone Beach
Makaha
Kunia Camp

3

Mililani Town

H2

Pokai Bay Beach Park
Waianae

Maili
▲ *Palikea*
Puu Manawahua ▲

99

750

2
Waipahu

Farrington
Nanakuli
93 *Hwy.*

H1

76

Kahe Point Beach Park (Electric Beach)

1 **2** **4**
1 **2**

Kahe

3

Ko Olina
Kapolei
Ewa

764

Ko Olina Beach

White Plains Beach Park

Ewa Beach

76

KEY
1 *Sights*
1 *Restaurants*
1 *Hotels*

0   4 mi
0   4 km

Sights ▼

1 Dole Plantation........... **E3**

2 Hawaii's Plantation Village..................... **E6**

3 Ko Hana Distillers....... **D5**

4 Kukaniloko Birthstones State Monument......... **E4**

Restaurants ▼

1 Makahiki — The Bounty of the Islands.............. **C7**

2 Mina's Fish House **C7**

3 Monkeypod by Merriman Ko Olina **C7**

4 Noe........................ **C7**

Hotels ▼

1 Aulani, A Disney Resort & Spa **C7**

2 Four Seasons Resort Oahu at Ko Olina......... **C7**

Sights

Hawaii's Plantation Village

HISTORY MUSEUM | FAMILY | Starting in the 1800s, immigrants seeking work on the sugar plantations came to the Islands like so many waves against the shore. At this museum 30 minutes from downtown Honolulu (without traffic), visit authentically furnished buildings, original and replicated, that re-create and pay tribute to the plantation era. See a Chinese social hall; a Japanese shrine, sumo ring, and saimin stand; a dental office; and historic homes. The village is open for guided tours only. ⊠ *Waipahu Cultural Gardens Park, 94-695 Waipahu St., Waipahu* ☎ *808/677–0110* ⊕ *hawaiiplantationvillage.org* ⊐ *$15* ⊘ *Closed Sun.*

Beaches

★ White Plains Beach

BEACH | FAMILY | Concealed from the public eye for many years as part of the former Barbers Point Naval Air Station, this beach is reminiscent of Waikiki but without the condos and the crowds. It is a long, sloping stretch with numerous surf breaks, but it is also mild enough at the shore for older children to play freely. It has views of Pearl Harbor and, over that, Diamond Head. Although the sand lives up to its name, the real impact of this beach comes from its history as part of a military property for the better part of a century. Expansive parking, great restroom facilities, and numerous tree-covered barbecue areas make it a great day-trip spot. As a bonus, a Hawaiian monk seal takes up residence here several months out of the year (seals are rare in the Islands). **Amenities:** lifeguards; parking (no fee); showers; toilets. **Best for:** surfing; swimming. ⊠ *Essex Rd. and Tripoli Rd., Kapolei* ⊕ *Take Makakilo Exit off H1 West, then turn left. Follow it into base gates, make left. Blue signs lead to beach.*

Performing Arts

LUAU

Chief's Luau at Wet 'n' Wild Hawaii

FOLK/TRADITIONAL DANCE | Chief Sielu and his *ohana* (family) perform at Wet 'n' Wild Hawaii waterpark. It's a top-rated luau with everything you'd expect from this island tradition: good food, rhythmic music, and interactive performances. The show ends with a high-energy fire-knife dance. The chef also heads the Fia Fia Luau at the Marriott in Ko Olina. ⊠ *Wet 'n' Wild Hawaii, 400 Farrington Hwy., Kapolei* ☎ *877/357–2480* ⊕ *www.chiefsluau.com* ⊐ *From $95.*

Germaine's Luau

THEMED ENTERTAINMENT | More than 3 million visitors have come to this luau, held about 45 minutes west of Waikiki in light traffic. Widely considered one of the most folksy and laid-back, Germaine's offers a tasty, multicourse, all-you-can-eat buffet. Admission includes the buffet and one drink to three drinks (depending on the package). It's held Tuesday to Sunday at 6. ⊠ *91-119 Olai St., Kapolei* ☎ *808/202–2528* ⊕ *www.germainesluau.com* ⊐ *From $85, transportation from $16.*

Shopping

Aloha Stadium Swap Meet & Marketplace

MARKET | This thrice-weekly outdoor bazaar attracts hundreds of vendors and even more bargain hunters. Every Hawaiian souvenir imaginable can be found here, from coral shell necklaces to bikinis, as well as a variety of ethnic wares, from Chinese brocaded dresses to Japanese pottery. There are also ethnic foods, silk flowers, and luggage in aloha floral prints. That said, be prepared to wade through the usual sprinkling of used and counterfeit goods to find value. Wear comfortable shoes, use sunscreen, and bring bottled water. The flea market takes place in the Aloha Stadium parking lot Wednesday and Saturday 8–3 and

Sunday 6:30–3. Admission is $1 per person ages 12 and up.

You can take either Uber or Lyft from your hotel. You might also ask your hotel concierge about shared shuttle services. For a cheaper but slower ride, take TheBus. The new Honolulu Rail trains will connect the Aloha Stadium with Kapolei when they start running (currently scheduled for late 2022). So you could shop at the swap meet and hop on the train to Ka Makana Alii to treasure-hunt even longer—all without a car! ⊠ *Aloha Stadium, 99-500 Salt Lake Blvd., Aiea* ☎ *808/486–6704* ⊕ *alohastadium.hawaii.gov/ aloha-stadium-swap-meet-marketplace.*

Waikele Premium Outlets

MALL | Armani Exchange, Calvin Klein, Coach, and Saks Fifth Avenue outlets anchor this discount destination of around 50 stores. ⊠ *94-790 Lumiaina St., Waipahu* ☎ *808/676–5656* ⊕ *www. premiumoutlets.com/outlet/waikele.*

Ko Olina

5 miles west of Kapolei, 25 miles west of downtown Honolulu.

For centuries, Hawaiian nobility rejuvenated at this pristine enclave on the island's southwestern edge. Today, Ko Olina is a major visitor hub, part of a decades-long master plan to attract jobs to the leeward side. The privately owned, 642-acre complex is a community unto itself, with one guarded public entrance/exit off Farrington Highway. It includes a golf course, three natural lagoons, a series of four man-made lagoons, three major resorts (each with a range of restaurants, shops, and activities), 4½ miles of walking paths, and a shopping area with additional restaurants and cafés. It's also home to the famed Paradise Cove Luau.

The Lanikuhonua Nature Preserve, with its pristine beach, edges the north end of the complex. The shoreline is public, but most of the 11-acre site belongs to the Lanikuhonua Cultural Institute, a nonprofit that preserves and promotes Hawaiian culture.

The lagoons are open to the public, but public parking is limited (first-come, first-served, sunrise to sunset). Come before 10 am to nab one of the prized spots. If you do manage to find a space, plan to walk at least a short bit to the lagoons along public access paths. Even resort guests pay hefty fees to park on-site.

🏖 Beaches

★ Ko Olina Beach

BEACH | **FAMILY** | This is the best spot on the island if you have small kids. The resort area commissioned a series of four man-made lagoons, but, as it has to provide public beach access, you are the winner. Huge rock walls protect the lagoons, making them perfect spots for the kids to get their first taste of the ocean without getting bowled over. The large expanses of seashore grass and hala trees that surround the semicircle beaches are made-to-order for nap time. A 1½-mile jogging track connects the lagoons. Due to its appeal for *keiki* (children), Ko Olina is popular, and the parking lot fills up quickly when school is out and on weekends, so try to get here before 10 am. The biggest parking lot is at the farthest lagoon from the entrance. There are actually three resorts here: Aulani (the Disney resort), Four Seasons Resort Oahu, and the Marriot's Ko Olina Beach Club (which has a time-share section as well). **Amenities:** food and drink; parking (no fee); showers; toilets. **Best for:** sunset; swimming; walking. ⊠ *92 Aliinui Dr., 23 miles west of Honolulu, Ko Olina* ⊹ *Take Ko Olina exit off H1 West and proceed to guard shack.*

Ko Olina, a planned resort community on the island's southwestern shore, is the biggest tourist area on Leeward Oahu.

🍴 Restaurants

Makahiki — The Bounty of the Islands

$$$$ | HAWAIIAN | FAMILY | The buffet restaurant at Disney's Aulani resort offers a wide variety of locally produced items, as well as familiar dishes from stateside and the rest of the world. You'll find sustainable Hawaiian seafood, Asian selections, familiar grilled meats and vegetables, and a kids' menu; an à la carte menu is also available. ■**TIP➔ Arrive early for dinner and have a drink at the adjacent Olelo Room, where the staff are fluent in Hawaiian; you can get a language lesson along with your libation. Known for:** wide array of food to please every member of the family; popular Disney character breakfasts (which book up weeks in advance); true reflection of Hawaii. $ *Average main: $65* ⊠ *Aulani, a Disney Resort & Spa, 92-1185 Aliinui Dr., Ko Olina* ☎ *808/674–6200* ⊕ *www.disneyaulani.com/dining/table-service/makahiki-buffet* ⊗ *No lunch.*

★ Mina's Fish House

$$$$ | SEAFOOD | Michael Mina, a James Beard Award winner, designed an exceptional line-to-table menu that celebrates the local catch and matches the panoramic views from indoor and lanai oceanfront tables. This might be the only restaurant in Hawaii (or the world) to have an on-site "fish sommelier," who guides you through the mind-boggling array of cooking techniques, flavorings, and portions—from fillet to whole fish— and helps you choose the best matches for your particular palate. **Known for:** Kona lobster dishes; daily happy hour; charbroiled Hawaiian seafood tower. $ *Average main: $51* ⊠ *Four Seasons Oahu Ko Olina Resort, 92-1001 Olani St., Ko Olina* ☎ *808/679–0079* ⊕ *www.michaelmina.net* ⊗ *No lunch weekdays.*

Monkeypod by Merriman Ko Olina

$$$ | HAWAIIAN | Local farm-to-table guru Peter Merriman is known throughout Hawaii for his inventive and popular

restaurants, and this one captures his creativity and locally inspired food mantra perfectly. Local slack-key guitar music and the gentle buzz of diners kicking back make this a nice stop for a leisurely lunch—that could easily slide into happy hour. **Known for:** indoor–outdoor setting; life-changing strawberry cream pie; lobster deviled eggs and fresh fish tacos. [$] *Average main: $28* ✉ *Ko Olina Resort, 92-1048 Olani St., Ko Olina* ☎ *808/380-4086* 🌐 *www.monkeypodkitchen.com.*

Noe

$$$$ | **ITALIAN** | Classic dishes from southern Italy's Amalfi Coast dominate the menu at this sleek Four Seasons restaurant, with seating indoors, in various intimate and more social spaces, and outdoors overlooking a nature preserve. Locals come to celebrate special occasions, while guests from throughout the Ko Olina community come to feast on house-made pastas—especially the signature tagliatelle with truffle pesto and mushrooms—and multiple dishes that showcase Kona lobster. **Known for:** extensive Italian wine list; weekend brunch; four-course tasting menu. [$] *Average main: $49* ✉ *Four Seasons Oahu at Ko Olina, 92-1001 Olani St., Ko Olina* ☎ *808/679-3347* 🌐 *www.fourseasons.com/oahu/dining/restaurants/noe* 🕑 *No lunch weekdays.*

Hotels

★ Aulani, A Disney Resort & Spa

$$$$ | **RESORT** | **FAMILY** | Disney's first property in Hawaii melds the Disney magic with breathtaking vistas, white sandy beaches, and sunsets that even Mickey stops to watch. **Pros:** tons to do on-site; family-friendly done right; Painted Sky: HI Style Studio makeovers for kids. **Cons:** Disney character breakfasts require advance reservation (book far in advance); areas and events can get really busy; a long way from Waikiki. [$] *Rooms from: $549* ✉ *92-1185 Aliinui Dr., Kapolei* ☎ *714/520-7001, 808/674-6200, 866/443-4763* 🌐 *www.disneyaulani.com* 🛏 *832 rooms* 🍴 *No Meals.*

★ Four Seasons Resort Oahu at Ko Olina

$$$$ | **RESORT** | At the first Four Seasons on the island, nearly every room or suite in the 17-story hotel offers floor-to-ceiling windows and a private lanai, all with an ocean view. **Pros:** luxurious and exclusive; secluded, even in the Ko Olina complex; amenities and options abound. **Cons:** luxury doesn't come cheap; it doesn't always measure up to other Four Seasons; an hour from Waikiki. [$] *Rooms from: $775* ✉ *92-1001 Olani St., in the Ko Olina complex, Ko Olina* ☎ *808/679-0079, 844/387-0308* 🌐 *www.fourseasons.com/oahu* 🛏 *371 rooms* 🍴 *No Meals.*

Performing Arts

LUAU

Fia Fia Luau

THEMED ENTERTAINMENT | Just after sunset at the Marriott Ko Olina Beach Club, the charismatic Chief Sielu Avea leads the Samoan-based Fia Fia, an entertaining show that takes guests on the journey through the South Pacific. Every show is different and unscripted, but always a good look at Polynesian culture. It's the only recurring show with eight fire-knife dancers in a blazing finale. It's held on Tuesday at 4:30. Admission includes a buffet dinner. ✉ *92-161 Waipahe Pl., Ko Olina* ☎ *808/679-4700,* 🌐 *www.marriott.com/hotels/hotel-information/restaurant/hnlko-marriotts-ko-olina-beach-club* 🎟 *From $105.*

Paradise Cove Luau

FOLK/TRADITIONAL DANCE | **FAMILY** | At one of the largest events on Oahu, you can stroll, drink in hand, through an authentic village, learn traditional arts and crafts, and play local games. The lively stage show includes a fire-knife dancer, singing emcee, and both traditional and contemporary hula and other Polynesian dances. A finale dance features participation from

In the summer, when the surf is calm, Makaha is a great snorkeling destination; in the winter, it's a popular surfing spot, especially for locals.

the audience. Admission includes the buffet, activities, and the show. You pay extra for table service, box seating, and shuttle transport to and from Waikiki—the stunning sunsets are free. It starts daily at 5. ⊠ *92-1089 Alii Nui Dr., Ko Olina* ☎ *808/842–5911* ⊕ *www.paradisecove. com* 🎫 *$125.*

Waianae

9 miles north of Ko Olina.

Waianae refers to both the town and the western (leeward) shores of Oahu, from Ko Olina up to Yokohama Bay and the end of the road near Kaena Point. It's mostly rural, without tourist traps and few restaurants apart from fast-food outlets, tiny cafés, and hole-in-the-wall poke shacks. Still, the Waianae coast is well worth a day trip, mostly to experience an area where "real" Hawaiians, descendants of natives who populated the coast centuries before the *haoles* (white people) arrived, live and play. The beaches boast

crystal clear water. Turtles and dolphins swim near the shores, and when surf's up, Oahu's finest shredders show up to have fun and wow the watchers on the sand.

 Beaches

Makaha Beach Park

BEACH | FAMILY | This beach provides a slice of local life that most visitors don't see. Families string up tarps for the day, fire up hibachis, set up lawn chairs, get out the fishing gear, and strum ukulele while they "talk story" (chat). Legendary waterman Buffalo Keaulana can be found in the shade of the palms playing with his grandkids and spinning yarns of yesteryear. In these waters, Buffalo not only invented some of the most outrageous methods of surfing, but also raised his world-champion son, Rusty. He also made Makaha the home of the world's first international surf meet in 1954, and it still hosts his Big Board Surfing Classic. With its long, slow-building waves, it's a great spot to try out longboarding. The swimming is generally decent in summer, but avoid the big winter waves. The only parking is along the highway, but it's free. **Amenities:** lifeguards; showers; toilets. **Best for:** surfing; swimming. ⊠ *84-450 Farrington Hwy., Waianae* ⊹ *Go 32 miles west of Honolulu on the H1, then exit onto Farrington Hwy. The beach will be on your left.*

Wahiawa

Approximately 20 miles northeast of Ko Olina, 20 miles north of downtown Honolulu.

Oahu's central plain is a patchwork of old towns and new residential developments, military bases, farms, ranches, and shopping malls, with a few noteworthy attractions and historic sites scattered about. Central Oahu encompasses the Moanalua Valley, residential Pearl City and Mililani, and the old plantation town of Wahiawa, on the uplands halfway to the North Shore.

James Dole first planted pineapples in the central plateau in the early 1900s, and the Dole Pineapple Plantation fields still border the northern limits of Wahiawa, a small town with a heavy military and working-class vibe. Lake Wilson (Wahiawa Reservoir) surrounds three sides of the town, and Highway 99 crosses two bridges (and several stoplights) to pass through.

Wahiawa is the commercial hub for several military bases, including Schofield Barracks, Wheeler Army Airfield, and the U.S. Naval Computer and Telecommunications Area Master Station Pacific. The main drag—a five-block stretch of Highway 99 where traffic often slows to a snail's pace—was once a fast-food mecca but in recent years has given birth to a handful of decent cafés and restaurants.

 # Sights

Dole Plantation

COLLEGE | FAMILY | Pineapple plantation days are nearly defunct in Hawaii, but you can still celebrate the state's famous golden fruit at this promotional center with exhibits, a huge gift shop, a snack concession, educational displays, and one of the world's largest mazes. Take the self-guided Garden Tour, or hop aboard the Pineapple Express for a 20-minute train tour to learn a bit about life on a pineapple plantation. Kids love the more than 3-acre Pineapple Garden Maze, made up of 14,000 tropical plants and trees. If you do nothing else, stop by the cafeteria in the back for a delicious pineapple soft-serve Dole Whip. This is about a 40-minute drive from Waikiki, a suitable stop on the way to or from the North Shore. ⊠ *64-1550 Kamehameha Hwy., Wahiawa* ☎ *808/621–8408* ⊕ *www.doleplantation.com* ⊿ *Plantation free, Pineapple Express $12, maze $9, garden tour $8.*

★ Ko Hana Distillers

DISTILLERY | Polynesians brought sugarcane to Hawaii more than 1,000 years ago, long before plantations were established on the Islands in the 1800s. Ko Hana grows 34 varieties of heirloom sugarcane and harvests it all by hand, then presses and distills the juice to make small-batch pure-cane rums. Stop by the tasting room at the farm in rural Kunia near Wahiawa, in the heart of the central valley for tastings. Standouts include Koho, a barrel-aged rum, and Kokoleka, made with pure cacao and raw honey. Sign up in advance for tours, which happen daily every hour until 4 pm and include a side-by-side tasting of white and barrel-aged rums. For a more in-depth experience, reserve a spot on a farm tour (Thursday morning at 10) and sample canes as well as rums. ⊠ *92-1770 Kunia Rd., Kunia* ☎ *808/649–0830* ⊕ *www.kohanarum.com/home* ⊿ *Tasting $10, tour and tasting $25, farm tours $45.*

Kukaniloko Birthstones State Monument

HISTORIC SIGHT | In the cool uplands of Wahiawa is haunting Kukaniloko, where noble chieftesses went to give birth to high-ranking children. One of the most significant cultural sites on the island, the lava-rock stones here were believed to possess the power to ease labor pains. The site is marked by approximately 180 stones covering about a half acre. It's a 40- to 45-minute drive from Waikiki. ⊠ *Kamehameha Hwy. and Whitmore Ave., Wahiawa* ✛ *The north side of Wahiawa town.*

The North Shore

An hour from town and a world away in atmosphere, Oahu's North Shore, roughly from Kahuku Point to Kaena Point, is about small farms and big waves, tourist traps, and otherworldly landscapes. Parks and beaches, roadside fruit stands and shrimp shacks, and a valley preserve offer a dozen reasons to stop between the onetime plantation town of Kahuku and the surf mecca of Haleiwa.

Haleiwa has had many lives, from resort getaway in the 1900s to plantation town through the 20th century to its life today as a surfer and tourist magnet. Beyond Haleiwa is the tiny village of Waialua; a string of beach parks; an airfield where gliders, hang gliders, and parachutists play; and, at the end of the road, Kaena Point State Park, which offers a brisk hike, striking views, and whale-watching in season. Pack wisely for a day's North Shore excursion: swim and snorkel gear, light jacket and hat (the weather is mercurial, especially in winter), sunscreen and sunglasses, bottled water and snacks, towels and a picnic blanket, and both sandals and closed-toe shoes for hiking. A small cooler is nice; you may want to pick up some fruit or fresh corn. As always, leave valuables in the hotel safe, and lock the car whenever you park.

GETTING HERE AND AROUND

From Waikiki, the quickest route to the North Shore is H1 west to H2 north, and then the Kamehameha Highway past Wahiawa. You'll hit Haleiwa in just under an hour. The windward route (H1 east, H3, Likelike or Pali Highway, through the mountains, or Kamehameha Highway north) takes at least 90 minutes to Haleiwa, but the drive is far prettier.

Waialua

30 miles northwest of Honolulu.

A tranquil, multicultural burg with sleepy residential areas, uncrowded beach parks, and small mom-and-pop businesses, Wailua provides refuge from neighboring (and often tourist-choked) Haleiwa. In the 1900s, the Waialua Sugar Company attracted workers from around the world, and their descendants continue to live and work here. The former sugar operation buildings now hold a General Store and eclectic, trendy shops, art studios, maker spaces for surfboard shapers and other craftspeople, and a coffee mill. Waialua is also the gateway to a wild and scenic coastline that includes Mokuleia Beach Park, Kaena Point State Park, and Kawaihapai Airfield (formerly known as Dillingham Airfield), where gliders and parachutists launch and land.

Sights

Kaena Point State Park

STATE/PROVINCIAL PARK | FAMILY | The name means "the heat," and, indeed, this windy, barren coast lacks both shade and fresh water (or any man-made amenities). Pack water, wear sturdy closed-toe shoes, don sunscreen and a hat, and lock the car. The hike is along a rutted dirt road, mostly flat and nearly 3 miles long (one-way), ending at a rocky, sandy headland. It is here that Hawaiians believed the souls of the dead met with their family gods and, if judged worthy to enter the

Kaena Point is remote and barren, but it's a beautiful place of religious significance: the ancient Hawaiians believed it was where the souls of the dead departed for the afterlife.

afterlife, leapt off into eternal darkness at Leina Kauhane, just south of the point.

In summer and at low tide, the small coves offer bountiful shelling; in winter, don't venture near the water. Rare native plants dot the landscape, and seabirds like the Laysan albatross nest here. If you're lucky, you might spot seals sunbathing on the rocks. From November through March, watch for humpbacks spouting and breaching. Binoculars and a camera are highly recommended. ⊠ 69-385 Farrington Hwy., Waialua ⊕ dlnr.hawaii.gov/dsp/parks/oahu/kaena-point-state-park.

 Beaches

Mokuleia Beach Park

BEACH | There is a reason why the producers of the TV show *Lost* chose this beach for their set: it's on the island's remote, northwest point and about 10 miles from the closest store or public restroom. Its beauty is in its lack of facilities and isolation—all the joy of being stranded on a deserted island without the trauma of the plane crash. The beach is wide and white, the waters bright blue (but a little choppy) and full of sea turtles and other marine life. Mokuleia is a great secret find; just remember to pack supplies and use caution, as there are no lifeguards. **Amenities:** parking (no fee). **Best for:** sunset, walking. ⊠ 68-67 Farrington Hwy., Waialua ⊕ West of Haleiwa town center, across from Dillingham Airfield.

Haleiwa

3 miles northeast of Waialua, 30 miles northwest of Honolulu.

The North Shore's shopping, dining, and surf-culture hub has preserved its historic plantation-era roots and melded it with a laid-back 1960s-era vibe. The town sits amid a picture-perfect setting on Waialua Bay, where the Anahulu River empties into the harbor.

In the 1920s, Waialua had a posh hotel at the end of a railroad line (both long gone).

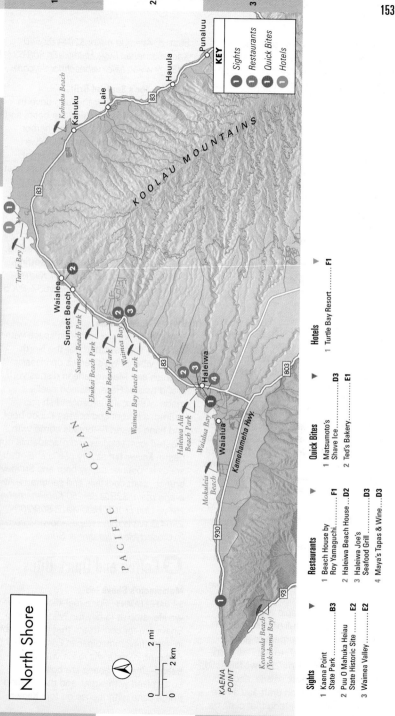

North Shore

2 mi
2 km

KEY
- Sights
- Restaurants
- Quick Bites
- Hotels

PACIFIC OCEAN

KOOLAU MOUNTAINS

KAENA POINT

Keawaula Beach (Yokohama Bay)
Mokuleia Beach
Waialua Bay
Haleiwa Alii Beach Park
Waimea Bay Beach Park
Pupukea Beach Park
Ehukai Beach Park
Sunset Beach Park
Turtle Bay
Kahuku Beach

Waialua
Haleiwa
Waimea Bay
Sunset Beach
Waialee
Kahuku
Laie
Hauula
Punaluu

Kamehameha Hwy.

Sights
1 Kaena Point State Park.........**B3**
2 Puu O Mahuka Heiau State Historic Site.........**E2**
3 Waimea Valley.........**E2**

Restaurants
1 Beach House by Roy Yamaguchi.........**F1**
2 Haleiwa Beach House.........**D2**
3 Haleiwa Joe's Seafood Grill.........**D3**
4 Maya's Tapas & Wine.........**D3**

Quick Bites
1 Matsumoto's Shave Ice.........**D3**
2 Ted's Bakery.........**E1**

Hotels
1 Turtle Bay Resort.........**F1**

During the '60s, hippies congregated here, followed by surfers from around the world. Today, the streets of historic Haleiwa Town reflect a fun mix of old and new, with charming general stores and contemporary boutiques, galleries, and eateries.

Haleiwa Alii Beach Park and Haleiwa Beach Park border the bay and provide endless opportunities for water sports and other activities. Be sure to stop in at Liliuokalani Protestant Church, founded by missionaries in the 1830s. It's fronted by a large, stone archway built in 1910 and covered with night-blooming cereus. Also check out the historic Rainbow Bridge, whose distinctive double arches appear in many local works of art.

Beaches

★ Haleiwa Alii Beach Park
BEACH | FAMILY | The winter waves are impressive here, but in summer, the ocean is like a lake, ideal for family swimming. The beach itself is big and tends to be full of locals. Its broad lawn off the highway is often the site of volleyball and Frisbee games, family barbecues, and art festivals and carnivals. This beach is also the opening break for the Triple Crown of Surfing. **Amenities:** lifeguards; parking (no fee); showers; toilets. **Best for:** surfing; swimming. ⊠ *66-167 Haleiwa Rd., Haleiwa* ✛ *North of Haleiwa town center and past harbor.*

 Restaurants

Haleiwa Beach House
$$ | AMERICAN | FAMILY | One of the newer restaurants on the North Shore takes full advantage of its epic water views. The menu is chock full of surf-and-turf options, from juicy burgers to grilled steaks, blackened fish to red Thai curry with lobster and shrimp. **Known for:** solid, reliable beef, seafood, salads, and kids options; craft beers on draft and a nice wine list; view and setting that can't be

beat. $ *Average main: $26* ⊠ *62-540 Kamehameha Hwy., Haleiwa* ☎ *808/637–3435* ⊕ *www.haleiwabeachhouse.com.*

Haleiwa Joe's Seafood Grill
$$$ | AMERICAN | After the long drive to the North Shore, watching the boats and surfers come and go from the harbor while you enjoy a mai tai on Haleiwa Joe's open-air lanai may be just what you need. This casual little joint, just past the Rainbow Bridge, rarely changes (to some, that might feel dated, but regulars appreciate the familiarity); a more upscale Kaneohe location overlooks the lush Haiku Gardens. **Known for:** crunchy coconut shrimp; good daily fish specials; reliable food with a nice harbor setting. $ *Average main: $29* ⊠ *66-011 Kamehameha Hwy., Haleiwa* ☎ *808/637–8005* ⊕ *www.haleiwajoes.com.*

Maya's Tapas & Wine
$$$ | TAPAS | A cozy, romantic space with a slightly sophisticated (for the North Shore) vibe, Maya's serves up classic Spanish and Mediterranean dishes with island twists. Here, seafood paella is made with local line-caught fish and shrimp, a burger showcases Kunoa beef, and hand-tossed flatbreads come with roasted local veggies and macadamia nut pesto. **Known for:** savory paella and other specials; popular happy hour and Sunday brunch; craft cocktails and sangria. $ *Average main: $28* ⊠ *66-250 Kamehameha Hwy., Unit D-101, Haleiwa* ☎ *808/200–2964* ⊕ *www.mayastapasandwine.com* ⊘ *Closed Mon. No dinner Sun.*

☕ Coffee and Quick Bites

Matsumoto's Shave Ice
$ | CAFÉ | FAMILY | For a real slice of Haleiwa life, stop at family-run Matsumoto's Shave Ice for cool treats that are available in every flavor imaginable. For something different, order a shave ice with adzuki beans—the red beans are boiled until soft, mixed with sugar, and then placed in the cone with the ice on top. **Known**

Malasadas

Malasadas are a contribution of the Portuguese, who came to the Hawaiian Islands to work on the plantations. Roughly translated, the name means "half-cooked," as these deep-fried, heavily sugared treats are said to have been created as a way to use up scraps of rich, buttery egg dough. They are similar to fluffy donuts and are offered in many flavors; some are filled with fruit or cream.

You'll find malasadas at farmers' markets, fairs, and carnivals. In addition, a handful of bakeries specialize in them, including **Leonard's Bakery** (✉ *933 Kapahulu Ave.*); **Kamehameha Bakery** (✉ *1284 Kalani St., Unit D-106*); and **Pipeline Bakeshop** (✉ *3632 Waialae Ave.*). Some Honolulu restaurants serve upscale versions, stuffed with fruit puree. Regardless, eat them fresh and hot or not at all.

for: the Matsumoto with lemon, pineapple, and coconut syrup; house-made adzuki beans; one of the most popular shave ice spots on Oahu. $ *Average main: $4* ✉ *66-111 Kamehameha Hwy., Suite 605, Haleiwa* ☎ *808/637–4827* ⊕ *www.matsumotoshaveice.com.*

 Shopping

The Growing Keiki
CHILDREN'S CLOTHING | FAMILY | Frequent visitors return to this store year after year for a fresh supply of unique, locally made, Hawaiian-style clothing for youngsters. ✉ *66-051 Kamehameha Hwy., Haleiwa* ☎ *808/637–4544* ⊕ *www. facebook.com/TheGrowingKeiki.*

★ Silver Moon Emporium
WOMEN'S CLOTHING | The small boutique carries everything from Brighton jewelry and European designer wear to fashionable T-shirts, shoes, and handbags. Expect attentive and personalized yet casual service. The stock changes frequently, and there's always something wonderful on sale. No matter what your taste, you'll find something for everyday wear or special occasions. ✉ *North Shore Marketplace, 66-250 Kamehameha Hwy., Haleiwa* ☎ *808/637–7710.*

Pupukea

6 miles northeast of Haleiwa.

Pupukea is a tiny village that anchors the Seven Mile Miracle—the legendary stretch of North Shore coast that faithfully serves up some of the world's best barrels and perfectly shaped waves every winter. It's also home to Foodland, the only grocery store between Kahuku/Laie and Haleiwa, which means you're likely to rub elbows in the checkout line with seasoned professional surfers and visiting celebrities, along with slipper-clad locals.

Across the street are Shark's Cove and Three Tables, both excellent snorkeling and scuba sites when the winter swells abate. The Banzai Pipeline and Sunset Beach are just a mile up the road. Drive up the hill behind Foodland to explore the sacred Puu o Mahuka Heiau, the largest shrine on the island.

◉ Sights

Puu o Mahuka Heiau State Historic Site
RUINS | Worth a stop for its spectacular views from a bluff high above the ocean overlooking Waimea Bay, this sacred spot spans 2 acres and is the largest *heiau* (place of worship) on the island. At

one time it was used as a *heiau luakini,* or a temple for human sacrifices. It's now on the National Register of Historic Places. Turn up the road at the Pupukea Foodland and follow it to the site. ☒ *Pupukea Rd., ½ mile north of Waimea Bay, Pupukea* ✚ *From Rte. 83, turn right on Pupukea Rd. and drive 1 mile uphill* ⊕ *dlnr.hawaii.gov/dsp/parks/oahu/ puu-o-mahuka-heiau-state-historic-site.*

★ Waimea Valley

GARDEN | FAMILY | Waimea may get lots of press for the giant winter waves in the bay, but the valley itself is a newsmaker and an ecological treasure in its own right, with a local nonprofit working to conserve and restore its natural habitat. Follow the Kamananui Stream up the valley through the 1,875 acres of gardens. The botanical collections here have more than 5,000 species of tropical flora, including a superb gathering of native Hawaiian and international plants. It's the best place on the island to see native species, such as the endangered Hawaiian moorhen.

You can also see the restored Hale o Lono *heiau* (shrine) along with other ancient archaeological sites; evidence suggests that the area was an important spiritual center. Daily activities include botanical walking tours and cultural tours. At the back of the valley, Waihi Falls plunges 45 feet into a swimming pond. ■TIP➡ **Bring your board shorts—a swim is the perfect way to end your hike, although the pond can get crowded. Be sure to bring mosquito repellent, too; it can get buggy.** ☒ *59-864 Kamehameha Hwy., Pupukea* ☎ *808/638–7766* ⊕ *www.waimeavalley. net* ☒ *$20.*

Beaches

Ehukai Beach Park

BEACH | What sets Ehukai apart is the view of the famous Banzai Pipeline. Here the winter waves curl into magnificent tubes, making it an experienced wave-rider's dream. It's also an inexperienced swimmer's nightmare. Spring and summer waves, on the other hand, are more accommodating to the average person, and there's good snorkeling. Except when the surf contests are happening, there's no reason to stay on the central strip. Travel in either direction from the center, and the conditions remain the same but the population thins out, leaving you with a magnificent stretch of sand all to yourself. **Amenities:** lifeguards; parking (no fee); showers; toilets. **Best for:** snorkeling; surfing. ☒ *59-337 Ke Nui Rd., Pupukea* ✚ *1 mile north of Foodland at Pupukea.*

★ Pupukea Beach Park (*Shark's Cove*)

BEACH | Surrounded by shade trees, Pupukea Beach Park is pounded by surf in the winter months but offers great diving and snorkeling in summer (March through October). Its cavernous lava tubes and tunnels are great for both novice and experienced snorkelers and divers, though it's imperative that you wear reef shoes at all times since there are a lot of sharp rocks. Sharp rocks also mean that this beach isn't the best for little ones. Some dive-tour companies offer round-trip transportation from Waikiki. Equipment rentals and dining options are nearby. **Amenities:** parking (no fee); showers; toilets. **Best for:** diving; snorkeling; swimming. ☒ *Pupukea* ✚ *3½ miles north of Haleiwa, across street from Foodland.*

★ Sunset Beach Park

BEACH | The beach is broad, the sand is soft, the summer waves are gentle—making for good snorkeling—and the winter surf is crashing. Many love searching this shore for the puka shells that adorn the necklaces you see everywhere. **Amenities:** lifeguards; parking (no fee); showers; toilets. **Best for:** snorkeling; sunset; surfing. ☒ *59-144 Kamehameha Hwy., Pupukea* ✚ *1 mile north of Ehukai Beach Park.*

While Waimea Bay is known for its big winter waves and surf culture, the Waimea Valley is an area of great historical significance. It's also known for its botanical specimens, including big tropical trees.

★ **Waimea Bay Beach Park**

BEACH | Made popular in that old Beach Boys song "Surfin' U.S.A.," this is a slice of big-wave (25 to 30 feet) heaven in winter. Summer is the time to swim and snorkel in the calm waters. The shore break is great for novice bodysurfers. Due to the beach's popularity, its postage-stamp parking lot is often full, but it's also possible to park along the side of the road and walk in. **Amenities:** lifeguards; parking (no fee); showers; toilets. **Best for:** snorkeling; surfing; swimming. ✉ *61-31 Kamehameha Hwy., Pupukea* ✣ *Across from Waimea Valley, 3 miles north of Haleiwa.*

Coffee and Quick Bites

Ted's Bakery

$ | **AMERICAN** | **FAMILY** | Sunburned tourists and salty surfers rub shoulders in their quest for Ted's famous chocolate *haupia* cream pie (layered coconut and dark chocolate puddings topped with whipped cream) and hearty plates—like garlic shrimp, gravy-drenched hamburger steak, and *mahimahi*. Parking spots and the umbrella-shaded tables are at a premium, so be prepared to grab and go; if you can't get enough of that haupia goodness, Foodland and other grocery chains typically stock a selection of the famous pies as well. **Known for:** reliable all-day dining; plate lunches; Ted's pies, which seem to show up at every Oahu potluck. [$] *Average main: $14* ✉ *59-024 Kamehameha Hwy., Pupukea* ☎ *808/638–8207* 🌐 *www.tedsbakery.com.*

Kahuku

Kawela Bay is 5½ miles northeast of Pupukea, Kahuku is about 9 miles northeast of Pupukea.

The Kahuku district, which stretches from Kahuku town to Kawela Bay, includes Kahuku Point, the northernmost point on Oahu. The area is best known for fresh fruits and veggies from local farms (watch for stands along the highway), shrimp shacks, and exceptional high school football stars who go on to play at top-tier colleges and in the NFL.

Kahuku town has a collection of brand-name stores and tiny mom-and-pop shops amid modest residential neighborhoods filled with longtime island residents. Multimillion-dollar homes line the shores of the gated Kawela Bay community, but there's public beach access off Kamehameha Highway at Kawela Camp. Park on the side of the road, and walk about ¼ mile along a trail to get there.

Beaches

Turtle Bay (*Kuilima Cove*)

BEACH | **FAMILY** | Now known more for its namesake resort than its magnificent beach at Kuilima Cove, Turtle Bay is mostly passed over on the way to the better-known beaches of Sunset and Waimea. But for those with average swimming capabilities, this is a good place to be. The crescent-shaped stretch is protected by a huge sea wall, so you can see and hear the fury of the northern swell while blissfully floating in cool, calm waters. The convenience of this spot is also hard to pass up—there is a concession selling sandwiches and sunblock right on the beach. The resort has free parking for beach guests. **Amenities:** food and drink; parking (no fee); showers; toilets. **Best for:** sunset; swimming. ✉ *57-20 Kuilima Dr., 4 miles north of Kahuku, Kahuku* ✥ *Turn into Turtle Bay Resort and follow signs to public parking lot and beach access spots.*

Restaurants

Beach House by Roy Yamaguchi

$$$$ | **MODERN HAWAIIAN** | Loyalists of Roy Yamaguchi's celebrated spots in Hawaii Kai and Waikiki are thrilled to find his North Shore outpost—a rustic, beam-and-concrete-floor pavilion literally on the sand at Turtle Bay. All the favorites are served at this more beach-casual spot, from the miso deep-water black cod to the beef short ribs, along with a more casual lunch menu. **Known for:** fresh North Shore ingredients; special-occasion celebrations; casual, romantic setting right on the beach. [$] *Average main: $42* ✉ *Turtle Bay Resort, 57-091 Kamehameha Hwy., Kahuku* ☎ *808/293–0801* 🌐 *www.royyamaguchi.com/beach-house-by-roy-yamaguchi.*

Hotels

★ **Turtle Bay Resort**

$$$$ | **RESORT** | **FAMILY** | Sprawling over nearly 1,300 acres of natural landscape on the edge of Kuilima Point in Kahuku, this resort has spacious guest rooms (averaging nearly 500 square feet) with lanai that showcase stunning peninsula views. **Pros:** fabulous open public spaces in a secluded area of Oahu; beautiful spa; excellent location for exploring the North Shore. **Cons:** hefty resort fee; 24/7 resort living isn't for everyone; very remote—even Haleiwa is a 20-minute drive. [$] *Rooms from: $759* ✉ *57-091 Kamehameha Hwy., Kahuku* ☎ *808/293–6000, 800/203–3650, 866/827–5321 for reservations* 🌐 *www.turtlebayresort.com* 🛏 *452 rooms* 🍴 *No Meals.*

Nightlife

★ **Off the Lip**

COCKTAIL LOUNGES | West-oriented views (particularly stellar at sunset), creative cocktails incorporating fresh fruit and herbs from neighboring farms, house-made syrups and spirits, and live entertainment most nights draw locals and visitors alike to this classy, surf-themed lobby bar at Turtle Bay Resort. It's also the only nightlife choice on the North Shore east of Haleiwa, and night crawlers should know that the bar usually stops serving by 10 pm. ✉ *57-091 Kamehameha Hwy., Kahuku* ☎ *866/475–2569* 🌐 *www.turtlebayresort.com/dining/lip.*

Windward (East) Oahu

Looking at Honolulu's topsy-turvy urban sprawl, you would never suspect the windward side existed. Here the pace is slower, and hiking, diving, surfing, boating, and lounging on the beach are the primary draws.

Oahuans like to keep the existence of the windward side a secret so they can watch the awe on the faces of their guests when the car emerges from tunnels through the mountains and the panorama of turquoise bays and emerald valleys is revealed. Jaws literally drop. Every time. And this just a 15-minute drive from downtown.

It's on this side of the island where many Native Hawaiians live. Evidence of traditional lifestyles is abundant in old fishponds, rock platforms that once were altars, taro patches still being worked, and throw-net fishermen posed stock-still above the water (though today, they're invariably wearing polarized sunglasses, the better to spot the fish).

The natural world on this side of the island beckons. But a visit to the Polynesian Cultural Center and poking through little shops and wayside stores are musts as well.

GETTING HERE AND AROUND

There are a couple of ways to reach the windward side. One possibility is to spend a day hugging the coast all the way to Laie, home of the Polynesian Cultural Center. First, head east on the H1 past Diamond Head until it becomes Kalanianaole Highway. Look for Kamehameha Highway upon reaching Kaneohe, and follow this two-lane road all the way to the North Shore.

Another option that's just as spectacular but much more direct is taking the H1 to either the Pali Highway, the Likelike Highway, or the H3 across the mountains and through the tunnels to Kaneohe

and beyond. Although the Pali Highway affords the opportunity to take in the view from its namesake lookout, the H3 offers the most breathtakingly beautiful arrival to this side of the island.

Hawaii Kai

Approximately 10 miles southeast of Waikiki.

Driving southeast from Waikiki on busy, four-lane Kalanianaole Highway, you'll pass a dozen bedroom communities tucked into the valleys at the foot of the Koolau Range, with fleeting glimpses of the ocean from a couple of pocket parks. Suddenly, civilization falls away, the road narrows to two lanes, and you enter the rugged coastline of Koko Head and Ka Iwi.

This is a cruel coastline: dry, windswept, and with rocky shores and untamed waves that are notoriously treacherous. While walking its beaches, do not turn your back on the ocean, don't venture close to wet areas where high waves occasionally reach, and be sure to heed warning signs.

At this point, you're passing through Koko Head Regional Park. On your right is the bulging remnant of a pair of volcanic craters that the Hawaiians called Kawaihoa, known today as Koko Head. To the left is Koko Crater and an area of the park that includes a hiking trail, a dryland botanical garden, a firing range, and a riding stable. Ahead is a sinuous shoreline with scenic pullouts and beaches to explore.

Named the Ka Iwi Coast (*iwi,* "ee-vee," are bones—sacred to Hawaiians and full of symbolism) for the channel just offshore, this area was once home to a ranch and small fishing enclave that were destroyed by a tidal wave in the 1940s.

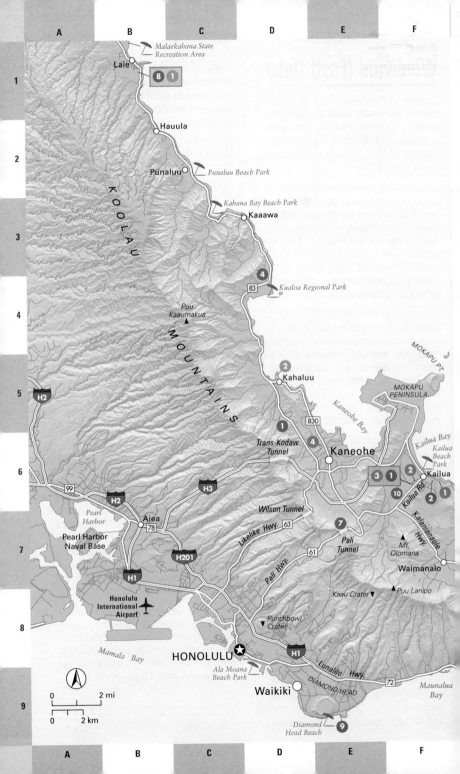

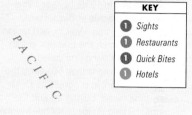

Windward (East) Oahu

KEY

1 *Sights*
1 *Restaurants*
1 *Quick Bites*
1 *Hotels*

PACIFIC

OCEAN

Lanikai Beach Park

Bellows Field
Beach Park

72

Waimanalo
Beach Park

MANANA ISLAND
(RABBIT ISLAND)

Makapuu Beach Park

6

Hawaii
Kai

3

▼Koko Crater

2

5

5

Sandy Beach Park

Halona Cove

Hanauma Bay
Nature Preserve

KOKO
HEAD

⊙ Sights

★ Halona Blowhole

VIEWPOINT | Below a scenic turnout along the Koko Head shoreline, this oft-photographed lava tube sucks the ocean in and spits it out. Don't get too close, as conditions can get dangerous. ■**TIP➜ Look to your right to see the tiny beach below that was used to film the wave-washed love scene in From Here to Eternity.**

In winter, this is a good spot to watch whales at play. Offshore, the island of Molokai calls like a distant siren, and, every once in a while, Lanai is visible in blue silhouette. Take your valuables with you, and lock your car, because this popular scenic location is a hot spot for petty thieves. ⊠ *Kalanianaole Hwy., Hawaii Kai* ⊹ *1 mile east of Hanauma Bay.*

Koko Crater Botanical Garden

GARDEN | If you've visited any of Oahu's other botanical gardens, this one will stand in stark contrast. Inside the tallest tuff cone on Oahu, in one of the hottest and driest areas on the island, Koko Crater Botanical Garden showcases dryland species of plants, including baobab trees, cacti, plumeria, and bougainvillea. ■**TIP➜ Bring plenty of water, sunscreen, and a hat. Though it's close to Oahu's more lush windward side, this is a scorching spot.** ⊠ *7491 Kokonani St., Hawaii Kai* ⊹ *Entrance at end of Kokonani St.* ☎ *808/768–7135* ⊕ *honolulu.gov/parks/ hbg.html* ⊠ *Free.*

Lanai Lookout

VIEWPOINT | A little more than a ½ mile past Hanauma Bay as you head toward Makapuu Point, you'll see a turnout on the ocean side with some fine views of the coastline. In winter, you'll have an opportunity to see storm-generated waves crashing against lava cliffs. This is also a popular place for winter whale-watching, so bring your binoculars, some sunscreen, and a picnic lunch, and join the small crowd scanning for telltale white spouts of water only a few hundred yards away. On clear days, you should be able to see the islands of Molokai and Lanai off in the distance, hence the name. ⊠ *Kalanianaole Hwy., Hawaii Kai* ⊹ *Just past Hanauma Bay.*

★ Shangri La Museum of Islamic Art, Culture & Design

HISTORIC HOME | In 1936, heiress Doris Duke bought 5 acres at Black Point, down the coast from Waikiki, and began to build and furnish the first home that would be all her own. She called it Shangri La. For more than 50 years, the home was a work in progress as Duke traveled the world, buying art and furnishings, picking up ideas for her Mughal Garden, for the Playhouse in the style of a 17th-century Irani pavilion, and for the water terraces and tropical gardens. When she died in 1993, Duke left instructions that her home was to become a public center for the study of Islamic art.

Outside of minor conservation-oriented changes and more extensive 2017 renovations to the courtyard and pool, the house and gardens have remained much as Duke left them. To walk through them is to experience the personal style of someone who saw everything as raw material for her art. With her trusted houseman, Jin de Silva, she helped build the elaborate Turkish Room, trimming tiles and painting panels to retrofit the existing space (including raising the ceiling and lowering the floor) and building a fountain of her own design.

Among many aspects of the home inspired by the Muslim tradition is the entry: an anonymous gate, a blank white wall, and a wooden door that bids you, "Enter herein in peace and security" in Arabic script. Inside, tiles glow, fountains tinkle, and shafts of light illuminate artwork through arches and high windows. In 2014, after years of renovation, Duke's bedroom (the Mughal Suite) opened to the public. This was her private world, entered only by trusted

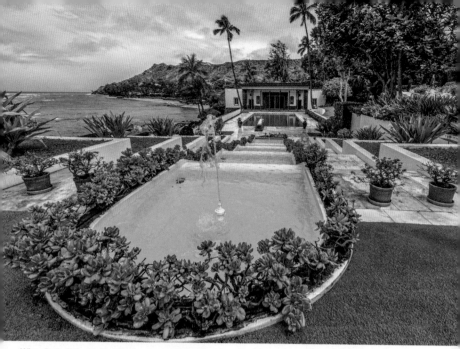

When Doris Duke died in 1993, her estate, Shangri La, became a museum of Islamic culture and art. Tours leave from the Honolulu Museum of Art in downtown Honolulu.

friends. ■TIP→ **The house is open only via the guided tours that depart from downtown's Honolulu Museum of Art, take about 2½ hours including transit time, and require reservations.** Book your spot as early as possible, and note that children under eight are not permitted. ⊠ *Hawaii Kai* ☎ *808/532–3853 for Honolulu Museum of Art* ✎ *tickets@honolulumuseum. org* ⊕ *www.shangrilahawaii.org* ✉ *$25* ⊘ *Closed Sun.–Tues.* ☞ *$5 parking at Honolulu Museum of Art.*

Beaches

★ Hanauma Bay Nature Preserve

BEACH | FAMILY | Picture this as the world's biggest open-air aquarium. You come to see fish, and fish you'll see. Due to their exposure to thousands of visitors every week, these fish are more like family pets than the skittish marine life you might expect. An old volcanic crater has created a haven from the waves where the coral has thrived. Note that there's a fee for nonresidents to enter the preserve; make reservations and prepay online ahead of time. You must also watch a nine-minute video about the nature preserve in its educational center before being allowed down to the bay. Snorkel equipment and lockers are available for rent, and you can walk the short distance from the parking lot or take a tram. ■TIP→ **It's best to visit early in the morning (around 7), as it's difficult to park later in the day.** Need transportation? Take TheBus each way from anywhere on the island. **Amenities:** food and drink; lifeguards; parking (fee); showers; toilets. **Best for:** snorkeling; swimming. ⊠ *7455 Kalanianaole Hwy., Hawaii Kai* ☎ *808/768–6861* ⊕ *hanaumabaystatepark.com* ✉ *Nonresidents $25 (excluding tram from parking lot); parking $3 (cash only); snorkel rental $20* ⊘ *Closed Mon. and Tues.* ⚓ *Reservations must be made in advance.*

★ Sandy Beach Park

BEACH | Very popular with locals, this broad, sloping beach is covered with sunbathers who come to soak up the

If you're a snorkeler, head straight for Hanauma Bay, the best and most popular place to snorkel on Oahu.

rays and watch "The Show"—a shore break that's like no other in the Islands. Monster ocean swells rolling into the beach combined with the sudden rise in the ocean floor causes waves to jack up and crash magnificently. Expert surfers and bodyboarders young and old brave the dangers to enjoy some of the biggest barrels around. ⚠ **Use extreme caution when swimming here. The stretch is nicknamed Break-Neck Beach for a reason: many neck and back injuries are sustained here each year.** **Amenities:** lifeguards; parking (no fee); showers; toilets. **Best for:** walking. ✉ *7850 Kalanianaole Hwy., Hawaii Kai* ✣ *Makai (toward ocean) of Kalanianaole Hwy., 2 miles east of Hanauma Bay.*

🍴 Restaurants

Roy's Hawaii Kai
$$$ | **MODERN HAWAIIAN** | Roy Yamaguchi is one of the 12 founding chefs of Hawaiian regional cuisine, a culinary movement that put the state on the food map back in 1991. Opened in 1988, his flagship restaurant across the highway from Maunalua Bay is still packed every night with food-savvy visitors and well-heeled residents, all of whom come for classics like smoked Szechuan baby back ribs or blackened ahi with soy mustard butter sauce. **Known for:** small and large portions available for many dishes; signature menu items like blackened ahi with a cultlike following; spectacular sunset views and a tiki torch–lit lanai and bar area. [$] *Average main: $34* ✉ *Hawaii Kai Corporate Plaza, 6600 Kalanianaole Hwy., Hawaii Kai* ☎ *808/396–7697* 🌐 *www.royyamaguchi.com/roys-hawaiikai* 🕒 *No lunch.*

Waimanalo

11 miles north of Hawaii Kai.

This modest little seaside town flanked by chiseled cliffs is worth a visit. Home to more Native Hawaiian families than Kailua to the north or Hawaii Kai to the south, Waimanalo's biggest draws are its beautiful beaches, offering glorious views to the windward side. Bellows Field Beach Park is great for swimming, bodysurfing, and camping, and Waimanalo Bay Beach Park is also safe for swimming.

Down the side roads, as you head *mauka* (toward the mountains), are little farms that grow a variety of fruits and flowers. Toward the back of the valley are small ranches with grazing horses. ■**TIP→ If you see any trucks selling corn, and you're staying at a place where you can cook it, be sure to get some. It may be the sweetest you'll ever eat, and prices are the lowest on Oahu.**

 Sights

★ **Makapuu Point**

VIEWPOINT | This spot has breathtaking views of the ocean, mountains, and the windward Islands. The point of land jutting out in the distance is Mokapu Peninsula, site of a U.S. Marine base. The spired mountain peak is Mt. Olomana. On the long pier is part of the Makai Undersea Test Range, a research facility that's closed to the public. Offshore is Manana Island (Rabbit Island), a picturesque cay said to resemble a swimming bunny with its ears pulled back. Ironically enough, Manana Island was once overrun with rabbits, thanks to a rancher who let a few hares run wild on the land. They were eradicated in 1994 by biologists who grew concerned that the rabbits were destroying the island's native plants.

Nestled in the cliff face is the Makapuu Lighthouse, which became operational in 1909 and has the largest lighthouse lens in America. The lighthouse is closed to the public, but near the Makapuu Point turnout you can find the start of a paved mile-long road (it's closed to vehicular traffic). Hike up to the top of the 647-foot bluff for a closer view of the lighthouse and, in winter, to do

some whale-watching. ⊠ *Ka Iwi State Scenic Shoreline, Kalanianaole Hwy., Waimanalo* ⊹ *At Makapuu Beach* ⊕ *dlnr.hawaii.gov/dsp/hiking/oahu/ makapuu-point-lighthouse-trail.*

 Beaches

★ **Bellows Field Beach Park**

BEACH | Bellows is the same beach as Waimanalo, but it's under the auspices of the military, making it more friendly for visitors—though that also limits public access on weekends. The park area is excellent for camping, and ironwood trees provide plenty of shade. There are no food concessions, but McDonald's and other takeout options are right outside the entrance gate; there's also a weekend farmers' market. ■**TIP→ The beach is best before 2 pm. After 2, trade winds bring clouds that get hung up on steep mountains nearby, causing overcast skies. Amenities:** lifeguards; parking (no fee); showers; toilets. **Best for:** solitude; swimming; walking. ⊠ *520 Tinker Rd., Waimanalo* ⊹ *Enter on Kalanianaole Hwy. near Waimanalo town center.*

Makapuu Beach Park

BEACH | A magnificent beach protected by Makapuu Point welcomes you to the windward side. Hang gliders circle above, and the water is filled with bodyboarders. Just off the coast you can see Bird Island, a sanctuary for aquatic fowl, jutting out of the blue. The currents can be heavy, so check with a lifeguard if you're unsure of safety. Before you leave, take the prettiest (and coldest) outdoor shower available on the island. Being surrounded by tropical flowers and foliage while you rinse off that sand will be a memory you will cherish from this side of the rock. **Amenities:** lifeguards; parking (no fee); showers; toilets. **Best for:** sunrise; walking. ⊠ *41-095 Kalanianaole Hwy., Waimanalo* ⊹ *Across from Sea Life Park, 2 miles south of Waimanalo.*

Did You Know?

Windward Oahu's Makapuu Beach is protected by Makapuu Point, but currents are still strong, so be cautious when in the water.

3

Waimanalo Bay Beach Park

BEACH | **FAMILY** | One of the most beautiful beaches on Oahu, Waimanalo is a local pick, busy with picnicking families and active sports fields. Expect a wide stretch of sand; turquoise, emerald, and deep-blue water; and gentle shore-breaking waves that are fun for all ages. Theft is an occasional problem, so lock your car. **Amenities:** lifeguards; parking (no fee); showers; toilets. **Best for:** sunrise; swimming; walking. ⊠ *41-849 Kalanianaole Hwy., Waimanalo* ✛ *South of Waimanalo town center.*

Kailua

6 miles north of Waimanalo.

Upscale Kailua is the most easily accessed town on the windward side. It has two of Oahu's best beaches as well as great shopping and dining opportunities in its central core. You could easily spend a day visiting the stunning beaches, kayaking, exploring a hidden *heiau* (shrine), picnicking, or dining out with locals.

 Sights

Ulupo Heiau State Historic Site

RUINS | Find this spot—where signs near a *heiau* (shrine) also explain Kailua's early history—tucked next to the Windward YMCA. Although they may look like piles of rocks to the uninitiated, *heiau* are sacred stone platforms for the worship of the gods and date from ancient times. *Ulupo* means "night inspiration," referring to the legendary Menehune, a mythical race of diminutive people who are said to have built the heiau under the cloak of darkness. ⊠ *Kalanianaole Hwy. and Kailua Rd., Kailua* ✛ *Behind Windward YMCA* ⊕ *dlnr.hawaii.gov/dsp/parks/oahu/ulupo-heiau-state-historic-site.*

 Beaches

★ Kailua Beach Park

BEACH | **FAMILY** | A cobalt-blue sea and a wide continuous arc of powdery sand make this one of the island's best beaches, as illustrated by the crowds of local families who spend their weekend days here. The water is calm, a line of palms and ironwoods provides shade on the sand, and a huge park has picnic pavilions where you can escape the heat. This is also the "it" spot for windsurfing or kiteboarding, and you can rent kayaks nearby at Kailua Beach Adventures (⊠ *130 Kailua Rd.*) for day trips to the Mokulua Islands. **Amenities:** lifeguards; parking (no fee); showers; toilets; water sports. **Best for:** swimming; walking; windsurfing. ⊠ *437 Kawailoa Rd., Kailua* ✛ *Near Kailua town, turn right on Kailua Rd. After Kalapawai Market, cross bridge, then turn left into beach parking lot.*

★ Lanikai Beach

BEACH | Think of the beaches you see in commercials: peaceful jade-green waters, powder-soft white sand, families and dogs frolicking, and offshore islands in the distance. It's an ideal spot for camping out with a book. Though the beach hides behind multimillion-dollar houses, by state law there is public access every 400 yards. Street parking is available but very difficult to find (and prohibited on holiday weekends). Consider parking at Kailua Beach Park and walking along the paved pathway into Lanikai. Just don't block the boat ramp stalls. There are no shower or bathroom facilities here—but you'll find both at Kailua Beach Park. ■ **TIP**➔ **Look for walled or fenced pathways every 400 yards, leading to the beach. Be sure not to park in the marked bike/jogging lane. Amenities:** none. **Best for:** sunrise; swimming; walking. ⊠ *974 Mokulua Dr., Kailua* ✛ *Past Kailua Beach Park.*

🍴 Restaurants

Buzz's Original Steak House

$$$ | STEAKHOUSE | Virtually unchanged since opening in 1967, this neighborhood institution opposite Kailua Beach Park is filled with the aroma of grilling steaks and plumeria blooms. It doesn't matter if you're a bit sandy and beach bedraggled (though bare feet are a no-no, as are tank tops after 4:30 pm)—just find a spot in the cozy maze of rooms; stop at the salad bar; and order a steak, a burger, teriyaki chicken, or the fresh fish special. **Known for:** the views from the lanai at lunch; excellent fruity beach cocktails, including very strong mai tais; local institution. [$] *Average main: $35* ✉ *413 Kawailoa Rd., Kailua* ☎ *808/261–4661* 🌐 *buzzsoriginalsteakhouse.com.*

Cinnamon's Restaurant

$ | AMERICAN | FAMILY | Known for uncommon variations on common breakfast themes, this neighborhood favorite is tucked into a hard-to-find Kailua office park (call for directions). Local-style lunch plates are good, but the main attraction is breakfast, when you don't want to miss the guava chiffon and red velvet pancakes or the signature cinnamon macadamia-nut rolls. (The Waikiki location in the Ilikai Hotel serves dinner, too.) Be prepared to wait. **Known for:** cinnamon rolls (of course); long waits; endless variations on pancakes, eggs Benedict, and waffles. [$] *Average main: $16* ✉ *315 Uluniu St., Kailua* ☎ *808/261–8724* 🌐 *cinnamons808.com* 🕒 *No lunch on Sun. and holidays. Takeout only on Wed. and Thurs.*

Kalapawai Cafe & Deli

$$ | ECLECTIC | FAMILY | This one-stop, green-and-white, Mediterranean-leaning café, wine bar, bakery, and gourmet deli is the creation of the Dymond family, two generations of restaurateurs who have shaken up the windward food scene. Come in on your way to the beach for a cup of coffee and bagel, and stop back for a gourmet pizza or bruschetta for lunch or a candlelight dinner at night. **Known for:** good coffee and sandwiches by day; impressive wine list for such a small spot; signature dishes by night. [$] *Average main: $20* ✉ *750 Kailua Rd., Kailua* ☎ *808/262–3354* 🌐 *kalapawaimarket.com.*

☕ Coffee and Quick Bites

★ Agnes' Portuguese Bake Shop

$ | BAKERY | This food truck in the Manuhealii parking lot serves delicious, made-to-order *malasadas* (Portuguese donuts) that are crispy and dark brown on the outside and soft, chewy, and sweet on the inside. They're also denser than those found at some other bakeries on the island. **Known for:** no-fuss takeout; authentic malasadas; convenient location. [$] *Average main: $15* ✉ *5 Hoolai St., Kailua* ✥ *In the parking lot of Manuhealii across from Kalapawai Cafe* 🕒 *Closed Sun.* ☞ *Just over $1 a malasada.*

Island Snow

$ | ICE CREAM | FAMILY | This hole-in-the-wall has been creating shave ice perfection in its tiny original spot since 1979, but when two young girls named Obama discovered the luscious flavors in 2008, it was really put on the map. A favorite spot for both locals and storied visitors (and these days lots of regular tourists), it makes a mean shave ice, whether you stick with standard flavors like cherry or go for *lilikoi* (passion fruit) guava with a snowcap on top. **Known for:** the Obama girls, who grew up on this stuff (look for their photos on the wall); long lines of locals and tourists; the best shave ice on the windward side. [$] *Average main: $6* ✉ *130 Kailua Rd., Kailua* ☎ *808/263–6339* 🌐 *islandsnow.com.*

🍸 Nightlife

Tap & Barrel

BREWPUBS | Lanikai Brewing Company's taproom features its island-centric beer, including seasonal varieties that

Windward Oahu Villages

Tiny villages—generally consisting of a sign, a store, a beach park, possibly a post office, and not much more—are strung along Kamehameha Highway on the windward side. Each has something to offer. In **Waiahole**, look for fruit stands and the Waiahole Poi Factory, which is worth a stop for Hawaiian food and their famous poi. In **Kaaawa**, there's a convenience store/gas station. In **Punaluu**, get a plate lunch at Keneke's, or visit the venerable Chings' General Store. **Hauula** has the gallery of fanciful landscape artist Lance Fairly; the Shrimp Shack; Hauula Gift Shop, a clothing shop where sarongs wave like banners; and, at Hauula Kai Shopping Center, Penny's Malasadas and Tamura's Market, with excellent seafood and the last liquor before Mormon-dominated Laie.

incorporate unusual ingredients like surname cherry, mushrooms, and white tea. It also serves Valentina's wood-fired pizza and sometimes has a food truck out front. In addition to beer, there are spirits from the brewery's new distillery line, house-made sangria, Paradise Ciders, and other sips from which to choose. Kids are welcome, and there are board games available to play. ⊠ *167 Hamakua Dr., Kailua ⊕ www.lanikaibrewing.com.*

🛍 Shopping

★ Bookends

BOOKS | FAMILY | Shop for gifts or yourself at this cozy, independent bookstore, which feels more like a small-town library, welcoming browsers to linger. It sells new and secondhand books, and its children's section is filled with both books and toys. ⊠ *600 Kailua Rd., Unit 126, Kailua ☎ 808/261–1996 ⊕ instagram. com/bookendskailua.*

Manuhealii

MIXED CLOTHING | For modern and authentic aloha attire made in Hawaii, Manuhealii is your place. The Kailua storefront is one of two physical locations (the other is in Honolulu). The clothes aren't inexpensive, but their quality is superb. ⊠ *5 Hoolai St., Kailua ☎ 808/261–9865 ⊕ manuhealii.com.*

★ Under a Hula Moon

HOUSEWARES | Exclusive tabletop items and Pacific home decor, such as shell wreaths, shell night-lights, Hawaiian beach sheets, frames, and unique one-of-a-kind gifts with an Islands influence, define this eclectic shop. ⊠ *Kailua Shopping Center, 600 Kailua Rd., Kailua ☎ 808/261–2200 ⊕ underahulamoonkailua.com.*

Kaneohe

6 miles west of Kailua.

The largest community on Oahu's windward side, Kaneohe (meaning "bamboo man" in Hawaiian) is a sprawling community with malls, car dealerships, and a few worthwhile restaurants. At the base of the Koolau Range, Kaneohe sees a lot more rain than neighboring Kailua and is the greener for it. Two noteworthy sights take advantage of their proximity to the mountains: the Byodo-In Temple and Hoomaluhia Botanical Garden.

👁 Sights

★ Byodo-In Temple

TEMPLE | Tucked away in the back of the Valley of the Temples Memorial Park is a replica of the 11th-century temple at Uji in Japan. A 2-ton, carved-wood statue of the Buddha presides inside the main building. Next to the temple are a meditation pavilion and gardens set dramatically against the sheer, green cliffs of the Koolau Mountains. You can ring the 5-foot, 3-ton brass bell for good luck; feed some of the hundreds of koi, ducks, and swans that inhabit the garden's 2-acre pond (buy fish food at the gift shop); and relax and enjoy the peaceful surroundings. Call ahead to schedule a guided tour. ✉ *47-200 Kahekili Hwy., Kaneohe* ☎ *808/239–9844* 🌐 *byodo-in.com* 🎟 *$5.*

★ Nuuanu Pali State Wayside

VIEWPOINT | This panoramic perch looks out to expansive views of Windward Oahu—from Kaneohe Bay to a small island off the coast called Mokolii ("little lizard," also known as Chinaman's Hat). It was in this region that King Kamehameha I drove defending forces over the edges of the 1,200-foot-high cliffs, thus winning the decisive battle for control of the island.

Temperatures at the summit are several degrees cooler than in warm Waikiki, so bring a jacket along. Hang on tight to any loose possessions, and consider wearing pants; it gets extremely windy at the lookout, which is part of the fun. After arriving in the pay-to-park lot, remove valuables from your car and lock it; break-ins have occurred here (this wayside is in the most trafficked state park in Hawaii). ✉ *Pali Hwy., Kaneohe* ✥ *at very top of Pali Hwy.* 🌐 *dlnr.hawaii.gov/dsp/parks/oahu/nuuanu-pali-state-wayside* 🎟 *Parking $7 per car.*

Beaches

Kahana Bay Beach Park

BEACH | **FAMILY** | Local parents often bring their children here to wade in safety in the very shallow, protected waters. This pretty beach cove, surrounded by mountains, has a long arc of sand that is great for walking and a cool, shady grove of tall ironwood and pandanus trees that is ideal for a picnic. An ancient Hawaiian fishpond, which was in use until the 1920s, is visible nearby. Note, though, that the water here is not generally a clear blue due to the runoff from heavy rains in the valley. **Amenities:** parking (no fee); showers; toilets. **Best for:** swimming; walking. ✉ *52-201 Kamehameha Hwy., Kaaawa* ✥ *North of Kualoa Park.*

Restaurants

Pah Ke's Chinese Restaurant

$ | **CHINESE** | **FAMILY** | If you happen to be on the windward side at dinner time, this out-of-the-ordinary Chinese restaurant—named for the local pidgin term for "Chinese" (literally translated, this is "Chinese's Chinese Restaurant")—is a good option. Ebullient owner and chef Raymond Siu, a former hotel pastry chef, focuses on healthier cooking techniques and local ingredients. **Known for:** house specials that are usually better than standard menu fare; a big dining room with bright lights and not much atmosphere; dependable spot for the family. [$] *Average main: $15* ✉ *46-018 Kamehameha Hwy., Kaneohe* ☎ *808/235–4505* 🌐 *pahke.com* ☞ *BYOB.*

Hotels

Paradise Bay Resort

$$ | **RESORT** | Right on picturesque Kaneohe Bay amid the junglelike fauna of the windward side, this resort offers apartment-style units ranging from cozy studios to spacious two-bedroom suites with breathtaking views of the majestic Koolau Mountains; there's also one stand-alone cottage in a remote area not generally frequented by tourists. **Pros:** local, authentic experience; beautiful views over the bay; en suite kitchens or kitchenettes. **Cons:** neighborhood is a bit run-down; rental car a necessity (but parking included in $35 nightly resort

Kualoa Point is in Kualoa Regional Park in Kaaawa, a beautiful but windy area overlooking Kaneohe Bay and the towering Koolau Mountains.

fee); remote location not near most other attractions. $ *Rooms from: $200* ✉ *47-039 Lihikai Dr., Kaneohe* ☎ *808/239–5711* ⊕ *www.paradisebayresort.com* ⏎ *46 rooms.*

Kaaawa

14 miles north of Kaneohe.

Less a village than a collection of homes, Kaaawa consists of little more than a post office, bus stop, and gas station—bookended by an elementary school and a fire station. Of course, there's a beach park, too.

Sights

★ Kualoa Ranch
FARM/RANCH | FAMILY | Encompassing 4,000 acres, about 45 minutes by car from Waikiki, this working ranch offers a wide range of activities—from ATV and horseback tours to zip-lining or expeditions into the valley on an electric bike. The mountains that serve as the backdrop here may seem familiar: the ranch has served as the set for movies such as *Jurassic Park* and *Windtalkers*, as well as TV shows like *Magnum P.I.* and *Lost* (and you can take a film sites tour). From the grounds, you'll have a wonderful view of the ocean and Mokolii (Chinaman's Hat). You can drop by the visitor center anytime, but it's best to book activities and tours two or three days in advance. ✉ *49-560 Kamehameha Hwy., Kaaawa* ☎ *808/237–7321* ⊕ *www.kualoa. com* ⏎ *From $48.*

Beaches

★ Kualoa Regional Park
BEACH | Grassy expanses border a long, narrow stretch of sand with spectacular views of Kaneohe Bay and the Koolau Mountains, making Kualoa one of the island's most beautiful picnic, camping, and beach areas. Dominating the view is an islet called Mokolii, better known

as Chinaman's Hat, which rises 206 feet above the water. You can swim in the shallow areas of this rarely crowded beach year-round. The one drawback is that it's usually windy here, but the wide-open spaces are ideal for kite flying. **Amenities:** lifeguards; showers; toilets. **Best for:** solitude; swimming. ✉ *49-479 Kamehameha Hwy., Kaaawa* ✣ *North of Waiahole.*

Laie

10 miles north of Kaaawa, 33 miles north of Honolulu.

Visiting Laie—over an hour by car and a world away from bustling Waikiki and Honolulu—is like taking a trip to another island. Home to a Mormon temple and the Mormon-founded Polynesian Cultural Center, Laie is a "dry town."

Sights

Polynesian Cultural Center

MUSEUM VILLAGE | **FAMILY** | Re-created individual villages showcase the lifestyles and traditions of Hawaii, Tahiti, Samoa, Fiji, the Marquesas Islands, New Zealand, and Tonga. In addition, the 42-acre center, which is 35 miles from Waikiki and which was founded in 1963 by the Church of Jesus Christ of Latter-day Saints, has restaurants, hosts luau, and demonstrates cultural traditions, such as hula, fire dancing, and ancient ceremonies. The Hukilau Marketplace carries Polynesian handicrafts.

There are multiple packages available, from basic admission to an all-inclusive deal. Every May, the Center hosts the World Fireknife Championships, an event that draws the top fireknife dance performers from around the world. Get tickets for that event in advance. ■ **TIP→ If you're staying in Honolulu, see the Center as part of a van tour so you won't have to drive home late at night after the two-hour evening show.** ✉ *55-370 Kamehameha Hwy., Laie* ☎ *800/367–7060* 🌐 *www.polynesia.com* 🎟 *From $70* 🕒 *Closed Sun. and Wed.*

Hotels

Courtyard Oahu North Shore

$$$ | **HOTEL** | **FAMILY** | This property offers reliable and affordable accommodations close to the Polynesian Cultural Center and a short drive to some of the North Shore's most iconic beaches and surfing spots. **Pros:** best bet for North Shore exploring; reliable, modern, and clean; near the beach. **Cons:** no alcohol served in the hotel or nearby establishments; a car is needed, and parking is not free; a long drive to the rest of Oahu's attractions. [$] *Rooms from: $270* ✉ *55-400 Kamehameha Hwy., Laie* ☎ *808/293–4900* 🌐 *marriott.com* 🛏 *144 rooms* 🍴 *No Meals.*

Performing Arts

DINNER CRUISES AND SHOWS

Ha: Breath of Life

THEATER | The Polynesian Cultural Center's long-running nightly show, *Ha: Breath of Life,* is a story of love, respect, and responsibility. *Ha,* which means "breath" in Hawaiian, follows the central character of Mana from his birth to the birth of his own child. The performances highlight ancient Hawaiian, Polynesian, Samoan, and Tahitian culture, music, and dance, including fire-knife dancers, and with more than 100 performers. Performances are Monday–Saturday at 7:30 pm. ✉ *Polynesian Cultural Center, 55-370 Kamehameha Hwy., Laie* ☎ *800/367–7060* 🌐 *www.habreathoflife.com* 🎟 *From $89.95.*

LUAU

★ **Polynesian Cultural Center Alii Luau**

THEMED ENTERTAINMENT | Although this elaborate luau has the sharpest production values, there is no booze allowed (it's a Mormon-owned facility in the heart of Laie—Mormon country). It's held amid the seven re-created villages at the Polynesian Cultural Center in the North Shore town of Laie, about a 1½-hour drive from Honolulu. The luau—considered one of the most authentic on the island—includes the *Ha: Breath of Life* show that has long been popular with both residents and visitors. Rates vary depending on activities and amenities that are included (personalized tours, reserved seats, or table service, for example). Waikiki transport is available. It's held Monday–Saturday at 5. ✉ *Polynesian Cultural Center, 55-370 Kamehameha Hwy., Laie* ☎ *808/293–3333, 800/367–7060* ⊕ *www. polynesia.com* ✉ *From $119.95.*

Activities and Tours

Although much is written about the water surrounding this little rock known as Oahu, there is as much to be said for the rock itself. It's a wonder of nature, thrust from the ocean floor thousands of millennia ago by a volcanic hot spot that is still spitting out islands today.

Hawaii is the most remote island chain on Earth, with creatures and plants that can be seen here and nowhere else. And there are dozens of ways for you to check them all out.

From the air, you can peer down into nooks and crannies in the mountains—where cars cannot reach and hikers don't dare. Whether flitting here and there amid a helicopter's rush and roar or sailing by in the silence of a glider's reverie, you glimpse sights that few have experienced. Or, if you would rather, take a step back in time and take off from the waters of Keehi Lagoon in a World War II–era seaplane. Follow the flight path flown by the Japanese Zeros as they attempted to destroy Pearl Harbor and the American spirit.

If you prefer to stay grounded, Oahu is covered in hiking trails that traverse everything from tropical rain forest to arid desert. Even when in the bustling city of Honolulu, you are but minutes from hidden waterfalls and bamboo forests. Out west, you can wander a dusty path that has long since given up its ability to accommodate cars but is perfect for hikers. You can admire sea arches and gape at caves opened by the rock slides that closed the road. You can also camp out on many of these treks and beaches.

If somewhat less rugged and less vigorous exploration is more your style, how about letting horses do your dirty work? You can ride them on the beaches and in the valleys, checking out ancient holy sites, movie sets, and brilliant vistas.

Finally, there is the ancient sport of Scotland. Why merely hike into the rain forest when you can slice a 280-yard drive through it and then hunt for your Titleist in the bushy leaves instead? Almost 40 courses cover this tiny expanse, ranging from the target jungle golf of the Royal Hawaiian Golf Club to the pro-style links of Turtle Bay. There is no off-season in the tropics, and no one here knows your real handicap.

Aerial Tours

Taking an aerial tour of the Islands opens up a world of perspective. Look down from the sky at the outline of the USS *Arizona,* where it lies in its final resting place below the waters of Pearl Harbor, or get a glimpse of the vast carved expanse of a volcanic crater—here are views only seen by an "eye in the sky." Don't forget your camera.

⚠ **All helicopter tour companies in Hawaii are under increasing legislative and regulatory scrutiny due to multiple fatal accidents since 2018, so it's possible that they will undergo further regulations and limitations in the near future.**

Take a helicopter tour for a unique perspective of the island.

Blue Hawaiian Helicopters

AIR EXCURSIONS | This company stakes its claim as Hawaii's largest helicopter operation, with tours on all the major Islands and more than two-dozen choppers in its fleet. The 45-minute Oahu tour seats up to six passengers and includes narration from your friendly pilot along with sweeping views of Waikiki, the beautiful windward coast, and the North Shore. If you like to see the world from above or are just pinched for time and want to get a quick overview of the whole island without renting a car, this is the way to go. Discounts are available if you book online in advance. ⊠ *99 Kaulele Pl., Airport Area* ☎ *808/831–8800, 800/745–2583* ⊕ *www. bluehawaiian.com* 🖃 *From $129.*

Magnum Helicopters

AIR EXCURSIONS | For the adventurous, this *Magnum P.I.*, doors-off helicopter tour offers sweeping views of Keehi Lagoon through urban Honolulu and the harbor, including the Aloha Tower and Waikiki Beach. Soar past and over Diamond Head Crater and up the scenic coast by Makapuu Lighthouse and Sandy Beach and over Windward Oahu's iconic Lanikai and Kailua Beaches. The breathtaking finale takes you inland to Sacred Falls, known for its stunning, 1,000-foot drop and its starring role in *Jurassic Park*, before returning to the airport via North Shore surf spots and a bird's-eye view of Pearl Harbor and the USS *Arizona* Memorial. If you're looking for more thrill (or a cool proposal site), opt for the exclusive mountain-top landing. And if water is your thing, your Navy SEAL guide will join you in plunging into the ocean for some scuba diving. ⊠ *130 Iolana Pl., Airport Area* ☎ *808/833–4354* ⊕ *www.magnum-helicopters.com* 🖃 *From $295.*

Honolulu Soaring — The Original Glider Rides

AIR EXCURSIONS | "Mr. Bill" has been offering piloted glider (sailplane) rides over the northwest end of Oahu's North Shore since 1970. Scenic rides for one or two passengers are in sleek, bubble-top, motorless aircraft with aerial views of mountains, shoreline, coral pools, windsurfing sails, and, in winter, humpback whales. Seeking more thrills? You can also take a more acrobatic ride or take control yourself in a mini-lesson. Flights run 15–60 minutes long. The company operates two days a week, and reservations are requested. ⊠ *Dillingham Airfield, 69-132 Farrington Hwy., Waialua* ☎ *808/637–0207* ⊕ *www.honolulusoaring.com* ⊠ *From $85.*

Paradise Helicopters

AIR EXCURSIONS | Paradise offers tours on several islands, with Oahu tours departing from two helipads: Kalaeloa (near the Ko Olina resorts on the west side) and Turtle Bay Resort on the North Shore. Kalaeloa options range from a one-hour trip over Diamond Head to a two-hour island circle (daytime and sunset) to specialized trips that focus on World War II history. Turtle Bay choices include several 1½-hour North Shore adventures, with vistas of beaches as well as inland waterfalls. ⊠ *Honolulu* ☎ *866/300–2294* ⊕ *paradisecopters.com* ⊠ *From $295.*

Boat Tours and Charters

Being on the water can be the best way to enjoy the Islands. Whether you want to see the fish in action or experience how they taste, there is a tour for you.

For a sailing experience, you need go no farther than the beach in front of your Waikiki hotel. Strung along the sand are several catamarans that offer one-hour rides during the day (about $35) and 90-minute sunset sails ($49–$120).

■ TIP➔ **Feel free to haggle, especially with the smaller boats.**

Some operators provide drinks for free, some charge for them, and some let you pack your own, so keep that in mind when pricing the ride. Or choose to go the ultraluxe route and charter a boat for a day or week. These run from less than

$100 per person per day to more than $1,000 *(see also, Deep-Sea Fishing).*

Hawaii Nautical

BOATING | With two locations—one in Waikiki and one on the Waianae coast—this outfitter offers a wide variety of cruise options, including guaranteed-sighting dolphin and whale-watching (in season), gourmet dinners, lunches, snorkeling, scuba diving, and sunset viewing. Three-hour cruises, including lunch and two drinks, depart from the Kewalo Basin Harbor just outside Waikiki. (The company's Port Waikiki Cruises sail from the Hilton Pier off the Hilton Hawaiian Village in Waikiki.) For those interested in leaving from the Waianae coast, snorkel tours are available from the Waianae Boat Harbor on Farrington Highway (⊠ *85-471 Farrington Hwy.*). Prices include all gear, food, and two alcoholic beverages. The dock in the Waianae Boat Harbor is a little more out of the way, but this is a much more luxurious option than what is offered in Waikiki. Both morning and afternoon snorkel tours include stops for observing dolphins from the boat and a visit to a snorkel spot well populated with fish. All gear, snacks, sandwiches, and two alcoholic beverages make for a more complete experience. Pickup in Ko Olina is free. ⊠ *Kewalo Basin Harbor, 1125 Ala Moana Blvd., Waikiki* ☎ *808/234–7245* ⊕ *www.hawaiinautical.com* ⊠ *From $59.*

Maitai Catamaran

BOATING | Taking off from the stretch of sand between the Sheraton Waikiki and The Halekulani, this 44-foot cat is the fastest and sleekest on the beach. There are a variety of tours to choose from, including a sunset sail and a snorkel excursion. If you have a need for speed and want a more upscale experience, this is the boat for you. ⊠ *Sheraton Waikiki, 2255 Kalakaua Ave., Waikiki* ✛ *On beach behind hotel* ☎ *808/922–5665, 800/462–7975* ⊕ *www.maitaicatamaran. net* ⊠ *From $49.*

Star of Honolulu Cruises

BOATING | FAMILY | Founded in 1957, this company anchors Oahu's dinner-cruise market with its 232-foot *Star of Honolulu*, featuring four floors of walk-around decks and a 60-foot-high observation deck. Enjoy views, live entertainment, cocktails, and dinner. The company also offers several cruise experiences—from casual to luxury—to fit your needs and whims. On some cruises you can even learn how to string lei, play ukulele, or dance hula. Transportation from all hotels on the island can be arranged. ☒ *Honolulu* ☎ *808/983–7827, 800/334–6191* ⊕ *starofhonolulu.com* ☒ *From $69.*

Tradewind Charters

BOATING | This company's half-day private excursions can include sailing, snorkeling, reef fishing, sunset dinner cruises, whale-watching, and even spa treatments, all on luxury yachts that can accommodate 2–49 people. Traveling on these vessels not only gets you away from the crowds, but also gives you the opportunity to take the helm if you wish. The cruises may include snorkeling at an exclusive anchorage, as well as hands-on snorkeling and sailing instruction. All charters are for the full ship. ☒ *Kewalo Basin Harbor, 1125 Ala Moana Blvd., Ala Moana* ☎ *808/227–4956, 800/829–4899* ⊕ *www.tradewindcharters.com* ☒ *From $495.*

Bodyboarding and Bodysurfing

Bodyboarding (or sponging) has long been a popular alternative to surfing for a couple of reasons. First, the start-up cost is much less—a usable board can be purchased for $30–$40 or rented on the beach for $5 an hour. Second, it's a whole lot easier to ride a bodyboard than a surfboard. All you have to do is paddle out to the waves, then turn toward the beach as the wave approaches and kick like crazy.

Most grocery and convenience stores sell bodyboards. Though these boards don't compare to what the pros use, beginners won't notice a difference in how they handle on smaller waves.

Though they are not absolutely necessary for bodyboarding, fins do give you a tremendous advantage when you're paddling. If you plan to go out into bigger surf, get a leash, which reduces the chance you'll lose your board. The smaller, sturdier versions of dive fins used for bodyboarding sell for $25–$60 at surf and sporting-goods stores. Most beach stands don't rent fins with the boards, so if you want them, you'll probably need to buy them.

Bodysurfing requires far less equipment—just a pair of swim fins with heel straps—but it can be a lot more challenging to master. Typically, surf breaks that are good for bodyboarding are good for bodysurfing.

If the direction of the current or dangers of the break are not readily apparent to you, don't hesitate to ask a lifeguard for advice.

BEST SPOTS

Bodyboarding and bodysurfing can be done anywhere there are waves, but due to the paddling advantage surfers have over spongers, it's usually more fun to go to surf breaks exclusively for bodyboarding. For more information on Oahu beaches, see the individual regional chapters.

Bellows Beach. On Oahu's windward side, Bellows Field Beach Park has shallow waters and a consistent break that makes it an ideal spot for bodyboarders and bodysurfers. (Surfing isn't allowed between the two lifeguard towers.) But take note: the Portuguese man-of-war, a blue jellyfishlike invertebrate that delivers painful and powerful stings, is often seen here. ⊠ *41-043 Kalanianaole Hwy., Waimanalo.*

Kuhio Beach. This beach park offers an easy spot for first-timers to check out the action. A break near the large pedestrian walkway that's called Kapahulu Groin is the quintessential bodyboarding spot. The soft, rolling waves make it perfect for beginners. Even during summer's south swells, it's relatively tame because of the outer reefs. ⊠ *Waikiki Beach, between Sheraton Moana Surfrider Hotel and Kapahulu Groin, Honolulu.*

Makapuu Beach. With its extended waves, this beach park is a sponger's dream. If you're a little more timid, go to the far end of the beach to Keiki's, where the waves are mellowed by Makapuu Point. Although the main break at Makapuu is much less dangerous than that at Sandy's, mind the ocean floor—the sands are always shifting, sometimes exposing coral heads and rocks. Always check (or ask lifeguards about) the currents, which can be strong. ⊠ *41-095 Kalanianaole Hwy., across from Sea Life Park.*

Sandy Beach. The best spot for advanced bodyboarding is Sandy Beach on Oahu's eastern shore. That said, even when the shore break here is small, it can be extremely dangerous. As lifeguards will attest, there are more neck injuries suffered here than at any other surf break in the United States. It's awesome for the advanced, but know its danger before paddling out. ⊠ *8800 Kalanianaole Hwy., 2 miles east of Hanauma Bay, Honolulu.*

Waimanalo Beach. With the longest sand beach on Oahu's windward side, Waimanalo Bay Beach Park has a shallow sandbar at the water's edge that provides good waves for bodyboarding and bodysurfing. It's an ideal break for novices because of its soft waves. Like Walls in Waikiki, this area is protected by an outer reef. And like Bellows, it's favored by the dangerous Portuguese man-of-war. ⊠ *Aloiloi St., Waimanalo.*

EQUIPMENT

The more than 30 rental spots along Waikiki Beach all offer basically the same prices. But if you plan to bodyboard for more than just an hour, consider buying an inexpensive board for $20–$40 at an ABC Store—there are almost 40 in the Waikiki area—and giving it to a kid at the end of your vacation. It will be more cost-effective for you, and you'll be passing along some aloha spirit in the process.

Deep-Sea Fishing

Fishing isn't just a sport in Hawaii, it's a way of life. A number of charter boats with experienced crews can take you on a sportfishing adventure throughout the year. Sure, the bigger yellowfin tuna (ahi) are generally caught in summer, and the coveted spearfish are more frequent in winter, but you can still hook them any day of the year. Plus, the dolphinfish (mahimahi), wahoo (ono), and skipjacks, not to mention the king—Pacific blue marlin—are ripe for the picking on any given day. The largest Pacific blue marlin ever caught, weighing in at 1,805 pounds, was reeled in along Oahu's coast.

When choosing a fishing boat in the Islands, look for veteran captains with decades of experience. Better yet, find those who care about Hawaii's fragile marine environment. Many captains now tag and release their catches to preserve the state's fishing grounds.

The general rule for the catch is an even split with the crew. Unfortunately, there are no "freeze-and-ship" providers in the state, so unless you plan to eat the fish while you're here, you'll probably want to leave it with the boat. Most boats do offer mounting services for trophy fish; ask your captain.

Prices vary greatly, but expect to pay from around $65 per person for a spot on a boat with more than 20 people to $2,000 for an overnight trip for up to six people. Besides the gift of fish, a gratuity of 10%–20% is standard, but use your own discretion based on the overall experience.

BOATS AND CHARTERS

Maggie Joe Sport Fishing

FISHING | The oldest sportfishing company on Oahu boasts landing one of the largest marlins ever caught out of Kewalo Basin. It offers a variety of offshore fishing packages, including exclusive or shared charters, and has a fleet of three boats. Half-day exclusives on the 41-foot *Sea Hawk* or the 38-foot *Ruckus* can accommodate up to six people and are the cheapest options for daytime fishing. The 53-foot *Maggie Joe* embarks on three-quarter- or full-day sails; can accommodate up to 15 anglers; and is equipped with air-conditioned cabins, hot showers, and cutting-edge gear. A marine taxidermist can mount the monster you reel in. ⊠ *Kewalo Basin, 1025 Ala Moana Blvd., Ala Moana* ☎ *808/591–8888, 877/806–3474* ⊕ *www.maggiejoe.com* ⊠ *From $200.*

Magic Sport Fishing

FISHING | This 50-foot Pacifica fishing yacht, aptly named *Magic,* boasts a slew of sportfishing records, including some of the largest marlins caught in local tournaments and the most mahimahi hooked during a one-day charter. The yacht, which can accommodate up to six passengers for both shared or full charters, is very comfortable, with air-conditioning, a cozy seating area, and a smooth ride thanks to twin diesel engines. ⊠ *Kewalo Basin Harbor, 1125 Ala Moana Blvd., Slip G, Ala Moana* ☎ *808/596–2998* ⊕ *www.magicsportfishing.com* ⊠ *From $220 per person for a shared charter; from $1,190 for a private charter.*

Golf

Unlike elsewhere in Hawaii, most of Oahu's golf courses aren't associated with hotels and resorts. In fact, of the island's more than three dozen courses, only five are tied to lodging, and none is in the tourist hub of Waikiki.

Although municipal courses are a good choice for budget-conscious golfers, they're more crowded than (and not always as well maintained as) private courses. Your best bet is to call the day you want to play and inquire about walk-on availability. Greens fees are standard at city courses: walking rate $66 for visitors, riding carts $20 for 18 holes, pull carts $4.

Greens fees listed here are the highest course rates per round on weekdays and weekends for U.S. residents. (Some courses charge non–U.S. residents higher prices.) Discounts are often available for resort guests and for those who book tee times online. Twilight fees are usually offered.

WAIKIKI

Ala Wai Golf Course

GOLF | Just across the Ala Wai Canal from Waikiki, this municipal golf course is said to host more rounds than any other U.S. course—up to 500 per day. Not that it's a great course, just really convenient. The best bet for a visitor is to show up and expect to wait at least an hour or call up to three days in advance for a tee time. (The jury is out on whether online reservations have made securing a time any easier.) The course itself is flat, though Robin Nelson did some redesign work in the 1990s, adding mounding, trees, and a lake. The Ala Wai Canal comes into play on several holes on the back nine, including the treacherous 18th. There's also an on-site restaurant and bar. ⊠ *404 Kapahulu Ave., Waikiki* ☎ *808/207– 6856 for reservations* ⊕ *www.honolulu.gov/*

des/golf/alawai.html ⊠ *$66* 🏌 *18 holes, 5861 yards, par 70.*

SOUTHEAST OAHU
Hawaii Kai Golf Course

GOLF | The Championship Golf Course (William F. Bell, 1973) winds through a Honolulu suburb at the foot of Koko Crater. Homes (and the liability of a broken window) come into play on many holes, but they are offset by views of the Pacific and a crafty routing of holes. With several lakes, lots of trees, and bunkers in all the wrong places, Hawaii Kai really is a "championship" golf course, especially when the trade winds howl. Greens fees for this course include a mandatory cart. The Executive Course (1962), a par-54 track, is the first of only three courses in Hawaii built by Robert Trent Jones Sr. Although a few changes have been made to his original design, you can find the usual Jones attributes, including raised greens and lots of risk-reward options. You may walk or use a cart on this course for an additional fee. ⊠ *8902 Kalanianaole Hwy., Hawaii Kai* ☎ *808/395–2358* ⊕ *hawaiikaigolf.com* ⊠ *Championship Course: $150. Executive Course: $50* 🏌 *Championship Course: 18 holes, 6207 yards, par 72. Executive Course: 18 holes, 2196 yards, par 54.*

WINDWARD OAHU
Olomana Golf Links

GOLF | Bob and Robert L. Baldock are the architects of record for this layout, but so much has changed since it opened in 1969 that they would recognize little of it. A turf specialist was brought in to improve fairways and greens, tees were rebuilt, new bunkers were added, and mangroves were cut back to make better use of natural wetlands. But what really puts Olomana on the map is that this is where wunderkind Michelle Wie learned the game. A cart is required at this course and is included in the greens fee. ⊠ *41-1801 Kalanianaole Hwy., Waimanalo* ☎ *808/259–7926* ⊕ *www.olomanalinks.*

com ⊠ *$75 from 2 pm to close, $105 for 18 holes* 🏌 *18 holes, 6306 yards, par 72.*

★ Royal Hawaiian Golf Club

GOLF | In the cool, lush Maunawili Valley, Pete and Perry Dye created what can only be called target jungle golf. In other words, the rough is usually dense jungle, and you may not hit a driver on three of the four par 5s, or several par 4s, including the perilous 18th that plays off a cliff to a narrow green protected by a creek. Mt. Olomana's twin peaks tower over the course. ■TIP➔ **The back nine wanders deep into the valley and includes an island green (par-3 11th) and perhaps the loveliest inland hole in Hawaii (par-4 12th).** ⊠ *770 Auloa Rd., at Luana Hills Rd., Kailua* ☎ *808/262–2139* ⊕ *royalhawaiiangc.com* ⊠ *$160* 🏌 *18 holes, 5541 yards, par 72.*

NORTH SHORE
Turtle Bay Resort

GOLF | When the Lazarus of golf courses, the Fazio Course (George Fazio, 1971), rose from the dead in 2002, Turtle Bay on Oahu's rugged North Shore became a premier golf destination. Two holes had been plowed under when the Palmer Course (Arnold Palmer and Ed Seay, 1992) was built, while the other seven lay fallow, and the front nine remained open. Then new owners came along and re-created holes 13 and 14 using Fazio's original plans, and the Fazio became whole again.

Check on the status of the temporarily closed Fazio Course. The gem at Turtle Bay, though, is the Palmer. The front nine is mostly open as it skirts Punahoolapa Marsh, a nature sanctuary, while the back nine plunges into the wetlands and winds along the coast. The short par-4 17th runs along the rocky shore, with a diabolical string of bunkers cutting diagonally across the fairway from tee to green. Carts are required and are included in the greens fee. ⊠ *57-091 Kamehameha Hwy., Kahuku* ☎ *808/293–8574* ⊕ *www.turtlebaygolf.com* ⊠ *$209*

($139 twilight, staring at 1PM) ✦. *Palmer Course: 18 holes, 7200 yards, par 72.*

CENTRAL OAHU
Royal Kunia Country Club

GOLF | At one time, the PGA Tour considered buying the Royal Kunia Country Club and hosting the Sony Open here. It's that dear. Robin Nelson's eye for natural sight lines and his dexterity with water features add to the visual pleasure. ■TIP→ **Every hole offers fabulous views from Diamond Head to Pearl Harbor to the nearby Waianae Mountains.** Carts are required and are included in the greens fee. ⊠ *94-1509 Anonui St., Waipahu* ☎ *808/688–9222* ⊕ *www.royalkuniacc. com* ✉ *From $85* ✦. *18 holes, 6507 yards, par 72.*

Waikele Country Club

GOLF | Outlet stores are not the only bargain in Waikele. The adjacent, daily-fee golf course offers a private club–like atmosphere and a terrific Ted Robinson (1992) layout. Robinson's water features are less distinctive here but define the short par-4 4th hole—with a lake running down the left side of the fairway and guarding the green—and the par-3 17th, which plays across a lake. The par-4 18th is a terrific closing hole, with a lake lurking on the right side of the green. Carts are required and are included in the greens fee. ⊠ *94-200 Paioa Pl., Waipahu* ☎ *808/676–9000* ⊕ *www.golfwaikele. com* ✉ *$170* ✦. *18 holes, 6261 yards, par 72.*

WEST (LEEWARD) OAHU
Coral Creek Golf Course

GOLF | On the Ewa Plain, 4 miles inland, this course is cut from ancient coral left from when this area was still underwater. Robin Nelson (1999) did some of his best work in making use of the coral—and of some dynamite—blasting out portions to create dramatic lakes and tee and green sites. They could just as easily call it Coral Cliffs because of the 30- to 40-foot cliffs Nelson created. They include the par-3 10th green's grotto and waterfall and

the vertical drop-off on the right side of the par-4 18th green. An ancient creek meanders across the course, but there's not much water, just enough to be a babbling nuisance. Carts are required and are included in the greens fee. ⊠ *91-1111 Geiger Rd., Ewa Beach* ☎ *808/441–4653* ⊕ *www.coralcreekgolfhawaii.com* ✉ *$80 for 9 holes, $155 for 18 holes* ✦. *18 holes, 6347 yards, par 72.*

Ko Olina Golf Club

GOLF | Hawaii's golden age of golf-course architecture came to Oahu when Ko Olina Golf Club opened in 1989. Ted Robinson, king of the water features, went splash-happy here, creating nine lakes that come into play on eight holes, including the par-3 12th, where you reach the tee by driving behind a Disney-like waterfall. Tactically, though, the most dramatic is the par-4 18th, where the approach is a minimum 120 yards across a lake to a two-tiered green guarded on the left by a cascading waterfall. Today Ko Olina has matured into one of Hawaii's top courses. You can niggle about routing issues—the first three holes play into the trade winds (and the morning sun), as do two consecutive par 5s on the back nine play—but Robinson does enough solid design to make those of passing concern. ■TIP→ **The course provides free transportation from Waikiki hotels.** ⊠ *92-1220 Aliinui Dr., Ko Olina* ☎ *808/676–5300* ⊕ *koolinagolf.com* ✉ *$115 for 9 holes, $225 for 18 holes* ✦. *18 holes, 6432 yards, par 72.*

Hiking

The trails of Oahu cover a full spectrum of environments: desert walks through cactus, slippery paths through bamboo-filled rain forest, and scrambling rock climbs up ancient volcanic calderas. The only thing you won't find is an overnighter, as even the longest of hikes won't take you more than half a day. In addition to being short in length, many

Did You Know?

Trekking to 150-foot Manoa Falls—a cascade or a trickle, depending on the rains—is more about the journey than the destination. The mile-long trail traverses an array of ecosystems, including a bamboo forest.

of the prime hikes are within 10 minutes of downtown Waikiki, meaning that you won't have to spend your whole day getting back to nature.

BEST SPOTS

Diamond Head State Monument

HIKING & WALKING | Every vacation has requirements that must be fulfilled, so that when your neighbors ask, you can say, "Yeah, did it." Climbing Diamond Head is high on that list of things to do on Oahu. It's a moderately easy hike if you're in good physical condition, but be prepared to climb many stairs along the way. Also be sure to bring a water bottle, because it's hot and dry. Only a mile up, a clearly marked trail with handrails scales the inside of this extinct volcano. At the top, the fabled final 99 steps take you up to the pillbox overlooking the Pacific Ocean and Honolulu. It's a breathtaking view and a lot cheaper than taking a helicopter ride for the same photo op. Last entry for hikers is 4:30 pm. ⊠ *Diamond Head Rd. at 18th Ave., Diamond Head* ✛ *Enter on east side of crater; there's limited parking inside, so most park on street and walk in* ☎ *808/587–0300* ⊕ *dlnr.hawaii.gov/dsp/parks/oahu/ diamond-head-state-monument* ⌨ *$5 per person, $10 to park.*

★ Kaena Point Trail

HIKING & WALKING | Kaena Point is one of the island's last easily accessible pockets of nature left largely untouched. For more than a quarter century, the state has protected nearly 60 acres of land at the point, first as a nature preserve and then, more recently, as an ecosystem restoration project for endangered and protected coastal plants and seabirds. The uneven 5-mile trail around the point can be accessed from two locations—Keawaula Beach (aka Yokohama Bay) at the end of Farrington Highway on Oahu's western coastline, or Mokuleia at the same highway's northern coast endpoint. It's a rugged coastline hike without much shade, so bring lots of water and

sunscreen. (Or, better yet, start early!) ■TIP➜ **Keep a lookout for the Laysan albatrosses, and don't be surprised if these enormous birds come in for a closer look at you, too.** ⊠ *81-780 Farrington Hwy., Waianae* ✛ *Take Farrington Hwy. to its end at Yokohama. Hike in on old 4x4 trail* ⊕ *dlnr.hawaii.gov/dsp/hiking/oahu/ kaena-point-trail.*

Makapuu Lighthouse Trail

HIKING & WALKING | For the less adventurous hiker and anyone looking for a great view, this paved trail that runs up the side of Makapuu Point in Southeast Oahu fits the bill. Early on, the trail is surrounded by lava rock, but as you ascend, foliage—the tiny white koa haole flower, the cream-tinged spikes of the kiawe, and, if you go early enough, the stunning night-blooming cereus—begins taking over the barren rock. At the easternmost tip of Oahu, where the island divides the sea, this trail gives you a spectacular view of the cobalt ocean meeting the land in a cacophony of white caps.

To the south is the lighthouse; to the east are the Manana (Rabbit) and Kaohikaipu islets, two bird sanctuaries just off the coast. The 2-mile round-trip hike is a great break on a circle-island trip. From late December to early May, this is a marvelous perch to see migrating humpback whales. Note that you can no longer access the tidal pools here. The trail to them is closed as the descent was treacherous (steep, rocky, and very slippery), and there were incidences of rogue waves sweeping people out to sea. ■TIP➜ **Heed trail closure signs. Also, don't leave valuables in your car; break-ins, even in the parking lot, are common.** ⊠ *Makapuu Lighthouse Rd., Hawaii Kai* ✛ *Take Kalanianaole Hwy. to base of Makapuu Point, then look for parking lot* ⊕ *dlnr.hawaii.gov/dsp/hiking/oahu/ makapuu-point-lighthouse-trail.*

★ Manoa Falls Trail

HIKING & WALKING | Travel up into the valley beyond Honolulu to make the Manoa

Falls hike. Though only a mile long, this well-trafficked path, with an estimated 100,000 visitors a year, passes through so many different ecosystems that you feel as if you're in an arboretum—and you're not far off. The beautiful Lyon Arboretum is right near the trailhead, if you want to make another stop. Walk among the elephant ear (ape) plants, ruddy fir trees, and a bamboo forest straight out of China. At the top is a 150-foot waterfall, which can be an impressive cascade or, if rains have been light, little more than a trickle, but this hike is more about the journey than the destination. Make sure you bring mosquito repellent because they grow 'em big up here. ⊠ 3998 Manoa Rd., Manoa ✛ West Manoa Rd. is behind Manoa Valley in Paradise Park. Take West Manoa Rd. to end, park on side of road or in parking lot for a small fee, follow trail signs ⊕ hawaiitrails. hawaii.gov/trails.

GUIDES

Hawaii Nature Center

HIKING & WALKING | FAMILY | This center in the upper Makiki Valley conducts a number of programs for both adults and children, including guided hikes into tropical settings that reveal hidden waterfalls and protected forest reserves. Activities aren't offered every day, so it's a good idea to check ahead and make reservations. ⊠ 2131 Makiki Heights Dr., Makiki Heights ☎ 808/955–0100 ⊕ hawaiinature-center.org.

North Shore Eco Tours

HIKING & WALKING | Native Hawaiians own and operate this business, the only one allowed to lead guided small-group adventures in private conservation lands. Options range from 2- and 3½-mile round-trip hikes to pools and waterfalls (lunch included) to an off-road expedition in all-terrain vehicles. Excursions, which are described in detail on the company's website, have minimum age requirements for children. The pickup point for hikes is the North Shore Marketplace in Haleiwa town; off-road tours begin in Waimea Valley. ⊠ North Shore Marketplace, 56-250 Kamehameha Hwy., Haleiwa ☎ 877/521–4453 ⊕ www.north-shoreecotours.com ⊠ From $95.

Oahu Nature Tours

HIKING & WALKING | Guides explain the native flora and fauna and history that are your companions on the various walking and hiking tours of the North Shore, Diamond Head, and Windward Oahu. The company also offers much more expensive private birding tours, perfect for those interested in spotting one of Hawaii's native honeycreepers. Tours include pickup at centralized Waikiki locations and are discounted if booked online in advance. ☎ 808/924–2473 ⊕ www. oahunaturetours.com ⊠ From $125.

Horseback Riding

A great way to see the island is atop a horse, leaving the direction to the pack while you drink in the views of mountains or the ocean. It may seem like a cliché, but there really is nothing like riding a horse with spectacular ocean views to put you in a romantic state of mind.

Happy Trails Hawaii

HORSEBACK RIDING | FAMILY | Take a guided horseback ride above the North Shore's Waimea Bay along trails that offer panoramic views from Kaena Point to the famous surfing spots. Groups are no larger than 10, and instruction is provided. The rides are particularly family-friendly, and children six and older are welcome. You can take either a 1½- or a 2-hour ride, which includes a 15-minute mini-lesson. Local fruits grown on the property are offered for tasting when available. Reservations are required. ⊠ 59-231 Pupukea Rd., Pupukea ✛ Go 1 mile mauka (toward mountain) up Pupukea Rd.; the office is on right ☎ 808/638–7433 ⊕ happytrailsha-waii.com ⊠ From $109.

The 4,000-acre Kualoa Ranch may look familiar to you; a popular film site, it's been featured in several movies, as well as other films and TV shows. You can even take a film sites tour of the ranch.

Kualoa Ranch

HORSEBACK RIDING | FAMILY | This 4,000-acre working ranch across from Kualoa Beach Park offers two-hour trail rides in the breathtaking Kaaawa Valley, which was the site of such movie back lots as *Jurassic Park, Godzilla,* and *50 First Dates,* as well as numerous television shows, including *Lost.* Kualoa has other activities—bus, boat, and Jeep tours; electric mountain bike tours; kayak adventure tours; ATV trail rides; canopy zip line tours; and children's activities—that may be combined for full-day package rates. The minimum age for horseback rides is 10. ✉ *49-479 Kamehameha Hwy., Kaneohe* ☎ *800/231–7321, 808/237–7321* ⊕ *www.kualoa.com* 🎟 *From $144.*

Turtle Bay Stables

HORSEBACK RIDING | FAMILY | Trail rides follow the 12-mile-long coastline and even step out onto sandy beaches fronting this luxe resort on Oahu's fabled North Shore. The stables here are part of the resort but can be utilized by nonguests. The sunset ride is a must. Private rides, group rides, and educational (horsemanship) classes are among the many options. A basic trail ride lasts 45 minutes and visits filming sites for ABC's *Lost* and the film *Pirates of the Caribbean.* ✉ *Turtle Bay Resort, 57-091 Kamehameha Hwy., Kahuku* ☎ *808/293–6024* ⊕ *turtlebaystables.com* 🎟 *From $85.*

Kayaking

Kayaking is an easy way, even for novices, to explore the ocean—and Oahu's natural beauty—without much effort or skill. It offers a vantage point not afforded by swimming or surfing and a workout you won't get lounging on a catamaran.

The ability to travel long distances can also get you into trouble. ■**TIP→ Experts agree that rookies should stay on the windward side.** Their reasoning is simple: if you get tired, break or lose an oar, or just plain pass out, the onshore winds will eventually blow you back to the beach.

The same cannot be said for breezes off the North Shore and West Oahu.

Kayaks are specialized: some are better suited for riding waves while others are designed for traveling long distances. Your outfitter can address your needs depending on your skill level. Sharing your plans with your outfitter can lead to a more enjoyable—and safer—experience. Expect to pay from $35 for a half-day single rental to $139 for a guided kayak tour with lunch. Some kayaking outfitters also rent stand-up paddleboards (see also Stand-Up Paddleboarding).

BEST SPOTS

Bellows Field Beach Park, near Waimanalo Town Center on the windward side, and **Mokuleia Beach Park,** across from Kawaihapai Airfield (formerly Dillingham Airfield) on the North Shore, are two great spots to try surf kayaking. Hard-to-reach breaks, the ones that surfers exhaust themselves trying to reach, are easily accessed by kayak. The buoyancy of the kayak also lets you catch the wave earlier and get out in front of the white wash. If you're green, stick to Bellows with those onshore winds. Also, you don't want to be catching waves where the surfers are (in Waikiki, however, pretty much anything goes).

Because of its calm waters and onshore winds, **Lanikai Beach,** tucked away in a windward side residential area, is popular with amateur kayakers. More adventurous paddlers can head to the Mokulua Islands, two islets less than a mile from the beach. You can land on Moku Nui, which has surf breaks and small beaches great for picnicking. Take a dip in Queen's Bath, a small saltwater swimming hole.

For something a little different, try Windward Oahu's Kahana Stream, which empties into the ocean at **Kahana Bay Beach Park.** The riverlike stream may not have the blue water of the ocean, but the majestic Koolau Mountains, with waterfalls during rainy months, make for a picturesque backdrop. It's a short jaunt, about 2 miles round-trip from the beach, but it's tranquil and packed with rainforest foliage. Bring mosquito repellent.

EQUIPMENT, LESSONS, AND TOURS

Go Bananas Kayaks

KAYAKING | Staffers make sure that you rent the appropriate kayak for your abilities and can also outfit your rental car with soft racks (included in the rental fee) to transport your boat to the beach. You can rent either a single or a double kayak. The store also carries clothing and kayaking accessories and rents stand-up paddleboards. A second location in Aiea is closer to the North Shore. ⊠ *799 Kapahulu Ave., Kapahulu* ☎ *808/737–9514* ⊕ *gobananaskayaks.com* ⌑ *From $35.*

Kailua Beach Adventures

KAYAKING | One of the best places for beginners to kayak is Kailua Beach, and this outfitter has an ideal location just across the street from it. The company offers two- and five-hour guided kayak tours (the longer tour includes lunch, time for kayaking, and time for the beach). More adventurous visitors can rent a kayak (double or single for a half or full day) and venture to the Mokulua Islands off Lanikai. Other rental options include snorkeling equipment, stand-up paddleboards, and bikes. Discounts are given if booked online. ⊠ *Kailua Beach Shopping Center, 130 Kailua Rd., Kailua* ☎ *808/262–2555* ⊕ *www.kailuasailboards.com* ⌑ *From $69 for rental, $179 for tours.*

Sun & Salt Adventures Hawaii

KAYAKING | The outfitter offers kayak rentals (single or double), lessons, and guided tours. Guides are trained in the history, geology, and birds of the area. Fully guided kayak excursions are either 2½ or 5 hours and include lunch, snorkeling gear, and transportation to and from Waikiki. ⊠ *134B Hamakua Dr., Kailua* ☎ *808/262–5656* ⊕ *www.twogoodkayaks.com* ⌑ *Rentals from $49, tours from $147.*

Scuba Diving

Not all of Hawaii's beauty is above water. What lurks below can be just as magnificent. Although snorkeling provides adequate access to this underwater world, nothing gives you the freedom—or depth, quite literally—as scuba.

The diving on Oahu is comparable with any you might do in the tropics, but its uniqueness comes from the isolated environment of the Islands. There are literally hundreds of species of fish and other marine life that you can find only in this chain. In fact, about 25% of Hawaii's marine life can be seen here only—nowhere else in the world. Adding to the singularity of diving off Oahu is the human history of the region. Military activities and tragedies of the 20th century filled the waters surrounding Oahu with wreckage that the ocean creatures have since turned into their homes.

Although instructors certified to license you in scuba are plentiful in the Islands, it's best to get your PADI certification before coming, as a week of classes may be a bit of a commitment on a short vacation. Expect to pay around $150 for a two-tank boat dive (provided that you are certified). ■ TIP→ **You can go on short, shallow introductory dives without the certification, but the best dives require it and cost a bit more.**

BEST SPOTS

Hanauma Bay Nature Preserve. On Oahu's southeast shore, about a 30-minute drive east of Waikiki, this preserve is home to more than 250 different species of fish, a quarter of which can be found nowhere else in the world. This has made this volcanic crater bay one of the state's most popular dive sites. It's a long walk from the parking lot to the beach—even longer lugging equipment—so consider hooking up with a licensed operator. Preservation efforts have aided the bay's delicate ecosystem, so expect to see

various butterfly fish, surgeonfish, tangs, parrot fish, and endangered Hawaiian sea turtles. ⊠ *7455 Kalanianaole Hwy., Hawaii Kai* ☎ *808/396–4229* 🖾 *$7.50 per person and $1 parking.*

Mahi Wreck. Hawaii's waters are littered with shipwrecks, but one of the most intact and accessible is this 165-foot minesweeper that was sunk in 1982 off the leeward coast. It lies upright in about 90 feet of calm, clear water, encrusted in coral and patrolled by white spotted eagle rays and millet seed butterfly fish. The wreck also serves as an artificial reef for such Hawaii aquatic residents as blue-striped snappers, puffer fish, lionfish, moray eels, and octopuses. Visibility averages about 100 feet, making this one of the most popular dives on the island. ⊠ *Waianae.*

Maunalua Bay. Stretching about 7 miles, from Portlock Point to Black Point, and teeming with marine life, this bay has several accessible dive sites of varying difficulty. The shallow-water Turtle Canyon is home to endangered Hawaiian green sea turtles. Fantasy Reef is another shallow dive, with three plateaus of volcanic rock lined with coral that is home to fish, eels, and sea turtles. In about 85 feet of water, *Baby Barge* is an easy-to-access sunken vessel encrusted in coral. An advanced dive, the wreck of a Vought F4U Corsair attracts garden eels and stingrays. ⊠ *Southeast Oahu.*

100 Foot Hole. Once an ancient Hawaiian fishing ground reserved for royalty, this cluster of volcanic boulders, which is accessible from shore, features ledges, caves, and a large open-ended cavern perfect for diving. The spot attracts octopuses, manta rays, and the occasional white-tip shark. ⊠ *Off Diamond Head, Honolulu.*

Shark's Cove. Oahu's best shore dive is accessible only during the summer months. Shark's Cove, on the North Shore, churns with monster surf during the winter, making this popular snorkeling and diving spot extremely dangerous. In summer, the cavernous lava tubes and tunnels are great for both novices and experienced divers. Some dive-tour companies offer round-trip transportation from Waikiki.✉ *Haleiwa*.

Three Tables. A short walk from Shark's Cove is Three Tables, named for a trio of flat rocks running perpendicular to shore. There are lava tubes to the right of these rocks that break the surface and extend out about 50 feet. Although this area isn't as active as Shark's Cove, you can still spot octopuses, moray eels, parrot fish, green sea turtles, and the occasional shark. ✉ *Haleiwa*.

EQUIPMENT, LESSONS, AND TOURS

Aaron's Dive Shop

SCUBA DIVING | This friendly and well-equipped dive shop caters to everyone. Take an "introductory" dive if you're not certified, get certified, or sign up for an offshore day or night dive excursion if you're experienced. In addition to organized group dives, the company's "dive concierge" can arrange private charters for those who want a completely customized experience. Snorkelers can go along on many dives as well. ✉ *307 Hahani St., Kailua* ☎ *808/262–2333* ⊕ *www.aaronsdiveshop.com* ✉ *From $140 for 2-tank dive.*

Surf N Sea

SCUBA DIVING | This is the North Shore headquarters for all things water-related, including diving. One interesting perk: upon request, the dive guides can shoot a video of your adventure. It's hard to see facial expressions under the water, but it still might be fun for those who want to prove that they took the plunge. Two-tank shore dives are the most economical choice (prices for noncertified divers are higher), but the company also offers boat dives, and in the summer, night dives are available for only slightly more. ✉ *62-595 Kamehameha Hwy., Haleiwa*

☎ *808/637–3483* ⊕ *www.surfnsea.com* ✉ *From $120 (2-tank shore dives).*

Snorkeling

If you can swim, you can snorkel. You don't need any formal training, and you can do it anywhere there's enough water to stick your face in. A mask, snorkel, and fins will run you about $35 at any corner ABC Store. At the other end of the price spectrum, luxurious snorkel cruises cost up to $175, including lunch and drinks.

Conditions at each snorkeling spot vary, depending on the weather and time of year, so consult with the purveyor of your gear for tips on where the best viewing is that day. Keep in mind that the North Shore should be attempted only when the waves are calm, namely in the summertime. Also, be sure to put plenty of sunscreen on your back (or better yet, wear a T-shirt): once you start gazing below, your head may not come back up for hours.

BEST SPOTS

Electric Beach. This haven for tropical fish is on the island's western side, directly across from an electricity plant—hence the name (aka Kahe Beach Park). The expulsion of hot water from the plant raises the temperature of the ocean, attracting Hawaiian green sea turtles, spotted moray eels, and spinner dolphins. Although visibility is not always the best, the crowds are small, and the fish are guaranteed. ✉ *Farrington Hwy., 1 mile west of Ko Olina Resort, Kapolei.*

Hanauma Bay Nature Preserve. What Waimea Bay is to surfing, Hanauma Bay in Southeast Oahu is to snorkeling. It's home to more than 250 different species of marine life. Due to the protection of the narrow mouth of the cove and the prodigious reef, you would be hard-pressed to find a place you would feel safer while snorkeling. ✉ *7455 Kalanianaole Hwy.,*

Did You Know?

Shark's Cove is a wonderful place for young snorkelers to spend time exploring the ocean's bottom in shallow waters, as the area is protected by a huge reef just offshore.

Honolulu ☎ 808/396–4229 *$7.50 per person and $1 parking.*

Queen's Surf Beach. On the edge of Waikiki, between the Kapahulu Groin and the Waikiki Aquarium, this marine reserve isn't as chock-full of fish as Hanauma Bay, but it has its share of colorful reef fish and the occasional Hawaiian green sea turtle. Just yards from shore, it's a great spot for an escape if you're stuck in Waikiki and have grown weary of watching the surfers. ✉ *Kalakaua Ave., Honolulu.*

Shark's Cove. Great shallows protected by a huge reef make Shark's Cove on the North Shore a prime spot for snorkelers, even young ones, in the summer. You'll find a plethora of critters, from crabs to octopuses, in water that's no more than waist deep. When the winter swells come, this area can turn treacherous. ✉ *Kamehameha Hwy., across from Foodland, Haleiwa.*

EQUIPMENT AND TOURS

★ Hanauma Bay Rental Stand

SNORKELING | FAMILY | You can rent masks, fins, and snorkels here. The stand also has lockers that are just large enough to stash your valuables. Bring ID or car keys as a deposit for rental. ✉ *Hanauma Bay Nature Preserve, 7455 Kalanianaole Hwy., Hawaii Kai* ☎ *808/396–3483* 🌐 *hanaumabaystatepark.com* *Rentals from $20, lockers from $10* ⏲ *Closed Mon. and Tues.*

Snorkel Bob's

SNORKELING | FAMILY | This place has all the stuff you'll need—and more—to make your water adventures more enjoyable. Bob makes his own gear and is active in protecting reef fish species. Feel free to ask the staff about good snorkeling spots, as the best ones can vary with weather and the seasons. You can either rent or buy gear (and reserve it in advance online). ✉ *700 Kapahulu Ave., Kapahulu* ☎ *808/735–7944* 🌐 *snorkelbob.com* *Rentals from $42 per wk.*

Spas

Excellent day and resort spas can be found throughout Oahu, primarily in the resorts of Waikiki but also downtown and on the North Shore. Individual treatments and day packages offer a wide choice of rejuvenating therapies, some of which are unique to the Islands. Try the popular *lomilomi* massage with kukui-nut oil (*lomi* meaning to rub, knead, and massage using palms, forearms, fingers, knuckles, elbows, knees, feet, even sticks). Add heated *pohaku* (stones) placed on the back to relieve sore muscles, or choose a facial using natural ingredients such as coconut, mango, papaya, ti leaf, Hawaiian honey, or ginger. Many full-service spas offer couples' private treatment rooms, fitness suites, yoga, and hydrotherapy pools.

HONOLULU

WAIKIKI

Mandara Spa at Hilton Hawaiian Village Beach Resort & Spa

SPAS | From its perch in the Kalia Tower, this outpost of the chain that originated in Bali overlooks the mountains, ocean, and downtown Honolulu. Hawaiian ingredients and traditional techniques are included in an array of services. Relieve achy muscles with a Thai poultice massage, perhaps with a reflexology or Balinese body polish add-on. This is one of the largest spas in Honolulu, with 25 treatment rooms, spa suites for couples, individual relaxation lounges with wet and dry saunas for men and women, Jacuzzis, traditional Japanese showers, a private infinity pool, fitness facilities, a salon, and a boutique. The delicately scented, candlelit foyer can fill up quickly with robe-clad conventioneers, so be sure to make a reservation. ✉ *Hilton Hawaiian Village Beach Resort & Spa, 2005 Kalia Rd., 3rd and 4th fl., Kalia Tower, Waikiki* ☎ *808/945–7721* 🌐 *www.mandaraspa.com.*

Na Hoola Spa at the Hyatt Regency Waikiki Resort & Spa

SPAS | The 16 rooms of Waikiki's premier resort spa are on two floors of the Hyatt on Kalakaua Avenue. Arrive early for your treatment to enjoy the serene, postcard-perfect beach views. You can choose from more than 15 different types of massages, including those for couples, and many of the treatments for body, face, and hair feature Hawaiian healing plants—noni, kukui, awa, and *kalo* (taro) . This spa also has various day packages that last three to six hours. The small exercise room, however, is for use by hotel guests only. ⊠ *Hyatt Regency Waikiki Resort & Spa, 2424 Kalakaua Ave., Waikiki* ☎ *808/923–1234, 808/237–6330 for reservations* ⊕ *www.hyatt.com/en-US/spas/Na-HoOla-Spa/home.*

SpaHalekulani

SPAS | Massages and body and facial therapies at this intimate, tranquil spa are influenced by the traditions of Pacific Island cultures. Try the Samoan Nonu, which uses warm stones and healing nonu gel to relieve muscle tension. The exclusive line of bath and body products is scented by maile, lavender orchid, or coconut passion. Facilities are specific to your treatment and may include a Japanese *furo* bath or a steam shower. ⊠ *Halekulani Hotel, 2199 Kalia Rd., Waikiki* ☎ *808/931–5322* ⊕ *www.halekulani.com/living/spahalekulani.*

ALA MOANA

Hoala Salon and Spa

SPAS | This Aveda concept spa has everything from Vichy showers to hydrotherapy rooms to customized aromatherapy. They'll even touch up your makeup for free before you leave. ⊠ *Ala Moana Shopping Center, 3rd fl., 1450 Ala Moana Blvd., Ala Moana* ☎ *808/947–6141* ⊕ *www.hoalasalonspa.com.*

THE NORTH SHORE

Nalu Spa at Turtle Bay

SPAS | Luxuriate at the ocean's edge in this lovely spa at Turtle Bay Resort.

Try one of the signature treatments, including a coconut-lava shell massage or a ginger-lime sugar scrub followed by a coconut-argan oil infusion. There are private spa suites, an outdoor treatment cabana that overlooks the surf, and a lounge area and juice bar. Spa guests may also join fitness classes for a fee. ⊠ *Turtle Bay Resort, 57-091 Kamehameha Hwy., Kahuku* ☎ *808/447–6868* ⊕ *www.turtlebayresort.com/wellness/spa.*

WEST (LEEWARD) OAHU

Laniwai — A Disney Spa

SPAS | At this spa, every staff member—or "cast member," as they call themselves—is extensively trained in Hawaiian culture and history to ensure they are projecting the right *mana*, or energy, in their work. To begin each treatment, you select a special *pohaku* (lava rock) with words of intent, then cast it into a reflective pool. Choose from about 150 spa therapies, and indulge in Kula Wai, the only outdoor hydrotherapy garden on Oahu—with private vitality pools, a reflexology path, six different "rain" showers, whirlpool jet spas, and more. ⊠ *Aulani, A Disney Resort & Spa, 92-1185 Aliinui Dr., Ko Olina* ☎ *808/674–6300* ⊕ *www.disneyaulani.com/spa-fitness/.*

Stand-Up Paddling

From the lakes of Wisconsin to the coast of Lima, Peru, stand-up paddleboarding (or SUP, for short) is taking the sport of surfing to the most unexpected places. Still, the sport remains firmly rooted in the Hawaiian Islands.

Back in the 1960s, Waikiki beachboys would paddle out on their longboards using a modified canoe paddle. It was longer than a traditional paddle, enabling them to stand up and stroke. It was easier this way to survey the ocean and snap photos of tourists learning how to surf. Eventually it became a sport unto itself, with professional contests at world-class surf breaks and long-distance races across treacherous waters.

Stand-up paddleboarding is easy to learn—though riding waves takes some practice—and most outfitters on Oahu offer lessons for all skill levels starting at about $55. It's also a great workout; you can burn off yesterday's dinner buffet, strengthen your core, and experience the natural beauty of the island's coastlines all at once. Once you're ready to head out on your own, half-day rentals start at $50.

If you're looking to learn, go where there's already a SUP presence. Avoid popular surf breaks, unless you're experienced, and be wary of ocean and wind conditions. You'll want to find a spot with calm waters, easy access in and out of the ocean, and a friendly crowd that doesn't mind the occasional stand-up paddleboarder.

BEST SPOTS

Ala Moana Beach Park. About a mile west of Waikiki, Ala Moana is the most SUP-friendly spot on the island. In fact, the state installed a series of buoys in the flat-water lagoon to separate stand-up paddlers and swimmers. There are no waves here, making it a great spot to learn, but beware of strong trade winds, which can push you into the reef.

Anahulu Stream. Outfitters on the North Shore like to take SUP beginners to Anahulu Stream, which empties into Waialua Bay near the Haleiwa Boat Harbor. This area is calm and protected from winds, plus there's parking at the harbor, and surf shops nearby rent boards.

Waikiki. Several south shore outfitters take beginners into the waters off Waikiki. Canoes, the surf break fronting the Duke Kahanamoku statue, and the channels between breaks are often suitable for people learning how to maneuver their boards in not-so-flat conditions. But south swells here can be menacing, and ocean conditions can change quickly.

Check with lifeguards before paddling out, and be mindful of surfers in the water.

White Plains Beach. If you've got a car with racks, you might want to venture to White Plains, a fairly uncrowded beach about 27 miles west of Waikiki. It's a long, sandy beach with lots of breaks and plenty of room for everyone. There are lifeguards, restrooms, and lots of parking, making this a great spot for beginners and those just getting comfortable in small waves.

EQUIPMENT AND LESSONS

Hawaiian Watersports
STAND UP PADDLEBOARDING | FAMILY | Paddle off the shore of picturesque Kailua Beach. This safety-conscious outfitter offers both equipment rentals and 90-minute and 3-hour group or individual lessons. The one-stop shop for water sports also offers kiteboarding, surfing, and windsurfing lessons as well as kayak tours and equipment rentals. Discounts are available online if you book ahead. ⌧ 171 Hamakua Dr., Kailua ☎ 808/262–5483 ⊕ hawaiianwatersports. com ⌦ Rentals from $59.

Rainbow Watersports Adventures
STAND UP PADDLEBOARDING | FAMILY | When you spot this company's colorful van at the bay near Haleiwa Beach Park, you'll know you're in the right place. You can get a two-hour private or group lesson on Oahu's North Shore. All lessons are held in a spot popular with the resident green sea turtles. The company also offers a 3½-hour coastal eco-adventure trip, including snorkeling and lunch. Its Twilight Glow Paddle lets you glide through calm waters illuminated by lights mounted to your board. ⌧ Haleiwa Beach Park, Kamehameha Hwy., Haleiwa ☎ 800/470–4964, 808/470-4332 ⊕ rainbowwatersports.com ⌦ Group lessons from $99; private lessons from $119.

This surfer is doing a stellar job of riding the infamous Banzai Pipeline on Oahu's North Shore.

Submarine Tours

Atlantis Submarines

BOATING | FAMILY | This is the underwater adventure for the unadventurous. Not fond of swimming, but want to see what you've been missing? Board this high-tech 64-passenger vessel for a ride past shipwrecks, turtle breeding grounds, and coral reefs. Little kids really seem to love it, though there's a 36-inch height minimum. The tours, which depart from the pier at the Hilton Hawaiian Village, are available in several languages, and discounts are available if booked online. ✉ *Hilton Hawaiian Village Beach Resort & Spa, 2005 Kalia Rd., Honolulu* ☎ *808/973–9800, 800/381–0237 for reservations* ⊕ *atlantisadventures.com* 🎫 *From $143.*

Surfing

Perhaps no word is more associated with Hawaii than surfing. Every year, the best of the best gather on Oahu's North Shore to compete in their version of the Super Bowl: the prestigious Vans Triple Crown of Surfing. The pros dominate the waves for a month, but the rest of the year belongs to folks just trying to have fun.

Oahu is unique because it has so many famous spots: Banzai Pipeline, Waimea Bay, Kaiser Bowls, and Sunset Beach. These spots, however, require experience. Waikiki is a great place for beginners to learn or for novice surfers to catch predictable waves. Group lessons on Waikiki Beach start at $50, but if you really want to fine-tune your skills, you can pay up to $500 for a daylong private outing with a former pro.

The island also has miles of coastline with surf spots that are perfect for everyday surfers. But remember this surfer's credo: when in doubt, don't go out. If you're unsure about conditions, stay on the beach, and talk to locals to get more info about surf breaks before trying yourself.

⚠ **To avoid a confrontation with local surfers, who can be very territorial about their favorite breaks, try some of the alternate spots listed below. They may not have the name recognition, but their waves can be just as great.**

BEST SPOTS

Makaha Beach Park. If you like to ride waves, try this west side beach. It has legendary, interminable rights that allow riders to perform all manner of stunts: from six-man canoes with everyone doing headstands to Bullyboards (oversize bodyboards) with whole families along for the ride. Mainly known as a longboarding spot, it's predominantly local but respectful to outsiders. Use caution in winter, as the surf can get huge. It's not called Makaha—which means "fierce"—for nothing. ⊠ *84-369 Farrington Hwy., Waianae.*

Sunset Beach Park. Impress your surfing buddies back home by catching a wave at the famous Sunset Beach on Oahu's North Shore. Two of the more manageable breaks are Kammie Land (or Kammie's) and Sunset Point. For the daring, Sunset is part of the Vans Triple Crown of Surfing for a reason. Thick waves and long rides await, but you'll need a thick board and a thicker skull. Surf etiquette here is a must, as it's mostly local. ⊠ *59-104 Kamehameha Hwy., 1 mile north of Ehukai Beach Park, Haleiwa.*

Ulukou Beach. In Waikiki you can paddle out to Populars—or Pops—a break at Ulukou Beach. Nice and easy, it never breaks too hard and is friendly to both newbies and veterans. It's one of the best places to surf during pumping south swells, as this thick wave breaks in open ocean, making it more rideable. The only downside is the long paddle out from Kuhio Beach, but that keeps the crowds manageable. ⊠ *Waikiki Beach, in front of Sheraton Waikiki hotel, Honolulu.*

White Plains Beach. Known among locals as "mini Waikiki," the surf at White Plains breaks in numerous spots, preventing the logjams that are inevitable at many of Oahu's more popular spots. It's a great break for novice to intermediate surfers, though you do have to watch for wayward boards. ⊠ *From the H1, take the Makakilo exit. Off H1, Kapolei.*

EQUIPMENT AND LESSONS

Aloha Beach Services

SURFING | FAMILY | It may sound like a cliché, but there's no better way to learn to surf than from the iconic beachboys in Waikiki, a Waikiki fixture since 1959. In fact, it's often where locals take their visitors who want to surf because it's really got it all. There's no one better than Harry "Didi" Robello, a second-generation beachboy and owner of Aloha Beach Services. Learn to surf in an hour-long group or semiprivate lesson or with just you and an instructor. You can also rent a board here. ⊠ *2365 Kalakaua Ave., on beach near Moana Surfrider, Waikiki* ☎ *808/922–3111 (ask for Aloha Beach Services)* ⊕ *www.alohabeachservices. com* 🖃 *Lessons from $100, board rentals from $20.*

Faith Surf School

SURFING | FAMILY | Professional surfer Tony Moniz started his own surf school in 2000, and since then, he and his wife, Tammy, have helped thousands of people catch their first waves in Waikiki. The Moniz family is iconic in Hawaii's surf culture, and their stories are as good as their lessons. The 90-minute group lessons include all equipment and are the cheapest option. You can pay more (sometimes a lot more) for semiprivate lessons with up to three people or for private lessons. You can also book an all-day surf tour with Moniz, riding waves with him at his favorite breaks. ✉ *Outrigger Waikiki Beach Resort, 2335 Kalakaua Ave., Waikiki* ☎ *808/931–6262* ⊕ *faithsurfschool.com* 🎫 *Lessons from $95, board rental from $20.*

Surf N Sea

SURFING | This is a one-stop shop for surfers (and other water-sports enthusiasts) on the North Shore. Rent a short or long board by the hour or for a full day. Two-hour group lessons are offered, as are four- to five-hour surf safaris for experienced surfers. ✉ *62-595 Kamehameha Hwy., Haleiwa* ☎ *800/899–7873* ⊕ *www.surfnsea.com* 🎫 *Lessons from $85, rentals from $35 per day.*

Whale-Watching

December is marked by the arrival of snow in much of North America, but in Hawaii it marks the return of the humpback whale. These migrating behemoths move south during the winter months for courtship and calving, and they put on quite a show. Watching males and females alike throwing themselves out of the ocean and into the sunset awes even the saltiest of sailors. Newborn calves riding gently next to their 2-ton mothers will stir you to your core. These gentle giants can be seen from the shore as they make a splash, but there's nothing like having a boat rock beneath you in the wake of a whale's breach.

Wild Side Specialty Tours

WILDLIFE-WATCHING | FAMILY | Boasting a marine-biologist/naturalist crew, this company takes you to undisturbed snorkeling areas. Along the way you may see dolphins and turtles. The company promises a sighting of migrating whales year-round on some itineraries. Tours may depart as early as 8 am from Waianae, so it's important to plan ahead. The three-hour deluxe wildlife tour is the most popular option. ✉ *Waianae Boat Harbor, 85-471 Farrington Hwy., Waianae* ☎ *808/306–7273* ⊕ *sailhawaii.com* 🎫 *From $205.*

Chapter 4

MAUI

Updated by Syndi Texeira and
Laurie Lyons-Makaimoku

◉ Sights	🍴 Restaurants	🛏 Hotels	🛍 Shopping	🍸 Nightlife
★★★★★	★★★☆☆	★★★☆☆	★★★☆☆	★★☆☆☆

WELCOME TO MAUI

TOP REASONS TO GO

★ **Beaches:** From black-sand beauties to palm-lined strands, each beach is unique.

★ **Resorts:** Opulent spas, pools, gardens, and golf courses deliver pampering aplenty.

★ **Hawaiian culture:** From hula to luau, you can experience Maui's diverse culture.

★ **Road to Hana:** This famed winding road offers stunning views of waterfalls and coast.

★ **Whale-watching:** Humpback whales congregate each winter right off Maui's shores.

★ **Water sports:** Surfing, snorkeling, and sailing are just a few top options.

1 West Maui. This sunny leeward area with excellent beaches is ringed by upscale resorts and condominiums as well as the busy, tourist-oriented town of Lahaina.

2 South Shore. The leeward side of Maui's eastern half is what most people mean when they say "South Shore."

3 Central Maui. Between Maui's two mountain areas is Central Maui, home to the county seat of Wailuku and the commercial center of Kahului along with Maui's airport.

4 Upcountry. Island residents have a name they use affectionately to describe the regions climbing up the slope of Haleakala Crater in Haleakala National Park: Upcountry.

5 North Shore. The North Shore has no large resorts, just plenty of picturesque, laid-back small towns like Paia and Haiku.

6 Road to Hana. The Island's windward northeastern side is largely one great rain forest, traversed by the stunning Road to Hana.

7 East Maui. Located between Hana and Upcountry, East Maui invites visitors to really get off the beaten path.

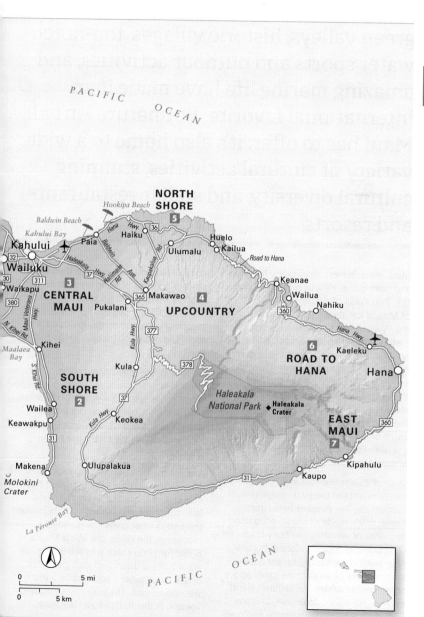

PACIFIC OCEAN

NORTH SHORE 5

Hookipa Beach

Baldwin Beach

Kahului Bay

Kahului

Wailuku

Waikapu

CENTRAL MAUI 3

Pukalani

Paia

Haiku

Ulumalu

Huelo

Kailua

Road to Hana

Keanae

Wailua

Nahiku

Makawao

UPCOUNTRY 4

Kihei

Maalaea Bay

SOUTH SHORE 2

Wailea

Keawakpu

Makena

Molokini Crater

La Pérouse Bay

Kula

Keokea

Ulupalakua

Haleakala National Park

Haleakala Crater

ROAD TO HANA 6

Kaeleku

Hana

EAST MAUI 7

Kaupo

Kipahulu

PACIFIC OCEAN

0   5 mi

0   5 km

Those who know Maui well understand why it's earned all its superlatives. The island's miles of perfect beaches, lush green valleys, historic villages, top-notch water sports and outdoor activities, and amazing marine life have made it an international favorite. But nature isn't all Maui has to offer: it's also home to a wide variety of cultural activities, stunning cultural diversity, and stellar restaurants and resorts.

Maui is much more than sandy beaches and palm trees; it's a land of water and fire. Puu Kukui, the 5,788-foot interior of Mauna Kahalawai, also known as the "West Maui Mountains," is one of Earth's wettest spots—an annual rainfall of 400 inches has sculpted the land into impassable gorges and razor-sharp ridges. On the opposite side of the island, the blistering lava fields at Ahihi-Kinau receive scant rain. Just above this desert-like landscape, *paniolo* (cowboys) herd cattle on rolling fertile ranchlands. On the island's rugged east side is the lush tropical Hawaii of travel posters.

In small towns like Paia and Hana you can see remnants of the past mingling with modern-day life. Ancient *heiau* (platforms, often made of stone, once used as places of worship) line busy roadways. Old coral-and-brick missionary homes now welcome visitors. The antique smokestacks of sugar mills tower above communities where the children blend English, Hawaiian, Japanese, Chinese, Portuguese, Filipino, and more into one colorful language. Hawaii is a melting pot like no other. Visiting an eclectic mom-and-pop shop—such as Makawao's T. Komoda Store & Bakery—can feel like stepping into another country or back in time. The more you look here, the more you find.

At 729 square miles, Maui is the second-largest Hawaiian Island, but it offers more miles of swimmable beaches than any of its neighbors. Despite rapid growth over the past few decades, the local population still totals less than 200,000.

Maui is made up of two volcanoes, one now extinct and the other dormant but that erupted long ago, joined into one island. The resulting depression between the two is what gives the island its nickname, the Valley Isle. West Maui's 5,788-foot Puu Kukui was the first volcano to form, a distinction that gives that area's mountainous topography a more weathered look. The Valley Isle's second volcano is the 10,023-foot Haleakala, where desertlike terrain abuts tropical forests.

Haleakala is one of few homes to the rare *ahinahina* (silversword plant). The plant's brilliant silver leaves are stunning against the red lava rock that blankets the walls of Haleakala's caldera—particularly during blooming season July–September. A distant cousin of the sunflower, the silversword blooms just once before it dies—producing a single towering stalk awash in tiny fragrant blossoms. Also calling Haleakala home are a few hundred nene, Hawaii's state bird (related to the Canada goose), currently fighting its way back from near extinction. Maui is the best Hawaiian island for whale-watching, and migrating humpbacks can be seen off the island's coast November–April, with peak season happening January–March.

Maui's history is full of firsts—Lahaina was the first capital of Hawaii and the first destination of the whaling industry (early 1800s), which explains why the town still has that seafaring vibe. Lahaina was also the first stop for missionaries on Maui (1823). Although they suppressed aspects of Hawaiian culture, the missionaries did help invent the Hawaiian alphabet and built a printing press—the first west of the Rockies—that rolled out the news in Hawaiian, as well as, not surprisingly, Hawaii's first Bibles. Maui also boasts the first sugar plantation in Hawaii (1849) and the first Hawaiian luxury resort (1946), now called the Travaasa Hana.

The Valley Isle's namesake, the demigod Maui, is a well-known Polynesian trickster. When his mother, Hina, complained of too few hours in the day to dry her *kapa* (traditional Hawaiian bark cloth, used for decoration and clothing), Maui promised to slow the sun. Hearing this, the god Moemoe teased Maui for boasting, but undeterred, the demigod wove a strong cord and lassoed the sun. Angry, the sun scorched the fields until an agreement was reached: During summer, the sun would travel more slowly. In winter, it would return to its quick pace. For ridiculing Maui, Moemoe was turned into a large rock that still juts from the water near Kahakuloa.

In the mid-1970s savvy marketers saw a way to improve Maui's economy by promoting the Valley Isle to golfers and luxury travelers. The strategy worked well; Maui's visitor count is about 2.6 million annually. Impatient traffic now threatens to overtake the ubiquitous aloha spirit, development encroaches on agricultural lands, and county planners struggle to meet the needs of a burgeoning population. But Maui is still carpeted with an eyeful of green, and for every tailgater there's a local on "Maui time" who stops for each pedestrian and sunset.

Planning

Getting Here and Around

AIR

Hawaii's major islands have their own airports, but Oahu's Daniel K. Inouye International Airport is the main stopover for most U.S. mainland and international flights. From Honolulu, daily flights to Maui leave from early morning until late evening. You can depart from the interisland or commuter terminals in two structures adjacent to the overseas terminal building. The Wiki Wiki Shuttle, a free bus service, can transport you between terminals. Flights from Honolulu into Lanai and Molokai are offered several times a day. In addition, several carriers offer nonstop service directly from the U.S. mainland to Maui.

Maui has two major airports. Kahului Airport handles major airlines and interisland flights; it's the only airport on Maui with direct service from the mainland. Kapalua–West Maui Airport is served by

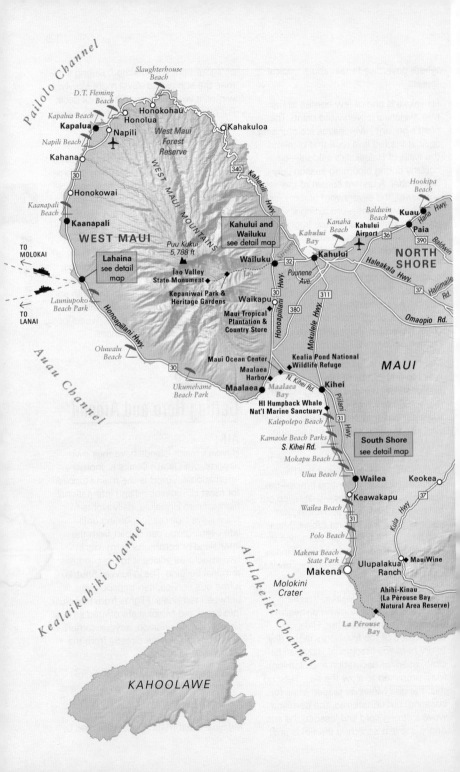

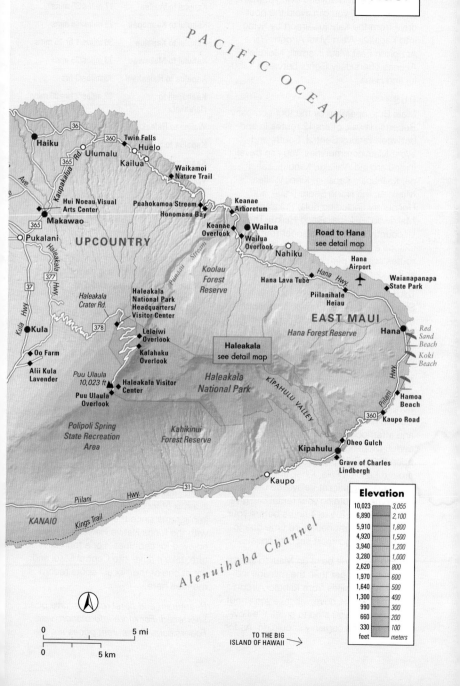

Maui

PACIFIC OCEAN

Haiku

36

360 Twin Falls
Huelo

Ulumalu

Kailua

Waikamoi
Nature Trail

365

Kaupakalua Rd.

Hui Noeau Visual
Arts Center

Puahokamoa Stream
Honomanu Bay

Keanae
Arboretum

Makawao

365

Keanae
Overlook

Wailua

Wailua
Overlook

Nahiku

Road to Hana
see detail map

Hana
Airport

Pukalini

UPCOUNTRY

Koolau
Forest
Reserve

Hana Lava Tube

Hana Hwy.

Waianapanapa
State Park

377

37

Piilanihale
Heiau

Kula Hwy.

Haleakala Hwy.

Haleakala
Crater Rd.

Haleakala
National Park
Headquarters/
Visitor Center

EAST MAUI

Hana Forest Reserve

Hana

Red
Sand
Beach

Kula

378

Leleiwi
Overlook

Haleakala
see detail map

Piilani Hwy.

Koki
Beach

Oo Farm

Kalahaku
Overlook

Haleakala
National Park

Alii Kula
Lavender

Puu Ulaula
10,023 ft

Puu Ulaula
Overlook

Haleakala Visitor
Center

Kahikinui
Forest Reserve

KIPAHULU VALLEY

Hamoa
Beach

360 Kaupo Road

Polipoli Spring
State Recreation
Area

Kipahulu

Oheo Gulch

Grave of Charles
Lindbergh

31

Kaupo

Piilani Hwy.

KANAIO

Kings Trail

Alenuihaha Channel

0   5 mi

0   5 km

TO THE BIG
ISLAND OF HAWAII →

Elevation

feet	meters
10,023	3,055
6,890	2,100
5,910	1,800
4,920	1,500
3,940	1,200
3,280	1,000
2,620	800
1,970	600
1,640	500
1,300	400
990	300
660	200
330	100

Hawaiian and Mokulele airlines. If you're staying in West Maui and flying in from another island, you can avoid the hour drive from the Kahului Airport by flying into Kapalua–West Maui Airport. Hana Airport in East Maui is small; Mokulele Airlines offers daily flights between Kahului and Hana.

BUS

Maui Bus, operated by the tour company Roberts Hawaii, offers 12 routes in and between various Central, South, and West Maui communities. You can travel in and around Wailuku, Kahului, Lahaina, Kaanapali, Kapalua, Kihei, Wailea, Maalaea, the North Shore (Paia), and Upcountry (including Kula, Pukalani, Makawao, Haliimaile, and Haiku). The Upcountry and Haiku Islander routes include a stop at Kahului Airport. All routes cost $2 per boarding; children five and under ride free.

CAR

Should you plan to do any sightseeing on Maui, it's best to rent a car. Even if all you want to do is relax at your resort, you may want to hop in the car to check out one of the Island's popular restaurants.

Many of Maui's roads are two lanes, so allow plenty of time to your next destination. Check the local traffic reports and Google Maps for delays. During morning and afternoon rush hours, traffic can be awful. Morning (6:30–9:30 am) and afternoon (3:30–6:30 pm) rush-hour traffic around Kahului, Paia, Kihei, and Lahaina can cause significant delays, so use caution. When returning your rental car, give yourself about 3½ to 4 hours before your transpacific flight departure time due to traffic and long airport security lines.

Driving from one point on Maui to another can take longer than the mileage indicates. It's 52 miles from Kahului Airport to Hana, but the drive will take you about three hours if you stop to smell the flowers, which you certainly should do. As for

Driving Times

Kahului to Wailea	17 miles/30 mins
Kahului to Kaanapali	25 miles/45 mins
Kahului to Kapalua	36 miles/1 hr 15 mins
Kahului to Makawao	13 miles/25 mins
Kapalua to Haleakala	73 miles/3 hrs
Kaanapali to Haleakala	62 miles/2 hrs 30 mins
Wailea to Haleakala	54 miles/2 hrs 30 mins
Kapalua to Hana	88 miles/5 hrs
Kaanapali to Hana	77 miles/5 hrs
Wailea to Hana	69 miles/4 hrs 30 mins
Wailea to Lahaina	20 miles/45 mins
Kapalua to Lahaina	12 miles/20 mins

driving to Haleakala, the 38-mile trip from sea level to the summit will take about two hours. The roads are narrow and winding; you must travel slowly. Kahului is the transportation hub—the main airport and largest harbor are here. Traffic on Maui's roads can be heavy, especially from 6 am–8:30 am and 3:30 pm–6:30 pm. Here are average driving times.

Restaurants

There's a lot going on for a place the size of Maui, from old-school holes-in-the-wall to fancy oceanfront fish houses. Much of it is excellent, but some of it is overpriced and touristy. Choose menu items made with products that are abundant on the island, including local fish. Local cuisine is a mix of foods brought by various immigrants since the late 1700s, blended with the foods Native Hawaiians have enjoyed for centuries. For a food adventure, take a drive into Central Maui and eat at one of the "local" spots recommended here.

Restaurant and hotel reviews have been shortened. For more information, visit Fodors.com. Restaurant prices are the

Where to Stay in Maui

Neighborhood	Local Vibe	Pros	Cons
West Maui	Popular and busy, West Maui includes the picturesque, touristy town of Lahaina and the upscale resort areas of Kaanapali and Kapalua.	A wide variety of shops, water sports, and historic sites provide plenty to do. To relax, there are great beaches and brilliant sunsets.	Traffic is usually congested; parking is hard to find; beaches can be crowded.
South Shore	The protected South Shore of Maui offers diverse experiences and accommodations, from comfortable condos to luxurious resorts—and golf, golf, golf.	Many beautiful beaches; sunny weather; great snorkeling.	Numerous strip malls; crowded with condos; there can be lots of traffic.
Upcountry	Country and chic come together in farms, ranches, and trendy towns on the cool, green slopes of Haleakala.	Cooler weather at higher elevations; panoramic views of nearby islands; distinctive shops, boutiques, galleries, and restaurants.	Fewer restaurants; no nightlife; can be very dark at night and difficult to drive for those unfamiliar with roads and conditions.
North Shore	A hub for surfing, windsurfing, and kiteboarding. When the surf's not up, the focus is on shopping: Paia is full of galleries, shops, and hip eateries.	Wind and waves are terrific for water sports; colorful small towns to explore without the intrusion of big resorts.	Weather inland may not be as sunny as other parts of the island, and coastal areas can be windy; little nightlife; most stores in Paia close early, around 6 pm.
Road to Hana and East Maui	Remote and rural, laid-back and tropical Hana and East Maui are special places to unwind.	Natural experience; rugged coastline and lush tropical scenery; lots of waterfalls.	Accessed by a long and winding road; no nightlife; wetter weather; few places to eat or shop.

average cost of a main course at dinner or, if dinner is not served, at lunch. Hotel prices are the lowest cost of a standard double room in high season or, for rentals, the lowest per-night cost for a one-bedroom unit in high season. Prices do not include 13.42% tax.

What It Costs in U.S. Dollars			
$	$$	$$$	$$$$
RESTAURANTS			
Under $18	$18–$26	$27–$35	Over $35
HOTELS			
Under $181	$181–$260	$261–$340	Over $340

Hotels

Maui is well known for its lovely resorts, some of them very luxurious; many cater to families. But there are other options, including abundant and convenient apartment and condo rentals for all budgets. The resorts and rentals cluster largely on Maui's sunny coasts, in West Maui and the South Shore. For a different, more local experience, you might spend part of your time at a small bed-and-breakfast. Check Internet sites and ask about discounts and packages.

Visitor Information

The Hawaii Visitors and Convention Bureau (HVCB) has a lot of general and vacation-planning information for Maui and all the Islands. HVCB also offers a free official vacation planner.

INFORMATION Maui Visitors Bureau. ⊠ *427 Ala Makani Street, Kahului* ⊕ *gohawaii.com/islands/maui.*

West Maui

Separated from the remainder of the Island by steep *pali* (cliffs), West Maui has a reputation for attitude and action. Once upon a time this was the haunt of whalers, missionaries, and the kings and queens of Hawaii.

Today the main drag, Front Street, is crowded with T-shirt and trinket shops, art galleries, and restaurants. Farther north is Kaanapali, Maui's first planned resort area. Its first hotel, the Sheraton, opened in 1963. Since then, massive resorts, luxury condos, and a shopping center have sprung up along the white-sand beaches, with championship golf courses across the road. A few miles farther up the coast is the ultimate in West Maui luxury, the resort area of Kapalua. In between, dozens of strip malls line both the *makai* (toward the sea) and *mauka* (toward the mountains) sides of the highway. There are gems here, too, like Napili Bay and its jaw-dropping crescent of sand.

In addition to Mele Mei musical events during May, Maui also plays host to some exciting culinary, cultural, and eco-driven festivals. Residents and visitors gather to partake in great food and drink, as well as family-friendly cultural festivities that usually span multiple days.

Lahaina

27 miles west of Kahului; 4 miles south of Kaanapali.

Lahaina is a bustling waterfront town packed with visitors from around the globe. Some may describe the area as tacky, with too many T-shirt vendors and not enough mom-and-pop shops, but this historic town houses some of Hawaii's best restaurants, boutiques, cafés, and galleries.

■ TIP→ **If you spend Friday afternoon exploring Front Street, hang around for Friday Night Is Art Night, when the galleries stay open late and offer entertainment, including artists demonstrating their work.**

Sunset cruises and other excursions depart from Lahaina Harbor. At the southern end of town is an important archaeological site known as Mokuula, which was once a spiritual and political center, as well as home to Maui's chiefs.

The town has been welcoming visitors for more than 200 years. In 1798, after waging war to unite the Hawaiian Islands, Kamehameha the Great chose Lahaina, then called *Lele,* as the seat of his monarchy. Warriors from Kamehameha's 800 canoes, stretched along the coast from Olowalu to Honokowai, turned inland and filled the lush valleys with networks of stream-fed *loi kalo,* or taro patches. For nearly 50 years Lahaina remained the capital of the Hawaiian Kingdom. During this period, the scent of Hawaiian sandalwood brought those who traded with China to these waters. Whaling ships followed, chasing sperm whales from Japan to the Arctic. Lahaina became known around the world for its rough-and-tumble ways.

Then, almost as quickly as it had come, the tide of foreign trade receded. The Hawaiian capital was moved to Honolulu in 1845, and by 1860 the sandalwood forests were empty and sperm whales nearly extinct. Luckily, Lahaina had already grown into an international, sophisticated (if sometimes rowdy) town, laying claim to the first printing press and high school west of the Rockies. Sugar interests kept the town afloat until tourism stepped in.

GETTING HERE AND AROUND

It's about a 45-minute drive from Kahului Airport to Lahaina (take Route 380 to Route 30), depending on the traffic on this heavily traveled route. Traffic can be slow around Lahaina, especially from 4

Walking Tours

Lahaina's side streets are best explored on foot. Both the Baldwin Home Museum and the Lahaina Visitor Center offer self-guided walking-tour brochures with a map for $2 each. The historic trail map is easy to follow; it details three short but enjoyable loops of the town.

4

Maui WEST MAUI

to 6 pm. Shuttles and taxis are available from Kahului Airport. The Maui Bus Lahaina Islander route runs from Queen Kaahumanu Center in Kahului to the Wharf Cinema Center on Front Street, Lahaina's main thoroughfare.

◉ Sights

Baldwin Home Museum

HISTORIC HOME | If you want some insight into 19th-century life in Hawaii, this informative museum is an excellent place to start. Begun in 1834 and completed the following year, the coral-and-stone house was originally home to missionary Dr. Dwight Baldwin and his family. The building has been carefully restored to reflect the period, and many of the original furnishings remain: you can view the family's grand piano, carved four-poster bed, and most interestingly, Dr. Baldwin's dispensary. Also on display is the "thunderpot"—learn how the doctor single-handedly inoculated 10,000 Maui residents against smallpox. ■ TIP→ **Self-guided tours run Tues.–Sun. from 10 am–4 pm, or come Friday at dusk for a special candlelight tour every half hour from 5–8 pm.** ⊠ *120 Dickenson St., Lahaina* ☎ *808/661–3262* ⊕ *lahainarestoration. org* ⊠ *$7* ⊗ *Closed Mon.*

★ Banyan Tree

CITY PARK | Planted in 1873, this massive tree is the largest of its kind in the United States and provides a welcome retreat and playground for visitors and locals,

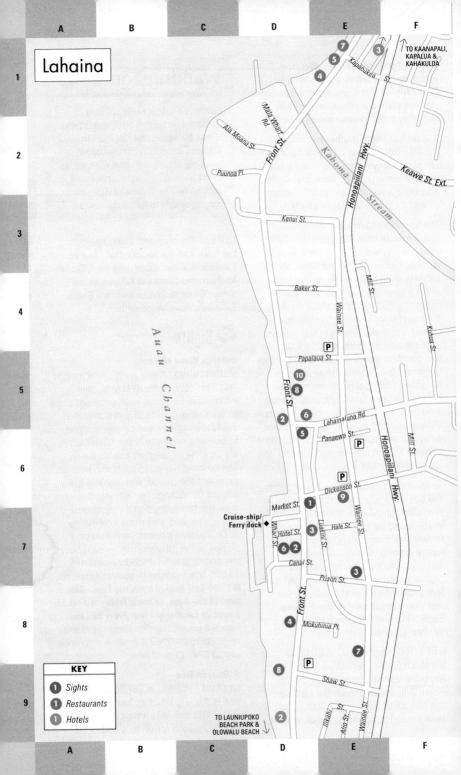

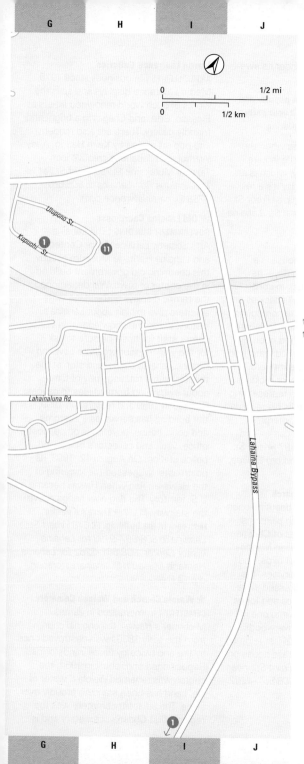

who rest and play music under its awesome branches.

■ TIP→ **The Banyan Tree is a popular and hard-to-miss meeting place if your party splits up for independent exploring.**

It's also a terrific place to be when the sun sets—mynah birds settle in here for a screeching symphony, which is an event in itself. During the day it's a respite for a variety of chickens. ⊠ *Front St. between Hotel St. and Canal St., Lahaina* ⊕ *lahainarestoration.org.*

Hale Paahao (Old Prison)

JAIL/PRISON | Lahaina's jailhouse is a reminder of rowdy whaling days. Its name literally means "stuck-in-irons house," referring to the wall shackles and ball-and-chain restraints. The compound was built in the 1850s by convict laborers out of blocks of coral that had been salvaged from the demolished waterfront fort. Most prisoners were sent here for desertion, drunkenness, or reckless horse riding. Today, a figure representing an imprisoned old sailor tells his recorded tale of woe. There are also interpretive signs for the botanical garden and whale boat in the yard. ⊠ *187 Prison St., Lahaina* ⊕ *lahainarestoration.org* ⊡ *Free, donation suggested.*

Holy Innocents Episcopal Church

CHURCH | Built in 1927, this beautiful open-air church is decorated with paintings depicting Hawaiian versions of Christian symbols (including a Hawaiian Madonna and child), rare or extinct birds, and native plants. At Sunday services, the congregation is typically dressed in traditional clothing from Samoa and Tonga. Anyone is welcome to slip into one of the pews, carved from native woods. Queen Liliuokalani, Hawaii's last reigning monarch, lived in a large grass house on this site as a child. ⊠ *561 Front St., near Mokuhina St., Lahaina* ⊞ *808/661–4202* ⊕ *holyimaui.org* ⊡ *Free.*

Martin Lawrence Galleries

ART GALLERIES | In business since 1975, Martin Lawrence displays and sells the works of such world-renowned artists as Picasso, Erté, and Chagall in a bright and friendly gallery. There are also modern and pop art pieces by Keith Haring, Andy Warhol, and Japanese creative icon Takashi Murakami. ⊠ *790 Front St., at Lahainaluna Rd., Lahaina* ⊞ *808/661–1788* ⊕ *martinlawrence.com.*

★ Old Lahaina Courthouse

GOVERNMENT BUILDING | The Lahaina Arts Society, Lahaina Visitor Center, and Lahaina Heritage Museum occupy this charming old government building in the center of town. Wander among the terrific displays and engage with an interactive exhibit about Lahaina's history, pump the knowledgeable visitor center staff for tips—be sure to ask for the walking-tour brochure covering historic Lahaina sites—and stop at the theater with a rotating array of films about everything from whales to canoes. Erected in 1859 and restored in 1999, the building has served as a customs and court house, governor's office, post office, vault and collector's office, and police station. On August 12, 1898, its postmaster witnessed the lowering of the Hawaiian flag when Hawaii became a U.S. territory. The flag now hangs above the stairway. ■ TIP→ **There's a public restroom in the building.** ⊠ *648 Wharf St., Lahaina* ⊞ *808/667–9193 for Lahaina Visitor Center, 808/661–3262 for Lahaina Heritage Museum* ⊕ *lahainarestoration. org* ⊡ *Free.*

★ Waiola Church and Wainee Cemetery

CEMETERY | Immortalized in James Michener's *Hawaii*, the original church from the early 1800s was destroyed once by fire and twice by fierce windstorms. Repositioned and rebuilt in 1954, the church was renamed Waiola ("water of life") and has been standing proudly ever since. The adjacent cemetery was the region's first Christian cemetery and is

Once a whaling center, Lahaina Harbor bustles with tour boats, fishing vessels, and pleasure craft.

the final resting place of many of Hawaii's most important monarchs, including Kamehameha the Great's wife, Queen Keopuolani, who was baptized during her final illness. ✉ *535 Wainee St., Lahaina* ☎ *808/661–4349* ⊕ *waiolachurch.org* 🎫 *Free.*

★ Wo Hing Museum

HISTORY MUSEUM | Smack-dab in the center of Front Street, this eye-catching Chinese temple reflects the importance of early Chinese immigrants to Lahaina. Built by the Wo Hing Society in 1912, the museum contains beautiful artifacts, historic photo displays of Dr. Sun Yat-sen, and a Taoist altar. Don't miss the films playing in the rustic cookhouse next door—some of Thomas Edison's first films, shot in Hawaii circa 1898, show Hawaiian wranglers herding steer onto ships. Ask the docent for some star fruit from the tree outside, for an offering or for yourself. ■ **TIP→ If you're in town in late January or early February, this museum hosts a nice Chinese New Year festival.**

✉ *858 Front St., Lahaina* ☎ *808/661–5553* ⊕ *lahainarestoration.org* 🎫 *$7.*

 Beaches

Launiupoko Beach Park

BEACH | FAMILY | This is the beach park of all beach parks: both a surf break and a beach, it offers a little something for everyone with its inviting stretch of lawn, soft white sand, and gentle waves. The shoreline reef creates a protected wading pool, perfect for small children. Outside the reef, beginner surfers will find good longboard rides. From the long sliver of beach, you can enjoy superb views of neighboring islands, and, landside, of deep valleys cutting through West Maui's mountain. Because of its endless sunshine and serenity—not to mention such amenities as picnic tables and grills—Launiupoko draws a crowd on the weekends, but there's space for everyone (and overflow parking across the street). **Amenities:** parking (no fee); showers; toilets. **Best for:** partiers; sunset; surfing; swimming. ✉ *Rte. 30,*

Lahaina ✣ At mile marker 18 🌐 maui-county.gov.

Olowalu

BEACH | More an offshore snorkel and stand-up paddling spot than a beach, Olowalu is also a great place to watch for turtles and whales in season. The beach is literally a pullover from the road, which can make for some unwelcome noise if you're looking for quiet. The entrance can be rocky (reef shoes help), but if you've got your snorkel gear it's a 200-yard swim to an extensive and diverse reef. Shoreline visibility can vary depending on the swell and time of day; late morning is best. Except for during a south swell, the waters are usually calm. You can find this rocky surf break a half mile north of mile marker 14. Snorkeling here is along pathways that wind among coral heads. Note: this is a local hangout and can be unfriendly at times. **Amenities:** none. **Best for:** snorkeling. ✉ *Rte. 30, Olowalu ✣ Look for mile marker 14, south of Olowalu General Store.*

🍴 Restaurants

Alchemy Maui

$$ | **ECLECTIC** | This cute, casual café by Valley Isle Kombucha is part kombucha tasting room, part eatery. Try one of the many kombucha flavors on tap, which is crafted in small batches using local ingredients, and comes in flavors like guava pineapple and Kula strawberry. **Known for:** fresh and local ingredients; vegetarian and vegan options; friendly staff. [$] *Average main: $19* ✉ *157 Kupuohi St., Lahaina* ☎ *808/793–2115* 🌐 *alchemymauibistro.com* ⏲ *Closed Sat. and Sun.*

Cheeseburger in Paradise

$$ | **BURGER** | A chain joint on Front Street, this place is known for—what else?—big beefy cheeseburgers, not to mention a great turkey burger, as well as healthier options such as smoothies and hearty salads. The second-floor balcony gives you a bird's-eye view of Lahaina's Front Street action. **Known for:** Island Style Burger with avocado, pineapple, and teriyaki glaze; great cocktails and local beers; generous portions. [$] *Average main: $18* ✉ *811 Front St., Lahaina* ☎ *808/661–4855* 🌐 *cheeseburgernation.com.*

★ Down the Hatch

$$ | **AMERICAN** | **FAMILY** | Located steps from Lahaina Harbor, this casual restaurant serves top-notch seafood with Southern flair. The shrimp po'boy, seared *ahi* (yellowfin tuna) tacos, and fish-and-chips are perennial favorites. **Known for:** daily happy hour from 2 to 5 pm; fun and lively atmosphere; expansive seafood menu. [$] *Average main: $21* ✉ *Wharf Cinema Center, 658 Front St., Lahaina* ☎ *808/661–4900* 🌐 *dthmaui.com.*

Frida's Mexican Beach House

$$$ | **MEXICAN FUSION** | No matter the cuisine, serial restaurateur Mark Ellman always delivers, as he does yet again with this oceanfront eatery along Front Street. The setting is reason enough to dine here, but the food—specializing in Latin-inspired dishes—attracts diners all on its own and 40 varieties of tequila dominate the bar. **Known for:** live music on Mon. and Tues. evenings; plenty of tasty vegetarian options; grilled Spanish octopus. [$] *Average main: $32* ✉ *1287 Front St., Lahaina* ☎ *808/661-1287* 🌐 *fridasmaui.com* ⏲ *Closed Sun.*

Honu Seafood & Pizza

$$$$ | **ECLECTIC** | This oceanfront fish house and pizza restaurant began as a way to showcase the work of celebrity chef Mark Ellman before recently changing ownership. Guests can expect a lot of their favorite dishes to remain on the menu, with some fun food and cocktail additions to come. **Known for:** fantastic selection of craft beers and cocktails; gluten-free options; unparalleled ocean views with sea turtle sightings. [$] *Average main: $36* ✉ *1295 Front St., Lahaina* ☎ *808/667–9390* 🌐 *honumaui.com* ⏲ *Closed Sun.*

Maui's Food Trucks: Movable Feasts 🍴

As in so many other places, food-truck culture has taken hold on Maui, but don't expect to find well-equipped, customized trucks like the ones you see on the Food Network. Most have no websites, Instagram accounts, or Facebook pages; some don't even have phones. Many have irregular days and hours of operation.

A group of trucks has formed a food court across from the Costco parking lot, just minutes from Kahului Airport. In Kihei, look for the food truck park behind the Azeka Mauka Center. Honokowai has developed a park of its own, which is located along Lower Honoapiilani Highway.

Lahaina Grill

$$$$ | **AMERICAN** | At the top of many "best restaurants" lists, this expensive upscale bistro is about as fashionably chic as it gets on Maui, and the interior is as pretty as the patrons. Wagyu beef ravioli, bufala salad with locally grown tomatoes, and Kona-coffee–roasted rack of lamb are a few of the classics customers demand; the full menu—including dessert—is available at the bar. **Known for:** downtown location; extensive dessert menu; romantic ambience. [$] *Average main: $60* ✉ *127 Lahainaluna Rd., Lahaina* ☎ *808/667–5117* 🌐 *lahainagrill.com* 🕒 *No lunch.*

★ Mala Ocean Tavern

$$$$ | **MODERN HAWAIIAN** | The menu at this oceanfront standout features interesting local-style Hawaiian food fusions. There's a focus on ingredients that promote local sustainability, and the cocktails and wine list are great, too. **Known for:** seafood brodo; friendly and attentive staff; seared ahi (yellowfin tuna) bruschetta. [$] *Average main: $38* ✉ *1307 Front St., Lahaina* ☎ *808/667–9394* 🌐 *malaoceantavern.com.*

PacificO

$$$$ | **MODERN HAWAIIAN** | Sophisticated outdoor dining on the beach (yes, truly *on* the beach) and creative Island cuisine using local, fresh-caught fish and greens and veggies grown in the restaurant's own Upcountry O'o Farm (and, quite possibly, picked that very morning)—this is the Maui dining experience you've been dreaming about. Start with a variety of fresh vegetable dishes on the appetizer menu, move on to any of the fantastic fresh fish dishes, and for dessert, finish with the banana bread ice cream sandwich. **Known for:** Hamakua mushroom risotto; exceptional wine list; lemongrass curry with tiger prawns. [$] *Average main: $45* ✉ *505 Front St., Lahaina* ☎ *808/667–4341* 🌐 *pacificomaui.com* 🕒 *Closed Sun. and Mon.*

Penne Pasta Cafe

$ | **ITALIAN** | A couple of blocks off Front Street in Lahaina, this small restaurant packs a powerhouse of a menu with reasonably priced pizzas, pastas, salads, and sandwiches. The name can be found on the menu in four dishes; two can easily split a salad and entrée and leave completely sated. **Known for:** fast and friendly service; fantastic desserts; gluten-free and vegan options. [$] *Average main: $12* ✉ *180 Dickenson St., Lahaina* ☎ *808/661–6633* 🌐 *pennepastacafe.net.*

Sale Pepe

$$ | **ITALIAN** | Aromas from a wood-fired oven lure you into this cozy Italian restaurant set just off of Front Street, and the wine list tempts you to stay awhile. Quality is paramount here—many of the ingredients are imported directly from

Italy, while farm-fresh produce and meats come from Maui. **Known for:** salumi and house-made focaccia; brick-oven pizzas; packaged handmade pasta and sauces to-go. $ Average main: $24 ✉ 878 Front St., Units 7 and 8, Lahaina ☎ 808/667-7667 ⊕ salepepemaui.com ⊘ Closed Sun.

★ Star Noodle

$ | ASIAN | This local favorite, one of Maui's most popular restaurants, recently moved to an oceanside locale. The expanse of the Pacific sets the scene for an eclectic Asian menu with must-try items like the *ahi* (yellowfin tuna) avo, tempura shrimp, and noodle dishes like the Lahaina fried soup that's served with fat chow fun, pork, and bean sprouts. **Known for:** shared, small-plate dining; house-made noodles; steamed pork buns. $ Average main: $16 ✉ 1285 Front St., Lahaina ☎ 808/667-5400 ⊕ starnoodle.com.

 ## Hotels

Lahaina doesn't have a huge range of accommodations, but it does make a great headquarters for active families or those who want to avoid spending a bundle on resorts. One major advantage is the proximity of restaurants, shops, and activities—everything is within walking distance. It's a business district, however, and won't provide the same peace and quiet as resorts or secluded vacation rentals. Still, Lahaina has a nostalgic charm, especially early in the morning before the streets have filled with visitors and vendors.

★ Hooilo House

$$$$ | B&B/INN | A luxurious intimate getaway without resort facilities, this stunning, 2-acre B&B in the foothills of West Maui's mountain, just south of Lahaina town, exemplifies quiet perfection. **Pros:** friendly, on-site hosts; beautiful furnishings; gazebo for special events. **Cons:** three-night minimum; far

from shops and restaurants; not good for families with younger children. $ Rooms from: $499 ✉ 138 Awaiku St., Lahaina ☎ 808/667-6669 ⊕ hooilohouse.com ⤳ 6 rooms ⦿ Free Breakfast.

Lahaina Shores Beach Resort

$$ | APARTMENT | You really can't get any closer to the beach than this seven-story rental property that offers panoramic ocean and mountain views, and fully equipped kitchens. **Pros:** right on the beach; historical sites, attractions, and activities are a short walk away; free parking, no additional costs and no resort fee. **Cons:** no posh, resort-type amenities; no restaurant on-site; older property. $ Rooms from: $250 ✉ 475 Front St., Lahaina ☎ 866/934-9176 ⊕ lahainashores.com ⤳ 199 rooms ⦿ No Meals.

Maui Garden Oasis

$$ | B&B/INN | In an older neighborhood just outside of busy Lahaina town lies a quiet place that welcomes you with light and clean rooms featuring pleasant island furnishings and private entrances. **Pros:** free use of chairs, coolers, boogie boards, and other beach toys; knowledgeable hosts; maid service. **Cons:** one-time $40 cleaning fee; no stores within safe, easy walking distance; not secluded. $ Rooms from: $199 ✉ 67 Kaniau Rd., Lahaina ☎ 808/661-8800 ⊕ mauigardenoasis.com ⤳ 6 rooms ⦿ No Meals.

 ## Nightlife

Cool Cat Café

LIVE MUSIC | You could easily miss this casual 1950s-style diner while strolling through Lahaina. Tucked in the second floor of the Wharf Cinema Center, its semi-outdoor area plays host to rockin' local music Thursday through Sunday nights. The entertainment lineup covers reggae, light rock, contemporary Hawaiian, and traditional island rhythms. It doesn't hurt that the kitchen dishes out specialty burgers, fish that's fresh from the harbor, and delicious house-made sauces from the owner's family recipes. ✉ *658 Front St., Lahaina* ☎ *808/667–0908* ⊕ *coolcatcafe.com.*

★ Slack Key Show: Masters of Hawaiian Music

LIVE MUSIC | Grammy-winning musician George Kahumoku Jr. hosts this program on Wednesday, as well as some Saturdays, which features a rotating lineup of the Island's finest slack-key artists as well as other traditional forms of Hawaiian music. The setup at Aloha Pavilion is humble, but you'll enjoy these beloved musicians in an intimate setting. ✉ *Napili Kai Beach Resort, 5900 Lower Honoapiilani Rd., Lahaina* ☎ *808/249–2125* ⊕ *slackkeyshow.com.*

 Performing Arts

★ Feast at Lele

THEMED ENTERTAINMENT | This place redefines the luau by crossing it with Islands-style fine dining in an intimate beach setting. Each course of this succulent sit-down meal represents the Pacific Island cultures—Hawaiian, Samoan, Maori, Tahitian—featured onstage. Wine, spirits, and cocktail options are copious and go beyond the usual tropical concoctions. Lahaina's gorgeous sunset serves as the backdrop to the show, which forgoes gimmicks and pageantry for an authentic expression of Polynesian chants and dances. Lele, by the way, is the traditional name for Lahaina. ✉ *505 Front St., Lahaina* ☎ *808/667–5353* ⊕ *feastatlele.com.*

★ Old Lahaina Luau

THEMED ENTERTAINMENT | FAMILY | Considered the best luau on Maui, it's certainly the most traditional. Sitting either at a table or on a *lauhala* (mat made of leaves), you can dine on Hawaiian cuisine such as pork *laulau* (wrapped with taro sprouts in ti leaves), *ahi* poke (raw yellowfin tuna salad), *lomi lomi* salmon (traditional Hawaiian diced side dish), and

Maui Midnight

If you want to see any action on Maui, head out early. Otherwise, you might be out past what locals call "Maui Midnight," where as early as 9 pm the restaurants close and the streets empty. What can you expect, though, when most people wake up with the sun? After a long salty day of sea and surf, you might be ready for some shut-eye yourself.

haupia (coconut pudding). At sunset, the historical journey touches on the arrival of the Polynesians, the influence of missionaries and, later, the advent of tourism. Talented performers will charm you with beautiful music, powerful chanting, and a variety of hula styles, from *kahiko*, the ancient way of communicating with the gods, to *auana*, the modern hula. You won't see fire dancers here, as they aren't considered traditional. ■ TIP→ **This luau sells out regularly, so make reservations before your trip to Maui.** ✉ *1251 Front St., near Lahaina Cannery Mall, Lahaina* ☎ *808/667–1998* ⊕ *oldlahainaluau.com.*

Kaanapali

4 miles north of Lahaina.

As you drive north from Lahaina, the first resort community you reach is Kaanapali, a cluster of high-rise hotels framing a world-class white-sand beach. This is part of West Maui's famous resort strip and is a perfect destination for families and romance seekers wanting to be in the center of the action.

The theatrical look of Hawaii tourism—planned resort communities where luxury homes mix with high-rise hotels, fantasy swimming pools, and a theme-park landscape—began right here in the 1960s, when clever marketers built this sunny shoreline into a playground for the world's vacationers. Three miles of uninterrupted white-sand beach and placid water form the front yard of this artificial utopia, with its many tennis courts and two championship golf courses.

In ancient times, the area near Sheraton Maui was known for its bountiful fishing (especially lobster) and its seaside cliffs. The sleepy fishing village was washed away by the wave of Hawaii's new economy: tourism. Puu Kekaa (today incorrectly referred to as Black Rock) was a *leina a ka uhane*, a place in ancient Hawaii believed to be where souls leaped into the afterlife.

A little farther up the road lie the condo-filled beach towns of Honokowai and Napili, followed by Kapalua. Each boasts its own style and flavor, though most rely on a low-key beach vibe for people wanting upscale vacation rentals.

GETTING HERE AND AROUND
Shuttles and taxis are available from Kahului and Kapalua (West Maui) airports. Resorts offer free shuttles between properties, and some hotels also provide complimentary shuttles into Lahaina. In the Maui Bus system, the West Maui Islander begins and ends at Wharf Cinema Center in Lahaina and stops at most condos along the coastal road as far north as Napili Bay.

 Beaches

★ Kaanapali Beach
BEACH | If you're looking for quiet and seclusion, this is not the beach for you. But if you want lots of action, spread out your towel here. Stretching from the northernmost end of the Sheraton Maui Resort & Spa to the Hyatt Regency Maui Resort & Spa at its southern tip, Kaanapali Beach is lined with resorts, condominiums, restaurants, and shops. Ocean activity companies launch from the shoreline fronting Whalers Village, making it one of Maui's best people-watching spots. A concrete pathway

weaves along the length of this 3-mile-long beach, leading from one astounding resort to the next.

The drop-off from Kaanapali's soft sugary sand is steep, but waves hit the shore with barely a rippling slap outside of winter months. The landmark promontory known as Puu Kekaa (nicknamed "Black Rock") was traditionally considered a *leina a ka uhane*, or jumping-off place for spirits. It's easy to get into the water from the beach to enjoy the prime snorkeling among the lava-rock outcroppings.

■ TIP→ **Strong rip currents are often present near Puu Kekaa; always snorkel with a companion.**

Throughout the resort, blue "Shoreline Access" signs point the way to a few free-parking stalls and public rights-of-way to the beach. Kaanapali Resort public beach parking can be found between the Hyatt and the Marriott, between the Marriott and the Kaanapali Alii, next to Whalers Village, and at the Sheraton. You can park for a fee at most of the large hotels and at Whalers Village. The merchants in the shopping village will validate your parking ticket if you make a purchase. **Amenities:** parking (no fee); showers; toilets. **Best for:** snorkeling; sunset; swimming; walking. ⊠ *Honoapiilani Hwy., Kaanapali* ✥ *Follow any of the 3 Kaanapali exits.*

★ Napili Beach
BEACH | FAMILY | Surrounded by sleepy condos, this round bay is a turtle-filled pool lined with a sparkling white crescent of sand. Sunbathers love this beach, which is also a terrific sunset spot. The shore break is steep but gentle, so it's great for bodyboarding and bodysurfing. It's easy to keep an eye on kids here as the entire bay is visible from everywhere. The beach is right outside the Napili Kai Beach Resort, a popular local-style resort for honeymooners and families, only a few miles south of Kapalua. **Amenities:** showers; toilets. **Best for:** sunset; surfing;

swimming; snorkeling. ⊠ *5900 Lower Honoapiilani Hwy., Napili* ⊕ *Look for Napili Pl. or Hui Dr.*

🍴 Restaurants

CJ's Deli & Diner

$ | **AMERICAN** | Chef Christian Jorgensen left fancy hotel kitchens behind to open a casual place serving simple, delicious food—mango-glazed ribs, burgers, and classic Reuben sandwich—at reasonable prices including a vegan menu and kombucha on tap. If you're staying in a condo, the Chefs to Go service is a great alternative to picking up fast food (run-of-the-mill and usually lousy) as everything is prepped and comes with easy cooking instructions. **Known for:** filling, affordable food; mochiko chicken plate (a traditional Hawaiian fried chicken dish); casual atmosphere with Wi-Fi. $ *Average main: $12* ⊠ *Fairway Shops, 2580 Kekaa Dr., Kaanapali* ☎ *808/667–0968* ⊕ *www.cjsmaui.com.*

Hula Grill

$$$ | **MODERN HAWAIIAN** | **FAMILY** | A bustling, family-oriented spot on Kaanapali Beach, this restaurant designed to look like a sprawling '30s beach house serves large dinner portions with an emphasis on fresh local fish. But if you're just in the mood for an umbrella-adorned cocktail and some tasty, more casual fare, head to the popular Barefoot Bar, where you can wiggle your toes in the sand. **Known for:** macadamia nut-crusted fresh catch; location along Kaanapali boardwalk; classic cocktails and lively bar scene. $ *Average main: $29* ⊠ *Whalers Village shopping center, 2435 Kaanapali Pkwy., Kaanapali* ☎ *808/667–6636* ⊕ *www.hulagrillkaanapali.com.*

★ Japengo

$$$$ | **ASIAN** | Located inside the Hyatt Regency, this spot sits atop a man-made pool grotto and offers stunning ocean views and a gorgeous glassed-in sushi bar. The views aside, it's the food that makes Japengo worth a visit; the fresh local fish is well prepared—as are the sushi and hand rolls—and the desserts are amazing. **Known for:** outstanding chef's specials; nice sake menu with flight options; live Hawaiian and acoustic entertainment. $ *Average main: $42* ⊠ *Hyatt Regency Maui Resort & Spa, 200 Nohea Kai Dr., Kaanapali* ☎ *808/667–4909* ⊕ *hyatt.com/en-US/hotel/hawaii/hyatt-regency-maui-resort-and-spa/oggrm/dining* ⊙ *No lunch.*

Pulehu, an Italian Grill

$$$$ | **ITALIAN** | This restaurant proves that good food doesn't need to be complicated, using many local Maui products to do what the Italians do best: craft simple, delicious food that lets the ingredients shine. Must-haves include the panfried gnocchi Genovese, risotto-crusted fresh catch, and the deconstructed tiramisu. **Known for:** lobster risotto; porcini-dusted lamb chops; excellent selection of Italian wines. $ *Average main: $36* ⊠ *The Westin Kaanapali Ocean Resort Villas, 6 Kai Ala Dr., Kaanapali* ☎ *808/667–3254* ⊕ *www.pulehurestaurantmaui.com* ⊙ *Closed Tues. and Wed. No lunch.*

★ Roy's Kaanapali

$$$$ | **MODERN HAWAIIAN** | Roy Yamaguchi is a James Beard Award–winning chef and the granddaddy of East-meets-West cuisine. His eponymous Maui restaurant, located next to the golf course clubhouse near Kaanapali's main entrance, features signature dishes like fire-grilled, Szechuan-spiced baby back ribs, Roy's original blackened ahi, and hibachi-style grilled salmon, as well as an exceptionally user-friendly wine list. **Known for:** classic Hawaiian regional cuisine; golf course setting; hot chocolate soufflé. $ *Average main: $42* ⊠ *2990 Kaanapali Pkwy., Kaanapali* ☎ *808/669–6999* ⊕ *www.royshawaii.com.*

★ Son'z Steakhouse

$$$$ | **STEAKHOUSE** | To enter the only steak house in West Maui, you descend a grand staircase into an amber-lighted

dining room with soaring ceilings and a massive artificial lagoon complete with swans, ducks, waterfalls, and tropical gardens. Chef Amy Mayers' classic menu features favorites like the bone-in rib eye and Tomahawk steaks with accompaniments including five house-made sauces and a variety of sides and seafood add-ons, as well as lighter plates like shrimp cocktail and the must-try black and blue *ahi* starter. **Known for:** astounding wine cellar; private, lagoon-front setting; 100% USDA-certified-prime steaks. $ *Average main: $40 ⊠ Hyatt Regency Maui, 200 Nohea Kai Dr., Kaanapali ☎ 808/667–4506 ⊕ sonzsteakhouse.com ◷ No lunch.*

Tiki Terrace

$$ | MODERN HAWAIIAN | Executive chef Tom Muromoto is a local boy who loves to cook modern, upscale Hawaiian food, and he augments the various fresh fish dishes on his menu with items influenced by Hawaii's ethnic mix. This casual, open-air restaurant is the only place on Maui—maybe in Hawaii—where you can have a Native Hawaiian combination plate that is as healthful as it is authentic. **Known for:** seafood lawalu (food wrapped in green ti leaves); Hawaiian laulau (pork wrapped in leaves that's cooked until tender); Native Hawaiian plate. $ *Average main: $26 ⊠ Kaanapali Beach Hotel, 2525 Kaanapali Pkwy., Kaanapali ☎ 808/667–0124 ⊕ www.kbhmaui.com ◷ No lunch.*

 Hotels

With its long stretch of beach lined with luxury resorts, shops, and restaurants, Kaanapali is a vacationers' playground. Expect top-class service here and everything you could want a few steps from your room, including the calm waters of sun-kissed Kaanapali Beach. Wandering along the beach path between resorts is a recreational activity unto itself. Weather is dependably warm, and for that reason as well as all the others, Kaanapali is a popular—at times, downright crowded—destination.

★ Hyatt Regency Maui Resort & Spa

$$$$ | RESORT | FAMILY | Splashing waterfalls, swim-through grottos, a lagoon-like swimming pool, and a 150-foot waterslide "wow" guests of all ages at this bustling Kaanapali resort; spacious standard rooms are another draw. **Pros:** Drums of the Pacific luau and the must-see rooftop astronomy Tour of the Stars; Hawaiian cultural programs and wildlife education; water wonderland will thrill families. **Cons:** might not offer the most peaceful escape; daily resort and parking fees; can be difficult to find a space in self-parking. $ *Rooms from: $733 ⊠ 200 Nohea Kai Dr., Kaanapali ☎ 808/661–1234 ⊕ hyattregencymaui.com ➷ 810 rooms ⦿ No Meals.*

Kaanapali Alii

$$$$ | APARTMENT | FAMILY | Amenities like maid service, an activities desk, a small store with complimentary DVDs for guests to borrow, and a 24-hour front-desk service—and no pesky resort fees—make this a winning choice for families and those wanting to play house on Maui's most stunning shores. **Pros:** large comfortable units on the beach; quiet compared to other hotels in the resort; free parking. **Cons:** no on-site restaurant; small pools can get crowded; parking can be crowded during high season. $ *Rooms from: $534 ⊠ 50 Nohea Kai Dr., Kaanapali ☎ 866/644–6410 ⊕ kaanapalialii.com ➷ 264 units ⦿ No Meals.*

★ Kaanapali Beach Hotel

$$$$ | HOTEL | This charming beachfront hotel is full of aloha—locals say it's one of the few resorts on the Island where you can get a true Hawaiian experience as the entire staff takes part in the hotel's Pookela program, which teaches guests about the history, traditions, and values of Hawaiian culture. **Pros:** no resort fee; friendly staff; diverse array of cultural activities. **Cons:** fewer amenities than other places along this beach; daily parking fee; property is older than neighboring modern resorts. $ *Rooms from:*

$350 ✉ *2525 Kaanapali Pkwy., Kaanapali* ☎ *808/661–0011, 800/262–8450* 🌐 *kbh-maui.com* 🛏 *432 rooms* 🍴 *No Meals.*

★ **Maui Eldorado Kaanapali**

$$$ | **APARTMENT** | The Kaanapali Golf Course's fairways wrap around this fine, well-priced, two-story condo complex that boasts spacious studios, one- and two-bedroom units with fully equipped kitchens, and access to a stocked beach cabana on a semiprivate beach. **Pros:** privileges at the Kaanapali Golf Courses; Wi-Fi in all units; friendly staff. **Cons:** some distance from attractions of the Kaanapali Resort; no housekeeping but checkout cleaning fee; not right on beach. [$] *Rooms from: $300* ✉ *2661 Kekaa Dr., Kaanapali* ☎ *808/633-8331* 🌐 *mauikaanapalivacationrentals.com* 🛏 *204 units* 🍴 *No Meals.*

Royal Lahaina Resort

$$$$ | **RESORT** | Built in 1962, this grand property on the uncrowded, sandy shore in North Kaanapali has hosted millionaires and Hollywood stars, and today it pleases families and budget seekers as well as luxury travelers with a variety of lodging styles. **Pros:** on-site luau; variety of lodgings and rates; tennis ranch with 11 courts and a pro shop. **Cons:** daily self-parking fee; evening luau noise can be loud; older property. [$] *Rooms from: $420* ✉ *2780 Kekaa Dr., Kaanapali* ☎ *800/447–6925* 🌐 *royallahaina.com* 🛏 *447 units* 🍴 *No Meals.*

★ **Sheraton Maui Resort & Spa**

$$$$ | **RESORT** | Set among dense gardens on Kaanapali's best stretch of beach, the Sheraton offers a quieter, more low-key atmosphere than its neighboring resorts, and sits next to and on top of Puu Kekaa, the site of a nightly torch-lighting and cliff-diving ritual. **Pros:** free shuttle to Lahaina and shopping malls; great snorkeling right off the beach; Maui Nui luau three times a week. **Cons:** daily resort and parking fees; beach subject to seasonal erosion; extensive property can mean a long walk from your room to lobby, restaurants, and beach. [$] *Rooms from: $759* ✉ *2605 Kaanapali Pkwy., Kaanapali* ☎ *808/661–0031* 🌐 *marriott.com/hnmsi* 🛏 *508 units* 🍴 *No Meals.*

The Westin Maui Resort & Spa

$$$$ | **RESORT** | **FAMILY** | This 12-acre beachfront paradise offers a setting that is both beautiful and calming. **Pros:** free shuttle to Lahaina town; excellent concierge desk; one adults-only pool. **Cons:** a lot going on; crowded pool and common areas; daily resort and parking fees. [$] *Rooms from: $797* ✉ *2365 Kaanapali Pkwy., Kaanapali* ☎ *808/667–2525* 🌐 *westinmaui.com* 🛏 *770 rooms* 🍴 *No Meals.*

Performing Arts

Drums of the Pacific Luau

THEMED ENTERTAINMENT | **FAMILY** | By Kaanapali Beach, this luau shines in every category—convenient parking, well-made food, and a nicely paced program that touches on Hawaiian, Samoan, Tahitian, Fijian, Tongan, and Maori cultures. Some guests get tickled by the onstage audience hula tutorial. The finale features three fire-knife dancers. You'll feast on delicious Hawaiian delicacies like teriyaki steak, oven-roasted *mahimahi* (dolphinfish), and Pacific *ahi* poke (pickled raw yellowfin tuna, tossed with herbs and seasonings). The dessert spread consists of chocolate and coconut indulgences. An open bar offers beer, seltzer, wine, and standard tropical mixes. ✉ *Hyatt Regency Maui, 200 Nohea Kai Dr., Kaanapali* ☎ *808/667–4727* 🌐 *drumsofthepacificmaui.com.*

★ **Hula Girl**

SAILING | **FAMILY** | This custom catamaran is one of the slickest and best-equipped boats on the Island, complete with a VIP lounge by the captain's fly bridge. The initial cost doesn't include the cooked-to-order meals, but guests can choose from a relatively extensive menu that includes filet mignon, daily fish specials,

With a central location almost midway between the Hyatt and Sheraton resorts in Kaanapali, Whalers Village offers a mix of upscale shopping, dining, and even live entertainment.

and crème brûlée. If you're willing to splurge a little for live music, an onboard chef, and upscale service, this is your best bet. From mid-December to early April the cruise focuses on whale-watching. Check-in is in front of Leilani's restaurant at Whalers Village. ⊠ *Whalers Village, 2435 Kaanapali Pkwy., Kaanapali* ☎ *808/665–0344, 808/667–5980* ⊕ *sailingmaui.com* 💰 *$90.*

🛍 Shopping

★ Whalers Village

MALL | **FAMILY** | Chic Whalers Village boasts wonderful oceanfront restaurants and shops in the heart of Kaanapali. Upscale haunts include Louis Vuitton and Tourneau, and beautyphiles can get their fix at Sephora. Elegant home accessories at Martin and MacArthur and Totally Hawaiian Gift Gallery are perfect Hawaii-made souvenirs, while the many great surf and swimwear shops will prepare you for a day at the beach. Kids will fall in love with the whimsical two-story

climbing structure at the lower courtyard. The outdoor mall also offers free weekly entertainment, lei-making classes, and hula lessons; check their website for a complete schedule. ⊠ *2435 Kaanapali Pkwy., Kaanapali* ☎ *808/661–4567* ⊕ *whalersvillage.com.*

Kapalua

Kapalua is 10 miles north of Kaanapali; 36 miles west of Kahului.

Beautiful and secluded, Kapalua is West Maui's northernmost resort community. First developed in the late 1970s, the resort now includes the Ritz-Carlton, posh residential complexes, two golf courses, and the surrounding former pineapple fields. The area's distinctive shops and restaurants cater to dedicated golfers, celebrities who want to be left alone, and some of the world's richest folks. In addition to golf, recreational activities include hiking and snorkeling. Mists regularly envelop the landscape

Beach Safety on Maui

Hawaii's beautiful beaches can be dangerous at times due to large waves and strong currents. Look for posted black and yellow hazard signs warning of high surf, jellyfish, sharks, and other dangers. Be especially cautious at beaches without lifeguards.

Generally, North Shore beaches (including Mokuleia and D. T. Fleming on the west side of the Island) can be rough in the winter and not good for swimming or beginner-level water sports. On the south side, large summer swells and Kona storms (which usually occur in winter) can cause strong rip currents and powerful shore breaks.

Swim only when there's a normal caution rating, never swim alone, and don't dive into unknown water or shallow breaking waves. If you're unable to swim out of a rip current, tread water and wave your arms in the air to signal for help.

Even in calm conditions, there are other dangerous things in the water to be aware of, including razor-sharp coral, jellyfish, eels, and the occasional shark. Jellyfish cause the most ocean injuries, and signs are posted along beaches when they're present. Box jellyfish swarm to Hawaii's leeward shores 9–10 days after a full moon. Portuguese man-of-war jellyfish are usually found when winds blow from the ocean onto land. Reactions to a sting are usually mild (burning sensation, redness); however, in some cases they can be severe (breathing difficulties). If you are stung, pick off the tentacles, rinse the affected area with water, and apply ice. Seek first aid from a lifeguard if you experience severe reactions.

According to state sources, the chances of getting bitten by a shark in Hawaiian waters are low. To reduce your shark-attack risk:

■ Swim, surf, or dive with others at beaches patrolled by lifeguards.

■ Avoid swimming at dawn, dusk, and night.

■ Don't enter the water if you have open wounds or are bleeding.

■ Avoid murky waters, harbor entrances, areas near stream mouths, channels, or steep drop-offs.

■ Don't wear high-contrast swimwear or shiny jewelry.

■ Leave the water quickly and calmly if you spot a shark.

of tall Cook pines and rolling fairways in Kapalua, which is cooler and quieter than its southern neighbors. The beaches here, including Kapalua and D. T. Fleming, are among Maui's finest.

GETTING HERE AND AROUND

Shuttles and taxis are available from Kahului and West Maui airports. The Ritz-Carlton, Kapalua, has a resort shuttle within the Kapalua Resort.

Beaches

D. T. Fleming Beach

BEACH | FAMILY | Because the current can be quite strong, this charming, mile-long sandy cove is better for sunbathing than for swimming or water sports. Still, it's one of the Island's most popular beaches. It's a perfect spot to watch the spectacular Maui sunsets, and there are picnic tables and grills. Part of the beach runs along the front of the Ritz-Carlton,

4

Maui WEST MAUI

Kapalua—a good place to grab a cocktail and enjoy the view. **Amenities:** lifeguards; parking (no fee); showers; toilets. **Best for:** sunset; walking. ✉ *Rte. 30, Kapalua* ✣ *About 1 mile north of Kapalua.*

★ Kapalua Bay Beach

BEACH | FAMILY | Over the years, Kapalua has been recognized as one of the world's best beaches, and for good reason: it fronts a pristine bay that is good for snorkeling, swimming, and general lazing. Just north of Napili Bay, this lovely sheltered shore often remains calm late into the afternoon, although currents may be strong offshore. Snorkeling is easy here, and there are lots of colorful reef fish. This popular area is bordered by the Kapalua Resort, so don't expect to have the beach to yourself. Walk through the tunnel from the parking lot at the end of Kapalua Place to get here. **Amenities:** parking (no fee); showers; toilets. **Best for:** snorkeling; sunset; swimming. ✉ *Rte. 30, Kapalua* ✣ *Turn onto Kapalua Pl.*

Mokuleia Bay (Slaughterhouse Beach)

BEACH | The Island's northernmost beach is part of the Honolua-Mokuleia Marine Life Conservation District. "Slaughterhouse" is the surfers' nickname for what is officially Mokuleia. Weather permitting, this is a great place for bodysurfing and sunbathing. Concrete steps and a railing help you get down the cliff to the sand, but it's generally a difficult area to access for younger children. The next bay over, Honolua, has no beach but offers one of the best surf breaks in Hawaii. Competitions are sometimes held there; telltale signs are cars pulled off the road and parked in the old pineapple field. **Amenities:** none. **Best for:** sunset; surfing; snorkeling. ✉ *Rte. 30, Kapalua* ✣ *At mile marker 32.*

🍴 Restaurants

Banyan Tree

$$$$ | ECLECTIC | This eclectic farm-to-table dinner spot is an open-air, ocean-view restaurant and lounge. Classic Hawaiian recipes combined with Mediterranean cooking techniques result in unique, fresh, coastal cuisine. **Known for:** creative presentation; island cuisine; local ingredients. [$] *Average main: $45* ✉ *The Ritz-Carlton, Kapalua, 1 Ritz-Carlton Drive, Kapalua* ☎ *808/669–6200* 🌐 *banyantreekapalua.com.*

The Gazebo Restaurant

$ | DINER | Breakfast is the reason to seek out this restaurant located poolside at the Napili Shores Resort. The food is standard diner fare, but the portions are big, the prices are low, and many folks think the pancakes—with bananas, macadamia nuts, or white chocolate chips—are the best in West Maui. **Known for:** create-your-own pancakes; enormous omelets; long but fast-moving lines. [$] *Average main: $13* ✉ *Napili Shores Maui, 5315 Lower Honoapiilani Hwy., Napili* ☎ *808/669–5621* 🕓 *No dinner.*

★ Merriman's Maui

$$$$ | MODERN HAWAIIAN | Perched above the postcard-perfect Kapalua Bay, this is the place to impress your date, as Chef Peter Merriman highlights the Islands' bounty by using fresh seafood and ingredients from local farms. A nightly changing prix-fixe menu ($120) features stunning dishes that represent land and sea options and a vegetarian option that abounds with local produce. **Known for:** exceptional wine list; fire pit on the outdoor lanai; panoramic ocean views. [$] *Average main: $120* ✉ *1 Bay Club Pl., Kapalua* ☎ *808/669–6400* 🌐 *merrimanshawaii.com* 🕓 *No lunch.*

Pizza Paradiso

$ | ITALIAN | When it opened in 1995 this was an over-the-counter pizza place, but it's evolved over the years into a local favorite, serving Mediterranean-style pizza and comfort food including pitas, gyros, and kabobs. **Known for:** gelato and Dole Whip for dessert; pizzas with local Maui produce; fresh, house-made pesto. [$] *Average main: $15* ✉ *Honokowai*

Marketplace, 3350 Lower Honoapiilani Hwy., Honokowai ☎ *808/667–2929* 🌐 *pizzaparadiso.com.*

★ **Sansei Seafood Restaurant & Sushi Bar**
$$$$ | **ASIAN** | With locations on three islands, Sansei takes sushi, sashimi, and contemporary Japanese food to a new level. If you're a fish or shellfish lover, this is the place for you. **Known for:** panko-crusted ahi (yellowfin tuna) sashimi; inventive rolls and sushi appetizers; award-winning Shrimp Dynamite (tempura shrimp with a garlic masago aioli). [$] *Average main: $36* ✉ *600 Office Rd., Kapalua* ☎ *808/669–6286* 🌐 *sanseihawaii.com* 🕒 *No lunch.*

Hotels

The neighborhoods north of Kaanapali—Honokowai, Mahinahina, Kahana, Napili, and finally, Kapalua—blend almost seamlessly into one another along Lower Honoapiilani Highway. Each has a few shops and restaurants and a secluded bay or two to call its own. Many visitors have found a second home here, at one of the condominiums nestled between beach-access roads and groves of mango trees. You won't get the stellar service of a resort (except at Kapalua), but you'll be among the locals here, in a relatively quiet part of the island. Be prepared for a long commute, though, if you're planning to do much exploring elsewhere on the island. Kapalua is the area farthest north, but well worth all the driving to stay at the elegant Ritz-Carlton, which is surrounded by misty greenery and overlooks beautiful D. T. Fleming Beach.

Honua Kai Resort & Spa
$$$$ | **APARTMENT** | **FAMILY** | Two high-rise towers contain these individually owned, eco-friendly (and family-friendly) units combining the conveniences of a condo with the full service of a hotel. **Pros:** large spacious rooms with full kitchens; upscale appliances and furnishings; beautiful, well-maintained grounds. **Cons:** housekeeping every other day; beach is small and rocky, not good for swimming; sometimes windy. [$] *Rooms from: $700* ✉ *130 Kai Malina Pkwy., Honokowai* ☎ *808/662–2800, 855/718–5789* 🌐 *honuakai.com* 🛏 *628 units* 🍴 *No Meals.*

Mahina Surf
$$$ | **APARTMENT** | Of the many condo complexes lining the ocean-side stretch of Honoapiilani Highway, this one offers friendly service, a saline oceanfront pool, and affordable units—some with million-dollar views. **Pros:** oceanfront barbecues; resident turtles hang out on the rocks below; no hidden fees. **Cons:** no housekeeping (and cleaning fee for stays fewer than seven nights); minimum three-night stay; rocky shoreline rather than a beach. [$] *Rooms from: $272* ✉ *4057 Lower Honoapiilani Hwy.* ☎ *808/669–6068, 800/544–0300* 🌐 *mahinasurf.com* 🛏 *56 units* 🍴 *No Meals.*

The Mauian on Napili Bay
$$$ | **APARTMENT** | If you're looking for a low-key place with a friendly staff, this small, delightful beachfront property on Napili Bay may be for you. **Pros:** reasonable rates; located on one of Maui's top swimming and snorkeling beaches; free parking and no resort fees. **Cons:** some may find motel-like design reduces privacy; few amenities; small units. [$] *Rooms from: $299* ✉ *5441 Lower Honoapiilani Hwy., Napili* ☎ *808/669–6205* 🌐 *mauian.com* 🛏 *44 rooms* 🍴 *No Meals.*

★ **Montage Kapalua Bay**
$$$$ | **RESORT** | **FAMILY** | This luxury resort caters to well-heeled travelers who want the comfort and privacy of a residential-style suite combined with resort service and amenities—elegantly furnished one- to four-bedroom units with gourmet kitchens, in-unit washers/dryers, and the largest lanai to be found. **Pros:** prime snorkeling; great kids clubs for children and teens; large, well-appointed rooms. **Cons:** large property means lots of walking; far from other Maui attractions;

pricey daily parking and resort fees. $ *Rooms from: $1200* ⊠ *1 Bay Dr., Kapalua* ☎ *808/662–6600* ⊕ *montagehotels.com/kapaluabay* ⤳ *50 units* ¶◎¶ *No Meals.*

★ Napili Kai Beach Resort

$$$$ | **RESORT** | **FAMILY** | Spread across 10 beautiful acres along one of the best beaches on Maui, the family-friendly Napili Kai with its "old Hawaii" feel draws a loyal following to its island-style rooms that open onto private lanai. **Pros:** weekly kids' hula performances and Hawaiian slack-key guitar concert; fantastic swimming and sunning beach; no resort fees. **Cons:** beach subject to periodic erosion; parking spaces tight for some; not as modern as other resorts in West Maui. $ *Rooms from: $355* ⊠ *5900 Lower Honoapi'ilani Hwy., Napili* ☎ *808/669–6271* ⊕ *napilikai.com* ⤳ *163 units* ¶◎¶ *No Meals.*

Papakea Resort

$$$$ | **APARTMENT** | **FAMILY** | All studios and one- and two-bedroom units at this casual, oceanfront condominium complex face the ocean and, because the units are spread out among 11 low-rise buildings on about 13 acres of land, there is built-in privacy and easy parking. **Pros:** large rooms; lovely garden landscaping; weekly mai tai party. **Cons:** pool can get crowded; busy, family-oriented property; no beach in front of property. $ *Rooms from: $365* ⊠ *3543 Lower Honoapiilani Hwy., Honokowai* ☎ *808/665–0880, 855/945–4047* ⊕ *astonatpapakea.com* ⤳ *364 units* ¶◎¶ *No Meals.*

★ The Ritz-Carlton, Kapalua

$$$$ | **RESORT** | This notable hillside property features luxurious service and upscale accommodations along with an enhanced Hawaiian sense of place. **Pros:** spa, golf, walking trails, and many other activities; AAA 4-Diamond Banyan Tree restaurant will please locavores; many cultural and recreational programs. **Cons:** far from major attractions such as Haleakala; daily parking and resort fees; can be windy

on grounds and at pool. $ *Rooms from: $1665* ⊠ *1 Ritz-Carlton Dr., Kapalua* ☎ *808/669–6200* ⊕ *ritzcarlton.com/kapalua* ⤳ *466 units* ¶◎¶ *No Meals.*

Sands of Kahana

$$$$ | **APARTMENT** | Meandering gardens, spacious rooms, and an on-site restaurant distinguish this large condominium complex—units on the upper floors benefit from the height, with unrivaled ocean views stretching away from private lanais. **Pros:** restaurant on premises; fitness center, tennis courts, and sand volleyball court; one-, two-, and three-bedroom units available. **Cons:** street-facing units can get a bit noisy; property a bit dated; may be approached about buying a time-share unit. $ *Rooms from: $494* ⊠ *4299 Lower Honoapiilani Hwy., Kahana* ☎ *808/669–0400 property phone, 855/386–4658* ⊕ *sandsofkahanaresort.com* ⤳ *196 units* ¶◎¶ *No Meals.*

Westin Nanea Ocean Villas

$$$$ | **RESORT** | **FAMILY** | It's rare to find a resort that so thoroughly incorporates authentic Hawaiian cultural symbols and traditions into its design, but this deluxe beachfront property in North Kaanapali carries this commitment into its native landscaping and the Puuhonua O Nanea cultural center that hosts artifacts, displays, activities, and talks. **Pros:** "zero-entry" family pool with sandy bottom and water slide; great location for snorkeling and water sports; free shuttle to Lahaina town and other Westin resorts. **Cons:** outside main Kaanapali resort; limited dining options; may be pitched to join time-share club. $ *Rooms from: $891* ⊠ *45 Kai Malina Pkwy., Kaanapali* ☎ *808/662–6300* ⊕ *marriott.com* ⤳ *390 units* ¶◎¶ *No Meals.*

 Nightlife

Alaloa Lounge

LIVE MUSIC | When ambience weighs heavy on the priority list, this spot at the

Ritz-Carlton, Kapalua, might just be the ticket. Live performances range from jazz to island rhythms on Tuesday through Saturday nights (6–9 pm), and the menu includes locally inspired cocktails and a fresh sushi station from 5–9 pm. Step onto the lanai for that plumeria-tinged tropical air and gaze at the deep blue of the Pacific.

You'll find an extensive menu of specialty cocktails, domestic and imported beers, premium spirits, and signature appetizers, including a fresh sushi station, open daily from 5–9 pm. The best sunsets can be viewed from here and, from December to April, enjoy whale-watching while having lunch. As the sun sets, relax and enjoy live entertainment Tuesday to Saturday from 6–9 pm. ⊠ *The Ritz-Carlton, Kapalua, 1 Ritz-Carlton Dr., Kapalua* ☎ *808/669–6200* ⊕ *ritzcarlton.com.*

The South Shore

Blessed by more than its fair share of sun, the southern shore of Haleakala was an undeveloped wilderness until the 1970s, when the sun worshippers found it. Now restaurants, condos, and luxury resorts line the coast from the world-class aquarium at Maalaea Harbor through working-class Kihei to lovely Wailea, a resort community rivaling its counterpart, Kaanapali, on West Maui. Farther south, the road disappears and unspoiled wilderness still has its way. Because the South Shore includes so many fine beach choices, a trip here—if you're staying elsewhere on the Island—is an all-day excursion, especially if you include a visit to the aquarium. Get active in the morning with exploring and snorkeling, then shower in a beach park, dress up a little, and enjoy the cool luxury of the Wailea resorts. At sunset, settle in for dinner at one of the area's many fine restaurants.

Kihei

9 miles south of Kahului; 20 miles east of Lahaina.

Traffic lights and shopping malls may not fit your notion of paradise, but Kihei offers dependably warm sun, excellent beaches, and a front-row seat to marine life of all sorts. Besides all the sun and sand, the town's relatively inexpensive condos and excellent restaurants make this a home base for many Maui visitors.

County beach parks, such as Kamaole I, II, and III, have lawns, showers, and picnic tables.

▓ TIP→ **Remember: beach park or no beach park, the public has a right to the entire coastal strand, but not to cross private property to get to it.**

GETTING HERE AND AROUND
Kihei is an easy 25-minute ride south of Kahului Airport, easily accessed via the four-lane Maui Veteran's Highway (Route 311). Once there, if you plan to plant yourself at the water's edge for most of your vacation, a car may not be necessary, especially if you're staying at a hotel or condo within walking distance of Kihei's fabulous beaches. For those wanting to explore beyond the beach, renting a car is a good idea.

◉ Sights

★ **Hawaiian Islands Humpback Whale National Marine Sanctuary**
COLLEGE | FAMILY | This nature center sits in prime humpback-viewing territory beside a restored ancient Hawaiian fishpond. Whether the whales are here or not, the education center is a great stop for youngsters curious to know more about underwater life, and for anyone eager to gain insight into the cultural connection between Hawaii and its whale residents. Interactive displays and informative naturalists explain it

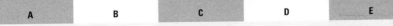

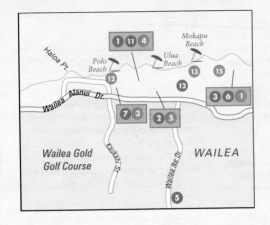

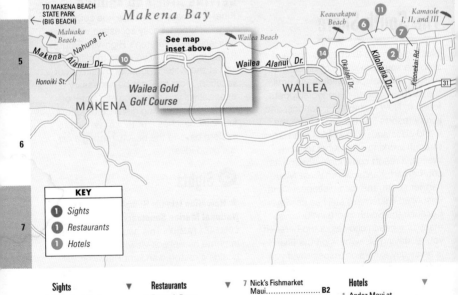

KEY

1 Sights

1 Restaurants

1 Hotels

Sights ▼

1 Hawaiian Islands
Humpback Whale
National Marine
Sanctuary................ **H4**

2 Kealia Pond National
Wildlife Refuge.......... **J3**

3 Maalaea Harbor **J2**

4 Maui Ocean Center..... **J2**

Restaurants ▼

1 Ferraro's Bar e
Ristorante................ **B2**

2 Humuhumunukunu-
kuapuaa.................. **B2**

3 Kaana Kitchen **C1**

4 Kihei Caffe.............. **F4**

5 Monkeypod Kitchen.... **C3**

6 Morimoto Maui **C1**

7 Nick's Fishmarket
Maui..................... **B2**

8 Pita Paradise
Mediterranean Bistro .. **J2**

9 Seascape
Restaurant.............. **J2**

10 South Shore
Tiki Lounge **F4**

11 Spago **B2**

12 Tommy Bahama......... **C2**

Hotels ▼

1 Andaz Maui at
Wailea Resort........... **C1**

2 Aston Maui Hill......... **E5**

3 Fairmont Kea Lani
Maui..................... **B2**

4 Four Seasons Resort
Maui at Wailea......... **B2**

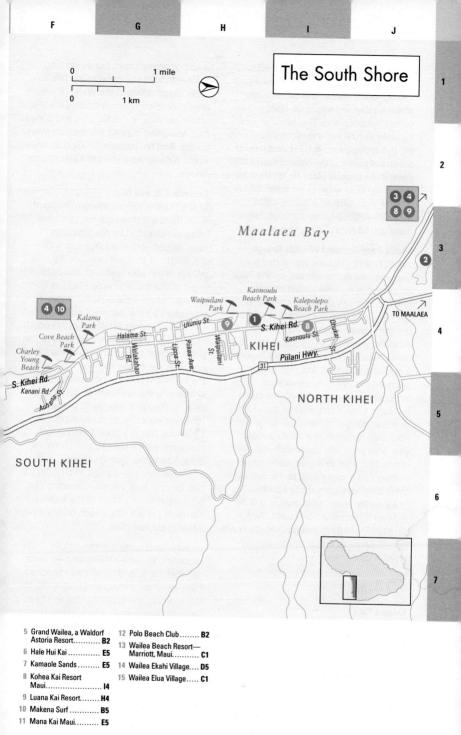

The South Shore

0   1 mile

0   1 km

Maalaea Bay

Waipuilani
Park

Kaonoulu
Beach Park

Kalepolepo
Beach Park

TO MAALAEA

Kalama
Park

Cove Beach
Park

Charley
Young
Beach

Uluniu St.

Halama St.

S. Kihei Rd.

Kaonoulu St.

KIHEI

Piilani Hwy.

31

Welakahao Rd.

Lipoa St.

Piikea Ave.

Waipuilani St.

Ohukai St.

NORTH KIHEI

S. Kihei Rd.

Kanani Rd.

Auhana St.

SOUTH KIHEI

all, including the sanctuary that acts as a breeding ground for humpbacks. Throughout the year, the center hosts activities that include talks, labs, and volunteer opportunities. The sanctuary itself includes virtually all the waters surrounding the archipelago. ■TIP→ **Just outside the visitor center is the ancient Koieie fishpond; it is a popular place for locals to bring their children to wade in the water.** ⊠ *726 S. Kihei Rd., Kihei* ☎ *808/879–2818, 800/831–4888* ⊕ *hawaiihumpbackwhale. noaa.gov* ⊠ *Free* ⊗ *Closed weekends.*

Kealia Pond National Wildlife Refuge

TRAIL | **FAMILY** | Natural wetlands have become rare in the Islands, so the 700 acres of this reserve attract migratory birds, such as Hawaiian coots and long-legged Hawaiian stilts that casually dip their beaks into the shallow waters as traffic shuttles by; it's also home to other wildlife. The visitor center provides a good introduction, and interpretive signs on the half-mile elevated boardwalk, which stretches along the coast by North Kihei Road, explain the journey of the endangered hawksbill turtles and how they return to the sandy dunes year after year. The boardwalk includes ramps that lead to the adjacent beach so visitors can explore tidal pools. Note that there's no restroom at the boardwalk. ⊠ *Mokulele Hwy., mile marker 6, Kihei* ⊕ *Main entrance on Mokulele Hwy.* ☎ *808/875–1582* ⊕ *fws.gov/refuge/kealia-pond* ⊠ *Free* ⊗ *Visitor center closed weekends.*

Beaches

Kalama Park

BEACH | **FAMILY** | Stocked with grills and picnic pavilions, this 36-acre beach park with plenty of shade is great for families and sports lovers. With its extensive lawns and sports fields, the park welcomes volleyball, basketball, baseball, and tennis players, and even has a playground, skateboard park, and a roller hockey rink. The beach itself is all but nonexistent, but swimming is fair—though you must brave the rocky steps down to the water. If you aren't completely comfortable with this entrance, stick to the burgers and bocce ball. **Amenities:** parking (no fee); showers; toilets. **Best for:** partiers. ⊠ *1900 S. Kihei Road, Kihei* ⊕ *Across from Kihei Kalama Village.*

Kamaole I, II, and III

BEACH | **FAMILY** | Three steps from South Kihei Road are three golden stretches of sand separated by outcroppings of dark, jagged lava rocks. You can walk the length of all three beaches if you're willing to get your feet wet. The northernmost of the trio, Kamaole I (across from the ABC Store—important to know if you forget your sunscreen) offers perfect swimming and an active volleyball court. There's also a great lawn, where you can spread out at the south end of the beach. Kamaole II is nearly identical except for the lawn, but there is no parking lot. The last beach, the one with all the people on it, is 10-acre Kamaole III, perfect for throwing a disk or throwing down a blanket. This is a great family beach, complete with a playground, barbecue grills, kite flying, and, frequently, rented inflatable castles—a must at birthday parties for cool kids. All three beach parks offer wheelchair ramps to the beach; Kamaole I is the only beach on Maui with a beach access chair.

Locally—and quite disrespectfully, according to Native Hawaiians—known as "Kam" I, II, and III, all three beaches have great swimming and lifeguards. In the morning the water can be as still as a lap pool. Kamaole III offers terrific breaks for beginning bodysurfers. **Amenities:** lifeguards; parking (no fee); showers; toilets. **Best for:** sunsets, surfing; swimming; walking. ⊠ *S. Kihei Rd., between Alii Ke Alanui and Hale Kamaole Condominiums, Kihei* ☎ *808/270–6136 for beach wheelchair availability.*

Did You Know?

Maui's South Shore beaches, generally white and sandy, get better as you go south. Wailea's beaches have great views. For wilder landscapes, keep heading south to Makena.

Keawakapu Beach

BEACH | FAMILY | Everyone loves Keawaka-
pu, with its long stretch of golden sand,
near-perfect swimming, and views of Puu
Olai cinder cone. It's great fun to walk or
jog this beach south into Wailea, as it's
lined with over-the-top residences. It's
best here in the morning—the winds pick
up in the afternoon (beware of sand-
storms). Keawakapu has three entrances: one is at the Mana Kai Maui resort
(look for the blue "Shoreline Access"
sign); the second is directly across from
the parking lot on Kilohana Street (the
entrance is unmarked); and the third is
at the dead end of Kihei Road. Toilets
are portable. **Amenities:** parking (no
fee); showers; toilets. **Best for:** sunset;
swimming; walking. ⊠ *S. Kihei Rd., near
Kilohana St., Kihei.*

 Restaurants

South Maui's dining scene begins at
Maalaea Harbor and wends its way
through the beach towns of Kihei and
Wailea. There are plenty of casual,
relatively inexpensive eateries along
the way—until you reach Wailea, where
most of the dining is pricey. Some of it,
fortunately, is worth it.

★ Kaana Kitchen

$$$$ | MODERN HAWAIIAN | This signature
restaurant at Maui's most stylish luxury
resort, Andaz Maui at Wailea, has it all:
ingredients sourced within the Islands,
marvelous wine list, stellar service, and
spectacular views from every table.
The whole space has been masterfully
designed with the gorgeous exhibition
kitchen as the focal point of the restaurant and both indoor and outdoor seating
wrapping around the space. **Known
for:** most ingredients locally sourced;
plantation flavors with a modern twist;
romantic setting for sunset dining.
Ⓢ *Average main: $44* ⊠ *Andaz Maui at
Wailea, 3550 Wailea Alanui Dr., Wailea*
☎ *808/879–1234* ⊕ *andazmaui.com* ⊗ *No
lunch.*

★ Kihei Caffe

$ | AMERICAN | This unassuming popular
spot across the street from Kalama
Beach Park has a breakfast menu that
runs the gamut from healthy yogurt-
filled papaya to the local classic *loco
moco*—two eggs, ground beef patty,
rice, and brown gravy—and everything
in between. Unique menu items include
corned beef hash and catfish at breakfast
and a calamari sandwich at lunch. **Known
for:** enormous portions; breakfast served
all day; killer cinnamon rolls. Ⓢ *Average
main: $15* ⊠ *1945 S. Kihei Rd., Kihei*
☎ *808/879–2230* ⊕ *kiheicaffe.com* ⊗ *No
dinner.*

★ Nick's Fishmarket Maui

$$$$ | SEAFOOD | Find some of the best
seafood on the Island at this elegant
eatery inside the Fairmont Kea Lani. This
dinner-only restaurant sources the freshest fish possible, and often has beautifully prepared offerings, like *opakapaka*
(pink snapper), that other fish restaurants
don't. **Known for:** outstanding levels of
service; strawberries panzini dessert
(flambéed with Grand Marnier); good
selection of gluten-free options. Ⓢ *Average main: $55* ⊠ *4100 Wailea Alanui Dr.,
Wailea* ⊕ *nicksfishmarketmaui.com.*

South Shore Tiki Lounge

$ | AMERICAN | This tiki bar—tucked into
Kihei Kalama Village—serves burgers,
sandwiches, and delicious specialty
pizzas that are crafted from scratch with
sauces made from fresh Roma tomatoes
and Maui herbs. **Known for:** all-day happy
hour; late-night dancing under the gaze of
the lounge's namesake tiki; kitchen open
until 10 pm. Ⓢ *Average main: $18* ⊠ *Kihei
Kalama Village, 1913-J S. Kihei Rd., Kihei*
☎ *808/874–6444* ⊕ *southshoretikilounge.
com.*

 Hotels

If you're a beach lover, you won't find
many disadvantages to staying in Kihei.
A string of welcoming beaches stretches

from tip to tip. Snorkeling, bodyboarding, and barbecuing find their ultimate expression here. Affordable condos line South Kihei Road; however, some find the busy traffic and the strip-mall shopping distinctly un-Maui and prefer quieter hideaways.

Aston Maui Hill

$$$$ | **APARTMENT** | **FAMILY** | Take in sweeping views of the ocean and Haleakala from the large lanai of the one- to three-bedroom units on this sprawling, well-maintained property just outside the swanky Wailea Resort. **Pros:** great option for large groups needing multiple units; no resort or parking fees; spacious layout makes property seem less crowded. **Cons:** units are not handicapped-accessible; stairs and walking distances may be challenging to guests with mobility issues; decor may seem dated. $ *Rooms from: $399 ⊠ 2881 South Kihei Rd., Kihei ☎ 808/879–6321, 855/945–4044 ⊕ aquaaston.com ⇨ 140 units ⦿ No Meals.*

Hale Hui Kai

$$$$ | **APARTMENT** | **FAMILY** | This modest three-story condo complex of mostly two-bedroom units is just steps away from the beach. **Pros:** far enough from noise and tumult of "central" Kihei; well-maintained grounds; free street parking. **Cons:** some units are dated; no daily housekeeping; most units have one-week minimum stays. $ *Rooms from: $350 ⊠ 2994 S. Kihei Rd., Kihei ☎ 808/879–1219 ⊕ bookings-bellorealty. escapia.com ⇨ 40 units ⦿ No Meals.*

Kamaole Sands

$$$ | **APARTMENT** | **FAMILY** | This South Kihei property sits across the street from Kamaole III beach and is perfect for active families. **Pros:** pleasant grounds and well-maintained units; elevators, unlike many low-rise condos; free assigned parking. **Cons:** lack of diversity among building facades; older property; large cleaning fee. $ *Rooms from: $269 ⊠ 2695 S. Kihei Rd., Kihei*

☎ *808/270–1200, 877/367–1912 ⊕ castleresorts.com/maui/kamaole-sands ⇨ 400 units ⦿ No Meals.*

Kohea Kai Resort Maui

$$$ | **HOTEL** | Located across the beach and in the quieter north end of Kihei, this relaxed, family-friendly property has 26 units—some with kitchens and kitchenettes—that range from standard rooms to three-bedroom, two-bath penthouses. **Pros:** no resort or parking fees; no minimum stay; free Wi-Fi and beach toy use. **Cons:** located next to busy South Kihei Road; most rooms lack views; small pool. $ *Rooms from: $298 ⊠ 551 S. Kihei Rd., Kihei ☎ 808/879–1261 ⊕ koheakai.com ⇨ 26 units ⦿ No Meals.*

★ Luana Kai Resort

$$ | **APARTMENT** | If you don't need everything to be totally modern, consider setting up house at this great value condominium-by-the-sea. **Pros:** meticulously landscaped grounds; excellent management team; free parking. **Cons:** no maid service; air-conditioning only available in some units for an additional fee; no elevators. $ *Rooms from: $229 ⊠ 940 S. Kihei Rd., Kihei ☎ 808/879–1268 ⊕ luanakai.com ⇨ 113 units ⦿ No Meals.*

Mana Kai Maui

$$$$ | **APARTMENT** | **FAMILY** | You simply cannot get any closer to gorgeous Keawakapu Beach than this unsung hero of South Shore hotels, offering both renovated hotel rooms and condos that may be older than its competitors but are well priced and have marvelous ocean views, especially during the winter humpback whale season; one- and two-bedroom condos have private lanai and kitchens. **Pros:** arguably the best beach on the South Shore; good for families; free reserved parking. **Cons:** interior design might not appeal to discerning travelers; some rooms are small; older property. $ *Rooms from: $485 ⊠ 2960 S. Kihei Rd., Kihei ☎ 808/879–1561, 800/525–2025 ⊕ manakaimaui.com ⇨ 98 units ⦿ No Meals.*

Food Shopping for Renters

Condo renters in search of food and takeout meals should try these great places around Maui.

West Maui

Foodland Farms. This large supermarket combines the best of gourmet selections and local products with all the familiar staples you need to stock your vacation kitchen. It also makes an excellent *poke* (diced raw fish). ⊠ *Lahaina Gateway Shopping Center, 345 Keawe St., Lahaina* ☎ *808/662–7088* ⊕ *foodland.com.*

South Shore

Safeway. Find everything you could possibly need at this 24-hour supermarket, located in the Piilani Village Shopping Center. There's also a deli, prepared-foods and seafood section, and bakery. ⊠ *277 Piikea Ave., Kihei* ☎ *808/891–9120* ⊕ *www.safeway.com.*

Times Supermarket. This locally owned and -operated grocery store chain is a community staple on Maui, with an outstanding seafood counter, locally made products, bakery, and a full grocery selection. ⊠ *1310 S. Kihei Rd., Kihei* ⊕ *timessupermarkets.com.*

Central Maui

Safeway. Located a minute from Kahului Airport, this gigantic 24-hour supermarket has all the essentials, and then some. The deli, prepared

foods, and seafood sections, and bakery are all fantastic. There's a good wine selection, tons of produce, and a flower shop where you can treat yourself to a fresh lei. ⊠ *1090 Hookele St., Kahului* ☎ *808/359–2970* ⊕ *safeway. com.*

Whole Foods Market. This busy supermarket carries local organic produce, and the seafood, bakery, beer and wine, and meat offerings are exceptional. The pricey prepared foods—including pizza, sushi, a salad bar, Asian bowls, and Mexican fare—attract crowds. ⊠ *70 E. Kaahumanu Ave., Kahului* ☎ *808/872–3310* ⊕ *wholefoodsmarket.com.*

Upcountry

Foodland. This branch of the local supermarket chain at the Pukalani Terrace Center is a full-service store with prepared foods, a deli, fresh sushi, local produce, and a good seafood section in addition to the usual fare. Sign up for a Maikai Rewards card for deep (and necessary) savings. ⊠ *55 Pukalani St., Pukalani* ☎ *808/572–0674* ⊕ *foodland.com.*

Pukalani Superette. Stop at this family-owned store on your way up or down Haleakala for fresh Maui-grown produce and meat, flowers, and a variety of made-in-Maui products. ⊠ *15 Makawao Ave., Pukalani* ☎ *808/572–7616* ⊕ *pukalanisuperette.com.*

 Nightlife

South Shore Tiki Lounge

COCKTAIL LOUNGES | Good eats are paired with cool tunes in this breezy tropical tavern. Local acts and DJs are featured from 4 to 6 pm most evenings, and DJs get the dance floor shaking at 10 pm

Thursday through Saturday. Happy hour specials run from 11 am to 6 pm. This is the bar where locals hang out, so if you'd like to mix with the local scene, this is the spot. ⊠ *Kihei Kalama Village, 1913-J S. Kihei Rd., Kihei* ☎ *808/874–6444* ⊕ *southshoretikilounge.com.*

Vibe Bar Maui

COCKTAIL LOUNGES | This speakeasy-style bar is smack dab in the middle of Kihei's nightlife scene, and it stands out for its lineup of specialty cocktails. It's the size of a living room, but mixology is given more consideration here than at other venues. ✉ *1913 S. Kihei Rd., Kihei* ☎ *808/891–1011.*

Shopping

Azeka Shopping Center

SHOPPING CENTER | Spread across two complexes on either side of South Kihei Road, this no-frills shopping center is in the heart of Kihei. The mall is comprised of more than 50 stores, including a scuba shop for rentals and dive bookings, a gas station, several great takeout and dine-in restaurants, a coffee shop, and a post office. Ample free parking makes this an easy stop to fulfill your basic needs. ✉ *1279 and 1280 S. Kihei Rd., Kihei* ☎ *808/879–5000* ⊕ *azekashoppingcenter. com.*

Kihei Kalama Village

MALL | Encompassing more than 40 specialty shops and restaurants, this area known as "the Triangle" attracts visitors and locals alike. In addition to the brick-and-mortar establishments, there are shaded outdoor stalls selling everything from printed and hand-painted T-shirts and sundresses to jewelry, pottery, wood carvings, fruit, and gaudily painted coconut husks—some, but not all, made by local craftspeople. ✉ *1941 S. Kihei Rd., Kihei* ☎ *808/879–6610* ⊕ *kiheikalamavillage.com.*

Maalaea

13 miles south of Kahului; 6 miles west of Kihei; 14 miles southeast of Lahaina.

Pronounced "Mah-*ah*-lye-*ah*," this spot is not much more than a few condos, an aquarium, and a wind-blasted harbor (where there are tour boats)—but that's more than enough for some visitors. Humpback whales seem to think Maalaea is tops for meeting mates, and green sea turtles treat it like their own personal spa, regularly seeking appointments with cleaner wrasses in the harbor. Surfers revere this spot for "freight trains," reportedly one of the world's fastest waves.

A small Shinto shrine stands at the shore here, dedicated to the fishing god Ebisu Sama; it's the only Shinto fishing shrine remaining in the world, other than in Japan. Across the street, a giant hook often swings heavy with the sea's bounty, proving the worth of the shrine. At the end of Hauoli Street (the town's sole road), a small community garden is sometimes privy to traditional Hawaiian ceremonies. There's not much else, but the few residents here like it that way.

Sights

Maalaea Harbor

MARINA/PIER | With so many good reasons to head out onto the water, this active little harbor is quite busy. Many snorkeling and whale-watching excursions depart from here. There was a plan to expand the facility, but surfers argued that would have destroyed the world-renowned surf breaks. The elusive spot to the left of the harbor, called "freight train," rarely breaks, but when it does, it's said to be the fastest anywhere. Shops, restaurants, and the Maui Ocean Center aquarium front the harbor. ✉ *101 Maalaea Boat Harbor Rd., off Honoapiilani Hwy., Maalaea.*

★ Maui Ocean Center

AQUARIUM | **FAMILY** | You'll feel as though you're walking from the seashore down to the bottom of the reef at this aquarium, which focuses on creatures of the Pacific. Vibrant exhibits let you get close to turtles, rays, sharks, and the unusual creatures of the tide pools; allow two hours or so to explore it all. A whale

At Maui Ocean Center, you'll see turtles, rays, and sharks.

exhibit includes interactive learning stations and a dome theater that uses 3-D technology to give viewers a whale's-eye-view. There's also a moving exhibit highlighting the history of Kahoolawe, a neighboring island that can be seen just across the Alalakeiki Channel. It's not an enormous facility, but it does provide an excellent introduction to the sea life that makes Hawaii special. The center is part of a complex of retail shops and restaurants overlooking the harbor. Enter from Honoapiilani Highway as it curves past Maalaea Harbor. ■ **TIP→ The Ocean Center's gift shop is one of the best on Maui for artsy souvenirs and toys.** ✉ *192 Maalaea Rd., off Honoapiilani Hwy., Maalaea* ☎ *808/270–7000* 🌐 *mauioceancenter.com* 🎫 *$45.*

🍴 Restaurants

Seascape Restaurant

$$ | SEAFOOD | FAMILY | Maui Ocean Center's signature restaurant is a great choice for seafood (aquarium admission is not required to dine here) and offers harbor and ocean views from its open-air perch. The restaurant promotes heart-healthy cuisine, using sustainable seafood and trans fat–free items, but still allows for indulgence in their well-priced cocktail menu. **Known for:** friendly service; excellent vegan options; certified "ocean-friendly restaurant." [$] *Average main: $23* ✉ *Maui Ocean Center, 192 Maalaea Rd., Maalaea* ☎ *808/270–7000* 🌐 *mauioceancenter.com/dine* 🕒 *Lunch only.*

🎫 Performing Arts

Pride of Maui

FOLK/TRADITIONAL DANCE | A 65-foot catamaran built specifically for Maui's waters, the *Pride of Maui* has a spacious cabin for live entertainment, a dance floor, and a large upper deck for unobstructed sightseeing. Evening cruises include Polynesian dance performances, top-shelf cocktails, and an impressive spread cooked onboard, including baby back ribs, stir-fried vegetables, and shoyu chicken, plus seasonal desserts.

The Plate Lunch Tradition

To experience Island history first-hand, take a seat at one of Hawaii's ubiquitous "plate lunch" eateries, where you'll be served a segmented plate piled with a protein—usually in an Asian-style preparation, like beef teriyaki—two scoops of rice, a scoop of macaroni salad, and maybe a pickled vegetable condiment. On the sugar plantations, immigrant workers from many different countries ate together in the fields, sharing food from their *kaukau* tins, the utilitarian version of the Japanese *bento* (a divided box filled with savory items). From this stir-fry of people came the vibrant pidgin language and its equivalent in food: the plate lunch.

At beaches and public parks you will probably see locals eating plate lunches from nearby restaurants, stands, or trucks. Favorite combos include deep-fried chicken *katsu* (rolled in Japanese panko flour and spices), marinated beef teriyaki, and miso butterfish. *Saimin*, a noodle soup with Japanese fish stock and Chinese red-tinted barbecue pork, is a distinctly local medley. Koreans have contributed spicy barbecue *kalbi* ribs, often served with chili-laden *kimchi* (pickled cabbage or, sometimes, cucumber). Portuguese bean soup and tangy Filipino *pinakbet* (a mixed-vegetable dish with eggplant, okra, and bitter melons in fish sauce) are also favorites. The most popular contribution to this genre is the Hawaiian plate, featuring *laulau*, a mix of meat and fish and young taro leaves, wrapped in ti leaves and steamed, *kalua* pork and cabbage, *lomi lomi* salmon, and chicken long rice, along with *haupia* (coconut pudding) for dessert.

✉ *Maalaea Harbor, 101 Maalaea Boat Harbor Rd., Maalaea* ☎ *808/242-0955* ⊕ *prideofmaui.com* 🛥 *$118.*

Wailea

15 miles south of Kahului, at the southern border of Kihei.

The South Shore's resort community, Wailea is slightly quieter and drier than its West Maui sister, Kaanapali. Many visitors cannot pick a favorite, so they stay at both. The luxury of the resorts and the simple grandeur of the coastal views make the otherwise stark landscape an outstanding destination. Take time to stroll the coastal beach path; a handful of perfect little beaches, all with public access, front the resorts.

The first two resorts were built here in the late 1970s. Soon a cluster of upscale properties sprang up, including the Four Seasons Resort Maui at Wailea and the Fairmont Kea Lani. Check out the Grand Wailea Resort's chapel, which tells a Hawaiian love story in stained glass.

GETTING HERE AND AROUND
From Kahului Airport, take Route 311 (Maui Veteran's Highway) to Route 31 (Piilani Highway) until it ends in Wailea. Shuttles and taxis are available at the airport.

Beaches

★ **Makena Beach State Park (Big Beach)**
BEACH | Locals successfully fought to turn Makena—one of Hawaii's most breathtaking beaches—into a state park. This stretch of deep golden sand abutting sparkling aquamarine water is 3,000

feet long and 100 feet wide. It's often mistakenly referred to as Big Beach, but natives prefer its Hawaiian name, Oneloa. The water is fine for swimming, but use caution.

■ TIP➔ **The shore drop-off is steep, and swells can get deceptively big.**

Despite the infamous "Makena cloud," a blanket that rolls in during the early afternoon and obscures the sun, it seldom rains here. For a dramatic view of the beach, climb Puu Olai, the steep cinder cone near the first entrance you pass if you're driving south. Continue over the cinder cone's side to discover "Little Beach"—clothing-optional by popular practice, although this is technically illegal. On Sunday, free spirits of all kinds crowd Little Beach's tiny shoreline for a drumming circle and bonfire. Little Beach has the Island's best bodysurfing (no pun intended). Skimboarders catch air at Makena's third entrance, which is a little tricky to find (it's just a dirt path with street parking). Access to all beaches now requires paid parking and an entrance fee for non-resident visitors. **Amenities:** lifeguards; parking ($10 fee for non-residents); toilets. **Best for:** surfing; swimming; walking. ⊠ *Makena* ⊹ *Off Wailea Alanui Dr.* ⊕ *www.hawaiistateparks.org.*

Mokapu and Ulua

BEACH | FAMILY | Look for a little road and public parking lot near the Wailea Beach Resort if you are heading to Mokapu and Ulua beaches. Although there are no lifeguards, families love this place. Reef formations create tons of tide pools for kids to explore, and the beaches are protected from major swells. Snorkeling is excellent at Ulua, the beach to the left of the entrance. Mokapu, to the right, tends to be less crowded. **Amenities:** parking (no fee); showers; toilets. **Best for:** snorkeling; swimming. ⊠ *Halealii Pl., Wailea* ⊹ *Before Shops of Wailea.*

Polo Beach

BEACH | FAMILY | Small and secluded, this crescent fronts the Fairmont Kea Lani. Swimming and snorkeling are great here, and it's a good place for whale-watching. As at Wailea Beach, private umbrellas and chaise lounges occupy the choicest real estate, but there's plenty of room for you and your towel. There's a nice grass picnic area, although it's a considerable distance from the beach. The pathway connecting the two beaches is a great spot to jog or to take in awesome views of nearby Molokini and Kahoolawe. Rare native plants grow along the ocean, or *makai,* side of the path—the honey-sweet-smelling one is *naio,* or false sandalwood. **Amenities:** parking (no fee); showers; toilets. **Best for:** snorkeling; swimming. ⊠ *Kaukahi St., Wailea* ⊹ *South of Fairmont Kea Lani entrance.*

Wailea Beach

BEACH | FAMILY | A road near the Grand Wailea Resort takes you to Wailea Beach, a wide, sandy stretch with snorkeling and swimming. If you're not a guest at the Grand Wailea or Four Seasons, the cluster of private umbrellas and chaise lounges can be a little annoying, but the calm unclouded waters and soft white sand more than make up for this. From the parking lot, walk to the right to get to the main beach; to the left is another, smaller section that fronts the Four Seasons Resort. There are picnic tables and grills away from the beach. **Amenities:** parking (no fee); showers; toilets. **Best for:** snorkeling; swimming. ⊠ *Wailea Alanui Dr., Wailea* ⊹ *South of Grand Wailea Resort entrance.*

🍴 Restaurants

Ferraro's Bar e Ristorante

$$$$ | ITALIAN | Overlooking the ocean from a bluff above Wailea Beach, this outdoor Italian restaurant at Four Seasons Resort Maui is Wailea's only oceanfront restaurant. For lunch, indulge in the catch of the day, artisanal sandwiches,

or one of a variety of stone-baked pizzas. **Known for:** excellent selection of Italian wines; classical music in the moonlight; romantic ambience. [$] *Average main: $47 ⊠ Four Seasons Resort Maui at Wailea, 3900 Wailea Alanui Dr., Wailea ☎ 808/874–8000 ⊕ fourseasons.com/maui.*

Humuhumunukunukuapuaa

$$$$ | **MODERN HAWAIIAN** | This Polynesian-style thatch-roof, open-air restaurant "floats" atop a saltwater lagoon, which gives it an exotic romantic feel that's suited for special occasions. Daily breakfast features hearty, yet elegant options. **Known for:** nightly live music; seasonal, farm-to-table dishes; macadamia-crusted catch of the day. [$] *Average main: $52 ⊠ Grand Wailea, 3850 Wailea Alanui Dr., Wailea ☎ 808/875–1234 ⊕ grandwailea.com/humuhumunukunukuapuaa ⊗ No lunch, closed for dinner Mon. and Tues.*

Monkeypod Kitchen

$$ | **ECLECTIC** | The wooden surfboards hanging above the bar and surf videos playing in the background set a decidedly chill vibe at this buzzing restaurant, the creation of local celebrity-chef Peter Merriman. He offers a menu that highlights local bounty, with such standout dishes as poke tacos, coconut corn chowder, and wood-fired pizzas. **Known for:** live music twice daily; pecan-crusted mahimahi (dolphinfish); fun cocktails such as Monkeypod mai tai. [$] *Average main: $26 ⊠ 10 Wailea Gateway Pl., Wailea ☎ 808/891–2322 ⊕ monkeypod-kitchen.com.*

★ Morimoto Maui

$$$$ | **ASIAN** | "Iron Chef" Masaharu Morimoto's eponymous restaurant, located at the Andaz Maui resort, has some of Maui's most creative presentations and, arguably, some of its best food. Poolside outdoor tables that sit directly under the stars, a bustling dining room, and a sushi bar all make it a lively choice, but the food is ultimately the reason to go. **Known for:** signature Morimoto dishes; excellent ambience; fantastic levels of service. [$] *Average main: $64 ⊠ Andaz Maui at Wailea, 3550 Wailea Alanui Dr., Wailea ☎ 808/243–4766 ⊕ morimotomaui.com.*

★ Pita Paradise Mediterranean Bistro

$$ | **MEDITERRANEAN** | Don't be fooled by its playful name; this place serves high-quality food that befits its chic surroundings. This restaurant's owner is a fisherman himself, so you know the fish here is the freshest available. **Known for:** baklava ice-cream cake with Roselani ice cream; lamb gnocchi, made in-house; Mediterranean chicken pita. [$] *Average main: $24 ⊠ Wailea Gateway Center, 34 Wailea Gateway Pl., A-108, Wailea ☎ 808/879–7177 ⊕ pitaparadisehawaii.com.*

Spago

$$$$ | **MODERN HAWAIIAN** | It's a marriage made in Hawaii heaven: the California cuisine of celebrity-chef Wolfgang Puck combined with Maui flavors and served lobby-level and oceanfront at the luxurious Four Seasons Resort Maui. Try the spicy *ahi* (yellowfin tuna) poke in sesame-miso cones to start and then see what the chef can do with some of Maui's fantastic local fish. **Known for:** show-stopping desserts; sunset views from the patio; exceptional wine list. [$] *Average main: $79 ⊠ Four Seasons Resort Maui at Wailea, 3900 Wailea Alanui Dr., Wailea ☎ 808/879–2999 ⊕ wolfgangpuck.com/dining/spago-maui ⊗ No lunch.*

★ Tommy Bahama

$$$$ | **MODERN AMERICAN** | It's more "Island-style" than Hawaii-style—and yes, it's a chain—but the food is consistently great, the service is filled with aloha, and the ambience is Island refined. The cocktails are among the best and most creative on the Island and include well-priced non-alcoholic options. **Known for:** filet mignon in a variety of preparations; festive bar scene; miso-glazed King Salmon. [$] *Average main: $40 ⊠ The*

Shave Ice and Ice Cream

🍴

The two most critical components in the making of the Islands' favorite frosty treat—shave ice—are the fineness of the shave and the quality of the syrup. The shave should be almost powdery, like snow. Top that ice with tropical flavors like mango, *lilikoi* (Hawaiian passion fruit), or guava. For a multipart taste sensation, start with a scoop of vanilla ice cream in the bottom (and maybe some Japanese adzuki beans), add shave ice and flavoring, and then top it with a drizzle of cream or a sprinkle of *li hing mui* (Chinese plum) powder for a salty-pungent kick. A great pick is **Ululani's Hawaiian Shave Ice**, which makes "gourmet" shave ice and has locations all over Maui. The Kihei location includes sister company Sugar Beach Bake Shop (✉ *61 S. Kihei Road* ☎ *808/757-8285*).

Prefer ice cream on its own? Maui's own Roselani has been made from scratch in Wailuku since 1932. Look for the brand's line of Tropics flavors, available at all Maui supermarkets. *Haupia* (coconut pudding) is the best-selling flavor. Some of the best ice cream parlors in South Maui are **Hula Cookies & Ice Cream** (✉ *300 Maalaea Road, Maalaea* ☎ *808/243-2271*), **Maui Gelato and Waffles** (✉ *2395 S. Kihei Rd., No. 120, Kihei* ☎ *808/419-6213*), and **Maui Sweet Shoppe** (✉ *1819 S. Kihei Road, Kihei* ☎ *808/214-5151*).

Shops at Wailea, 3750 Wailea Alanui Dr., Wailea ☎ *808/875-9983* 🌐 *tommybahama.com* 🕒 *Closed Mon.*

🛏 Hotels

Warm, serene, and luxurious, Wailea properties offer less "action" than West Maui resorts. The properties here tend to focus on ambience, thoughtful details, and natural scenery. Nightlife is pretty much nil, save for a few swanky bars. However, you have your choice of sandy beaches with good snorkeling. Farther south, Makena is a little less developed. Expect everything—even bottled water—to double in price when you cross the line from Kihei to Wailea.

★ Andaz Maui at Wailea Resort

$$$$ | **RESORT** | Sophisticated travelers and romance-seeking couples will swoon at the sleek luxury of this eco-friendly, beachfront resort. **Pros:** outstanding service and dining; one-of-a-kind resort on Maui; free shuttle service around Wailea. **Cons:** not the best resort for families; slick design style might feel cold to some; rooms on the small side. [$] *Rooms from: $1,033* ✉ *3550 Wailea Alanui Dr., Wailea* ☎ *808/573-1234* 🌐 *andazmaui.com* 🛏 *321 units* 🍴 *No Meals.*

Fairmont Kea Lani Maui

$$$$ | **RESORT** | **FAMILY** | Gleaming white spires and tiled archways are the hallmark of this stunning resort that's particularly good for families with its spacious suite and villa options. **Pros:** all rooms are suites; 22,000-square-foot water complex; located on almost-private Polo Beach. **Cons:** daily resort and parking fees; lounge chairs in high demand; noisy families at play may be a turnoff for some. [$] *Rooms from: $1089* ✉ *4100 Wailea Alanui Dr., Wailea* ☎ *808/875-4100, 866/540-4456* 🌐 *fairmont.com/kealani* 🛏 *450 suites* 🍴 *No Meals.*

★ Four Seasons Resort Maui at Wailea

$$$$ | **RESORT** | "Impeccably stylish" and "extravagant" describe most Four Seasons properties, and this elegant one fronting Wailea Beach is no exception, with its beautiful courtyards and luxuries

The Four Seasons Maui in Wailea is one of the island's best resort hotels.

such as 24-hour room service, twice-daily housekeeping, excellent restaurants, on-site spa, and adults-only serenity pool with outstanding views. **Pros:** no resort fee; complimentary kids' club, snorkeling, tennis, and cultural activities; great shopping and local crafts and artwork market. **Cons:** a bit ostentatious for some; when fully booked facilities can seem crowded; adults-only pool chairs fill up fast. $ *Rooms from: $1,045* ✉ *3900 Wailea Alanui Dr., Wailea* ☎ *808/874–8000, 800/311–0630* ⊕ *fourseasons.com/maui* ⇆ *383 rooms* ⦿ *No Meals.*

Grand Wailea, a Waldorf Astoria Resort

$$$$ | **RESORT** | **FAMILY** | "Grand" is no exaggeration for this opulent, sunny 40-acre resort that's wildly entertaining due to its elaborate water features such as the Wailea Activity Pool with enclosed "lava tube," slides, caves, a Tarzan swing, and the world's only water elevator. **Pros:** set on beautiful Wailea Beach; offers one of the largest varieties of cultural programs on Maui; many shops. **Cons:** sprawling property can be difficult

to traverse; limited poolside chairs; daily resort and parking fees. $ *Rooms from: $1,222* ✉ *3850 Wailea Alanui Dr., Wailea* ☎ *808/875–1234, 800/888–6100* ⊕ *grand-wailea.com* ⇆ *776 rooms* ⦿ *No Meals.*

Makena Surf

$$$$ | **APARTMENT** | For travelers who've done all there is to do on Maui and just want simple but luxurious relaxation at a condo that spills onto a private beach, this is the spot. **Pros:** away from it all, yet still close enough to "civilization"; great snorkeling right off the beach; laundry facilities in every unit and daily housekeeping. **Cons:** split-level units may be difficult for guests with mobility issues; check-in at a different location; too secluded and "locked-up" for some. $ *Rooms from: $964* ✉ *4850 Makena Alanui, Makena* ☎ *808/891–6200 guest services, 800/367–5246 reservations* ⊕ *destinationresidenceswailea.com* ⇆ *105 units* ⦿ *No Meals.*

Polo Beach Club

$$$$ | **APARTMENT** | Lording over a hidden section of Polo Beach, this wonderful,

older eight-story rental property's charm somehow manages to stay under the radar. **Pros:** ocean-view grills and herb garden you can pick from; beautiful beach fronting the building; daily housekeeping. **Cons:** split-level units potentially challenging for those with impaired mobility; check-in at a different location; some may feel isolated. $ *Rooms from: $809* ✉ *4400 Makena Alanui Rd., Makena* ☎ *808/891–6200 guest services, 808/495-4491 reservations* ⊕ *destinationresidencesmaui.com* ↗ *71 units* �‖ *No Meals.*

★ Wailea Beach Resort—Marriott, Maui

$$$$ | **RESORT** | **FAMILY** | The Wailea Beach Resort, which sits closer to the crashing surf than most resorts, promises not only dramatic views but luxurious amenities and spacious accommodations. **Pros:** hosts the only Starbucks in Wailea; short walk to The Shops at Wailea; Te Au Moana Luau four nights a week. **Cons:** foot traffic on coastal beach walk; daily resort fee and daily self-parking fee (valet also available); rocky shore that is not quite beachfront. $ *Rooms from: $1175* ✉ *3700 Wailea Alanui Dr., Wailea* ☎ *808/879–1922* ⊕ *waileamarriott.com* ↗ *547 units* �‖ *No Meals.*

Wailea Ekahi Village

$$$$ | **RESORT** | Overlooking Keawakapu Beach, this family-friendly vacation resort features studios and one- and two-bedroom suites in low-rise buildings that span 34 acres of tropical gardens and won't cost your child's entire college fund. **Pros:** convenient access to a great beach; en-suite kitchen and laundry facilities; daily housekeeping. **Cons:** check-in at a different location; decor in individually owned units may differ; large complex can be tricky to find your way around. $ *Rooms from: $419* ✉ *3300 Wailea Alanui Dr., Wailea* ☎ *808/891–6200 guest services, 800/367–5246 reservations* ⊕ *destinationresidenceswailea.com* ↗ *289 units* �‖ *No Meals.*

Wailea Elua Village

$$$$ | **RESORT** | Located on Ulua Beach, one of the Island's most beloved snorkeling spots, these upscale one-, two-, and three-bedroom condo suites have spectacular views and 24 acres of manicured lawns and gardens. **Pros:** easy access to the designer boutiques and upscale restaurants at The Shops at Wailea; daily housekeeping; on-site naturalist and organic herb garden. **Cons:** hard to find your way around; check-in at a different location; large complex. $ *Rooms from: $669* ✉ *3600 Wailea Alanui Dr., Wailea* ☎ *808/891–6200, 800/367–5246* ⊕ *destinationresidenceswailea.com* ↗ *152 suites* �‖ *No Meals.*

Nightlife

Luau—Grand Wailea

THEMED ENTERTAINMENT | **FAMILY** | Grand Wailea's spectacular luau features traditional ceremonies, music, and dishes such as poi, kalua pig, poke, and haupia. Guests can sit at their own private table overlooking Wailea Beach for an unforgettable evening filled with interactive entertainment, hula lessons, and amazing performances that showcase the myths and legends of Maui all in their colorful, fiery glory. Seating includes standard and Alii premium seating. ✉ *Grand Wailea Resort & Spa, 3850 Wailea Alanui Dr., Wailea* ☎ *808/875–1234* ⊕ *grandwailea. com* ⊙ *Closed select days.*

The Feast at Mokapu

THEMED ENTERTAINMENT | Held on the grounds of the posh Andaz, it's no surprise that this oceanfront luau is elevated to luxurious heights. A live band sets the soundtrack for an evening of storytelling, traditional and modern dance from across Polynesia, and an energetic fire-knife dance. The onstage performance is matched by eye-catching culinary creations delivered directly to your table and served family style. Indeed, standard luau fare goes gourmet with a multicourse dinner that blends traditional foods with modern flare. Preshow cultural activities, an open bar, and a complimentary printed photo are additional perks. ⊠ *Andaz Maui at Wailea Resort, 3550 Wailea Alanui Dr., Wailea* ☎ *808/573–1234* ⊕ *www. feastatmokapu.com* ✉ *$200.*

★ Lobby Lounge at Four Seasons Resort Maui

LIVE MUSIC | This lofty resort's lobby lounge is perfect when you want live Hawaiian music, a bit of hula, and freshly prepared sushi all in one sitting. If you're not in the mood for a ceremonious sit-down meal but still crave something out of the ordinary, the place is perfect for a quick bite. The artisanal cocktails are well done and highlight locally distilled spirits. The contemporary beachfront space, which boasts a stunning view of the Pacific, west Maui, and neighboring island of Lanai, is beautifully appointed with natural tones and textiles inspired by the destination, rare ivory cane palms, and locally made art. Food is served 5–10 pm; cocktails 5–11 pm. ⊠ *Four Seasons Resort Maui at Wailea, 3900 Wailea Alanui Dr., Wailea* ☎ *808/874–8000* ⊕ *fourseasons.com/maui.*

Te Au Moana

THEMED ENTERTAINMENT | Te Au Moana means "ocean tide," which is all you need to know about the simply breath-taking backdrop for this South Maui luau at Wailea Beach Resort. The tasty family-style dinner serves a three-course dinner that includes variety of local staples and desserts, as well as an open bar. Longtime local entertainment company Tihati Productions seamlessly intertwines ancient Hawaiian stories and contemporary songs with traditional hula and Polynesian dances, concluding with a jaw-dropping solo fire-knife dance. ⊠ *Wailea Beach Resort—Marriott, Maui, 3700 Wailea Alanui, Wailea* ☎ *877/827–2740* ⊕ *teaumoana.com* ⊗ *Closed Sun.*

Shopping

The Shops at Wailea

MALL | Stylish, upscale, and close to most of the resorts, this mall brings high fashion to Wailea. Luxury boutiques such as Gucci, Cos Bar, and Tiffany & Co. are represented, as are less expensive chains like Billabong, Lululemon, and Tommy Bahama. Daily events include lei making, ukulele lessons, hula performances, and more. Dining options include elevated pub food at Pint & Cork, along with the hip and trendy Lineage. Island Gourmet Markets offers everything from grocery essentials to locally made food products, plus a wide selection of takeaway food options. ⊠ *3750 Wailea Alanui Dr., Wailea* ☎ *808/891–6770* ⊕ *shopsatwailea.com.*

Wailea Gateway Center

MALL | Located at the top of tony Wailea, this center is comprised of commercial offices and a handful of fantastic dining options. Although lunch at chef Peter Merriman's Monkeypod is reason enough to venture here, you might also be enticed by eateries including Pita Paradise, Sprout Vegan Cafe, and the Market Maui. ⊠ *34 Wailea Gateway Pl., Wailea.*

Central Maui

Some visitors bypass Central Maui in favor of towns that cater to fun-in-the-sun activities. However, there's still plenty to see and do here—from learning to windsurf or kiteboard at Kanaha Beach Park, exploring nature and taking an ice-cold dip in lush Iao Valley, and catching a world-class concert at the Maui Arts & Cultural Center.

Kahului, where you most likely landed when you arrived on Maui, is the industrial and commercial center of the island. West of Kahului is Wailuku, the county seat since 1950 and the most charming town in Central Maui, with some good inexpensive restaurants. Outside these towns are attractions ranging from museums and historical sites to gardens.

You can combine sightseeing in Central Maui with shopping at the Queen Kaahumanu Center, Maui Mall, and Wailuku's Market Street. This is one of the best areas on the island to stock up on groceries and supplies, thanks to major retailers, including Safeway, Target, and Costco. Note that grocery prices are much higher than on the mainland.

Kahului

3 miles west of Kahului Airport; 9 miles north of Kihei; 31 miles east of Kaanapali; 51 miles west of Hana.

With the Island's largest airport and commercial harbor, Kahului is Maui's commercial hub. But it also offers plenty of natural and cultural attractions. The town was developed in the early 1950s to meet the housing needs of the large sugarcane interests here, specifically those of Alexander & Baldwin. The company was tired of playing landlord to its many plantation workers and sold land to a developer who promised to create affordable housing. The scheme worked, and "Dream City," the first planned city in Hawaii, was born.

GETTING HERE AND AROUND
From the airport, take Keolani Place to Route 36 (Hana Highway), which becomes Kaahumanu Avenue, Kahului's main drag. Run by Maui Bus, the Kahului Loop route traverses all of the town's major shopping centers; the fare is $2.

 Sights

Alexander & Baldwin Sugar Museum
HISTORY MUSEUM | Maui's largest landowner, A&B was one of the "Big Five" companies that spearheaded the planting, harvesting, and processing of sugarcane. At this museum, historic photos, artifacts, and documents explain the introduction of sugarcane to Hawaii. Exhibits reveal how plantations brought in laborers from other countries, forever changing the Islands' ethnic mix. Although sugarcane is no longer being grown on Maui, the crop was for many years the mainstay of the local economy. You can find the museum in a small, restored plantation manager's house across the street from the post office and the still-operating sugar refinery, where smoke billows up when the cane is being processed. Their gift shop sells plantation-themed memorabilia, coffee, and a selection of history books. ⊠ *3957 Hansen Rd., Puunene* ☏ *808/871–8058* ⊕ *sugarmuseum.com* ⊡ *$7* ⊙ *Closed Fri., Sat., Sun.*

Maui Nui Botanical Gardens
GARDEN | FAMILY | Hawaiian and Polynesian species are cultivated at this fascinating 7-acre garden, including Hawaiian bananas; local varieties of sweet potatoes and sugarcane; and native poppies, hibiscus, and *anapanapa,* a plant that makes a natural shampoo when rubbed between your hands. Reserve ahead for the weekly ethnobotany tours. Self-guided tour booklets and an audio tour wand are included with admission (docent tours must be arranged online in advance). ⊠ *150 Kanaloa Ave., Kahului* ☏ *808/249–2798* ⊕ *mnbg.org* ⊡ *$10 admission; docent tour $10* ⊙ *Closed Sun. and Mon.*

 Restaurants

Bistro Casanova
$$ | MEDITERRANEAN | The location of this Mediterranean restaurant is smack-dab in the middle of Kahului, making it a convenient choice for lunch or dinner. The menu features everything from salads to pasta, and the tapas menu (available from 4–9 pm) changes weekly and always has an excellent selection of dishes. **Known for:** beautiful desserts; perfect place for dinner before heading to the airport; paella with saffron rice,

The Maui Nui Botanical Gardens have acres of fascinating plant species from Hawaii and Polynesia.

scallop linguine. $ *Average main: $26* ✉ *33 Lono Ave., Kahului* ☎ *808/873–3650* ⊕ *bistrocasanova.com* ⊗ *Closed Sun.*

Marco's Grill & Deli

$$ | ITALIAN | One of the go-to places for airport comers and goers, this popular Italian restaurant also draws a steady crowd of local residents, mostly for business lunches. Meatballs, sausages, and sauces are all made in-house, there's a long list of sandwiches that are available all day, and the affordable salads are big enough to share; substitutions or special requests are not recommended. **Known for:** chicken Parmesan; great selection of breakfasts; gluten-free options. $ *Average main: $18* ✉ *444 Hana Hwy., Kahului* ☎ *808/877–4446* ⊕ *marcosgrillanddeli. com.*

★ Tin Roof

$ | MODERN HAWAIIAN | Celebrity chef Sheldon Simeon has taken the fame he earned on *Top Chef* and opened this trendy lunch counter in a small Kahului warehouse. You can't miss this spot; look for the line of people waiting in the parking lot. **Known for:** fresh poke bowl; plantation-inspired "kau kau tins"; decadent treats such as mochi birthday cake bites. $ *Average main: $10* ✉ *360 Papa Pl., Suite Y, Kahului* ☎ *808/868–0753* ⊕ *tinroofmaui.com* ⊗ *No dinner. Closed Sun.*

Hotels

Courtyard by Marriott Maui Kahului Airport

$$$ | HOTEL | At the entrance to Kahului Airport, this hotel offers many amenities for business travelers and tourists. **Pros:** great for business and pleasure; central location; conference and banquet rooms available. **Cons:** airport and city noise; daily parking fee; not on the beach. $ *Rooms from: $289* ✉ *532 Keolani Pl., Kahului* ☎ *808/871–1800, 877/852–1880* ⊕ *marriott.com* ➷ *138 rooms* ⦿ *No Meals.*

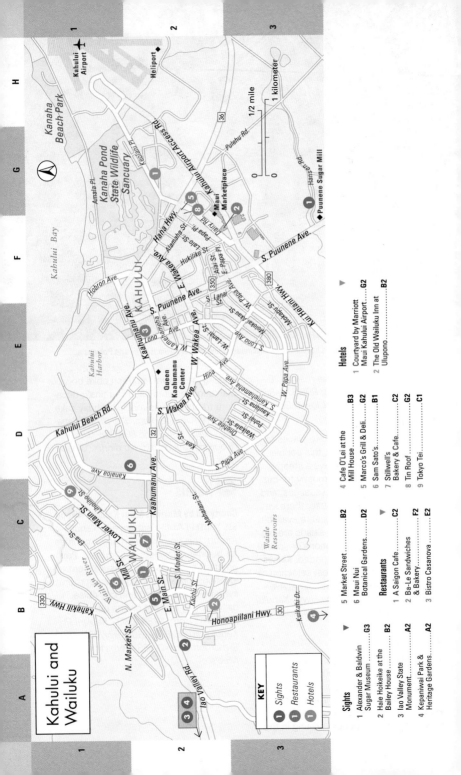

Kahului and Wailuku

KEY
- ① Sights
- ① Restaurants
- ① Hotels

Sights ▶
1 Alexander & Baldwin
  Sugar Museum...............**G3**
2 Hale Hoikeike at the
  Bailey House..................**B2**
3 Iao Valley State
  Monument......................**A2**
4 Kepaniwai Park &
  Heritage Gardens..........**A2**
5 Market Street..................**B2**
6 Maui Nui
  Botanical Gardens..........**D2**

Restaurants ▶
1 A Saigon Cafe..................**C2**
2 Ba-Le Sandwiches
  & Bakery.........................**F2**
3 Bistro Casanova.............**E2**
4 Cafe O'Lei at the
  Mill House......................**B3**
5 Marco's Grill & Deli.........**G2**
6 Sam Sato's......................**B1**
7 Stillwell's
  Bakery & Cafe................**C2**
8 Tin Roof...........................**G2**
9 Tokyo Tei.........................**C1**

Hotels ▶
1 Courtyard by Marriott
  Maui Kahului Airport......**G2**
2 The Old Wailuku Inn at
  Ulupono..........................**B2**

🛍 Shopping

⭐ Hi-Tech

MIXED CLOTHING | This locally owned shop is a favorite among stylish surfers and landlubbers alike. Stop here immediately after deplaning to stock up on surf trunks, windsurfing gear, bikinis, or sundresses. You can also rent a surfboard or sign up for windsurfing or kiteboarding lessons while you're at it. You'll find additional branches in Kihei and Paia. ⊠ 425 Koloa St., Kahului 🕾 808/877–2111 ⊕ surfmaui.com.

Maui Coffee Roasters

FOOD | It's the best stop in Kahului for 100% Kona, Kau, and Maui coffee from the best coffee farms in Hawaii. This café and roasting house is near Kahului Airport. Sales associates are very helpful and friendly, and they will ship items. You can get a free cup of joe in a signature to-go cup when you buy a pound of coffee. Order online or call in your food or drink order and the barista will meet you at the door or bring it to your car! ⊠ 444 Hana Hwy., Kahului 🕾 808/877–2877 ⊕ mauicoffeeroasters.com ⊗ Closed Sun.

Maui Swap Meet

MARKET | Crafts, T-shirts, fresh produce, flowers, souvenirs that range from authentic to average make this enormous flea market—operating since 1981—the Island's biggest bargain. Maui-made food product vendors and freshly cracked coconuts can be found next to the food trucks serving fresh, affordable, authentic local food. ⊠ 310 W Kaahumanu Ave., Kahului ⚓ UH Maui College, rear parking lot. 🕾 808/244–3100 ⊕ mauihawaii.org/maui-shopping/swap-meet ⊗ Closed Sun.-Fri.

Pu'unene Shopping Center

MALL | This newer shopping center is near Kahului Airport. It is anchored by a Target store that includes a supermarket, making it convenient to purchase necessities and groceries after landing on Maui. Other retailers include Planet Fitness, Ulta, Maui Tacos, Petco, Starbucks, and the popular farm-to-table takeout joint Fork & Salad. ⊠ 100 Hookele St., Kahului.

Queen Kaahumanu Center

MALL | Maui's largest shopping center has more than 100 stores and restaurants, a movie theater, and a food court. The mall's attractive rooftop is easily spotted, composed of a series of manta ray-like umbrella shades. Stop at Camellia Seeds for what locals call "crack seed," a snack made from dried fruits, or swing by 180 Boardshop for Hawaii-based streetwear like 808 All Day or In4mation. For surf-inspired gear, stop by The Foam Company and Shapers. Other stops include Macy's, PacSun, Bath & Body Works, and American Eagle Outfitters. Beyond retail therapy, the mall also hosts a creative lineup of events throughout the month, including a farmers' market, live music, and car shows. ⊠ 275 W. Kaahumanu Ave., Kahului 🕾 808/877–3369 ⊕ queen-kaahumanucenter.com.

Wailuku

4 miles west of Kahului; 12 miles north of Kihei; 21 miles east of Lahaina.

Wailuku is peaceful now, although it wasn't always. Its name means "Water of Destruction," after the fateful battle in Iao Valley that pitted King Kamehameha the Great against Maui warriors. Wailuku was a politically important town until the sugar industry declined in the 1960s and tourism took hold. Businesses left the cradle of the West Maui mountains and followed the new market (and tourists) to the shores. Wailuku houses the county government but has the feel of a town that's been asleep for several decades.

The shops and offices now inhabiting Market Street's plantation-style buildings serve as reminders of a bygone era, and continued attempts at gentrification, at the very least, open the way for unique eateries, shops, and galleries.

GETTING HERE AND AROUND

Heading to Wailuku from the airport, Hana Highway turns into Kaahumanu Avenue, the main thoroughfare between Kahului and Wailuku. Maui Bus system's Wailuku Loop stops at shopping centers, medical facilities, and government buildings; the fare is $2.

Sights

★ Hale Hoikeike at the Bailey House

HISTORIC HOME | This repository of the largest and best collection of Hawaiian artifacts on Maui includes objects from the sacred island of Kahoolawe. Erected in 1833 on the site of the compound of Kahekili (the last ruling chief of Maui), the building was occupied by the family of missionary teachers Edward and Caroline Bailey until 1888. Edward Bailey was something of a Renaissance man: not only a missionary, but also a surveyor, a naturalist, and an excellent artist. The museum contains missionary-period furniture and displays a number of Bailey's landscape paintings, which provide a snapshot of the island during his time. The grounds include gardens with native Hawaiian plants and a fine example of a traditional canoe. The gift shop is one of the best sources on Maui for items that are actually made in Hawaii. Before visiting, check their website for current hours of operation. ⊠ *2375A Main St., Wailuku* ☎ *808/244–3326* ⊕ *mauimuseum.org* 💰 *$10* ◔ *Closed Sun.*

★ Iao Valley State Monument

NATURE SIGHT | When Mark Twain saw this park, he dubbed it the Yosemite of the Pacific. Yosemite, it's not, but it is a lovely deep valley with the curious Iao Needle, a spire that rises more than 2,000 feet from the valley floor. You can walk from the parking lot across Iao Stream and explore the thick, jungle-like topography. This park has some lovely short strolls on paved paths, where you can stop and meditate by the edge of a stream or marvel at the native plants. Mist often rises if there has been raining, making it even more magical. Be aware that this area is prone to flash flooding; stay out of the water if it's been raining. ⊠ *Western end of Rte. 32, Wailuku* ⊕ *hawaiistateparks. org* 💰 *$5 per person; $10 parking per vehicle.*

Kepaniwai Park & Heritage Gardens

CITY PARK | FAMILY | Picnic facilities dot the landscape of this county park, a memorial to Maui's cultural roots. Among the interesting displays are an early-Hawaiian *hale* (house), a New England–style saltbox, a Portuguese-style villa with gardens, and dwellings from such other cultures as China and the Philippines.

The peacefulness here belies the history of the area. In 1790, King Kamehameha the Great from the Island of Hawaii waged a successful bloody battle against Kahekili, the son of Maui's chief. An earlier battle at the site had pitted Kahekili himself against an older Hawaii Island chief, Kalaniopuu. Kahekili prevailed, but the carnage was so great that the nearby stream became known as *Wailuku* (Water of Destruction), and the place where fallen warriors choked the stream's flow was called *Kepaniwai* (Damming of the Waters). ⊠ *870 Iao Valley Rd., Wailuku* ☎ *808/270–7980* ⊕ *mauicounty.gov* 💰 *Free.*

Market Street

HISTORIC DISTRICT | A unique assortment of historic buildings, stylish boutiques, coffee shops, antique stores, and restaurants make Wailuku's Market Street a delightful place for a stroll. Brown-Kobayashi and the Bird of Paradise Unique Antiques are the best shops for interesting collectibles and furnishings. Brown Eyed Bella has stylish bikinis and island wear. Wailuku Coffee Company holds works by local artists and occasionally offers live entertainment in the evening. ⊠ *Market St., Wailuku* ⊕ *wailukulive.com* 💰 *Free.*

🍴 Restaurants

A Saigon Cafe

$$ | VIETNAMESE | Locals have been flocking to this off-the-beaten-path gem for years, lured in by the reliably delicious Vietnamese cuisine served family-style at decent prices. It's tucked behind a nondescript overpass—and only recently did they put a sign on its building—but you can't go wrong with the green papaya salad, mixed fondue, and the make-your-own Vietnamese burritos. **Known for:** authentic Com Tay Cam (rice in a clay pot); known locally as "Jennifer's"; strong cocktails well mixed. $ *Average main: $19* ⊠ 1792 Main St., Wailuku ☎ 808/243–9560 ⊕ asaigoncafe.com.

★ Ba-Le Sandwiches & Bakery

$ | VIETNAMESE | This popular spot began as a French-Vietnamese bakery on Oahu and has branched into popular small restaurants sprinkled throughout the Islands. Some are kiosks in malls; others are stand-alone with some picnic tables out front, as is the case at this location. **Known for:** boba teas in fun flavors like taro or pineapple; opakapaka (pink snapper) with garlic shrimp; affordable Vietnamese cuisine. $ *Average main: $10* ⊠ 1824 Oihana St., Wailuku ☎ 808/249–8833 ⊕ balemaui.com ⊙ Closed Sun. 🏛 Casual.

Cafe O'Lei at the Mill House

$$$ | FUSION | The food is so fresh at this Waikapu standout that you can see the fields where the food was grown while seated at your mountain view table. This family-owned restaurant creates rich cuisine from *mauka* (mountain) to *makai* (ocean), boasting seasonal produce. **Known for:** bold flavors and farm-to-table freshness; ulu and sweet potato enchiladas; robust happy hour. $ *Average main: $27* ⊠ 1670 Honoapiilani Hwy., Waikapu ☎ 808/270–0333 ⊕ millhousemaui.com ⊙ Closed Mon.

★ Sam Sato's

$ | HAWAIIAN | Sam Sato's is a local favorite for noodles, *manju* (Japanese pastry filled with sweet bean paste), and plate lunches. Open for breakfast and lunch; the menu includes favorites like "dry noodles," beef tomato, omelets, and fried rice. **Known for:** huge portions of flavorful food; affordable local hideout; amazing spare ribs. $ *Average main: $8* ⊠ The Millyard, 1750 Wili Pa Loop, Wailuku ☎ 808/244–7124 ⊟ No credit cards ⊙ Closed Sun.

★ Stillwell's Bakery & Cafe

$ | BAKERY | Stillwell's is one of the best bakeries in Maui, so this is the place to come for coffee and an outrageously good strawberry florentine or a renowned cream horn. Their breakfast and lunch offerings are exceptional, from a fried egg sandwich to mouthwatering pancakes and gourmet sandwiches on house-made bread to their famous Chinese chicken salad. **Known for:** amazing pies (try the coconut cream); towering Rubens and BLTs; friendly staff who love to share local tips. $ *Average main: $12* ⊠ 1740 Kaahumanu Ave., Wailuku ☎ 808/243–2243 ⊕ stillwellsbakery.com.

Tokyo Tei

$ | JAPANESE | FAMILY | Tokyo Tei is worth seeking out for local-style Japanese food. At lunch, you can rub elbows with bankers and construction workers, and at dinner, three generations might be celebrating *tutu's* (grandma's) birthday at the next table. **Known for:** misoyaki-glazed fish; unlikeliest of locations for great food; local institution that's been around for more than eight decades. $ *Average main: $12* ⊠ Puuone Plaza, 1063 Lower Main St., Wailuku ☎ 808/242–9630 ⊙ Closed Mon.–Sat. 1:30–5 pm; Sun. dinner only.

Hotels

★ The Old Wailuku Inn at Ulupono

$$ | **B&B/INN** | Built in 1924 and listed on the State of Hawaii Register of Historic Places, this home with knowledgeable innkeepers offers the charm of old Hawaii, including authentic decor and architecture. **Pros:** walking distance to civic center, restaurants, historic Wailuku Town; lovely garden setting; immaculately maintained. **Cons:** traffic noise at certain times; parking can be tight; closest beach is a 15-minute drive away. [$] *Rooms from: $185* ✉ *2199 Kahookele St., Wailuku* ☎ *808/244–5897 local, 800/305–4899 toll free* 🌐 *mauiinn.com* 🛏 *10 rooms* 🍴 *Free Breakfast.*

Shopping

ARTS AND CRAFTS

★ Mele Ukulele

MUSIC | For a professional-quality, authentic ukulele, skip the souvenir shops. Mele's handcrafted beauties are made of koa or mahogany and strung and finished by expert craftsmen on the Island. Owner Michael Rock has consciously observed the cultural significance and importance of the ukulele to the Hawaiian people and their music, by creating instruments for everyone from *kupuna* to *keiki* (grandparents to children). There is a location at The Shops at Wailea and in Paia. ✉ *1750 Kaahumanu Ave., Wailuku* ☎ *808/244–3938* 🌐 *meleukulele.com* 🕒 *Closed Sun.*

★ Native Intelligence

OTHER SPECIALTY STORE | This store in the heart of Wailuku champions cultural traditions and craftsmanship. It has curated Hawaiian and Polynesian works of art that include traditional wear, jewelry, weaponry, photography, books, music, hula instruments, and even surfboards. ✉ *1980 Main St., Wailuku* ☎ *808/249–2421* 🌐 *native-intel.com* 🕒 *Closed Sun.*

CLOTHING

Ha Wahine

WOMEN'S CLOTHING | At this women's clothing store, statement Polynesian prints are redefined in vibrantly colored blouses, *pareos* (beach wraps), dresses, and aloha shirts. All clothing is designed and made locally, as is most of the jewelry. ✉ *53 N. Market St., Wailuku* ☎ *808/344–1642* 🌐 *facebook.com/hawahine* 🕒 *Closed Sun.*

Upcountry

The west-facing upper slope of Haleakala is considered "Upcountry" by locals and is a hidden gem by most accounts. Although this region is responsible for most of Maui's produce—lettuce, tomatoes, strawberries, sweet Maui onions, and more—it is also home to innovators, renegades, artists, and some of Maui's most interesting communities. It may not be the Maui of postcards, but some say this is the real Maui and is well worth exploring for at least a day or two.

Upcountry is also fertile ranch land; *paniolo* (cowboys) still work the historic 18,000-acre Ulupalakua Ranch fields and the 30,000-acre Haleakala Ranch.

TIP→ Take an agricultural tour and learn more about the Island's bounty. Lavender and wine are among the offerings.

Up here cactus thickets mingle with purple jacaranda, wild hibiscus, and towering eucalyptus trees. Keep an eye out for *pueo*, Hawaii's native owl, which hunts these fields during daylight hours.

A drive to Upcountry Maui from Wailea (South Shore) or Kaanapali (West Maui) can be an all-day outing if you take the time to visit MauiWine and the tiny but entertaining town of Makawao. You may want to cut these side trips short and combine your Upcountry tour with a visit to Haleakala National Park—it's a Maui must-see. Suppose you leave early enough to catch the sunrise from the summit of Haleakala. In that case, you should have plenty of time to explore the mountain, have lunch in Kula or at Ulupalakua Ranch, and end your day with dinner in Makawao.

Makawao

27 miles from Kahului.

Despite its easygoing pace and small-town feel, Makawao remains the center of Upcountry action. The area is synonymous with the rugged *paniolo* (cowboy) lifestyle, and cowboys and cowgirls still work the fields and care for the livestock as the generations before have. Festivities abound when the Makawao Rodeo and Parade trots into town, an annual tradition now more than 60 years in the making. Spend an afternoon in Makawao Town, centered at the crossroads of Makawao and Baldwin Avenues browsing upscale clothing boutiques and gift shops or talking to a local artist at one of the many galleries. Of course, no visit to Makawao is complete without a stop at Maui's famous mom-and-pop landmark, T. Komoda Store and Bakery. Grab a cream puff or two and don't forget the butter rolls.

GETTING HERE AND AROUND

From Kahului, take Route 37 (Haleakala Highway) until you reach Makawao Avenue. Locate the center of Makawao Town by traveling along Makawao Avenue until you reach Baldwin Avenue.

Sights

Hui Noeau Visual Arts Center

ARTS CENTER | The grande dame of Maui's visual arts scene, "the Hui," hosts exhibits that are always satisfying. Located just outside Makawao, the center's main building is an elegant two-story Mediterranean-style villa designed in 1917 by Hawaii's architect of the era, C. W. Dickey. Explore the grounds, see locally made products, and experience community enrichment through art. Crafts, drawing, photography, and glass blowing are some of the classes offered. ✉ *2841 Baldwin Ave., Makawao* ☎ *808/572–6560* 🌐 *huinoeau.com* 🎟 *Free to visit; self-guided tour booklets are $6* 🕒 *Closed Sun., Mon., and Tues.*

Maui Pineapple Tours

FARM/RANCH | The quintessence of sun-blessed tropical flavor, pineapple exudes tropical happiness. It just so happens Maui boasts the only tour of a working pineapple plantation in the United States. You'll join a worker on a stroll through the sunny fields and hear all about the especially sweet Maui Gold pineapples (and sample its various stages of maturity along the way). The best part? Everyone gets a free pineapple at the end!

TIP→ Maui Pineapple Tours partners with Haliimaile Distilling Company, inviting guests after the plantation tour to visit the distillery and taste such island treats as Pau Maui Vodka, the world's only pineapple vodka.

For an additional cost, your tour can also include lunch at Haliimaile General Store just across the street. ✉ *883 Haliimaile Rd., Makawao* ☎ *808/665–5491* 🌐 *mauipineappletour.com* 🎟 *From $75.*

Restaurants

Casanova Italian Restaurant

$$$ | **ITALIAN** | An authentic Italian ristorante, Casanova is smack dab in the middle of Maui's *paniolo* (cowboy) town of Makawao. Imported from Italy, the brick wood-burning oven has turned out perfect pies and steaming-hot focaccia for more than 20 years. **Known for:** attentive staff and friendly atmosphere; decadent desserts; outstanding calamari. [$] *Average main: $30* ✉ *1188 Makawao Ave., Makawao* ☎ *808/572–0220* 🌐 *casanovamaui.com.*

Grandma's Coffee House
$ | **AMERICAN** | **FAMILY** | If you're taking a drive through the gorgeous Upcountry, this is a great place to stop for a truly homegrown, organic cup of coffee. The Franco family has been perfecting their coffee since 1918, growing the beans, handpicking, drying them under the Maui sun, then roasting them at the coffeehouse. **Known for:** tasty, generously portioned breakfasts; idyllic country location best viewed from the back deck; fresh-pressed juices. [$] *Average main: $12* ✉ *9232 Kula Hwy., Keokea* ☎ *808/878–2140* 🌐 *grandmascoffeehousemaui.com* 👔 *Casual.*

Kula Bistro
$$ | **ITALIAN** | **FAMILY** | Nestled on the slopes of Haleakala, this bistro's atmosphere is reminiscent of trattorias in northern Italy. Serving up home-style food with a splash of Italian, this eatery makes the scenic drive worth it. **Known for:** family- and group-friendly; impressive desserts; BYOB. [$] *Average main: $25* ✉ *4566 Lower Kula Rd., Kula* ☎ *808/871–2960* 🌐 *kulabistro.com* 🕒 *No breakfast on Mon.*

Polli's Mexican Restaurant
$ | **MEXICAN** | A Makawao staple since 1981, Polli's is set in the town's only intersection. Polli's is a lively Mexican restaurant that serves up the best fish tacos on the Island. **Known for:** huge dishes and family-style dining; tasty mango, strawberry, and lilikoi (Hawaiian passion fruit) margaritas; fun and friendly atmosphere. [$] *Average main: $16* ✉ *1202 Makawao Ave., Makawao* ☎ *808/572–7808* 🌐 *pollismexicanrestaurant.com* 🕒 *Closed Wed.*

★ **T. Komoda Store and Bakery**
$ | **BAKERY** | One of Makawao's landmarks is T. Komoda Store and Bakery, a mom-and-pop shop that has changed very little over the last century. **Known for:** amazing guava malasadas (Portuguese cream puffs); cool store with historic vibe; long but fast-moving lines. [$] *Average main: $4* ✉ *3674 Baldwin Ave., Makawao* ☎ *808/572–7261* 🕒 *Closed Wed. and Sun.* ☞ *Small parking lot to the right of building.*

Hotels

★ **The Banyan Tree Bed and Breakfast Retreat**
$ | **B&B/INN** | **FAMILY** | If a taste of rural Hawaii life in plantation days coupled with quiet time and privacy is what you crave, you can find it at this 2-acre property: it's awash in tropical foliage, dotted with banyan trees, and has a 50-foot, saltwater pool and in-ground spa that afford views of Maui's northern coast and Molokai. **Pros:** one cottage and the pool are outfitted for travelers with disabilities; free on-site parking; you can walk to quaint Makawao town for dining and shopping. **Cons:** not all units have air-conditioning; some daytime traffic noise; cottages have pretty basic furniture and few amenities. [$] *Rooms from: $175* ✉ *3265 Baldwin Ave., Makawao* ☎ *808/572–9021* 🌐 *www.bed-breakfast-maui.com* 🛏 *7 cottage suites* 🍴 *Free Breakfast.*

Hale Hookipa Inn
$ | **B&B/INN** | A handsome, 1924, Craftsman-style house in the heart of Makawao town is on both the Hawaii and the National Historic Registers, and provides a great base for excursions to Haleakala, Hana, or North Shore beaches. **Pros:** genteel rural setting; price includes buffet breakfast with organic fruit from the garden; charming architecture and decor. **Cons:** no food allowed in rooms; this is not the sun, sand, and surf surroundings of travel posters; a 20-minute drive to the nearest beach. [$] *Rooms from: $140* ✉ *32 Pakani Pl., Makawao* ☎ *808/281-2074* 🌐 *www.maui-bed-and-breakfast.com* 🛏 *4 units* 🍴 *Free Breakfast.*

Nightlife

Stopwatch Bar & Grill

BARS | This friendly dive bar hosts a popular karaoke night on Thursday from 7:30 to 10:30 pm. On tap, you'll find local Maui and Kona Brewing Company beers and happy hour from 3 to 6 pm daily. ✉ *1127 Makawao Ave., Makawao* ☎ *808/572–1380* ⊕ *stopwatchbarandgrill.com.*

Shopping

Designing Wahine Emporium and Hale Zen

HOUSEWARES | This Upcountry haven is a shopper's delight of beach luxe, wrapped in aloha, and sprinkled with zen. Featuring Hawaiian merchandise and Balinese imports, you'll find endless gift options like authentic aloha shirts, jams and jellies, children's clothes and books, bath and beauty products, and home decor. Find products from Capri Blue, Maka Sea, Velvet, Dolce Vita, and more. ✉ *3640 Baldwin Ave., Makawao* ☎ *808/573–0990* ⊕ *halezen.com.*

Maui Master Jewelers

JEWELRY & WATCHES | The shop's exterior is as rustic as all the old buildings of Makawao and belies the elegance of the handcrafted jewelry displayed by more than 30 fine art jewelers. Each artist is unique, and expresses their designs using gold, silver, and platinum with colored gemstones, diamonds, and pearls. ✉ *3655 Baldwin Ave., Makawao* ☎ *808/573–5400* ⊕ *mauimasterjewelers. com* ☾ *Closed Sun. and Mon.*

Pink By Nature

MIXED CLOTHING | In 2004, Desiree Martinez established Pink By Nature in Makawao. She keeps her rustic store stocked with beautiful local jewelry and feminine pieces from brands such as Indah, Bella Dahl, and Novella Royale. Versatile plaid shirts from Rails are popular, along with stylish menswear and home decor. ✉ *3663 Baldwin Ave., Makawao* ☎ *808/572–9576.*

Viewpoints Gallery

ART GALLERIES | This friendly gallery is co-owned by local artists and offers eclectic paintings, sculptures, photography, ceramics, and glass, along with locally made jewelry and quilts that celebrate Hawaii. Located in a cozy courtyard, the gallery's free monthly exhibits feature artists from various disciplines. ✉ *3620 Baldwin Ave., Makawao* ☎ *808/280–2845* ⊕ *viewpointsgallerymaui.com.*

Kula

15 miles east of Kahului; 44 miles east of Kaanapali; 28 miles east of Wailea.

Kula: most Mauians say it with a hint of a sigh. Why? It's just that much closer to heaven. On the broad shoulder of Haleakala, this is blessed country. From the Kula Highway most of Central Maui is visible—from the lava-scarred plains of Kanaio to the cruise ship–lighted waters of Kahului Harbor. Beyond the central valley's sugarcane fields, the plunging profile of the West Maui Mountains can be seen in its entirety, wreathed in ethereal mist. If this sounds too dramatic a description, you haven't been here yet. These views, coveted by many, continue to drive real-estate prices further skyward. Luckily, you can still have them for free—just pull over on the roadside and inhale the beauty. Explore it for yourself on some of the area's agricultural tours.

GETTING HERE AND AROUND

From Kahului, take Route 37 (Haleakala Highway), which runs into Route 377 (Kula Highway). Upper and Lower Kula highways are both numbered 377, but join each other at two points.

Sights

Alii Kula Lavender

FARM/RANCH | Created by Alii Chang, master horticulturist and visionary, Alii Kula Lavender farm has a falcon's view: it's *the* relaxing remedy for those suffering from too much sun, shopping, or golf. You can explore on your own or reserve a spot for the 30–40 minute tour that winds through paths of therapeutic lavender varieties, protea, and succulents. The gift shop has many locally made lavender products, such as honey, moisturizing lotions, and scone mixes. ✉ *1100 Waipoli Rd., Kula* ☎ *808/878–3004* 🌐 *aklmaui.com* 🎟 *$3, walking tours $12 (reservations recommended)* 🕒 *Closed Tues. to Thurs.*

★ **MauiWine**

WINERY | Maui's only winery in Ulupalakua is located on the former Rose Ranch on historical grounds. Stop by to learn about its history—which includes visits by monarchs, sugar production, and cattle ranching—and to sample its coveted wines. The King's Cottage was built in the late 1800s for frequent appearances from King Kalakaua, but today, tastings are held daily. A more intimate tasting held in the Old Jail building sometimes includes unreleased wines or special bottlings. Naturally, the winery's top seller is the pineapple wine Maui Blanc. ✉ *'Ulupalakua Vineyards, 14815 Piilani Hwy., Kula* ☎ *808/878–6058* 🌐 *mauiwine.com* 🎟 *Free* 🕒 *Closed Mon.*

★ **Oo Farm**

FARM/RANCH | About a mile from Alii Kula Lavender are 8 acres of organic salad greens, herbs, vegetables, coffee, cocoa, fruits, and berries—and the public is welcome to enjoy the bounty. Oo Farm is owned and operated by the restaurateurs responsible for one of Maui's finest dining establishments, PacificO, and more than 300 pounds of produce end up on diners' plates every week. Reserve a space for the breakfast or lunch tours that include an informational walk around the pastoral grounds and an alfresco meal prepared by an on-site chef. Cap off the experience with house-grown roasted and brewed coffee. Reservations are required. ✉ *651 Waipoli Rd., Kula* ☎ *808/856–0965* 🌐 *oofarm.com* 🎟 *Lunch tour from $125* 🕒 *Closed weekends.*

🍴 Restaurants

★ **Haliimaile General Store**

$$$$ | **MODERN HAWAIIAN** | Chef-restaurateur Beverly Gannon's first restaurant remains a culinary destination after more than 30 years, serving exquisite dishes like Bev's Famous Crab Pizza, sashimi napoleon, BBQ pork sandwich, and the macadamia nut–crusted fresh catch. There are daily and nightly specials, hand-crafted cocktails, and local beers as well. **Known for:** exquisite dining in an unlikely location; Hawaii regional cuisine; Bev Gannon's classic recipes. [$] *Average main: $40* ✉ *900 Haliimaile Rd., Haliimaile* ✣ *Take exit on the left halfway up Haleakala Hwy.* ☎ *808/572–2666* 🌐 *hgsmaui.com* 🕒 *Closed Sun. and Mon.*

Haleakala National Park

15 miles from Kula.

From the tropics to the moon! Two hours, 38 miles, 10,023 feet—those are the unlikely numbers involved in reaching Maui's highest point, the summit of the volcano Haleakala. Haleakala Crater is the park's centerpiece, though it's not actually a crater; technically, it's an erosional valley flushed out by water pouring from the summit through two enormous gaps. The mountain has excellent camping and hiking, including a trail that loops through the crater, but the chance to witness this unearthly landscape is reason enough for a visit. Another section of the park, Oheo Gulch in Kipahulu, can be reached only via the Road to Hana.

Exploring Haleakala Crater is one of the best hiking experiences on Maui. The volcanic terrain offers an impressive diversity of colors, textures, and shapes—as if the lava has been artfully sculpted. The barren landscape is home to many plants, insects, and birds that exist nowhere else on earth and has developed intriguing survival mechanisms, such as the sun-reflecting, hairy leaves of the silversword, which allow it to survive the intense climate.

GETTING HERE AND AROUND

To reach Haleakala National Park and the mountain's breathtaking summit, take Route 36 east of Kahului to the Haleakala Highway (Route 37). Head east, up the mountain to the unlikely intersection of Haleakala Highway and Haleakala Highway. If you continue straight the road's name changes from Kula Highway (still Route 37). Instead, turn left onto Haleakala Highway—this is now Route 377. After about 6 miles, make a left onto Crater Road (Route 378). After several long switchbacks (look out for downhill bikers), you'll come to the park entrance.

VISITOR INFORMATION
Haleakala Visitor Center

VISITOR CENTER | Located at the crater summit, the visitor center has exhibits inside and a trail that leads to Pa Kaoao (White Hill)—a short, easy walk with even better views of the valley. Call ahead for hours of operation. ⊠ *Haleakala Hwy., Makawao* ☎ *808/572–4459* ⊕ *nps. gov/hale* 🎫 *Free; parking is $30 per vehicle.*

Sights

★ Haleakala National Park

NATIONAL PARK | Nowhere else on Earth can you drive from sea level to 10,023 feet in only 38 miles. And what's more shocking: in that short vertical ascent to the summit of the volcano Haleakala you'll journey from lush, tropical island landscape to the stark, moon-like basin of the volcano's enormous, otherworldly crater.

Established in 1916, Haleakala National Park covers an astonishing 33,222 acres, with the Haleakala Crater as

its centerpiece. There's terrific hiking, including trails for one-hour, four-hour, eight-hour, and overnight hikes, one of which goes through the Waikamoi Cloud Forest on Monday and Thursday only and requires reservations (call the park line no more than a week in advance). No other hikes require reservations. There is also on-site camping.

■**TIP**→ **Before you head up Haleakala, call for the latest weather conditions. Extreme gusty winds, heavy rain, and even snow in winter are not uncommon. Because of the high altitude, the mountaintop temperature is often as much as 30°F cooler than that at sea level, so bring a jacket.**

There's a $30-per-car fee to enter the park, good for three days. Hold on to your receipt—it can also be used at Oheo Gulch in Kipahulu. Once inside the park, stop at the Park Headquarters to learn about the volcano's history, and pick up trail maps (and memorabilia, if you want) at the gift shop. Campers and hikers must check in here.

If you're planning to view the sunrise from the summit, you must make reservations (⊕ *recreation.gov*) up to 60 days before your visit. This allows you to enter the summit area between 3 and 7 am. A limited number of last-minute tickets are released online two days beforehand, but these can be difficult to secure. If you don't snag one of these coveted spots, consider visiting for sunset, which, on most days, offers equally stunning views. ■**TIP**→ **The air is thin at 10,000 feet. Don't be surprised if you feel a little breathless while walking around the summit. Take it easy, and drink lots of water. Anyone who has been scuba diving within the last 24 hours should not make the trip up Haleakala.** ⊠ *Haleakala Crater Rd., Makawao* ☎ *808/572–4400, 866/944–5025 for weather conditions* ⊕ *nps.gov/hale* 🎫 *$30 per vehicle.*

Haleakala Visitor Center

VISITOR CENTER | Located at the crater summit, the visitor center has exhibits inside and a trail that leads to Pa Kaoao (White Hill)—a short, easy walk with even better views of the valley. Call ahead for hours of operation. ⊠ *Haleakala Hwy., Makawao* ☎ *808/572–4459* ⊕ *nps. gov/hale* ⌦ *Free; parking is $30 per vehicle.*

Leleiwi Overlook

VIEWPOINT | Located at about the 8,800-foot level, the Leleiwi Overlook offers your first awe-inspiring view of the crater. The small hills in the basin are *puu* (cinder cones). If you're here in the late afternoon, it's possible you'll see yourself reflected on the clouds and encircled by a rainbow—a phenomenon called the Brocken Specter. Don't wait long for this, because it's not a daily occurrence. ⊠ *Off Haleakala Hwy., Makawao.*

Puuulaula Overlook

VIEWPOINT | The highest point on Maui is this 10,023-foot summit, where a glass-enclosed lookout provides a 360-degree view. The building is open 24 hours a day, and this is where many visitors gather to view the sunrise. Bring jackets, warm layers, hats, and blankets to stay warm on the cold and windy summit. On a clear day, you can see the islands of Molokai, Lanai, Kahoolawe, and Hawaii Island; on a crystal clear day, you can even spot Oahu glimmering in the distance. ⊠ *Makawao.*

The North Shore

Blasted by winter swells and wind, Maui's North Shore draws water-sports thrill seekers from around the world. But there's much more to this area of Maui than coastline. Inland, a lush, waterfall-fed Garden of Eden beckons. In forested pockets, wealthy hermits have carved out a little piece of paradise for themselves. North Shore action centers on the colorful town of Paia and the windsurfing mecca of Hookipa Beach. It's a far cry from the more developed resort areas of West Maui and the South Shore. Paia is also a starting point for one of the most popular excursions in Maui, the Road to Hana. Waterfalls, phenomenal views of the coast and the ocean, and lush rainforest are all part of the spectacular 55-mile drive into East Maui. Many of the people you see jaywalking in Paia sold everything they owned to come to Maui and live a beach bum's life. Beach culture abounds on the North Shore. But these folks aren't sunbathers; they're big-wave riders, windsurfers, or kiteboarders, and the North Shore is their challenging sports arena. Beaches here face the open ocean and tend to be rougher and windier than beaches elsewhere on Maui—but don't let that scare you off. On calm days the reef-speckled waters are truly beautiful and offer a quieter and less commercial beach-going experience than the leeward shore. Be sure to leave your locked car in a paved parking area so that it doesn't get stuck in soft sand.

Paia

9 miles east of Kahului; 4 miles west of Haiku.

At the intersection of Hana Highway and Baldwin Avenue, Paia has eclectic boutiques that supply everything from high fashion to hemp-oil candles. Some of Maui's best shops for surf trunks, Brazilian bikinis, and other beachwear are here. Restaurants provide excellent people-watching opportunities and an array of dining and takeout options, from flatbread to fresh fish. The abundance is helpful because Paia is the last place to snack before the pilgrimage to Hana and the first stop for the famished on the return trip. Its popularity has led to a bit of overcrowding, however, so bring

Continued on page 259

HALEAKALA NATIONAL PARK

From the Tropics to the Moon! Two hours, 38 miles, 10,023 feet—those are the unlikely numbers involved in reaching Maui's highest point, the summit of the volcano Haleakala. Nowhere else on earth can you drive from sea level (Kahului) to 10,023 feet (the summit) in only 38 miles. And what's more shocking—in that short vertical ascent, you'll journey from lush, tropical-island landscape to the stark, moonlike basin of the volcano's enormous, otherworldly crater.

Established in 1916, Haleakala National Park covers an astonishing 33,222 acres. Haleakala "Crater" is the centerpiece of the park though it's not actually a crater. Technically, it's an erosional valley, flushed out by water pouring from the summit through two enormous gaps. The mountain has terrific camping and hiking, including a trail that loops through the crater, but the chance to witness this unearthly landscape is reason enough for a visit.

THE CLIMB TO THE SUMMIT

To reach Haleakala National Park and the mountain's breathtaking summit, take Route 36 east of Kahului to the Haleakala Highway (Route 37). Head east, up the mountain to the unlikely intersection of Haleakala Highway and Haleakala Highway. If you continue straight the road's name changes to Kula Highway (still Route 37). Instead, turn left onto Haleakala Highway—this is now Route 377. After about 6 miles, make a left onto

Map Labels

378

Hosmer Grove
(6,800 ft)

KEANAE VALLEY

Visitor Center
(7,000 ft)

Halemauu Trailhead

Leleiwi Overlook
(8,800 ft)

Holua Cabin

KOOLAU GAP

Kalahaku Overlook

Hanakauhi
8,907 ft

Puu Kumu

Mauna Hina

Haleakala National Park

Halemauu Trail

Halalii

Puu Naue

Kaluaiki

Puu o Maui

Puu o Maui

Visitor Center
(9,740 ft)

Ka Luu o kaOo

Kamoalii

Na Mana o ke Akua

Halemauu Trail

Oilipuu

Keoneheehee (Sliding Sands) Trailhead

Ka Moa o Pele

Puu Ulaula
10,028 ft

Puu Ulaula Overlook

Puu o Pele

Puu Maile

Magnetic Peak
10,008 ft

Science City

Haupaakea
9,159 ft

Keoneheehee Trail
(aka Sliding Sands Trail)

Kapalaoa Cabin

KAUPO VALLEY

Hosmer Grove
0.5 miles loop trail

▶ At entrance to park

Ten minutes down the trail you can spy honeycreepers, some of the world's rarest birds, hopping from branch to branch.

Keoneheehee (a.k.a. Sliding Sands) Trail
4.0 miles round-trip

▶ Haleakala Visitor Center parking lot

This trail descends 2,500 feet to the crater floor. Allow twice the time to hike out as it takes to hike in.

Halemauu Trail
2.25 miles round-trip

▶ Parking lot 3.5 miles above Park Headquarters at mile marker 14.

The cliffside, snaking switchbacks of this trail offer views stretching across the crater's floors to its far walls.

Crater Road (Route 378). After several long switchbacks (look out for downhill bikers!) you'll come to the park entrance.

■TIP→ **Before you head up Haleakala, call for the latest park weather conditions (☎ 866/944–5025). Extreme gusty winds, heavy rain, and even snow in winter are not uncommon. Because of the high altitude, the mountaintop temperature is often as much as 30 degrees cooler than that at sea level. Be sure to bring a jacket. Also make sure you have a full tank of gas. No service stations exist beyond Kula.**

There's a car fee to enter the park; but it's good for three days and can be used at Oheo Gulch (Kipahulu), so save your receipt.

6,800 feet, Hosmer Grove. Just as you enter the park, Hosmer Grove has campsites and interpretive trails. Park rangers maintain a changing schedule of talks and hikes both here and at the top of the mountain. Call the park for current schedules.

7,000 feet, Park Headquarters/Visitor Center. Not far from Hosmer Grove, the Park Headquarters/Visitor Center has trail maps and displays about the volcano's origins and eruption history. Hikers and campers should check-in here before

KALAPAWILI RIDGE

K A L A P A W I L I

▲ Paliku Cabin

Kipahulu Valley
Biological Reserve
(no public access)

KIPAHULU VALLEY

Kaupo Trail

Waimoku
Falls

31

Makahiku
Falls

Kuloa Point

Visitor Center

◆ **Oheo
Gulch**

PACIFIC OCEAN

0 ————— ½ mi
0 ————— ½ km

SUNRISE AT THE SUMMIT

Sunrise at the summit has become the thing to do. You need an hour and a half from the bottom of **Haleakala Highway** (Route 37) to Puu Ulaula Overlook. Add to that the time of travel to the highway—at least 45 minutes from Lahaina or Kīhei. *The Maui News* posts the hour of sunrise every day. Remember the Alpine-Aeolian summit is *freezing* at dawn (Alpine indicates cold, Aeolian indicates windy). Bring hotel towels, blankets—anything you can find to stay warm. Also keep in mind, the highly touted colors of sunrise are weather-dependent. Sometimes they're spectacular and sometimes the sun just comes up without the fanfare.

heading up the mountain. Maps, posters, and other memorabilia are available at the gift shop.

8,800 feet, Leleiwi Overlook. Continuing up the mountain, you come to Leleiwi Overlook. A short walk to the end of the parking lot reveals your first awe-inspiring view of the crater. The small hills in the basin are volcanic cinder cones (called *puu* in Hawaiian), each with a small crater at its top, and each the site of a former eruption.

If you're here in the late afternoon, it's possible you'll experience a phenomenon called the Brocken Specter. Named after

a similar occurrence in East Germany's Harz Mountains, the "specter" allows you to see yourself reflected on the clouds and encircled by a rainbow. Don't wait all day for this because it's not a daily occurrence.

9,000 feet, Kalahaku Overlook. The next stopping point is Kalahaku Overlook. The view here offers a different perspective of the crater, and at this elevation the famous silversword plant grows amid the cinders. This odd, endangered beauty grows only here and at the same elevation on the Big Island's two peaks. It begins life as a silver, spiny-leaf rosette and is the sole home of a variety of native

insects (it's the only shelter around). The silversword reaches maturity between 7 and 17 years, when it sends forth a 3- to 8-foot-tall stalk with several hundred tiny sunflowers. It blooms once, then dies.

9,740 feet, Haleakala Visitor Center. Another mile up is the Haleakala Visitor Center, open daily from sunrise to 3 pm except Christmas and New Year's. There are exhibits inside, and a trail from here leads to White Hill—a short easy walk that will give you an even better view of the valley.

10,023 feet, Puu Ulaula Overlook. The highest point on Maui is the Puu Ulaula Overlook, at the 10,023-foot summit. Here you find a glass-enclosed lookout with a 360-degree view. The building is open 24 hours a day, and this is where visitors gather for the best sunrise view. Dawn begins between 5:45 and 7, depending on the time of year. On a clear day you can see the islands of Molokai, Lanai, Kahoolawe, and Hawaii (the Big Island). On a *really* clear day you can even spot Oahu glimmering in the distance.

■TIP➔ The air is very thin at 10,000 feet. Don't be surprised if you feel a little breathless while walking around the summit. Take it easy and drink lots of water. Anyone who has been scuba diving within the last 24 hours should not make the trip up Haleakala.

On a small hill nearby, you can see **Science City**, an off-limits research and communications center straight out of an espionage thriller. The University of Hawaii maintains an observatory here, and the Department of Defense tracks satellites.

HIKING AND CAMPING

Exploring Haleakala Crater is one of the best hiking experiences on Maui. The volcanic terrain offers an impressive diversity of colors, textures, and shapes—almost as if the lava has been artfully sculpted. The barren landscape is home to many plants, insects, and birds that exist nowhere else on earth and have developed intriguing survival mechanisms, such as the sun-reflecting, hairy leaves of the silversword, which allow it to survive the intense climate.

Stop at park headquarters to register and pick up trail maps on your way into the park.

1-Hour Hike. Just as you enter Haleakala National Park, Hosmer Grove offers a short 10-minute hike and an hour-long, ½-mile loop trail that will give you insight into Hawaii's fragile ecology. Anyone can go on these hikes, whereas a longer trail through the Waikamoi Cloud Forest is accessible only with park ranger–guided hikes. Call park headquarters for the schedule. Facilities here include six campsites (no permit needed, available on a first-come, first-served basis), pit toilets, drinking water, and cooking shelters.

4-Hour Hikes. Two half-day hikes involve descending into the crater and returning the way you came. The first, Halemauu Trail (trailhead is between mile markers 14 and 15), is 2.25 miles round-trip. The cliffside, snaking switchbacks of this trail offer views stretching across the crater's puu-speckled floor to its far walls. On clear days you can peer through the Koolau Gap to Hana. Native flowers and shrubs grow along the trail, which is typically misty and cool (though still exposed to the sun). When you reach the gate at the bottom, head back up.

The other hike, which is 5 miles round-trip, descends down Keoneheehee (aka Sliding Sands) Trail (trailhead is at the Haleakala Visitor Center) into an alien landscape of reddish black cinders, lava bombs, and silverswords. It's easy to imagine life before humans in the solitude and silence of this place. Turn back when you hit the crater floor.

■ TIP→ **Bring water, sunscreen, and a reliable jacket. These are demanding hikes. Take it slowly to acclimate, and allow additional time for the uphill return trip.**

8-Hour Hike. The recommended way to explore the crater in a single, but full day is to go in two cars and ferry yourselves back and forth between the head of Halemauu Trail and the summit. This way, you can hike from the summit down Keoneheehee Trail, cross the crater's floor, investigate the Bottomless Pit and Pele's Paint Pot, then climb out on the switchback trail (Halemauu). When you emerge, the shelter of your waiting car will be very welcome (this is an 11.2-mile hike). If you don't have two cars, hitching a ride from Halemauu back to the summit should be relatively safe and easy.

TIP→ Take a backpack with lunch water, sunscreen, and a reliable jacket for the beginning and end of the 8-hour hike. This is a demanding trip, but you will never regret or forget it.

Overnight Hike. Staying overnight in one of Haleakala's three cabins or two wilderness campgrounds is an experience like no other. You'll feel like the only person on earth when you wake up inside this enchanted, strange landscape. The cabins, each tucked in a different corner of the crater's floor, are equipped with 12 bunk beds, wood-burning stoves, fake logs, and kitchen gear.

Holua cabin is the shortest hike, less than 4 hours (3.7 miles) from Halemauu Trail. *Kapalaoa* is about 5 hours (5.5 miles) down Keoneheehee Trail. The most cherished cabin is *Paliku*, an eight-hour (9.3-mile) hike starting from either trail. It's nestled against the cliffs above Kaupo Gap. Cabin reservations can be made up to 90 days in advance. Tent campsites at Holua and Paliku are free and easy to reserve on a first-come, first-served basis.

TIP→ Toilets and nonpotable water are available—bring iodine tablets to purify the water. Open fires are not allowed and packing out your trash is mandatory.

For more information on hiking or camping, contact the National Park Service (✉ *Box 369, Makawao 96768* ☎ *808/572–4400* ⊕ *www.nps.gov/hale*).

OPTIONS FOR EXPLORING

If you're short on time you can drive to the summit, take a peek inside, and drive back down. But the "House of the Sun" is really worth a day, whether you explore by foot, horseback, or helicopter.

BIKING

At this writing, all guided bike tours inside park boundaries were suspended indefinitely. However, the tours continue but now start outside the boundary of the park. These can provide a speedy, satisfying downhill trip. The park is still open to individual bikes for a fee. There are no bike paths, however—just the same road that is used by vehicular traffic. Whether you're on your own or with a tour, be careful!

HELICOPTER TOURS

Viewing Haleakala from above can be a mind-altering experience, if you don't mind dropping $229+ per person for a few blissful moments above the crater. Most tours buzz Haleakala, where airspace is regulated, then head over to Hana in search of waterfalls.

HORSEBACK RIDING

Several companies offer half-day, full-day, and even overnight rides into the crater. On one half-day ride you descend into the crater on Keoneheehee Trail and have lunch before you head back.

your patience and be sure to leave plenty of time for parking (there are only a few public parking lots and they fill up quickly) and for navigating crowds. Lunchtime is an especially busy time.

This little town on Maui's North Shore was once a sugarcane enclave, with a mill, plantation camps, and shops. The old sugar mill finally closed, but the town continues to thrive. In the 1970s Paia became a hippie town, as dropouts headed for Maui to open boutiques, galleries, and unusual eateries. In the 1980s, windsurfers—many of them European—discovered nearby Hookipa Beach and brought an international flavor to Paia. Today this historic town is hip and happening.

GETTING HERE AND AROUND

Route 36 (Hana Highway) runs directly though Paia; if you're journeying there from Upcountry, Route 37 can get you there, but not directly. You can take the Maui Bus from the airport and Queen Kaahumanu Shopping Center in Kahului to Paia.

 Beaches

Those beautiful North Shore swells make the beaches in the area more likely to have water sports enthusiasts than swimmers on some days, but that doesn't mean that you can't enjoy a great beach day by lingering in the sand, soaking in the panoramic views, and taking walks along the surf.

Baldwin Beach

BEACH | FAMILY | A local favorite, this approximately 1-mile stretch of golden sand is a good place to stretch out, jog, or swim, although the waves can sometimes be choppy and the undertow strong. Don't be alarmed by those big brown blobs floating beneath the surface; they're just pieces of seaweed awash in the surf. You can find shade along the beach beneath the ironwood trees. Though there is a pavilion, it's not

the safest place to hang out. Instead, take your picnics to the tree line and enjoy visits from friendly birds and dogs. Because this is a beach park there are picnic tables, grills, and a large playing field, as well.

The long, shallow pool at the Kahului end of the beach is known as Baby Beach. Separated from the surf by a flat reef wall, this is where ocean-loving families bring their kids (and sometimes puppies) to practice a few laps. Take a relaxing stroll along the water's edge from one end of Baldwin Beach to Baby Beach and enjoy the scenery. The view of the West Maui Mountains is hauntingly beautiful. **Amenities:** lifeguard; parking (no fee); showers; toilets. **Best for:** swimming; walking. ⊠ *Hana Hwy., Paia* ⊕ *About 1 mile west of Baldwin Ave.*

★ Hookipa Beach

BEACH | To see some of the world's finest windsurfers, hit this beach along the Hana Highway. It's also one of Maui's hottest surfing spots, with waves that can reach 20 feet. Hookipa is not necessarily a good swimming beach; however, there are a few spots that have protected reef areas that provide a shore break and places to play in the water, so getting wet isn't completely out of the question. It's also not the place to learn windsurfing, but it's great for hanging out and watching the pros. There are picnic tables and grills, though the pavilion area isn't particularly inviting. **Amenities:** lifeguard; parking (no fee); showers; toilets. **Best for:** surfing; windsurfing. ⊠ *Hana Hwy, Paia* ⊕ *At mile marker 9, about 2 miles east of Paia.*

Kanaha Beach

BEACH | Windsurfers, kiteboarders, joggers, and picnicking families like this long, golden strip of sand bordered by a wide grassy area with lots of shade that is within walking distance of Kahului Airport. The winds pick up in the early afternoon, making for the best kiteboarding and windsurfing conditions—if you

Did You Know?

In the 1980s, many windsurfers came from Europe and "discovered" Hookipa Beach. Today you can see some fine windsurfing here.

know what you're doing, that is. The best spot for watching kiteboarders is at the far left end of the beach. A picnic paired with surf-watching makes a great option for a farewell activity before getting on a departing flight. **Amenities:** lifeguard; parking (no fee); showers; toilets. **Best for:** walking; windsurfing. ✉ *Amala Pl., Kahului* ✥ *From Kaahumanu Ave., turn makai onto Hobron St., then right onto Amala Pl. Drive just over a mile through an industrial area and take any of three entrances into Kanaha.*

🍴 Restaurants

Cafe Mambo

$$ | **ECLECTIC** | Paia is one of Maui's most interesting food towns, and this colorful, airy, and brightly painted hangout is right in the thick of things. The menu features everything from burgers and fish to three different preparations of duck, and aside from the great food, the people-watching is fascinating. **Known for:** unique fajitas and salads; locally inspired tapas; fabulous breakfasts. [$] *Average main: $19* ✉ *30 Baldwin Ave., Paia* ☎ *808/579–8021* 🌐 *cafemambomaui.com.*

Flatbread Company

$$ | **PIZZA** | **FAMILY** | This Vermont-based company marched right into Paia in 2007 and instantly became a popular restaurant and a valued addition to the community as it gives back to local nonprofits. The bustling restaurant uses organic, local, sustainable products, including 100% organically grown wheat for the made-fresh-daily dough, and it's a good spot to take the kids. **Known for:** small but lively bar and jam-packed Tuesday benefit nights; wood-fired, clay-oven pizzas; Mopsy's Kalua Pork Pizza served with kiawe (mesquite)-smoked free-range pork shoulder and house-made organic mango barbecue sauce. [$] *Average main: $22* ✉ *89 Hana Hwy., Paia* ☎ *808/579–8989* 🌐 *flatbreadcompany.com.*

★ **Paia Fishmarket Restaurant**

$ | **SEAFOOD** | If you're okay with communal picnic tables, or taking your meal to a nearby beach, this place in funky Paia town serves, arguably, the best fresh fish for the best prices on this side of the island. Four preparations are offered and, on any given day, there are at least four to six fresh fishes from which to choose; there are burgers, chicken, and pasta options for the non-fish fans. **Known for:** grilled opah; local fish and local beer at low, local prices; delectable side dishes. [$] *Average main: $15* ✉ *100 Hana Hwy., Paia* ☎ *808/579–8030* 🌐 *paiafishmarket.com.*

★ **Ululani's Hawaiian Shave Ice**

$ | **ICE CREAM** | **FAMILY** | This Maui institution is a must-visit for interesting shave ice flavors featuring natural, hand-made syrups and a variety of toppings including Roselani's ice cream. The menu is extensive but features some popular combos to make your choice easier. **Known for:** decadent "snow cap" condensed milk or coconut cream topping; long but fast-moving lines to get served; unique and very delicious ube (purple yam) syrup. [$] *Average main: $6* ✉ *115 Hana Hwy., Paia* 🌐 *ululanishawaiianshaveice.com.*

🛏 Hotels

Paia Inn

$$$$ | **B&B/INN** | Located in the former plantation town of Paia, along Hana Highway, this chic inn with Southeast Asian influences is surprisingly quiet and includes oceanfront accommodations. **Pros:** unique and varied shops and dining just steps away in funky beach town; well-maintained property; excellent on-site restaurant. **Cons:** limited on- and off-site parking; lots of street action; some rooms are very small. [$] *Rooms from: $429* ✉ *93 Hana Hwy., Paia* ☎ *808/579–6000* 🌐 *paiainn.com* 🛏 *15 units* 🍴 *No Meals.*

🛍 Shopping

★ Mana Foods

FOOD | At this bustling health food store you can stock up on local fish and grass-fed beef for your barbecue. You'll find the best selection of organic produce on the Island, as well as a great bakery and deli. The health and beauty room has a dizzying selection of products that promise to keep you glowing. ⊠ 49 Baldwin Ave., Paia 🕾 808/579–8078 ⊕ manafoodsmaui. com.

★ Maui Crafts Guild

ART GALLERIES | One of the Island's only artist cooperatives, Maui Crafts Guild is crammed with treasures. Resident artists produce lead-glazed pottery, basketry, glass and feather art, photography, ceramics, and woodwork pieces. The prices are surprisingly low, making this a great place to find gifts and one-of-a-kind items to take home. ⊠ 120 Hana Hwy., Paia 🕾 808/579–9697 ⊕ mauicraftsguild. com.

★ Maui Girl Swimwear

WOMEN'S CLOTHING | This is *the* place on Maui for swimwear, cover-ups, beach hats, and sandals. Maui Girl designs its own suits, which have been spotted in *Sports Illustrated* fashion shoots and on celebrities. Tops and bottoms can be purchased separately, increasing your chances of finding the perfect fit. ⊠ 12 Baldwin Ave., Paia 🕾 808/579–9266 ⊕ maui-girl.com.

★ Maui Hands

ART GALLERIES | This gallery shows work by more than 300 local artists: exquisite woodwork, lovely ceramics, authentic Niihau shell lei, wave metal etchings, and whimsical clay figures. There are locations in Lahaina, Makawao, and at The Shops at Wailea. At each location, the gallery offers a unique Artists in Residence program that connects the public to the artists at local "talk story" sessions each month. ⊠ 84 Hana Hwy., Paia 🕾 808/579–9245 ⊕ mauihands.com.

Haiku

13 miles east of Kahului; 4 miles east of Paia.

At one time this area centered around a couple of enormous pineapple canneries, before they shuttered. Both have since been transformed into rustic warehouse malls. Because of the post office next door, Old Haiku Cannery earned the title of town center. Here you can try eateries offering everything from plate lunches to vegetarian dishes to juicy burgers and fantastic sushi. Follow windy Haiku Road to Pauwela Cannery, the other defunct factory-turned-hangout. This jungle hillside is a maze of flower-decked roads that seem to double back on themselves.

GETTING HERE AND AROUND

Route 36 (Hana Highway) runs directly through Paia; 4 miles east of town, follow the sign to Haiku, a short detour off the highway. You can take the Maui Bus from the airport and Queen Kaahumanu Shopping Center in Kahului to Paia and on to Haiku.

Haiku is a short detour off Hana Highway (Route 36) just past Hookipa Beach Park on the way to Hana. Haiku Road turns into Kokomo Road at the post office.

TOURS

★ Leilani Farm Sanctuary

SPECIAL-INTEREST TOURS | For a chance to snuggle a sheep or hug a cow in paradise, an hour-long tour of Leilani Farm Sanctuary is just the thing. Visitors must make reservations and be at least seven years old to participate in these personalized, guided tours. While the tours are a crucial part of the sanctuary, visitors can really give back by volunteering during morning rounds on Monday and Wednesday (reservations preferred). ⊠ 260 East Kuiaha St., Haiku-Pauwela 🕾 808/298–8544 ⊕ leilanifarmsanctuary.org 🖘 $50 tax-deductible donation ⟟ Tours Mon., Wed., at 12 pm, Sat. at 10 am.

Above the rain forests of Haiku are views of the Pacific.

🍴 Restaurants

★ Colleen's at the Cannery

$$ | **AMERICAN** | You'd never guess what's inside by the nondescript exterior and the location in an old pineapple cannery-cum-strip-mall, but this is one of Maui's most overlooked and underrated restaurants. Popular with locals for breakfast, lunch, and a daily happy hour, at night during dinner is when the candles come out and it's time for martinis and fresh fish; you'll feel like you're at a hip urban eatery. **Known for:** specialty artisan pizzas and enormous salads; eggs Benedict (available every day) and Bloody Marys; excellent food featuring Upcountry's best produce. $ *Average main: $24 ⊠ Haiku Cannery Marketplace, 810 Haiku Rd., Haiku-Pauwela ☎ 808/575–9211 ⊕ colleensinhaiku.com.*

Nuka

$$ | **ASIAN FUSION** | This off-the-beaten-path izakaya-style Japanese eatery is worth the trek to sleepy Haiku. Diners flock here for the eclectic menu that includes everything from specialty French fries and fusion sushi rolls to sashimi and some of the best tempura around—all based on what's fresh from local farmers and fishermen. **Known for:** house-made green tea and black sesame ice cream; exceptional sushi and sashimi; hard to get a table (no reservations). $ *Average main: $18 ⊠ 780 Haiku Rd., Haiku-Pauwela ☎ 808/575–2939 ⊕ nukamaui.com ⊘ Closed daily 2:30–4:30 pm. No lunch on weekends.*

Kuau

Kuau is a small neighborhood just off the Road to Hana, home to a few standout spots for dining, swimming, grabbing a cup of coffee, and taking in the views. You may consider skipping this area in favor of getting an early start to Hana, but it's worth the extra time to visit.

Beaches

★ Hookipa Beach

BEACH | To see some of the world's finest windsurfers, hit this beach along the Hana Highway. It's also one of Maui's hottest surfing spots, with waves that can reach 20 feet. Hookipa is not necessarily a good swimming beach; however, there are a few spots that have protected reef areas that provide a shore break and places to play in the water, so getting wet isn't completely out of the question. It's also not the place to learn windsurfing, but it's great for hanging out and watching the pros. There are picnic tables and grills, though the pavilion area isn't particularly inviting. **Amenities:** lifeguard; parking (no fee); showers; toilets. **Best for:** surfing; windsurfing. ✉ *Hana Hwy, Paia* ✣ *At mile marker 9, about 2 miles east of Paia.*

Restaurants

Mama's Fish House

$$$$ | **SEAFOOD** | Set in an intimate location on the beach, Mama's has been *the* Maui destination for special occasions for almost four decades. A path of gecko-shape stones leads to an ever-changing fantasyland of Hawaiian kitsch, where savvy servers can explain the various fish types and preparations, and you'd be wise to heed their recommendation; the fish is so fresh that the daily menu lists who caught it that morning. **Known for:** Polynesian Black Pearl dessert; exceptionally fresh fish; ambience and romance. [$] *Average main: $50* ✉ *799 Poho Pl., Kuau* ☎ *808/579–8488* 🌐 *www.mamasfishhouse.com.*

Hotels

★ The Inn at Mama's Fish House

$$$$ | **B&B/INN** | Nestled in gardens adjacent to one of Maui's most popular dining spots (Mama's Fish House) and fronting a small beach known as Kuau Cove, these well-maintained studios, suites, and one- and two-bedroom cottages have been recently renovated with high-end appliances and furnishings and decorated with local artwork to provide contemporary beach house luxury. **Pros:** easy access to Kuau Cove; free parking and Wi-Fi; near Hookipa Beach and Paia town shops and restaurants. **Cons:** limited swimming at beach; not a full-service hotel with concierge; restaurant can get crowded during the evening. [$] *Rooms from: $395* ✉ *799 Poho Pl., Kuau* ☎ *808/579–9764* 🌐 *innatmamas.com* 🍴 *No Meals.*

Road to Hana

The Road to Hana is a 55-mile journey into the unspoiled heart of Maui. Tracing a centuries-old path, the road begins as a well-paved highway in Kahului and ends in the tiny rustic town of Hana on the island's rain-gouged windward side, spilling into a backcountry rarely visited by humans. Many travelers venture beyond Hana to Oheo Gulch in East Maui, where one can cool off in basalt-lined pools and waterfalls.

This drive is a Hawaii pilgrimage for those eager to experience what glossy magazines consider the "real" Hawaii. To most, the lure of Hana is its timelessness, and paired with the spectacular drive (which brings to life the old adage: the journey *is* the destination), this is one of Hawaii's best experiences. The Road to Hana is undoubtedly one of the most beautiful drives on the planet.

The challenging part of the road takes only an hour and a half, but the drive begs to be taken at a leisurely pace. You'll want to slow the passage of time to take in foliage-hugged ribbons of road and roadside banana bread and food stands, to swim beneath a waterfall, and to inhale the lush Maui tropics in all their

Photo Ops Along the Road to Hana

The entire Road to Hana features postcard-worthy views. You'll be craning your neck to take in the lush landscape that seems to swallow your car, and every turnoff offers another striking photo opportunity, each one seemingly better than the last. However, there are some pit stops you'll kick yourself for skipping.

For jaw-dropping views, pull into the Huelo Lookout near mile marker 5, order a smoothie, and drink in the expanse of the Pacific Ocean and the historic Huelo township below.

If you are a banana bread fan, be sure to stop in the small community of Keanae for some of the best loaves you're likely to try at Aunty Sandy's Banana Bread. Just be sure to arrive early since the stand sells out frequently.

At mile marker 24, Hanawi Falls is another picturesque spot. The best way to see the falls is from the bridge, and we advise against hiking beyond that point.

At mile marker 31, turn onto Ulaino Road to explore the vast cave network of Kaeleku Caverns. Afterward, make your way to nearby Piilanihale Heiau, a beautiful 16th-century temple. While there, you can also amble through the lovely Kahanu Garden.

Near mile marker 32 you should carve out time to hike the 3-mile trail from Waianapanapa State Park to Hana Bay. You'll scramble over lava rock and along a stunning coastline rarely seen by travelers.

After you arrive in Hana, motor straight to Hamoa Beach, one of Hawaii's most beautiful strands. But the road does not end in Hana. In fact, for many travelers, the payoff comes at Oheo Gulch's abundant hiking trails—don't miss the inland hike through the bamboo forest. After you're done, you can travel a mile past Oheo Gulch and pay your respects at the grave of Charles Lindbergh.

glory. You'll also want to stop often and let the driver enjoy the view, too.

Huelo

10 miles east of Haiku.

As the Road to Hana begins its journey eastward, the slopes get steeper and the Pacific Ocean pops into view. The first waterfall you see, Twin Falls, is around mile marker 2, and farther up the road is the Koolau Forest Reserve. Embedded in the forest are two townships, Huelo and Kailua, both of which are great places to pull over and take in the dramatic landscape.

GETTING HERE AND AROUND
Just after Haiku, the mile markers on the Hana Highway change back to 0. The town of Huelo is at mile marker 4. To reach the township, follow the signs toward the *mauka* (ocean) side of the road.

 Sights

Twin Falls
WATERFALL | Keep an eye out for the Twin Falls Farm Stand just after mile marker 2 on the Hana Highway. Stop here and treat yourself to some fresh sugarcane juice. If you're feeling adventurous, follow the path beyond the stand to the

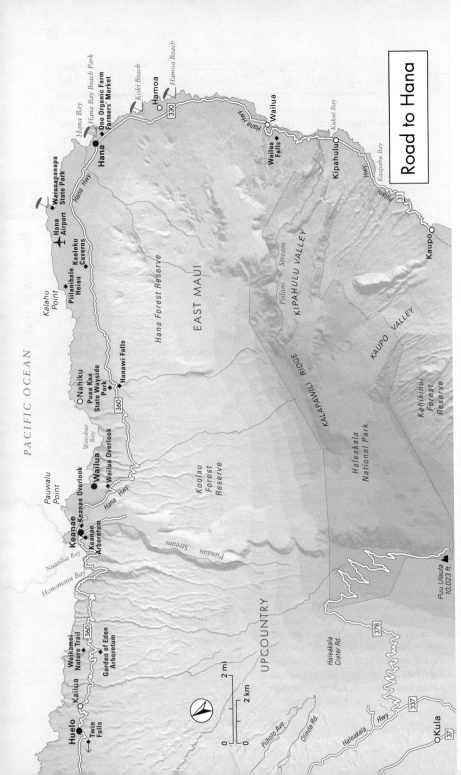

Road to Hana

PACIFIC OCEAN

Pauwalu Point

Pailolo Point

Kalahu Point

Waiohue Bay

Nuaailua Bay

Honomanu Bay

Hana Bay

Hana Bay Beach Park

Koki Beach

Hamoa Beach

Kukui Bay

Kaapahu Bay

Huelo

Twin Falls

Waikamoi Nature Trail

Garden of Eden Arboretum

Kailua

360

Keanae

Keanae Overlook

Keanae Arboretum

Wailua

Wailua Overlook

Nahiku

Puaa Kaa State Wayside Park

Hanawi Falls

360

Piilanihale Heiau

Kaeleku Caverns

Hana Airport

Waianapanapa State Park

Hana

Ono Organic Farm Farmers' Market

Hamoa

330

Wailua

Wailua Falls

Hana Hwy

Hana Hwy

Kipahulu

Piilani Stream

31

Piilani Hwy

Kaupo

KIPAHULU VALLEY

KAUPO VALLEY

KALAPAWILI RIDGE

Kahikinui Forest Reserve

Haleakala National Park

Koolau Forest Reserve

Puohokamoa Stream

Hana Forest Reserve

EAST MAUI

Puu Ulaula 10,023 ft.

378

Haleakala Crater Rd

337

Haleakala Hwy

Kula

37

Piiholo Ave.

Olinda Rd.

UPCOUNTRY

2 mi

2 km

0

Tropical Delights

The drive to Hana wouldn't be as enchanting without a stop or two at one of the countless fruit and flower (and banana bread) stands by the highway. Every so often a thatch hut tempts passersby with apple bananas (a smaller, firmer variety), *lilikoi* (passion fruit), avocados, or star fruit just plucked from the tree. Leave a few dollars in the can for the folks who live off the land. Huge bouquets of tropical flowers are available for a handful of change, and some farms will ship.

One standout is **Aunty Sandy's Banana Bread Stand,** in the blink-and-you'll-miss-it community of Keanae. This legendary banana-bread shop is just past the coral-and-lava-rock church. Aunty Sandy's sweet loaves lure locals and tourists alike, but be sure to arrive early, because once the stand runs out (it's also closed on Sundays), you'll have to scurry back up the main road to the **Halfway to Hana Fruit Stand** to find a tasty replacement.

paradisiacal waterfalls known as Twin Falls. Although it's still private property, the "no trespassing" signs have been replaced by colorfully painted arrows pointing toward the easily accessible falls. Several deep, emerald pools sparkle beneath waterfalls and offer excellent (and a little cold) swimming and photo opportunities. In recent years, this natural attraction has become a tourist hot spot. Although the attention is well deserved, those who wish to avoid crowds may want to keep driving. The family who owns the property recently implemented a paid parking system to help manage the overcrowding; parking costs $10 per car and is available on a first-come, first-served basis. ⊠ *6300 Hana Hwy., past mile marker 2, Haiku-Pauwela* ⊕ *twinfalls-maui.net* ⊠ *$10.*

Huelo

TOWN | When you see the colorful mailboxes on the *makai* (toward the ocean) side of the road just past mile marker 4 on the Hana Highway, follow the windy road to the rural area of Huelo—a funky community that includes a mix of off-the-grid inhabitants and vacation rentals. The town features two picturesque churches, one of which is Kaulanapueo Church, constructed in 1853 out of coral blocks.

If you linger a while, you may meet local residents and learn about a rural lifestyle you might not have expected to find on the Islands. The same can be said for nearby Kailua (mile marker 6). ■ **TIP→ When you're back up on Hana Highway, pull into the Huelo Lookout Fruit Stand for yummy smoothies and killer views of the Pacific below.** ⊠ *Hana Hwy., near mile marker 4, Huelo.*

Waikamoi Nature Trail

TRAIL | Slightly after the town of Huelo, the Hana Highway enters the Koolau Forest Reserve. Vines wrap around street signs, and waterfalls are so abundant that you don't know which direction to look. A good start is between mile markers 9 and 10, where the Waikamoi Nature Trail sign beckons you to stretch your car-weary limbs. A short (if muddy) trail leads through tall eucalyptus trees to a coastal vantage point with a picnic table. Signage reminds visitors: "Quiet, Trees at Work" and "Bamboo Picking Permit Required." *Awapuhi,* or Hawaiian shampoo ginger, sends up fragrant shoots along the trail. ■ **TIP→ The area has picnic tables and a restroom.** ⊠ *Hana Hwy., between mile markers 9 and 10.*

Keanae

13 miles east of Huelo.

Officially, Keanae is the halfway point to Hana, and for many, this is where the drive offers the most rewarding vistas. The greenery seems to envelop the skinny road, forcing drivers to slow to a crawl as they "ooh" and "aah" at the landscape. Around the village of Wailua, one of the most fiercely native Hawaiian regions on the Island, there seem to be waterfalls at every turn.

Sights

★ Garden of Eden Arboretum

GARDEN | Just beyond mile marker 10 on the Hana Highway, the Garden of Eden Arboretum offers interpretive trails through 26 acres of manicured gardens. Anyone with a green thumb will appreciate the care and attention given to the more than 500 varieties of tropical plants—many of them native. Trails lead to views of the lovely Puohokamoa Falls and provide a glimpse into the botanical wonders that thrive in this lush region. Be sure to stop by the gift shop on the way out for a wide variety of gifts made by local artisans and to hang out with the ducks and peacocks. To avoid lines and crowds, visit in the morning at opening time or in the afternoon after 2 pm. ☒ *10600 Hana Hwy., past mile marker 10, Haiku-Pauwela* ☏ *808/572–9899* ⊕ *mauigardenofeden.com* ☒ *$20.*

Keanae Arboretum

GARDEN | Here you can add to your botanical education or enjoy a challenging hike into the forest. Signs help you learn the names of the many plants and trees now considered native to Hawaii. The meandering Piinaau Stream adds a graceful touch to the arboretum and provides a swimming pond when there is enough water. You can take a fairly rigorous hike from the arboretum if you can find the trail at one side of the large taro patch. Be careful not to lose the trail once you're on it. A lovely forest waits at the end of the 25-minute hike. ☒ *13385 Hana Hwy., past mile marker 16, Keanae* ☒ *Free.*

Keanae Overlook

NATURE SIGHT | Near mile marker 17 along the Hana Highway, you can stop at the Keanae Overlook. From this observation point you can take in the patchwork effect the taro patches create against the dramatic backdrop of the ocean. In the other direction, there are awesome views of Haleakala through the foliage. This is a great spot for photos, but it is not recommended that you fly your drones over the inhabited areas. ☒ *Hana Hwy., near mile marker 17, Keanae.*

Puaa Kaa State Wayside Park

NATURE SIGHT | For a leg-stretching break, visitors will find a respite and real bathrooms at this small roadside park. This is one of the few places on the highway with plenty of parking, so take some time to linger and enjoy the short hike to a small waterfall and pool across the highway from the bathrooms. There are also picnic tables and friendly cats to welcome you. ☒ *Hana Hwy., Wailua (Maui County)* ✛ *½ mile past mile marker 22.*

Hanawi Falls

WATERFALL | At mile marker 24 of the Hana Highway, just as you approach the bridge, look toward the mountains to catch a glimpse of Hanawi Falls. This lush spring-fed stream travels 9 miles to the ocean, and the waterfalls are real crowd-pleasers, even when rains have been light. The best views are from the bridge. ⚠ **It is not safe to hike to the falls, and you must cross private property to get there. We strongly advise against this.** ☒ *Hana Hwy., near mile marker 24, Keanae.*

Wailua

1 mile from Keanae.

This tiny town filled with one of the highest concentrations of Hawaiian blood in any island community (around 94% of the residents have at least partial Hawaiian blood) is best viewed from above at the overlook. The town below prefers not to have visitors, as tourists often trespass to get a better view. From above visitors will be able to enjoy the quilt of the taro patches and Saint Gabriel's Church. Just before the overlook, enjoy some time at the concrete arches of the beautiful Waikani Stream Bridge past mile marker 18.

Sights

Wailua Overlook

SCENIC DRIVE | From the parking lot on the side of the Hana Highway near mile marker 20, you can see Wailua Canyon in one direction and Wailua Village in the other. Photos are spectacular in the morning light of the verdant expanse below. Also from your perch, you can see Wailua Village's landmark 1860 church, which was allegedly constructed of coral that washed up onto the shore during a storm. You'll want to take photos, but flying a drone over the populated area is strongly discouraged. ⊠ *Hana Hwy., near mile marker 20, Wailua (Maui County).*

Hana and Nearby

15 miles east of Keanae.

Even though Hana is a very small town with limited offerings, the relaxed pace of life that Hana residents enjoy will likely have you in its grasp. Hana is one of the few places where the slow pulse of the Island is still strong. The town centers on its lovely circular bay, dominated on the right-hand shore by a *puu* (volcanic cinder cone) called Kauiki. A short trail here leads to a cave, the birthplace of Queen Kaahumanu. Two miles beyond town, another puu presides over a loop road that passes Hana's two best beaches—Koki and Hamoa. The hill is called Ka Iwi O Pele (Pele's Bone). Offshore here, at tiny Alau Island, the demigod Maui supposedly fished up the Hawaiian Islands.

Although sugar was once the mainstay of Hana's economy, the last plantation shut down in the 1940s. In 1946 rancher Paul Fagan built the Hotel Hana-Maui and stocked the surrounding pastureland with cattle. The hotel became a Travaasa experiential resort in 2011, before changing hands in 2020. Now Hana-Maui Resort, the Mani Brothers Real Estate Group purchased the hotel and Hyatt was brought on in 2020 as the management company. The brothers also bought various other associated parcels of real estate in Hana. It's pleasant to stroll around this beautifully rustic property. The cross you can see on the hill above the hotel was put there in memory of Fagan.

◉ Sights

Kaeleku Caverns

CAVE | **FAMILY** | If you're interested in spelunking, take the time to explore Kaeleku Caverns (aka Hana Lava Tube), just after mile marker 31 on the Hana Highway. The site is a mile down Ulaino Road. The friendly folks at the cave give a brief orientation and promptly send nature enthusiasts into Maui's largest lava tube, accented by colorful underworld formations. You can take a self-guided, 30- to 40-minute tour daily 10:30 am until 4 pm. LED flashlights are provided. For those who don't want to explore the caverns, this still makes for a great stop to check out the world's only red ti leaf maze on the grounds. ⊠ *205 Ulaino Rd., off Hana Hwy., past mile marker 31, Hana* ☎ *808/248–7308* ⊕ *mauicave.com* ⊠ *$15.*

Did You Know?

At Waianapanapa State Park, the tide pools turn red several times a year. Legend claims the color represents the blood of Popoalaea, said to have been murdered in one of the caves by her husband, Chief Kakae.

Ono Organic Farms Farmers' Market

MARKET | The family-owned Ono Farms offers certified organic produce at this roadside market at an old gas station. Depending on the season, you'll find such unusual delicacies as *rambutan* (resembling grapes), jackfruit (tastes like bananas), and *lilikoi* (passion fruit). Gordon Ramsay even gave the farm a visit while filming his show *Uncharted* for National Geographic. ■**TIP→ For a memorable on-farm experience, check out their Exotic Tropical Fruit Tasting Adventure, held on Tuesday by reservation.** ⊠ *Hana Hwy., near Hasegawa General Store, Hana* ☎ *808/248–7779* ⊕ *onofarms.com.*

Piilanihale Heiau

GARDEN | This temple, the largest *heiau* in Polynesia, was built for a great 16th-century Maui king named Piilani and his heirs. Hawaiian families continue to maintain and protect this sacred site as they have for centuries, and they have not been eager to turn it into a tourist attraction. However, there is now a brochure, so you can tour the property yourself. The *heiau* is situated within the 122-acre Kahanu Garden, a research center focusing on the ethnobotany of the Pacific. ⊠ *650 Ulaino Rd., Hana* ⊹ *To get here, turn left onto Ulaino Rd. at Hana Hwy. mile marker 31; the road turns to gravel; continue 1½ miles* ☎ *808/248–8912* ⊕ *ntbg.org* ⊡ *$16* ⊙ *Closed Sat. and Sun.*

★ Waianapanapa State Park

BEACH | Home to one of Maui's few black-sand beaches and freshwater caves for adventurous swimmers to explore, this park is right on the ocean. It's a lovely spot to picnic, hike, or swim. To the left you'll find the volcanic sand beach, picnic tables, and cave pools; to the right is an ancient trail that snakes along the ocean past blowholes, sea arches, and archaeological sites. Bird lovers could linger for hours watching the comings and goings of seabirds on the ocean outcroppings. The tide pools here turn red several times a year. Scientists say it's explained by the arrival of small shrimp, but legend claims the color represents the blood of Popoalaea, said to have been murdered in one of the caves by her husband, Chief Kakae. In either case, the dramatic landscape is bound to leave a lasting impression. There is a private cemetery on the grounds of the park, so be mindful to keep out of this area. ■**TIP→ With a permit, you can stay in a state-run cabin or campsite for a steal. It's wise to reserve as early as possible, as these spots book up quickly.** ⊠ *Hana Hwy., near mile marker 32, Hana* ☎ *808/984–8109* ⊕ *hawaiistateparks.org* ⊡ *Free.*

★ Wailua Falls

WATERFALL | Once you've made it past Hana town, you're rewarded with views of what many consider to be the most beautiful and most photographed waterfall in Maui. The best part is that you don't even have to get off of the highway to see the stunning 80-foot falls that end in a gorgeous pool. Look for local food and gift vendors in the parking area. ⊠ *Piilani Hwy., Hana* ⊹ *Mile marker 45.*

Beaches

Red, black, and salt-and-pepper colored beaches welcome visitors to some of the most visually stunning beaches you'll find. These aren't your white-sand resort beaches, rather ones where nature and civilization smash into one another to create truly memorable places.

★ Hamoa Beach

BEACH | FAMILY | Why did James Michener describe this stretch of salt-and-pepper sand as the most "South Pacific" beach he'd come across, even though it's in the North Pacific? Maybe it was the perfect half-moon shape, speckled with the shade of palm trees. Perhaps he was intrigued by the jutting black coastline, often outlined by rain showers out at sea, or the pervasive lack of hurry he felt here. Whatever it was, many still feel the lure. The beach can be crowded, yet it is

Hamoa Beach is one of Maui's most beautiful stretches of sand.

nonetheless relaxing. Early mornings and late afternoons are best for swimming. At times the churning surf might intimidate swimmers, but the bodysurfing can be great. Though there are beach chairs and a pavilion at the beach, they are strictly for the use of Travaasa Hana guests. Hamoa is half a mile past Koki Beach on Haneoo Loop Road, 2 miles south of Hana Town. **Amenities:** showers; toilets. **Best for:** surfing; swimming. ⊠ *Haneoo Loop Rd., Hana.*

Hana Bay Beach Park
CITY PARK | FAMILY | This family-friendly park situated around an old pier offers the calmest swimming opportunities in the area. The black-sand beach is a favorite among local families and canoe clubs, especially thanks to the picnic tables and showers available. Keep cash handy, as you can occasionally find craft vendors in the parking lot. Residents prefer that Sundays be left for local families to enjoy the facilities. **Amenities**: picnic tables, free parking. **Best for**: families. ⊠ *150 Keawa Pl., Hana* ☎ *808/248–7022* ⊕ *mauicounty. gov.*

Koki Beach
BEACH | You can tell from the trucks parked alongside the road that this is a favorite local surf spot.

■ **TIP →** **Swimming is not recommended here, as there are no lifeguards, and the rip currents are powerful.**

Look for awesome views of the rugged coastline and a sea arch on the left end.

Iwa, or white-throated frigate birds, dart like pterodactyls over the offshore Alau Islet. Though it's not a swimming beach, the grassy area and picnic tables are cozy and allow visitors to watch the surfers navigate the waves, while the small red-sand beach is good for walks if the tide allows. **Amenities:** picnic tables. **Best for:** surfing. ⊠ *Haneoo Loop Rd., Hana* ⊹ *About 2 miles south of Hana Town.*

🍴 Restaurants

★ Hana Farms Bamboo Hale Grill & Pizzeria
$$ | **AMERICAN** | Just outside of Hana is this small food truck that has been transformed into a permanent location with a large, covered patio, real restrooms, and beautiful wood-fired pizzas, calzones, and salads that highlight the vegetables from Hana Farms. While you wait for your food enjoy the free Wi-Fi (very rare in the area) and peruse the shelves of the farm stand for tropical fruits, banana bread, home and bath gifts, and more. **Known for:** farm-grown veggies included in every dish; a beautiful outdoor eatery; sides vibrantly flavored and colored with turmeric and curry powder. [$] *Average main: $20* ✉ *2910 Hana Hwy., Hana* ☎ *808/248–4047* 🌐 *hanafarms.com* 🕒 *No dinner Sun.–Thurs.*

★ Hana Ranch Restaurant
$$ | **AMERICAN** | The variety of abundance from local Hana farms is on display here with fresh produce highlighting plates with tasty American fare and a few local favorites like *loco moco* (white rice, burger patty, fried egg, and brown sauce) and *ahi* (yellowfin tuna) poke. The quality of meals and the prices are reflective of a more upscale restaurant, but customers can keep it casual here (no swimwear allowed, however). **Known for:** epic burgers and upscale plate lunches; generous portions; refreshing passion fruit lemonade. [$] *Average main: $24* ✉ *1752 Mill Pl., Hana* ☎ *808/270–5280* 🌐 *hanamauiresort.com/dining.*

Maui's Best Omiyage

Omiyage is the Japanese term for souvenirs or small gifts you take home to family and friends.

- Lavender-salt seasoning from **Alii Kula Lavender**
- Peaberry beans from **Maui Coffee Company**
- Jeff's jams and jellies from **Paia Gelato**
- Hot sauces from **HI Spice**

🛏 Hotels

★ Bamboo Inn on Hana Bay
$$ | **B&B/INN** | A thatched-roof gate opens to the courtyard of this informal Balinese-inspired guesthouse with a sweeping view of Hana Bay. The ground-floor studio has a private outdoor shower and the other two units have private whirlpool hot tubs on their second-floor decks. **Pros:** fall asleep to the sound of waves lapping at the rocky coast; close to town center; large BBQ available for grilling. **Cons:** no air-conditioning; no nightlife in this early-to-bed, early-to-rise town; two-night minimum, though one-night fillers may be available. [$] *Rooms from: $265* ✉ *4869 Uakea Rd., Hana* ☎ *808/248–7718* 🌐 *bambooinn.com* 🛏 *3 rooms* 🍴 *No Meals.*

★ Hana Kai Maui
$$$$ | **HOTEL** | Perfectly situated on Hana Bay, this two-story "condotel" has an excellent reputation for cleanliness and visitor hospitality—and the ocean views are stunning. **Pros:** 10-minute walk to Hana Bay; one-night rentals are accepted, except oceanfront units; Wi-Fi available in all units. **Cons:** no elevator; no air-conditioning or TV; tight parking lot can be a little difficult to manage. [$] *Rooms from: $465* ✉ *4865 Uakea Rd., Hana* ☎ *808/248–8426, 800/346–2772* 🌐 *hanakaimaui.com* 🛏 *17 units* 🍴 *No Meals.*

Hana-Maui Resort
$$$$ | **RESORT** | After Travaasa-Hana resort was purchased by new owners in 2019, with Hyatt brought in to manage in 2020, Hana-Maui Resort began focusing on major renovations and updates to this

remote oceanside getaway that features bungalows and villas set on sprawling lawns with all of the resort amenities, including a focus on cultural experiences. Expect various closures during its first few years as the property gently incorporates modern touches and environmentally friendly upgrades. **Pros:** welcoming and attentive staff; romantic spot perfect for honeymooners; fun program of traditional activities. **Cons:** construction noise can be bothersome; some suites still in desperate need of an upgrade; disparity in quality of accommodations. [$] *Rooms from: $749* ✉ *5031 Hana Hwy., Hana* ☎ *808/400–1234* 🌐 *hanamauiresort.com* 🛏 *75 bungalows, villas* 🍴 *No Meals.*

Shopping

★ Hana Coast Gallery
ART GALLERIES | One of the most well-curated galleries on the Island, this 3,000-square-foot facility has handcrafted koa furniture, marble sculptures, photography, and jewelry on consignment from local artists as well as artists from across Polynesia. The gallery makes a wonderful effort to give voice to the artists and to teach visitors about them. ✉ *Hana-Maui Resort, 5031 Hana Hwy., Hana* ☎ *808/248–8636* 🌐 *hanacoast.com.*

East Maui

East Maui defies definition. Part hideaway for renegades, part escape for celebrities, this funky stretch of Maui surprises at every turn. You might find a smoothie shop that powers your afternoon bike ride, or a hidden restaurant–artist gathering off a backcountry road serving organic cuisine that could have been dropped in from San Francisco. Farms are abundant, and the dramatic beauty seems to get better the farther you get from Hana. This route leads through stark ocean vistas rounding the back side of Haleakala and into Upcountry. If you plan to meander this way, be sure to check the weather and road conditions.

Kipahulu

11 miles east of Hana.

Most know Kipahulu as the resting place of Charles Lindbergh. Kipahulu devotes its energy to staying under the radar. There is not much for tourists, save an organic farm stand and astounding natural landscapes, particularly those in the back side of Haleakala National Park. Beaches in the area are full of rough surf and strong currents, making them off-limits for swimming. This area was also home to many ancient Hawaiians, making it rife with ruins. Be sure not to touch them when you see them, but do take the time to learn more by talking with park rangers. Maui's wildest wilderness might not beg for your tourist dollars, but it is a tantalizing place to escape just about everything.

GETTING HERE AND AROUND

To access Kipahulu from Hana, continue on Hana Highway, also known as 360, for 11 miles southeast. You can also reach the area from Upcountry's Highway 37, which turns into Highway 31, although this route can take up to two hours and is a bit rough on your rental car.

Sights

Grave of Charles Lindbergh
CEMETERY | Many people travel the mile past Oheo Gulch to see the grave of Charles Lindbergh. The world-renowned aviator chose to be buried here because he and his wife, writer Anne Morrow Lindbergh, spent a lot of time living in the area in a home they'd built. He was buried here in 1974, next to Palapala Hoomau Congregational Church. The simple one-room church sits on a bluff over the sea, with the small graveyard on the ocean side and gorgeous views. Since this is a churchyard, be considerate

and leave everything exactly as you found it. Next to the churchyard on the ocean side is a small county park, a good place for a peaceful picnic. ⊠ *Palapala Hoomau Congregational Church, Piilani Hwy., Kipahulu* ⊕ *palapalahoomau.org.*

Kaupo Road

SCENIC DRIVE | Also called Piilani Highway, this road winds through what locals say is one of the last parts of real Maui. It goes all the way around Haleakala's back side through Ulupalakua Ranch and into Kula. The desert-like area, with its grand vistas, is unlike anything else on the Island. This road has a reputation for being treacherous, and while narrow sections and steep cliffs can be intimidating for some drivers, recent road improvements have made this a much smoother ride.

⚠ Some car-rental agencies call the area off-limits for their passenger cars, and they won't come to your rescue if you need emergency assistance. However, four-wheel drive isn't necessary.

The small communities around East Maui cling tenuously to the old ways—please be respectful of that if you do pass this way. Between Kipahulu and Kula may be a mere 38 miles, but the twisty road makes the drive take up to two hours. If you must drive this road at night, keep an eye out for free-range cattle crossing your path.

■TIP➔ Fill up on gas and food before departing, as the only stop out here is Kaupo General Store, which hawks a few pricey necessities.

Oheo Gulch

WATERFALL | One branch of Haleakala National Park runs down the mountain from the crater and reaches the sea here, 12 miles past Hana at mile marker 42 on the Hana Highway, where a basalt-lined stream cascades from one pool to the next. Some tour guides still incorrectly call this area Seven Sacred Pools, but in truth there are more than seven, and they've never been considered sacred.

⚠ While you may be tempted to take a dip, know that the pools are often closed because of landslides and flash flooding. If you see a closure notice, take it seriously, as people have died here.

The place gets crowded, as most people who drive the Hana Highway make this their last stop. It's best to get here early to soak up the solace of these waterfalls. ■TIP➔ The $30 entrance fee per car is good for three days and includes entry to Haleakala's Summit District. ⊠ *Hana Hwy., 12 miles south of Hana, Hana* ⊕ *nps.gov/hale* 🖃 *$15–$30 National Park entry fee.*

★ Waimoku Falls

WATERFALL | If you enjoy hiking, go up the stream from the Pools of Oheo on the 2-mile hike to Waimoku Falls via Pipiwai Trail. The trail crosses a spectacular gorge, then turns into a boardwalk that takes you through an amazing bamboo forest. The hike also includes a giant banyan tree, views of Makahiku Falls, and forests of tropical plant life. After returning from your hike you can pitch a tent in the grassy campground down by the sea if you've made reservations in advance. ⊠ *Piilani Hwy., Hana* 🕾 *808/572–4400* ⊕ *nps.gov/hale* 🖃 *$15 per person on foot, $30 per vehicle.*

Activities and Tours

Aerial Tours

Helicopter flight-seeing excursions can take you over the West Maui Mountains, Haleakala Crater, or the Island of Molokai. Flying is a beautiful, thrilling way to see the Island and the *only* way to see some of its most scenic areas and waterfalls. Tour prices usually include a digital video of your trip so you can relive the experience at home. Fees run about $250 for a half-hour flight and more than $350 for a

75-minute tour with an ocean or cliffside landing. Discounts may be available online or if you're willing to take a chance by calling at the last minute.

Tour operators come under sharp scrutiny for passenger safety and equipment maintenance. Don't be shy; ask about a company's safety record, flight paths, age of equipment, and level of operator experience. Generally, though, if it's still in business, it's doing something right.

Air Maui Helicopters

AIR EXCURSIONS | Priding itself on a perfect safety record, Air Maui provides 45-minute flights covering Haleakala Crater and Hana ($229). A deluxe package ($303) includes a cliffside landing. Discounts are available online. Charter flights are also available. ✉ *1 Kahului Airport Rd., Hangar 110, Kahului* ☎ *877/238–4942, 808/877–7005* ⊕ *airmaui.com.*

Sunshine Helicopters

AIR EXCURSIONS | The 45-minute Hana-Haleakala tour soars past Haleakala National Park, revealing its many faces, including the arid moonlike crater and lush eastern edge dripping with waterfalls and rain forests. First-class seating is available for an additional fee. Charter flights can be arranged. A pilot-narrated digital record of your actual flight is available for purchase. ✉ *Kahului Airport Rd., Hangar 107, Kahului* ☎ *808/270–3999, 866/501–7738* ⊕ *sunshinehelicopters. com* 🖅 *Tours start at $254.*

Biking

Long distances and mountainous terrain keep biking from being a practical mode of travel on Maui. Still, painted bike lanes enable cyclists to travel from Makena to Kapalua, and you'll see hardy souls battling the trade winds under the hot Maui sun.

Several companies offer guided bike tours down Haleakala. This activity is a great way to enjoy an easy, gravity-induced bike ride but isn't for those not confident on a bike. The ride is inherently dangerous due to the slope, sharp turns, and the fact that you're riding down an actual road with cars on it. That said, the guided bike companies take every safety precaution. A few companies offer unguided (or, as they like to say, "self-guided") tours where they provide you with the bike and transportation to the mountain, and then you're free to descend at your own pace. Most companies offer discounts for Internet bookings.

Haleakala National Park no longer allows commercial downhill bicycle rides within the park's boundaries. As a result, tour amenities and routes differ by company. Ask about sunrise viewing from the Haleakala summit (be prepared to leave *very* early in the morning) if this is an essential feature for you. Some lower-price tours begin at the 6,500-foot elevation just outside the national park boundaries, where you will be unable to view the sunrise over the crater. Weather conditions on Haleakala vary greatly, so a visible sunrise can never be guaranteed. Sunrise is downright cold at the summit, so be sure to dress in layers and wear closed-toe shoes.

Each company has age and weight restrictions, and pregnant women are discouraged from participating, although they are generally welcome in the escort van. Reconsider this activity if you have difficulty with high altitudes, have recently been scuba diving, or take medications that may cause drowsiness.

BEST SPOTS

Thompson Road in Keokea and Polipoli Spring State Recreation Area in Kula are popular areas for cycling in Maui, and Makawao Forest Reserve is attracting riders of all ages and ability levels with its well-maintained, clearly marked trails.

Thompson Road

BIKING | Street bikers will want to head out to scenic Thompson Road. It's quiet, gently curvy, and flanked by gorgeous views on both sides. Because it's at a higher elevation, the air temperature is cooler and the wind lighter. The coast back down toward Kahului on the Kula Highway is worth the ride up. ⊠ *Kula Hwy., off Rte. 37, Keokea.*

EQUIPMENT AND TOURS

★ Cruiser Phil's Volcano Riders

BIKING | In the downhill bicycle industry since 1983, "Cruiser" Phil Feliciano offers both group and private tours that include hotel transfers, coffee and snacks, and a guided 23-mile ride down the mountain. Participants should be older than 12, at least five feet tall, weigh less than 280 pounds, and have ridden a bike in the past year. Feliciano also offers structured independent bike tours, van-only tours, and packages that include a zip-lining experience. Discounts are available for online bookings. ⊠ *810 Haiku Rd. #120, Haiku-Pauwela* ☎ *808/575–9575* ⊕ *cruiserphils.com* ✉ *Tours start at $130 per person.*

Island Biker

BIKING | Maui's premier bike shop for rentals, sales, and service offers standard front-shock bikes, road bikes, and full-suspension mountain bikes. Rental prices include a helmet, pump, water bottle, cages, tire-repair kit, and spare tube. Car racks are included with weekly rentals. The staff can suggest routes appropriate for mountain or road biking. ⊠ *415 Dairy Rd. Suite C, Kahului* ☎ *808/877–7744* ✉ *Daily rentals start at $75. Weekly rates start at $250.*

Krank Cycles

BIKING | Krank Cycles is located in Kahului and Upcountry Maui, close to the Makawao Forest Reserve. They offer full-day and weekly rentals of high-end road and mountain bikes. Owner Moose will provide you with maps and trail reports, in addition to your rental bike and gear. ⊠ *1120 Makawao Ave., Makawao* ☎ *808/572–2299* ⊕ *krankmaui.com* ✉ *Daily rental $59 and up.*

West Maui Cycles

BIKING | Serving the island's west side, West Maui Cycles offers a range of bikes, including cruisers, hybrids, and performance road bikes. They offer discounted rates for longer-term rentals. Sales and service are also available. ⊠ *1087 Limahana Pl., No. 6, Lahaina* ☎ *808/661–9005* ⊕ *westmauicycles.com* ✉ *Cruisers $20 per day, hybrids $40 per day, and performance road bikes $60–$100 per day.*

Bodyboarding and Bodysurfing

Bodysurfing and "sponging" (as bodyboarding is called by the regulars; "boogie boarding" is another variation) are great ways to catch some waves without having to master surfing—and there's no balance or coordination required. A bodyboard (or "sponge") is softer than a hard fiberglass surfboard, which means you can ride safely in the rough-and-tumble surf zone. If you get tossed around—which is half the fun—you don't have a heavy surfboard nearby to bang your head on but you do have something to hang onto. Serious spongers invest in a single short-clipped fin to help propel them into the wave.

BEST SPOTS

In West Maui, **D. T. Fleming Beach** offers great surf almost daily along with some nice amenities: ample parking, restrooms, a shower, grills, picnic tables, and a daily lifeguard. Caution is advised, especially during winter months, when the current and undertow can get rough.

Between Kihei and Wailea on the South Shore, **Kamaole III** is a good spot for bodysurfing and bodyboarding. It has a sandy floor, with one- to three-foot waves breaking not too far out. It's often crowded late in the day, especially on weekends when local kids are out of school. Don't let that chase you away; the waves are wide enough for everyone.

If you don't mind public nudity (officially illegal but practiced nonetheless), Puu Olai **(aka Little Beach)** on the South Shore is the best break on the island for bodyboarding and bodysurfing. The shape of the sandy shoreline creates waves that break a long way out and tumble into shore. Because it's sandy, you only risk stubbing a toe on the few submerged rocks. Don't try bodyboarding at neighboring Oneloa **(aka Big Beach)**—waves will slap you onto the steep shore. To get to Little Beach, take the first entrance to Makena State Beach Park; climb the rock wall at the north end of the beach.

On the North Shore, **Paia Bay** has waves suitable for spongers and bodysurfers. The beach is just before Paia town, beyond the large community building and grass field.

EQUIPMENT

Most condos and hotels have bodyboards available to guests—some in better condition than others (beat-up boards work just as well for beginners). You can also pick up a bodyboard from any discount shop, such as Target or Longs Drugs (now owned by CVS), for upwards of $30.

Auntie Snorkel

WATER SPORTS | You can rent decent bodyboards and all types of affordable watersport equipment at Auntie Snorkel. Check online for specials and discounts. ⊠ *2439 S. Kihei Rd., Kihei* ☎ *808/298–3021* ⊕ *auntiesnorkel.com* ☜ *Bodyboard rentals $6.95 a day or $20 a week.*

West Maui Sports and Fishing Supply

WATER SPORTS | This old country store has been around since 1987 and has some of the best prices on the west side for surfboards and bodyboards. Snorkel and fishing gear, beach chairs, and umbrellas are also available. ⊠ *843 Wainee St.,*

Lahaina ☎ *808/661–6252* ⊕ *westmauisports.com* ☜ *Surfboards $70 per week. Bodyboards $3 per day, $15 per week.*

Deep-Sea Fishing

If fishing is your sport, Maui is your island. In these waters, you'll find *ahi* (yellowfin tuna), *aku* (skipjack tuna), barracuda, bonefish, *kawakawa* (bonito), *mahimahi* (dolphinfish), Pacific blue marlin, *ono* (wahoo), and *ulua* (giant trevally). You can fish year-round, and you don't need a license.

Plenty of fishing boats run out of Lahaina and Maalaea harbors. If you charter a private boat, expect to spend in the neighborhood of $700 to $1,000 for an exciting half day in the swivel seat. You can share a boat for much less if you don't mind close quarters with a stranger. Before you sign up, you should know that some boats keep the catch. Most will, however, fillet a nice piece for you to take home. And if you catch a real beauty, you might even be able to have it professionally mounted.

■ **TIP**➔ **Because boats fill up fast during busy seasons, make reservations before coming to Maui.**

You're expected to bring your lunch and beverages in unbreakable containers. (Shop the night before; it's hard to find snacks at 5 am.) Boats supply coolers, ice, and bait. A 7.5% tax is added to the cost of a trip, and a 15%–20% tip for the crew is suggested.

BOATS AND CHARTERS

Die Hard Sportfishing

FISHING | Captain Fuzzy Alboro runs a highly recommended operation on the 33-foot *Die Hard*. Check-in times vary between 10 pm and 3 am, depending on the moon's location, and trips range from four to eight hours. He takes a minimum of four and a maximum of six people. ⊠ *Lahaina Harbor, 654 Wharf St., Slip 9, Lahaina* ☎ *808/344–5051*

⊕ *diehardsportfishing.com* ✉ *$300 for shared boat or $1,520 for private charter.*

Finest Kind Sportfishing

FISHING | A record 1,118-pound pacific blue marlin was reeled in by the crew aboard *Finest Kind,* a lovely 37-foot Merritt kept so clean you'd never guess the action it's seen. Captain David Hudson has been around these waters for about 40 years, long enough to befriend other expert fishers. This three-generation family-run company operates three boats and specializes in skilled trolling. No bananas on board, please; the captain thinks they're bad luck for fishing. ⊠ *Lahaina Harbor, 675 Wharf St., Slip 7, Lahaina* ☎ *808/661–0338* ⊕ *finestkindsportfishingmaui.com* ✉ *Shared charters $300 for 4 hours, $475 for full day. Full-day private charter $2,300.*

Golf

Maui's natural beauty and surroundings offer some of the most jaw-dropping vistas imaginable on a golf course; add a variety of challenging, well-designed courses, and it's easy to explain the Island's popularity with golfers. Holes run across small bays, past craggy lava outcrops, and up into cool forested mountains. Most courses have mesmerizing ocean views, some close enough to feel the salt in the air. Although many golf courses are affiliated with resorts (and therefore a little pricier), the general-public courses are no less impressive. Playing on Lanai is another option.

Greens Fees: Golf can be costly on Maui. Greens fees listed here are the highest course rates per round on weekdays and weekends for U.S. residents. (Some courses charge non-U.S. residents higher prices.) Rental clubs may or may not be included with the greens fee. Discounts are often available for resort guests, for twilight tee times, and for those who book online.

■ TIP → Resort courses, in particular, offer more than the usual three sets of tees, so bite off as much or as little challenge as you like. Tee it up from the tips and you can end up playing a few 600-yard par 5s and see a few 250-yard forced carries.

★ The Dunes at Maui Lani

GOLF | Robin Nelson is at his minimalist best here, creating British-style links in the middle of the Pacific. Holes run through ancient, lightly wooded sand dunes, 5 miles inland from Kahului Harbor. Thanks to the natural humps and slopes of the dunes, Nelson had to move very little dirt and created a natural beauty. During the design phase, he visited Ireland, and not so coincidentally the par-3 3rd looks a lot like the Dell at Lahinch: a white dune on the right sloping down into a deep bunker and partially obscuring the right side of the green—just one of several blind to semi-blind shots here. ⊠ *1333 Maui Lani Pkwy., Kahului* ☎ *808/873–0422* ⊕ *dunesatmauilani.com* ✉ *$99 (prices drop later in the day)* ⚑ *18 holes, 6841 yards, par 72.*

Kaanapali Golf Courses

GOLF | In 1962, the Royal Kaanapali (North) Course opened and was one of three in Hawaii designed by Robert Trent Jones Sr., the godfather of modern golf architecture. The greens average a whopping 10,000 square feet, necessary because of the often-severe undulation. The par-4 18th hole course is challenging (the prevailing trade breezes, with out-of-bounds on the left and a lake on the right). Designed by Arthur Jack Snyder, the Kaanapali Kai (South) Course (opened in 1976) shares similar seaside-into-the-hills terrain. Still, it is rated a couple of strokes easier, mainly because putts are less treacherous. ⊠ *2290 Kaanapali Pkwy., Lahaina* ☎ *808/661–3691, 866/454–4653* ⊕ *kaanapaligolfcourses.com* ✉ *Royal Kaanapali (North) Course $255, Kaanapali Kai (South) Course $205* ⚑ *Royal Kaanapali (North) Course: 18 holes, 6700 yards,*

Tips for Golfing on Maui

Golf is golf, and Hawaii is part of the United States, but Island golf has its quirks. Here are a few tips to make your golf experience in the Islands more pleasant.

■ Sunscreen: Buy it, apply it (we're talking a minimum of 30 SPF). The subtropical rays of the sun are intense, even in December. Good advice is to apply sunscreen, at a minimum, on the 1st and 10th tees.

■ Stay hydrated. Spending four-plus hours in the sun and heat means you'll sweat away many fluids and energy.

■ All resort courses and many daily-fee courses provide rental clubs. In many cases, they're the latest lines from top manufacturers. Valid both for men and women and for left-handers, which means you don't have to schlep clubs across the Pacific.

■ Pro shops at most courses are well stocked with balls, tees, and other accoutrements, so it doesn't weigh a ton even if you bring your bag.

■ Come spikeless—few Hawaii courses still permit metal spikes. Also, most of the resort courses require a collared shirt.

■ Maui is notorious for its trade winds. Consider playing early or at twilight if you want to avoid the breezes, and remember that although they will frustrate you at times and make club selection difficult, you may well see some of your longest drives ever.

■ In theory, you can play golf in Hawaii 365 days a year, but there's a reason the Hawaiian Islands are so green: an umbrella and light jacket can come in handy.

■ Unless you play a muni or specific daily-fee courses, plan on taking a cart. Riding carts are mandatory at most courses and are included in the greens fee.

par 71; Kaanapali Kai (South) Course: 18 holes, 6400 yards, par 70.

★ Kapalua Golf

GOLF | Perhaps Hawaii's best-known golf resort and the crown jewel of golf on Maui, Kapalua hosts the PGA Tour's first event each January: the Sentry Tournament of Champions at the Plantation Course. On this famed course, Ben Crenshaw and Bill Coore (1991) tried to incorporate traditional shot values in a nontraditional site, taking into account slope, gravity, and the prevailing trade winds. The par-5 18th hole, for instance, plays 663 yards from the back tees (600 yards from the resort tees). The hole drops 170 feet in elevation, narrowing as it goes to a partially guarded green, and

plays downwind and down-grain. Despite the longer-than-usual distance, the slope is great enough and the wind at your back usually brisk enough to reach the green with two well-struck shots—a truly unbelievable finish to a course that will challenge, frustrate, and reward the patient golfer.

The Bay Course (Arnold Palmer and Francis Duane, 1975) is the more traditional of Kapalua's courses, with gentle rolling fairways and generous greens. The most memorable hole is the par-3 5th hole, with a tee shot that must carry over a turquoise inlet of Oneloa Bay. Each of the courses has a separate clubhouse. ⊠ *2000 Plantation Club Dr., Kapalua* ☎ *808/669–8044, 877/527–2582*

⊕ *golfatkapalua.com* ✉ *Plantation Course $329, Bay Course $229* 🏌 *Plantation Course: 18 holes, 7411 yards, par 73. Bay Course: 18 holes, 6600 yards, par 72.*

Kapalua Golf Academy

GOLF | It is a state-of-the-art golf school and training facility designed by three-time U.S. Open Champion Hale Irwin. With 23 acres of practice turf, an 18-hole putting course, and a three-hole walking course, the Kapalua Golf Academy offers individual lessons, corporate clinics, golf schools, daily clinics, and custom off-site instruction by its renowned staff of PGA professionals. ✉ *1000 Office Rd., Kapalua* ☎ *808/665–5455, 877/527–2582* ⊕ *golfat-kapalua.com* ✉ *Private instruction starts at $185 for a 50-minute lesson.*

Pukalani Country Club

GOLF | At 1,110 feet above sea level, Pukalani (Bob Baldock, 1980) provides one of the finest vistas in all Hawaii. Holes run up, down, and across the slopes of Haleakala. The trade winds tend to come up in the late morning and afternoon. Winds combined with frequent elevation change, makes club selection a test. The fairways tend to be wide, but greens are undulating and quick. ✉ *360 Pukalani St., Pukalani* ☎ *808/572–1314* ⊕ *pukalanigolf.com* ✉ *$89; Twilight rate $69 from 11 am - 1 pm* 🏌 *18 holes, 6962 yards, par 72.*

Wailea Blue Course

GOLF | Wailea's original course, the Blue Course (1971), nicknamed "The Grand Lady of Wailea," is operated from a separate clubhouse from the Gold and Emerald courses, its newer siblings. Here, judging elevation change is key. Fairways and greens tend to be wider and more forgiving than on the newer courses, and they run through colorful flora that includes hibiscus, wiliwili, bougainvillea, and plumeria. ✉ *100 Wailea Ike Dr., Wailea* ☎ *808/875–7450, 888/328–6284* ⊕ *waileagolf.com* ✉ *$190* 🏌 *18 holes, 6765 yards, par 71.*

★ Wailea Golf Club

GOLF | Wailea is the only Hawaii resort to offer three courses: Gold, Emerald, and Blue—the latter at a different location with another pro shop. Designed by Robert Trent Jones Jr. (Gold and Emerald) and Arthur Jack Snyder (Blue), these courses share similar terrain, carved into the leeward slopes of Haleakala. Although the ocean does not come into play, its beauty is visible on almost every hole.

■ TIP→ **Remember, putts break dramatically toward the ocean.**

Jones refers to the Gold Course at Wailea (1994) as the "masculine" course. It's all trees and lava, and regarded as the hardest of the three courses. The trick here is to note even subtle changes in elevation. The par-3 8th, for example, plays from an elevated tee across a lava ravine to a large, well-bunkered green framed by palm trees, the blue sea, and tiny Molokini. The course demands strategy and careful club selection. The Emerald Course (1994) is the "feminine" layout with lots of flowers and bunkering away from greens. Although this may seem to render the bunker benign, the opposite is true. A bunker well in front of a green disguises the distance to the hole. Likewise, the Emerald's extensive flower beds are dangerous distractions because of their beauty. The Gold and Emerald courses share a clubhouse, practice facility, and 19th hole. ✉ *100 Wailea Golf Club Dr., Wailea* ☎ *808/875–7450, 888/328–6284* ⊕ *waileagolf.com* ✉ *Gold Course $279, Emerald Course $279* 🏌 *Gold Course: 18 holes, 7078 yards, par 72; Emerald Course: 18 holes, 6825 yards, par 72.*

Hang Gliding and Paragliding

If you've always wanted to know what it feels like to fly, hang gliding or paragliding might be your perfect Maui adventure. You'll get open-air, bird's-eye views of the Valley Isle that you'll likely never forget. And you don't need to be a daredevil to participate.

LESSONS AND TOURS

Hang Gliding Maui

HANG GLIDING & PARAGLIDING | Armin Engert will take you on an instructional powered hang-gliding trip out of Hana Airport in East Maui. With more than 13,000 hours in the air and a perfect safety record, Armin flies you over Maui's most beautiful coast. Snapshots of your flight from a wing-mounted camera cost an additional $50, and a 34-minute DVD of the flight from a wing-mounted camera is available for $100. Reservations are required. ⊠ *Hana Airport, Alalele Pl., off Hana Hwy., Hana* ☎ *808/264–3287* ⊕ *hangglidingmaui.com* 🖭 *30-minute flight lesson $240, 45-minute lesson $320, and 60-minute lesson $400.*

Paraglide Maui

HANG GLIDING & PARAGLIDING | The only paragliding outfit on Maui to offer solo, tandem, and instruction is at Polipoli Spring State Recreation Area. The leeward slope of Haleakala lends itself to paragliding with breathtaking scenery and air currents that increase during the day. Polipoli creates tremendous thermals that allow you to descend 3,000 feet peacefully to land. Solo paragliding certification is also available. ⊠ *1100 Waipoli Rd., Kula* ☎ *808/874–5433* ⊕ *paraglidemaui.com* 🖭 *Tandem instruction prices $175 to $295.*

Hiking

Hikes on Maui include treks along the coastal seashore, verdant rain forest, and alpine desert. Orchids, hibiscus, ginger, heliconia, and anthuriums grow wild on many trails, and exotic fruits like mountain apple, *lilikoi* (passion fruit), and strawberry guava provide refreshing snacks for hikers. During your hike, don't hike alone, wear bright clothing, stay on the trail, and be aware that you may encounter hunters who are hunting off the trail.

■ TIP➜ **Hawaii possesses some of the world's rarest plants, insects, and birds. Pocket field guides are available at most grocery or drug stores and can really illuminate your walk.**

BEST SPOTS

HALEAKALA NATIONAL PARK

★ **Haleakala Crater**

NATURE SIGHT | The park's main attraction is the eroded depression found at the Summit District known as Haleakala Crater. And, undoubtedly, the island's best hiking is found here. If you're in good shape, do a day hike descending from the summit along Keoneheehee Trail (Sliding Sands Trail) to the crater floor. You might also consider spending several days here amid the cinder cones, lava flows, and all that loud silence. Entering the crater is like landing on a different planet. In the early 1960s, NASA brought moon-suited astronauts here to practice what it would be like to "walk on the moon." Tent camping and cabins are available with permits. On the 30 miles of trails, you can traverse black sand and wild lava formations, follow the blooming *ahinahina* (silverswords) path, and take in tremendous views of the big sky and burned-red cliffs.

The best time to go into the crater is summer when the conditions are generally more predictable. Be sure to bring layered clothing—and plenty of warm clothes if you're staying overnight.

It may be scorching hot during the day, but it gets mighty chilly after dark. Bring drinking water, as potable water is available only at the two visitor centers. Overnight visitors must get a permit at park headquarters before entering the crater. ⊠ *Haleakala Crater Rd., Haleakala National Park* ☏ *808/572–4400* ⊕ *www. nps.gov/hale* ✉ *$30 entrance fee per vehicle (good for 3 days).*

IAO VALLEY STATE MONUMENT

In Hawaiian, Iao means "supreme cloud." When you enter this mystical valley in the middle of an unexpected rain forest near Wailuku in West Maui, you'll know why. At 750 feet above sea level, the 10-mile valley clings to the clouds as if it's trying to cover its naked beauty. One of Maui's great wonders, the valley is the site of a famous battle to unite the Hawaiian Islands. Out of the clouds, the Iao Needle, a tall chunk of volcanic rock, stands as a monument to the long-ago lookout for Maui warriors. Today, the valley is a peaceful land of lush tropical plants, clear pools and a running stream, and easy enjoyable strolls.

To get to Iao Valley State Monument, head to the western end of Route 32. The road dead-ends into the parking lot ($25 per car). The park is open daily 7 am–6 pm with an entrance fee ($5 per person). Facilities are available, but there is no drinking water.

★ Iao Needle Lookout Trail & Ethnobotanical Loop

HIKING & WALKING | Anyone can do this short walk from the parking lot at Iao Valley State Monument. On your choice of two paved walkways, you can cross the Iao Stream and explore the junglelike area. Ascend the stairs up to the Iao Needle for spectacular views of Central Maui. Be sure to stop at the lovely Kepaniwai Heritage Gardens, which commemorate the cultural contributions of various immigrant groups. Open daily from 7 am–6 pm. *Easy.* ⊠ *Trailhead: Iao Valley State Monument parking lot, Rte. 32, Wailuku*

⊕ *dlnr.hawaii.gov/dsp/parks/maui/iao-valley-state-monument* ✉ *$5 per person; $25 parking per car.*

OHEO GULCH

A branch of Haleakala National Park, Oheo Gulch is famous for its pools (Seven Sacred Pools). There are more than seven pools when the water levels are up. A former owner of the Travaasa Hotel in Hana started calling the area Seven Sacred Pools to attract the masses to sleepy old Hana. His plan worked, and the name stuck, much to the chagrin of many locals.

The best time to visit the pools is in the morning before the crowds and tour buses arrive. Start your day with a vigorous hike. Oheo has some fantastic trails to choose from, including our favorite, the Pipiwai Trail. At the end of your walk, nothing could be better than going to the pools, lounging on the rocks, and cooling off in the freshwater reserves. Keep in mind that the park periodically closes the pools when the potential for flash flooding exists.

You can find Oheo Gulch on Route 31, 10 miles past Hana town. To visit, you must pay the $30-per-car National Park fee, which is valid for three days and can be used at Haleakala's summit (keep your receipt). For information about scheduled orientations and cultural demonstrations, be sure to visit Haleakala National Park's Kipahulu Visitor Center, 10 miles past Hana. Note that there is no drinking water here—plan accordingly.

★ Pipiwai Trail

TRAIL | This popular 2-mile trek upstream reveals two magnificent waterfalls: Makahiku Falls at about half a mile in, and the grand finale 400-foot Waimoku Falls, pounding down in all its power and glory. Following signs from the parking lot, head across the road and uphill into the forest. The trail borders a stunning gorge and passes onto a boardwalk through an impenetrable forest of giant bamboo. This stomp through muddy and rocky terrain takes around three hours to enjoy fully. Although this trail is never truly crowded, it's best done early in the morning before the tours arrive. Be sure to bring mosquito repellent. *Moderate.* ✉ *Hana Hwy., Hana* ✛ *Trailhead: Near mile marker 42* ⊕ *nps.gov/hale* ✉ *$30 entrance fee per vehicle (good for 3 days).*

THE SOUTH SHORE AND WEST MAUI

In addition to the trails listed below, the Kapalua Resort offers free access to 100 miles of self-guided hikes. Trail information and maps are available at the Kapalua Adventure Center.

Hoapili Trail (King's Trail)

HIKING & WALKING | This 5½-mile coastal trail beyond the Ahihi-Kinau Natural Area Reserve offers a challenging hike through eye-popping scenery. Named after a king, it follows the shoreline, threading through the remains of ancient villages. King Hoapili created an islandwide road, and this broad path of stacked lava rocks is a marvel to look at and walk on. (It's not the easiest surface for the ankles and feet, so wear sturdy shoes.) The trail takes you through brutal territory with little shade and no facilities, and extra water is a must. To get here, follow Makena Road to La Perouse Bay. The trail can be a challenge to find—walk south along the ocean through the *kiawe* (mesquite, or algaroba) trees, where you'll encounter numerous wild goats (don't worry—they're gentle), and past a scenic little bay. The trail begins just around the corner to the left. *Difficult.* ✉ *Trailhead: La Perouse Bay, Makena Rd., Makena.*

Kapalua Resort

HIKING & WALKING | The resort offers free access to miles of hiking trails as a self-guided experience. Trail information and maps are available at the Kapalua Village Center. The Village Walking Trails offer a network of exercise opportunities on former golf cart paths, including the 3.6-mile Lake Loop, which features sweeping views and a secluded lake

populated with quacking ducks. The Coastal Trail provides views of the ocean and wildlife as it crosses the golden sand dunes of Oneloa Bay and past Ironwood Beach and the Ritz-Carlton, Kapalua, to its terminus at D. T. Fleming Beach Park. Sightings of green sea turtles, dolphins, and humpback whales (in season) are likely, along with wedge-tailed sheerwater seabirds called *uau kani*. Guided 1½-mile hikes on the coastal trail that include tide pool exploration are available for $100 through the Jean-Michel Cousteau Ambassadors of the Environment program at the Ritz-Carlton, Kapalua. ✉ *2000 Village Rd., corner of Office Rd., Kapalua* ☎ *808/665–4386 Kapalua Village Center concierge, 808/665–7292 Jean-Michel Cousteau Ambassadors of the Environment* ⊕ *kapalua.com.*

GUIDES

Guided hikes can help you see more than you might on your own. If the company is driving you to the site, be sure to ask about drive times; they can be fairly lengthy for some hikes.

★ Friends of Haleakala National Park

HIKING & WALKING | This nonprofit offers overnight trips into the volcanic crater. The purpose of your trip, the service work itself, isn't too much—mostly native planting, removing invasive plants, and light cabin maintenance. But participants are asked to check the website to learn more about the trip and certify readiness for service work. A knowledgeable guide accompanies each trip, taking you to places you'd otherwise miss and teaching you about the native flora and fauna. ✉ *Makawao* ☎ *808/876–1673* ⊕ *fhnp.org.*

★ Hike Maui

HIKING & WALKING | Started in 1983, the area's oldest hiking company remains extremely well regarded for its hikes led by enthusiastic, highly trained guides who weave botany, geology, ethnobotany, culture, and history into the outdoor experience. The seven-hour Haleakala tour includes two hikes, each revealing vastly different environments that make up this national park. The 11-hour Hana excursion takes you to the park's remote eastern edge, where you'll explore a bamboo forest that leads to a stunning 400-foot waterfall, among other stops. Hike Maui supplies day packs, rain gear, mosquito repellent, first-aid supplies, bottled water, snacks, lunch, and transportation to and from the site. ⊠ *Kahului* ☎ *808/784–7992* ⊕ *hikemaui.com* ⌑ *Tours start at $109.*

Sierra Club

HIKING & WALKING | One great avenue into the island's untrammeled wilderness is Maui's chapter of the Sierra Club. Join one of the club's hikes into pristine forests, along ancient coastal paths, to historic sites, and to Haleakala Crater. Some outings require volunteer service, but most are just for fun. Bring your own food and water, rain gear, sunscreen, sturdy shoes, and a suggested donation of $5 for hikers over age 14 ($3 for Sierra Club members). This is a true bargain. ⊠ *Paia* ☎ *808/867–6001* ⊕ *mauisierraclub.org.*

Horseback Riding

Mendes Ranch

HORSEBACK RIDING | Family-owned and -run, Mendes Ranch operates out of the beautiful ranch land of Kahakuloa on the windward slopes of the West Maui Mountains. Morning and afternoon trail rides lasting 1½ hours are available. Paniolos take you cantering up rolling pastures into the lush rain forest, and then you'll descend all the way down to the ocean for a photo op with a dramatic backdrop. Don't expect a Hawaiian cultural experience here—it's all about the horses and the ride. Mendes also offers a horseback riding and helicopter tour in partnership with Sunshine Helicopters. ⊠ *3530 Kahekili Hwy., Wailuku* ☎ *800/871–5222* ⊕ *mendesranch.com* ⌑ *Rides start at $135.*

Kayaking

Kayaking is a fantastic and eco-friendly way to experience Maui's coast up close. Floating aboard a "plastic Popsicle stick" is easier than you might think, and it allows you to cruise out to vibrant, living coral reefs and waters where dolphins and even whales roam. Kayaking can be a leisurely paddle or a challenge of heroic proportions, depending on your ability, the location, and the weather.

■ **TIP→ Although you can rent kayaks independently, we recommend hiring a guide.**

A calm surface can hide powerful ocean currents. Most guides are naturalists who will steer you away from surging surf, lead you to pristine reefs, and point out camouflaged fish, like the stalking hawkfish. Not having to schlep your gear on top of your rental car is a bonus. A half-day tour runs around $75.

If you decide to strike out on your own, tour companies will rent kayaks for the day with paddles, life vests, and roof racks, and many will meet you near your chosen location. Ask for a map of good entries and plan to avoid paddling back to shore against the wind (schedule extra time for the return trip regardless). Read weather conditions, bring binoculars, and take a careful look from the bay before heading in. Get there early before the trade wind kicks in, and stick close to shore. When you're ready to snorkel, secure your belongings in a dry pack on board and drag your kayak by its bowline behind you. (This isn't as hard as it sounds.)

BEST SPOTS

Makena Landing is an excellent starting point for a South Shore adventure. Enter from the paved parking lot or the small sandy beach a little south. The shoreline is lined with million-dollar mansions. The bay itself is virtually empty, but the right edge is flanked with brilliant coral heads and juvenile turtles. If you round the point on the right, you come across Five Caves, a system of enticing underwater arches. In the morning you may see dolphins, and the arches are havens for lobsters, eels, and spectacularly hued butterfly fish.

In West Maui, past the steep cliffs on the Honoapiilani Highway, there's a long stretch of inviting coastline that includes **Ukumehame Beach.** This is a good spot for beginners; entry is easy, and there's much to see in every direction. Pay attention if trade winds pick up from the late morning onward; paddling against them can be challenging. If you want to snorkel, the best visibility is farther out at Olowalu Beach. Watch for sharp *kiawe* (mesquite) thorns buried in the sand on the way into the water. Water shoes are recommended.

EQUIPMENT AND TOURS
Kelii's Kayak Tours

KAYAKING | One of the highest-rated kayak outfitters on the Island, Kelii's offers kayaking trips and combo adventures where you can also surf, snorkel, or hike to a waterfall. Leading groups of up to eight people, the guides show what makes each reef unique. Most popular is the kayak and snorkel combo to Turtle Town—explore colorful reefs, endangered green sea turtles, and you might see a dolphin or two. Trips are available on the Island's north, south, and west shores. ⊠ *1993 S. Kihei Rd., Suite 12, Kihei* ☎ *808/874–7652* ⊕ *keliiskayak.com* 🖃 *$84 and up.*

★ South Pacific Kayaks

KAYAKING | These guys pioneered recreational kayaking on Maui, so they know their stuff. Guides are friendly, informative, and eager to help you get the most out of your experience; we're talking genuine, fun-loving, kayak geeks who will maneuver away from crowds when exploring prime snorkel spots. South Pacific stands out as adventurous and environmentally responsible, plus their gear and equipment are well maintained. They offer a variety of trips leaving from both West Maui and South Shore locations. ⊠ *95 Halekuai St., Kihei* ☎ *808/875–4848* ⊕ *southpacifickayaks. com* 🖃 *From $85.*

Parasailing

Parasailing is an easy, exhilarating way to earn your wings: strap on a harness attached to a parachute, and a power-boat pulls you up and over the Pacific ocean from a launching dock or a boat's platform.

■ TIP➜ **Parasailing is limited to West Maui, and "thrill craft"—including parasails—are prohibited in Maui waters during humpback-whale calving season, December 15–May 15.**

LESSONS AND TOURS
West Maui Parasail

HANG GLIDING & PARAGLIDING | Soar at 800 feet above the ocean for a bird's-eye view of Lahaina, or be daring at 1,200 feet for smoother rides and even better views. The captain will be glad to let you experience a "toe-dip" or "freefall" if you request it. Hour-long trips from Lahaina Harbor and Kaanapali Beach include 8- to 10-minute flights. ■ TIP➜ **No paras-ailing during whale season.** ⊠ *Lahaina Harbor, 675 Wharf St., Slip 15, Lahaina* ☎ *808/661–4060* ⊕ *westmauiparasail. com* 🖃 *Starting at $125.*

Rafting

The high-speed, inflatable rafts you find on Maui are nothing like the raft that Huck Finn used to drift down the Mississippi. While passengers grip straps, these rafts fly, skimming and bouncing across the sea. Because they're so maneuverable, they go where the big boats can't—secret coves, sea caves, and remote beaches.

■ TIP➔ **Although safe, these trips are not for the faint of heart. If you have back or neck problems or are pregnant, you should reconsider this activity.**

TOURS

Blue Water Rafting

BOATING | One of the few ways to get to the stunning Kanaio Coast (the roadless southern coastline beyond Ahihi-Kinau), this rafting tour begins conveniently at the Kihei Boat Ramp on the South Shore. Dolphins, turtles, and other marine life are the highlight of this adventure, along with majestic sea caves, lava arches, and views of Haleakala. The Molokini stop is usually timed between the bigger cata-marans, so you can enjoy the crater without the usual massive crowd. If condi-tions permit, you'll be able to snorkel the back wall, which has much more marine life than the inside. ⊠ *Kihei Boat Ramp, S. Kihei Rd., Kihei* ☎ *808/879–7238* ⊕ *bluewaterrafting.com* ✉ *From $60.*

Ocean Riders

BOATING | Start the day with a spectacular view of the sun rising above the West Maui Mountains, then cross the Auau Channel to Lanai's Kaiolohia (commonly referred to as Shipwreck Beach). After a short swim at a secluded beach, this tour circles Lanai, allowing you to view the Island's 70 miles of remote coast. The "back side" of Lanai is one of Hawaii's unsung marvels, and you can expect to stop at three protected coves for snorkeling. You might chance upon *honu* (sea turtles), monk seals, and a friendly reef shark, as well as rare varieties of angelfish and butterflyfish. Guides are knowledgeable and slow down long enough for you to marvel at sacred burial caves and interesting rock formations. Sit toward the backbench if you are sensitive to motion sickness. Tours include snorkel gear, a fruit breakfast, and a satisfying deli lunch. ⊠ *Mala Wharf, Front St., Lahai-na* ☎ *808/661–3586* ⊕ *mauioceanriders. com* ✉ *From $186.*

★ Redline Rafting

WATER SPORTS | This company's raft tours begin with a trip to Molokini Crater for some snorkeling. If weather permits, the raft explores the crater's back wall, too. There's a quick stop at La Perouse Bay to spot dolphins, and then it's off to Makena for more underwater fun and a deli lunch. The rafts provide great seating, comfort, and shade. ⊠ *Kihei Boat Ramp, 2800 S. Kihei Rd., Kihei* ☎ *808/201–7450* ⊕ *redlinerafting.com* ✉ *Whale-watching excursions start at $85, snorkel trips at $139.*

Sailing

With the islands of Molokai, Lanai, Kahoolawe, and Molokini a stone's throw away, Maui's waters offer visually arresting backdrops for sailing adven-tures. Sailing conditions can be fickle, so some operations throw in snorkeling or whale-watching, and others offer sunset cruises. Winds are consistent in summer but variable in winter, and afternoons are generally windier throughout the year.

■ TIP➔ **You won't be sheltered from the ele-ments on the trim racing boats, so be sure to bring a hat that won't blow away, a light jacket, sunglasses, and sunscreen.**

BOATS AND CHARTERS

Paragon Sailing Charters

SAILING | If you want to snorkel and sail, this is your boat. Many snorkel cruises claim to sail, but motor most of the way—Paragon is an exception. Both Paragon vessels (one catamaran in Lahaina, the other in Maalaea) are shipshape, and crews are accommodat-ing and friendly. Its mooring in Molokini Crater is particularly good, and tours will often stay after the masses have left. The Lanai trip includes a picnic lunch at Manele Bay, snorkeling, and a quick afternoon blue-water swim. Extras on the trips to Lanai include mai tais, sodas, dessert, and champagne. Hot and cold appetizers come with the sunset sail, which departs daily from Lahaina Harbor ⊠ *Maalaea Harbor, Maalaea* ☎ *808/244–2087* ⊕ *www.sailmaui.com* ⊠ *Sunset sail starts at $85, snorkel at $160.*

★ Trilogy Excursions

SAILING | With more than four decades of experience and some good karma from their reef-cleaning campaigns, Trilogy has an excellent reputation in the community. It's one of only two companies that sail to Molokini Crater rather than motor. Their two-hour sunset sail includes appetizers, beer, wine, champagne, margaritas, and mai tais. Tours depart from Lahaina Harbor, Maalaea Harbor, and, in West Maui, in front of the Kaanapali Beach Hotel. ⊠ *Lahaina Harbor, 675 Wharf St., Lahaina* ☎ *808/874–5649, 888/225–6284* ⊕ *sailtrilogy.com* ⊠ *Starts at $99.*

Scuba Diving

Maui has been rated one of the top 10 dive spots in the United States. It's common to see huge sea turtles, eagle rays, and small reef sharks, not to mention many varieties of angelfish, parrotfish, eels, and octopuses. Most of the species are unique to this area, unlike other popular dive destinations. In addition, the terrain itself is different from other dive spots. Here you can find ancient and intricate lava flows full of nooks where marine life hide and breed. Although the water tends to be a bit rougher—not to mention colder—divers are given an incredible thrill during the humpback-whale season, when you can hear whales singing underwater. Be sure to check conditions before you head out.

Some of the finest diving spots in all of Hawaii lie along the Valley Isle's western and southwestern shores. Dives are best in the morning when visibility can hold a steady 100 feet. If you're a certified diver, you can rent gear at any Maui dive shop simply by showing your PADI or NAUI card. Unless you're familiar with the area, however, it's probably best to hook up

with a dive shop for an underwater tour. Shops also offer introductory dives for those who aren't certified.

■ **TIP→ Before signing on with any outfitter, it's a good idea to ask a few pointed questions about your guide's experience, the weather outlook, and the condition of the equipment.**

BEST SPOTS

Honolua Bay, a marine preserve in West Maui, is alive with many varieties of coral and tame tropical fish, including large *ulua* (giant trevally), *kahala* (jack fish family), barracuda, and manta rays. With depths of 20–50 feet, this is a popular summer dive spot, good for all levels.

■ **TIP→ High surf often prohibits winter dives.**

On the South Shore, one of the most popular dive spots is **Makena Landing** (also called Nahuna Point, Five Graves, or Five Caves). You can revel in underwater delights—caves, ledges, coral heads, and an outer reef home to a large green–sea turtle colony called Turtle Town.

■ **TIP→ Entry is rocky lava, so be careful where you step. This area is for more experienced divers.**

Three miles offshore from Wailea on the South Shore, **Molokini Crater** is world-renowned for its deep, crystal clear, fish-filled waters. A crescent-shape islet formed by the eroding top of a volcano, the crater is a marine preserve ranging 10–80 feet deep. The numerous tame fish and brilliant coral within the crater make it a popular introductory dive site. On calm days, the back side of Molokini Crater (called Back Wall) can be a dramatic sight for advanced divers, with visibility of up to 150 feet. The enormous drop-off into the Alalakeiki Channel offers awesome seascapes, black coral, and chance sightings of larger fish and sharks.

Some of the southern coast's best diving is at **Ahihi Bay,** part of the Ahihi-Kinau Natural Area Reserve. The area frequently closes due to shark sightings; call ahead before visiting. The area is best known for its "Fishbowl," a small cove right beside the road, next to a hexagonal house. Here you can find excellent underwater scenery, with many types of fish and coral.

■ TIP→ **Be careful of the rocky-bottom entry (wear reef shoes if you have them).**

The Fishbowl can get crowded, especially in high season. If you want to steer clear of the crowds, look for a second entry ½ mile farther down the road—a gravel parking lot at the surf spot called Dumps. Entry into the bay here is trickier, as the coastline is all lava.

Formed from the last lava flow two centuries ago, **La Perouse Bay** brings you the best variety of fish—more than any other site. The lava rock provides a protective habitat, and all four types of Hawaii's angelfish can be found here. To dive into the spot called Pinnacles, enter anywhere along the shore, just past the private entrance to the beach. Wear your reef shoes, as entry is sharp. To the right, you'll be in the Ahihi-Kinau Natural Area Reserve; to the left, you're outside. Look for the white sandy bottom with massive coral heads. Pinnacles is for experienced divers only.

EQUIPMENT, LESSONS, AND TOURS

Extended Horizons

DIVING & SNORKELING | This eco-friendly dive boat stands apart by being the only commercial vessel on Maui to run on 100% locally made biodiesel. Its popular Lanai charter has divers swimming through dramatic archways and lava structures, while other trips venture along West Maui. Shore and night dives are also available. Tours are run by enthusiastic and professional guides who are keen at not only identifying underwater creatures but also interpreting their behavior. ⊠ Mala Boat Ramp, Lahaina ☎ 808/667–0611 ⊕ extendedhorizons. com ☒ From $179.

Maui Dive Shop

SCUBA DIVING | Maui Dive Shop offers scuba charters, diving instruction, and equipment rental at its Kihei location. Excursions go to Molokini, Shipwreck Beach, and Cathedrals on Lanai. Intro dives are done offshore. Night dives, scooter dives, and customized trips are available, as are full SSI and PADI certificate programs. ⊠ 1455 S. Kihei Rd., Kihei ☎ 808/875–0333 local, 800/542–3483 toll free ⊕ mauidiveshop.com ☒ From $189.

★ Mike Severns Diving

SCUBA DIVING | This popular and reliable company has been around for more than four decades and takes groups of up to seven certified divers, with two dive masters, to both popular and off-the-beaten-path dive sites. Marine biologists or naturalists offer informative briefings, and boat trips leave from Kihei Boat Ramp and go wherever conditions are best: the Molokini Marine Life Conservation District, Molokini Crater's Back Wall, Makena, or beyond La Perouse Bay. ⊠ Kihei Boat Ramp, 2988 S. Kihei Rd., Kihei ☎ 808/879–6596 ⊕ mikesevernsdiving.com ☒ Dives from $224 (BYO gear) or $269 (gear included).

Shaka Divers

SCUBA DIVING | Since 1983, owner Doug Corbin has led personalized dives, including great four-hour intro dives, refresher courses, scuba certifications, and south shore dives to Ulua, Nahuna Point or Turtle Town (also called Five Caves or Five Graves), and Bubble Cave. Typical dives last about an hour. Dives can be booked on short notice, with afternoon tours available (hard to find on Maui). Shaka also offers night dives and torpedo-scooter dives. The twilight two-tank dive is nice for day divers who want to ease into night diving. ⊠ 24 Hakoi Pl., Kihei ☎ 808/250–1234 ⊕ www.shakadivers. com ☒ From $59.

Snorkelers can see adorable green sea turtles around Maui.

Snorkeling

There are two ways to approach snorkeling—by land or by sea. At around 7 am daily, a parade of boats heads out to Lanai or to Molokini Crater, that ancient cone of volcanic cinder off the coast of Wailea. Boat trips offer some advantages—deeper water, seasonal whale-watching, crew assistance, lunch, and gear. But much of Maui's best snorkeling is found just steps from the road. Nearly the entire leeward coastline from Kapalua south to Ahihi-Kinau offers opportunities to ogle fish and turtles. If you're patient and sharp-eyed, you may glimpse eels, octopuses, lobsters, eagle rays, and even a rare shark or monk seal.

■TIP→ **Visibility is best in the morning, before the trade winds pick up.**

BEST SPOTS
Snorkel sites are listed from north to south, starting at the northwest corner of the Island. The **Honolua Bay Marine Life Conservation District** *has a superb reef for snorkeling just north of Kapalua.*

■TIP→ **Bring a fish key with you, as you're sure to see many species of triggerfish, filefish, and wrasses.**

The coral formations on the right side of the bay are particularly dramatic, with pink, aqua, and orange varieties. On a lucky day, you might even be snorkeling with a pod of dolphins nearby. Take care entering the water; there's no beach, and the rocks and concrete ramp can be slippery. The northeast corner of this windward bay periodically gets hammered by big waves in winter. Avoid the bay then, as well as after heavy rains.

Minutes south of Honolua Bay, dependable **Kapalua Bay** beckons. As beautiful above the water as it is below, Kapalua is exceptionally calm, even when other spots get testy. Needle and butterfly fish dart just past the sandy beach, which is why it's sometimes crowded.

■TIP→ **The sand can be particularly hot here—watch your toes!**

Puu Kekaa (nicknamed Black Rock), in front of the Sheraton Maui Resort & Spa at the northernmost tip of **Kaanapali Beach,** is great for snorkelers of any skill level. The entry couldn't be easier—dump your towel on the sand and in you go. Beginners can stick close to shore and still see lots of action. Advanced snorkelers can swim to the tip of Puu Kekaa to see larger fish and eagle rays. One of the underwater residents here is a turtle whose hefty size earned him the name Volkswagen. He sits very still, so you have to look closely. Equipment can be rented on-site. Parking, which is in a small lot adjoining the hotel, is the only hassle.

Along Honoapiilani Highway, there are several favorite snorkel sites, including the area just out from the cemetery at **Hanakaoo Beach Park.** At depths of 5 and 10 feet, you can see a variety of corals, especially as you head south toward Wahikuli Wayside Park.

South of Olowalu General Store, the shallow coral reef at **Olowalu** is good for a quick underwater tour, but if you're willing to venture out about 50 yards, you'll have easy access to an expansive coral reef with abundant turtles and fish—no boat required. Swim offshore toward the pole sticking out of the reef. Except for during a south swell, this area is calm, and good for families with small children. Boats sometimes stop here (they refer to this site as Coral Gardens) when conditions in Honolua Bay are not ideal. During low tide, be extra cautious when hovering above the razor-sharp coral.

Excellent snorkeling is found down the coastline between Kihei and Makena on the South Shore.

■TIP→ **The best spots are along the rocky fringes of Wailea's beaches—Mokapu, Ulua, Wailea, and Polo—off Wailea Alanui Drive.**

Find one of the public parking lots sandwiched between Wailea's luxury resorts (look for a blue sign reading "Shoreline Access" with an arrow pointing to the lot). Enjoy the sandy and calm waters with relatively good visibility and a variety of fish. Of the four beaches, Ulua has the best reef. You may listen to snapping shrimp and parrotfish nibbling on coral.

In South Maui, the end of the paved section of Makena Road is where you'll find the **Ahihi-Kinau Natural Area Reserve.** Despite its lava-scorched landscape, the area is very popular, especially with sharks, causing the area to be closed quite frequently. Call ahead to make sure it's open. It's difficult terrain and the area sometimes gets crowded, but it's worth visiting to experience some of the reserve's outstanding treasures, such as the sheltered cove known as the Fish Bowl.

■TIP→ **Be sure to bring water: this is a hot and unforgiving wilderness.**

Between Maui and neighboring Kahoolawe you'll find the world-famous **Molokini Crater.** Its crescent-shape rim acts as a protective cove from the wind and provides a sanctuary for birds and colorful marine life. Most snorkeling tour operators offer a Molokini trip, and it's not unusual for your charter to share this dormant volcano with five or six other boats. The journey to this sunken crater takes more than 90 minutes from Lahaina, an hour from Maalaea, and less than half an hour from the South Shore.

EQUIPMENT

Most hotels and vacation rentals offer complimentary use of snorkel gear. Beachside stands fronting the major resort areas rent equipment by the hour or day. If you're squeamish about using someone else's gear (or need a prescription lens), pick up your own at any discount shop. Costco and Longs Drugs have better prices than ABC Stores; dive shops have superior equipment.

■ TIP→ **Don't shy away from asking for instructions; a snug fit makes all the difference in the world. A mask fits if it sticks to your face when you inhale deeply through your nose. Fins should cover your entire foot (unlike diving fins, which strap around your heel).**

Maui Dive Shop

SNORKELING | You can rent pro gear (including optical masks, bodyboards, and wet suits) at their Kihei location. Daily and weekly rates are available. Pump these guys for weather info before heading out; they'll know better than last night's news forecaster, and they'll give you the real deal on conditions. ✉ *1455 S. Kihei Rd., Kihei* ☎ *808/875–0333* ⊕ *mauidiveshop.com.*

Snorkel Bob's

SNORKELING | Here you can rent fins, masks, and snorkels, and Snorkel Bob's will throw in a carrying bag, map, and snorkel tips. Avoid the circle masks and go for the split-level or premium snorkel package; it's worth the extra money. There are seven Snorkel Bob's locations on Maui, including Kihei, Wailea, Lahaina, Kahana, and Napili. ✉ *5425 C Lower Honoapiilani Hwy., Napili* ☎ *808/669–9603* ⊕ *snorkelbob.com* ✉ *Weekly rentals from $10–$72.*

SNORKELING TOURS

The same boats that offer whale-watching, sailing, and diving also offer snorkeling excursions. Trips usually include visits to two locales, lunch, gear, instruction, and possible whale or dolphin sightings. Some captains troll for fish along the way.

The most popular snorkel cruise destination is Molokini Crater, a crescent about 3 miles offshore from Wailea. You can spend half a day floating above the fish-filled crater for about $80. Some say it's not as good as it's made out to be and that it's too crowded, but others consider it one of the best spots in Hawaii. Visibility is generally outstanding, and fish are

incredibly tame. Your second stop will be somewhere along the leeward coast, either Turtle Town near Makena or Coral Gardens toward Lahaina.

■ TIP→ **On windy mornings, there's a good chance the waters will be too rough to moor in Molokini Crater, and you'll end up snorkeling somewhere off the shore, where you could have driven for free.**

If you've tried snorkeling and are tentatively thinking about scuba, you may want to try "snuba," a cross between the two. With snuba, you dive 20 feet below the surface; only you're attached to an air hose from the boat. Many boats now offer snuba (for an extra fee of $45–$65) and snorkeling.

Snorkel cruises vary—some serve mai tais and steaks, whereas others offer beer and cold cuts. You might prefer a large ferryboat to a smaller sailboat, or vice versa. Be sure you know where to go to board your vessel; getting lost in the harbor at 6 am is a lousy start to your day.

■ TIP→ **Bring sunscreen, an underwater camera (they're double the price onboard), a towel, and a cover-up for the windy return trip.**

Even tropical waters get chilly after hours of swimming, so consider wearing a rash guard or renting wetsuits for a fee.

Alii Nui Maui

SNORKELING | On this 65-foot luxury catamaran, you can come as you are (with a bathing suit, of course); towels, sunblock, and all your gear are provided. Because the owners also operate Maui Dive Shop, snorkel and dive equipment are top-of-the-line. Wet-suit tops are available to use for sun protection or to keep extra warm in the water. The boat, which holds a maximum of 60 people, is nicely appointed. A morning snorkel sail (there's a diving option, too) heads to

Continued on page 298

SNORKELING IN HAWAII

Molokini Crater

The waters surrounding the Hawaiian Islands are filled with life—from giant manta rays cruising off the Big Island's Kona Coast to humpback whales giving birth in the waters around Maui. Dip your head beneath the surface to experience a spectacularly colorful world: pairs of milletseed butterflyfish dart back and forth, redlipped parrotfish snack on coral algae, and spotted eagle rays flap past like silent spaceships. Sea turtles bask at the surface while tiny wrasses give them the equivalent of a shave and a haircut. The water quality is typically outstanding; many sites afford 30-foot-plus visibility. On snorkel cruises, you can often stare from the boat rail right down to the bottom.

Certainly few destinations are as accommodating to every level of snorkeler as Hawaii. Beginners can tromp in from sandy beaches while more advanced divers descend to shipwrecks, reefs, craters, and sea arches just offshore. Because of Hawaii's extreme isolation, the island chain has fewer fish species than Fiji or the Caribbean—but many of the fish that live here exist nowhere else. The Hawaiian waters are home to the highest percentage of endemic fish in the world.

The key to enjoying the underwater world is slowing down. Look carefully. Listen. You might hear the strange crackling sound of shrimp tunneling through coral, or you may hear whales singing to one another during winter. A shy octopus may drift along the ocean's floor beneath you. If you're hooked, pick up a waterproof fishkey from Long's Drugs. You can brag later that you've looked the Hawaiian turkeyfish in the eye.

Picasso Triggerfish	Milletseed Butterflyfish*	Yellow Tang
Moorish Idol	Hawaiian Whitespotted Toby*	Saddleback Wrasse*
Redlip Parrotfish	Hawaiian Turkeyfish*	Zebra Moray Eel
Stocky Hawkfish	Green Sea Turtle (Honu)	Spotted Eagle Ray

*endemic to Hawaii

POLYNESIA'S FIRST CELESTIAL NAVIGATORS: HONU

Honu is the Hawaiian name for two native sea turtles, the hawksbill and the green sea turtle. Little is known about these dinosaur-age marine reptiles, though snorkelers regularly see them foraging for *limu* (seaweed) and the occasional jellyfish in Hawaiian waters. Most female honu nest in the uninhabited Northwestern Hawaiian Islands, but a few sociable ladies nest on Maui and Big Island beaches. Scientists suspect that they navigate the seas via magnetism—sensing the earth's poles. Amazingly, they will journey up to 800 miles to nest—it's believed that they return to their own birth sites. After about 60 days of incubation, nestlings emerge from the sand at night and find their way back to the sea by the light of the stars.

SNORKELING

Many of Hawaii's reefs are accessible from the shore.

The basics: Sure, you can take a deep breath, hold your nose, squint your eyes, and stick your face in the water in an attempt to view submerged habitats . . . but why not protect your eyes, retain your ability to breathe, and keep your hands free to paddle about when exploring underwater? That's what snorkeling is all about.

Equipment needed: A mask, snorkel (the tube attached to the mask), and fins. In deeper waters (any depth over your head), life jackets are advised.

Steps to success: If you've never snorkeled before, it's natural to feel a bit awkward at first, so don't sweat it. Breathing through a mask and tube, and wearing a pair of fins take getting used to. Like any activity, you build confidence and comfort through practice.

If you're new to snorkeling, begin by submerging your face in shallow water or a swimming pool and breathing calmly through the snorkel while gazing through the mask.

Next you need to learn how to clear water out of your mask and snorkel, an essential skill since splashes can send water into tube openings and masks can leak. Some snorkels have built-in drainage valves, but if a tube clogs, you can force water up and out by exhaling through your mouth. Clearing a mask is similar: lift your head from water while pulling forward on mask to drain. Some masks have built-in purge valves, but those without can be cleared underwater by pressing the top to the forehead and blowing out your nose (charming, isn't it?), allowing air to bubble into the mask, pushing water out the bottom. If it sounds hard, it really isn't. Just try it a few times and you'll soon feel like a pro.

Never touch or stand on coral.

Now your goal is to get friendly with fins—you want them to be snug but not too tight—and learn how to propel yourself with them. Fins won't help you float, but they will give you a leg up, so to speak, on smoothly moving through the water or treading water (even when upright) with less effort.

Flutter stroking is the most efficient underwater kick, and the farther your foot bends forward the more leg power you'll be able to transfer to the water and the farther you'll travel with each stroke. Flutter kicking movements involve alternately separating the legs and then drawing them back together. When your legs separate, the leg surface encounters drag from the water, slowing you down. When your legs are drawn back together, they produce a force pushing you forward. If your kick creates more forward force than it causes drag, you'll move ahead.

Submerge your fins to avoid fatigue rather than having them flailing above the water when you kick, and keep your arms at your side to reduce drag. You are in the water—stretched out, face down, and snorkeling happily away—but that doesn't mean you can't hold your breath and go deeper in the water for a closer look at some fish or whatever catches your attention. Just remember that when you do this, your snorkel will be submerged, too, so you won't be breathing (you'll be holding your breath). You can dive head-first, but going feet-first is easier and less scary for most folks, taking less momentum. Before full immersion, take several long, deep breaths to clear carbon dioxide from your lungs.

If your legs tire, flip onto your back and tread water with inverted fin motions while resting. If your mask fogs, wash condensation from the lens and clear water from your mask.

TIPS FOR SAFE SNORKELING

- Snorkel with a buddy and stay together.
- Plan your entry and exit points prior to getting in the water.
- Swim into the current on entering and then ride the current back to your exit point.
- Carry your flippers into the water and then put them on, as it's difficult to walk in them, and rocks may be slippery.
- Make sure your mask fits properly and is not too loose.
- Pop your head above the water periodically to ensure you aren't drifting too far out, or too close to rocks.
- Think of the water as someone else's home—don't take anything that doesn't belong to you, or leave any trash behind.
- Don't touch any sea creatures; they may sting.
- Wear a T-shirt over your swimsuit to help protect you from being fried by the sun.
- When in doubt, don't go without a snorkeling professional; try a guided tour.
- Don't go in if the ocean seems rough.

Green sea turtle (Honu)

Turtle Town or Molokini Crater and includes a continental breakfast, lunch, and post-snorkel alcoholic drinks. The three-, five-, or six-hour snorkel trip offers transportation from your hotel. Videography and huka (similar to snuba) are available for a fee. ⊠ *Maalaea Harbor, Slip 56, Maalaea* ☎ *800/542–3483, 808/875–0333* ⊕ *aliinuimaui.com* ✉ *From $109.*

Maui Classic Charters

SNORKELING | FAMILY | Hop aboard the *Four Winds II*, a 55-foot, glass-bottom catamaran (great fun for kids), for one of the most dependable snorkel trips around. You'll spend more time than other charter boats at Molokini Crater and enjoy turtle-watching on the way home. The trip includes optional snuba ($62 extra), continental breakfast, barbecue lunch, beer, wine, and soda. With its reasonable price, the trip can be popular and crowded. The crew works hard to keep everyone happy, but if the trip is fully booked, you will be cruising with more than 100 new friends. For a more intimate experience, opt for the *Maui Magic*, Maalaea's fastest PowerCat, which holds fewer people than some of the larger vessels. ⊠ *Maalaea Harbor, Slips 55 and 80, Maalaea* ☎ *808/879–8188, 800/736–5740* ⊕ *mauiclassiccharters.com* ✉ *From $65.*

Teralani Sailing Charters

SNORKELING | Choose between a standard or premier snorkel trip with a deli lunch or a top-of-the-line excursion that's an hour longer and includes two snorkel sites and a barbecue-style lunch. The company's cats could hold well over 100 people, but 49 is the maximum per trip. The boats are kept in pristine condition. Freshwater showers are available, as is an open bar after the second snorkel stop. A friendly crew provides all your gear, a flotation device, and a quick course in snorkeling. During whale season, only the premier trip is available. Boarding is right off Kaanapali Beach, fronting the Westin Maui Hotel. ⊠ *Kaanapali Beach, Kaanapali* ☎ *808/661–7245* ⊕ *teralani.net* ✉ *From $139.*

★ Trilogy Excursions

SNORKELING | Many people consider a trip with Trilogy Excursions to be a highlight of their vacation. Maui's longest-running operation has comprehensive offerings, with six beautiful 54- to 65-foot sailing vessels at three departure sites. All excursions are staffed by energetic crews who will keep you well-fed and entertained with local stories and corny jokes. A full-day catamaran cruise to Lanai includes a continental breakfast and barbecue lunch, a guided tour of the island, a "Snorkeling 101" class, and time to snorkel in the waters of Lanai's Hulopoe Marine Preserve (Trilogy Excursions has exclusive commercial access). The company also offers Molokini Crater and Olowalu snorkel cruises that are top-notch. Tours depart from Lahaina Harbor, Maalaea Harbor, and, in West Maui, in front of the Kaanapali Beach Hotel. ⊠ *Lahaina Harbor, 675 Wharf St., Lahaina* ☎ *808/874–5649, 888/225–6284* ⊕ *sailtrilogy.com* ✉ *From $135.*

Spas

WEST MAUI

The Ritz-Carlton Spa, Kapalua

SPAS | At this gorgeous 17,500-square-foot spa, you enter a blissful maze where floor-to-ceiling riverbed stones lead to serene treatment rooms, couples' *hales* (cabanas), and a rain forest–like grotto with a Jacuzzi, dry cedar sauna, and eucalyptus steam rooms. Hang out in the coed waiting area, where sliding-glass doors open to a whirlpool overlooking a taro-patch garden. Exfoliate any rough spots with an alaea salt (Hawaiian red sea salt) scrub, then wash off in a private outdoor shower garden before indulging in a lomilomi massage. High-end beauty treatments include advanced oxygen technology to tighten and nourish mature skin. The boutique has a highly coveted collection of organic, local, and high-end beauty products, fitness wear, and Maui-made Nina Kuna jewelry and natural skin-care lines. ⊠ *The Ritz-Carlton, Kapalua, 1 Ritz-Carlton Dr., Kapalua* ☎ *808/665–7079* ⊕ *ritzcarlton.com* ⊠ *$190 for 50-min massage, $350 spa packages.*

Spa Montage Kapalua Bay

SPAS | FAMILY | This spa's grand entrance opens onto an airy, modern beach house with panoramic island and ocean views. With amenities including a movement studio, fitness center, and coed infinity pool you can easily spend a day meandering about the spa's expansive layout without feeling cooped up. The spa menu includes therapies that incorporate local ingredients and calming ingredients from the sea. This spa is for the whole family, with treatments available for kids as young as four. ⊠ *1 Bay Dr., Kapalua* ☎ *808/665–8282* ⊕ *montagehotels. com/kapaluabay/spa* ⊠ *$215 for 60-min massage.*

SOUTH SHORE

Awili Spa and Salon, Andaz Maui at Wailea Resort

SPAS | At Awili Spa and Salon's apothecary or blending bar (*awili* means "to mix"), consultants assist in creating your personalized body products made from local ingredients. Set aside an extra hour to fully indulge in the blending bar, or opt for ready-made concoctions. The cool, soothing interior of this spa is an extension of the minimalist, monochromatic style of the Andaz Maui at Wailea Resort. Relaxation lounges are stocked with thoughtful amenities and the full salon takes care of pampering your hair and nails. ⊠ *Andaz Maui at Wailea Resort, 3550 Wailea Alanui Dr., Wailea* ☎ *808/573–1234* ⊕ *andazmaui.com* ⊠ *$200 for 60-min massage.*

★ Spa & Wellness Center at Four Seasons Resort Maui

SPAS | A wide array of beauty and health and wellness services are offered here including Hawaiian traditional massage,

innovative facials, and a full hair and nail salon with barber, along with some services you won't find anywhere else on Maui. For the ultimate indulgence, reserve one of the seaside open-air *hale hau* (traditional thatch-roof houses), one of the best outdoor massage experiences on the Island. Recently added to the Health & Wellness lineup is California-based Next/Health, providing IV and Ozone Therapy services, as well as biomarker testing, in a lounge near the spa. ⊠ *Four Seasons Resort Maui at Wailea, 3900 Wailea Alanui Dr., Wailea* ☎ *808/874–2925* ⊕ *fourseasons.com/ maui* ⊠ *$205 for 50-minute massage.*

Willow Stream Spa, Fairmont Kea Lani

SPAS | This spa makes meticulous use of Hawaii's natural elements to replenish your Zen. Give a full hour to enjoy the fascinating amenities, two if you plan to work out. Upon arrival, rinse off in a high-tech shower that combines color, sound, and hydrotherapy to mimic different types of Hawaiian rain. A heated stone bench and foot bed awaits to deepen the relaxation before the treatment. The spa has 17 indoor treatment rooms with a poolside and oceanside option for outdoor treatments. ⊠ *4100 Wailea Alanui, Wailea* ☎ *808/875–2229* ⊕ *fairmont-kea-lani.com* ⊠ *$200 for 60-min massage.*

ROAD TO HANA

★ The Spa at Hana-Maui Resort

SPAS | A bamboo gate opens into an outdoor sanctuary with a lava-rock basking pool and hot tub. At first glimpse, this spa seems to have been organically grown, not built. Ferns still wet from Hana's frequent downpours nourish the spirit as you rest with a cup of Hawaiian herbal tea, take an invigorating dip in the cold plunge pool, or enjoy the views while enjoying a soak. Luxurious skin-care treatments feature local products from Oshan and Malie Organics, and body treatments incorporate organic Maui-made Ala Lani Bath and Body products. ⊠ *Hana-Maui Resort, 5031 Hana*

Hwy., Hana ☎ *808/400–1234* ⊕ *han-amauiresort.com* ✉ *$180 for 60-minute massage.*

Stand-Up Paddling

Also called stand-up paddle surfing or paddleboarding, stand-up paddling is the "comeback kid" of surf sports; you stand on a longboard and paddle out with a canoe oar. While stand-up paddling requires even more balance and coordination than regular surfing, it is still accessible to every skill level. Most surf schools now offer stand-up paddle lessons. Advanced paddlers can amp up the adrenaline with a downwind coastal run that spans almost 10 miles from North Shore's Maliko Gulch to Kahului Harbor, sometimes reaching speeds up to 30 mph.

The fun thing about stand-up paddling is that you can enjoy it whether the surf is good or the water is flat. However, as with all water sports, being attentive and reading the environment is essential. Look at the sky and assess the wind by how fast the clouds move. Note where the whitecaps are going, and always point the nose of your board perpendicular to the wave.

■ TIP→ **Because of the size and speed of a longboard, stand-up paddling can be dangerous, so lessons are highly recommended, especially if you intend to surf.**

LESSONS

Stand-Up Paddle Surf School

WATER SPORTS | Maui's first school devoted solely to stand-up paddling was founded by the legendary Maria Souza, the first woman to surf the treacherous waves of Peahi (nicknamed "Jaws") on Maui's North Shore. Although most surf schools offer stand-up paddling, Maria's classes are in a league of their own. They include a proper warm-up with a hula-hoop and balance ball and a cool-down with yoga. Locations vary depending on conditions.

✉ *185 Paka Pl., Kihei* ☎ *808/579–9231* ✆ *Lessons from $199* ☞ *standuppaddle-surfschool.com.*

Surfing

Maui's coastline has surf for every skill level, beginners included. Waves on leeward-facing shores (West and South Maui) tend to break in gentle sets all summer long. Surf instructors in Kihei and Lahaina can rent you boards, give you onshore instruction, and then lead you out through the channel, where it's safe to enter the surf. They'll shout encouragement while you paddle like mad for the thrill of standing on the water—most will give you a helpful shove. These areas are great for beginners; the only danger is whacking a stranger with your board or stubbing your toe against the reef.

The North Shore is another story. Winter waves pound the windward coast, attracting water champions from every corner of the world. Jet Skis tow in adrenaline addicts to "Jaws," the legendary deep-sea break. Waves here periodically tower upward of 40 feet. The only spot for viewing this phenomenon (which happens just a few times a year) is on private property so, if you hear the surfers next to you crowing about "Jaws going off," cozy up and get them to take you with them.

Whatever your skill, there's a board, a break, and even a surf guru to accommodate you. A two-hour lesson is a good intro to surf culture.

You can get the wave report each day by checking page 2 of the *Maui News*, logging on to the Glenn James weather site (⊕ *hawaiiweathertoday.com*), or by calling ☎ *808/871–5054* (for the weather forecast) or ☎ *808/877–3611* (for the surf report).

BEST SPOTS

On the South Shore, beginners can hang ten at Kihei's **Cove Park,** a sometimes crowded but reliable one- to two-foot break. Boards can easily be rented across the street or neighboring Kalama Park's parking lot. Balancing the nine-plus-foot board on your head while crossing busy South Kihei Road is the only bummer.

For advanced wave riders, **Hookipa Beach Park** on the North Shore boasts several well-loved breaks, including "Pavilions," "Lanes," "the Point," and "Middles." Surfers have priority until 11 am when windsurfers move in on the action.

■ TIP→ **Competition is stiff here. If you don't know what you're doing, consider watching.**

Long- or shortboarders in West Maui can paddle out at **Launiupoko Beach Park.** The east end of the park has an easy break, suitable for beginners.

Also called Thousand Peaks, **Ukumehame** is one of the better beginner spots in West Maui. You'll soon see how the spot got its name—the waves here break again and again in wide and consistent rows, giving lots of room for beginning and intermediate surfers.

Good surf spots in West Maui include "Grandma's" at **Papalaua Park,** just after the *pali* (cliff), where waves are so easy a grandma could ride them. **Puamana Beach Park** for a mellow longboard day and **Lahaina Harbor** offers an excellent inside wave for beginners (called Breakwall) and the more advanced outside (a great lift if there's a big south swell).

EQUIPMENT AND LESSONS

Maui is the perfect place to learn to surf, with plenty of fantastic surf schools offering lessons that guarantee you'll catch a wave on your first day. Surf camps are becoming increasingly popular. One- or two-week camps offer a terrific way to build muscle and self-esteem simultaneously.

Big Kahuna Adventures

SURFING | Rent soft-top longboards here for $35 for two hours. Weekly rates are $160. Call ahead to make an appointment. This company also offers surf lessons and rents kayaks, stand-up paddleboards, plus snorkel and beach gear. Look for the Big Kahuna truck at Kalama Park; lessons take place at Cove Park. ✉ *Kalama Park, 1900 S Kihei Rd., Kihei* ☎ *808/875–6395* ⊕ *bigkahunaadventures. com* ▣ *Lessons start at $95.*

Goofy Foot

SURFING | Surfing "goofy foot" means putting your right foot forward. They might be goofy, but we like the right-footed gurus here. This shop is just plain cool and only steps away from "Break-wall," a great beginner's spot in Lahaina. A two-hour class with five or fewer students is $85, and you're guaranteed to be standing by the end or it's free. ✉ *505 Front St., Suite 123, Lahaina* ☎ *808/244–9283* ⊕ *goofyfootsurfschool. com* ▣ *Group classes start at $85; private two-hour lessons $170.*

★ Hi-Tech Surf Sports

SURFING | Hi-Tech has some of the best boards, advice, and attitude around. It rents even its best surfboards—choose from longboards, shortboards, and hybrids—starting at $25 per day. There's another shop in Paia and a third location in Kihei across of Cove Park, a popular surf spot for beginners. ✉ *425 Koloa St., Kahului* ☎ *808/877–2111* ⊕ *surfmaui.com.*

★ Maui Surf Clinics

SURFING | **FAMILY** | Instructors here will get even the shakiest novice riding with the school's beginner program. They offer two-hour group lessons (up to five students) and private lessons with the patient and meticulous instructors. The company provides boards, rash guards, and water shoes, all in impeccable condition—and it's tops in the customer-service department. ✉ *505 Front St., Suite 201, Lahaina* ☎ *808/244–7873*

Humpback whale calves are plentiful in winter; this one is breaching off West Maui.

⊕ *mauisurfclinics.com* ✉ *Group lessons $85; private lessons $180.*

Maui Surfer Girls

SURFING | Maui Surfer Girls started in 2001 with surf camps for teen girls, but quickly branched out to offer surfing lessons year-round. Located away from the crowds, Maui Surfer Girls specializes in private lessons and small groups, and their ratio of four students per instructor is the smallest in the industry. ✉ *Ukumehame Beach Park, Lahaina* ☎ *808/670–3886* ⊕ *mauisurfergirls.com* ✉ *Group lesson $99, Semi-Private $145, Private $209.*

Whale-Watching

From December into May, whale-watching becomes one of the most popular activities on Maui. During the season, *all* outfitters offer whale-watching in addition to their regular activities, and most do an excellent job. Boats leave the wharves at Lahaina and Maalaea in search of humpbacks, allowing you to enjoy the awe-inspiring size of these creatures in closer proximity. From November through May, the Pacific Whale Foundation sponsors the Maui Whale Festival, a variety of whale-related events for locals and visitors; check the calendar at ⊕ *maui-whalefestival.org.*

As it's almost impossible *not* to see whales in winter on Maui, you'll want to prioritize: is an adventure or comfort your aim? If close encounters with the giants of the deep are your desire, pick a smaller boat that promises sightings. Those who think "green" usually prefer the smaller, quieter vessels that produce the least amount of negative impact on the whales' natural environment. If you want to sip mai tais as whales cruise by, stick with a sunset cruise ($50 and up) on a boat with an open bar and *pupus* (appetizers).

■ TIP➔ **Afternoon trips are generally rougher because the wind picks up, but some say this is when the most surface action occurs.**

The Humpbacks' Winter Home

The humpback whales' attraction to Maui is legendary, and seeing them from December to May is a highlight for many visitors. More than half the Pacific's humpback population winters in Hawaii, especially in the waters around the Valley Isle, where mothers can be seen just a few hundred feet offshore, training their young calves in the fine points of whale etiquette. From shore, it's easy to catch sight of whales spouting or even breaching—when they leap almost entirely out of the sea, slapping back onto the water with a huge splash.

There were thousands of giant mammals, but a history of overhunting and marine pollution reduced the world population to about 1,500. In 1966, humpbacks were put on the endangered-species list. Hunting or harassing whales is illegal in the waters of most nations, and in the United States, boats and airplanes are prohibited from getting too close. However, the jury is still out on the effects of military sonar testing on marine mammals.

Marine biologists believe the humpbacks (much like humans) keep returning to Hawaii because of its warmth. Having fattened themselves in subarctic waters all summer, the whales migrate south in the winter to breed, and a rebounding population of thousands cruises Maui waters. Winter is calving time, and the young whales probably couldn't survive in the frigid Alaskan waters. No one has ever seen a whale give birth here, but experts know that calving is their main winter activity because the 1- and 2-ton youngsters suddenly appear while the whales are in residence.

Each season, the first sighting of a humpback whale spouts is exciting for locals on Maui. A collective sigh of relief can be heard: "Ah, they've returned." Flukes and flippers can rise above the ocean's surface at a not-so-far distance. It's hard not to anthropomorphize the tail waving; it looks like a friendly gesture. Each fluke is uniquely patterned, like a human's fingerprint, and is used to identify the giants as they travel halfway around the globe and back.

Every captain aims to please during whale season, getting as close as legally possible (100 yards). Crew members know when a whale is about to dive (after several waves of its heart-shaped tail) but can rarely predict breaches (when the whale hurls itself up and almost entirely out of the water). Prime viewing space (on the upper and lower decks, around the railings) is limited, so boats can feel crowded even when half full. Opt for a smaller boat with fewer bookings if you don't want to squeeze in beside strangers. Don't forget to bring sunscreen, sunglasses, a light long-sleeve cover-up, and a hat you can

secure. Winter weather is less predictable and, at times, can be extreme, especially as the wind picks up. Arrive early to find parking.

BEST SPOTS

The northern end of **Keawakapu Beach** on the South Shore seems to be a whale magnet. Situate yourself on the sand or at the nearby restaurant and watch mamas and calves at play. From mid-December to mid-April, the Pacific Whale Foundation has naturalists at Ulua Beach and the scenic viewpoint at **Papawai Point Lookout.** You can spot whales along the *pali* of West Maui's Honoapiilani Highway all day long. Make sure to park safely before trying to take that perfect photo.

BOATS AND CHARTERS
Maui Adventure Cruises
WILDLIFE-WATCHING | Whale-watching from this company's raft puts you right above the water surface and on the same level as the whales. You'll forgo the cocktail in your hand, but you won't have to deal with crowds, even if the vessel is at max capacity with 36 people. The whales can get up close if they like, and when they do, it's spectacular. These rafts can move faster than a catamaran, so you don't spend much time motoring between whales or pods. Refreshments are included; no children under five. ✉ *Lahaina Harbor, Slip 11, Lahaina* ☎ *808/661–5550* ⊕ *mauiadventurecruises.com* 🖃 *Adults $64; Children 5–12 years old $49.*

★ Pacific Whale Foundation
WILDLIFE-WATCHING | FAMILY | This nonprofit organization pioneered whale-watching back in 1979. The crew includes a certified marine naturalist who offers insights into whale behavior and suggests ways for you to help save marine life worldwide. One of the best things about these trips is the underwater hydrophone that allows you to hear the whales sing. Trips meet at the organization's store, which sells whale-theme and local souvenirs. You'll share the boat with a large group of people in stadium-style seating. If you prefer a smaller crowd, book their small-group experience instead. ✉ *612 Front St., Lahaina* ☎ *808/650–7056* ⊕ *pacificwhale.org* 🖃 *From $70.*

Windsurfing

Windsurfing, invented in the 1950s, found its true home at Hookipa on Maui's North Shore in 1980. Seemingly overnight, windsurfing pros from around the world flooded the area. Equipment evolved, amazing film footage was captured, and a new sport was born.

If you're new to the action, you can get lessons from the experts islandwide. For a beginner, the best thing about windsurfing is that (unlike surfing) you don't have to paddle. Instead, you have to hold on tight to a flapping sail as it whisks you into the wind. Needless to say, you're going to need a little coordination and balance to pull this off. Instructors start you out on a beach at Kanaha. Lessons range from two-hour introductory classes to five-day advanced "flight school."

BEST SPOTS
After **Hookipa Bay** was discovered by windsurfers four decades ago, this windy North Shore beach 10 miles east of Kahului gained an international reputation. The spot is blessed with optimal wave-sailing wind and sea conditions and offers the ultimate aerial experience.

In the summer, the windsurfing crowd heads to **Kalepolepo Beach** on the South Shore. Trade winds build in strength, and by afternoon a swarm of dragonfly sails can be seen skimming the whitecaps, with Mauna Kahalawai (the West Maui Mountains) as a backdrop.

An excellent site for speed, **Kanaha Beach Park** is dedicated to beginners in the morning hours before the waves and wind get roaring. After 11 am, the professionals choose the size and shape best suited for the day's demands. This beach tends to have smaller waves and forceful winds—sometimes sending sailors flying at 40 knots. If you aren't ready to go pro, this is a great place for a picnic while you watch from the beach. To get here, use any of the three entrances on Amala Place, which runs along the shore just north of Kahului Airport.

EQUIPMENT AND LESSONS
Action Sports Maui
WINDSURFING | The quirky, friendly professionals will meet you at Kanaha Beach Park on the North Shore, outfit you with your sail and board, and guide you through your first "jibe," or turn.

They promise that your learning time for windsurfing will be cut in half. Lessons begin at 9 am every day except Sunday. ✉ *96 Amala Pl., Kahului* ☎ *808/283–7913* ⊕ *actionsportsmaui.com* 💲 *Lessons from $250.*

★ Hawaiian Sailboarding Techniques

WINDSURFING | Considered one of Maui's finest windsurfing schools, Hawaiian Sailboarding Techniques brings you quality instruction by skilled sailors. Founded by Alan Cadiz, an accomplished World Cup Pro, the school sets high standards for a safe, quality windsurfing experience. The company is inside Hi-Tech Surf Sports, which offers excellent equipment rentals. ✉ *Hi-Tech Surf Sports, 425 Koloa St., Kahului* ☎ *808/871–5423* ⊕ *hstwindsurfing.com* 💲 *Lessons start at $189.*

Zip Line Tours

Zip-lining on one of Maui's several courses lets you satisfy your inner Tarzan by soaring high above deep gulches and canyons—for a price that can seem steep. A harness keeps you fully supported on each ride. Each course has age minimums and weight restrictions, but generally, you must be at least 10 years old and weigh a minimum of 60–80 pounds and a maximum of 230–250 pounds. You should wear closed-toe athletic-type shoes and expect to get dirty.

■ **TIP →** **Reconsider this activity if you are pregnant, uncomfortable with heights, or have serious back or joint problems.**

★ Flyin' Hawaiian Zipline

ZIP-LINING | These guys have the longest line in the state (a staggering 3,600 feet) and a unique course layout. You build confidence on the first line, then board a four-wheel-drive vehicle that takes you 1,500 feet above the town of Waikapu to seven more lines that carry you over 11 ridges and nine valleys. The total distance covered is more than 2½ miles, and the views are astonishing. You must be able to hike over steep, sometimes slippery terrain while carrying a 10-pound metal trolley. Must be at least 10 years old or older and between 75–230 lbs. ✉ *Maui Tropical Plantation, 1670 Honoapiiani Hwy., Wailuku* ☎ *808/463–5786* ⊕ *flyinhawaiianzipline.com* 💲 *$219.*

Kapalua Ziplines

ZIP-LINING | Begin with a 20-minute ride in a four-wheel-drive van through pineapple fields to the Mountain Outpost, a 3,000 square-foot observation deck boasting panoramic ocean and mountain views. If you're on the seven-line zip, you'll climb even higher above the Pacific Ocean in a Polaris Ranger to experience 2 miles of parallel zipping plus snacks. The shorter five-line zip and full moon zip are great if you're short on time. Must be 10 years old or older and between 60–250 lbs. ✉ *500 Office Rd., Kapalua* ☎ *808/756–9147* ⊕ *kapaluaziplines.com* 💲 *Starting at $160.*

THE BIG ISLAND OF HAWAII

Updated by Karen Anderson
and Kristina Anderson

👁 Sights	🍴 Restaurants	🛏 Hotels	🛍 Shopping	🍸 Nightlife
★★★★★	★★★☆☆	★★★☆☆	★★★☆☆	★★☆☆☆

WELCOME TO THE BIG ISLAND OF HAWAII

TOP REASONS TO GO

★ **Hawaii Volcanoes National Park:** The world's most active volcano is an amazing sight.

★ **Fun towns:** Humming Kailua-Kona, cowboy country Waimea, rainbow-streaked Hilo.

★ **Stargazing:** Maunakea's peak is the best place on Earth to stare out into space.

★ **Beaches:** The Big Island offers sand in many shades—black, white, and even green.

★ **Wildlife:** You can watch sea turtles on the beach and humpback whales in the waves.

★ **Kona coffee:** Farm tours, smooth sips, and a coffee cultural festival are all memorable.

1 Kailua-Kona and the Kona Coast. This quaint seaside town is packed with restaurants, shops, and a busy waterfront. The Kona Coast is the place to taste samples of world-famous Kona coffee.

2 The Kohala Coast and Waimea. The sparkling coast is home to all those long, white-sand beaches and the expensive resorts that go with them. Ranches sprawl across the cool, upland meadows of Waimea, known as *paniolo* (cowboy) country.

3 The Hamakua Coast. Waterfalls, dramatic cliffs, ocean vistas, ancient hidden valleys, rain forests, and the stunning Waipio Valley are just a few of the treats here.

4 Hilo. Known as the City of Rainbows for all its rain, Hilo is what many consider the "real" Hawaii.

5 Hawaii Volcanoes National Park, Puna, and Kau. The spectacular Halemaumau Crater is not to be missed, especially during eruptions. The remote Puna district is home to the quirky, hippie town of Pahoa as well as the island's most recent lava flows. Round the southernmost part of the island to Kau for two of the Big Island's most unusual beaches.

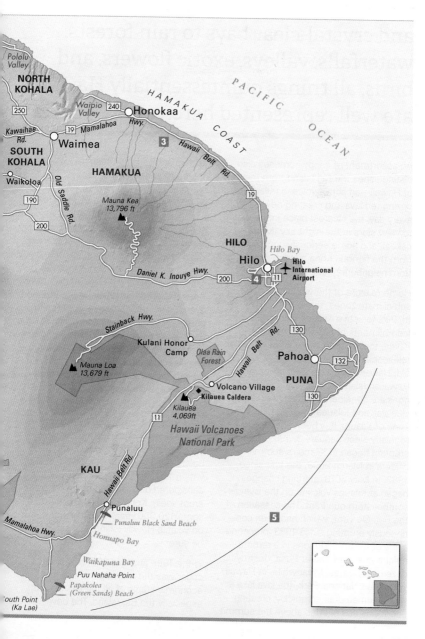

Nicknamed "the Big Island," Hawaii Island is a microcosm of Hawaii the state. From long white-sand beaches and crystal-clear bays to rain forests, waterfalls, valleys, exotic flowers, and birds, all things quintessentially Hawaii are well represented here.

An assortment of happy surprises also distinguishes the Big Island from the rest of Hawaii—an active volcano (Kilauea) oozing red lava and creating new earth every day, the clearest place in the world to view stars in the night sky (Maunakea), and some seriously good coffee from the famous Kona district, as well as from neighboring Kau.

Home to eight of the world's 13 sub-climate zones, this is the land of fire (thanks to active Kilauea volcano) and ice (compliments of not-so-active Maunakea, topped with snow and expensive telescopes). At just under a million years old, Hawaii is the youngest of the main Hawaiian Islands. Three of its five volcanoes are considered active: Mauna Loa, Hualalai, and Kilauea. The Southeast Rift Zone of Kilauea has been spewing lava regularly since January 3, 1983; another eruption began at Kilauea's summit caldera in March 2008, the first since 1982. In May 2018, startling changes began at Kilauea Volcano on the island's southeastern quadrant. The cessation of the Puu Oo vent, which had been continuously erupting since 1983, preceded a line of fissure eruptions in a remote neighborhood of Lower Puna, destroying dozens of homes. Meanwhile, in Hawaii Volcanoes National Park, the lava lake at Halemaumau drained quickly, creating enormous ash plumes above the summit caldera and causing steam explosions and earthquakes as it collapsed. The dramatic events claimed several beloved beaches in Lower Puna, including the Kapoho tide pools and the Ahalanui warm ponds. Those same forces also created a brand-new, black-sand beach at Pohoiki, which continues to expand as more black sand builds up on the shore. Hawaii Volcano Observatory (HVO) scientists have since declared this phase of the eruption over, but in late 2020, a new summit eruption began in the caldera, lasted for a few months, paused, and then restarted in September 2021. The current eruption is fully contained in the caldera and can be safely viewed from inside the park from several vantage points.

Back in 1984, Mauna Loa's eruptions crept almost to Hilo, and it could fire up again any minute—or not for years. Hualalai last erupted in 1801, and geologists say it will definitely do so again within 100 years. Maunakea is currently considered dormant but may very well erupt again. Kohala, which last erupted some 120,000 years ago, is inactive, but on volatile Hawaii Island, you can never be sure.

In the 19th- and mid-20th centuries, sugar was the main agricultural and economic staple of all the Islands, but especially the Big Island. The drive along the Hamakua Coast, from Hilo or Waimea, illustrates diverse agricultural developments on the island. Sugarcane stalks have been replaced by orchards of macadamia-nut trees, eucalyptus, and specialty crops from lettuce to strawberries. Macadamia-nut orchards on the Big Island supply 90% of the state's yield, while coffee continues to be big business, dominating the mountains above Kealakekua Bay. Orchids keep farmers from Honokaa to Pahoa afloat, and small organic farms produce meat, fruits, vegetables, and even goat cheese for high-end resort restaurants.

Hawaii's history is deeply rooted in its namesake island, which was home to the first Polynesian settlements and has the state's best-preserved *heiau* (temples) and *puuhonua* (refuges). Kamehameha, the greatest king in Hawaiian history and the man credited with uniting the Islands, was born here, raised in Waipio Valley, and died peacefully in Kailua-Kona. The other man who most affected Hawaiian history, Captain James Cook, spent the bulk of his time in the Islands here, docked in Kealakekua Bay. (He landed first on Kauai, but had little contact with the residents there.) Thus it was here that Western influence was first felt, and from here that it spread to the rest of Hawaii.

Planning

Getting Here and Around

AIR

Daniel K. Inouye International Airport (HNL) on Oahu is the main gateway for most domestic and international flights into Hawaii. From Honolulu, interisland flights to the Big Island depart regularly from early morning through mid-evening. From Honolulu, the travel time is about 35 minutes. From Maui, it's about 20 minutes. Those flying to the Big Island regularly land at one of two fields. Ellison Onizuka Kona International Airport at Keahole, on the west side, serves Kailua-Kona, Keauhou, the Kohala Coast, North Kohala, Waimea, and points south. There are Visitor Information Program (VIP) booths by all baggage-claim areas to assist travelers. Additionally, the airport offers news and lei stands, Laniakea by Centerplate (a café), and a small gift and sundries shop. A modernization project joined the two terminals (previously separate) so that baggage and passenger screening can be streamlined and retail options enhanced. Hilo International Airport is more appropriate for those planning visits based on the east side of the island. VIP booths are across from the Centerplate Coffee Shop near the departure lobby and in the arrival areas at each end of the terminal. In addition to the coffee shop, services include a Bank of Hawaii ATM, a gift shop, newsstands, and lei stands. Waimea-Kohala Airport, called Kamuela Airport by residents, is used primarily for private flights between islands but offers daily flights via Mokulele Airlines.

BUS

Although public transportation isn't very practical for the average vacationer, depending on where you're staying, you can take advantage of the affordable Hawaii County Mass Transit Agency's Hele-On Bus, which travels several routes throughout the island. Mostly serving local commuters, the Hele-On Bus costs $2 per person (students and senior citizens pay $1). Just wait at a scheduled stop for the next bus. A one-way journey between Hilo and Kona takes about four hours. There's regular service in and around downtown Hilo, Kailua-Kona, Waimea, North and South Kohala, Honokaa, and Pahoa. Nevertheless, some routes are served only once a day, so if you are planning on using the bus, study up carefully before assuming the bus serves your area.

Visitors staying in Hilo can take advantage of the Transit Agency's Shared Ride Taxi program, which provides door-to-door transportation in the area. A one-way fare is $2, and a book of 15 coupons can be purchased for $30. Visitors to Kona can also take advantage of free trolleys operated by local shopping centers.

CAR

It's essential to rent a car when visiting the Big Island. As the name suggests, it's a very big island, and it takes a while to get from one destination to another.

Fortunately, when you circle the island by car, you are treated to miles and miles of wondrous vistas of every possible description. In addition to using standard compass directions such as east and west, Hawaii residents often refer to places as being either *mauka* (toward the mountains) or *makai* (toward the ocean).

It's difficult to get lost along the main roads of the Big Island. Although their names may challenge the visitor's tongue, most roads are well marked; in rural areas look for mile marker numbers. Free publications containing basic road maps are given out at car rental agencies, but if you are doing a lot of driving, invest about $4 in the standard Big Island map available at local retailers. GPS might be unreliable in remote areas.

Driving the roads on the Big Island can be dangerous, as there's no margin for error to avoid a head-on collision. Distracted drivers are all too common. Most roads and main highways are two lanes with no shoulders; if there is a shoulder to access, it might be riddled with rocks, debris, and potholes. Speeding and illegal passing are frequent occurrences along winding, remote roads. In addition, most roads are not well lit at night. Fatalities can happen at a moment's notice, whether on the main highway from the airport to the resorts, the Saddle Road, the upper road from Waimea to Hawi, or on the Hawaii Belt Road that wraps around

Island Driving Times

Kailua-Kona to Kealakekua Bay	14 miles/25 min
Kailua-Kona to Kohala Coast	32 miles/40 min
Kailua-Kona to Waimea	40 miles/1 hr
Kailua-Kona to Hamakua Coast	53 miles/1 hr, 40 min
Kailua-Kona to Hilo	75 miles/2 hrs
Kohala Coast to Waimea	16 miles/20 min
Kohala Coast to Hamakua Coast	29 miles/55 min
Hilo to Volcano	30 miles/40 min

the island. During Ironman week, cyclists pose additional potential hazards on all roads in West Hawaii. Use extreme caution when driving on the Big Island, and of course, do not drive after drinking.

For those who want to travel from the west side to the east side, or vice versa, the rerouted and repaved Saddle Road, known as the Daniel K. Inouye Highway, is a nice shortcut across the middle of the island. This is especially convenient if you are staying on the west side of the island and wish to visit the east side. Hazardous conditions such as fog and speeding are common.

Before you embark on your day trip, it's a good idea to know how long it will take you to get to your destination. Some areas, like downtown Kailua-Kona and Waimea, can become congested at certain times of day. For those traveling to South Kona, a bypass road between Keauhou and Kealakekua alleviates congestion considerably during rush hour. In general, you can expect the following average driving times.

Beaches

Don't believe anyone who tells you that the Big Island lacks beaches. It's just one of the myths about Hawaii's largest island. It's not so much that the Big Island has fewer beaches than the other islands, just that there's more island, so getting to the beaches can be slightly less convenient. That said, there are plenty of those perfect white-sand stretches you think of when you hear "Hawaii," plus the added bonus of black-and green-sand beaches, thanks to the relative young age of the island and its active volcanoes. New beaches appear and disappear at times, created and/or destroyed by volcanic activity or surf.

Hawaii's largest coral reef systems lie off the Kohala Coast. Waves have battered them over millennia to create abundant white-sand beaches on the northwest side of the island. Black-, mixed-, and green-sand beaches lie in the southern regions and along the coast nearest the volcano. On the eastern side of the island, beaches tend to be of the rocky-coast–surging-surf variety, but there are still a few worth visiting, and this is where the Hawaii shoreline is at its most picturesque.

Restaurants

Between star chefs and myriad local farms, the Big Island restaurant scene has become a destination for foodies. Food writers praise chefs of the Big Island for their ability to turn the local bounty into inventive blends inspired by the island's cultural heritage. Resorts along the Kohala Coast have long invested in culinary programs offering memorable dining experiences that include inventive entrées, spot-on wine pairings, and customized chef's table options. But great food on the Big Island doesn't begin and end with the resorts. A handful of chefs have retired from the fast-paced hotel world and opened their own small bistros in upcountry Waimea or other places off the beaten track. Unique and wonderful restaurants have cropped up in Hawi, Kainaliu, and Waikoloa Village, and on the east side of the island in Hilo. In addition to restaurants, festivals devoted to island products draw attendees to learn about everything from breadfruit and mango to avocado, chocolate, and coffee. Agritourism has turned into a fruitful venture for farmers as farm tours afford the opportunity to meet with and learn from local producers. Some tours conclude with a meal of items sourced from the same farms. Whether a tour includes Puna goat farms churning creamy, savory goat cheese, or farms in Waimea producing row after row of bright tomatoes, or high-tech aquaculture operations at the Natural Energy Lab of Hawaii Authority (NELHA), visitors can see exactly where their next meal comes from.

Hotels

Our recommendation is to stay on both sides of the island. Each offers a different range of accommodations, restaurants, and activities. Consider staying at one of the upscale resorts along the Kohala Coast or in a condo in Kailua-Kona for half of your trip. Then, shift gears and check into a romantic bed-and-breakfast on the Hamakua Coast, South Kona, Hilo, or near the volcano. If you've got children in tow, opt for a vacation home or a stay at one of the island's many family-friendly hotels. On the west side, explore the island's most pristine beaches or try some of the fine-dining restaurants; on the east side, hike through rain forests, witness majestic waterfalls, or go for a plate lunch.

Some locals like to say that the east is "more Hawaiian," but we argue that King Kamehameha himself made Kailua-Kona his final home during his sunset years.

Another reason to try a bit of both: your budget. You can justify splurging on a stay at a Kohala Coast resort for a few nights because you'll spend the rest of your time paying far less at a cozy cottage in Volcano or a vacation rental on Alii Drive. And although food at the resorts is very expensive, you don't have to eat every meal there. Condos and vacation homes can be ideal for a family trip or for a group of friends looking to save money and live like *kamaainas* (local residents) for a week or two. Many of the homes also have private pools and hot tubs, lanai, ocean views, and more—you can go as budget or as high-end as you like.

If you choose a B&B, inn, or out-of-the-way hotel, explain your expectations fully to the proprietor and ask plenty of questions before booking. Be clear about your travel and location needs. Some places require stays of two or three days.

Hotel reviews have been shortened. For full information, visit Fodors.com.

CONDOS AND VACATION RENTALS

Renting a condo or vacation house gives you much more living space than the average hotel, plus the chance to meet more people (neighbors are usually friendly). You'll also pay lower nightly rates and have the option of cooking or barbecuing rather than eating out. When booking, remember that most properties are individually owned, with rates and amenities that differ substantially depending on the place. Some properties are handled by rental agents or agencies, while many are handled through the owner.

The booking agencies may specialize in various lodging types or locations, so be sure to call and ask questions before booking. Big Island Villas lists condos attached to a number of resorts. Hawaiian Beach Rentals is an excellent source for high-end homes. Keauhou Property Management has condos along the Kona Coast, as do Kona Coast Vacations and

Knutson and Associates. Kona Hawaii Vacation Rentals is known for affordable Kailua-Kona condos. Kolea Vacations lists high-end condos in Waikoloa, and Kona Vacation Rentals focuses on luxury Kohala Coast condos. Hawaii Vacation Rentals has some properties in Puako, near the Kohala Coast resorts. South Kohala Management handles everything from family-friendly condos to larger homes in the Kohala Coast resort areas.

CONTACTS Big Island Villas. ⊠ *Waimea (Hawaii County)* ☎ *808/936–3870, 808/443–6991* ⊕ *www.bigislandvillas. com.* **Hawaiian Beach Rentals.** ⊠ *Honolulu* ☎ *844/261–0464* ⊕ *www.hawaiianbeachrentals.com.* **Hawaii Vacation Rentals.** ⊠ *Waimea (Hawaii County)* ☎ *808/882–7000* ⊕ *www.vacationbigisland.com.* **Keauhou Property Management.** ⊠ *Keauhou* ☎ *808/326–7053* ⊕ *www.konacondo.net.* **Kolea Vacations.** ⊠ *Waikoloa* ☎ *808/987–4519* ⊕ *www.waikoloavacationrentals.com/kolea-rentals.* **Kona Coast Vacations.** ⊠ *Kailua-Kona* ☎ *808/329–2140* ⊕ *www.konacoastvacations.com.* **Kona Hawaii Vacation Rentals.** ⊠ *Kailua-Kona* ☎ *808/326–4137* ⊕ *www.konahawaii. com.* **Kona Vacation Rentals.** ⊠ *Kailua-Kona* ☎ *808/334–1199* ⊕ *www.konarentals. com.* **Knutson and Associates.** ⊠ *Kailua-Kona* ☎ *808/329–1010* ⊕ *www.konahawaiirentals.com.* **South Kohala Management.** ⊠ *Waimea (Hawaii County)* ☎ *808/883–8500* ⊕ *www.southkohala.com.*

Restaurant and hotel reviews have been shortened. For more information, visit Fodors.com. Restaurant prices are for a main course at dinner. Hotel prices are for two people in a standard double room in high season. Condo price categories reflect studio and one-bedroom rates. Prices do not include 13.42% tax.

What It Costs in U.S. Dollars			
$	$$	$$$	$$$$
RESTAURANTS			
Under $17	$17–$26	$27–$35	Over $35
HOTELS			
Under $180	$180–$260	$261–$340	Over $340

Shopping

Residents like to complain that there isn't a lot of great shopping on the Big Island, but unless you're searching for winter coats, you can find plenty to deplete your pocketbook.

Dozens of shops in Kailua-Kona offer a range of souvenirs from far-flung corners of the globe and plenty of local coffee and foodstuffs to take home to everyone you left behind. Housewares and artworks made from local materials (lauhala, coconut, koa, and milo wood) fill the shelves of small boutiques and galleries throughout the island. Upscale shops in the resorts along the Kohala Coast carry high-end clothing and accessories, as do a few boutiques scattered around the island. Galleries and gift shops, many showcasing the work of local artists, fill historical buildings in Waimea, Kainaliu, Holualoa, and Hawi. Hotel shops generally offer the most attractive and original resort wear, but, as with everything else at resorts, the prices run higher than elsewhere on the island.

Tours

Kona Historical Society Walking Tour
SELF-GUIDED TOURS | The society, based in Kealakekua, sells a 24-page *Historic Kailua Village Map* booklet with a map and more than 40 historical photos. You can take a self-guided walking tour to learn more about the village's fascinating past. Order the booklet online before you travel so you have it in hand for your tour. ✉ *81-6551 Mamalahoa Hwy., Kealakekua* ☎ *808/323–3222* ⊕ *www.konahistorical. org* ⌧ *$15 for booklet.*

Visitor Information

CONTACTS Island of Hawaii Visitors Bureau. ✉ *68-1330 Mauna Lani Dr., Puako* ⊕ *In Shops at Mauna Lani* ☎ *808/885–1655* ⊕ *www.gohawaii.com/islands/hawaii-big-island.*

Kailua-Kona and the Kona Coast

More laid-back than the tonier Kohala Coast to the north, the Kona Coast and its largest town, Kailua-Kona, are great if you want to get away from resort crowds and resort pricing. A handful of small beaches, a fun surf town vibe, and some oceanfront hot spots for sunset and a mai tai are just a few good reasons to spend time here.

Except for the rare deluge, the sun shines year-round. Mornings offer cooler weather, smaller crowds, and more birds singing in the banyan trees; you'll see tourists and locals out running on Alii Drive, the town's main drag, by about 5 am every day. Afternoons sometimes bring clouds and light rain, but evenings often clear up so you can enjoy cool drinks, brilliant sunsets, gentle trade winds, and lazy hours spent gazing out over the ocean. Though there are better beaches north of town on the Kohala Coast, Kailua-Kona is home to a few gems, including a sweet snorkeling beach (Kahaluu Beach Park) and a tranquil bay perfect for kids (Kamakahonu Beach, in front of the Courtyard King Kamehameha's Kona Beach Hotel).

South Kona is quiet and relatively rural. Much of the farmland is in leasehold

Where to Stay on the Big Island

Neighborhood	Local Vibe	Pros	Cons
Kailua-Kona	A bustling little village; Alii Drive brims with hotels and condo complexes.	Plenty to do, day and night; everything within easy walking distance of most hotels; many grocery stores in the area.	More traffic than anywhere else on the island; limited number of beaches; traffic noise on Alii Drive.
South Kona and Kau	Kealakekua Bay and Captain Cook have plenty of B&Bs and vacation rentals; a few more are farther south in Kau.	Kealakekua Bay is popular for kayaking and snorkeling; Captain Cook and Kainaliu have some good restaurants and coffee farms.	Few sandy beaches; not as many restaurant options; Kau is quite remote.
The Kohala Coast	Home to most of the Big Island's major resorts. Blue sunny skies prevail here. Has the island's best beaches.	Beautiful beaches; high-end shopping and dining; lots of activities for adults and children.	Pricey; long driving distances to Volcano, Hilo, and Kailua-Kona.
Waimea	Though it seems a world away, upcountry Waimea is only about a 15- to 20-minute drive from the Kohala Coast.	Striking scenery; *paniolo* (cowboy) culture; home to some exceptional local restaurants.	Can be cool and rainy year-round; nearest beaches are a 20-minute drive away.
The Hamakua Coast	A nice spot for those seeking peace, tranquility, and an alternative to the tropical-beach-vacation experience.	Close to Waipio Valley; foodie and farm tours in the area; good spot for honeymooners seeking low-key vibe.	Beaches are an hour's drive away; convenience shopping is limited, as are lodging options.
Hilo	Hilo is on the wet and lush eastern side of the Big Island. It's less touristy than the west side but retains much local charm.	Proximity to waterfalls, rain forest hikes, museums, zoo, and botanical gardens; also many good restaurants.	The best white-sand beaches are on the other side of the island; noise from coqui frogs can be distracting at night.
Puna	Puna doesn't attract as many visitors as other regions, so you'll find good deals on rentals here.	A few black-sand beaches; off the beaten path and fairly wild; lava has flowed into the sea here in years past.	Few dining and entertainment options; no resorts or resort amenities; noisy coqui frogs at night.
Hawaii Volcanoes National Park and Vicinity	There are any number of enchanting B&B inns in fern-shrouded Volcano Village, near the park.	Great for hiking, nature tours, and bike riding; close to Hilo and Puna.	Just a few dining options; not much nightlife; can be cold and wet.

status, which explains why this part of the Big Island has remained rather untouched by development. Tour one of the coffee farms to find out what the big deal is about Kona coffee, and enjoy a free sample while you're at it. A 20-minute drive off the highway from Captain Cook leads to beautiful Kealakekua Bay, where Captain James Cook arrived in 1778, dying here not long after. Hawaiian spinner dolphins visit the bay, now a Marine Life Conservation District, nestled alongside high green cliffs that jut dramatically out to sea. Snorkeling is superb here, so you may want to bring your gear and devote an hour or so to exploring the coral reefs. The bay is normally extremely calm. ■ TIP→ **One of the best ways to spend a morning is to kayak in the pristine waters of Kealakekua Bay, paddling over to see the spot where Cook died. Guided tours are your best bet, and you'll likely see plenty of dolphins along the way.**

North of Kona International Airport, along Mamalahoa Highway, brightly colored bougainvillea stands out in relief against miles of jet-black lava fields stretching from the mountain to the sea. Sometimes visitors liken it to landing on the moon when they first see it. True, the dry barren landscape may not be what you'd expect to find on a tropical island, but it's a good reminder of the island's evolving volcanic nature.

Kailua-Kona

Kailua-Kona is about 7 miles south of the Kona airport.

The largest town on the Kona Coast, Kailua-Kona offers plenty to accommodate the needs of locals and visitors, but it also has some significant historic sites. Scattered among the shops, restaurants, and condo complexes of Alii Drive are Ahuena Heiau, a temple complex restored by King Kamehameha the Great and the spot where he spent his last days (he died here in 1819); the last royal

palace in the United States (Hulihee Palace); and a battleground dotted with the graves of ancient Hawaiians who fought for their way of life and lost. It was also in Kailua-Kona that Kamehameha's successor, King Liholiho, broke with the ancient *kapu* (roughly translated as "forbidden," it was the name for the strict code of conduct that islanders were compelled to follow) system by publicly sitting and eating with women. The following year, on April 4, 1820, the first Christian missionaries came ashore here, changing life in the Islands forever.

GETTING HERE AND AROUND
Most first-time visitors to the island are startled by the seemingly endless black lava fields that make up the airport area and immediate surroundings. But just a 10-minute drive on Queen Kaahumanu Highway heading south takes you into the seaside town of Kailua-Kona and nearby retail centers. To get to town, take a right onto Palani Road and a left on Kuakini, and find one of the free lots along Kuakini Highway. You can park and walk right to the village and the seawall. You can also get to the restaurant row area by taking Kuakini Highway and turning right into the Coconut Grove Marketplace's parking lot. From there, you can walk to oceanfront establishments such as Humpy's Big Island Alehouse and Island Lava Java. Alii Drive, the town's main street, runs north and south along the water and is popular for walking, with plenty of shops and restaurants. Sunsets here are spectacular.

 Sights

★ Holualoa
TOWN | Hugging the hillside above the Kona Coast, the artsy village of Holualoa has galleries that feature all types of artists. Painters, woodworkers, jewelers, gourd makers, and potters work in their studios in back and sell their wares up front. Look for frequent town-wide events such as art strolls and block

parties, and relax with a cup of coffee in one of the cafés or galleries. Formerly the exclusive domain of coffee plantations, Holualoa still boasts quite a few coffee farms offering free tours and inviting cups of Kona. The town is 3 miles up winding Hualalai Road from Kailua-Kona. ⊠ *Holualoa* ⊕ *www.holualoahawaii.com.*

Hula Daddy Kona Coffee

FARM/RANCH | On a walking tour of this working coffee farm (by advance reservation only), visitors can witness the workings of a small plantation, pick and pulp their own coffee beans, watch a roasting demonstration, and savor a tasting. The gift shop carries whole beans and logo swag including bags, T-shirts, and mugs. Coffee brewing workshops and one-on-one tours with a master roaster are also offered. ⊠ *74-4944 Mamalahoa Hwy., Holualoa* ☎ *808/327–9744, 888/553–2339* ⊕ *www.huladaddy.com* 🖻 *$30* ⊙ *Closed weekends.*

★ Hulihee Palace

CASTLE/PALACE | On the National Register of Historic Places, this lovely two-story oceanfront home, surrounded by jewel-green grass and elegant coconut palms and fronted by an elaborate wrought-iron gate, is one of only three royal palaces in America (the other two are in Honolulu). The royal residence was built by Governor John Adams Kuakini in 1838, a year after he completed Mokuaikaua Church. During the 1880s, it served as King David Kalakaua's summer palace.

Built of lava rock and coral lime mortar, it features vintage koa furniture, weaving, European crystal chandeliers, giant four-poster beds, royal portraits, tapa cloth, feather work, and Hawaiian quilts. After the overthrow of the Hawaiian monarchy in 1893, the property fell into disrepair. Set to be torn down for a hotel, it was rescued in 1920 by the Daughters of Hawaii, a nonprofit organization dedicated to preserving the culture and royal heritage of the Islands. The organization oversees and operates the site to this day; visitors see it on a guided tour. ⊠ *75-5718 Alii Dr., Kailua-Kona* ☎ *808/329–1877* ⊕ *www.daughtersofhawaii.org* 🖻 *$22 includes guided tour.*

Kailua Pier

MARINA/PIER | Though most fishing boats use Honokohau Harbor in Kailua-Kona, this pier dating from 1918 is still a hub of ocean activity where outrigger canoe teams practice and race, shuttles transport cruise ship passengers to and from town, and tour boats depart from the docks. Along the seawall, children and old-timers cast their lines and hope for the best. For youngsters, a bamboo pole and hook are easy to come by, and plenty of locals are willing to give pointers. September brings the world's largest long-distance outrigger canoe race, and in October, nearly 2,000 elite athletes depart the pier to swim 2.4 miles in the first leg of the famous Ironman World Championship triathlon. ⊠ *Alii Dr., Kailua-Kona* ⊕ *Across from Courtyard King Kamehameha's Kona Beach Hotel* 🖻 *Free.*

★ Kamakahonu and Ahuena Heiau

HISTORIC SIGHT | In the early 1800s, King Kamehameha the Great built a large royal compound at Kamakahonu, the bay fronting what is now the Courtyard King Kamehameha's Kona Beach Hotel; today it is one of the most revered and historically significant sites in all of Hawaii. Kamakahonu, meaning "eye of the turtle," was named for a prominent turtle-shaped rock there, covered in cement when the hotel and pier were built. The Ahuena Heiau, an impressive *heiau* (temple), was dedicated to Lono, the Hawaiian god of peace and prosperity. It was also used as a seat of government. The compound features a scaled-down replica of the temple and is a National Historic Landmark. You can't go inside the *heiau*, but you can view it from the beach or directly next door at the hotel's luau grounds. ⊠ *75-5660 Palani Rd., Kailua-Kona* ☎ ⊕ *www.nps.gov/places/kamakahonu.htm.*

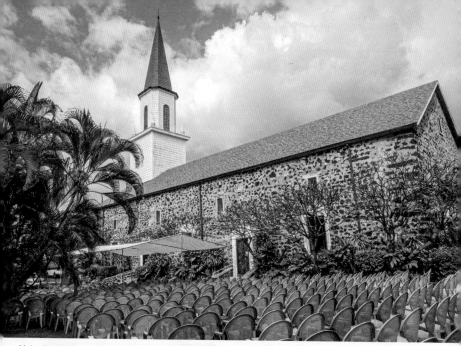

Mokuaikaua Church in Kailua-Kona, completed in 1837, was the first Christian church on the Hawaiian Islands.

★ Mokuaikaua Church

CHURCH | Site of the first Christian church in the Hawaiian Islands, this solid lava-rock structure, completed in 1837, is mortared with burned lime, coral, and *kukui* (candlenut) oil and topped by an impressive steeple. The ceiling and interior were crafted of timbers harvested from a forest on Hualalai and are held together with wooden pegs, not nails. Inside, behind a panel of gleaming koa wood, rests a model of the brig *Thaddeus* as well as a koa-wood table crafted by Henry Boshard, pastor for 43 years. At this writing, the building is closed due to renovations, but you may still stop and admire it from the outside. ⊠ *75-5713 Alii Dr., Kailua-Kona* ☎ *808/329–0655* ⊕ *www.mokuaikaua.org* ⊴ *Free.*

Beaches

Kahaluu Beach Park

BEACH | Shallow and easily accessible, this salt-and-pepper beach is one of the Big Island's most popular swimming and snorkeling sites, thanks to the fringing reef that helps keep the waters calm, visibility high, and reef life—especially *honu* (green sea turtles) and colorful fish—plentiful. Kahaluu was a favorite of the Hawaiian royal family, too. Because it is so protected, it's great for first-time snorkelers. Outside the reef, very strong rip currents can run, so caution is advised. Never hand-feed the unusually tame reef fish here; it upsets the balance of the reef.

Experienced surfers find good waves beyond the reef, and scuba divers like the shore dives—shallow ones inside the breakwater, deeper ones outside. Snorkel equipment and boards are available for rent nearby, and surf schools operate here. A community group has provided reef-safe sunscreen dispensers on-site. **Amenities:** food and drink; lifeguards; parking (no fee); showers; toilets. **Best for:** snorkeling; surfing; swimming. ⊠ *78-6720 Alii Dr., Kailua-Kona* ↔ *5½ miles south of Kailua-Kona, across from Beach Villas* ☎ *808/961–8311* ⊴ *Free.*

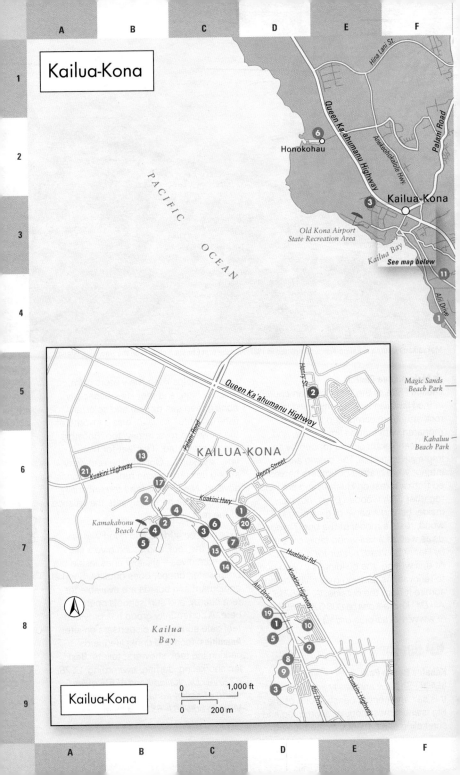

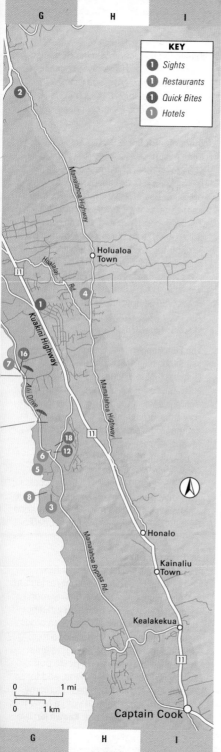

KEY

1 *Sights*
1 *Restaurants*
1 *Quick Bites*
1 *Hotels*

Kamakahonu Beach

BEACH | FAMILY | This beach is where King Kamehameha spent his final days—the replica of the Ahuena Heiau sits on a platform across from the sand. Adjacent to Kailua Pier, the scenic crescent of white sand is one of the few beaches in downtown Kailua-Kona. The water here is almost always calm and the beach clean, making this a perfect spot for kids. For adults, it's a great place for swimming, stand-up paddling (SUP), watching outrigger teams practice, or enjoying a lazy beach day. It can get crowded on weekends. Snorkeling can be good north of the beach, and snorkeling, SUP, and kayaking equipment can be rented nearby. There's lots of grass and shade, and free parking in county lots is a short stroll away. **Amenities:** food and drink; showers; toilets; water sports. **Best for:** snorkeling; swimming. ✉ *75-5660 Palani Rd., at Alii Dr., Kailua-Kona* 🎫 *Free.*

🍴 Restaurants

Big Island Grill

$ | HAWAIIAN | FAMILY | This beloved local-style restaurant has switched to drive-up only and serves huge portions of pork chops, diet-busting *loco moco* (meat, rice, and eggs smothered in gravy), and an assortment of fish specialties at very reasonable prices. At this writing, the drive-up window is open until 2 pm, but you can call to confirm. **Known for:** succulent Kalbi short ribs; large saimin portions; authentic local vibe. [$] *Average main: $15* ✉ *75-5702 Kuakini Hwy., Kailua-Kona* ☎ *808/326–1153* 🕒 *Closed weekends.*

★ Big Kahuna Beach Grill

$ | AMERICAN | FAMILY | From its upstairs, open-air dining room decorated with kitschy surfer chic, this new restaurant invites customers to enjoy views of the pier and a bustling corner of Alii Drive. Fortunately, an excellent, extensive menu makes it well worth a stop; fresh fish plates including fish tacos are a sure bet. **Known for:** five types of eggs Benedict; full bar menu of island-style cocktails; clam chowder. [$] *Average main: $15* ✉ *75-5663 Palani Rd., Kailua-Kona* ☎ *808/731–5055* 🌐 *bigkahunabeachgrill.com.*

Don's Mai Tai Bar & Restaurant at Royal Kona Resort

$$ | HAWAIIAN | The largest open-air tiki bar in Kona has the absolute best view of Kailua Bay in town. This is the perfect spot to relax with a *pupu* (appetizer) such as the coconut-crusted shrimp or "Hapa" poke bowl, or to dig into something more substantial like the kiawe wood–smoked prime rib. **Known for:** worthy desserts and dessert coffees; Hawaiian performers weekly; 10 types of mai tais. [$] *Average main: $25* ✉ *Royal Kona Resort, 75-5852 Alii Dr., Kailua-Kona* ☎ *808/329–3111* 🌐 *www.royalkona.com.*

The Fish Hopper

$$ | SEAFOOD | FAMILY | In the heart of Historic Kailua Village, the open-air Hawaii location of the popular Monterey, California, restaurant offers an expansive menu for breakfast, lunch, and dinner in a vintage building with a bayfront view. Inventive fresh-fish specials as well as simple fish-and-chips are among the local favorites. **Known for:** good lunch menu; signature Volcano flaming cocktail; award-winning clam chowder. [$] *Average main: $24* ✉ *75-5683 Alii Dr., Kailua-Kona* ☎ *808/326–2002* 🌐 *www.fishhopperkona.com.*

★ Foster's Kitchen

$$ | AMERICAN | Ocean breezes flow through this open-air, bayfront restaurant on Alii Drive, known for a quality menu infused with Cajun and island influences; almost all dishes are made to order and feature non-GMO, hormone-free, or USDA-certified organic ingredients. A must-try is the seafood pesto puff pastry on the appetizer menu, and for dinner, the steak house pasta (creamy mushroom pasta topped with a New York strip steak) is a good bet. **Known for:** live

entertainment nightly; great happy hour prices; scratch-made food and cocktails. $ *Average main: $23* ⊠ *75-5805 Alii Dr., Kailua-Kona* ☎ *808/326–1600* ⊕ *www. fosterskitchen.com.*

★ Harbor House

$ | AMERICAN | On the docks at Kona's sleepy harbor, this open-air restaurant is an authentic place to grab a beer and a bite after a long day fishing, beach-going, or diving. The venue is nothing fancy, but it's one of the best spots in Kona for fresh-fish sandwiches, a variety of fried fish-and-chip combos, and even burgers. **Known for:** fresh fish right off the incoming boats; fun waterfront dining on the way to or from the airport; chilled schooners of Kona Brewing Co. lager. $ *Average main: $10* ⊠ *Honokohau Harbor, 74-425 Kealakehe Pkwy., Suite 4, Kailua-Kona* ☎ *808/326–4166* ⊕ *harbor-houserestaurantkona.com.*

★ Hayashi's You Make the Roll

$ | JAPANESE | Tiny and locally owned, this sushi shack in the heart of town has gained an incredible following and specializes in "reverse" (rice on the outside, nori on the inside) rolls, filled with three or four ingredients of your choice. It's super popular and gets crazy crowded, so expect a long wait—but it's worth it. (Wait times can exceed an hour, but they let you know how long before you order.) Hayashi's has been in take-out mode only since COVID-19 (call to confirm this), so you have to phone your order in. **Known for:** small, low-key location; local favorite; affordable, take-out sushi rolls. $ *Average main: $7* ⊠ *75-5725 Alii Dr., Suite D101, Kailua-Kona* ☎ *808/326–1322* ⊗ *Closed Sun.*

Huggo's

$$$$ | HAWAIIAN | A Kona icon since 1969, family-owned Huggo's is one of the few restaurants in town with prices and atmosphere comparable to the splurge restaurants at the Kohala Coast resorts. Dinner offerings sometimes fall short, considering the prices, but the *pupus*

(appetizers) and small plates are usually a good bet. **Known for:** next-door bar with toes-in-the sand dining; nightlife hot spot; fine dining at the water's edge. $ *Average main: $36* ⊠ *75-5828 Kahakai Rd., off Alii Dr., Kailua-Kona* ☎ *808/329–1493* ⊕ *www.huggos.com.*

Humpy's Big Island Alehouse

$ | AMERICAN | This place is usually packed for a reason: the more than 36 craft brews on tap, plus an upstairs and downstairs bar with plenty of outdoor seating. Take in the oceanfront view with amazing sunsets while chowing down on stone-baked pizza, fresh salads, fish-and-chips, fish tacos, burgers, stone-baked subs, and lots of appetizers. **Known for:** great steamed clams; good nightlife (for Kona); largest selection of craft beer on the island. $ *Average main: $15* ⊠ *Coconut Grove Marketplace, 75-5815 Alii Dr., Kailua-Kona* ☎ *808/324–2337* ⊕ *humpys-kona.com.*

Island Lava Java

$$ | AMERICAN | With cocktail bars both upstairs and downstairs, oceanfront Island Lava Java serves eggs Benedict for breakfast, fresh fish tacos for lunch, and pasta, Big Island beef, and seafood for dinner, plus towering, fresh bistro salads. There are also pizzas, sandwiches, and plenty of choices for both vegetarians and meat eaters. **Known for:** bar with extensive cocktail menu; 100% Kona coffee; large portions using mostly local organic ingredients. $ *Average main: $20* ⊠ *Coconut Grove Marketplace, 75-5801 Alii Dr., Kailua-Kona* ☎ *808/327–2161* ⊕ *www.islandlavajava.com.*

Jackie Rey's Ohana Grill

$$ | AMERICAN | FAMILY | The brightly decorated, open-air restaurant is a favorite lunch and dinner destination of visitors and residents, thanks to generous portions and a nice variety of chef's specials, steaks, and seafood dishes. The lunchtime menu offers such diversity as beer-battered fish-and-chips, *kalua* (earth oven–baked) pork quesadilla, and

guava-glazed baby-back ribs. **Known for:** great-value lunch menu; $5 happy hour; strong local following. $ *Average main: $23* ⊠ *Pottery Terrace, 75-5995 Kuakini Hwy., Kailua-Kona* ☎ *808/327–0209* ⊕ *www.jackiereys.com* ⊙ *No lunch weekends.*

Kenichi Pacific

$$$ | JAPANESE | With black-lacquer tables and lipstick-red banquettes, Kenichi offers a more sophisticated dining atmosphere than what's normally found in Kona. This is where residents go when they feel like splurging on top-notch sushi, sashimi, steak, and Asian-fusion cuisine. **Known for:** happy hour discounts on sushi; cheaper lounge menu of small plates; upscale dining at much less than resort prices. $ *Average main: $30* ⊠ *Keauhou Shopping Center, 78-6831 Alii Dr., Suite D-125, Kailua-Kona* ☎ *808/322–6400* ⊕ *www.kenichipacific. com* ⊙ *Closed Mon. No lunch.*

★ Kona Brewing Co.

$ | AMERICAN | FAMILY | An ultrapopular destination with an outdoor patio, Kona Brewing offers an excellent, varied menu, including famous brews, pulled-pork quesadillas, gourmet pizzas, and a killer spinach salad with Gorgonzola cheese and macadamia nuts. The sampler tray, a good value, offers four of the 10 available microbrews. **Known for:** live music; selling growlers of to-go beer from taps; Longboard Lager and other famous brews made on-site. $ *Average main: $12* ⊠ *74-5612 Pawai Pl., Kailua-Kona* ⊕ *Off Kaiwi St. at end of Pawai Pl.* ☎ *808/329–2739* ⊕ *www.konabrewingco.com.*

Kona Inn Restaurant

$$ | AMERICAN | This vintage open-air restaurant at the historical Kona Inn Shopping Village offers a beautiful oceanfront setting on Kailua Bay. The view and the bar are Kona icons, and it's a great place to have a mai tai and some appetizers later in the day, or to enjoy a calamari sandwich, clam chowder, or salad at lunch. **Known for:** nice bar and lounge at

all times; inconsistent food at dinner; sunset-watching spot. $ *Average main: $20* ⊠ *Kona Inn Shopping Village, 75-5744 Alii Dr., Kailua-Kona* ☎ *808/329–4455* ⊕ *konainnrestaurant.com.*

Kona Taeng on Thai

$ | THAI | A hidden gem, the open-air eatery is on the second floor of an oceanfront shopping center. Patrons can watch the scene below on bustling Alii Drive while enjoying freshly prepared Thai specialties, including plenty of vegetarian options and delicious Thai iced tea. **Known for:** lunch specials; large portions; uncrowded, spacious layout. $ *Average main: $11* ⊠ *Kona Inn Shopping Center, 75-5744 Alii Dr., #208, 2nd fl., Kailua-Kona* ☎ *808/329–1994.*

Magics Beach Grill

$$$ | HAWAIIAN | In a vintage building dating from 1965, Magics offers an exhilarating oceanfront location overlooking the famous Disappearing Sands Beach, also known as Magic Sands. From fried *ulu* (breadfruit) wedges in umami truffle oil aioli to griddled crab cakes and shoyu-and-coconut-braised pork belly, the eclectic menu features intriguing choices with contemporary island flair. **Known for:** spicy dragonfruit margarita; great happy hour 2–4 pm; sunset beach views. $ *Average main: $33* ⊠ *77-6452 Alii Dr., Kailua-Kona* ☎ *808/662–4427* ⊕ *magicsbeachgrill.com.*

★ Quinn's Almost by the Sea

$ | AMERICAN | FAMILY | With the bar in the front and the dining patio in the back, Quinn's may seem like a bit of a dive at first glance, but this venerable restaurant serves the best darn cheeseburger and fries in town. The menu has many other tasty options, such as fish-and-chips and beef tenderloin tips. **Known for:** comfort food like meatballs; old Kona vibe; strong cocktails. $ *Average main: $15* ⊠ *75-5655 Palani Rd., Kailua-Kona* ☎ *808/329–3822* ⊕ *www.quinnsalmostbythesea.com* ⊙ *Closed Wed.*

Sam Choy's Kai Lanai

$$ | **HAWAIIAN** | **FAMILY** | Perched above a shopping center with a million-dollar panoramic view, this open-air "fast casual" restaurant offers customers the chance to enjoy cocktail service table side and then order entrées directly from the counter. The ahi wrap is the star of the show, and the macadamia nut–encrusted ono is a close second. **Known for:** fast-casual concept useful if you have limited time; the best views in town; limited parking for such a popular place. [$] *Average main: $22* ✉ *Keauhou Shopping Center, 78-6831 Alii Dr., Suite 1000, Kailua-Kona* ☎ *808/333–3434* 🌐 *www.samchoyskailanai.com* 🕒 *Closed Mon.*

Thai Rin Restaurant and Bar

$$ | **THAI** | **FAMILY** | Everything is cooked to order at this low-key oceanfront restaurant with an excellent selection of Thai food at decent prices. The menu brims with choices, including five curries, a green-papaya salad, and deep-fried fish. **Known for:** appetizer platters for sharing; convenient to village shops; great views with both indoor and outdoor seating. [$] *Average main: $18* ✉ *75-5799 Alii Dr., Kailua-Kona* ☎ *808/329–2929* 🌐 *www.thairin.com* 🕒 *Closed Tues.*

TK Noodle House

$ | **ASIAN FUSION** | Former resort chef T. K. Keosavang serves inventive Asian fusion cuisine with the emphasis on noodles. Generous portions are beautifully plated, like the crispy pork belly sauté with Chinese greens and garlic sauce, and noodle soups and abundant salads don't disappoint. **Known for:** seafood yentafo soup; lunch specials; ample parking. [$] *Average main: $12* ✉ *75 Hanama Pl., Kailua-Kona* ✣ *Near Big Island Grill* ☎ *808/327–0070* 🌐 *www.cheftk.com.*

★ **Umekes Fish Market Bar & Grill**

$ | **HAWAIIAN** | **FAMILY** | Locals flock to this downtown Kailua-Kona restaurant for good reason: the poke is the most *ono-licious* (superdelicious) in town, and the many other seafood offerings are just as stellar. Poke does not get more authentic than this, and you can get it by the bowl or the pound. **Known for:** locally sourced ingredients; authentic Kona experience; daily specials using the freshest fish. [$] *Average main: $12* ✉ *74-5599 Pawai Pl., Kailua-Kona* ☎ *808/238–0571* 🌐 *umekesrestaurants.com.*

Coffee and Quick Bites

Kanaka Kava

$ | **HAWAIIAN** | This is a popular local hangout, and not just because the kava drink makes you mellow. The Hawaiian proprietors also serve traditional Hawaiian food, including fresh poke, bowls of healthy organic greens, *opihi* (limpets), and traditional Hawaiian *laulau* (pork or chicken wrapped in taro leaves and steamed). **Known for:** pulled kalua pork; squid luau (the leaf from a taro plant); kava served in coconut cups. [$] *Average main: $12* ✉ *Coconut Grove Marketplace, 75-5803 Alii Dr., Space B6, Kailua-Kona* ☎ *808/327–1660* 🌐 *www.kanakakava.bar/bar-1.*

★ **Poi Dog Deli**

$ | **AMERICAN** | With vintage memorabilia and a bluesy soundtrack as a background, this cool deli in a tiny strip mall has a lot more to offer than the average sandwich shop. Yes, there are gourmet sandwiches, salads, and wraps, but Poi Dog's wide-ranging menu extends to an impressive list of wines, craft beers, ales, and pilsners from all over the world. **Known for:** salads featuring house-made Cajun croutons and house dressings; Ranch House Reuben; house-made soups. [$] *Average main: $9* ✉ *75-1022 Henry St., Kailua-Kona* ✣ *Across from Walmart* ☎ *808/329–2917* 🌐 *poidogdeli.com* 🕒 *No dinner.*

Ultimate Burger

$ | **DINER** | **FAMILY** | Located in the Office Max shopping complex in Kailua-Kona, this excellent burger joint may look like a chain, but it's an independent, locally owned and operated eatery that serves 100% organic, grass-fed Big Island beef. Be sure to order a side of seasoned Big Daddy fries served with homemade aioli dipping sauce. **Known for:** supporting local farmers and ranchers; locally made buns; organic, hormone-free ingredients. [$] *Average main: $8* ✉ *Kona Commons Shopping Center, 74-5450 Makala Blvd., Kailua-Kona* ☎ *808/329–2326* 🌐 *www.ultimateburger.net.*

Hotels

Aston Kona by the Sea

$$$$ | **APARTMENT** | **FAMILY** | Complete modern kitchens, tiled lanai, and washer-dryer units are found in every suite of this comfortable oceanfront condo complex with a welcoming entry lobby and reception area that feels like a hotel. **Pros:** lobby and activities desk; near delis and convenience stores; ocean-fed saltwater pool next to the property. **Cons:** not walking distance to Kailua Village; individually owned units, so prices may vary; no beach access (2 miles away). [$] *Rooms from: $669* ✉ *75-6106 Alii Dr., Kailua-Kona* ☎ *808/327–2300, 877/997–6667* 🌐 *www.astonhotels.com* 🛏 *86 units* 🍴 *No Meals.*

Courtyard by Marriott King Kamehameha's Kona Beach Hotel

$$$$ | **HOTEL** | **FAMILY** | Right on the beach in the heart of Historic Kailua Village, this landmark hotel built in 1975 offers good vibrations and authentic local hospitality—all for less than the price of a Kohala Coast resort. **Pros:** easy access to shops and restaurants; deep historical ambience includes Hawaiian artifacts; on-site restaurant and poolside bar. **Cons:** some rooms face the parking lot; often sold out; most rooms have partial ocean views. [$] *Rooms from: $469* ✉ *75-5660 Palani Rd., Kailua-Kona* ☎ *808/329–2911* 🌐 *marriott.com* 🛏 *452 rooms* 🍴 *No Meals.*

★ **Holualoa Inn**

$$$$ | **B&B/INN** | Six spacious rooms and suites—plus two vintage, one-bedroom cottages perfect for honeymooners—are available at this 30-acre coffee-country estate, a few miles above Kailua Bay in the heart of the artists' village of Holualoa. **Pros:** within walking distance of art galleries and cafés; everything necessary for hosting a wedding or event; luxurious, Zen-like vibe. **Cons:** unheated swimming pool; books up far in advance; not kid friendly. [$] *Rooms from: $440* ✉ *76-5932 Mamalahoa Hwy., Holualoa* ☎ *808/324–1121, 800/392–1812* 🌐 *www.holualoainn.com* 🛏 *8 units* 🍴 *Free Breakfast.*

Holua Resort at Mauna Loa Village

$$$$ | **RESORT** | Tucked away by Keauhou Bay amid a plethora of coconut trees, this well-maintained enclave of blue-roofed villas offers lots of amenities, including an 11-court tennis center (with a center court, pro shop, and lights), swimming pools, hot tubs, a fitness center, waterfalls, and covered parking. **Pros:** manicured gardens; upscale feeling; walking distance to major resort restaurants. **Cons:** partial ocean views; no on-site restaurant; no beach. [$] *Rooms from: $599* ✉ *78-7190 Kaleiopapa St., Kailua-Kona* ☎ *808/324–1550* 🌐 *www.shellhospitality.com* 🛏 *73 units* 🍴 *No Meals.*

Kanaloa at Kona by Outrigger

$$$$ | **APARTMENT** | The 18-acre grounds provide a peaceful and verdant background for this low-rise condominium complex bordering the Keauhou-Kona Country Club and within a five-minute drive of the nearest beaches (Kahaluu and Magic Sands). **Pros:** within walking distance of Keauhou Bay; three pools with hot tubs; shopping center and restaurants nearby. **Cons:** mandatory cleaning fee at check-in; air-conditioning available only by paying a daily fee; no elevators. [$] *Rooms from: $479* ✉ *78-261 Manukai St., Kailua-Kona* ☎ *808/322–9625, 800/688–7444* 🌐 *www.outrigger.com* 🛏 *63 units* 🍴 *No Meals.*

Kona Condo Comforts

Safeway Kona at the brand-new Niumalu Marketplace (⊠ *75-971 Henry St., Kailua-Kona* ☎ *808/339–9155*) offers an excellent inventory of groceries and produce, although prices can be steep. Delivery and curbside pickup are available.

Longs Drugs at Lanihau Center (⊠ *75-5595 Palani Rd., Kailua-Kona* ☎ *808/329–1632*) is the place to pick up personal care items, rubber slippers, a snorkel, and sunscreen. They also have a good selection of liquor at competitive prices.

For pizza, **Kona Crust** in the Kona Coast Shopping Center (⊠ *74-5586 Palani Rd., Kailua Kona* ☎ *808/731–7553*) is the best bet; order online and pick up. Otherwise, for delivery, try **Domino's** (☎ *808/329–9500*).

Kona Coast Resort

$$$$ | TIMESHARE | FAMILY | Just below Keauhou Shopping Center, this resort offers furnished condos on 21 acres with pleasant ocean views and a host of on-site amenities, including two swimming pools, beach volleyball, a cocktail bar, barbecue grills, a hot tub, tennis courts, a fitness center, hula classes, equipment rentals, and children's activities. **Pros:** all rooms updated in 2018; good amenities for kids; away from the bustle of downtown Kailua-Kona. **Cons:** not on the beach; time-share salespeople; some units have parking lot views. Ⓢ *Rooms from: $509* ⊠ *78-6842 Alii Dr., Keauhou* ☎ *808/324–1721* ⊕ *www. shellhospitality.com* ↪ *268 units* ⦿ *No Meals.*

Kona Magic Sands

$$ | APARTMENT | Cradled between a lovely grass park and Magic Sands Beach Park, this older condo complex is great for swimmers, surfers, and sunbathers. **Pros:** lanai in most units; affordable studios; oceanfront view from all units. **Cons:** some units are dated; popular complex, but booked through a third-party site; studios only. Ⓢ *Rooms from: $180* ⊠ *77-6452 Alii Dr., Kailua-Kona* ☎ *808/329–9393, 800/622–5348* ↪ *15 units* ⦿ *No Meals.*

Outrigger Kona Resort and Spa at Keauhou Bay

$$$ | RESORT | FAMILY | What the hotel's concrete architecture lacks in intimacy, it makes up for with its beautifully manicured grounds, historical sense of place, stylish interiors, and stunning location on Keauhou Bay. Many rooms have great views of the bay and feel like they're right on the water, and each is decorated in a modern Polynesian style. **Pros:** cool pool that's great for kids; manta rays on view nightly; resort style at lower price. **Cons:** long walk from parking area; Wi-Fi can be spotty; no beach. Ⓢ *Rooms from: $299* ⊠ *78-128 Ehukai St., Keauhou* ☎ *808/930–4900* ⊕ *outrigger.com* ↪ *484 rooms* ⦿ *No Meals.*

Royal Kona Resort

$$$ | HOTEL | FAMILY | If you're on a budget, this is a great option: the location is central; the bar, lounge, pool, and restaurant are right on the water; and the rooms feature contemporary Hawaiian decor with Polynesian accents. **Pros:** convenient location by shops and restaurants; waterfront pool; restaurant and bar with great views. **Cons:** $18 per day parking fee; grounds have dated feel; can be crowded. Ⓢ *Rooms from: $275* ⊠ *75-5852 Alii Dr., Kailua-Kona* ☎ *808/329–3111, 800/222–5642* ⊕ *www.royalkona.com* ↪ *430 rooms* ⦿ *No Meals.*

Nightlife

BARS

★ Ola Brew Co

BREWPUBS | There's an enticing and creative array of beers, ales, ciders, and hard seltzers at this employee-owned brewing company. Ola Brew is committed to community investment and support of local farmers and merchants. Take a barstool at a picture window facing the main brewing operation and enjoy a fresh, on-tap draft and an appetizer. There's plenty of outdoor seating as well. The taproom menu features reasonably priced tacos, salads, flatbreads, and poke bowls. Ask about their brewery tours. Popular local bands entertain on a regular basis. ✉ *74-5598 Luhia St., Kailua-Kona* ☎ *808/339–3599* ⊕ *www.olabrewco.com.*

CLUBS

★ Gertrude's Jazz Bar

LIVE MUSIC | You know you're in the right place when you climb the stairs to this little gem and notice that the steps are painted like piano keys. With a location in the heart of town, including a perfect view of Kailua Bay, this open-air club presents an incredible variety of music (jazz, Latin, country, classical) and special events such as dance lessons, wine tastings, and themed dress-up parties. One of the proprietors is a renowned jazz musician and plays with his own group or guest musicians. The menu of crepes is straightforward and a tad overpriced. A small cover charge helps pay the musicians a living wage. Note that Gertrude's is closed Monday and Tuesday. ✉ *75-5699 Alii Dr., 2nd fl., Kailua-Kona* ☎ *808/327–5299* ⊕ *gertrudesjazzbar.com.*

Huggo's on the Rocks

COCKTAIL LOUNGES | Jazz, Island, and classic-rock bands perform here nightly, and outside you may see people dancing in the sand. It's best for a tropical cocktail and an appetizer such as a poke bowl or kalua pork quesadilla. The location, on the waterfront right next to their flagship restaurant, doesn't get any better than this in town. Happy hour is 3 to 5. ✉ *75-5824 Kahakai Rd., at Alii Dr., Kailua-Kona* ☎ *808/329–1493* ⊕ *huggosontherocks.com.*

Laverne's Sports Bar

DANCE CLUBS | They call themselves Kona's "dive" bar, but we're not sure we agree. It's fun and kitschy, and locals know this is the best place to dance and drink in Kailua-Kona. With 32 TVs, there's not a sports event you will miss, either. Sometimes Hawaiian and island music headliners perform here, such as local recording artists Anuhea or Rebel Souljahz. Local musicians with followings also draw their "groupies." After 10, DJs spin tunes on the ocean-breeze-cooled dance floor, located upstairs with killer views of the water. The food is decent and includes full meals, such as cheeseburgers or fish-and-chips. ✉ *Coconut Grove Marketplace, 75-5819 Alii Dr., Kailua-Kona* ☎ *808/331–2633* ⊕ *laverneskona.com.*

Performing Arts

FESTIVALS

★ King Kamehameha Day Celebration Parade

FESTIVALS | Each summer on the Saturday nearest to King Kamehameha Day (June 11), at least 100 regal riders on horseback parade through Historic Kailua Village, showing off the colorful flora and aloha spirit of Hawaii. This spectacular free event is one of the highlights of summer. The traditional royal *pau* riders (women dressed in long skirts) include a queen and princesses representing the major Hawaiian Islands. A cultural festival with live music and a *houlaulea* (local fundraiser) always follow on the historic grounds of Hulihee Palace, Hawaii Island's only royal palace. ✉ *Historic Kailua Village, Alii Dr., Kailua-Kona* ⊕ *www.konaparade.org* ⬤ *Free.*

★ Kona Brewers Festival

FESTIVALS | The lively festival showcases island-based brewers and chefs on the luau grounds of the Courtyard King Kamehameha's Kona Beach Hotel. A fashion show, live music, and community fundraisers are all part of the fun. Check the date and get tickets early online, as this event always sells out. ⊠ *Courtyard King Kamehameha's Kona Beach Hotel, 75-5660 Palani Rd., Kailua-Kona* ☎ *808/331–3033* ⊕ *www.konabrewersfestival.com.*

★ Kona Coffee Cultural Festival

FESTIVALS | Held over 10 days in early November, on the Kona side, the longest-running food festival in Hawaii celebrates world-renowned Kona coffee. The highly anticipated festival includes coffee contests, serious cupping (tasting) competitions, a lecture series, label contests, farm tours, and a colorful community parade featuring the newly crowned Miss Kona Coffee. During the Holualoa Village Coffee and Art Stroll, you can meet artists and sample estate coffees. ⊠ *Kailua-Kona* ☎ *808/323–2006* ⊕ *www.konacoffeefest.com.*

LUAU

Feast & Fire Luau at the Outrigger Kona Resort and Spa

CULTURAL FESTIVALS | On the graceful grounds of the Outrigger Kona Resort and Spa, this popular luau (Mondays and Thursdays) takes you on a journey of song and dance, celebrating the culture and history of the islands. The excellent buffet is a feast of local favorites, including *kalua* (earth oven–baked) pig, poi, ahi poke, chicken long rice, fish, and mango chutney. Generous mai tai refills are a plus, and a highlight is the dramatic fire-knife dance finale. ⊠ *Sheraton Kona Resort and Spa at Keauhou Bay, 78-128 Ehukai St., Kailua-Kona* ☎ *808/930–4900* ⊕ *outrigger.com* 🍽 *$160.*

Island Breeze Luau

CULTURAL FESTIVALS | With traditional dancing showcasing the interconnected Polynesian roots of Hawaii, Samoa, Tahiti, and New Zealand, the "We Are Ohana" luau is not a hokey, tourist-trap event; these performers take their art seriously, and it shows. The historic oceanfront location—on the Courtyard King Kamehameha's Kona Beach Hotel's luau grounds and directly next to the king's former royal compound and Ahuena Heiau—adds to the authenticity of the event, which takes place daily except Monday and Saturday. The bounty of food includes *kalua* (earth oven–baked) pig cooked. The hotel validates parking. ⊠ *75-5660 Palani Rd., Kailua-Kona* ☎ *866/482–9775* ⊕ *www.islandbreezeluau.com* 🍽 *$149.*

🛍 Shopping

ARTS AND CRAFTS

★ Hula Lamps of Hawaii

CRAFTS | Located near Costco in the Kaloko Light Industrial complex, this one-of-a-kind shop features the bronze creations of artist Charles Moore. Inspired by the vintage hula-girl lamps of the 1930s, Moore creates art pieces (both dancing and non-dancing) sought by visitors and residents alike. Mix and match with an array of hand-painted lampshades. ⊠ *73-5613 Olowalu St., Suite 2, Kailua-Kona* ⊹ *Near Costco on upper road* ☎ *808/326–9583* ⊕ *www.hulalamps.com.*

Just Ukes

MUSIC | As the name suggests, this place is all about ukuleles—from music books to T-shirts and accessories like cases and bags. The independently owned shop carries a variety of ukuleles ranging from low-priced starter instruments to high-end models made of koa and mango. ⊠ *Kona Inn Shopping Village, 75-5744 Alii Dr., Suite 187, Kailua-Kona* ☎ *808/769–5101* ⊕ *justukes.com.*

★ Kimura's Lauhala Shop

CRAFTS | Originally a general store built in 1914, this shop features handmade products crafted by local lauhala weavers, who use the leaves of the hala tree. Among the offerings are hats, baskets, containers, and mats, many of which are woven by the proprietors. Owner Alfreida Kimura-Fujita was born in the house behind the shop, and her daughter Renee is also an accomplished weaver. The shop is closed Sunday–Tuesday. ✉ *77-996 Hualalai Rd., Holualoa* ☎ *808/324–0053.*

CLOTHING AND SHOES
Mermaids Swimwear
WOMEN'S CLOTHING | Local residents know that Mermaids is one of the best places in Kona to buy fashion-forward ladies' swimwear, cover-ups, sandals, hats, sunglasses, and other stylish beach accessories. Although on the pricey side, the swimwear is mostly name brand and high quality. There's a beautiful selection of *pareau* (sarongs), which are island-style wraps in tropical prints and colors. The owner's husband, Tony, is a famous surfboard maker whose World Core surf shop is just around the corner. ✉ *Kona Inn Shopping Village, 75-5744 Alii Dr., Kailua-Kona* ☎ *808/329–6677.*

FOOD AND WINE
★ Kona Butcher Shop
FOOD | Locally sourced meats from all over the state are showcased at this specialty market owned by two former executive chefs. Lamb, chicken, venison, and dry-aged, grass-fed beef are among the gourmet offerings, along with imported fresh black truffles. The shop also hosts cutting classes, agriculture lectures, and cooking competitions. ✉ *Kopiko Plaza, Kailua-Kona* ☎ *808/796–6636* ⊕ *konabutchershop.com.*

★ Kona Wine Market
WINE/SPIRITS | Near Costco, this long-time local wine store carries both local and imported varietals (with more than 600 high-end wines), specialty liquors, champagnes, 150 craft beers, gourmet foods, and cigars. There are even some accessories for home brewers. As a bonus, the market delivers wine and gift baskets to hotels and homes, and it offers complimentary tastings Fridays from 3 to 6. ✉ *73-5613 Olowalu St., Kailua-Kona* ☎ *808/329–9400* ⊕ *www. konawinemarket.com.*

★ Mrs. Barry's Kona Cookies
FOOD | Since 1980, Mrs. Barry and her family have been serving yummy home-made cookies, including macadamia nut, white chocolate–macadamia nut, oatmeal raisin, and coffee crunch. Packaged in beautiful gift boxes or bags, the cookies make excellent gifts. She even makes cookies for the family dog. Stop by on your way to Costco or the airport and pick up a bag or two or three—or just ask Mrs. Barry to ship your stash instead. ✉ *73-5563 Maiau St., Kailua-Kona* ✛ *By Costco in the Kaloko Light Industrial Area* ☎ *808/329–6055* ⊕ *www.konacookies. com.*

★ Westside Wines
WINE/SPIRITS | Tucked away in a small downtown Kona retail center below Longs, this nifty gourmet wine and spirits shop offers restaurant-quality "wine list" wines at affordable prices. It's also the place to find large-format craft beers, Champagne from France, single-malt whiskies, organic vodka, small-batch bourbon, rye whiskey, fresh bread, and artisan cheeses from around the world. George Clooney's Casamigos tequila is the store's house tequila. A certified wine specialist, proprietor Alex Thropp was one of the state's top wholesale wine reps for decades. Wine tastings take place Friday and Saturday afternoons from 3 to 6. ✉ *75-5660 Kopiko St., #4, Kailua-Kona* ✛ *Below Longs Drugs in Kopiko Plaza* ☎ *808/329–1777.*

Continued on page 334

BIRTH OF THE ISLANDS

How did the volcanoes of the Hawaiian Islands come to be here, in the middle of the Pacific Ocean? The ancient Hawaiians believed that the volcano goddess Pele's hot temper was the key to the mystery; modern scientists contend that it's all about plate tectonics and one very hot spot.

Plate Tectonics and the Hawaiian Question: The theory of plate tectonics says that the Earth's surface is comprised of plates that float around slowly over the planet's hot interior. The vast majority of earthquakes and volcanic eruptions occur near plate boundaries—the San Francisco earthquakes in 1906 and 1989, for example, were the result of activity along the nearby San Andreas Fault, where the Pacific and North American plates meet. Hawaii, more than 1,988 miles from the nearest plate boundary, is a giant exception. For years scientists struggled to explain the island chain's existence—if not a fault line, what caused the earthquakes and volcanic eruptions that formed these islands?

What's a hot spot? In 1963, J. Tuzo Wilson, a Canadian geophysicist, argued that the Hawaiian volcanoes must have been created by small concentrated areas of extreme heat beneath the Pacific Plate. Wilson hypothesized that there is a hot spot beneath the present-day position of Hawaii Island (the "Big Island") and its heat produced a persistent source of magma. Magma is produced by rising-but-solid mantle rock that melts when it reaches about 100 km. At that depth, the lower pressure can no longer stop the rock from melting, and the magma rises to erupt onto the sea floor, forming an active seamount. Each flow caused the seamount to grow until it finally emerged above sea level as an island volcano. Plausible so far, but why then, is there not one giant Hawaiian island?

THE JOURNEY OF PELE

Holo Mai Pele, often told through hula, is the Hawaiian story of how volcano goddess Pele sends her sister Hiiaka on an epic quest from the Big Island to fetch her lover Lohiau, living on Kauai. Overcoming many obstacles, Hiiaka reaches full goddess status and falls in love with Lohiau herself. When Pele finds out, she destroys everything dear to her sister, killing Lohiau and burning her sister's ohia groves. Each time lava flows from a volcano, ohia trees sprout shortly after, in a constant cycle of destruction and renewal.

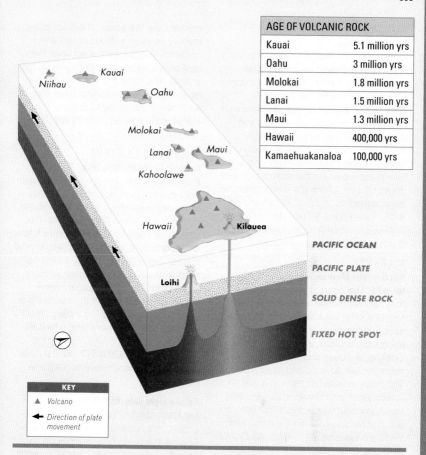

AGE OF VOLCANIC ROCK	
Kauai	5.1 million yrs
Oahu	3 million yrs
Molokai	1.8 million yrs
Lanai	1.5 million yrs
Maui	1.3 million yrs
Hawaii	400,000 yrs
Kamaehuakanaloa	100,000 yrs

PACIFIC OCEAN

PACIFIC PLATE

SOLID DENSE ROCK

FIXED HOT SPOT

KEY

▲ Volcano

◄ Direction of plate movement

Volcanoes on the Move: Wilson further suggested that the movement of the Pacific Plate itself eventually carries the island volcano beyond the hot spot. Cut off from its magma source, the island volcano becomes dormant. As the plate slowly moved to the northwest, one island volcano would become extinct just as another would develop over the hot spot. After several million years, there is a long volcanic trail of islands and seamounts across the ocean floor. The oldest islands are those farthest from the hot spot. The exposed rocks of Kauai, for example, are about 5.1 million years old, but those on the Big Island are less than half a million years old, with new volcanic rock still being formed.

An Island on the Way: Off the coast of the Big Island of Hawaii, another volcano is still submerged but erupting. Geologists long believed it to be a retired seamount volcano, but in the 1970s they discovered both old and new lava on its flanks, and in 1996 it erupted with a vengeance. It is believed that thousands of generations from now, it will be the newest addition to the Hawaiian archipelago, so in July 2021 was given the name Kamaehuakanaloa, "the red child of Kanaloa."

HOUSEWARES
The Spoon Shop
HOUSEWARES | Williams-Sonoma has nothing on this excellent gourmet kitchenware store that brims with every manner of accoutrement for the avid cook. There's also a great selection of gourmet seasonings, olive oils, dressings, and condiments. If you're planning a party, the Spoon Shop has items for every occasion. Cooking classes with guest chefs take place weekly in the store's high-end demo kitchen; check the website for the latest schedule. ⊠ 73-4976 Kamanu St., #105, Kailua-Kona ✛ Near Home Depot in New Industrial Area ☎ 808/887–7666 ⊕ www.thespoonshopkona.com.

MARKETS
Alii Gardens Marketplace
MARKET | The outdoor stalls at this mellow, parklike market, open daily except Monday, offer tropical flowers, produce, soaps, kettle corn, coffee, coconut postcards, cookies, jewelry, koa wood, clothing, antiques and collectibles, handmade lei, silk flowers, and kitschy crafts. The made on-site barbecue is a real hit. A food kiosk also serves shave ice, fish tacos, coconut water, fresh-fruit smoothies, and hamburgers. Free parking and Wi-Fi are available. ⊠ 75-6129 Alii Dr., Kailua-Kona ✛ 1½ miles south of Kona Inn Shopping Village ☎ 808/937–8844.

Keauhou Farmers Market
MARKET | FAMILY | Held in the parking lot at Keauhou Shopping Center, this cheerful market is the place to go on Saturday morning for live music, local produce (much of it organic), goat cheese, honey, island-raised meat, flowers, macadamia nuts, fresh-baked pastries, Kona coffee, and plenty of local color. ⊠ Keauhou Shopping Center, 78-6831 Alii Dr., Kailua-Kona ⊕ www.keauhoufarmersmarket.com.

Kona Farmers' Market
MARKET | FAMILY | An awesome flower vendor creates custom arrangements while you wait at this touristy farmers' market near the ocean. There are more than 40 vendors with souvenirs and crafts for sale, as well as some of the best prices on fresh produce and orchids in Kona. The market is held in a parking lot at the corner of Hualalai Road and Alii Drive, Wednesday to Sunday 7 to 4. Parking is free. ⊠ 75-7544 Alii Dr., Kailua-Kona.

SHOPPING CENTERS
Coconut Grove Marketplace
SHOPPING CENTER | The meandering oceanfront marketplace includes gift shops, cafés, restaurants (Outback Steakhouse, Humpy's Big Island Alehouse, Thai Rin, Lava Java, Foster's Kitchen, Fumi's Kitchen), sports bars, sushi, boutiques, crystal stores, Jack's Diving Locker, a running shop, and several art galleries. At night, locals gather to watch outdoor sand volleyball games held in the courtyard or grab a beer and enjoy live music. Directly adjacent is Ali'i Sunset Plaza, which is served by the same large parking lot. ⊠ 75-5795–75-5825 Alii Dr., Kailua-Kona ⊕ www.thecoconutgrovemarketplace.com.

Kaloko Light Industrial Park
SHOPPING CENTER | Located south of the airport, this large retail complex includes Costco, the best place to stock up on food if you're staying at a vacation rental. Kona Wine Market and the Spoon Shop feature gourmet finds, and Mrs. Barry's Kona Cookies sells beautifully packaged, delicious "souvenirs." ⊠ Off Hwy. 19 and Hina Lani St., Kailua-Kona ✛ Near Kona airport.

Keauhou Shopping Center
SHOPPING CENTER | About 5 miles south of Kailua Village, this neighborhood shopping center includes KTA Superstore, Longs Drugs, Kona Stories bookstore, and a multiplex movie theater. Kenichi Pacific, an upscale sushi restaurant, and Peaberry & Galette, a café that serves excellent crepes, are favorite eateries, joined by Bianelli's Pizza and Sam Choy's Kai Lanai, which is perched above the

center. You can also grab a quick bite at Los Habaneros, Subway, or L&L Hawaiian Barbecue. ⊠ *78-6831 Alii Dr., Kailua-Kona* ☎ *808/322–3000* ⊕ *www.keauhoushoppingcenter.com.*

Kona Commons

SHOPPING CENTER | This downtown center features a Ross Dress for Less (for suitcases, shoes, swimsuits, and aloha wear) and Hawaiian Island Creations (for a great selection of surf gear, clothing, and accessories). There's also an Old Navy and Office Max and a number of other smaller clothing retailers. Food and drink options include fast-food standbys like Dairy Queen, Subway, and Panda Express, as well as Ultimate Burger, for local beef and delicious house-made fries, and Genki Sushi, where the goods are delivered via conveyor belt. ■ TIP➔ **Across the street, Target has fresh-flower lei for a fraction of the cost of local florists.** ⊠ *75-5450 Makala Blvd., Kailua-Kona* ⊕ *www.konacommons.com.*

Kona Inn Shopping Village

SHOPPING CENTER | Originally a hotel, the Kona Inn was built in 1928 to woo a new wave of wealthy travelers. As newer condos and resorts opened along the Kona and Kohala Coasts, it was transformed into a low-rise, outdoor shopping village with shops and island-style eateries. Although quite a few longtime shops did not survive the pandemic, new ones are expected to take their place. Broad lawns with coconut trees on the ocean side provide a lovely setting for an afternoon picnic. The iconic Kona Inn is best for drinks and appetizers. ⊠ *75-5744 Alii Dr., Kailua-Kona.*

South Kona

Kealakekua is 14 miles south of Kailua-Kona.

Between its coffee plantations, artsy havens, and Kealakekua Bay—one of the most beautiful spots on the Big Island—South Kona has plenty of activities to occupy a day. Bring a swimsuit and snorkel gear, and hit Kealakekua Bay first thing in the morning. You'll beat the crowds, have a better chance of a dolphin sighting, and see more fish. After a morning of swimming or kayaking, head to one of the homey cafés in nearby Captain Cook to refuel.

The meandering road leading to Kealakekua Bay is home to a historic painted church, as well as coffee-tasting spots and several reasonably priced B&Bs with great views. The communities surrounding the bay (Kealakekua and Captain Cook) are brimming with local and transplanted artists. These towns are great places to shop for gifts or antiques, have some coffee, or take an afternoon stroll.

Several coffee farms around the Kona coffee-belt area welcome visitors to watch all or part of the coffee-production process, from harvest to packaging. Some tours are self-guided and many are free, with the exception of the Kona Coffee Living History Farm.

GETTING HERE AND AROUND

To get to Kealakekua Bay, follow the signs off Highway 11 and park at Napoopoo Beach Park. It's not much of a beach (it used to be before Hurricane Iniki washed it away in 1992), but it provides access into the water. Use caution if waters are rough; it can be difficult to exit the water due to the boulders.

◉ Sights

★ Captain James Cook Monument

MONUMENT | On February 14, 1779, famed English explorer Captain James Cook was killed here during an apparent misunderstanding with local residents, and this 27-foot-high obelisk marks the spot where he died. He had chosen Kealakekua Bay as a landing place in November 1778. Arriving during the celebration of Makahiki, the harvest

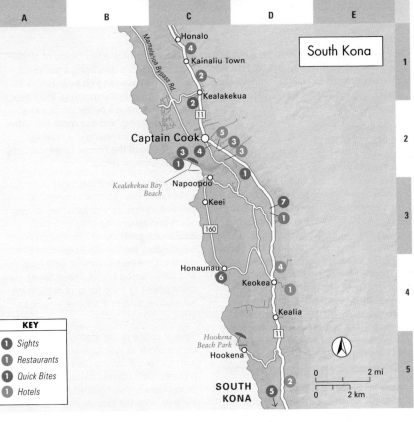

South Kona

KEY
- **1** Sights
- **1** Restaurants
- **1** Quick Bites
- **1** Hotels

0 ___ 2 mi
0 ___ 2 km

SOUTH KONA

Sights ▼
1 Captain James Cook Monument................ **C2**
2 Greenwell Farms......... **C2**
3 Kealakekua Bay State Historical Park **C2**
4 Kona Coffee Living History Farm **C2**
5 Kona RainForest Farms..................... **D5**
6 Puuhonua O Honaunau National Historical Park **C4**
7 Royal Kona Coffee Center and Coffee Mill............... **D3**

Restaurants ▼
1 Kaaloa's Super J's Authentic Hawaiian Food **D3**
2 Keei Cafe at Hokukano................ **C1**
3 Manago Hotel Restaurant................ **C2**
4 Teshima's Restaurant............... **C1**

Quick Bites ▼
1 The Coffee Shack **D2**

Hotels ▼
1 Aloha Guest House..... **D4**
2 Horizon Guest House... **D5**
3 Kaawa Loa Plantation................ **C2**
4 Kane Plantation Guesthouse............. **D4**
5 Manago Hotel........... **C2**

Kealakekua Bay is generally considered the best snorkeling spot on the Big Island.

season, Cook was welcomed at first. Some Hawaiians saw him as an incarnation of the god Lono. Cook's party sailed away in February 1779, but a freak storm forced his damaged ship back to Kealakekua Bay. Believing that no god could be thwarted by a mere rainstorm, the Hawaiians were not so welcoming this time. The theft of a longboat brought Cook and an armed party ashore to reclaim it. Shots were fired, daggers and spears were thrown, and Captain Cook fell, mortally wounded. A white obelisk monument to the man is located at Kaawaloa, at the north end of the bay. ✉ *Captain Cook.*

★ Greenwell Farms
FARM/RANCH | FAMILY | Depending on the season, the 20-minute walking tour of this working farm takes in various stages of coffee production, including a look at the 100-year-old coffee trees. The Greenwell family played a significant role in the cultivation of the first commercial coffee in the Kona area (as well as the first grocery store). No reservations are required,

unless you are booking for a private party, which does have a cost. Sample a cup of their famous Kona coffee at the end; the gift shop stays open until 5. ✉ *81-6581 Mamalahoa Hwy., Kealakekua* ⊕ *Ocean side, between mile markers 112 and 111* ☎ *808/323–2295* ⊕ *www.greenwell-farms.com* ✉ *Free.*

★ Kealakekua Bay State Historical Park
STATE/PROVINCIAL PARK | One of the most beautiful spots in the state, this underwater marine reserve has dramatic cliffs that surround super deep, crystal clear, turquoise water chock-full of stunning coral pinnacles and tropical fish. The protected dolphins that frequent the sanctuary should not be disturbed, as they use the bay to sleep and escape predators. There's very little sand at west-facing Napoopoo Beach, but this is a nice place to enter the water and swim (when the water is calm) as it's well protected from currents. At times, you may feel tiny jellyfish stings. There are no lifeguards, but there are bathrooms, a pavilion, shower, and (limited) parking. The Captain James

Cook Monument, marking where the explorer died, is at the northern edge of the bay. Stay at least 300 feet from the shoreline along the cliffs, which have become unstable during recent earthquakes. A limited number of tour operators offer snorkeling and kayaking tours here, a good and very popular option. ⊠ *Beach Rd., off Government Rd. from Puuhonua Rd. (Hwy. 160), Captain Cook* ⊕ *dlnr.hawaii.gov/dsp* 🖃 *Free.*

★ Kona Coffee Living History Farm

FARM/RANCH | On the National Register of Historic Places, this perfectly preserved farm was completely restored by the Kona Historical Society. It includes a 1913 farmhouse first homesteaded by the Uchida family and is surrounded by coffee trees, a Japanese bathhouse, a *kuriba* (coffee-processing mill), and a *hoshidana* (traditional drying platform). Caretakers still grow, harvest, roast, and sell the coffee exactly as they did more than 100 years ago. All admission proceeds directly help the nonprofit's educational efforts. ■**TIP**➔ **Call ahead to confirm hours, as they have been limited and varied.** ⊠ *82-6199 Mamalahoa Hwy., mile marker 110, Captain Cook* 🕿 *808/323–2006* ⊕ *www.konahistorical. org* 🖃 *$20* ⊗ *Closed weekends.*

Kona RainForest Farms

FARM/RANCH | At this family-owned business, the commitment to growing 100% organic coffee starts even before the plants are in the ground, with organic mulch and naturally developed fertilizers that they also sell throughout Hawaii. No pesticides or commercial fertilizers are used on the 80-acre farm. Because it's such an exacting process, only 2% of Kona coffee can claim to be 100% certified organic. They process coffee from cherry to roasted on a solar-powered mill. The farm does private tours (with tastings) by appointment only and even offers a guesthouse should you wish to stay a little longer than a day. At this writing, plans are under way for building a

visitor center in 2022. ■**TIP**➔ **The property can be accessed only by four-wheel-drive vehicles.** ⊠ *87-2854 Mamalahoa Hwy., Captain Cook* 🕿 *808/328–1941* ⊕ *www. mawahocoffee.com* 🖃 *Free* ⊗ *Tours by appointment only.*

★ Puuhonua O Honaunau National Historical Park (*Place of Refuge*)

NATIONAL PARK | The 420-acre National Historical Park has the best preserved *puuhonua* (place of refuge) in the state, and an aura of ancient sacredness and serenity still imbues the place. Providing a safe haven for noncombatants, *kapu* (taboo) breakers, defeated warriors, and others, the *puuhonua* offered protection and redemption for anyone who could reach its boundaries, by land or sea. The oceanfront, 960-foot stone wall built over 400 years ago still stands and is one of the park's most prominent features. A number of ceremonial temples, including the restored Hale o Keawe Heiau (circa 1700), have served as royal burial chambers. Bring a picnic to the back of the park, where there are tables and bathrooms. ⊠ *Rte. 160, Honaunau* ⊕ *About 20 miles south of Kailua-Kona* 🕿 *808/328–2288* ⊕ *www.nps.gov/puho* 🖃 *$20 per vehicle.*

Royal Kona Coffee Center and Coffee Mill

FACTORY | Come here to learn how growers create the perfect cup of Kona coffee through a multilayered process, with coffee cherries getting pulped, sorted, and dried in preparation for roasting, both by hand and with machinery. Take an easy, self-guided tour of this mill by following the descriptive plaques around the property. Then stop off at the coffee center to see coffee-making relics, peruse the gift shop, and watch an informational film. Visitors can also enjoy the beautiful views and stroll through a real lava tube on the grounds. ⊠ *83-5427 Mamalahoa Hwy., Captain Cook* ⊕ *Next to the tree house* 🕿 *808/328–2511* ⊕ *www. royalkonacoffee.com* 🖃 *Free* ⊗ *Closed weekends.*

Kona Coffee

The Kona coffee belt, some 16 miles long and about a mile wide, has been producing smooth, aromatic coffee for more than a century. The slopes of massive Mauna Loa at this elevation provide the ideal conditions for growing coffee: sunny mornings; cloudy, rainy afternoons; and rich, rocky, volcanic soil. More than 600 farms, most just 3 to 7 acres in size, grow the delicious—and luxurious, at generally more than $40 per pound—gourmet beans. Only coffee from the North and South Kona districts can be called Kona (labeling requirements are strict and fiercely defended), and Hawaii is the only state in the United States that produces commercially grown coffee.

The caffeine goodness began in 1828, when the Reverend Samuel Ruggles, an American missionary, brought a cutting over from the Oahu farm of Chief Boki, Oahu's governor. That coffee plant was a strain of Ethiopian coffee called Arabica, which is still produced today, although a Guatemalan strain of Arabica introduced in the late 1800s is produced in far higher quantities.

In the early 1900s, the large Hawaiian coffee plantations subdivided their lots and began leasing parcels to local tenant farmers, a practice that continues today. Many tenant farmers were Japanese families. In the 1930s, local schools switched summer vacation to "coffee vacation," August to November, so that children could help with the coffee harvest, a practice that held until 1969.

When coffee trees are flowering, the white blossoms are fondly known as "Kona snow." Once ripened, coffee is harvested as "cherries"—beans encased in a sweet, red shell. Kona coffee trees are handpicked several times each season to guarantee the ripest product. The cherries are shelled, their parchment layer sun-dried and removed, and the beans roasted to perfection. Today most farms—owned and operated by Japanese-American families, West Coast mainland transplants, and descendants of Portuguese and Chinese immigrants—control production from cultivation to cup.

🏖 Beaches

★ Kealakekua Bay Beach

BEACH | Gorgeous and undeveloped, this area in the state historical park offers extraordinary vistas and protected swimming. The shoreline is rocky, but the area is surrounded by high green cliffs, creating calm conditions for superb swimming, snorkeling, and diving (beware of jellyfish). Protected Hawaiian spinner dolphins come to rest and escape predators during the day. Captain James Cook first landed in Hawaii here in 1778, but a year later he was killed in a skirmish with Hawaiians, now marked by a monument on the bay's north end. Rocky but walkable trails lead to Hikiau Heiau, a sacred place for the Hawaiian people. Please proceed respectfully and do not walk on it or enter it. Parking is very limited. Be aware of the off-limits area (in case of rockfalls) marked by orange buoys. **Amenities:** parking (no fee); showers; toilets. **Best for:** snorkeling; swimming. ⊠ *Kealakekua Bay State Historical Park, Napoopoo Rd. off Hwy. 11, just south of mile marker 111, Kealakekua* ☎ *808/961–9544* ⊕ *dlnr.hawaii.gov/dsp* 🆓 *Free.*

🍴 Restaurants

★ Kaaloa's Super J's Authentic Hawaiian Food

$ | **HAWAIIAN** | It figures that the best *laulau* (pork or chicken wrapped in taro leaves and steamed) in West Hawaii can be found at a roadside hole-in-the-wall rather than at an expensive resort luau; in fact, this humble family-run eatery was featured on the Food Network's *The Best Thing I Ever Ate*. Plate lunches to go include tender chicken or pork *laulau*, steamed for up to 10 hours. **Known for:** friendly and welcoming proprietors; lomilomi salmon; tasty kalua pig and cabbage. [$] *Average main: $9* ✉ *83-5409 Mamalahoa Hwy., between mile markers 106 and 107, Honaunau* ☎ *808/328–9566* 🕓 *Closed Sun.*

Keei Cafe at Hokukano

$$ | **ECLECTIC** | Just 20 minutes south of Kailua-Kona, this nicely appointed restaurant with a warm, woodsy vibe serves delicious dinners with Brazilian, Asian, and European flavors, highlighting fresh ingredients from local farmers. Favorites are the Brazilian seafood chowder or peanut-miso salad, followed by pasta primavera smothered with a basil-pesto sauce. **Known for:** live dinner music; cash-only place and reservations are essential; most upscale restaurant in South Kona. [$] *Average main: $20* ✉ *79-7511 Mamalahoa Hwy., Kealakekua* ✥ *½ mile south of Kainaliu* ☎ *808/322–9992* 💳 *No credit cards* 🕓 *Closed Sun. and Mon. No lunch.*

Manago Hotel Restaurant

$ | **HAWAIIAN** | **FAMILY** | The historic Manago Hotel is like a time warp, complete with a vintage neon sign, TV room, and old photos. T-shirts brag (and it's not false advertising) that the restaurant has the best grilled pork chops in the world; the fresh fish and New York steak are excellent as well. **Known for:** mains come with a variety of side dishes; local hospitality; one of the only places in Kona serving opelu, a local fish. [$] *Average main: $12* ✉ *82-6155 Mamalahoa Hwy., Captain Cook* ☎ *808/323–2642* 🌐 *www.managohotel.com* 🕓 *Closed Mon.*

Hawaii Cherries 🍴

Don't scratch your head too much when you see signs advertising "cherries" as you drive around South Kona. They aren't about the cherries used in cherry pie; these signs refer to coffee cherries. Coffee beans straight off the tree are encased in fleshy, sweet red husks that make them look like bright little cherries. These husks are removed in the pulping process, and then the beans are sun-dried. Farmers who don't process their own can coffee sell 100-pound bags of just-picked cherries to the roasters.

Teshima's Restaurant

$ | **JAPANESE** | **FAMILY** | It doesn't look like much, either inside or out, but Teshima's has been a *kamaaina* (local) favorite since 1929 for a reason. Locals gather at this small landmark restaurant whenever they're in the mood for fresh sashimi, puffy shrimp tempura, or *hekka* (beef and vegetables cooked in an iron pot). **Known for:** long-standing family-owned establishment; authentic local flavor; excellent tempura combos. [$] *Average main: $15* ✉ *79-7251 Mamalahoa Hwy., Honalo* ☎ *808/322–9140* 🌐 *www.teshimarestaurant.com.*

☕ Coffee and Quick Bites

The Coffee Shack

$ | **AMERICAN** | Visitors enjoy stopping here before or after a morning of snorkeling at Kealakekua Bay, and for good reason: the views of the Honaunau Coast from this roadside restaurant are nothing short of drop-dead stunning. This place is best for breakfast or a quick bite, as overpriced mains can miss; but if you're in the mood for a Hawaiian smoothie, iced honey-mocha latte, or scone, it's worth the stop. **Known for:** its own brand of Kona coffee; popular spot with limited parking; house-baked luau bread. $ *Average main: $12* ✉ *83-5799 Mamalahoa Hwy., Captain Cook* ☎ *808/328–9555* 🌐 *www.coffeeshack.com* 🕒 *Closed Tues. and Wed.*

Hotels

Aloha Guest House

$$ | **B&B/INN** | In the hills above Puuhonua O Honaunau National Historical Park, this guesthouse offers quiet elegance, complete privacy, and beautiful ocean views from every room. **Pros:** eco-conscious option; delicious full breakfast; kitchenette in common area. **Cons:** 40 minutes from downtown; four-wheel drive recommended; remote location up a bumpy 1-mile dirt road. $ *Rooms from: $236* ✉ *Old Tobacco Rd., off Hwy. 11, near mile marker 104, Honaunau* ☎ *808/328–8955* 🌐 *www.alohaguesthouse.com* 🛏 *5 rooms* 🍴 *Free Breakfast.*

Horizon Guest House

$$$$ | **B&B/INN** | Surrounded by McCandeless Ranch on 40 acres in South Kona, this place may seem remote, but it's actually just a short drive from some of the best water attractions on the island, including Puuhonua O Honaunau, Kealakekua Bay, and Hookena Beach. **Pros:** private and quiet; heated pool with Jacuzzi; lovely ocean views. **Cons:** 40 minutes from Kailua-Kona; pricier option considering the location; not on the beach. $ *Rooms from: $375* ✉ *86-3992 Mamalahoa Hwy., between mile markers 101 and 100, Captain Cook* ☎ *808/938–7822* 🌐 *www.horizonguesthouse.com* 🛏 *4 suites* 🍴 *Free Breakfast.*

★ Kaawa Loa Plantation

$$ | **B&B/INN** | On a 5-acre coffee farm above Kealakekua Bay, proprietors Mike Martinage and Greg Nunn operate a grand yet very reasonably priced B&B in a home featuring a 2,000-square-foot wraparound veranda with excellent views of the bay and the entire Honaunau Coast. **Pros:** gracious and friendly hosts; excellent breakfast; Hawaiian steam room. **Cons:** some rooms share a bath; slightly steep turnoff; not within walking distance of bay. $ *Rooms from: $209* ✉ *82-5990 Napoopoo Rd., Captain Cook* ☎ *808/323–2686* 🌐 *www.kaawaloaplantation.com* 🛏 *5 rooms* 🍴 *Free Breakfast.*

Kane Plantation Guesthouse

$$$ | **B&B/INN** | The former home of the late, legendary artist Herb Kane, this luxury boutique guesthouse occupies a 16-acre avocado farm overlooking the South Kona coastline. **Pros:** sauna, hot tub, massage therapy room; upscale amenities; beautiful artwork. **Cons:** off the beaten track; 25 minutes to downtown; not on the beach. $ *Rooms from: $335* ✉ *84-1120 Telephone Exchange Rd., off Hwy. 11, Honaunau* ✥ *¼ mile past mile marker 105, south of Captain Cook* ☎ *808/328–2416* 🌐 *www.kaneplantationhawaii.com* 🛏 *3 suites* 🍴 *Free Breakfast.*

Manago Hotel

$ | **HOTEL** | If you are on a budget but still want to be close to the water and attractions like Kealakekua Bay and Puuhonua O Honaunau National Historical Park, this historical hotel is a good option. **Pros:** authentic local color; rock-bottom prices; terrific on-site restaurant. **Cons:** cheapest rooms share a community bath; some rooms have highway noise; not the best sound insulation between rooms. $ *Rooms from: $78* ✉ *81-6155 Mamalahoa Hwy., Captain Cook* ☎ *808/323–2642* 🌐 *www.managohotel.com* 🛏 *64 rooms* 🍴 *No Meals.*

ⓨ Nightlife

★ Korner Pocket

BARS | A favored haunt of the South Kona crowd, Korner Pocket is tucked in the back of an office plaza and looks like a dive at first glance. But don't let appearances fool you. They serve fantastic, affordable food, ranging from scrumptious burgers to a killer prime rib. Popular local bands frequently perform, with no cover, and everyone gets up to dance. You can also play pool. It's one of the only places open late down south. ⊠ *81-970 Halekii St., Kealakekua* ☎ *808/322–2994* ⊕ *kornerpocketkona.com.*

North Kona

The North Kona district is characterized by vast lava fields, dotted with turnoff points from Highway 19 leading to some of the most beautiful beaches in the world. Most lava flows here originate from the last eruptions of Hualalai, in 1800 and 1801, although some flows by the resorts (primarily Mauna Lani, to the north) hail from Mauna Loa. The stark black lavascapes contrast spectacularly with luminous azure waters framed by coconut palms and white-sand beaches. Some of the turnoffs will take you to state parks with parking lots and bathrooms, while others are simply a park-on-the-highway-and-hike-in adventure.

GETTING HERE AND AROUND

Head north from Kona International Airport and follow Highway 19 along the coast. Take caution driving at night between the airport and where resorts begin on the Kohala Coast; it's extremely dark, and there are few road signs or traffic lights on this two-lane road. Wild donkeys may appear on the roadway without warning.

⊙ Sights

★ Kaloko–Honokohau National Historical Park

NATIONAL PARK | FAMILY | The trails at this sheltered 1,160-acre coastal park near Honokohau Harbor, just north of Kailua-Kona, are popular with walkers and hikers, and it's a good place to observe Hawaiian archaeological history and intact ruins. These include a *heiau* (temple), house platforms, ancient fishponds, and numerous petroglyphs along a boardwalk. The park's wetlands provide refuge to waterbirds such as the endemic Hawaiian stilt and coot. Two beaches here are good for swimming, sunbathing, and sea turtle spotting: Aiopio, a few yards north of the harbor, is small and calm, with protected swimming areas (good for kids); Honokohau Beach, also north of the harbor, is a ¾-mile stretch with ruins of ancient fishponds. Of the park's three entrances, the middle one leads to a visitor center with helpful rangers and lots of information. Local docents with backgrounds in geology or other subjects give nature talks. To go directly to the beaches, take the harbor road north of the Gentry retail center, park in the gravel lot, and follow the signs. ⊠ *74–425 Kealakehe Pkwy., off Hwy. 19 near airport, Kailua-Kona* ✛ *3 miles south of Kona International Airport* ☎ *808/329–6881* ⊕ *www.nps.gov/kaho* ⊠ *Free.*

Mountain Thunder

FARM/RANCH | This coffee producer offers hourly "bean-to-cup" tours, including a tasting and access to the processing plant, which shows dry milling, sizing, coloring, sorting, and roasting. For $10, take the lava tube/nature walk in the cloud forest ecosystem. There's a small retail store where you can purchase coffee and souvenirs. Remember that afternoon rains are common at this elevation, so bring an umbrella and sturdy shoes. ⊠ *73-1944 Hao St., Kailua-Kona* ☎ *808/325–5566* ⊕ *www.mountainthunder.com* ⊠ *Free; nature walk $10.*

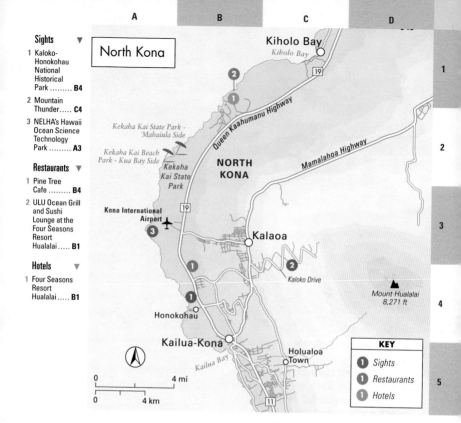

North Kona

Kiholo Bay
Kiholo Bay

19

*Kekaha Kai State Park -
Mahaiula Side*

*Kekaha Kai Beach
Park - Kua Bay Side*

*Kekaha
Kai State
Park*

**NORTH
KONA**

Queen Kaahumanu Highway

Mamalahoa Highway

19

**Kona International
Airport**

Kalaoa

Kaloko Drive

▲
*Mount Hualalai
8,271 ft*

Honokohau

Kailua-Kona

Kailua Bay

Holualoa
Town

11

0   4 mi
0   4 km

KEY

🔵 Sights

🔵 Restaurants

🔵 Hotels

★ NELHA's Hawaii Ocean Science Technology Park

OTHER ATTRACTION | Just south of Kona International Airport, a big building with a large photovoltaic (solar) panel installation resembles a top-secret military station, but it's actually the site of the Natural Energy Lab of Hawaii Authority's (NELHA) Hawaii Ocean Science Technology Park and worth a visit. Tours offered by the nonprofit Keahole Center for Sustainability, which helps administer the park, start with the innovative Gateway building and encompass the center's history, finishing with a visit to some of the park's tenants. Here, scientists, researchers, and entrepreneurs make use of a cold, deep-sea pipeline to develop and market everything from desalinated, mineral-rich drinking water and super-nutritious algae products to energy-efficient air-conditioning systems to environmentally friendly aquaculture techniques. Seahorses, abalone, *kampachi* (a type of yellowtail), Dungeness crab, and Maine lobsters are raised here, too. There's also a natural history tour that takes visitors along the shoreline to learn about seabirds, tide pool denizens, and other marine inhabitants. ✉ *73-4485 Kahilihili St., Kailua-Kona* ☎ *808/329–8073* ⊕ *kcshi.org* 💲 *$53* ☽ *Closed weekends.*

🏖 Beaches

Kekaha Kai State Park—Kua Bay Side

BEACH | **FAMILY** | On the northernmost stretch of the park's coastline, this lovely beach fronts an absolutely beautiful bay with crystal-clear, deep aquamarine water. It's peaceful in summer, but the park's paved entrance, amenities, and parking lot make the beach very accessible and, as a result, often crowded.

Beautiful Kua Bay in North Kona is known for its white sand and clear, aquamarine water.

Fine white sand sits in stark contrast to old black lava flows, and there's little shade—bring umbrellas. Rocky shores on either side protect the beach from afternoon winds and offer some fabulous snorkeling spots. Gates open daily from 8 to 7. In winter, surf can get rough, and often the sand washes away. **Amenities:** parking (no fee); showers; toilets. **Best for:** surfing; swimming. ✉ *Hwy. 19, north of mile marker 88, Kailua-Kona* ✣ *Across from Veterans Cemetery* ⊕ *dlnr.hawaii. gov/dsp* 🎫 *Free.*

★ Kekaha Kai State Park—Mahaiula Side

BEACH | It's slow going down a 1.8-mile, bumpy but partially paved road off Highway 19 to this beach park, but the lovely beaches are worth it when you reach the end. Very low-profile rentals may have some trouble making the drive. This state park encompasses three beaches: from south to north, Mahaiula, Makalawena, and Kua Bay, which has its own entrance. Mahaiula and Makalawena are classically beautiful expanses of white sand with dunes. Makalawena has great swimming

and bodyboarding. (Note: Makalawena, sandwiched between the two state parks, is private property and falls under the jurisdiction of Kamehameha Schools Bishop Estates.) Watch out for rough surf and strong currents. From Makalawena, a 4½-mile trail leads to Kua Bay. If you're game, work your way on foot to the top of Puu Kuili, a 342-foot-high cinder cone with a fantastic coastline view. But be prepared for the heat and bring water, as none is available. Gates at the highway entrance close promptly at 7, so you must leave the lot by about 6:30. **Amenities:** toilets. **Best for:** swimming. ✉ *Hwy. 19, Kailua-Kona* ✣ *Turnoff is about 2 miles north of Kona International Airport* ☎ *808/974–6200* ⊕ *dlnr.hawaii.gov/dsp* 🎫 *Free.*

🍴 Restaurants

Pine Tree Cafe

$ | **HAWAIIAN** | **FAMILY** | Named for a popular nearby surf spot, the low-key, no-frills café offers local plate lunch options and classics such as *loco moco* (meat, rice, and eggs smothered in gravy), alongside new inventions like crab curry bisque. The fresh-fish plate is decent, and all meals are served with fries or rice and macaroni salad. **Known for:** fresh fish; popular with locals; early-morning breakfast. $ *Average main: $12* ⊠ *Kohanaiki Plaza, 73-4354 Mamalahoa Hwy. (Hwy. 11), Kailua-Kona* ☎ *808/327–1234* ⊕ *pinetreecafehi.com.*

★ **ULU Ocean Grill and Sushi Lounge at the Four Seasons Resort Hualalai**

$$$$ | **MODERN HAWAIIAN** | Casual elegance takes center stage at the resort's flagship oceanfront restaurant, one of the most upscale restaurants on the Big Island. Breakfast can be à la carte or buffet, but nighttime is when the magic happens, with diverse menu choices—roasted beet salad, flame-grilled prime New York steak, Kona lobster, shrimp pad Thai, and more—that make deciding what to order a challenge. **Known for:** ingredients sourced from 160 local purveyors; impressive wine list; sushi lounge. $ *Average main: $45* ⊠ *Four Seasons Resort Hualalai, 72-100 Kaupulehu Dr., Kailua-Kona* ☎ *808/325–8000* ⊕ *www.fourseasons.com* ☻ *No lunch.*

 ## Hotels

★ **Four Seasons Resort Hualalai**

$$$$ | **RESORT** | **FAMILY** | Beautiful views everywhere, polished wood floors, custom furnishings and linens in warm earth and cool white tones, and Hawaiian fine artwork make this oceanfront resort a peaceful, luxurious retreat. **Pros:** beautiful location; gourmet restaurants; renowned service. **Cons:** quite pricey; 20-minute drive to Kailua-Kona; not the best beach among the resorts. $ *Rooms from: $1965* ⊠ *72-100 Kaupulehu Dr., Kailua-Kona* ☎ *808/325–8000, 888/340–5662* ⊕ *www.fourseasons.com/hualalai* ⇌ *243 rooms* ❏ *No Meals.*

The Kohala Coast and Waimea

If you had only a weekend to spend on the Big Island, this is probably where you'd want to be. The Kohala Coast is a mix of the island's best beaches and swankiest hotels, and it's also not far from ancient valleys and temples, waterfalls, and funky artist enclaves.

This area is home to almost all of the Big Island's megaresorts. Dotting the coastline are manicured lawns and golf courses, restaurants, and destination spas. But the real attraction here is the area's glorious beaches. On a clear day, you can see Maui, and during the winter months, numerous glistening humpback whales cleave the waters just offshore. Many visitors to the Big Island check in here and rarely leave the Kohala Coast. If you're looking to be pampered and lounge on the beach or by the pool all day with an umbrella drink in hand, this is where you need to be. You can still see the rest of the island since most of the hiking and adventure-tour companies offer pickups at the Kohala Coast resorts, and many hotels have connections to car rental agencies (though the number of cars is limited, and you will need to book ahead).

Rounding the northern tip of the island, the arid coast shifts rather suddenly to green villages and hillsides, leading to lush Pololu Valley in North Kohala, where the hot sunshine along the coast gives way to cooler temperatures. In this area are Hawi and Kapaau, quaint sugar-plantation towns turned artsy villages. New galleries are interspersed with charming reminders of old Hawaii—wooden boardwalks, quaint local storefronts, ice cream shops, delicious neighborhood restaurants, friendly locals, and a delightfully slow pace. There's great shopping for everything from antiques and designer beachwear to authentic Hawaiian crafts.

A short drive from the resorts, Waimea's upcountry, pastoral countryside is sprinkled with well-tended vintage homes with picket fences and flower beds. There's a gentle *paniolo* (Hawaiian cowboy) vibe throughout the town, which boasts a number of excellent restaurants worth seeking out.

GETTING HERE AND AROUND

Two days (or three, if your schedule allows) is sufficient time for experiencing each unique side of Kohala—one day for the resort perks, including the beach, the spa, the golf, and the restaurants; one day for hiking and admiring the waterfalls and valleys of North Kohala, coupled with a wander around Hawi and Kapaau. In addition, don't miss a quick drive up to explore the rustic town of Waimea, with its restaurants, galleries, and bucolic scenery.

The best way to explore the valleys of North Kohala is with a hiking tour. Look for one that includes lunch, maybe a zip line, and a dip in one of the area's waterfall pools.

While some resort guests enjoy staying at a single property for their entire trip, others appreciate having a rental car to sightsee and explore the island's wide diversity at their own pace. There are many rental options at the airport, but if you change your mind mid-trip and want to rent a car, the rental companies operate a satellite office from the Fairmont Orchid Hotel and one in Waikoloa Village.

VISITOR INFORMATION

CONTACTS North Kohala Welcome Center.
⊠ *55-3393 Akoni Pule Hwy., Hawi* ✛ *Just past the "Welcome to Kohala" sign* ☏ *808/889–5523* ⊕ *www.northkohala. org.*

Waikoloa

25 miles north of Ellison Onizuka Kona International Airport.

Waikoloa is a region known for its two large resort properties (one a bit outlandish), excellent golf, and eclectic shopping at both the Kings' Shops and Queens' MarketPlace. Sushi, local grills, food courts, small markets, and pricey restaurants all combine to give you abundant eating choices in Waikoloa. The natural gem here is the stunning, classically tropical Anaehoomalu Bay, once the site of royal fishponds and today an ideal spot to soak up some sun, explore along the trails, or try windsurfing. Waikoloa Village, a few miles inland and up the hill to the northeast, offers golf and rental condos for a fraction of the cost of the big resorts.

 Beaches

★ Anaehoomalu Bay

BEACH | FAMILY | This gorgeous, expansive stretch of white sand, fringed with coconut palms, fronts the Waikoloa Beach Marriott and is a perfect spot for swimming, windsurfing, snorkeling, and diving. Unlike some Kohala Coast beaches near hotel properties, this one is very accessible to the public and offers plenty of free parking. The bay is well protected, so even when the surf is rough or the trade winds are blasting, it's fairly calm here. (Mornings are calmest.) Snorkel gear, kayaks, and bodyboards are available for rent at the north end.

■ **TIP** → **Locals will appreciate your efforts to use the proper name rather than simply its nickname, "A-Bay."**

Behind the beach are two ancient Hawaiian fishponds, Kuualii and Kahapapa, that once served ancient Hawaiian royalty. A walking trail follows the coastline to the Hilton Waikoloa Village next door, passing by tide pools, ponds, and a turtle sanctuary where sea turtles can often be spotted sunbathing on the sand. Footwear is recommended for the trail. **Amenities:** food and drink; parking (no fee); showers; toilets; water sports. **Best for:** snorkeling; sunset; swimming; walking. ✉ *69-275 Waikoloa Beach Dr., Waikoloa* ✣ *Just south of Waikoloa Beach Marriott; turn left at Kings' Shops* 🎫 *Free.*

🍴 Restaurants

★ A-Bay's Island Grill
$ | MODERN HAWAIIAN | Beachy yet upscale, the restaurant has an in-house beer sommelier who advises on the perfect pairing with your food choice, which can range from fresh catch, steak, burgers, and sandwiches to crab cakes and escargots; many dishes incorporate Hawaiian touches. This sports bar offers a 24-tap digital beer tower and 10 TV screens. **Known for:** patio seating available; great tapas menu; fish tacos. [$] *Average main: $14* ✉ *Kings' Shops, 250 Waikoloa Beach Dr., Waikoloa* ☎ *808/209–8494* 🌐 *www.a-bays.com.*

KPC (Kamuela Provision Company) at the Hilton Waikoloa Village
$$$$ | MODERN HAWAIIAN | The breezy lanai has the most spectacular view of the leeward coast of any restaurant on the Big Island, and it's the perfect accompaniment to the elegant yet down-to-earth Hawaii Regional Cuisine and specialty cocktails. Entrées are on the pricey side, but the ginger-steamed *monchong* (a deep-water Hawaiian fish) is a winner, and the Keahole lobster chowder does not disappoint. **Known for:** the island's best sunset dinner spot; decadent Kona Coffee Mud Slide dessert; specialty cocktails, such as the Island Passion mango martini. [$] *Average main: $50* ✉ *Hilton Waikoloa Village, 69-425 Waikoloa Beach Dr., Waikoloa* ☎ *808/886–1234* 🌐 *www.hiltonwaikoloavillage.com* ⏲ *No lunch.*

★ Lava Lava Beach Club Restaurant
$$$ | HAWAIIAN | FAMILY | Dig your toes into the sand and enjoy one of the most happening, entertaining, and memorable bar/restaurants on the Kohala Coast. There's something for everybody here, whether you want cocktails and *pupus* (appetizers) for sunset or a fine-dining experience; highlights include Black Angus truffled New York steak and the chef's signature gazpacho topped with macadamia nut pesto. **Known for:** great Parmesan lava tots and coconut shrimp; signature Sandy Toes cocktail; live entertainment. [$] *Average main: $30* ✉ *69-1081 Kuualii Pl., Waikoloa* ☎ *808/769–5282* 🌐 *lavalavabeachclub.com/bigisland.*

Pueo's Osteria
$$$ | ITALIAN | Hidden in a shopping center in residential Waikoloa Village, this late-night destination serves dinner from 5 until 10 pm: *pueo* means "owl" in Hawaiian, and refers to the restaurant's "night owl" concept. Renowned executive chef James Babian (Four Seasons Hualalai, Fairmont Orchid) serves multiregional Italian offerings that combine farm-fresh ingredients with fine imported Italian products like prosciutto from Parma. **Known for:** late-night bar menu until 1 am; Tuscan-inspired dining room; Early Owl specials dinner daily from 5 to 6. [$] *Average main: $27* ✉ *Waikoloa Village Highlands Center, 68-1845 Waikoloa Rd., Waikoloa* ✣ *Near Subway* ☎ *808/339–7566* 🌐 *www.pueososteria.com* ⏲ *No lunch.*

Sansei Seafood Restaurant and Sushi Bar
$$ | JAPANESE | FAMILY | Creative sushi and contemporary Asian cuisine take center stage at this entertaining restaurant at Queens' MarketPlace, where you can make a meal out of appetizers and sushi rolls or feast on great entrées from both land and sea. Though it has tried-and-true mainstays, the menu is consistently updated to include options such as Hawaiian *moi* (a local fish)

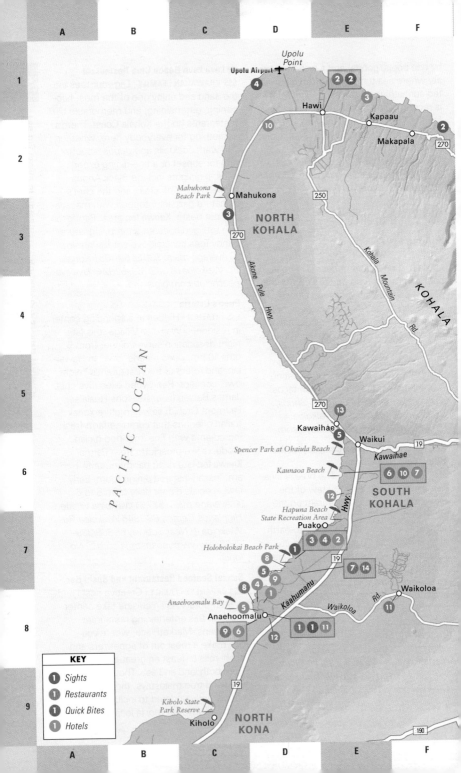

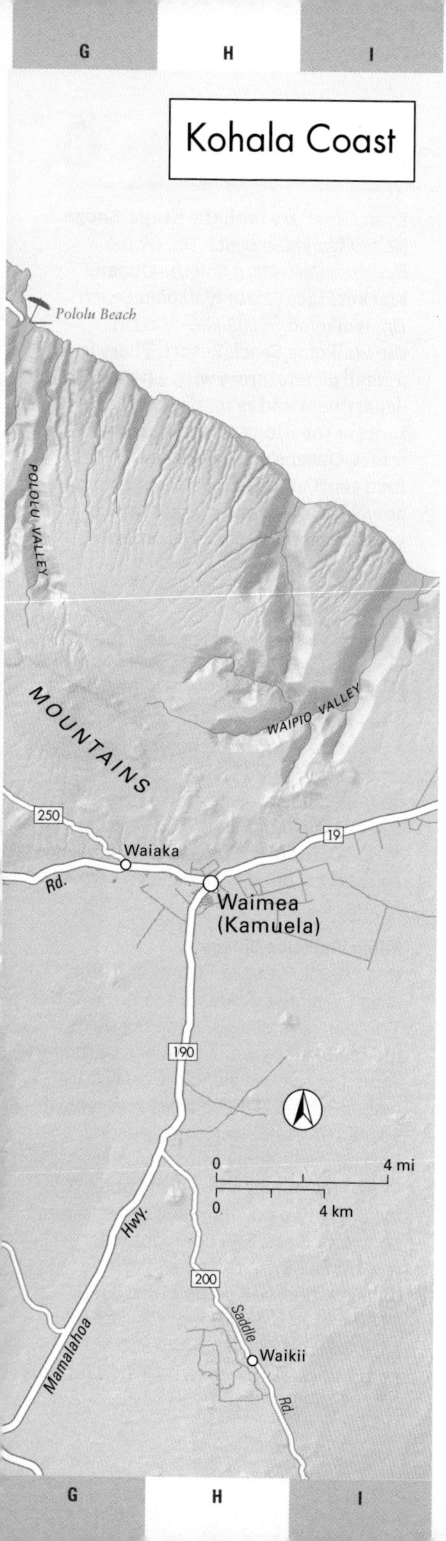

Kohala Coast

Sights ▼

1 Holoholokai Beach Park and Petroglyph Trail **D7**
2 Keokea Beach Park **F2**
3 Lapakahi State Historical Park **C3**
4 Mookini Heiau **D1**
5 Puukohola Heiau National Historic Site.... **E6**

Restaurants ▼

1 A-Bay's Island Grill **D8**
2 Bamboo Restaurant & Gallery **E1**
3 Binchotan Bar and Grill **D7**
4 Brown's Beach House at the Fairmont Orchid Hawaii **D7**
5 CanoeHouse at the Mauna Lani, Auberge Resorts Collection **D7**
6 Hau Tree **E6**
7 Knead & Bake **D7**
8 KPC (Kamuela Provision Company) at the Hilton Waikoloa Village **D8**
9 Lava Lava Beach Club Restaurant **D8**
10 Manta at the Mauna Kea Beach Hotel **E6**
11 Pueo's Osteria **F8**
12 Sansei Seafood Restaurant and Sushi Bar **D8**
13 Seafood Bar and Grill **E5**
14 Tommy Bahama Restaurant and Bar..... **D7**

Quick Bites ▼

1 Island Fish and Chips... **D8**
2 Kohala Coffee Mill and Tropical Dreams **E2**

Hotels ▼

1 Aston Shores at Waikoloa **D8**
2 Fairmont Orchid Hawaii **D7**
3 Hawaii Island Retreat at Ahu Pohaku Hoomaluhia **E1**
4 Hilton Waikoloa Village **D8**
5 Kolea at Waikoloa Beach Resort **D8**
6 Lava Lava Beach Club Cottages **D8**
7 Mauna Kea Beach Hotel, Autograph Collection.... **E6**
8 Mauna Lani, Auberge Resorts Collection **D7**
9 Mauna Lani Point and the Islands at Mauna Lani **D7**
10 Puakea Ranch **D2**
11 Waikoloa Beach Marriott Resort and Spa **D8**
12 The Westin Hapuna Beach Resort **E6**

Pololu Beach

POLOLU VALLEY

MOUNTAINS

WAIPIO VALLEY

250

19

Waiaka

Rd.

Waimea (Kamuela)

190

0   4 mi
0   4 km

200

Saddle

Waikii

Rd.

Hwy.

Mamalahoa

Kohala Condo Comforts

Renting a resort condo is a great way to relax near the beach with many of the comforts of home. The upside is that you get all the pluses of being near a resort with all the privacy of your own place. Most condos have kitchens or a place to barbecue, so you'll want to stock up on groceries. The nearest full-service market is **KTA Super Stores** (✉ *68-3916 Paniolo Ave., Waikoloa Village* ☎ *808/883–1088*), no more than a half hour from the resorts.

Even closer are both the **Kings' Shops** (✉ *250 Waikoloa Beach Dr., Waikoloa* ☎ *808/886–8811*) and the **Queens' MarketPlace** (✉ *201 Waikoloa Beach Dr., Waikoloa* ☎ *808/886–8822*) in the Waikoloa Beach Resort. There is a small general store with a liquor department and several nice restaurants at the Kings' Shops. Across the street, Queens' MarketPlace also has a food court and sit-down restaurants, as well as a gourmet market where you can get pizza baked to order.

---

sashimi rolls and Japanese yellowtail nori aioli poke. **Known for:** panko-encrusted ahi sashimi roll; karaoke on the weekends; sushi bar specials. $ *Average main: $20* ✉ *Queens' MarketPlace, 201 Waikoloa Beach Dr., Suite 801, Waikoloa* ☎ *808/886–6286* ⊕ *www.sanseihawaii.com* ☺ *No lunch.*

Coffee and Quick Bites

Island Fish and Chips
$ | **AMERICAN** | **FAMILY** | Hidden lakeside at the Kings' Shops, this little takeout place is a best-kept secret in the Waikoloa Beach Resort. The combo baskets brim with tempura fresh-catch fish, chicken, shrimp, and more. **Known for:** local ownership since 2000; great fish-and-chips to go; breakfast options such as loco moco (meat, rice, and eggs smothered in gravy), laden with tempura fish fillet. $ *Average main: $12* ✉ *Kings' Shops, 69-250 Waikoloa Beach Dr., #D3, Waikoloa* ☎ *808/886–0005.*

🛏 Hotels

Aston Shores at Waikoloa
$$ | **RESORT** | **FAMILY** | Villas with terra-cotta–tile roofs are set amid landscaped lagoons and waterfalls at the edge of the championship Waikoloa Village Golf Course. **Pros:** good prices for the area; great location; kid-friendly option with a pool and in-room kitchens. **Cons:** daily resort fee; older decor in some rooms; no restaurants on-site. $ *Rooms from: $247* ✉ *69-1035 Keana Pl., Waikoloa* ☎ *808/886–5001, 800/922–7866* ⊕ *www.aquaaston.com* ☞ *120 suites* ❍| *No Meals.*

Hilton Waikoloa Village
$$$$ | **RESORT** | **FAMILY** | Gondola trams glide by, pint-size guests zoom down the 175-foot waterslide, a bride poses on the grand staircase, a fire-bearing runner lights the torches along the seaside path at sunset—these are some typical scenes at this 62-acre megaresort. **Pros:** family-friendly saltwater lagoon; lots of restaurant and activity options, including two golf courses; close to retail shopping. **Cons:** $45 per night resort fee; restaurants are pricey; gigantic and crowded. $ *Rooms from: $690* ✉ *69-425 Waikoloa Beach Dr., Waikoloa* ☎ *808/886–1234, 800/445–8667* ⊕ *www.hiltonwaikoloavillage.com* ☞ *1,241 rooms* ❍| *No Meals.*

★ Kolea at Waikoloa Beach Resort

$$$$ | RESORT | FAMILY | These modern, impeccably furnished condos offer far more high-end amenities than the average condo complex, including both an infinity pool and a sand-bottom children's pool at its oceanside Beach Club, a fitness center, and a hot tub. **Pros:** can walk to beach; close to activities; resort amenities of nearby Hilton. **Cons:** no on-property restaurants; limited view from some units; pricey for not being directly on the beach. $ *Rooms from: $496 ⊠ Waikoloa Beach Resort, 69-1000 Kolea Kai Circle, Waikoloa ☎ 808/987–4519 ⊕ www.kolea. com ⊐ 53 units* ❍| *No Meals.*

★ Lava Lava Beach Club Cottages

$$$$ | HOUSE | FAMILY | Spend the day swimming at the beach just steps away from your private lanai and fall asleep to the sound of the ocean at one of four artfully decorated, one-room cottages on the sandy beach at Anaehoomalu Bay. These cottages are among the few beachfront rentals you will find anywhere on the island. **Pros:** one of the island's few beachfront rentals; fully air-conditioned; fun, Hawaii-themed decor. **Cons:** quite expensive; often booked up; beach is public, so there may be people in front of cottage. $ *Rooms from: $595 ⊠ 69-1081 Kuualii Pl., Waikoloa ☎ 808/769–5282 ⊕ www.lavalavabeachclub.com ⊐ 4 cottages* ❍| *No Meals.*

Waikoloa Beach Marriott Resort and Spa

$$$$ | RESORT | FAMILY | Encompassing 15 acres replete with ancient fishponds, historic trails, and petroglyph fields, the Marriott has rooms with sleek modern beds, bright white linens, Hawaiian art, and private lanai. **Pros:** more low-key than the Hilton Waikoloa; sunset luau Wednesday and Saturday; sand-bottom pool for kids. **Cons:** expensive daily parking charge; resort fee of $30 per day; some rooms lack views. $ *Rooms from: $693 ⊠ 69-275 Waikoloa Beach Dr., Waikoloa ☎ 808/886–6789, 800/228–9290 ⊕ www. marriott.com ⊐ 297 rooms* ❍| *No Meals.*

🎭 Performing Arts

LUAU

Legends of Hawaii Luau at Hilton Waikoloa Village

CULTURAL FESTIVALS | FAMILY | Presented outdoors at the Kamehameha Court, the aptly subtitled "Our Big Island Story" features song and a fire-knife dance as well as a delicious buffet with Big Island–grown luau choices and more familiar fare and tropical drinks. Pay a small fee and upgrade to Alii seating for a front-row vantage; unlimited cocktails, beer, and wine; and your own buffet station. A children's station has kid favorites. Delicious desserts such as *haupia* (with coconut milk) cream puffs and Kona-coffee cheesecake top it all off. ⊠ *Hilton Waikoloa Village, 69-425 Waikoloa Beach Dr., Waikoloa ☎ 808/886–1234 ⊕ www. hiltonwaikoloavillage.com/luau ⊒ $146.*

Waikoloa Beach Marriott Resort and Spa Sunset Luau

CULTURAL FESTIVALS | In a setting overlooking the white sands of Anaehoomalu Bay, this Polynesian luau includes a spectacular Samoan fire-dance performance as well as traditional music and dances from Pacific Island cultures. Making use of island ingredients such as Waipio Valley poi and Keahole shrimp, Pulehu steaks, the menu by executive chef Jayson Kanekoa treats guests to authentic island flavors. There's also an open bar. ⊠ *Waikoloa Beach Marriott Resort and Spa, 69-275 Waikoloa Beach Dr., Waikoloa ☎ 808/886–8111 ⊕ www. waikoloabeachresort.com ⊒ $173.*

🛍 Shopping

ARTS AND CRAFTS

Hawaiian Quilt Collection

CRAFTS | The Hawaiian quilt is a work of art that is prized and passed down through generations. At this store, the oldest quilt retailer in Hawaii, you'll find everything from hand-quilted purses and bags to wall hangings and blankets.

Hawaiian Music on the Big Island

It's easy to forget that Hawaii has its own style of music until you step off a plane onto the Islands—and then there's no escaping it. It's a unique blend of the strings and percussion imported by early Portuguese settlers and the chants and rituals of the ancient Hawaiians, reflecting the unique mixed heritage of this special place. Hawaiian music today includes Island-born tunings of acoustic guitar—slack key and steel guitar—along with the ukulele and vocals.

This is one of the few folk music traditions in the United States that is fully embraced by the younger generation, with no prodding from their parents or grandparents. A good many radio stations on the Big Island play Hawaiian/"island"/reggae music, and concerts performed by Island favorites like Makana or L. T. Smooth are filled with fans of all ages.

The best introduction is one of the annual festivals: the free **Hawaiian Slack Key Guitar Festival** (Labor Day weekend), with a handful of greats performing at the Outrigger Kona Resort and Spa; the **Great Waikoloa Ukulele Festival** (March), which features prominent players and everything ukulele; and the **KWXX Hoolaulea** (September), a popular Island music jam with big names performing on four stages in downtown Hilo.

You can also catch live performances most nights at a handful of local bars and clubs, including **Big Kahuna, Huggo's on the Rocks, Laverne's**, and the **Kona Brewing Co.** in Kailua-Kona; **Korner Pocket** in Kealakekua; and **Cronies Bar and Grill** in Hilo.

More than likely, a friendly Hawaiian *tutu* (grandma) will be in the shop talking story. You can even get a take-home kit and sew your own Hawaiian quilt. ✉ *Queens' MarketPlace, 69-201 Waikoloa Beach Dr., #305, Waikoloa* ☎ *808/886–0494* ⊕ *www.hawaiian-quilts.com.*

Island Pearls by Maui Divers

JEWELRY & WATCHES | Among the fine jewelry at this boutique is a wide selection of high-end pearl jewelry, including Tahitian black pearls, South Sea white and golden pearls, and chocolate Tahitian pearls. It also sells freshwater pearls in the shell, black coral (the Hawaii state gemstone), and diamonds. Creations in 14K gold showcasing Hawaii themes such as traditional heirloom designs and flora and fauna are also on display. Prices are high but so is the quality. ✉ *Queens' MarketPlace, 69-201 Waikoloa Beach Dr., #J-11, Waikoloa* ☎ *808/886–4817* ⊕ *www.mauidivers.com.*

CLOTHING AND SHOES
Blue Ginger

MIXED CLOTHING | The Waikoloa branch of this fashion veteran offers really sweet matching aloha outfits for the entire family in tropical batik prints. Handbags, shoes, robes, jewelry, and lotions are also sold here. ✉ *Queens' MarketPlace, 69-201 Waikoloa Beach Dr., #K2, Waikoloa* ☎ *808/886–0022* ⊕ *www.blueginger.com.*

SHOPPING CENTERS
Kings' Shops at Waikoloa Beach Resort

SHOPPING CENTER | Stores here include Martin & MacArthur, featuring koa furniture and accessories, and Tori Richard, which offers upscale resort wear, as well as high-end retailers Tiffany & Co. and Michael Kors. Gourmet offerings include A-Bay's Island Grill, Foster's Kitchen, and Island Fish & Chips. Shuttles run from the resorts to the center daily from noon to 8. ✉ *Waikoloa Beach Resort,*

250 Waikoloa Beach Dr., Waikoloa ☎ *808/339–7145* 🌐 *www.kingsshops.com.*

Queens' MarketPlace

SHOPPING CENTER | The largest shopping complex on the Kohala Coast houses fashionable clothing stores, jewelry boutiques, galleries, gift shops, and restaurants such as Sansei Seafood Restaurant & Sushi Bar, Kuleana Rum Shack, and Romano's Macaroni Grill. Island Gourmet Markets, Starbucks, and an affordable food court are other options. Waikoloa Luxury Cinemas offers the ultimate movie experience and includes a restaurant called Bistro at the Cinemas, which is a worth a stop even if you don't hit a show with dinner. ✉ *Waikoloa Beach Resort, 201 Waikoloa Beach Dr., Waikoloa* ☎ *808/886–8822* 🌐 *www.queensmarketplace.net.*

Mauna Lani

8 miles north of Waikoloa.

Mauna Lani is known for its expensive resorts, but fortunately, it's so much more. In addition to cooling trade winds, black lava landscapes, and turquoise seas, the region offers numerous historical sites, including ancient fishponds, petroglyphs, and historical trails that invite lovers of history and culture to explore numerous spots along this stunning coast.

Sights

Holoholokai Beach Park and Petroglyph Trail

TRAIL | While mostly rocky topography makes swimming and snorkeling a bit difficult here, this little park is still scenic and relaxing. Take the short trail over to the petroglyph trail; interpretive signs will guide you. There are showers, picnic tables, and restrooms; public parking is limited ✉ *Holoholokai Beach Park Rd., Waimea (Hawaii County)* ✥ *Near the end of N. Kaniku Dr.* ☎ *808/657–3293* 🎟 *Free.*

Restaurants

Binchotan Bar and Grill

$$$ | **ASIAN FUSION** | In a sophisticated setting that includes open-air patio seating, this restaurant offers contemporary Asian dishes made with meats, prawns, peppers, and more grilled over an open flame in the traditional style. Blending locally sourced ingredients with Japanese and Hawaiian influences, chef Justin Kalaluhi creates a menu that pays homage to multiple cultures. **Known for:** okonomiyaki (savory Japanese-style pancakes) featuring Kona lobster and macadamia nut shrimp; reservations strongly recommended; Robatayaki Experience (chef's selection of grilled items). [$] *Average main: $28* ✉ *Fairmont Orchid Hawaii, 1 N. Kaniku Dr., Waimea (Hawaii County)* ☎ *808/885–5778* 🌐 *www.fairmont.com* 🕒 *Closed Tues. and Wed. No lunch.*

Brown's Beach House at the Fairmont Orchid Hawaii

$$$$ | **MODERN HAWAIIAN** | Sitting right on the resort's sandy Pauoa Bay, the Fairmont's signature restaurant Brown's Beach House offers beautiful sunset dining and innovative cuisine. Attention to detail is evident in the sophisticated menu, which may include crab-crusted Kona *kampachi* or other dishes with sea fish, roasted duck breast, or Kona coffee–crusted venison, as well as local produce and ingredients. **Known for:** tiki torches and live Hawaiian music beneath starry skies; reservations highly recommended; Dungeness crab and lobster tail. [$] *Average main: $40* ✉ *Fairmont Orchid Hawaii, 1 N. Kaniku Dr., Waimea (Hawaii County)* ☎ *808/885–2000* 🌐 *www.fairmont.com* 🕒 *No lunch.*

★ CanoeHouse at the Mauna Lani, Auberge Resorts Collection

$$$$ | **MODERN HAWAIIAN** | One of the most romantic settings on the Kohala Coast, this landmark, oceanfront restaurant showcases traditional Hawaiian flavors, artful presentations, and locally grown or raised products. The progressive menu spotlights standout entrées such as roasted beef tenderloin, lamb, fish caught locally, shellfish, island-fresh greens, and local goat cheese. **Known for:** customized dining program by the chef offered at the Captain's Table; reservations essential far in advance; memorable sunsets with tiki torches. [$] *Average main: $48* ✉ *Mauna Lani, Auberge Resorts Collection, 68-1400 Mauna Lani Dr., Waimea (Hawaii County)* ☎ *808/885-6622* 🌐 *aubergeresorts.com/maunalani* 🕒 *No lunch.*

★ Knead & Bake

$$ | **PIZZA** | This authentic little pizzeria with tables inside and outdoors might just make the best hand-tossed pizza on the Kohala Coast, if not the whole island. The New York–born owner does not scrimp and has even imported special pizza ovens and dough machines from New York, as well as Fontanini-brand ingredients, to give his pizzas that extra pizzazz. **Known for:** good prices; fresh local ingredients; innovative pizza toppings. [$] *Average main: $20* ✉ *Shops at Mauna Lani, 68-1330 Mauna Lani Dr., Waimea (Hawaii County)* ☎ *808/731-4490* 🌐 *kneadandbake.com.*

Tommy Bahama Restaurant and Bar

$$$$ | **MODERN HAWAIIAN** | **FAMILY** | Upstairs at the Shops at Mauna Lani, this breezy, open-air restaurant offers an excellent roster of appetizers, including seared-scallop sliders and coconut-crusted crab cakes, as well as meat and fish mains and decadent desserts. The chef here has freedom to cook up his own daily specials, and the seared ahi is a standout. **Known for:** popular cocktail bar and lounge; house-baked breads and specialty butters; the chain's reliable cuisine and relaxed vibe. [$] *Average main: $38* ✉ *The Shops at Mauna Lani, 68-1330 Mauna Lani Dr., Suite 102, Waimea (Hawaii County)* ☎ *808/881-8686* 🌐 *www.tommybahama.com.*

Hotels

★ Fairmont Orchid Hawaii

$$$$ | **RESORT** | **FAMILY** | This first-rate resort overflows with tropical gardens, cascading waterfalls, a sandy beach cove, a meandering pool, a lagoon for the kids, and all the luxury amenities. **Pros:** oceanfront location; excellent pool; aloha hospitality. **Cons:** $35 resort fee; not the best beach among Kohala Coast resorts; central pool can get very crowded. [$] *Rooms from: $722* ✉ *1 N. Kaniku Dr., Waimea (Hawaii County)* ☎ *808/885-2000, 800/845-9905* 🌐 *www.fairmont.com* 🛏 *540 rooms* 🍴 *No Meals.*

★ Mauna Lani, Auberge Resorts Collection

$$$$ | **RESORT** | Popular with honeymooners and anniversary couples for decades, this elegant Kohala Coast classic is still one of the island's most beautiful resorts, highlighted by a breathtaking, open-air lobby with cathedral-like ceilings, Zen-like koi ponds, and illuminated sheets of cascading water. **Pros:** beautiful design; award-winning spa; many Hawaiian cultural programs. **Cons:** limited dining selection on-site; highest-priced resort on the island; no luau. [$] *Rooms from: $1049* ✉ *68-1400 Mauna Lani Dr., Waimea (Hawaii County)* ☎ *808/885-6622, 808/657-3293* 🌐 *aubergeresorts.com/maunalani* 🛏 *338 rooms* 🍴 *No Meals.*

Mauna Lani Point and the Islands at Mauna Lani

$$$$ | **RESORT** | Surrounded by the emerald greens of a world-class oceanside golf course, the private, independent, luxury condominiums at Islands at Mauna Lani offer spacious two-story suites, while Mauna Lani Point's villas are closer to the beach. **Pros:** friendly front desk; stellar

The Big Island of Hawaii THE KOHALA COAST AND WAIMEA

views; extra-large units. **Cons:** individually owned units vary in decor and amenities; some units are a distance from the barbecue/pool area; quite pricey. $ *Rooms from: $691 ⊠ Mauna Lani Point, 68-1050 Mauna Lani Point Dr., Waimea (Hawaii County)* ☎ *808/885–5022, 800/642–6284* ⊕ *www.classicresorts.com* ⟿ *66 units* ⫿⊙⫿ *No Meals.*

 Nightlife

BARS
Luana Lounge
COCKTAIL LOUNGES | The contemporary lounge in the Fairmont Orchid has a large terrace and an impressive water view. Bartenders are skilled at mixology, and service is impeccable. The crowd is mellow, so it's a nice place for an early evening cocktail or after-dinner liqueur. Happy hour is from 8 to 10, and live music begins at sunset and continues until 9. ⊠ *Fairmont Orchid Hawaii, 1 N. Kaniku Dr., Waimea (Hawaii County)* ☎ *808/885–2000* ⊕ *www.fairmont.com.*

 Performing Arts

LUAU
Hawaiiloa Luau
CULTURAL FESTIVALS | Slickly produced and well choreographed, this gorgeous show incorporates both traditional and contemporary music and dance, along with an array of beautiful costumes. It tells the tale of Hawaiiloa, the great navigator from Tahiti, and of the celestial object—*Hokulea,* "Star of Gladness"—that guided him to the islands later named Hawaii. Presented under the stars at the Fairmont Orchid Hawaii on Saturdays, the luau offers several stations with a variety of Hawaiian and Hawaii Regional Cuisine dishes, and there's an open full bar for mai tais and other tropical libations. ⊠ *Fairmont Orchid Hawaii, 1 N. Kaniku Dr., Waimea (Hawaii County)* ☎ *808/885–2000, 808/326–4969* ⊕ *fairmont.com/orchid-hawaii* ⫿ *$159.*

 Shopping

SHOPPING CENTERS
The Shops at Mauna Lani
SHOPPING CENTER | Some shops here have closed because of the pandemic and recent nearby hotel renovation, but this pleasant complex is sure to recover as economic conditions improve. Pizza does not get better than at Knead & Bake, where you can dine in or order online for pickup. A small market lets you stock up on basics, and coffee, smoothie, and sandwich shops are still around, as well as a couple of nice surf shops, jewelry stores, and upscale clothing boutiques. Tommy Bahama Restaurant and Bar is one spot favored by locals for a *pau hana* (after work) cocktail and *pupu* (appetizer). ⊠ *68-1330 Mauna Lani Dr., Waimea (Hawaii County)* ☎ *808/885–9501* ⊕ *www.shopsatmaunalani.com.*

Mauna Kea and Hapuna

6 miles north of Mauna Lani.

Every visitor to the Big Island should put Hapuna Beach State Recreation Area on an itinerary, especially if you're not staying at the Westin Hapuna Beach Resort, located beachfront. This glorious stretch of white-sand beauty will not fail to take your breath away, no matter what the season or time of day. Sheer enchantment also defines the luminous waters and curve of white sand at Kaunaoa, also called Mauna Kea Beach, but it's more difficult to access due to the Mauna Kea Beach Hotel's control of the parking area.

 Beaches

★ Hapuna Beach State Recreation Area
BEACH | **FAMILY** | One of Hawaii's most breathtaking beaches, Hapuna is a ½-mile-long stretch of white perfection, with turquoise water that is calm in summer, so it's good for kids, with just enough rolling waves to make

Hapuna Beach State Recreation Area protects the island's largest white-sand beach. At the northern end sits the Westin Hapuna Beach Resort.

bodysurfing and bodyboarding fun. Watch for the undertow; in winter it can be very rough. There is excellent snorkeling around the jagged rocks that border the beach on either side, but high surf brings strong currents. Known for awesome sunsets, this is one of the island's best places to see the "green flash" as the sun dips below a clear horizon.

Parking is ample, although the lot can fill up by midday and the beach can get crowded on holidays. Plenty of picnic tables overlooking the beach offer shady respite on a hot day. Lifeguards are on duty during peak hours. **Amenities:** food and drink; lifeguards; parking (fee); showers; toilets; water sports. **Best for:** sunset; surfing; swimming; walking. ⊠ Hwy. 19 near mile marker 69, Mauna Kea ✛ Just south of the Westin Hapuna Beach Resort ☎ 808/961–9544 ⊕ dlnr. hawaii.gov/dsp/parks ☞ $10 parking fee per vehicle.

★ **Kaunaoa Beach** (Mauna Kea Beach)
BEACH | FAMILY | Hands down one of the most beautiful beaches on the island, if not the whole state, Kaunaoa features a short crescent of pure white sand framed by coconut palms. The beach, which fronts the Mauna Kea Beach Hotel, slopes very gradually, and there's great snorkeling along the rocks. Classic Hawaii postcard views abound, especially in winter, when snow tops Maunakea to the east. When conditions permit, waves are good for body- and board surfing also. Currents can be strong in winter, so be careful. Get a cocktail at the beach cabana and enjoy the sunset. ■TIP➔ **Public parking is limited to a few spaces, so arrive before 10 am or after 4 pm. If the lot is full, head to nearby Hapuna Beach, where there's a huge parking lot ($10 per vehicle). Try this spot again another day—it's worth it!** **Amenities:** parking (no fee); showers; toilets; water sports. **Best for:** snorkeling; sunset; swimming; walking. ⊠ 62-100 Mauna Kea Beach Dr., Mauna Kea ✛ Entry through gate to Mauna Kea Beach Hotel ☞ Free.

🍽 Restaurants

Hau Tree

$$$ | **MODERN HAWAIIAN** | Though it sits on a patio by the pool, this beachside restaurant and beach bar with gazebo is not just for pupus and cocktails. The island-infused dinner menu features excellent entrées, such as the grass-fed Kulana beef tenderloin brochettes, plus plentiful seafood dishes and greens from local farms. **Known for:** great sunset views; reasonable prices for a resort restaurant; famous Fredrico cocktail. $ *Average main: $27* ✉ *Mauna Kea Beach Hotel, 62-100 Mauna Kea Beach Dr., Mauna Kea* ☎ *808/882–5707* ⊕ *www.maunakeabeachhotel.com.*

★ Manta at the Mauna Kea Beach Hotel

$$$$ | **MODERN HAWAIIAN** | Perched on the edge of a bluff overlooking the sparkling waters of Kaunaoa Beach, the resort's flagship restaurant is a compelling spot for a romantic meal at sunset, especially at one of the outside tables. The culinary team's take on Hawaii Regional Cuisine highlights locally sourced, sustainable fish, chicken, and beef. **Known for:** exhibition kitchen; Sunday brunch with prime rib, smoked salmon, and omelet station; beachfront balcony dining. $ *Average main: $40* ✉ *Mauna Kea Beach Hotel, 62-100 Mauna Kea Beach Dr., Mauna Kea* ☎ *808/882–5707* ⊕ *www.maunakeabeachhotel.com* ⊗ *No lunch.*

🛏 Hotels

Mauna Kea Beach Hotel, Autograph Collection

$$$$ | **RESORT** | The grande dame of the Kohala Coast has long been regarded as one of the state's premier vacation resort hotels, and it borders one of the world's finest white-sand beaches, Kaunaoa. **Pros:** good dining options; premier tennis center; no resort fees. **Cons:** $30 daily valet parking fee; 27 miles from airport; some oceanfront rooms are noisy. $ *Rooms from: $629* ✉ *62-100 Mauna Kea Beach Dr., Mauna Kea* ☎ *808/882–7222, 866/977–4589* ⊕ *www.maunakeabeachhotel.com* ⇱ *252 rooms* ⦿ *No Meals.*

The Westin Hapuna Beach Resort

$$$$ | **RESORT** | **FAMILY** | Known for its direct access to the Big Island's largest white-sand beach, this massive hotel has enormous columns and a terraced, open-air lobby with rotunda ceiling, curved staircases, and skylights. **Pros:** extra-large rooms, all ocean-facing; helpful staff; resort has 18-hole championship golf course. **Cons:** $37 daily resort fee; 30 miles from Kailua-Kona; fitness center a five-minute walk from the hotel. $ *Rooms from: $874* ✉ *62-100 Kaunaoa Dr., Mauna Kea* ☎ *808/880–1111, 866/774–6236* ⊕ *www.marriott.com* ⇱ *249 rooms* ⦿ *No Meals.*

 Performing Arts

LUAU

★ Mauna Kea Beach Luau

CULTURAL FESTIVALS | **FAMILY** | On the oceanfront North Side Luau Grounds, you can indulge in the best of island cuisine—a traditional feast of *kalua* (earth oven–baked) pig roasted in an *imu* (oven), island fish, lomilomi salmon, and sashimi—while enjoying entertainment by renowned local performers. The luau, originally premiering in 1960 for *Newsweek* magazine and going strong ever since, includes an amazing fire-knife dance, spirited chanting, and traditional hula. *Keiki* (children) can learn the *hukilau* (a traditional song and dance), and you can relax right on the beach, under the stars. If you choose one luau during your visit to the Big Island, this should be the one, and it's surprisingly affordable. ■ **TIP→ You can elect to see only the show for a reasonable fee.** ✉ *Mauna Kea Beach Hotel, Autograph Collection, 62-100 Mauna Kea Beach Dr., Mauna Kea* ☎ *808/882–5810, 808/882–7222* ⊕ *www.maunakeabeachhotel.com* ⦿ *$160, $110 show only.*

Kawaihae

6 miles north of Hapuna.

This no-frills industrial harbor, where in 1793 the first cattle landed in Hawaii, is a hub of commercial and community activity. It's also where King Kamehameha and his men launched their canoes when they set out to conquer the neighboring islands. Kawaihae is especially busy on weekends, when paddlers, surfers, tourist charters, and local fishing boats share the waters. Second in size only to Hilo Harbor, the port serves interisland cargo carriers and often shelters the *Makalii*, one of three traditional Hawaiian sailing canoes. Kawaihae Village has several restaurants with nice sunset views.

◉ Sights

★ Puukohola Heiau National Historic Site

HISTORIC SIGHT | Quite simply, this is one of the most historic and commanding sites in all of Hawaii: here, in 1810, on top of Puukohola (Hill of the Whale), Kamehameha the Great built the war *heiau*, or temple, that would serve to unify the Hawaiian Islands, ending 500 years of warring chiefdoms. The oceanfront, fortresslike site is foreboding and impressive. A paved ½-mile, looped trail runs from the visitor center to the main temple sites. An even older temple, dedicated to the shark gods, lies submerged just offshore, where sharks can be spotted swimming, usually first thing in the morning. A museum displays ancient Hawaiian weapons, including clubs, spears, a replica of a bronze cannon that warriors dragged into battle on a Hawaiian sled, and three original paintings by artist Herb Kane. Rangers are available to answer questions, or you can take a free audio tour on your smartphone. Plan about an hour to see everything. ✉ *62-3601 Kawaihae Rd., Kawaihae* ☎ *808/882–7218* ⊕ *www.nps. gov/puhe* ⛱ *Free.*

Beaches

Spencer Park at Ohaiula Beach

BEACH | FAMILY | Popular with local families because of its reef-protected waters, this white-sand beach is probably the safest beach in West Hawaii for young children. It's also generally safe for swimming year-round, which makes it a reliable spot for a lazy day at the beach. There is a little shade, plus a volleyball court and pavilion, and the soft sand is perfect for sand castles. It does tend to get crowded with families and campers on weekends, but the beach is mostly clean. Although you won't see a lot of fish if you're snorkeling here, in winter you can often catch sight of a breaching whale or two. The beach park lies just below Puukohola Heiau National Historic Site, the location of the historic war temple built by King Kamehameha the Great in 1810 after uniting the Islands. **Amenities:** lifeguards (weekends and holidays only); parking (no fee); showers; toilets. **Best for:** sunset; swimming. ✉ *Hwy. 270, Kawaihae* ✛ *Toward Kawaihae Harbor, just after road forks from Hwy. 19* ☎ *808/961–8311* ⛱ *Free.*

🍴 Restaurants

★ Seafood Bar and Grill

$$ | SEAFOOD | Upstairs in a historical building, this seafood tiki bar has been a hot spot for years, known for a dynamite and well-priced bar menu with tasty pupus, signature seafood dishes such as the coconut shrimp and poke burger, and even a prime rib special on Tuesday. Don't let the retro appearance deter you; this place is frequented by legacy celebrities whose names you know or whose records you've bought. **Known for:** seafood quesadilla; excellent service; funky tiki theme. $ *Average main: $23* ✉ *61-3642 Kawaihae Harbor (Hwy. 270), Kawaihae* ☎ *808/880–9393* ⊕ *www. seafoodbarandgrill.com.*

🛍 Shopping

GALLERIES

Harbor Gallery

ART GALLERIES | Since 1990, this gallery has been enticing visitors with a vast collection of paintings and sculptures by more than 200 Big Island artists. There are also antique maps and prints, wooden bowls, paddles, koa furniture, jewelry, and glasswork. The shop hosts two annual wood shows and actively supports the local arts community. ⊠ *Kawaihae Harbor Shopping Center, 61-3665 Akoni Pule Hwy., Kawaihae* ☎ *808/882–1510* ⊕ *www.harborgallery.biz.*

SHOPPING CENTERS

Kawaihae Harbor Shopping Center

SHOPPING CENTER | This almost-oceanfront shopping plaza houses the exquisite Harbor Gallery, which represents many Big Island artists. Try the Big Island–made ice cream and shave ice (the best in North Hawaii) at local favorite Anuenue. Also here are Kohala Burger and Taco, Mountain Gold Jewelers, and Kohala Divers. ⊠ *61-3665 Akoni Pule Hwy., Kawaihae.*

Hawi and Kapaau

18 miles north of Kawaihae.

These North Kohala towns have an interesting history, and today they are full of lovingly restored vintage buildings housing fun and funky shops and galleries, as well as eateries worth a stop for a quick bite. Near the birthplace of King Kamehameha, the towns thrived during the plantation days, once bustling with hotels, saloons, and theaters—even a railroad. They took a hit when "Big Sugar" left the island, but both are blossoming again, thanks to strong local communities, tourism, athletic events, and an influx of artists keen on honoring the towns' past. Hawi is internationally known as the turnaround point for the cycling portion of the Ironman World Championship triathlon event.

◉ Sights

Keokea Beach Park

CITY PARK | A pavilion welcomes visitors to this 7-acre county beach park fronting the rugged shore in North Kohala. This is a popular local spot for picnics, fishing, and surfing. It's a nice rest stop on your way to Pololu Valley. ■ TIP➔ **Enjoy the scenery, but don't try to swim here—the water is very rough. Be careful on the hairpin curve going down.** ⊠ *Hwy. 270, Kapaau* ✛ *On the way to Pololu Valley, near mile marker 27* ☑ *Free.*

Lapakahi State Historical Park

HISTORIC SIGHT | A self-guided, 1-mile walking tour leads through the ruins of the once-prosperous fishing village of Koaie, which dates as far back as the 15th century. Displays illustrate early Hawaiian fishing and farming techniques, salt gathering, games, and legends. Because the shoreline near the state park is an officially designated Marine Life Conservation District (and part of the site itself is considered sacred), swimming, swim gear, and sunscreen are not allowed in the water. Portable restrooms are available but not drinking water. ■ TIP➔ **Gates close promptly at 4 pm, and they mean business!** ⊠ *Hwy. 270 at mile marker 14, between Kawaihae and Mahukona, Kapaau* ☎ *808/327–4958* ⊕ *www.hawaiistateparks.org* ☑ *Free.*

Mookini Heiau

HISTORIC SIGHT | Dating from as early as AD 480, this parallelogram-shaped structure is a stunning example of a *luakini heiau*, used for ritualized human sacrifice to the Hawaiian war god Ku. The isolated National Historic Landmark within Kohala Historical Sites State Monument is so impressive in size and atmosphere that it's guaranteed to give you what locals call "chicken skin" (goose bumps). The place feels haunted, and even more so if you are the only visitor and the skies are dark and foreboding. Visit with utmost care and respect. Nearby is Kapakai

Royal Housing Complex, the birthplace of Kamehameha the Great. Although it is now under the care of the National Park Service, family descendants still watch over the site. ■ **TIP→ Don't drive out here if it's been raining; even with a four-wheel drive, you could easily get stuck.** ⊠ *Coral Reef Pl./Upolu Point Rd., off Upolu Airport Rd. and Hwy. 270 (Akoni Pule Hwy.), Hawi* ⊹ *Turn at sign for Upolu Airport, near Hawi, and hike or drive 1½ miles southwest* ☎ *808/961–9540* ⊕ *www.nps.gov* ☞ *Free* ⊘ *Closed Wed.*

Beaches

Pololu Valley Beach

BEACH | At the tip of North Kohala, this is one of the Big Island's most scenic beaches. Rain and erosion over millennia have created a stunning, deep-cut windward valley with a windswept gray-sand beach that is piled with large, round boulders and driftwood and backed by ironwood trees and sheer green cliffs. The trail is steep and rocky; it can also be muddy and slippery, so use caution. As of 2021, a Pololu Trail Steward program stations local "stewards" at the trailhead to share historical and cultural perspectives of the valley. Please visit with respect for the land and for all area residents. This is not a safe swimming beach even though locals swim, bodyboard, and surf here. Rip currents and usually rough surf pose a real hazard. Because this is an isolated area far from emergency help, extreme caution is advised. **Amenities:** none. **Best for:** solitude. ⊠ *Hwy. 270 at end of road, Kapaau* ☞ *Free.*

 Restaurants

Bamboo Restaurant & Gallery

$$ | **HAWAIIAN** | In the heart of Hawi, this popular restaurant provides a historical setting in which to enjoy a menu brimming with Hawaiian country flair. Most of the entrées feature fish and chicken prepared several ways, although if the kitchen gets busy, you might get a mediocre plate. **Known for:** passion fruit margaritas; weekend entertainment; fresh catch with ginger, cilantro, and peanuts. $ *Average main: $25* ⊠ *55-3415 Akoni Pule Hwy., Hawi* ☎ *808/889–5555* ⊕ *www.bamboorestauranthawaii.com* ⊘ *Closed Mon. No dinner Sun.*

Coffee and Quick Bites

Kohala Coffee Mill and Tropical Dreams

$ | **CAFÉ** | If you're looking for something sweet—or savory—this busy café in downtown Hawi serves breakfast (bagels, espresso machine–steamed eggs), and lunch (hot dogs, burgers, chili, salads) until 6. Sit outside and watch the world go by as you enjoy locally made ice cream that is *ono* (delicious), as well as other sweet treat specialties. **Known for:** sometimes crowded; outstanding local coffee; vegan soup. $ *Average main: $4* ⊠ *55-3412 Akoni Pule Hwy., Hawi* ☎ *808/889–5577* ⊘ *No dinner.*

🛏 Hotels

★ Hawaii Island Retreat at Ahu Pohaku Hoomaluhia

$$$$ | **B&B/INN** | Here, above the sea cliffs in North Kohala, sustainability meets luxury without sacrificing comfort: the resort generates its own solar and wind-turbine power, harnesses its own water, and grows much of its own food. **Pros:** stunning location; emphasis on organic food; affordable yurts are one lodging option. **Cons:** yurts don't have in-unit showers; four-night minimum; somewhat isolated and not within walking distance of restaurants. $ *Rooms from: $460* ⊠ *250 Maluhia Rd., Kapaau* ⊹ *Off Hwy. 270 in Hawi* ☎ *808/889–6336* ⊕ *www.hawaii-islandretreat.com* ⊅ *20 rooms* ⦿ *Free Breakfast.*

★ Puakea Ranch

$$$ | **HOUSE** | **FAMILY** | Four beautifully restored ranch houses and bungalows occupy this historic country estate in

Pololu Valley Beach is one of the island's most beautiful, but you may want to enjoy it from the lookout at the top; it's a steep, 15-minute climb down to reach the light gray sand.

Hawi, where guests enjoy their own private swimming pools, horseback riding, round-the-clock concierge availability, and plenty of fresh fruit from the orchards. **Pros:** charmingly decorated; washer and dryer in each house; private swimming pools. **Cons:** spotty cell-phone coverage; sometimes windy; 15 minutes to the beach. Ⓢ *Rooms from: $289* ✉ *56-2864 Akoni Pule Hwy., Hawi* ☎ *808/315–0805* ⊕ *www.puakearanch.com* ⮑ *4 houses* ⦿ *No Meals.*

🛍 Shopping

ARTS AND CRAFTS

Elements Jewelry and Fine Crafts

CRAFTS | The beautiful little shop carries lots of original jewelry handmade by local artists, as well as carefully chosen gifts, including unusual ceramics, paintings, prints, glass items, baskets, fabrics, bags, and toys. ✉ *55-3413 Akoni Pule Hwy., Hawi* ⊹ *Next to Bamboo Restaurant* ☎ *808/889–0760* ⊕ *www.elements-jewelryandcrafts.com.*

CLOTHING AND SHOES

★ As Hawi Turns

WOMEN'S CLOTHING | Housed in the 1932 Toyama Building, this landmark North Kohala shop stocks sophisticated women's resort wear made of hand-painted silk or high-quality cotton in tropical designs by local artists. There are also plentiful vintage treasures, jewelry, gifts, hats, bags, and toys, plus handmade ukuleles by local luthier David Gomes. ✉ *55-3412 Akoni Pule Hwy., Hawi* ☎ *808/889–5023.*

GALLERIES

Ackerman Galleries

ART GALLERIES | Kapaau-based artist Gary Ackerman features his oil paintings and multimedia art in an impressionistic and abstract style at this small gallery. ✉ *54-3878 Akoni Pule Hwy., Kapaau* ☎ *808/889–5138* ⊕ *www.ackermangalleries.com.*

Rankin Gallery

ART GALLERIES | Watercolorist and oil painter Patrick Louis Rankin showcases his own work at his shop in a restored plantation store next to the bright-green Chinese community and social hall. The building sits right at a curve in the road on the way to Pololu Valley, at the first gulch past Kapaau. ✉ *53-4380 Akoni Pule Hwy., Kapaau* ☎ *808/889–6849* ⊕ *www. patricklouisrankin.net.*

Waimea

10 miles east of the Kohala Coast, 23 miles southeast of Kapaau, 40 miles northeast of Kailua-Kona.

Thirty minutes over the mountain from Kohala, Waimea (sometimes called "Kamuela" to distinguish it from the similarly named places on Kauai and Oahu) offers a completely different experience than the rest of the island. Rolling green hills, large open pastures, light rain, cool evening breezes, and morning mists, along with abundant cattle, horses, and regular rodeos, are just a few of the surprises you'll stumble upon here in *paniolo* (cowboy) country. Parker Ranch, one of the largest privately held cattle ranches in the United States, surrounds this attractive little town.

Waimea is also where some of the island's top Hawaii Regional Cuisine chefs practice their art using local ingredients, which makes it an ideal place to find yourself at dinnertime. In keeping with the restaurant trend toward featuring local farm-to-table ingredients, a handful of Waimea farms and ranches supply most of the restaurants on the island, and many sell to the public as well. With its galleries, coffee shops, brewpubs, restaurants, beautiful countryside, and *paniolo* culture, Waimea is well worth a stop if you're heading to Hilo or Maunakea. ■ **TIP → The short highway, or mountain road, that connects Waimea to North Kohala (Highway 250) affords some of our favorite Big Island views.**

GETTING HERE AND AROUND

From the Kohala Coast, it's a reasonable drive to Waimea. From the Mauna Kea and Hapuna resorts, it's about 12 miles; from the Waikoloa resorts, it's about 19 miles via Waikoloa Road. You can see most of what Waimea has to offer in one day, but if you're heading up to Maunakea for stargazing—which you should—it could easily be stretched to two. If you stay in Waimea overnight (there are many B&B options), spend the afternoon browsing through town or touring some of the area's ranches and historic sites, and then indulging in a delicious meal.

Sights

★ **Anna Ranch Heritage Center**

HISTORIC SIGHT | On the National and State Registers of Historic Places, this stunning heritage property belonged to the "first lady" of Hawaii ranching, Anna Lindsey Perry-Fiske, and now provides a rare opportunity to see a fully restored cattle ranch compound and learn about the life of this fascinating woman. She rounded up and butchered cattle by day and threw lavish parties by night. Wander the picturesque grounds and gardens on a self-guided walk, watch a master saddlemaker and an ironsmith in action, and take a guided tour (by appointment only) of the historic house, where Anna's furniture, gowns, and elaborate *pau* (parade riding) costumes are on display. The knowledgeable staff shares anecdotes about Anna's life. (Some staff and visitors have even reported strange goings-on in the main house, suggesting that Anna may still be "hanging around.") ✉ *65-1480 Kawaihae Rd., Waimea (Hawaii County)* ☎ *808/885–4426* ⊕ *www.annaranch. org* ✉ *Grounds and Discovery Trail free, historic home tours $10* ⊗ *Closed Sat.–Mon.*

Kohala Mountain Road Lookout

VIEWPOINT | The road between North Kohala and Waimea is one of the most scenic drives in Hawaii, passing Parker

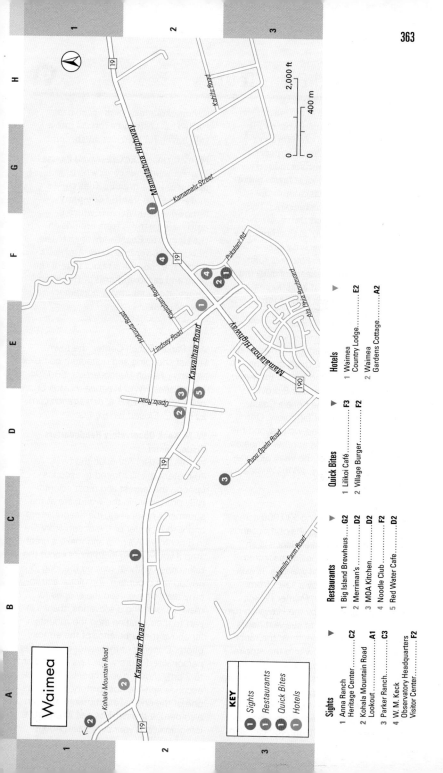

Waimea

KEY

- 1 Sights
- 1 Restaurants
- 1 Quick Bites
- 1 Hotels

Sights

1 Anna Ranch Heritage Center.........**C2**
2 Kohala Mountain Road Lookout.........**A1**
3 Parker Ranch.........**C3**
4 W. M. Keck Observatory Headquarters Visitor Center.........**F2**

Restaurants

1 Big Island Brewhaus.........**G2**
2 Merriman's.........**D2**
3 MOA Kitchen.........**D2**
4 Noodle Club.........**F2**
5 Red Water Cafe.........**D2**

Quick Bites

1 Lilikoi Café.........**F3**
2 Village Burger.........**F2**

Hotels

1 Waimea Country Lodge.........**E2**
2 Waimea Gardens Cottage.........**A2**

2,000 ft

400 m

Big Island Farm Tours

As local ingredients continue to play a more prominent role on Big Island menus, chefs and farmers are working together to support a burgeoning agritourism industry in Hawaii. Several local farms make specialty items that cater to the island's gourmet restaurants. The **Hawaii Island Goat Dairy** (⊕ hawaiiislandgoatdairy.com) on the Hamakua Coast produces specialty cheese; **Big Island Bees** (⊕ bigislandbees.com) boasts its own beekeeping museum and tasting room at Kealakekua Bay; and **Hamakua Mushrooms** (⊕ hamakuamushrooms.com) has turned harvested koa forests into a safe haven for gourmet mushrooms.

Many farms—like **Greenwell Farms** (⊕ greenwellfarms.com), which produces 100% organic Kona coffee, and **Hawaiian Vanilla Company** (⊕ hawaiianvanilla.com), which is cultivating vanilla from orchids on the Hamakua Coast—are open to the public and offer free tours. And don't forget the chocolate: take a tour of the farm and cacao orchards at **Honokaa Chocolate Company** (⊕ honokaachocolateco.com).

Ranch, open pastures, rolling hills, and tree-lined mountains. There are a few places to pull over and take in the view; the lookout at mile marker 8 provides a splendid vista of the Kohala Coast and Kawaihae Harbor far below. On clear days, you can see well beyond the resorts to Maui, while at other times an eerie mist drifts over the view. ⊠ *Kohala Mountain Rd. (Hwy. 250), Waimea (Hawaii County).*

★ Parker Ranch

FARM/RANCH | Exceeding 130,000 acres and regularly running tens of thousands of head of cattle, Parker Ranch is an impressive and compelling backdrop for the scenic town of Waimea. It was established in 1847 by a sailor from Massachusetts, John Palmer Parker, who was permitted by the Hawaiian ruler King Kamehameha I to cull vast herds of out-of-control cattle; thus, the ranch was born. It later grew into the empire it is today, and the foundation started by Parker's descendants supports community health care and education. In addition to taking self-guided tours of two of the ranch's historic homes—Hale Mana and Puuopelu—free of charge, you can also

visit Parker Ranch Center, the town's largest shopping and restaurant complex. ⊠ *Parker Ranch Headquarters, 66-1304 Mamalahoa Hwy., Waimea (Hawaii County)* ☎ *808/885–7311* ⊕ *parkerranch.com* 🎟 *Free* ☉ *Closed weekends.*

W. M. Keck Observatory Headquarters Visitor Center

VISITOR CENTER | Although the twin, 10-meter optical/infrared telescopes (among the largest and most scientifically productive in the world) are at the summit of Maunakea, the headquarters and visitor center of the observatory are in downtown Waimea and make a great stop if you want to learn more about the telescopes without making the long journey up the mountain. Top global astronomy teams have used the scopes to make astounding discoveries, thanks in part to their location atop the mountain, far above the turbulence of the atmosphere. Docents at the visitor center offer personalized tours weekdays from 10 am to 2 pm, showing you models of the telescopes and the observatory, as well as one of the original instruments. You can also peruse the exhibits and interpretive infographics at your own pace. About six times each year, highly renowned speakers, including Nobel Prize laureates, give free astronomy talks to the public. ✉ *65-1120 Mamalahoa Hwy., Waimea (Hawaii County)* ✣ *Across from hospital* ☎ *808/885–7887* 🌐 *www.keckobservatory.org* 🎟 *Free* ⏲ *Closed weekends.*

🍴 Restaurants

Big Island Brewhaus

$ | **AMERICAN** | A hands-down island favorite, this casual brewpub from owner and veteran brewmaster Tom Kerns churns out premium ales, lagers, and specialty beers from his on-site brewery in Waimea. With a focus on fresh ingredients, the brewpub's menu includes burgers, poke, fish tacos, burritos, and quesadillas fresh to order. **Known for:** affordable sampler with six beer choices; amazing grass-fed burgers; coconut-infused White Mountain porter. [$] *Average main: $12* ✉ *64-1066A Mamalahoa Hwy., Waimea (Hawaii County)* ☎ *808/887–1717* 🌐 *www.bigislandbrewhaus.com.*

Merriman's

$$$$ | **MODERN HAWAIIAN** | The signature restaurant of Peter Merriman, one of the pioneers of Hawaii Regional Cuisine, is the home of the original wok-charred ahi: it's seared on the outside, leaving sashimi on the inside. Although lunch prices are reasonable, dinner is "resort pricey," so prepare to splurge. **Known for:** locally raised Kahua Ranch braised lamb; reservations essential; grilled-to-order New York steak. [$] *Average main: $45* ✉ *Opelo Plaza, 65-1227 Opelo Rd., Waimea (Hawaii County)* ☎ *808/885–6822* 🌐 *www.merrimanshawaii.com.*

MOA Kitchen

$ | **JAPANESE** | Just like an authentic Japanese *izakaya* (bar/restaurant), this hip little place serves *yakatori* (skewered chicken) grilled on a *binchotan* (grill) that the restaurant imported from Japan. Ramen is served with a variety of broths—regular shoyu, spicy, and vegetarian. **Known for:** Hawaiian spicy ramen; island-grown ingredients; uni nigiri. [$] *Average main: $12* ✉ *65-1298 Kawaihae Rd., Waimea (Hawaii County)* ☎ *808/339–7887* ⏲ *Closed Mon. No lunch Sun.*

Noodle Club

$ | **JAPANESE FUSION** | **FAMILY** | Star Wars toys and action figures line the shelves of Noodle Club, a fun destination with serious food in the Parker Ranch Center. Veteran resort chef Edwin Goto simmers his broths for up to 36 hours to create the noodle, or saimin, dishes such as the savory Bowl of Seoul or the All Things Pork Ramen. **Known for:** bao buns with Hamakua Alii mushrooms; delicious desserts, including dairy-free chocolate mousse; house-made pork, beef, and vegetable broths. [$] *Average main: $14* ✉ *Parker Ranch Center, 67-1185 Mamalahoa Hwy., #A106, Waimea (Hawaii County)* ☎ *808/885–8825* 🌐 *www.noodleclubwaimea.com* ⏲ *Closed Mon.*

Red Water Cafe

$$$$ | **ECLECTIC** | **FAMILY** | Chef David Abraham serves upscale café fare with a twist and a side of aloha. Although it opens fairly early (at 2 pm Tuesday–Friday, noon on Saturday), there's only a single, all-day menu, and this place is busy, so reserve ahead. **Known for:** Kansas City rib-eye steak, Berkshire pork chops, and short ribs; sushi menu; worthy saketini (sake martini). [$] *Average main: $36* ✉ *65-1299 Kawaihae Rd., Waimea (Hawaii County)* ☎ *808/885–9299* 🌐 *www.redwatercafe.com* ⏲ *Closed Sun. and Mon. No lunch.*

☕ Coffee and Quick Bites

Lilikoi Café

$ | **AMERICAN** | **FAMILY** | Locals love this gem of a café, tucked away in the back of the Parker Ranch Center, in part because it's hard to find and they want to keep its delicious breakfast crepes, freshly made soups, and croissants Waimea's little secret. It's just as good for lunch:

owner and chef John Lorda creates an impressive selection of salad choices daily, including chicken curry, beet, fava bean, chicken pesto, and Mediterranean pasta. **Known for:** Israeli couscous with tomato, red onion, and cranberry; creative sandwiches and hot lunch entrées; handpainted murals. [$] *Average main: $9* ✉ *Parker Ranch Center, 67-1185 Mamalahoa Hwy. (Hwy. 11), Waimea (Hawaii County)* ☎ *808/887–1400* 🌐 *lilikoicafe.com* 🕓 *Closed Sun. No dinner.*

Village Burger

$ | **AMERICAN** | **FAMILY** | At this little eatery that brings a whole new meaning to gourmet hamburgers, locally raised, grass-fed, hormone-free beef is ground fresh, hand-shaped daily on-site, and grilled to perfection right before your eyes. Top your burger (be it ahi, veal, Kahua Ranch Wagyu beef, Hamakua mushroom, or Waipio taro) with everything from local avocados, baby greens, and chipotle goat cheese to tomato marmalade. **Known for:** order online for quicker service; ice cream for milkshakes made fresh in Waimea; brioche buns baked fresh in nearby Hawi. [$] *Average main: $10* ✉ *Parker Ranch Center, 67-1185 Mamalahoa Hwy. (Hwy. 11), Waimea (Hawaii County)* ☎ *808/885–7319* 🌐 *www.villageburgerwaimea.com.*

Hotels

Waimea Country Lodge

$ | **HOTEL** | In the heart of cowboy country, this quaint ranch house–style lodge offers views of the green, rolling slopes of Waimea and a distant view of Maunakea. **Pros:** large rooms; kitchenettes in some rooms; free coffee in morning. **Cons:** no pool; no on-site restaurant; not near the beach. [$] *Rooms from: $145* ✉ *65-1210 Lindsey Rd., Waimea (Hawaii County)* ☎ *808/885–4100, 800/367–5004* 🌐 *www.waimeacountrylodge.com* 🛏 *22 rooms* 🍴 *No Meals.*

Waimea Gardens Cottage

$$ | **HOUSE** | Surprisingly luxe yet cozy and quaint, the three charming country cottages and one suite at this historical Hawaiian homestead are surrounded by flowering private gardens and a backyard stream. **Pros:** charming, self-contained units; lush, bird-filled grounds; kitchens include food for breakfast. **Cons:** only personal or bank checks accepted; three-night minimum stay; 50% deposit within two weeks of booking and payment in full six weeks before arrival. [$] *Rooms from: $205* ✉ *Waimea (Hawaii County)* ✥ *Located off Kawaihae Rd., 2 miles from Waimea Town* ☎ *808/885–8550* 🌐 *www.waimeagardens.com* 💳 *No credit cards* 🛏 *4 units* 🍴 *Free Breakfast.*

Performing Arts

THEATER

Kahilu Theatre

ARTS CENTERS | The intimate theater regularly hosts internationally acclaimed performers and renowned Hawaiian artists such as Jake Shimabukuro, Kealii Reichel, and the Brothers Cazimero. They share the calendar with regional and national modern-dance troupes, community theater and dance groups, ukulele festivals, and classical music performances. The theater also supports the community by welcoming local artists to exhibit in its lobby, which doubles as a gallery. ✉ *Parker Ranch Center, 67-1185 Mamalahoa Hwy., Waimea (Hawaii County)* ☎ *808/885–6868* 🌐 *kahilutheatre.org.*

Shopping

ARTS AND CRAFTS

★ Gallery of Great Things

ART GALLERIES | You might lose yourself exploring the trove of fine art and collectibles in every price range at this gallery, which represents hundreds of local artists and has a low-key, unhurried atmosphere. The "things" include hand-stitched quilts, ceramic sculptures, vintage kimonos, original paintings, koa-wood bowls and furniture, etched glassware, Niihau shell lei, and feather art by local artist Beth McCormick. ⊠ *Parker Square, 65-1279 Kawaihae Rd., Waimea (Hawaii County)* ☎ *808/885–7706* ⊕ *www.gallery-ofgreatthingshawaii.com.*

Wishard Gallery

ART GALLERIES | A Big Island–born artist whose verdant landscapes, sea views, and *paniolo* (cowboy)-themed paintings have become iconic throughout the state, Harry Wishard showcases his original oils at this gallery, along with works by other renowned local artists like Kathy Long, Edward Kayton, and Lynn Capell. ⊠ *55-498 Hawi Rd., Hawi* ☎ *808/731–6556* ⊕ *www.wishardgallery.com.*

FOOD AND WINE

Kamuela Liquor Store

WINE/SPIRITS | From its plain name and exterior, this store doesn't look like much, but it sells the best selection of premium spirits, wines, and gourmet items on the island. Alvin, the owner, is a collector of fine wines, as evidenced by his multiple cellars. Wine tastings take place Friday afternoon from 3 to 6 and Saturday at noon. ⊠ *64-1010 Mamalahoa Hwy., Waimea (Hawaii County)* ☎ *808/885–4674.*

★ Waimea General Store

GENERAL STORE | Since 1970, this Waimea landmark at Parker Square has been a favorite of locals and visitors alike. Although specialty kitchenware takes center stage, the shop brims with local gourmet items, books, kimonos, and Hawaiian gifts and souvenirs. ⊠ *Parker Square, 65-1279 Kawaihae Rd., Suite 112, Waimea (Hawaii County)* ☎ *808/885–4479* ⊕ *www.waimeageneralstore.com.*

SHOPPING CENTERS

Parker Ranch Center

SHOPPING CENTER | With a welcoming, ranch-style motif, this shopping hub includes a supermarket, some great local eateries (Village Burger, Noodle Club,

and Lilikoi Café), a coffee shop, a natural foods store, galleries, and clothing boutiques. The Parker Ranch Store and Parker Ranch Visitors Center and Museum are also here, but at this writing, they are under renovation. ⊠ *67-1185 Mamalahoa Hwy. (Hwy. 11), Waimea (Hawaii County)* ⊕ *parkerranchcenter.com.*

Parker Square

SHOPPING CENTER | Although the Gallery of Great Things, known for art and collectibles, is this shopping center's star attraction, it's also worth looking into the Waimea General Store; Sweet Wind, for books, chimes, and beads; Bentley's, which sells locally crafted and imported home decor and gifts; and Hula Moon, for upscale women's fashions. Waimea Coffee Company satisfies with salads, sandwiches, and Kona coffee. ⊠ *65-1279 Kawaihae Rd., Waimea (Hawaii County).*

The Hamakua Coast

The spectacular waterfalls, jungles, emerald slopes, and ocean vistas along Highway 19 northwest of Hilo are referred to as the Hilo–Hamakua Heritage Coast. Brown road signs featuring a sugarcane tassel reflect the area's history: thousands of former acres of sugarcane sat idle after "King Sugar" left the island in the early 1990s, but today diversified agriculture is growing. This is a great place to wander off the main road and see "real" Hawaii—untouched valleys, overgrown banyan trees, tiny coastal villages, and little plantation towns such as Honomu, Laupahoehoe, and Honokaa. Some small communities are still hanging on quite nicely after the demise of the big sugar plantations that first engendered them. The towns have homey cafés, gift shops, galleries, and a way of life from a time gone by. Plenty of farmers here use premium agricultural lands serviced by former cane roads and the restored and repaired Hamakua Ditch, growing crops such as Hamakua mushrooms, sweet

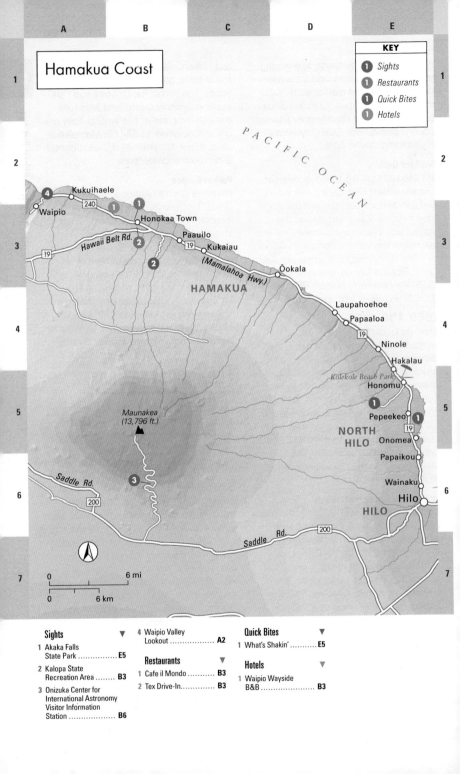

Hamakua Coast

KEY

- **1** Sights
- **1** Restaurants
- **1** Quick Bites
- **1** Hotels

PACIFIC OCEAN

Kukuihaele

Waipio

Honokaa Town

Hawaii Belt Rd.

Paauilo

Kukaiau

(Mamalahoa Hwy.)

Ōokala

HAMAKUA

Laupahoehoe

Papaaloa

Ninole

Hakalau

Kolekole Beach Park

Honomu

Maunakea
(13,796 ft.)

Pepeekeo

NORTH
HILO

Onomea

Papaikou

Saddle Rd.

Wainaku

Hilo

HILO

Saddle Rd.

| 0 | | 6 mi |
| 0 | | 6 km |

potatoes, tomatoes, vanilla, coffee, and lettuce. The dramatic Akaka Falls is only one of the area's hundreds of waterfalls, many of which tumble into a series of cascading pools. The falls may expand or retract depending on inclement weather. The pristine Waipio Valley was once a favorite getaway spot for Hawaiian royalty. Residents of the isolated valley floor have maintained the ways of old Hawaii, with taro patches, wild horses, and a handful of homes. The view from the lookout is breathtaking. Before you head out to the coast, consider taking a side trip to Maunakea, the tallest peak in the Hawaiian Islands and home to 11 powerful telescopes that are co-managed by a consortium of nations, universities, and researchers. You can go with a licensed guide to the summit (recommended) or just drive up to the visitor center at 9,200 feet to peruse exhibits and check out the stars above for yourself.

GETTING HERE AND AROUND

Most visitors to the Hamakua Coast fly into Ellison Onizuka Kona International Airport on the west side, which is about 1¼ hours away.

A car is by far the best and most efficient way to see the Hamakua Coast. You will want the freedom to leisurely stop off at various lookouts to take in the scenery or pause in a little town to grab a snack or lunch.

TOURS

A guided tour from a locally owned and operated company is one of the best (and easiest) ways to see Waipio Valley. You can walk down and up the steep, narrow road yourself, but you need to be in good shape and you may not see as much. And as locals say, it's 15 minutes to walk down but about 45 minutes to walk back up. The cost for a tour depends on both the company and the transport mode.

Waipio Naalapa Stables

GUIDED TOURS | Friendly horses and friendly guides take guests on tours of the valley floor, where they are treated to unforgettable sights of taro fields, waterfalls, lush trails, and freshwater streams. The 2½-hour tours run Monday through Saturday (the valley rests on Sunday), with check-in times of 9 and 12:30. Riders meet at Waipio Valley Artworks, near the lookout, where they are transported to the valley floor in a four-wheel-drive van. ✉ *Waipio Valley Artworks Bldg., 48-5416 Kukuihaele Rd., Kukuihaele* ☎ *808/775–0419* ⊕ *www.naalapastables. com* ✍ *From $115.*

Waipio on Horseback

GUIDED TOURS | On guided, 2½-hour horseback-riding tours on the Waipio Valley floor, riders experience lush tropical foliage, curving rivers, flowering trees, a scenic beach, tranquil streams, and 2,000-foot-tall cliff walls. Local *paniolo* (cowboy) guides share the history, culture, and mythology of this magical valley and give you a peek into a traditional family farm where the owners tend Hawaiian staples such as taro. You'll also get to see the stunning Naalapa Falls. ✉ *Hwy. 240 at mile marker 7.5, Honokaa* ⊹ *Northwest of Honokaa* ☎ *808/775–7291* ⊕ *www. waipioonhorseback.com* ✍ *From $150.*

Waipio Valley Shuttle

GUIDED TOURS | Not up for hiking in and out of the valley on foot? Informative and affordable, these 1½- to 2-hour, four-wheel-drive tours do the driving for you, exploring the valley with lots of stops Monday through Saturday. The windows on the van are removed, allowing you to snap unobstructed photos. You have the option to stay at the beach for two to four hours and come back up with the next tour. ✉ *48-5416 Kukuihaele Rd., Kukuihaele* ☎ *808/775–7121* ⊕ *www. waipiovalleyshuttle.com* ✍ *From $65.*

Did You Know?

The Waipio River flows through the verdant Waipio Valley to the ocean. The valley used to be a favorite getaway spot for Hawaiian royalty.

Waipio Valley

24 miles east and then north of Waimea.

Bounded by 2,000-foot cliffs, the "Valley of the Kings" was once a favorite retreat of Hawaiian royalty, and it remains one of the most picturesque spots in all of Hawaii. Waterfalls drop thousands of feet from the North Kohala watershed to the Waipio Valley floor. The lush valley is breathtaking in every way and from every vantage, with tropical foliage, abundant flowers, wild horses, misty pastures, curving rivers, stands of ironwood trees and a wide, gray, boulder-strewn shore. Though almost completely off the grid today, Waipio (the word means "curved water") was once a center of Hawaiian life. Somewhere between 4,000 and 20,000 people made it their home between the 13th and 17th centuries. In addition, this highly historic and culturally significant area housed *heiau* (temples) and *puuhonua* (places of refuge) in addition to royal residences. King Kamehameha the Great launched a great naval battle from here, which marked the start of his unification of (some would say conquest) and reign over the Hawaiian Islands. To preserve this pristine part of the island, commercial transportation permits are limited—only a few outfitters offer organized valley floor trips.

A treacherous paved road leads down from the Waipio Valley Lookout, but no car rental companies on the island allow their cars to be driven down. Please don't try, even if you rented a four-wheel drive. You can walk it, and you should if you can. The distance is actually less than a mile from the lookout point—just keep in mind that the climb back gains 1,000 feet in elevation and is highly strenuous, so bring water and a walking stick. Area landowners do not look kindly on public trespassing to access Hiilawe Falls at the back of the valley, so stick to the front by the beach. Hike all the way to the end of the beach for a glorious vantage point.

Swimming (for experienced swimmers only), surfing, and picnics are all popular here, conditions permitting; exercise caution. You can also take the King's Trail from the end of the beach to access another waterfall not far down the trail. Keep in mind that waterfalls can come and go depending on the level of recent rains. If you do visit here, kindly respect this area, as it is considered highly sacred to Hawaiians and is still home to several hundred full-time residents who cultivate taro on family farms.

■ TIP➔ **At time of writing, the Waipio Valley Road was closed to visitors because of repairs; only essential uses by residents and businesses or farms were being allowed. Check ahead and with any outfitters before visiting. The Waipio Valley Lookout remains open.**

◉ Sights

★ Waipio Valley Lookout

VIEWPOINT | An easily accessible access point to see the beauty of the Waipio Valley, this lookout offers a stunning view of the valley and the high cliffs that surround it. Not surprisingly, it's a popular spot, but there's plenty of parking to handle the cars on most days; Hawaii County maintains the park at the top. A treacherous paved road leads down (Big Island car-rental companies don't allow their cars to be driven down because it's so steep, but you can walk down if you wish, though it's 1,000 feet back up). Your best bet for seeing the wonders of the valley floor is with a guided four-wheel-drive tour. ■ TIP➔ **Due to repair work, Waipio Valley Road going down to the valley was closed at the time of writing for all but essential uses. Check ahead and confirm with outfitters.** ✉ *Hwy. 240, 8 miles west of Honokaa, Kukuihaele* 🖾 *Free.*

Shopping

ART GALLERIES

Waipio Valley Artworks

ART GALLERIES | In a vintage home, this quaint gallery showcases finely crafted wooden bowls, koa furniture, paintings, and jewelry—all made by local artists. There's also a great little café where you can pick up a sandwich or house-made ice cream before descending into Waipio Valley. ✉ *48-5416 Kukuihaele Rd., Kukuihaele* ☎ *808/775–0958* 🌐 *www.waipiovalleyartworks.com.*

Honokaa

8 miles east of Waipio Valley Lookout, 15 miles northeast of Waimea.

Cool antiques shops, a few interesting galleries, funky gift shops, and good cafés abound in this quaint, cliff-top village fronting the ocean. It was built in the 1920s and 1930s by Japanese and Chinese workers who quit the nearby plantations to start businesses that supported the sugar economy. The intact historical character of the buildings, bucolic setting, and friendliness of the merchants provide a nice reason to stop and stroll. There's even a vintage theater that often showcases first-rate entertainment. Most restaurants close by 8 pm.

Sights

★ Kalopa State Recreation Area

STATE/PROVINCIAL PARK | **FAMILY** | Northwest of the old plantation town of Paauilo, at a cool elevation of 2,000 feet, lies this sweet 100-acre state park with a lush forested area with picnic tables and restrooms. There's an easy.7-mile loop trail with additional paths in the adjacent forest reserve. Small signs identify some of the plants, including the Gothic-looking native ohia and the rare loulu palm. It's chilly and damp here, making it a good escape from the heat at sea level. Three campground areas with full-service kitchens, as well as four cabins, can be reserved online. ✉ *44-3375 Kalopa Mauka Rd., Honokaa* ✣ *12 miles north of Laupahoehoe and 3 miles inland off Hwy. 19* ☎ *808/775–8852* 🌐 *dlnr.hawaii.gov* 🎟 *Free.*

Restaurants

★ Cafe il Mondo

$ | **ITALIAN** | Unquestionably the fanciest spot in Honokaa, this cozy Italian bistro known for its pizza and other options feels like you've taken a step into Florence. Wood details, a full bar, travertine finishes, antique furnishings, pendant lighting, and a fantastic stone pizza oven combine to create a thoroughly welcoming atmosphere. **Known for:** pasta primavera; Paauilo penne; variety of house-made calzones. [$] *Average main: $11* ✉ *3580 Mamane St., Honokaa* ☎ *808/775–7711* 🌐 *cafeilmondo.com.*

★ Tex Drive-In

$ | **DINER** | A local institution, this casual place is famous for its *malasadas,* the puffy, doughy, deep-fried Portuguese doughnuts without a hole, best eaten hot; there are also cream-filled versions, including vanilla, chocolate, and coconut. For more than a snack, go for the Hawaiian burger, with a fat, juicy slice of sweet pineapple on top, the overstuffed burrito, or some decent house-made pizza. **Known for:** food cooked to order; long waits; the island's best malasadas. [$] *Average main: $6* ✉ *45-690 Pakalana St., at Hwy. 19, Honokaa* ☎ *808/775–0598* 🌐 *www.texdriveinhawaii.com.*

Hotels

Waipio Wayside B&B

$ | **B&B/INN** | Nestled amid the avocado, mango, coffee, and kukui trees of a historical plantation estate (circa 1932), this serene home provides a retreat close to the Waipio Valley. **Pros:** ocean views from many of the rooms; gracious owner;

full breakfast served in the dining room. **Cons:** close quarters; no lunch or dinner on property; remote location. [$] *Rooms from: $155* ✉ *42-4226 Waipio Rd. (Hwy. 240), Honokaa* ☎ *808/775–0275* 🌐 *www.waipiowayside.com* 🛏 *5 rooms* 🍴 *Free Breakfast.*

Laupahoehoe

19 miles southeast of Honokaa.

After the devastating events of 1946, in which a tsunami raged ashore and 24 people were killed, the once-thriving railway town of Laupahoehoe was relocated to higher ground. Now all that's there is a small museum, convenience store, and beach park. It's a quick turn off the highway and well worth it to see the memorial to the schoolteachers and children who died here.

Honomu

12 miles southeast of Laupahoehoe.

Bordering Akaka Falls State Park, this tiny town did not die when sugar did, and its sugar-plantation past is reflected in its wooden boardwalks and metal-roofed buildings. You can check out homemade baked goods, have an espresso, or browse the local art at one of the fine galleries. It's also fun to browse through some old, dusty shops filled with little treasures such as antique bottles.

Sights

★ Akaka Falls State Park

WATERFALL | A paved, 10-minute loop trail (approximately ½ mile) takes you to the best spots to see the spectacular cascades of Akaka, including the majestic upper Akaka Falls, which drops more than 442 feet. It tumbles far below into a pool drained by Kolekole Stream amid a profusion of fragrant white, yellow, and red torch ginger and other tropical foliage. Another 400-foot falls is on the lower end of the trail. Restroom facilities are available but no drinking water. The park is 4 miles inland, and vehicle parking closes at 6. Visitors are encouraged to reserve parking online in advance at this popular spot. **■ TIP→ A series of steps along parts of the trail may prove challenging for some visitors, and they are not wheelchair accessible.** ✉ *875 Akaka Falls Rd., Honomu* ✣ *At the end of Akaka Falls Rd. (Hwy. 220)* ☎ *808/974–6200* 🌐 *dlnr.hawaii.gov* 🎫 *$5 per vehicle; parking $10.*

Coffee and Quick Bites

What's Shakin'

$ | AMERICAN | A cute vintage shack, painted a cheery yellow, is the home of the best smoothies and shakes on the Hamakua Coast. Order at the counter and take away, or sit awhile under the canopy while you indulge in a Mango Tango, Lava Java, Bananarama, or any of about 15 selections of creative smoothies; you can pair it with tasty turkey, fish, or chicken roll-ups and other wraps. **Known for:** smoothies made from fruit grown on location; one of the few places to stop on the way to Honokaa; healthy vegetarian and vegan wraps. [$] *Average main: $10* ✉ *27-999 Old Mamalahoa Hwy., Pepeekeo* ☎ *808/964–3080* 🌐 *whatsshakinbigisland.com* 🕒 *No dinner.*

Shopping

ARTS AND CRAFTS

Glass from the Past

ANTIQUES & COLLECTIBLES | A fun place to shop for a quirky gift or just to browse before or after a visit to Akaka Falls, the store is chock-full of old Hawaiian bottles, antiques, vintage clothing, Japanese collectibles, and interesting ephemera. There's often even a "free" table out front to add to the discovery. ✉ *28-1672 Old Mamalahoa Hwy., Honomu* ☎ *808/963–6449.*

Did You Know?

The dramatic Akaka Falls is only one of hundreds of waterfalls on the Hamakua Coast. Many falls tumble into pristine pools, so bring your camera for some incredible shots.

GALLERIES
Woodshop Gallery

ART GALLERIES | Run by local artists Peter and Jeanette McLaren, the gallery showcases their woodwork and photography collections along with beautiful ceramics, photography, glass, and paintings from other Big Island artists. The historical building still has a working soda fountain dating from 1935. ⊠ *28-1690 Old Government Rd., Honomu* ☎ *808/963–6363.*

Maunakea

Maunakea's summit is 18 miles southeast of Waimea and 34 miles northwest of Hilo.

Maunakea ("white mountain"), a major attraction for stargazers, offers the antithesis of the typical tropical island experience: freezing temperatures and arctic conditions are common at the summit, and snow can fall year-round. You can even snowboard or ski up here, though you should be in very good shape and a close-to-expert boarder or skier to get down the slopes near the summit and then up again in the thin air—with no lifts.

Winter sports, however, are the least of the reasons that most people visit this starkly beautiful mountain, a dormant volcano. From its base below the ocean's surface to its summit, Maunakea is the tallest island mountain on the planet. It's also home to little Lake Waiau, one of the highest natural lakes in the world.

Maunakea's summit—at 13,796 feet—is the world's best place for viewing the night sky. For this reason, the summit is home to the largest and most productive astronomical observatories in the world—and $1 billion worth of equipment. Research teams from 11 different countries operate 11 telescopes. There are actually 13, but two are decommissioned now. Decommissioning takes time, so while they aren't doing science, the telescopes are still there. On Maunakea, several telescopes are record holders: the world's largest optical-infrared telescopes (the dual Keck telescopes), the world's largest dedicated infrared telescope (UKIRT), and the largest submillimeter telescope (the JCMT). The still-larger Thirty Meter Telescope (TMT) had been cleared for construction and was slated to open its record-breaking eye to the heavens until it was delayed by protests in 2019. The project's future is unknown.

Maunakea is tall, but there are higher mountains in the world, so what makes this spot so superb for astronomy? It has more to do with atmosphere than with elevation. A tropical-inversion cloud layer below the summit keeps moisture from the ocean and other atmospheric pollutants down at the lower elevations. As a result, the air around the Maunakea summit is extremely dry, which helps in the measurement of infrared and submillimeter radiation from stars, planets, and other astronomical points of interest. There are also rarely clouds up here; the annual number of clear nights here blows every other place out of the water. In addition, because the mountain is far away from any interfering artificial lights (not a total coincidence—in addition to the fact that the nearest town is nearly 30 miles away, there's an official ordinance limiting certain kinds of streetlights on the island), skies are dark for the astronomers' research. To quote the staff at the observatory, astronomers here are able to "observe the faintest galaxies that lie at the very edge of the observable universe."

Teams from various nations and universities around the world must submit proposals years in advance to get the chance to use the telescopes on Maunakea. They have made major astronomical discoveries, including several about the nature of black holes, new satellites around Jupiter and Saturn, new Trojans (asteroids that orbit, similar to moons) around Neptune, new moons and rings around Uranus, and new moons around Pluto. Their studies of galaxies are changing the way scientists think about time and the evolution of the universe.

What does all this mean for you? A visit to Maunakea is a chance to see more stars than you've likely ever seen before and an opportunity to learn more about mind-boggling scientific discoveries in the very spot where these discoveries are being made. Only the astronomers, though, are allowed to use the telescopes and other equipment, but the scenery is available to all. (You must leave the summit before dark for your safety.) We recommend going with a licensed summit tour company that takes care of the details.

If you're in Hilo, be sure to visit the Imiloa Astronomy Center. It offers presentations and planetarium films about the mountain and the science being conducted there, as well as exhibits describing the deep knowledge of the heavens possessed by the ancient Hawaiians. You can also visit the W. M. Keck Observatory Headquarters Visitor Center in Waimea to learn about the important work astronomers are conducting on the summit.

GETTING HERE AND AROUND

The summit of Maunakea isn't terribly far, but the drive takes about 90 minutes from Hilo and an hour from Waimea thanks to the steep road. Between the ride there, sunset on the summit, and stargazing, allot at least five hours for a Maunakea visit.

To reach the summit, you must take Saddle Road (Highway 200, the Daniel K. Inouye Highway), which is a beautiful shortcut across the middle of the island. At mile marker 28, John A. Burns Way, the access road to the visitor center (9,200 feet), is fine, but the road from there to the summit is a lot more precarious because it's unpaved washboard

and steep. As of 2022, new rules have restricted the road to true four-wheel-drive vehicles. These must have a 4-low or a 4-high on the transfer case; all-wheel-drive and two-wheel-drive vehicles are no longer allowed. Every vehicle will be inspected, and those deemed unsuitable will be turned away by rangers and prohibited past Hale Pohaku.

If you haven't rented a four-wheel-drive vehicle from Harper or Big Island Jeep Rentals—the only rental companies that allow their vehicles on the summit— the best thing to do is book a commercial tour. Operators provide transportation to and from the summit led by expert guides; they also provide parkas, gloves, telescopes, dinner, hot beverages, and snacks. All give their own star talks a few thousand feet below the summit, which is actually a better spot to view stars for amateur stargazers than the actual summit. Companies that offer summit tours are headquartered in Hilo and Kona.

Although you can park at the visitor center and hike to the summit if you are in good shape, the trip takes approximately seven hours one way, and no camping is allowed. That means you must leave in the predawn hours in order to be back before dark; a permit is also required for this hike.

The last potential obstacle to visiting the summit: it's cold—as in freezing—usually with significant wind chill, ice, and snow. Winds have been clocked exceeding 135 miles per hour. This is a wilderness area and there are no services or rangers, except in an absolute emergency.

SAFETY

Maunakea's extreme altitude can cause altitude sickness, leading to disorientation, headaches, and light-headedness. Keeping hydrated is crucial. Scuba divers must wait at least 24 hours before traveling to the summit. Children under 16, pregnant women, and those with heart,

The world's largest optical and infrared telescopes are located at the Keck Observatory on Maunakea's summit.

respiratory, or weight problems should not go higher than the visitor center.

TOURS

Arnott's Lodge and Hiking Adventures

SPECIAL-INTEREST TOURS | This outfitter takes small tours (maximum nine guests) to the summit of Maunakea for sunset and then stops on the way down the mountain, where guides give visual lectures (dependent on clear skies) using handheld lasers. They focus on major celestial objects and Polynesian navigational stars. The excursion departs from Hilo, offers pickup from Hilo hotels, and includes hot beverages. The company also offers a traveler's lodge and a number of volcano park and Puna eruption site adventure hikes. Private tours are available, as are alternate trips to the mountain for sunrise, when the summit is far less crowded. ✉ *98 Apapane Rd., Hilo* ☎ *808/339–0921* ⊕ *www. arnottslodge.com* ✉ *From $228.*

★ Hawaii Forest & Trail

SPECIAL-INTEREST TOURS | The ultracomfortable, highly educational Summit &

Stars tour packs a lot of fun into a few hours. Guides are knowledgeable about astronomy and Hawaii's geologic and cultural history, and the small group size (maximum of 12) encourages camaraderie while attending to safety. Included in the tour are dinner at an old ranching station, sunset on the summit, and a private star show midmountain. The company's powerful 11-inch Celestron Schmidt-Cassegrain telescope reveals many celestial objects. Everything from water bottles, parkas, and gloves to hot chocolate and brownies is included.

The company's Maunakea Sunrise tour begins in the wee hours before the sun comes up and includes a hike among the endangered silverswords as well as breakfast at the visitor center. Of course the main event is a spectacular sunrise on the summit. The company also offers a daytime version of the summit tour. ✉ *73-5593 Olowalu St., Kailua-Kona* ☎ *808/331–8505, 800/464–1993* ⊕ *www. hawaii-forest.com* ✉ *From $255.*

Mauna Kea Summit Adventures

SPECIAL-INTEREST TOURS | The first company to specialize in tours to the mountain is a small outfit that focuses on stars. Cushy vans with panoramic windows journey first to the visitor center, where participants eat dinner on the lanai and acclimatize for 45 minutes before donning hooded arctic-style parkas and ski gloves for the sunset trip to the 14,000-foot summit. With the help of knowledgeable guides, stargazing through a powerful Celestron telescope happens midmountain, where the elevation is more comfortable and skies are just as clear. The tour includes dinner, hot cocoa and biscotti, and west-side pickup; it runs 364 days a year, weather permitting. ■**TIP**→ **Book at least one month in advance, as these tours sell out fast.** ✉ Kailua-Kona ☎ 808/322–2366, 888/322–2366 ⊕ www.maunakea.com 💰 From $263.

 Sights

★ **Onizuka Center for International Astronomy Visitor Information Station**

VISITOR CENTER | At 9,200 feet, this excellent amateur observation site is a great way to get a sense of the mountain and the observatory work without going all the way to the summit. It's open daily from 11:30 am to 7 pm, and although the center is not offering stargazing activities at night due to COVID-19, this could change in the future. It's also a good place to stop to acclimatize yourself to the altitude if you're heading for the summit. Peruse the gift shop and exhibits about ancient Hawaiian celestial navigation, the mountain's significance as a quarry for the best basalt in the Hawaiian Islands, and Maunakea as a revered spiritual destination. You'll also learn about modern astronomy and ongoing projects at the summit. Nights are clear 90% of the year, so the chances are good of seeing some amazing sights in the sky. Surprisingly, stargazing here is actually better than at the summit itself

because of reduced oxygen there. The parking lot can get crowded. ✉ Maunakea Access Rd. ☎ 808/934–4550 visitor center, 808/935–6268 current road conditions ⊕ hilo.hawaii.edu/maunakea 💰 Free, donations welcome.

Hilo

In comparison to Kailua-Kona, Hilo is often deemed "the old Hawaii." With significantly fewer visitors than the resort areas of Kona and the Kohala Coast, more historic buildings, and a much stronger identity as a long-established community, this working-class, traditional town does seem more authentically "local."

The town stretches from the banks of the Wailuku River to Hilo Bay, where hotels line stately Banyan Drive. The vintage buildings that make up Hilo's downtown have been spruced up as part of a revitalization effort. Nearby, the 30-acre Liliuokalani Park and Gardens, a formal Japanese garden with arched bridges, stepping-stones and waterways, was created in the early 1900s to honor the beloved Queen Liliuokalani as well as the area's Japanese sugar plantation laborers. The park provides a serene setting for strolls, exercise, photography, and events, including an annual hula performance in September to honor Queen Liliuokalani's birthday.

With a population of almost 50,000 in the entire district, Hilo is the fourth-largest city in the state and home to the University of Hawaii at Hilo. Although it is the center of government and commerce for the island, Hilo is clearly a residential town. Mansions with yards of lush tropical foliage share streets with older, plantation-era houses with rusty corrugated roofs. It's a friendly community, populated by Native Hawaiians and descendants of the contract laborers—Japanese, Chinese, Filipino,

Mauna Loa

Mauna Loa is the world's largest active volcano, making up more than 50% of the Big Island of Hawaii. This shield volcano is so massive and heavy that it creates a depression in the sea floor (part of the Pacific tectonic plate) of 8 kilometers (5 miles). In fact, if measured from its base on the ocean floor, Mauna Loa would dwarf Everest. Its sheer size is difficult to quantify, but you could fit all the other Hawaiian islands within its mass. It's been erupting for nearly 700,000 years and shows no signs of stopping, although it's currently in a long "quiet" period.

The volcano remains fairly enigmatic to visitors (and locals) and is not often visited. On the rare days when the summit is visible from the southeast highway, the view of its gentle shield formation does not appear very commanding. You might drive by and either not notice that you are seeing the world's largest active volcano—or simply think it's just a rather large hill.

Looks can be deceiving. Mauna Loa is one of 16 "Decade Volcanoes," so designated by the International Association of Volcanology and Chemistry of Earth's Interior. These volcanoes are particularly dangerous to populated areas. Needless to say, the volcano looms large in the history and the daily life of Hawaii residents.

Visiting Mauna Loa

Despite its size, Mauna Loa is often forgotten in the typical visitor's itinerary. One reason for this is the long drive on a single-lane road to reach the summit. A paved, 17½-mile road, accessed from mile marker 28 on the Daniel K. Inouye Highway (Highway 200, also called the Saddle Road), takes you to the Mauna Loa Observatory at 11,500 feet, where the road ends. It's then a steep, rugged 6.4-mile hike (which can take all day) to the summit, a trek recommended only for the fit, the well-prepared, and the adventurous. There is a cabin at the summit caldera, called Mokuaweoaweo Caldera (13,250 feet), and you may sleep there if you obtain a permit (available from the Kilauea Visitor Center at Hawaii Volcanoes National Park). The other way to access the summit is even more difficult and takes a minimum of three to four days. It's a 19½-mile journey, during which you ascend in altitude by some 6,600 feet to reach the crater. Most hikers stop to acclimatize properly and camp in one of two basic cabins. You need a backcountry wilderness permit for this hike. But there are no services whatsoever in this subfreezing wilderness environment. It was from this vantage that several campers were awakened with the shock of their lives in 1984, when the summit erupted and sent lava flows within 6 miles of Hilo.

and Portuguese—brought in to work the sugarcane fields during the 1800s.

With the district's average rainfall of 130 inches per year, it's easy to see why Hilo's yards are so green and its buildings so weatherworn. Outside town, the Hilo District boasts scenic beach valleys, rain forests, and waterfalls. Although Hilo can get a lot of rain, when the sun does shine—usually part of nearly every day—the town sparkles; during winter, the snow glistens on the summit of Maunakea, 25 miles in the distance. The most magical time of all is when the sun appears while it's still misty, producing spectacular *anuenue* (rainbows) that earn Hilo its nickname: the City of Rainbows.

For a week every year in April, Hilo becomes the epicenter of the hula world when the Merrie Monarch Festival attracts tens of thousands of people to the renowned international event, steeped in traditions that represent the essence of Hilo's pioneering spirit. If you're planning a stay in Hilo during this time, be sure to book your room and car rentals at least eight months in advance.

GETTING HERE AND AROUND

Hilo International Airport is one of the island's two international airports, although flights to and from Kailua-Kona are more frequent. Still, this is the best airport to fly into if your main goal is to visit Hilo and Hawaii Volcanoes National Park.

The Hele-On (⊕ *www.heleonbus.org*) public bus offers intra-Hilo transit service throughout town, but buses don't operate at night. For ultra-budget travelers, the Hele-On bus is a cost-effective way to visit Hawaii Volcanoes National Park or Pahoa Town without having to rent a car. The cost is $2.

Your best bet for getting around Hilo is renting a car. The rental car companies at the Hilo airport include Advantage, Alamo, Budget, Dollar, Hertz, and National. Off-site rental car companies in Hilo include Harper (⊕ *www.harpershawaii. com*) and Enterprise. Daily rates average $125 a day, not including taxes and fees. Reserve early, as fleets in Hilo are not as large as on the Kona side. If you're coming during the Merrie Monarch Festival, rental cars will be in short supply.

Downtown

Local flavor abounds in downtown Hilo, where vintage homes are the norm and businesses occupy older buildings, some historic. The Hilo Farmers Market, in full swing on Wednesday and Saturday, is a must-see. Also downtown are the Pacific Tsunami Museum, the historic Palace Theater, and the Mokupapapa Discovery Center. Visitors to downtown Hilo might wonder why the bayfront shops, galleries, and businesses are located such a distance from the actual bayfront. That's because the devastating tsunamis of 1946 and 1960 decimated the populated shoreline areas of Hilo's former downtown center.

 ## Sights

★ Hilo Farmers Market

MARKET | The 200 vendors here—stretching a couple of blocks at the bayfront—sell a profusion of tropical flowers, locally grown produce, aromatic honey, tangy goat cheese, hot breakfast and lunch items; and fresh baked specialties at extraordinary prices. This colorful, open-air market—the largest and most popular on the island—opens for business Wednesday and Saturday from 6 am to 4 pm. A smaller version on the other days features more than 30 vendors. ✉ *Kamehameha Ave. and Mamo St., Hilo* ☎ *808/933–1000* ⊕ *www.hilofarmersmarket.com* 🎟 *Free.*

★ Lyman Museum and Mission House

HISTORY MUSEUM | Built in 1839 by a missionary couple from New England, Sarah and David Lyman, the beautifully restored Lyman Mission House is the island's oldest wood-frame building and displays household utensils, artifacts, tools, and furniture used by the family, giving visitors a peek into the day-to-day lives of Hawaii's first missionaries. The Lymans hosted such literary dignitaries as Isabella Bird and Mark Twain here. The home is on the State and National Registers of Historic Places, and docent-guided tours are offered. An adjacent museum has wonderful exhibits on volcanoes, island formation, island habitats and wildlife, marine shells, and minerals and gemstones. It also showcases Native Hawaiian culture and the culture of immigrant ethnic groups. On permanent exhibit is a full-size replica of a traditional 1930s Korean home. The gift shop sells great Hawaiian-made items. ✉ *276 Haili St., Hilo* ☎ *808/935–5021* 🌐 *www.lymanmuseum.org* 🎟 *$7, $2 kids 6–17* 🕓 *Closed weekends.*

Mokupapapa Discovery Center for Hawaii's Remote Coral Reefs

SCIENCE MUSEUM | **FAMILY** | This is a great place to learn about the stunning Papahanaumokuakea Marine National Monument, which encompasses nearly 140,000 square miles in the northwestern Hawaiian Islands and is the only mixed UNESCO World Heritage site (meaning one that has both natural and cultural significance) in the United States. Giant murals, 3-D maps, and hands-on interactive kiosks depict the monument's extensive wildlife, including millions of birds and more than 7,000 marine species, many of which are found only in the Hawaiian archipelago. Knowledgeable staff and volunteers are on hand to answer questions. A 3,500-gallon aquarium and short films give insight into the unique features of the monument, as well as threats to its survival. Located in the refurbished F. Koehnen Building, the center is worth a stop just to get an up close look at its huge stuffed albatross with wings outstretched or the monk seal exhibit. The price is right, too. ✉ *F. Koehnen Bldg., 76 Kamehameha Ave., Hilo* ☎ *808/933–8180* 🌐 *www.papahanaumokuakea.gov/education/center.html* 🎟 *Free* 🕓 *Closed Sun. and Mon.*

🍴 Restaurants

★ Bears' Coffee

$ | **DINER** | **FAMILY** | A fixture downtown since the late 1980s, this favorite, cozy breakfast spot is much loved for its fresh-fruit waffles and tasty morning coffee. For lunch the little diner serves huge deli sandwiches and decent entrée-size salads, plus specials like hearty meatloaf, roasted chicken, and pot roast. **Known for:** bear wallpaper and decor; specialty coffee such as the iced toddy cold brew; reliable breakfasts. [$] *Average main: $10* ✉ *106 Keawe St., Hilo* ☎ *808/935–0708* 🕓 *No dinner.*

Café Pesto

$$ | **ITALIAN** | Located in a beautiful high-ceiling venue in the vintage S. Hata Building, Café Pesto offers creative pizzas with ingredients such as fresh Hamakua mushrooms, artichokes, and Gorgonzola. **Known for:** wood-fired pizza; featured on the Food Network; use of local farm produce. [$] *Average main: $20* ✉ *308 Kamehameha Ave., Hilo* ☎ *808/969–6640* 🌐 *www.cafepesto.com.*

★ Hilo Burger Joint

$ | **AMERICAN** | **FAMILY** | What this casual pub-turned-burger-joint lacks in space and parking is more than made up for in burger choices: more than 22 varieties of gourmet burgers, from a bacon ranch burger to a southern BBQ burger. Many of the ingredients come straight from the Big Island, and non-beef selections such as fish burgers are available as well, so it's definitely worth checking out. **Known for:** grass-fed local beef; more than 21 beers on tap; live entertainment. [$] *Average main: $14* ✉ *776 Kilauea Ave., Hilo* ☎ *808/935–8880* 🌐 *www.hiloburgerjoint.com.*

Moon and Turtle

$$$ | **INTERNATIONAL** | This sophisticated, intimate restaurant in a bayfront building offers a classy selection of international fare with the focus on locally sourced meats, produce, and seafood. The menu changes daily (see their Facebook page), but mushroom pappardelle is a highlight, along with seafood chowder, spicy *kajiki* (marlin) tartare, and crispy whole-fried *moi* (Pacific threadfin). **Known for:** lychee martinis infused with Hawaiian influences; reservations essential; smoky ahi sashimi. [$] *Average main: $30* ✉ *51 Kalakaua St., Hilo* ☎ *808/961–0599* 🌐 *facebook.com/moonandturtle* 🕓 *Closed Sun. and Mon.*

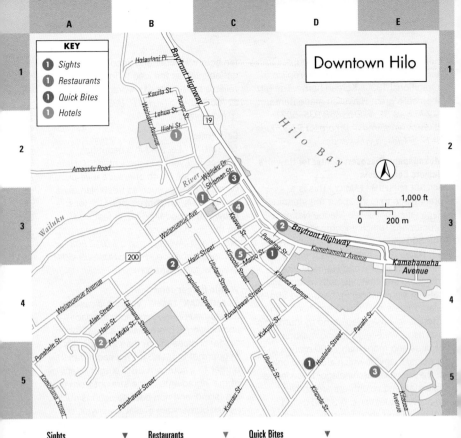

Downtown Hilo

KEY
1 Sights
1 Restaurants
1 Quick Bites
1 Hotels

Sights ▼
1 Hilo Farmers Market **C3**
2 Lyman Museum and
Mission House **B4**
3 Mokupapapa Discovery
Center for Hawaii's
Remote Coral Reefs **C2**

Restaurants ▼
1 Bears' Coffee **C3**
2 Café Pesto **C3**
3 Hilo Burger Joint......... **E5**
4 Moon and Turtle **C3**
5 Pineapples Island
Fresh Cuisine............ **C3**

Quick Bites ▼
1 K's Drive-In **D5**

Hotels ▼
1 Dolphin Bay Hotel **B2**
2 Hilo Honu Inn............ **A5**

Pineapples Island Fresh Cuisine

$ | **AMERICAN** | **FAMILY** | If you expect that a restaurant named Pineapples would serve tropical beverages in hollowed-out pineapples, you'd be exactly correct. Always packed, this open-air bistro looks like a tourist trap, but there is a fine-dining component to the menu, which includes fresh catch, *kalbi* ribs (grilled, Korean-style), teriyaki flank steak, burgers, wraps, and sandwiches. **Known for:** great pineapple salsa; live entertainment Thursday–Sunday; surprisingly inventive island cuisine. $ *Average main: $14* ✉ *332 Keawe St., Hilo* ☎ *808/238–5324* ◌ *Closed Mon.*

☕ Coffee and Quick Bites

K's Drive-In

$ | **HAWAIIAN** | Unassuming from the outside, this small, local-style plate-lunch eatery serves top-quality, genuine Hawaiian specialties in Hilo. All the staples are here, from *kalua* pork (slow-cooked and pulled) to *shoyu* chicken (cooked in a sauce including fermented soy sauce), *loco moco* (meat, rice, and eggs smothered in gravy), and pork adobo. **Known for:** extremely affordable prices; favorite among locals since 1964; daily specials like oxtail soup. $ *Average main: $8* ✉ *194 Hualalai St., Hilo* ☎ *808/935–5573* ⊕ *www.ksdrivein.com.*

Hotels

Dolphin Bay Hotel

$ | **HOTEL** | **FAMILY** | Units in this circa-1950s motor lodge are modest but charming, as well as clean and inexpensive; a glowing lava-flow sign marks the office and testifies to owner John Alexander's passion for the volcano. **Pros:** great value; full kitchens in all units; helpful and pleasant staff. **Cons:** no phones in the rooms; dated decor; no pool. $ *Rooms from: $129* ✉ *333 Iliahi St., Hilo* ☎ *808/935–1466* ⊕ *www.dolphinbayhotel.com* ⤳ *18 rooms* ◉ *No Meals.*

Hilo Honu Inn

$ | **B&B/INN** | A charming old Craftsman home lovingly restored by a friendly and hospitable couple from North Carolina, the inn offers quite a bit of variety in guest room size and decor, though every room has a fridge. **Pros:** spectacular Hilo Bay views; historical setting; within walking distance of Hilo bayfront. **Cons:** not on the beach; a/c in only two of the three rooms; no toddlers in the upstairs suite. $ *Rooms from: $175* ✉ *465 Haili St., Hilo* ☎ *808/935–4325* ⊕ *www.hilohonu.com* ⤳ *3 rooms* ◉ *Free Breakfast.*

▼ Nightlife

BARS

Cronies Bar and Grill

BARS | A sports bar by night and a good hamburger joint by day, Cronies is a local favorite. When the lights go down, the bar gets packed. ✉ *11 Waianuenue Ave., Hilo* ☎ *808/935–5158* ⊕ *www.cronieshawaii.com.*

Performing Arts

★ Merrie Monarch Festival

CULTURAL FESTIVALS | The mother of all Hawaii festivals, the world-class Merrie Monarch in Hilo celebrates all things hula for one fantastic week every April with competitions, activities, a parade, and more. The esteemed event honors the legacy of King David Kalakaua (1836–1891), the man responsible for reviving fading Hawaiian cultural traditions including hula. The three-day hula competition is staged at the Edith Kanakaole Multi-Purpose Stadium during the first week following Easter Sunday. Hula *halau* (studios) worldwide come to perform both *kahiko* (ancient) and *auana* (modern) dance styles, solo and in groups. Tickets are not expensive, but they are hard to get. ■**TIP**➔ **You should reserve accommodations and rental cars up to a year in advance. Ticket requests must be mailed and postmarked after December 1**

of the preceding year. ✉ *Edith Kanakaole Multi-Purpose Stadium, 350 Kalanikoa St., Hilo* ☎ *808/935–9168* ⊕ *www.merriemonarch.com.*

Shopping

CLOTHING AND SHOES

Sig Zane Designs

MIXED CLOTHING | The acclaimed boutique for women and men sells island wearables with bold colors and motifs designed by the legendary Sig Zane, known for his artwork honoring Hawaii's native flora and fauna. All apparel is handcrafted in Hawaii and is often worn by local celebrities and businesspeople. ✉ *122 Kamehameha Ave., Hilo* ☎ *808/935–7077* ⊕ *www.sigzanedesigns.com.*

FOOD

★ Sugar Coast Candy

CANDY | Located on the bayfront in downtown Hilo, this beautifully decorated candy boutique is a blast from the past, featuring an amazing array of nostalgic candies, artisan chocolates, and wooden barrels overflowing with saltwater taffy and other delights. ✉ *274 Kamehameha Ave., Hilo* ☎ *808/935–6960.*

★ Two Ladies Kitchen

CANDY | This hole-in-the-wall confections shop has made a name for itself thanks to its pillowy mochi. The proprietors are best known for their huge, ripe strawberries wrapped in a white mochi covering, which won't last as long as a box of chocolates—most mochi items are good for only two or three days. To guarantee you get your fill, call and place your order ahead of time. ✉ *274 Kilauea Ave., Hilo* ☎ *808/961–4766.*

Liliuokalani Gardens and Reeds Bay

The hotel district near Banyan Drive is within walking distance of nearby scenic Liliuokalani Gardens. To the east, Reeds Bay is small and idyllic, surrounded by a tiny sand beach and some parks with picnic tables. There's a lot of local activity here, including kayaking, fishing, swimming, and stand-up paddleboarding. Several bayside restaurants are within walking distance of the hotels, some with spectacular bayfront views.

Sights

Liliuokalani Gardens

GARDEN | Designed to honor Hawaii's first Japanese immigrants and named after Hawaii's last reigning monarch, Liliuokalani Gardens' 30 acres of fish-filled ponds, stone lanterns, half-moon bridges, elegant pagodas, and a ceremonial teahouse make it a favorite Sunday destination. You'll see weddings, picnics, and families as you stroll. The surrounding area, once a busy residential neighborhood on Waiakea Peninsula, was destroyed by a devastating 1960 tsunami that killed 61 people. ✉ *Banyan Dr., at Lihiwai St., Hilo* ☒ *Free.*

🍴 Restaurants

Happy Valley Seafood Restaurant

$ | **CHINESE** | Hilo's best Chinese restaurant specializes in seafood but also offers many other Cantonese treats, including salt-and-pepper pork, Mongolian lamb, and vegetarian specialties like garlic eggplant and crispy green beans. The food is good, portions are large, and the price is right, but don't come here expecting any ambience—this is a funky, no-frills Chinese restaurant, with random pieces of artwork tacked up here and there. **Known for:** salt-and-pepper prawns; good soups; authentic Cantonese Chinese food.

Liliuokalani Gardens, a 30-acre ornamental Japanese garden, was built in 1917 to honor the island's first Japanese immigrants.

$ *Average main: $12* ✉ *1263 Kilauea Ave., Suite 320, Hilo* ☎ *808/933–1083.*

★ Hilo Bay Cafe

$$ | JAPANESE FUSION | Overlooking Hilo Bay from its towering perch on the waterfront, this popular, upscale restaurant with great water views has a sophisticated second-floor dining room that looks like it's straight out of Manhattan. A sushi bar complements the excellent selection of fresh fish, pork, beef, and vegan options. **Known for:** Blue Bay burger with shoestring fries; Hilo's most upscale restaurant; creative use of fresh local produce. $ *Average main: $22* ✉ *123 Lihiwai St., Hilo* ☎ *808/935–4939* ⊕ *www.hilobaycafe.com* ⊗ *Closed Sun.*

Ken's House of Pancakes

$ | DINER | FAMILY | For years, this legendary diner near Banyan Drive between the airport and the hotels has been a gathering place for Hilo residents and visitors. Breakfast is the main attraction: Ken's serves 11 types of pancakes, plus all kinds of fruit waffles (banana, peach) and popular omelets, like Da Bradda, teeming with meats. **Known for:** extensive menu of Hawaiian and diner fare; weekly special nights like Sunday spaghetti and Tuesday tacos; local landmark with old-fashioned vibe. $ *Average main: $16* ✉ *1730 Kamehameha Ave., Hilo* ☎ *808/935–8711* ⊕ *www.kenshouseofpancakes.com.*

Ponds Hilo

$$ | AMERICAN | FAMILY | Perched on the waterfront overlooking a scenic pond at Reeds Bay Beach Park, this restaurant has the look and vibe of an old-fashioned, harborside steak house and bar. The menu features a good range of burgers and salads, steak, and seafood. **Known for:** excellent fish-and-chips; popular Sunday brunch; Thursday lobster night. $ *Average main: $20* ✉ *135 Kalanianaole Ave., Hilo* ☎ *808/934–7663* ⊕ *www.pond-shilo.com* ⊗ *Closed Tues. and Wed.*

★ Sombat's Fresh Thai Cuisine

$$ | THAI | There's a reason why locals flock to this hideaway for the best Thai cuisine in Hilo. Fresh local ingredients highlight proprietor Sombat Saenguthai's menu (many of the herbs come from

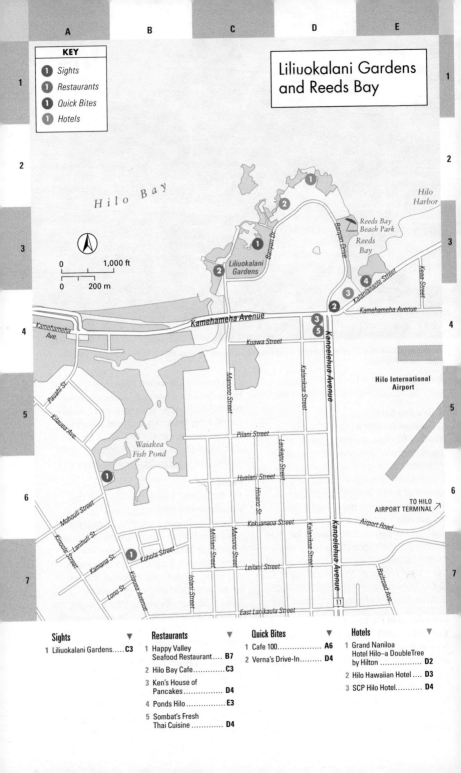

Liliuokalani Gardens and Reeds Bay

KEY

- ● Sights
- ● Restaurants
- ● Quick Bites
- ● Hotels

Hilo Bay

Hilo Harbor

Reeds Bay Beach Park

Reeds Bay

0 — 1,000 ft
0 — 200 m

Liliuokalani Gardens

Kamehameha Avenue

Kamehameha Ave.

Kuawa Street

Manono Street

Kalanikoa Street

Kanoelehua Avenue

Hilo International Airport

Pauahi St.

Kilauea Ave.

Waiakea Fish Pond

Pilani Street

Leukapu Street

Hualani Street

Hinano St.

TO HILO AIRPORT TERMINAL ↗

Mohouli Street

Kekuanaoa Street

Airport Road

Kinoole Street

Lanihuli St.

Kamana St.

Kohola Street

Mililani Street

Manono Street

Leilani Street

Railroad Ave.

Lono St.

Kilauea Avenue

Iolani Street

East Lanikaula Street

11

Sights ▼	Restaurants ▼	Quick Bites ▼	Hotels ▼
1 Liliuokalani Gardens..... **C3**	1 Happy Valley Seafood Restaurant.... **B7**	1 Cafe 100.................. **A6**	1 Grand Naniloa Hotel Hilo–a DoubleTree by Hilton **D2**
	2 Hilo Bay Cafe............. **C3**	2 Verna's Drive-In......... **D4**	2 Hilo Hawaiian Hotel **D3**
	3 Ken's House of Pancakes................. **D4**		3 SCP Hilo Hotel........... **D4**
	4 Ponds Hilo................. **E3**		
	5 Sombat's Fresh Thai Cuisine **D4**		

her own garden) to create authentic and tasty Thai treats like coconut curries, fresh basil rolls, eggplant stir-fry, and green papaya salad. **Known for:** friendly service; single owner and chef; famous pad Thai sauce available for purchase. *[$] Average main: $17 ✉ Waiakea Kai Plaza, 88 Kanoelehue Ave., Hilo ✣ Close to Ken's House of Pancakes ☎ 808/969–9336 🌐 www.sombats.com ⏲ Closed Sun. No lunch.*

Coffee and Quick Bites

Cafe 100

$ | **HAWAIIAN** | **FAMILY** | Established in 1948, this casual spot is famous for its tasty loco moco, prepared in more than three dozen ways (with different meats, chicken, vegetables, and fish), and its low-priced breakfast and lunch specials. The word "restaurant," or even "café," is used loosely—you order at a window and eat on one of the outdoor benches provided—but you come here for the food, prices, and authentic, old-Hilo experience. **Known for:** the Super Loco Moco; generous portions; family-owned eatery. *[$] Average main: $6 ✉ 969 Kilauea Ave., Hilo ☎ 808/935–8683 🌐 www.cafe100.com ⏲ Closed weekends.*

Verna's Drive-In

$ | **HAWAIIAN** | Verna's is tried-and-true among locals, who come for the juicy house-made burgers and filling plate lunches, and the price is right with a burger combo that includes fries and a drink. If you're hungry for more, try the traditional Hawaiian plate with either laulau, beef stew, chicken long rice, or lomilomi salmon (salted salmon with onions, tomatoes, and green pepper). **Known for:** smoked meat plate lunch; superlow prices; local grindz (food) 24/7 with outdoor seating. *[$] Average main: $6 ✉ 1765 Kamehameha Ave., Hilo ☎ 808/935–2776 ⏲ Closed Sun.*

Hotels

Grand Naniloa Hotel Hilo–a DoubleTree by Hilton

$$$$ | **HOTEL** | **FAMILY** | Hilo isn't known for its fancy resort hotels, but the Grand Naniloa, built in 1939, attempts to remedy that situation in grand fashion, paying homage to hula, Hawaiian culture, and Big Island adventures. **Pros:** walking distance to Japanese gardens and Coconut Island; rental kayaks, paddleboards, and bikes; free golf at adjacent 9-hole course and driving range. **Cons:** limited parking spaces; small swimming pool; some rooms don't have ocean views. *[$] Rooms from: $370 ✉ 93 Banyan Dr., Hilo ☎ 808/969–3333 🌐 www.grandnaniloahilo.com 🛏 388 rooms 🍴 No Meals.*

Hilo Hawaiian Hotel

$ | **HOTEL** | **FAMILY** | This renovated landmark hotel has large bayfront rooms offering spectacular views of Maunakea and Coconut Island on Hilo Bay; streetside rooms overlook the golf course, and the hotel is within walking distance of Liliuokalani Gardens. **Pros:** private lanai in most rooms; Hawaiian-style furniture; free parking. **Cons:** some rooms don't have bayfront views; no beach; pricey breakfast buffet. *[$] Rooms from: $169 ✉ 71 Banyan Dr., Hilo ☎ 808/935–9361, 800/367–5004 from mainland, 800/272–5275 interisland 🌐 www.castleresorts.com 🛏 286 rooms 🍴 No Meals.*

SCP Hilo Hotel

$$ | **HOTEL** | Formerly known as the Hilo Seaside Hotel, this boutique hotel features a minimalist Zen style combined with Hawaiiana accents; it's a decided upgrade from its previous incarnation as a no-frills accommodation. **Pros:** fantastic location across from Reeds Bay; complimentary bikes and stand-up paddleboards; walking distance to several restaurants. **Cons:** no TVs in rooms; no hot tub; parking lot can be tight. *[$] Rooms from: $240 ✉ 126 Banyan Way,*

Hilo ☎ *808/935–0821* ⊕ *scphotel.com/
hilo* ⇨ *128 rooms* ❏ *No Meals.*

🎭 Performing Arts

FESTIVALS
★ Merrie Monarch Festival
CULTURAL FESTIVALS | The mother of all Hawaii festivals, the world-class Merrie Monarch in Hilo celebrates all things hula for one fantastic week every April with competitions, activities, a parade, and more. The esteemed event honors the legacy of King David Kalakaua (1836–1891), the man responsible for reviving fading Hawaiian cultural traditions including hula. The three-day hula competition is staged at the Edith Kanakaole Multi-Purpose Stadium during the first week following Easter Sunday. Hula *halau* (studios) worldwide come to perform both *kahiko* (ancient) and *auana* (modern) dance styles, solo and in groups. Tickets are not expensive, but they are hard to get. ■TIP→ **You should reserve accommodations and rental cars up to a year in advance. Ticket requests must be mailed and postmarked after December 1 of the preceding year.** ✉ *Edith Kanakaole Multi-Purpose Stadium, 350 Kalanikoa St., Hilo* ☎ *808/935–9168* ⊕ *www.merriemonarch.com.*

🛍 Shopping

BOOKS AND MAGAZINES
★ Basically Books
BOOKS | The legendary shop stocks one of Hawaii's largest selections of maps, including topographical and relief maps, and Hilo's largest selection of Hawaiian music (feel free to ask for advice about your selection). It also has a wealth of books about Hawaii, with great choices for children. If you need an umbrella on a rainy Hilo day, this bookstore has plenty of them. ✉ *334 Kilauea Ave., Hilo* ✛ *Across from Ben Franklin's Crafts* ☎ *808/961–0144* ⊕ *www.basicallybooks.com.*

Greater Hilo

Sights beyond the downtown area spread out in every direction and are often interspersed among residential neighborhoods and industrial parks. Be sure to check out Panaewa Rainforest Zoo with its Hawaiian animals and hundreds of species of tropical plants. Above the University of Hawaii at Hilo campus, the Imiloa Astronomy Center has a planetarium and gift shop. For other things to do, Big Island Candies is a must-visit destination for world-class confections.

👁 Sights

Boiling Pots
WATERFALL | Four separate streams fall into a series of circular pools here, fed by Peepee Falls just above, and the resulting turbulent action—best seen after a good rain—has earned this scenic stretch of the Wailuku River the nickname Boiling Pots. Swimming is not allowed at Boiling Pots or anywhere in the Wailuku River, due to extremely dangerous currents and undertows. The falls are 3 miles northwest of downtown Hilo off Waianuenue Avenue; keep to the right when the road splits and look for the sign. The gate opens at 7 am and closes at 6 pm. You may want to combine a drive to this site with a visit to Rainbow Falls, a bit closer to downtown. ■TIP→ **You may be tempted, as you watch others ignore the signs and climb over guardrails, to jump in, but resist. Swimming is prohibited and unsafe, and people have died here.** ✉ *Wailuku River State Park, off Waianuenue Ave., Hilo* ✛ *At the end of Peepee Falls Dr.* ⊕ *dlnr.hawaii.gov/dsp/parks/hawaii* ⌨ *Free.*

★ Hawaii Tropical Bioreserve & Garden
GARDEN | Stunning coastline views appear around each curve of the 4-mile scenic jungle drive that accesses this privately owned nature preserve next to Onomea Bay. Paved pathways in the 17-acre botanical garden lead past ponds,

waterfalls, and more than 2,000 species of plants and flowers, including palms, bromeliads, torch ginger, heliconia, orchids, and ornamentals. The garden is well worth a stop, and your entry fee helps the nonprofit preserve plants, seeds, and rain forests. ■ **TIP→ Trails can get slippery when it's raining.** ⊠ *27-717 Old Mamalahoa Hwy., Papaikou* ✛ *8 miles north of downtown Hilo* ☎ *808/964–5233* ⊕ *www.htbg.com* 🖾 *$25.*

★ Imiloa Astronomy Center

SCIENCE MUSEUM | Part Hawaiian cultural center, part astronomy museum, part planetarium, this center provides community outreach for the astronomy program at the University of Hawaii at Hilo. With its interactive exhibits, full-dome planetarium shows, and regularly scheduled talks and events, the center is a must-see for anyone interested in the stars and planets, Hawaiian cultural history, and early Polynesian navigation. Admission includes one planetarium show and an all-day pass to the exhibit hall, which features more than 100 interactive displays. The lunch buffet at the adjoining Sky Garden Restaurant is popular and affordable. A five-minute drive from downtown Hilo, the center is located above the main campus at the university's Science and Technology Park. ⊠ *University of Hawaii at Hilo Science and Technology Park, 600 Imiloa Pl., off Nowelo and Komohana Sts., Hilo* ☎ *808/969–9700* ⊕ *www.imiloahawaii. org* 🖾 *$19* ⊗ *Closed Mon.*

★ Panaewa Rainforest Zoo and Gardens

ZOO | FAMILY | Billed as "the only natural tropical rain forest zoo in the United States," this 12-acre county zoo features native Hawaiian species such as the nene goose and the io (hawk), as well as many other rare birds such as the highly endangered Hawaiian crow, or alala. Two Bengal tigers are also part of the collection. The white-faced whistling tree ducks are a highlight, along with monkeys, sloths, and lemurs, and there's a petting zoo on Saturdays from 1:30 to 2:30. Hundreds of species of lush, unusual tropical plants fill the grounds. To get here, turn left on Mamaki off Highway 11; it's just past the "Kulani 19, Stainback Hwy." sign. ⊠ *800 Stainback Hwy., Hilo* ☎ *808/959–7224* 🖾 *Free, donations encouraged.*

Rainbow Falls

WATERFALL | After a hard rain, these impressive falls thunder into the Wailuku River gorge, often creating magical rainbows in the mist. Rainbow Falls, sometimes known as the "Hilo Town Falls," are located just above downtown Hilo in Wailuku River State Park. Take Waianuenue Avenue west for a mile; when the road forks, stay right and look for the Hawaiian warrior sign. The falls remain open during daylight. If you're visiting the falls, drive up to Boiling Pots, also inside the park but a bit farther up the road. At Boiling Pots, four streams fall into turbulent pools that resemble cauldrons. ⊠ *Wailuku River State Park, Rainbow Dr., Hilo* ⊕ *dlnr.hawaii.gov/dsp/ parks/hawaii* 🖾 *Free.*

 Beaches

Onekahakaha Beach Park

BEACH | FAMILY | Shallow, rock-wall-enclosed tide pools and an adjacent grassy picnic area make this park a favorite among Hilo families with small children. The protected pools are great places to look for Hawaiian marine life like crabs and opihi (limpets). There isn't much white sand, but access to the water is easy. The water is usually rough beyond the line of large boulders protecting the inner tide pools, so be careful if the surf is high. This beach gets crowded on weekends. **Amenities:** lifeguards (weekends, holidays, and summer only); parking (no fee); showers; toilets. **Best for:** swimming. ⊠ *Onekahakaha Rd. and Kalanianaole Ave., Hilo* ✛ *3 miles east of Hilo* ☎ *808/961–8311.*

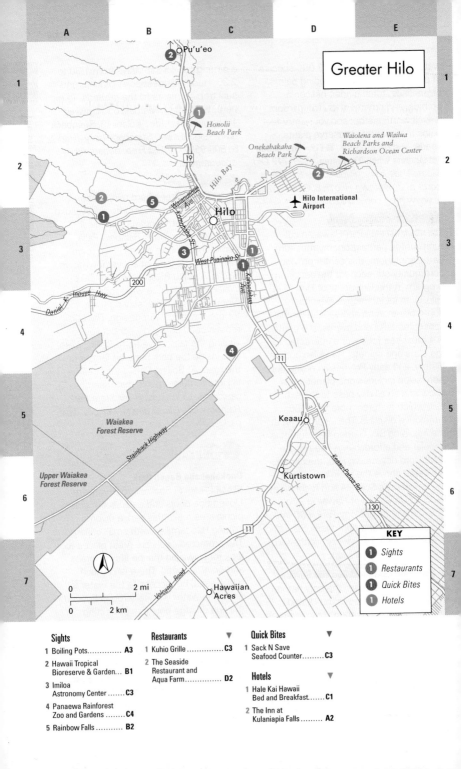

Greater Hilo

KEY

- **1** Sights
- **1** Restaurants
- **1** Quick Bites
- **1** Hotels

Richardson Ocean Park and Leleiwi Beach Park

BEACH | FAMILY | Just east of Hilo, almost at the end of the road, is one of the best snorkeling sites on this side of the island, as rocky outcrops provide shelter for schools of reef fish and sea turtles. Richardson Ocean Park is also the only beach in Hilo with black and green sand. Don't get close to turtles or disturb them; they are protected from harassment by federal and state law. The shaded grassy areas are great for picnics. The surrounding area unfolds into bays, protected inlets, fishponds, and lagoons, as well as the adjacent Leleiwi Beach Park. Local kids use the small black-sand beach for bodyboarding. **Amenities:** lifeguards (weekends, holidays, and summer only); parking (no fee); showers; toilets. **Best for:** snorkeling; walking. ✉ *2349 Kalanianaole Ave., Hilo* ✣ *4 miles east of Hilo* ☎ *808/961–8311.*

🍴 Restaurants

Kuhio Grille

$ | HAWAIIAN | There's no atmosphere to speak of at this diner, and water is served in unbreakable plastic tumblers, but if you're searching for local fare—that undefinable fusion of ethnic cuisines—this is the place. Choose from "grindz" that include *loco moco* (meat, rice, and eggs smothered in gravy), oxtail soup, plate lunches, pork chops, steaks, saimin, stir-fry, and daily specials. **Known for:** good plate lunches; award-winning one-pound laulau; authentic Hawaiian experience. [$] *Average main: $12* ✉ *80 Pauahi St., Hilo* ☎ *808/959–2336* 🌐 *www.kuhiogrille.com* 🕒 *Closed Tues.*

The Seaside Restaurant and Aqua Farm

$$ | SEAFOOD | FAMILY | Owned and operated by the Nakagawi family since the early 1920s, this landmark restaurant features three separate dining rooms that overlook a 30-acre natural brackish fishpond, making this one of the most interesting places to eat in Hilo. Some highlights are *paniolo* (cowboy) prime rib, New York steak, and shrimp scampi. **Known for:** ocean and pond views at sunset; fried aholehole (young Hawaiian flagtail); authentic local experience. [$] *Average main: $23* ✉ *1790 Kalanianaole Ave., Hilo* ☎ *808/935–8825* 🌐 *seasidehilo.square.site* 🕒 *Closed Mon. and Tues. No lunch.*

☕ Coffee and Quick Bites

Sack N Save Seafood Counter

$ | HAWAIIAN | FAMILY | It may sound strange, but the takeout seafood counter tucked in the back of this grocery store serves some of the finest poke in Hilo. For $10 a bowl, you get enough seafood on a steaming pile of rice to feed two people. **Known for:** house-made sauces; good-value grab-and-go lunch spot; variety of fresh, Hawaiian-style poke offerings. [$] *Average main: $10* ✉ *Puainako Center, 2100 Kanoelehua Ave., Suite 101, Hilo* ☎ *808/959–5831* 🌐 *www.foodland.com/stores/sack-n-save-puainako.*

🛏 Hotels

Hale Kai Hawaii Bed and Breakfast

$$ | B&B/INN | On a bluff above Honolii surfing beach, this modern, 5,400-square-foot home is 2 miles from downtown Hilo and features four rooms—each with patio, deluxe bedding, and grand ocean views within earshot of the surf. **Pros:** continental breakfast on outdoor deck; intimate, romantic vibe; smoke-free property. **Cons:** just outside walking distance to downtown Hilo; occasional coqui frog noise; no kids under 13. [$] *Rooms from: $199* ✉ *111 Honolii Pl., Hilo* ☎ *808/935–6330* 🌐 *www.halekaihawaii.com* 🛏 *4 rooms* 🍽 *Free Breakfast.*

The Inn at Kulaniapia Falls

$ | B&B/INN | Overlooking downtown Hilo and the ocean beyond, this inn sits next to a 120-foot waterfall that tumbles into a 300-foot-wide natural pond—enticing for swimming, conditions permitting. **Pros:** guest rooms in different buildings;

delicious full breakfast (not included with cabins); eco-friendly option. **Cons:** paved road is dark at night (drive slow); no air-conditioning; isolated location. [$] *Rooms from: $160* ✉ *100 Kulaniapia Dr., Hilo* ☎ *808/935–6789* 🌐 *www.waterfall.net* 🛏 *14 rooms* 🍴 *Free Breakfast.*

Shopping

ARTS AND CRAFTS

Most Irresistible Shop in Hilo

SOUVENIRS | FAMILY | Living up to its name, the store stocks unique gifts from around the Pacific, be it pure Hawaiian ohia lehua honey, Kau coffee, aloha wear, or tinkling wind chimes. ✉ *256 Kamehameha Ave., Hilo* ☎ *808/935–9644* 🌐 *www.mostirresistibleshop.com.*

FOOD

★ Big Island Candies

CHOCOLATE | A local legend in the cookie- and chocolate-making business, Big Island Candies is a must-see for connoisseurs of fine chocolates. The packaging is first-rate, which makes these world-class confections the ideal gift or souvenir. Enjoy a free cookie sample and a cup of Kona coffee as you watch through a window as sweets are being made. The store has many interesting products, but it is best known for its chocolate-dipped shortbread cookies. ✉ *585 Hinano St., Hilo* ☎ *808/935–8890* 🌐 *www.bigislandcandies.com.*

SHOPPING CENTERS

Prince Kuhio Plaza

MALL | FAMILY | The Big Island's most comprehensive mall has indoor shopping, entertainment (a multiplex), and dining, including KFC, Hot Dog on a Stick, Cinnabon, Genki Sushi, IHOP, and Maui Tacos. The kids might like the arcade (near the food court), while you enjoy the stores, anchored by Macy's and Old Navy. ✉ *111 E. Puainako St., Hilo* ☎ *808/959–3555* 🌐 *www.princekuhioplaza.com.*

Hawaii Volcanoes National Park, Puna, and Kau

Dynamic, dramatic, and diverse, Hawaii Volcanoes National Park encompasses 333,308 acres across two active shield volcanoes: Kilauea and Mauna Loa. The sparsely populated areas of the Puna and Kau districts surround the park to the northeast and southwest, respectively. One of the state's most popular visitor destinations, Hawaii Volcanoes National Park—a UNESCO World Heritage site and International Biosphere Reserve—beckons visitors to explore the sacred home of the fire goddess Pele, whose active presence shapes the primordial landscape. Presenting incomparable scenic, geological, and ecological attractions, the park is a must-see destination, whether for a half-day trek or a weeklong deep dive into this unique place. The area and the park have recovered from the damaging events of the 2018 Kilauea eruption that rocked the region for months, beginning with the collapse of the Puu Oo Vent in the lower East Rift Zone on April 30, 2018. Soon thereafter, the famed lava lake at Halemaumau Crater, known for its ethereal nighttime glow, disappeared for several years, only to return once more in December 2020. It has been putting on a show intermittently ever since. The seismic events of 2018 at the summit did cause permanent damage, however, to the Jaggar Museum and the Hawaii Volcano Observatory facility that overlooked the crater; both are closed. Visitors can explore almost all the sights and trails that were open prior to the 2018 eruption. While the dramatic changes to the Summit Caldera are evident to anyone who visited the park before the 2018 eruption, most of the park's favorite attractions survived intact including Thurston Lava Tube, Devastation Trail, and Kilauea Iki Trail. Although it's hard to keep up with the on-again, off-again nature of Kilauea when eruptions within Halemaumau Crater come to a pause, there are always plenty of activities such as hiking, biking, and picnicking to enjoy at any given time. Located just outside Hawaii Volcanoes National Park, the artsy, forested enclave of Volcano Village features galleries, glassblowing studios, cafés, restaurants, boutiques, and a Sunday farmers' market. Accommodations are plentiful here. When visiting Volcano Village, you can partake in wine tastings and tours at a local winery, go bird-watching, or ride a bike along quiet, flat streets. Nearby but inside the park, the Kilauea Military Camp has an arcade, bowling alley, a general store, and the Lava Lounge cocktail bar, all open to the public. And of course, you can always take in the nighttime celestial sights or the ever-changing daytime skies unveiling random rain showers, rainbows, rolling clouds, or crystal clear, sunny weather. The districts of Kau and Puna lie adjacent to each other and are big and sparse, requiring lots of drive time to get to the places of most interest. The Kau area is known for its wide-open spaces, vast desert regions, rugged coastline, dense macadamia groves, and windswept ranchlands. The Puna district encompasses Lower and Upper Puna.

GETTING HERE AND AROUND

The 27-mile drive on Highway 19 from Hilo to Volcano (all through Upper Puna) takes about 40 minutes. From downtown Kailua-Kona, the drive requires traversing Saddle Road to Hilo and then heading up to Volcano; the one-way drive takes approximately 2½ hours. Heading from South Kona through South Point to the park, the drive along Highway 11 takes about two hours. The park itself is easy to drive around, as there are only two main roads: Chain of Craters Road and Crater Rim Drive.

TOURS

Volcano Art Center Forest Tour

WALKING TOURS | Volcano Art Center offers a free Monday morning forest tour where visitors can learn about old-growth koa and ohia rain forests. These hour-long walks take place on easily traversed gravel trails, rain or shine. No reservations are required, but they are recommended for groups of five or more. The center offers additional customized rain forest tours, as well as forest restoration activities. ⊠ *Volcano Art Center, 99-150 Crater Rim Dr., Hawaii Volcanoes National Park* ☎ *866/967–8222 for administration, 808/967–7565 for gallery* ⊕ *www. volcanoartcenter.org* ⛴ *From $10.*

VISITOR INFORMATION

Hawaii Volcanoes National Park is open 24/7. When you arrive at the park entrance during normal visiting hours, you'll receive a complimentary, detailed map and brochure about the park. The park entrance fee (good for seven days) is $30 per vehicle, $15 per pedestrian, and $25 per motorcycle. Inside the Kilauea Visitor Center, trail guide booklets written by park geologists are available for less than $3 each. Operated by Hawaii Pacific Parks, the park store features educational materials, apparel, gifts, books, and art. A small theater plays educational films about the history of the park, and park rangers are available to answer questions. There is always an itinerary of ranger-led activities. ■TIP➔ **Purchase the Hawaii Tri-Park Annual Pass for $55, which allows full access to Hawaii Volcanoes National Park and Puuhonua O Honaunau National Historical Park on the Big Island, and Haleakala National Park on Maui.**

Volcano Village

Located right outside the park boundary and surrounded by rain forest, Volcano Village is a residential neighborhood that offers vacation rental accommodations, B&B inns, a gas station, a post office,

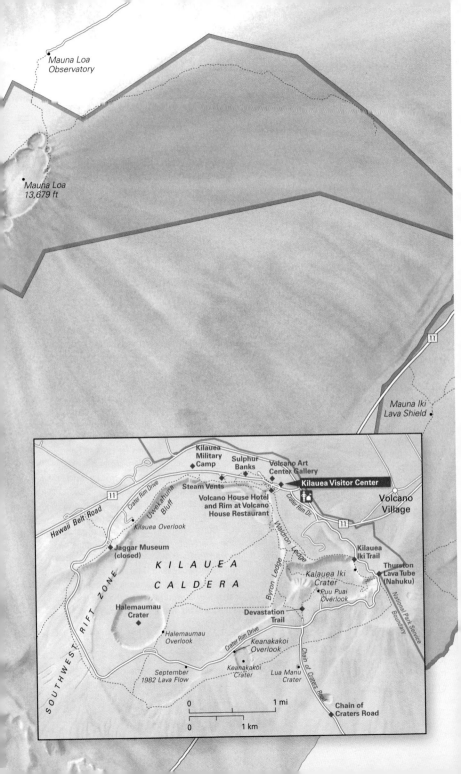

Mauna Loa
Observatory

Mauna Loa
13,679 ft

Mauna Iki
Lava Shield

Kilauea
Military
Camp

Sulphur
Banks

Volcano Art
Center Gallery

Kilauea Visitor Center

Steam Vents

Volcano House Hotel
and Rim at Volcano
House Restaurant

Volcano
Village

Crater Rim Drive

Uwekahuna Bluff

Kilauea Overlook

Hawaii Belt Road

Jaggar Museum
(closed)

K I L A U E A

C A L D E R A

Byron Ledge

Waldron Ledge

Kilauea
Iki Trail

Thurston
Lava Tube
(Nahuku)

Kalauea Iki
Crater

Puu Puai
Overlook

Halemaumau
Crater

Devastation
Trail

Halemaumau
Overlook

Keanakakoi
Overlook

Crater Rim Drive

Lua Manu
Crater

Keanakakoi
Crater

September
1982 Lava Flow

Chain of Craters Road

National Park Service Boundary

S O U T H W E S T   R I F T   Z O N E

Chain of
Craters Road

| 0 | | 1 mi |

| 0 | | 1 km |

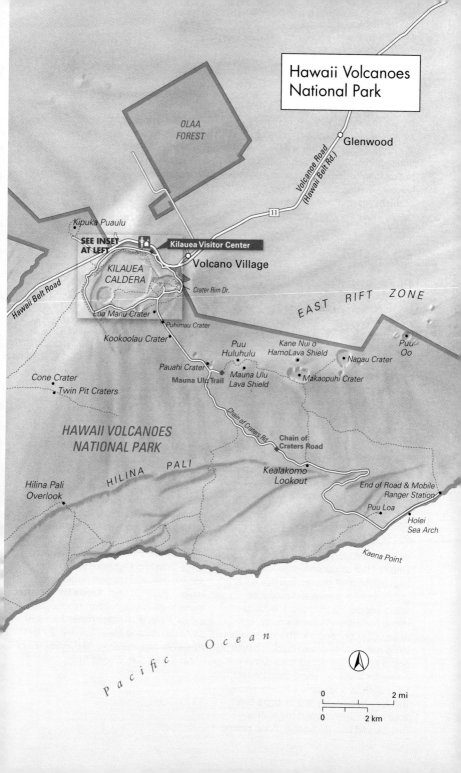

Hawaii Volcanoes National Park

OLAA FOREST

Volcanoe Road (Hawaii Belt Rd.)

Glenwood

11

Kipuka Puaulu

SEE INSET AT LEFT

Kilauea Visitor Center

Volcano Village

KILAUEA CALDERA

Hawaii Belt Road

Crater Rim Dr.

EAST RIFT ZONE

Lua Manu Crater

Puhimau Crater

Kookoolau Crater

Puu Huluhulu

Kane Nui o HamoLava Shield

Puu Oo

Pauahi Crater

Napau Crater

Makaopuhi Crater

Cone Crater

Twin Pit Craters

Mauna Ulu Trail

Mauna Ulu Lava Shield

HAWAII VOLCANOES NATIONAL PARK

Chain of Craters Rd

Chain of Craters Road

HILINA PALI

Kealakomo Lookout

Hilina Pali Overlook

End of Road & Mobile Ranger Station

Puu Loa

Holei Sea Arch

Kaena Point

Pacific Ocean

0   2 mi

0   2 km

an art school, galleries, shops, a general store, and a fun Sunday farmers' market. The immediate area also has a country club and golf course (as of this writing, not yet reopened under its new ownership), along with the popular Volcano Winery. Next door to the winery, the Keauhou Bird Conservation Center is not open to the public, but if you listen closely, you may be able to hear the call of the highly endangered *alala* (Hawaiian crow), a species being bred in captivity at the center.

Sights

Volcano Garden Arts

ART GALLERY | Located on beautifully landscaped grounds dotted with intriguing sculptures, this delightful gallery and garden lend credence to Volcano Village's reputation as an artists' haven. The complex includes an eclectic gallery representing more than 100 artists, an excellent organic café in redwood buildings built in 1908, and a cute, one-bedroom vacation cottage, available for rent. If you're lucky, you'll get to meet the award-winning owner/"caretaker" of this enclave, the multitalented Ira Ono, known for his mixed-media art, recycled trash creations, and friendly personality. ✉ *19-3834 Old Volcano Rd., Volcano* ☎ *808/985–8979* 🌐 *www.volcanogardenarts.com* 🎟 *Free* 🕑 *Garden closed Sun. and Mon.*

★ Volcano Winery

WINERY | Not all volcanic soils are ideal for the cultivation of grapes, but this winery grows its own grapes and produces some interesting vintages. The Macadamia Nut Honey Wine is a nutty, very sweet after-dinner drink. The Infusion Tea Wine pairs estate-grown black tea with South Kona's fermented macadamia nut honey for a smooth concoction perfect for brunch through early evening. Though this isn't Napa Valley, the vintners take their wine seriously, and the staff is friendly and knowledgeable. Wine tasting and flights are available; you can also enjoy wine and cheese inside or in a shaded picnic area. A gift store carries a selection of local crafts. ✉ *35 Pii Mauna Dr., Volcano* ✥ *Past entrance to Hawaii Volcanoes National Park, by golf course* ☎ *808/967–7772* 🌐 *www.volcanowinery.com* 🎟 *Free; tastings from $15 for a flight of 6 wines.*

Restaurants

Kilauea Lodge Restaurant

$$$ | **MODERN AMERICAN** | At this historic lodge in the heart of Volcano Village, the fare ranges from gourmet grass-fed Big Island beef burgers and locally sourced lamb burgers to Cajun shrimp and sausage pasta, catch of the day, and farm-fresh salads. The koa-wood tables and intimate lighting are in keeping with the ambience. **Known for:** fine dining with prices to match; popular Sunday brunch; Fireplace of Friendship. [$] *Average main: $30* ✉ *19-3948 Old Volcano Rd., Volcano* ☎ *808/967–7366* 🌐 *www.kilauealodge.com.*

Lava Rock Cafe

$ | **DINER** | **FAMILY** | This is an affordable place to grab a sandwich or a coffee and check your email (Wi-Fi is free with purchase of a meal) before heading to Hawaii Volcanoes National Park. The homey, sit-down diner caters to families, serving up heaping plates of comfort food like pancakes and French toast for breakfast; on the lunch menu, burgers range from bacon-cheese to turkey and *paniolo* (cowboy) burgers made with Hawaii grass-fed beef. **Known for:** live music in evenings; full bar; roadhouse atmosphere. [$] *Average main: $10* ✉ *19-3972 Old Volcano Hwy., Volcano* ✥ *Next to Kilauea General Store* ☎ *808/967–8526* 🕑 *No dinner Sun. Closed Mon.*

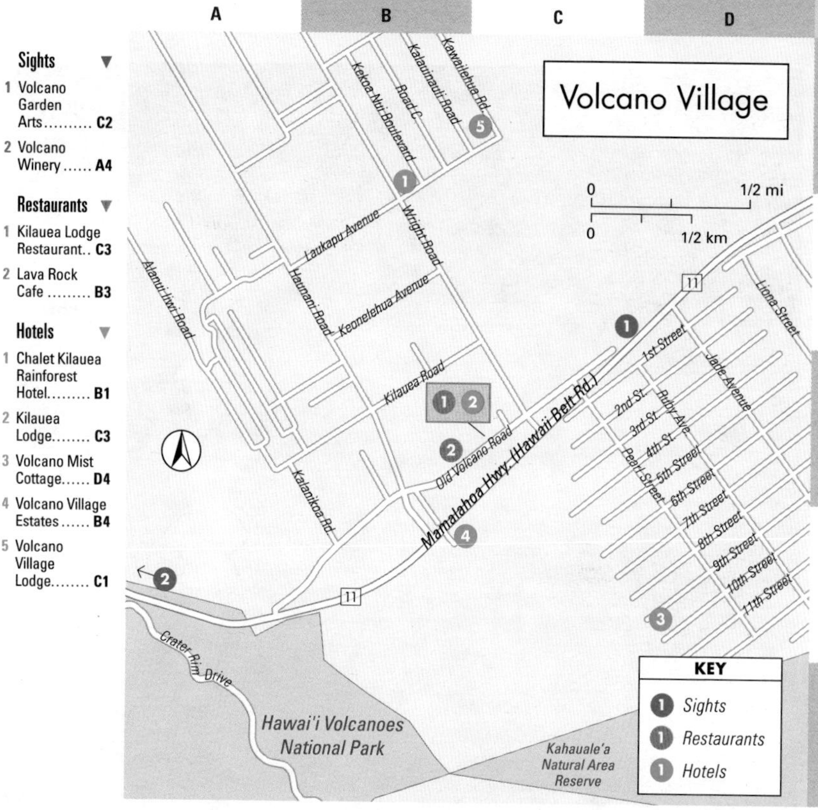
Volcano Village
Sights
1 Volcano Garden Arts.......... C2
2 Volcano Winery...... A4
Restaurants
1 Kilauea Lodge Restaurant.. C3
2 Lava Rock Cafe B3
Hotels
1 Chalet Kilauea Rainforest Hotel......... B1
2 Kilauea Lodge........ C3
3 Volcano Mist Cottage...... D4
4 Volcano Village Estates...... B4
5 Volcano Village Lodge........ C1
A
B
C
D
1
2
3
4
5
0
1/2 mi
0
1/2 km
Kawailehua Rd.
Kalaninauli Road
Road C
Kekoa Nui Boulevard
Laukapu Avenue
Wright Road
Alanui Iiwi Road
Haunani Road
Keonelehua Avenue
Kilauea Road
Old Volcano Road
Mamalahoa Hwy. (Hawaii Belt Rd.)
Kalanikoa Rd.
Liona Street
1st Street
Jade Avenue
2nd St.
3rd St.
Ruby Ave.
4th St.
Pearl Street
5th Street
6th Street
7th Street
8th Street
9th Street
10th Street
11th Street
11
Crater Rim Drive
Hawai'i Volcanoes National Park
Kahauale'a Natural Area Reserve
KEY
Sights
Restaurants
Hotels

Hotels

Chalet Kilauea Rainforest Hotel

$ | **B&B/INN** | Quirky yet upscale, this accommodation features four artistically distinctive rooms that unveil beautiful views of the rain forest from a great location five minutes from Hawaii Volcanoes National Park. **Pros:** unique decor; friendly front desk; hot tub on property. **Cons:** not close to the beach; can get cold at night; space heaters. [$] *Rooms from: $169* ✉ *19-4178 Wright Rd., Volcano* ☎ *808/967–7786, 800/937–7786* 🌐 *www.volcano-hawaii.com* 🛏 *4 rooms* 🍴 *No Meals.*

Kilauea Lodge

$$$ | **HOTEL** | A mile from the entrance to Hawaii Volcanoes National Park, this lodge built as a YMCA camp in the 1930s is now a pleasant inn, tastefully furnished with European antiques, photographs, and authentic Hawaiian quilts. **Pros:** great restaurant; close to volcano; historic ambience. **Cons:** 45 minutes to downtown Hilo; pricey; no TV or phone in lodge rooms. [$] *Rooms from: $300* ✉ *19-3948 Old Volcano Rd., Volcano* ✣ *1 mile northeast of national park* ☎ *808/967–7366* 🌐 *www.kilauealodge.com* 🛏 *12 rooms* 🍴 *No Meals.*

Volcano Mist Cottage

$$$$ | **HOUSE** | Both rustic and Zen, this magical cottage in the rain forest features cathedral ceilings, spruce walls, cork flooring, and amenities not usually found at Volcano vacation rentals, like bathrobes, a Bose home theater system, and Trek mountain bikes. **Pros:** isolated and private cottage; outdoor Jacuzzi tub;

Continued on page 404

HAWAII VOLCANOES NATIONAL PARK

Exploring the surface of the world's most active volcano—from the moonscape craters at the summit to the red-hot lava flows on the coast to the kipuka, pockets of vegetation miraculously left untouched—is the ultimate ecotour and one of Hawaii's must-dos.

The park sprawls over 520 square miles and encompasses Kilauea and Mauna Loa, two of the five volcanoes that formed the Big Island nearly half a million years ago. Kilauea, youngest and most rambunctious of the Hawaiian volcanoes, erupted at its summit from the 19th century through 1982. Since then, the top of the volcano had been more or less quiet, frequently shrouded in mist; an eruption in the Halemaumau Crater in 2008 ended this period of relative inactivity. A major eruption in 2018 has caused further changes in the park.

Kilauea's eastern side sprang to life on January 3, 1983, shooting molten lava four stories high. This eruption has been ongoing, and lava flows are generally steady and slow, appearing and disappearing from view. Over 500 acres have been added to Hawaii's eastern coast since the activity began, and scientists say this eruptive phase is not likely to end anytime soon. However, the famed lava lake at Halemaumau Crater, which drained in 2018, began to refill by 2020.

The damaging events of 2018 have now subsided, and you can see the effects of creation elemental—when molten lava meets the ocean, cools, and solidifies into brand-new stretches of coastline. Although some popular park sights have had to close, you can hike 150 miles of trails and camp amid wide expanses of *aa* (rough) and *pahoehoe* (smooth) lava. There's nothing quite like it.

✉ 1 Crater Rim Dr., Hawaii Volcanoes National Park, HI 96718

☎ 808/985-6000

🌐 www.nps.gov/havo

💵 $30 per vehicle; $15 for pedestrians and bicyclists. Ask about passes. Admission is good for seven consecutive days.

🕓 The park is open daily, 24 hours. Kilauea Visitor Center: 9 am–5 pm. Volcano Art Center Gallery: 9–5.

(top) Kilauea Iki Trail
(left) Solidified lava flow in Hawaii Volcanoes National Park

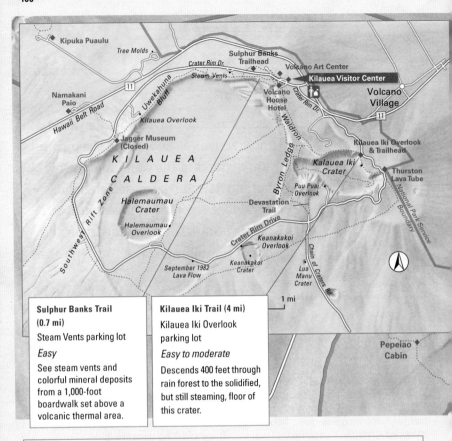

Sulphur Banks Trail (0.7 mi)

Steam Vents parking lot

Easy

See steam vents and colorful mineral deposits from a 1,000-foot boardwalk set above a volcanic thermal area.

Kilauea Iki Trail (4 mi)

Kilauea Iki Overlook parking lot

Easy to moderate

Descends 400 feet through rain forest to the solidified, but still steaming, floor of this crater.

SEEING THE SUMMIT

The best way to explore the summit of Kilauea is to cruise along Crater Rim Drive to Kilauea Overlook. From Kilauea Overlook you can see all of Kilauea Caldera and Halemaumau Crater, an awesome depression in Kilauea Caldera measuring 3,000 feet across and nearly 300 feet deep. It's a huge and breathtaking view with pluming steam vents. Halemaumau Crater's most recent on-and-off eruption has been taking place since December 2020, creating a lake that has risen within view of several observation points accessible to the public.

Regrettably, the events of 2018 damaged the Thomas A. Jaggar Museum beyond repair, and it is now permanently closed. You can visit the nearby Kilauea Military Camp, with its recreational activities and general store, and the park's star attractions, the Thurston Lava Tube, which you can walk through.

Other Highlights along Crater Rim Drive include sulfur and steam vents, fractures, and gullies along Kilauea's flanks. Kilauea Iki Crater, on the way down to Chain of Craters Road, is smaller, but just as fascinating when seen from Puu Pai Overlook.

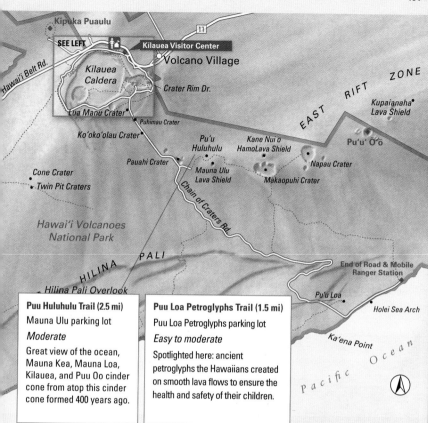

Kipuka Puaulu

SEE LEFT

Kīlauea Visitor Center

Volcano Village

Kīlauea Caldera

Crater Rim Dr.

Hawai'i Belt Rd.

Loa Manu Crater

Puhimau Crater

Koʻokoʻolau Crater

Pauahi Crater

Pu'u Huluhulu

Kane Nui o HamoLava Shield

EAST RIFT ZONE

Kupaianaha Lava Shield

Pu'u' Ōʻo

Napau Crater

Cone Crater

Twin Pit Craters

Mauna Ulu Lava Shield

Mākaopuhi Crater

Hawai'i Volcanoes National Park

HILINA PALI

Chain of Craters Rd.

Hilina Pali Overlook

End of Road & Mobile Ranger Station

Pu'u Loa

Holei Sea Arch

Ka'ena Point

Pacific Ocean

Puu Huluhulu Trail (2.5 mi)

Mauna Ulu parking lot

Moderate

Great view of the ocean, Mauna Kea, Mauna Loa, Kilauea, and Puu Oo cinder cone from atop this cinder cone formed 400 years ago.

Puu Loa Petroglyphs Trail (1.5 mi)

Puu Loa Petroglyphs parking lot

Easy to moderate

Spotlighted here: ancient petroglyphs the Hawaiians created on smooth lava flows to ensure the health and safety of their children.

SEEING LAVA

Lava flows have never been guaranteed, but for the first time since May 2021, lava is flowing in the park again at this writing. You can also still see steam vents and sulfur banks, as well as the effects of millennia of past lava flows.

There are three guarantees about lava flows in HVNP. First: They constantly change. Second: Because of that, you can't predict when and where you'll be able to see them. Third: New land formed when lava meets the sea is highly unstable and can collapse at any time. Never go into areas that have been closed.

■**TIP→** Even without flowing lava, Chain of Craters Road is a magnificent drive, and the park's best hiking trails have now reopened fully.

PLANNING YOUR TRIP TO HVNP

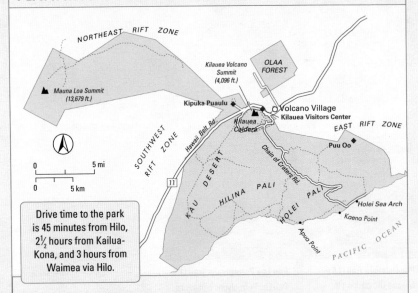

NORTHEAST RIFT ZONE

Kilauea Volcano Summit (4,096 ft.)

OLAA FOREST

▲ Mauna Loa Summit (13,679 ft.)

Kipuka Puaulu ◆

○ Volcano Village
Kilauea Visitors Center

Kilauea Caldera

EAST RIFT ZONE

Puu Oo ◆

SOUTHWEST RIFT ZONE

Hawaii Belt Rd.

11

KAU DESERT

HILINA PALI

Chain of Craters Rd.

HOLEI PALI

Holei Sea Arch

Kaena Point

Apua Point

PACIFIC OCEAN

0   5 mi
0   5 km

Drive time to the park is 45 minutes from Hilo, 2½ hours from Kailua-Kona, and 3 hours from Waimea via Hilo.

Lava entering the ocean

WHERE TO START

Begin your visit at the Visitor Center, where you'll find maps and books; information on trails, ranger-led walks, and special events; and current weather, road, and lava-viewing conditions. Free volcano-related film showings, lectures, and other presentations are regularly scheduled.

WEATHER

Weather conditions fluctuate daily, sometimes hourly. It can be rainy and chilly even during the summer; the temperature usually is 14° cooler at the 4,000-foot-high summit of Kilauea than at sea level.

Expect hot, dry, and windy coastal conditions at the end of Chain of Craters Road. Bring rain gear, and wear layered clothing, sturdy shoes, sunglasses, a hat, and sunscreen.

Visitors stand on cooled lava flows.

FOOD

It's a good idea to bring your own favorite snacks and beverages; stock up on provisions in Volcano Village, 1½ miles away. Kilauea Military Camp, near the summit, has a general store as well as casual dining options, and all are open to the public.

PARK PROGRAMS

Rangers lead daily walks at 10:30 and 1:30 into different areas; check with the Visitor Center for details as times and destinations depend on weather conditions and eruptions.

Over 60 companies hold permits to lead hikes at HVNP. Good choices are Hawaii Forest & Trail (⊕ www.hawaii-forest.com) and KapohoKine Adventures (⊕ www.kapohokine.com).

CAUTION

"Vog" (volcanic smog) can cause headaches; breathing difficulties; lethargy; irritations of the skin, eyes, nose, and throat; and other health problems. Pregnant women, young children, and people with asthma and heart conditions are most susceptible, and should avoid areas such as Halemaumau Crater where fumes are thick.

Wear long pants and boots or closed-toe shoes with good tread for hikes on lava. Stay on marked trails and step carefully. Lava is composed of 50% silica (glass) and can cause serious injury if you fall.

Carry at least 2 quarts of water on hikes. Temperatures near lava flows can rise above 100°F, and dehydration, heat exhaustion, and sunstroke are common consequences of extended exposure to intense sunlight and high temperatures.

Remember that these are active volcanoes, and eruptions can cause parts of the park to close at any time. Check the park's website or call ahead for last-minute updates before your visit.

Pay for and download a digital park entrance pass from ⊕ recreation.gov to save time at the entry gate. The pass can be downloaded to your smart phone or printed.

upscale amenities. **Cons:** 45 minutes from downtown Hilo; pricey for the area; not large enough for families. [$] *Rooms from: $425* ✉ *11-3932 9th St., Volcano* ☎ *808/895–8359* 🌐 *www.volcanomistcottage.com* 🛏 *1 cottage* 🍴 *Free Breakfast.*

Volcano Village Estates

$$$ | **B&B/INN** | **FAMILY** | A stately and comfortable Queen Anne–style mansion, the Dillingham House is the centerpiece of the property and was built in the 1930s as a summer home for a wealthy Scotsman (the property is listed on the State Historic Register). **Pros:** unique architecture; extraordinary setting; private location. **Cons:** simple breakfast offerings; can get cold at night; no TVs. [$] *Rooms from: $275* ✉ *11-3968 Hale Ohia Rd., Volcano* ☎ *808/967–7986, 800/455–3803* 🌐 *volcanovillageestates.com* 🛏 *18 units* 🍴 *Free Breakfast.*

★ **Volcano Village Lodge**

$$$ | **B&B/INN** | Hospitality abounds at this luxurious B&B in a secluded rain forest, where the separate suites (connected by paths) offer amenities including fine furnishings, dining niches, jetted bathtubs, heated blankets, and private forest entrances. **Pros:** secluded and quiet; hospitable staff; outdoor hot tub. **Cons:** far from Hilo town; no restaurants within walking distance; no covered parking (bring an umbrella in case of rain). [$] *Rooms from: $280* ✉ *19-4183 Kawailehua Rd., Volcano* ☎ *808/985–9500* 🌐 *www.volcanovillagelodge.com* 🛏 *5 suites* 🍴 *Free Breakfast.*

Summit Area

In the heart of Hawaii Volcanoes National Park, a primeval landscape unfolds at the summit of Kilauea volcano, where steam rises continuously from cracks in the earth and volcanic gases create malodorous sulfur banks. Here, Halemaumau Crater's most recent on-and-off eruption has been taking place since December 2020, creating a lake that has risen within view of several observation points accessible to the public. In addition to the many geological sights, the summit area of the park includes Kilauea Visitor Center, Volcano Art Center Gallery, and Volcano House—a landmark hotel perched above the rim of Kilauea Caldera. The visitor center is a good place to begin your park adventure.

Sights

Devastation Trail

TRAIL | A paved pathway takes visitors across a barren lavascape strewn with chunky cinders that descended from towering lava fountains during the 1959 eruption of nearby Kilauea Iki Crater. The easy 1-mile (round-trip) hike ends at the edge of the Kilauea Iki Crater. This must-see view of the crater could yield such memorable sights as white-tailed tropic birds gliding in the breeze or a rainbow stretching above the crater's rim after a sunlit rain shower. *Easy.* ✉ *Hawaii Volcanoes National Park* ✣ *Trailhead: 4 miles from visitor center at intersection of Crater Rim Dr. and Chain of Craters Rd.* ☎ *808/985–6101* 🌐 *www.nps.gov/havo.*

★ **Halemaumau Crater**

VOLCANO | For Native Hawaiians, Halemaumau Crater is the sacred home of Pele, the fire goddess; for scientists at the Hawaiian Volcano Observatory, this mighty pit crater within the massive Kilauea Caldera is an ever-changing force to be reckoned with. Prior to Kilauea's 2018 eruption, Halemaumau's visible lava lake awed visitors for 10 consecutive years. Then Puu Oo Vent, which had been erupting farther away in the East Rift Zone for 35 years, collapsed in April 2018. As lava from the vent drained, so did the lava lake at Halemaumau Crater. A relentless series of seismic events at the summit followed, doubling the diameter of Halemaumau Crater and deepening it by 1,300 feet, and a lake of water began forming, eventually growing to 160 feet deep. On December 20, 2020, an eruption within the crater instantly vaporized the water lake, sending molten lava cascading into the crater from vents within the walls and commencing the return of an active lava lake to Halemaumau intermittently throughout 2021. There are many places in the park to view the magnificent crater, including at the Steaming Bluff Overlook and at Volcano House hotel. To get a glimpse of the lava lake during an eruption phase, there is a lookout area between the Steam Vents and the former Jaggar Museum area; another lookout point is on the crater's other side near the Devastation Trail parking lot. ■TIP➔ **For the best lava-viewing experience of Halemaumau Crater during an eruption phase, visit the park after 10 pm when crowds are smaller.** ⊠ *Crater Rim Dr., Hawaii Volcanoes National Park* ☏ *808/985–6101* ⊕ *www.nps.gov/havo.*

★ Kilauea Iki Trail

TRAIL | The stunning 4-mile loop hike descends 400 feet into a massive crater via a forested nature trail. When you hike across the crater floor, you're actually walking on a solidified lava lake. Still steaming in places, the crater is dotted with baby ohia trees emerging from the cracks. Venture across the crater floor to the Puu Puai cinder cone that was formed by spatter from a towering lava fountain during the 1959 Kilauea Iki eruption. There are three different trailheads for Kilauea Iki; the main one, which takes two or three hours, begins at the Kilauea Iki Overlook parking lot off Crater Rim Drive. You can also access the crater from Devastation Trail or Puu Puai on the other side. *Easy.* ■TIP➔ **Bring water, snacks, a hat, sunscreen, and hooded rain gear, as weather can change at a moment's notice.** ⊠ *Crater Rim Dr., Hawaii Volcanoes National Park* ⊹ *Trailhead: 3 miles from visitor center* ☏ *808/985–6011* ⊕ *www.nps.gov/havo.*

Kilauea Military Camp

BUSINESS DISTRICT | **FAMILY** | Located inside the park, Kilauea Military Camp, established in 1916, offers visitor accommodations to members of the military and their families but also has places open to the public, including an arcade, bowling alley, diner, buffet, general store, and gas station. The Lava Lounge cocktail bar features live music on weekends. ⊠ *99-252 Crater Rim Dr., Hawaii Volcanoes National Park* ☏ *808/967–8333* ⊕ *www.kilaueamilitarycamp.com.*

Kilauea Visitor Center

VISITOR CENTER | **FAMILY** | Rangers and volunteers greet people and answer all questions at this visitor center, located just beyond the park entrance. There are lots of educational murals and displays, maps, and guidebooks. Also check out the daily itinerary of ranger-led activities and sign up for some. The gift shop operated by the Hawaii Pacific Park Association stocks excellent art, books, apparel, and more. A small theater plays documentaries about the park. ⊠ *1 Crater Rim Dr., Hawaii Volcanoes National Park* ☏ *808/985–6011* ⊕ *www.nps.gov/havo.*

Steam Vents and Sulphur Banks

VOLCANO | A short walk from the Kilauea Visitor Center leads to the pungent yet fascinating Sulphur Banks, where gases composed of hydrogen sulfide produce a smell akin to rotten eggs. Most of the rocks surrounding the vents have been dyed yellow due to constant gas exposure. Throughout the surrounding landscape, dozens of active steam vents emit white, billowing vapors that originate from groundwater heated by volcanic rocks. Located on the caldera's edge, Steaming Bluff is a short walk from a nearby parking area. ■TIP➔ **The best steam vents are across the road from the main steam vent parking area; they vary in size and are scattered alongside the dirt trails.** ⊠ *Crater Rim Dr., Hawaii Volcanoes National Park* ⊹ *Within walking distance* *of Kilauea Visitor Center* ☎ *808/985–6101* 🌐 *www.nps.gov/havo.*

Thurston Lava Tube (Nahuku)

NATURE SIGHT | FAMILY | One of the park's star attractions, the Thurston Lava Tube (named "Nahuku" in Hawaiian) spans 600 feet underground. The massive cavelike tube, discovered in 1913, was formed by hot molten lava traveling through the channel. To reach the entrance of the tube, visitors descend a series of stairs surrounded by lush foliage and the sounds of native birds. The Kilauea eruption of 2018 resulted in an almost two-year closure of the tube. During the closure, the drainage system was improved to reduce standing water on the cave's floor, and electrical lines were replaced. Visitors should not touch the walls or delicate tree root systems that grow down through the ceiling. **■ TIP→ Parking is limited near the tube. If the lot is full, you can park at the Kilauea Iki Overlook parking lot, ½ mile away.** ✉ *Crater Rim Dr., Hawaii Volcanoes National Park* ✥ *1½ miles from the park entrance* ☎ *808/985–6101* 🌐 *www.nps.gov/havo.*

🍴 Restaurants

The Rim at Volcano House

$$ | HAWAIIAN | FAMILY | This fine-dining restaurant overlooks the rim of Kilauea Caldera and the expansive Halemaumau Crater. Featuring two bars (one of which is adjacent to a lounge) and live entertainment nightly, the restaurant highlights island-inspired cuisine and locally sourced ingredients. **Known for:** Hilo coffee–rubbed rack of lamb; well-priced Taste of Hawaii lunch special; views of Halemaumau Crater. [$] *Average main: $25* ✉ *Volcano House, 1 Crater Rim Dr., Hawaii Volcanoes National Park* ☎ *808/756–9625* 🌐 *www.hawaiivolcanohouse.com.*

🛏 Hotels

★ Volcano House

$$ | HOTEL | Hawaii's oldest hotel—and the only one in Hawaii Volcanoes National Park—is committed to sustainable practices and promoting local Hawaiian culture and history through its locally sourced restaurants, artisan-crafted decor, and eco-focused guest programs. **Pros:** unbeatable location; views of crater; sense of place and history. **Cons:** books up quickly; some rooms have parking lot views; basic facilities. [$] *Rooms from: $220* ✉ *1 Crater Rim Dr., Hawaii Volcanoes National Park* ☎ *808/756–9625* 🌐 *www.hawaiivolcanohouse.com* 🔑 *33 rooms* 🍽 *No Meals.*

Greater Park Area

Spanning landscapes from sea level to the summits of two of the most active volcanoes in the world, Hawaii Volcanoes National Park boasts a diverse landscape with rain forests, rugged coastlines, surreal lava fields, and sacred cultural sites. There's also a sense of peace and tranquility here, despite the upheavals of nature. A drive down Chain of Craters Road toward the ocean allows you to access the greater area of the park, affording opportunities for exploration beyond the summit destinations. Along the way are birding trails, backcountry hikes, two campgrounds, pit craters, and a dramatic sea arch at the coast.

👁 Sights

★ Chain of Craters Road

SCENIC DRIVE | The coastal region of Hawaii Volcanoes National Park is accessed via the spectacularly scenic Chain of Craters Road, which descends 18.8 miles to sea level. You could drive it without stopping, but it's well worth spending a few hours or a day exploring the stops and trails. Winding past ancient craters and modern eruption sites, this scenic road was realigned in 1979 after parts of it were buried by the Mauna Ulu eruption. Marked stops along the way include Lua Manu Crater, Hilina Pali Road, Pauahi Crater, the Mauna Ulu eruption site, Kealakomo Lookout, and Puu Loa Petroglyphs. As you approach the coast, panoramic ocean vistas prevail. The last marked stop features views of the stunning natural Holei Sea Arch from an overlook. In recent decades, many former sights along the coast have been covered in lava, including a black-sand beach and the old campground. ⊠ *Hawaii Volcanoes National Park* ☎ *808/985–6101* ⊕ *www.nps.gov/havo.*

★ Mauna Ulu Trail

TRAIL | The Mauna Ulu lava flow presents an incredible variety of geological attractions within a moderate, 2½-mile round-trip hike. The diverse lava landscape was created during the 1969–74 Mauna Ulu flow, which produced enormous "lava falls" the size of Niagara Falls. Visitors can see everything from lava tree molds and fissure vents to cinder cones and portions of the old highway still exposed under the flow. Hawaiian nene geese roam the area, feeding on ripe ohelo berries. Hike to the top of a small hill that survived the flow for incredible views of the distant geological landmarks. On clear days, you can see Mauna Loa, Maunakea, and the Pacific Ocean from atop this hill, known as Puu Huluhulu. *Moderate.* ∎ TIP➔ **Purchase the Mauna Ulu trail booklet at the Kilauea Visitor Center for under $3. This excellent resource includes trailside attractions, trail maps, history, and photographs.** ⊠ *Chain of Craters Rd., Hawaii Volcanoes National Park* ↔ *Trailhead: 7 miles from Kilauea Visitor Center* ☎ *808/985-6101* ⊕ *www.nps.gov/havo.*

Puna

The Puna District begins 6 miles from the town of Hilo; Pahoa is 19 miles south of downtown Hilo.

The Puna District is wild in every sense of the word, with a jagged black coastline that is changing all the time. The albizzia trees grow out of control, forming canopies over roads; the residential areas are remote; and the people—well, there's something about living in an area that could be destroyed by lava at any moment (as Kalapana was in 1990, or Kapoho in 1960, or parts of Pahoa Town in 2014, or Kapoho Vacationland in 2018) that makes the norms of modern society seem silly. Vets, surfers, hippies, yoga teachers, and other free spirits abound. And there are also a few ruffians. So it is that Puna has its well-deserved reputation as an "outlaw" region of the Big Island. That said, it's well worth a detour, especially if you're near this part of the island. Some mighty fine people-watching opportunities exist in Pahoa, a funky little town that the "Punatics" call home.

This is also farm country for an array of agricultural products. Local farmers grow everything from orchids and anthuriums to papayas, bananas, and macadamia nuts. Several of the island's larger, rural, residential subdivisions are nestled between Keaau and Pahoa, including Hawaiian Paradise Park, Orchidland Estates, Hawaiian Acres, and Hawaiian Beaches. When dusk falls here, the air fills with the high-pitched symphony of thousands of coqui frogs. Though they look cute and seem harmless, the invasive frogs are considered pests by local residents weary of their shrieking, all-night calls.

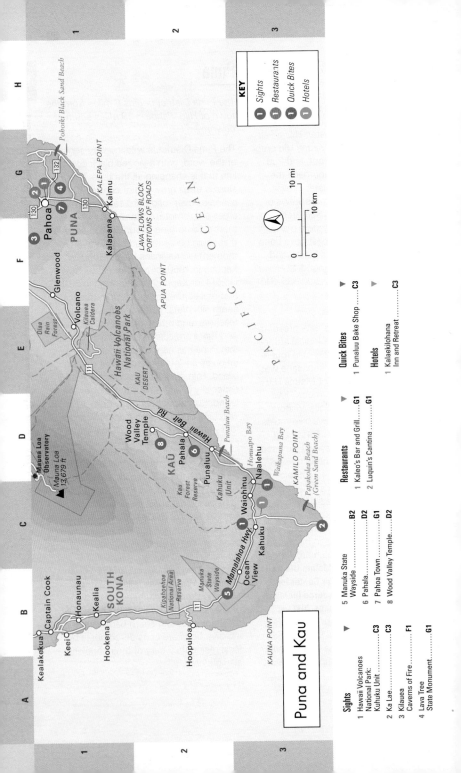

Puna and Kau

KEY

1 Sights
1 Restaurants
1 Quick Bites
1 Hotels

GETTING HERE AND AROUND

The sprawling Puna District stretches from the mountain to the sea. If you're staying in Hilo for the night, driving around Lower Puna is a great way to spend a morning.

Sights

★ Kilauea Caverns of Fire

CAVE | This way-out adventure explores the underbelly of the world's most active volcano via the Kazamura Lava Tube system. The world's longest lava tube system—more than 40 miles long, with sections up to 80 feet wide and 80 feet tall—is 500 to 700 years old and filled with bizarre lava formations and mind-blowing colors. Tours, customized to groups' interests and skill levels, focus on conservation and education and take visitors through beautiful lava caves unlike any others in the world. The tours are by reservation only and are well worth the extra detour (about 40 minutes off the main highway) and planning. Equipment is included. ■ TIP➜ **When you make your reservation, you will be given detailed directions to the location.** ⊠ *Hawaiian Acres, off Hwy. 11, between Kurtistown and Mountain View* ☎ *808/217–2363* ⊕ *www.kilaueacavernsoffire.com* 🎫 *$29 for 1-hour walking tour; $89 for 3-hour adventure tour; $239 day in the cave.*

Lava Tree State Monument

STATE/PROVINCIAL PARK | Tree molds that rise like blackened smokestacks formed here in 1790, when a lava flow swept through the ohia forest. Some reach as high as 12 feet. A meandering trail provides close-up looks at some of Hawaii's tropical plants and trees, and there are restrooms and a couple of picnic pavilions and tables. ■ TIP➜ **Mosquitoes live here in abundance, so be prepared.** ⊠ *Hwy. 132, Pahoa* ☎ *808/974–6200* ⊕ *dlnr. hawaii.gov/dsp* 🎫 *Free.*

Pahoa Town

TOWN | Founded to serve the sugar plantation community, this little town is reminiscent of the Wild West, with its wooden boardwalks and vintage buildings. Secondhand stores, tie-dye/hemp clothing boutiques, smoke shops, and art and antiques galleries add to the "trippy" experience. In 2014, lava flows from Kilauea almost intruded into the town, destroying a couple of buildings. Residents packed up as smoke from the flows billowed in the near distance and the flows glowed after dark. Then it all stopped within 500 yards of Pahoa Village Road, again ensuring the town's status as a survivor—until 2018, when Pahoa became command central for disaster assistance, Hawaii County Civil Defense, and reporters covering the nearby dramatic eruption of Kilauea. Today Pahoa's funky main street—with buildings dating from 1910—boasts a handful of excellent, local-style eateries. (In 2017, a fire swept through parts of the boardwalk and some buildings, which have been rebuilt.) To get here, turn southeast onto Highway 130 at Keaau, and drive 11 miles and follow signs to the Village. ⊠ *Pahoa.*

 Restaurants

Kaleo's Bar and Grill

$ | AMERICAN | Pahoa Town isn't known for gourmet dining choices, but Kaleo's is pretty sophisticated for a small-town restaurant and remains a local favorite with very good food. Hawaiian-inspired fare blends the gamut of the island's international influences with tempura ahi rolls, grilled burgers, and banana spring rolls. **Known for:** nightly entertainment; kalua (baked in an earth oven) pork wontons; good people-watching from the porch. 💲 *Average main: $15* ⊠ *15-2969 Pahoa Village Rd., Pahoa* ☎ *808/965–5600* ⊕ *www.kaleoshawaii.com.*

Luquin's Cantina

$ | **MEXICAN** | **FAMILY** | Long an island favorite for tasty, albeit greasy, Mexican grub, this landmark has made a comeback in funky Pahoa in a different space after a fire destroyed the original restaurant in 2017. Tacos are great (go for crispy), especially when stuffed with grilled, seasoned local fish on occasion. **Known for:** affordable fare; delicious huevos rancheros; good chips. [$] *Average main: $9* ✉ *15-1448 Kahakai Blvd., Pahoa* ☎ *808/333–3390* 🌐 *www.luquins.com.*

Kau

South Point in the District of Kau is 50 miles south of Kailua-Kona.

Perhaps the most desolate region of the island, the Kau District is nevertheless home to some spectacular sights. Mark Twain wrote some of his finest prose here, where macadamia nut farms, remote green-sand beaches, and tiny communities offer rugged, largely undiscovered beauty. The drive from Kailua-Kona to windswept South Point winds away from the ocean through a surreal moonscape of lava plains and patches of scrub forest. Coming from Volcano, as you near South Point, the barren lavascape gives way to lush vistas from the ocean to the hills. At the end of the 12-mile, two-lane road to South Point, you can park and hike about an hour to Papakolea (Green Sand Beach). Back on the highway, the coast passes the village of Naalehu, verdant cattle pastures, and sheer cliffs on the way to the black-sand beach of Punaluu, a nesting place of the Hawaiian hawksbill turtle.

GETTING HERE AND AROUND

Kau is usually combined with a quick trip to Hawaii Volcanoes National Park from Kona. This is probably cramming too much into one day, however. Visiting the volcano fills up at least a day (two is better), and the sights of this southern end of the island are worth more time. Instead, make Green Sand Beach or Punaluu a full beach day, and see some other sights on the way there or back. Bring sturdy shoes, water, and a sun hat if Green Sand Beach is your choice (reaching the beach requires a hike). It's much calmer and you can sometimes snorkel at Punaluu, but use caution at all Hawaii beaches.

Sights

Hawaii Volcanoes National Park: Kahuku Unit

NATIONAL PARK | Located off Highway 11 at mile marker 70.5, the Kahuku section of the park takes visitors over many trails through ancient lava flows and native forests. Ecological wonders abound in this beautiful but isolated region that encompasses more than 116,000 acres. Guided hikes with knowledgeable rangers are a regularly scheduled highlight. ✉ *Hwy. 11, at mile marker 70.5, Kahuku* ☎ *808/985-6101* 🌐 *www.nps.gov/havo* 🎟 *$30 per car, $15 for pedestrians* 🕒 *Closed Mon. and Tues.*

Ka Lae (*South Point*)

NATURE SIGHT | It's thought that the first Polynesians came ashore at this southernmost point of land in the United States, also a National Historic Landmark, and today people travel here for the views and access to Green Sand Beach. Old canoe-mooring holes, still visible, were carved through the rocks, possibly by settlers from Tahiti as early as AD 750. To get here, drive 12 miles down the turnoff road, past rows of giant electricity-producing windmills powered by the nearly constant winds sweeping across this coastal plain. Bear left when the road forks, and park in the lot at the end. Walk past the boat hoists toward the little lighthouse. South Point is just past the lighthouse at the southernmost cliff. You may see brave locals jumping off the cliffs and then climbing up rusty old ladders, but swimming here is not recommended. Don't leave anything of value in your car. The area is isolated and without services. Green Sand Beach is a 40-minute hike down the coast. ⊠ *South Point Rd. off Mamalahoa Hwy., near mile marker 70, Naalehu* 🖾 *Free.*

Manuka State Wayside

STATE/PROVINCIAL PARK | FAMILY | This lowland forest reserve spreads across several relatively recent lava flows, and a semirugged trail follows a 2-mile loop past a pit crater, winding around interesting trees such as hau and *kukui* (candlenut). You can wander through the well-maintained arboretum, snap photos of the eerie forest, and let the kids scramble around trees so large they can't get their arms around them. The pathways can get muddy and rough, so bring appropriate shoes if you plan to hike. Large populations of the Hawaiian hoary bat inhabit the area, which, in totality, encompasses 25,000 acres of forest reserve. Restrooms and picnic areas are available. ⊠ *Hwy. 11, north of mile marker 81, Naalehu* 🖾 *808/974–6200* ⊕ *dlnr.hawaii.gov/dsp* 🖾 *Free.*

Pahala

TOWN | About 16 miles east of Naalehu, beyond Punaluu Beach Park, Highway 11 passes directly by this sleepy little town, once a booming sugar plantation company town but still inhabited by retired cane workers and their descendants. You'll miss it if you blink. There is a Longs Pharmacy, a gas station, and a small supermarket, but not much else in terms of conveniences. Beyond the town, past a wide, paved cane road, is Wood Valley, known for a Buddhist temple set amid a peaceful area. ⊠ *Pahala.*

Wood Valley Temple (*Nechung Temple*)

TEMPLE | Behind the remote town of Pahala, this serene and beautiful Tibetan Buddhist temple, established in 1973, has hosted more than 50 well-known lamas, including the Dalai Lama on two occasions. Known as Nechung Dorje Drayang Ling (Immutable Island of Melodious Sound), this peaceful place welcomes all creeds. You can visit and meditate, leave an offering, walk the lush gardens shared by strutting peacocks, browse the gift shop, or stay in the temple's guesthouse. ⊠ *96-2285 Wood Valley Rd., Pahala* 🖾 *808/928–8539* ⊕ *www. nechung.org* 🖾 *$5.*

😊 Beaches

The rocky coasts of Kau don't have sparkling white-sand beaches, but the black-and green-sand beaches here are well worth the visit. There's also the chance to see endangered hawksbill or Hawaiian green sea turtles.

Papakolea Beach (*Green Sand Beach*)
BEACH | Those tired of the same old white- or black-sand beach can lace up good hiking shoes or sneakers to get to this olive-green crescent, one of the most unusual beaches on the island. It lies at the base of Puu O Mahana, at Mahana Bay, where a cinder cone formed during an early eruption of Mauna Loa. The greenish tint is caused by an accumulation of olivine crystals that form in volcanic eruptions. The dry, barren landscape is totally surreal but stunning, as aquamarine waters lap on green sand against reddish cliffs. Drive down to South Point; at the end of the 12-mile paved road, take the road to the left and park at the end. To reach the beach, follow the 2¼-mile coastal trail, which ends in a steep and dangerous descent down the cliffside on an unimproved trail. The hike takes about two hours each way and can get hot and windy, so bring lots of drinking water. Four-wheel-drive vehicles are no longer permitted on the trail. The surf is often rough and swimming can be hazardous due to strong currents, so caution is advised. **Amenities:** none. **Best for:** solitude; walking. ⊠ *Hwy. 11, Naalehu* ✛ *2½ miles northeast of South Point.*

Did You Know?

You can see turtles at the Big Island's Punaluu Black Sand Beach Park, a popular resting and feeding spot for endangered Hawaiian hawksbill sea turtles. There's absolutely no touching the animals—it's a hefty fine.

★ Punaluu Black Sand Beach Park
BEACH | A must-do on a south–south-east–bound trip to the volcano, this easily accessible black-sand beach is backed by low dunes, brackish ponds, and tall coco palms. The shoreline is jagged, reefed, and rocky. Most days, large groups of sea turtles nap on the sand—a stunning sight. Resist the urge to get too close or disturb them; they're protected by federal and state law, and fines for harassment can be hefty. Removing black sand is also prohibited. **■ TIP→ Extremely strong rip currents prevail, so only experienced ocean swimmers should consider getting in the water here.** A popular stop for locals and tour buses alike, this beach park can get busy, especially on weekends (the north parking lot is usually quieter). Shade from palm trees provides an escape from the sun, and at the northern end of the beach, near the boat ramp, lie the ruins of Kaneeleele Heiau, an old Hawaiian temple. The area was a sugar port until the 1946 tsunami destroyed the buildings. **Amenities:** parking (no fee); showers; toilets. **Best for:** walking. ✉ *Hwy. 11, between mile markers 55 and 56, Naalehu* ✣ *27 miles south of Hawaii Volcanoes National Park* ☎ *808/961–8311* 🎟 *Free.*

Coffee and Quick Bites

Punaluu Bake Shop
$ | **CAFÉ** | **FAMILY** | Billed as the southernmost bakery in the United States, it's a good spot to grab a snack or lunch. Hawaiian sweetbread is the specialty here. **Known for:** all goods baked on-site; malasada (Portuguese doughnuts) glazed with lilikoi (passion fruit); plate lunches. [$] *Average main: $8* ✉ *5642 Mamalahoa Hwy., Naalehu* ☎ *808/929–7343* 🌐 *www.bakeshophawaii.com* 🕒 *No dinner.*

Hotels

Kalaekilohana Inn and Retreat
$$$$ | **B&B/INN** | You wouldn't expect to find a top-notch B&B in Kau, but just up the road from South Point, this grand residence offers large private suites with locally harvested hardwood floors and private lanai with ocean and mountain views. **Pros:** big, comfy beds with down comforters; beautiful decor reminiscent of old Hawaii; delicious breakfast. **Cons:** no pool; very limited nearby shopping; not for children under 12. [$] *Rooms from: $349* ✉ *94-2152 South Point Rd., Naalehu* ☎ *808/939–8052* 🌐 *www.kau-hawaii.com* 🛏 *4 suites* 🍴 *Free Breakfast.*

Activities and Tours

With the Big Island's predictably mild year-round climate, it's no wonder you'll find an emphasis on outdoor activities. After all, this is the home of the annual Ironman World Championship triathlon and numerous other world-class athletic events. Whether you're an avid hiker or a beginning bicyclist, a casual golfer or a serious scuba diver, there are plenty of adventures to lure you away from your resort or condo.

You can explore by bike, helicopter, ATV, zip line, or horse, or you can put on your hiking boots and use your own horsepower. No matter how you get around, you'll be treated to breathtaking backdrops along the Big Island's 266-mile coastline and within its 4,028 square miles (and still growing!). Aerial tours take in any eruption activity and lava flows, as well as the island's gorgeous tropical valleys, gulches, and coastal plains. Trips into the backcountry wilderness explore the rain forest, private ranchlands, and coffee farms, while sleepy sugar plantation villages offer a glimpse of Hawaii's bygone days. Golfers will find acclaimed championship golf courses at the Kohala Coast resorts—Mauna Kea Beach Hotel,

Autograph Collection; the Westin Hapuna Beach Resort; Mauna Lani, Auberge Resorts Collection; and the Waikoloa area resorts, among others.

The ancient Hawaiians, who took much of their daily sustenance from the ocean, also enjoyed playing in the water, so it follows that visitors want to get out onto the water as well. In fact, surfing was the sport of kings, born in the Hawaiian Islands. Though it's easy to be lulled into whiling away the day baking in the sun on a white-, gold-, black-, or green-sand beach, getting into or onto the water is a highlight of most trips.

All the Hawaiian Islands are surrounded by the Pacific Ocean and blessed with a temperate latitude, making them some of the world's greatest natural playgrounds. Still, certain experiences are even better on the Big Island of Hawaii: nighttime diving trips to see manta rays; deep-sea fishing in Kona's fabled waters, where dozens of Pacific blue marlin of 1,000 pounds or more have been caught; and kayaking in pristine bays, to name a few.

From almost any point on the Big Island, the ocean is not far. From bodyboarding and snorkeling to kayaking and surfing, there is a water sport for everyone. For most activities, you can rent gear from a local vendor and go it alone. Or book a group excursion with experienced guides who offer convenience and security, as well as special insights into Hawaii's marine life, ecology, history, and culture. Want to try surfing? Contrary to what you may have heard, there *are* waves on the Big Island. You can take lessons from pros who take you to special spots and promise to have you standing the first day out.

The Kona and Kohala Coasts of West Hawaii have the largest number of ocean sports outfitters and tour operators. They operate from the small-boat harbors and piers in Kailua-Kona, Keauhou, and Kawaihae, and out of the Kohala Coast resorts. There are also several outfitters in East Hawaii.

As a general rule, the waves are gentler here than on the other Islands, especially in summer, but there are a few things to be aware of. First, never turn your back on the ocean. It's unlikely, but if conditions are right, a wave could come along and push you face-first into the sand or drag you out to sea. Second, when the Big Island does experience high surf, dangerous conditions prevail nearly everywhere and can change rapidly. Watch the ocean for a few minutes before going out to scan for waves, which arrive in sets, and wait for three to go by. If it looks too rough, don't chance it. Third, realize that ultimately you must keep yourself safe. We strongly encourage you to obey lifeguards and high surf advisories, and heed the advice of outfitters from whom you rent equipment, and even advice from locals on shore. If you are not a strong swimmer, find a baby beach and use a life vest. It could save your trip—or even your life.

Aerial Tours

There's nothing quite like the aerial view of a waterfall crashing down a couple of thousand feet into cascading pools. You can get this and other bird's-eye views from a helicopter or a fixed-wing small plane. All operators pay strict attention to safety and will take off only if conditions are safe. So how to get the best experience for your money? ■ TIP→ **Before you choose a company, be a savvy traveler, read up on the experience offered, and ask the right questions. What kind of aircraft do they fly? What is their safety record?**

Big Island Air Tours

AIR EXCURSIONS | This small charter company, in business since the 1980s, offers fixed-wing tours of the Big Island that include Kilauea Volcano and its various rift zones. Because a fixed-wing plane

Did You Know?

A helicopter tour is a great way to see the Big Island's most inaccessible areas. It's hard to beat aerial views, whether of the coast and its rocky cliff faces or a waterfall plunging into the valley below.

is allowed to fly above the altitude restrictions at Hawaii Volcanoes National Park, Big Island Air Tours can take you directly over Halemaumau Crater for rare views of the crater not available with a helicopter tour. You'll also be able to soar above such sights as the infamous (now dead) Puu Oo vent, as well as the devastated areas of lower Puna inundated by lava in 2018. A Twilight tour gets you back to the airport just in time for sunset. All tours depart from Kona International Airport. ✉ *Kona International Airport, 73-103 Ulu St., Kailua-Kona* ☎ *808/329–4868* ⊕ *www.bigislandair.com* ✈ *From $492.*

Blue Hawaiian Helicopters

AIR EXCURSIONS | Hawaii Island's premier aerial tour is on Blue Hawaiian's roomy Eco-Star helicopters—so smooth and quiet you hardly realize you're taking off. There are no worries about what seat you get because each has great views. Pilots are State of Hawaii–certified tour guides, too, so they are knowledgeable and experienced but not overly chatty. In the breathtaking Waimanu Valley, the helicopter hovers close to 2,600-foot cliffs and cascading waterfalls. Departing from Waikoloa, the two-hour Big Island Spectacular also takes in the incredible landscapes of Hawaii Volcanoes National Park, as well as the stunning valleys; you can even choose an optional waterfall landing. Leaving from Hilo, the more affordable, 50-minute Circle of Fire tour showcases Kilauea Volcano and other major island sites. ✉ *Waikoloa Heliport, Hwy. 19, Waikoloa* ☎ *808/961–5600* ⊕ *www.bluehawaiian.com* ✈ *From $369.*

★ **Paradise Helicopters**

AIR EXCURSIONS | Even in areas where the volcano is not actively flowing, there's plenty to see from the air, with great options from this locally owned and operated company. Departing from Kona, the Circle Island Experience and Experience Hawaii tours both fly over the Hawaii Volcanoes National Park area including the once-active Puu Oo vent. Departing from

Hilo, the Doors-Off Lava and Rainforest Adventure offers an unforgettable excursion in a Hughes 500 helicopter for unobstructed views of Kilauea Volcano. There are also options in which you land, take a hike through rugged rain forests, or enjoy a guided tour in Hawaii Volcanoes National Park with experts Keawe Adventures. ■ **TIP→ The only helicopter company in Hawaii certified by the Hawaii Ecotour Association, Paradise offers the option to offset your tour's carbon footprint by having a tree planted in Hawaii for each ride you take.** ✉ *Kailua-Kona* ☎ *808/969–7392, 866/876–7422* ⊕ *www.paradisecopters. com* ✈ *From $399.*

Biking

The Big Island's biking trails and road routes range from easy to moderate coastal rides to rugged backcountry wilderness treks that challenge the most serious cyclists. You can soak up the island's storied scenic vistas and varied geography—from tropical rain forest to rolling ranch country, from high-country mountain meadows to dry lava deserts. It's dry, windy, and hot on Kona's and Kohala's coastal trails, mountainous through South Kona, and cool, wet, and muddy in the upcountry Waimea and Volcano areas, as well as in lower Puna. There are long distances between towns, few bike lanes, narrow single-lane highways, and scanty services in the Kau, Puna, South Kona, and Kohala Coast areas, so plan accordingly for your weather, water, food, and lodging needs before setting out. ■ **TIP→ Your best bet is to book with an outfitter who has all the details covered.**

BEST SPOTS
★ **Kulani Trails**

BIKING | It has been called the state's best mountain bike ride—if you want to get gnarly. The technically demanding ride, which passes majestic eucalyptus trees, is for advanced cyclists; muddy conditions prevail. To reach the trailhead from the intersection of Highway 11 and Highway 19 in Hilo, take Highway 19 south about 4 miles, turn right on Stainback Highway, and continue 2½ miles. Turn right at the Waiakea Arboretum and park near the gate. A permit is required, available from the Department of Land and Natural Resources at Kawili Street and Kilauea Avenue in Hilo. ⊠ *Stainback Hwy., Hilo.*

EQUIPMENT AND TOURS

Bike shops around the island offer daily or weekly rentals, and many resorts rent beach cruisers that can be used around the properties. Most outfitters can provide a bicycle rack for your car, and all have reduced rates for rentals longer than one day. All retailers offer excellent advice about where to go; they know the areas well. **Hawaii Island Bikeshare** (⊕ *hawaiiislandbikeshare.org*) offers access to bikes across the island at their well-placed stations, using a subscription key. One of the best and easiest ways to see the island is to take a bike tour.

★ Volcano Bike Tours

BIKING | This friendly outfitter leads reasonably priced three- or five-hour e-bike tours through Hawaii Volcanoes National Park that take in fantastic sights from rain forests to craters. With an e-bike you can opt to use the pedal assist or not, depending on whether you want more of a workout. After meeting at their bike shop in Volcano Village, you will follow the guides over to the park, embark on the tour together, and wrap it up back at the shop. As long as Halemaumau is erupting, they will run sunset crater tours as well. The outfitter also offers e-bike rentals with a self-guided map. ⊠ *19-3972 Old Volcano Rd., Volcano* 📞 *808/934–9199* ⊕ *www.bikevolcano. com* 🚲 *Guided bike tours from $239; sunset lava tour $269; rentals from $100/ day.*

Mid Pacific Wheels

BIKING | The oldest bike shop on the Big Island, this community-oriented shop near the university carries a full line of bikes and accessories and rents mountain bikes for exploring the Hilo area. The friendly staff provides expert advice on where to go and what to see and do on a self-guided tour. They also carry a large selection of cycling accessories, bikes, and repair parts. ⊠ *1133C Manono St., Hilo* 📞 *808/935–6211* ⊕ *www.midpacificwheelsllc.com* 🚲 *From $35/day.*

Bodyboarding and Bodysurfing

According to the movies, in the Old West there was always friction between cattle ranchers and sheep ranchers. A similar situation has been known to exist between surfers and bodyboarders (and between surfers and stand-up paddleboarders). That's why they generally keep to their own separate areas. Often the bodyboarders, who lie on their stomachs on shorter boards, stay closer to shore and leave the outside breaks to the board surfers. Or the board surfers may stick to one side of the beach and the bodyboarders to the other. The truth is, bodyboarding (often called "boogie boarding," in homage to the first commercial manufacturer of this slick, little, flexible-foam board) is a blast. Most surfers also sometimes carve waves on a body board, no matter how much of a purist they claim to be.

You'll need a pair of short fins to get out to the bigger waves offshore, though novice bodyboarders should catch shorebreak waves only. Ask lifeguards or locals for the best spots. As for bodysurfing, just catch a wave and make like Superman going faster than a speeding bullet.

BEST SPOTS

Hapuna Beach State Recreation Area. Often considered one of the top 10 beaches in the world, Hapuna Beach offers fine white sand, turquoise water, and easy rolling surf on most days, making it great for bodysurfing and bodyboarding at all levels. Ask the lifeguards—who only cover areas south of the rocky cliff that juts out near the middle of the beach—about conditions before heading into the water, especially in winter. Sometimes northwest swells create a dangerous undertow, so use caution here. ⊠ *Hwy. 19, near mile marker 69, just south of Mauna Kea Beach Hotel, Kohala Coast* ⊕ *dlnr. hawaii.gov/dsp.*

Honolii Cove. North of Hilo, this is the best bodyboarding spot on the east side of the island. ⊠ *Off Hwy. 19, near mile marker 4, Hilo.*

Magic Sands Beach Park (White Sands Beach). This white-sand, shorebreak cove is great for beginning to intermediate bodysurfing and bodyboarding. Sometimes, randomly, much of the sand here washes out to sea and forms a sandbar just offshore, creating fun wave conditions, only to "reappear" a few days later. Also known as White Sands, the beach is popular and can get crowded with locals, especially when school is out. Watch for large, overwhelming surf and nasty rip currents at high tide. Listen to lifeguards when they tell you to get out of the water. ■ TIP➜ **If you're not using fins, wear reef shoes for protection against sharp rocks.** ⊠ *Alii Dr., just north of mile marker 4, Kailua-Kona.*

EQUIPMENT

Equipment rental shacks are located at many beaches and boat harbors, along the highway, and at most resorts. Bodyboard rental rates are around $12–$15 per day and around $60 per week. You can also buy snorkeling equipment at one of the big-box retailers if you plan to be out every day, want to ensure sanitation, or need a perfect fit. Most also carry bodyboards.

★ Orchidland Surfboards and Surf Shop

WATER SPORTS | This venerable shop in historic downtown Hilo—in business since 1972—carries a wide variety of surf and other water sports equipment for sale or rent. It stocks professional custom surfboards, bodyboards, and surf apparel. Owner Stan Lawrence, famous for his "Drainpipe" legacy, was one of the last people to surf that famous break before lava flows claimed the entire Kalapana area. Old photos and surfing posters on the walls celebrate the sport and add to the nostalgia. Through the shop, Stan hosts surfing contests and does the daily surf report for local radio stations. Orchidland, the longest continually operating surf shop on the Big Island, is as authentic as it gets. ⊠ *262 Kamehameha Ave., Hilo* ☎ *808/935–1533* ⊕ *www.orchidland-surfshop.com* ⌅ *From $15 body board/day, $25 surfboard/day.*

★ Pacific Vibrations

SURFING | Family-owned, this surf shop—in business since 1978—holds the distinction of being the world's oldest, smallest surf shop. Even at a compact, sub-500 square feet, this place stocks tons of equipment, surf wear and gear, sunglasses, and GoPro cameras. Located oceanfront in downtown Kailua Town, it is tucked in a vintage building and is worth a stop just to soak in the cool Hawaii surf vibe and to talk story with the friendly owners. The owners are activists in protecting local surf spots from development, and their grassroots efforts have been very successful. ⊠ *75-5702B Likana La., at Alii Dr., Kailua-Kona* ☎ *808/329–4140.*

Caving

The Kanohina Lava Tube system is about a thousand years old and was used by the ancient Hawaiians for water collection and for shelter. More than 56 miles of braided lava tubes have been mapped so far in the Kau District of the Big Island, near Ka Lae (South Point). About 45 miles south of Kailua-Kona, these lava tubes are a great experience for cavers of all age levels and abilities.

★ Kula Kai Caverns

SPELUNKING | Expert cave guides lead groups into the fantastic underworld of these caverns near South Point in Kau. The braided lava-tube system attracts scientists from around the world, who come to study and map them (more than 56 miles so far). Tours range from the Lighted Trail (in the lighted show cave, which is easy walking) to the Two Hour, a deep-down-under spelunking adventure that often takes closer to three hours and allows you to see archaeological evidence of the ancient Hawaiians. Longer, customized tours are available; all gear is provided. Tours start at an Indiana Jones–style expedition tent and divulge fascinating details about the caves' geological and cultural history. Reservations are required. ⊠ Kula Kai Estates, Lauhala Dr., at Kona Kai Blvd., Ocean View ☎ 808/929–9725 ⊕ www.kulakaicaverns. com ☑ From $28.

Deep-Sea Fishing

The Kona Coast boasts some of the world's most exciting "blue-water" fishing. The island's steep, sloping underwater geography means that just three miles out to sea, the ocean plunges to depths of more than 6,000 feet, making it a sportfisher's dream. Although July, August, and September are peak months, with the best fishing and a number of tournaments, charter fishing goes on year-round. Some 60 charter boats, averaging 26 to 58 feet in length, are available for hire, all of them out of **Honokohau Harbor,** north of Kailua-Kona.

The Kona Coast is world-famous for the presence of large marlin, particularly the Pacific blue. In fact, it's also known as

"Grander Alley" for the fish caught here that weigh more than 1,000 pounds. The largest blue marlin on record was caught in 1984 and weighed 1,649 pounds. In total, more than 60 granders have been reeled in here by top sportfishing teams.

For an exclusive charter, prices generally range from $700 to $950 for a half-day trip (about four hours) and $800 to $1,700 for a full day at sea (about eight hours). For share charters, rates are about $100 to $140 per person for a half day and $200 for a full day. If fuel prices increase, expect charter costs to rise. Most boats are licensed to take up to six passengers, in addition to the crew. Tackle, bait, and ice are furnished, but you usually have to bring your own lunch. You won't be able to keep your catch, although if you ask, many captains will send you home with a few fillets.

Honokohau Harbor's Fuel Dock

FISHING | Show up around 11 am and watch the weigh-in of the day's catch from the morning charters, or around 3:30 for the afternoon charters, especially during the summer tournament season. Weigh-ins are fun when the big ones come in, but these days, with most of the marlin being released, it's not a sure thing. ■TIP→ **In the foyer of the Kona Inn in Kailua-Kona, look for some of the "granders" on display.** ⊠ Honokohau Harbor, Kealakehe Pkwy. at Hwy. 11, Kailua-Kona.

BOATS AND CHARTERS
Bwana Sportfishing

FISHING | Half-, three-quarter-, and full-day charters, as well as overnight charters, are available on the 46-foot Bwana, a boat with the latest electronics, top-of-the-line equipment, and air-conditioned cabins. You get outstanding, quality tackle and lots of experience here. Captain Teddy comes from a fishing family; father Pete was a legend on Kona waters for decades. ⊠ Honokohau Harbor, Slip H-17, 74-381 Kealakehe Pkwy., Kailua-Kona

⊕ *Just south of Kona airport* ☎ *808/936–5168* 🌐 *From $1,250.*

Charter Locker

FISHING | Half- and full-day charter fishing trips on 36- to 53-foot vessels are offered by this experienced company. Featured boats include *Kona Blue, JR's Hooker, Strong Persuader,* and *Kila Kila.* Rates depend on the boat. ⊠ *Honokohau Harbor, 74-381 Kealakehe Pkwy., #16, Kailua-Kona* ⊕ *Just south of Kona airport* ☎ *808/326–2553* 🌐 *www.charterlocker. com* 🌐 *From $600.*

Humdinger Sportfishing

FISHING | The father-son team here brings more than five decades of fishing experience in Kona waters, and the expert crew are marlin specialists. Their 37-foot Rybovich, the *Humdinger,* features the latest in electronics and top-line rods and reels. ■TIP→ **They will let you keep your catch (except for billfish) and will even fillet it for you.** Book online for discounts and specials; they sell out quickly, so plan ahead. ⊠ *Honokohau Harbor, 74-381 Kealakehe Pkwy., Slip B-4, Kailua-Kona* ☎ *808/425–9225, 800/926–2374, 808/425–9228 boat phone* 🌐 *www.humdingersportfishing.com* 🌐 *From $599.*

Jeff Rogers Charters

FISHING | One of Kona's friendliest "old salts," Captain Jeff has been leading personalized big game and other fishing charters since 1982. Using a few tricks of the trade (including targeting the bottom), he's able to find the right fish in the right place, nearly without fail. You may ask him to fillet part of your catch. Holder of six world records and six state records, Jeff has caught his share of marlin granders (over 1,000 pounds). Guests (no more than two) may share a charter to save costs through his special program, so check online for the list of available shares. ⊠ *73-4345 Oneone St., Kailua-Kona* ☎ *808/895–1852* 🌐 *www. fishinkona.com* 🌐 *From $400.*

Golf

For golfers, the Big Island is a big deal—starting with the Mauna Kea Golf Course, which opened in 1964 and remains one of the state's top courses. Black lava and deep blue sea are the predominant themes on the island. In the roughly 40 miles from the Kona Country Club to the Mauna Kea resort, nine courses are carved into sunny seaside lava plains, with four more in the hills above. Indeed, most of the Big Island's best courses are concentrated along the Kohala Coast, statistically the sunniest spot in Hawaii. Vertically speaking, the majority of courses are seaside or at least near sea level, and three are located above 2,000 feet. This is significant because in Hawaii temperatures drop 3°F for every 1,000 feet of elevation gained.

Greens fee: Greens fees listed here are the highest course rates per round on weekdays for U.S. residents. (Some courses charge non–U.S. residents higher prices.) Courses with varying weekend rates are noted in the individual listings. ■TIP→ **Discounts are often available for resort guests and for those who book tee times online, as well as for those willing to play in the afternoon. Twilight rates are also usually offered.**

Hapuna Golf Course

GOLF | Hapuna's challenging play and environmental sensitivity make it one of the island's most unusual courses. Designed by Arnold Palmer and Ed Seay, it nestles into the natural contours of the land from the shoreline to about 700 feet above sea level. There are spectacular views of mountains and sea; Maui is often visible in the distance. Holes wind through kiawe scrub, beds of jagged lava, and tall fountain grasses. Hole 12 is favored for its beautiful views and challenging play. The course is within walking distance of the Westin Hapuna Beach Resort. ⊠ *Westin Hapuna Beach Resort, 62-100 Kanunaoa Dr., Mauna Kea*

Most of the Big Island's top golf courses are located on the sunny Kona Coast.

☎ 808/880–3000 ⊕ marriott.com 🖃 $200, cart required 👤 18 holes, 6875 yards, par 72.

Hilo Municipal Golf Course

GOLF | Hilo Muni is proof that you don't need sand bunkers to create a challenging course. Trees and several meandering creeks are the danger here. The course, which offers views of Hilo Bay from most holes, has produced many of the island's top players over the years. Taking a divot reminds you that you're playing on a volcano—the soil is dark-black crushed lava. Due to heavy demand, tee time reservations (required) are by phone only. ✉ 340 Haihai St., Hilo ☎ 808/959–7711 🖃 $40 weekdays, $47 weekends; $24 cart 👤 18 holes, 6325 yards, par 71.

Makani Golf Club

GOLF | At 2,000 feet above sea level on the slopes of Hualalai, this course is out of the way but well worth the drive. In 1997, Pete and Perry Dye created a gem that plays through upland woodlands— more than 2,500 trees line the fairways. On the par-5 16th, a giant tree in the

middle of the fairway must be avoided with the second shot. Five lakes and a meandering natural mountain stream bring water into play on nine holes. The most dramatic is the par-3 17th, where Dye created a knockoff of his infamous 17th at the TPC at Sawgrass. ✉ 71-1420 Hawaii Belt Rd., Kailua-Kona ☎ 808/325–5044 ⊕ makanigolfclub.com 🖃 $119 with cart, bottled water; $99 after noon 👤 18 holes, 7075 yards, par 72.

★ Mauna Kea Golf Course

GOLF | Originally opened in 1964, this golf course is one of the state's most revered. In 2008, it underwent a tee-to-green renovation by Rees Jones, son of the original architect, Robert Trent Jones Sr. Hybrid grasses were planted, the number of bunkers increased, and the overall yardage expanded. The par-3 third is one of the world's most famous holes—and one of the most photographed. You play from a cliffside tee across a bay to a cliffside green. Getting across the ocean is half the battle because the green is surrounded by seven bunkers, each one large and undulated. The course is a shot-maker's paradise and follows Jones's "easy bogey, tough par" philosophy. ⊠ *62-100 Kaunaoe Dr., Mauna Kea* ☎ *808/882–5400* ⊕ *maunakeabeachhotel. com* ⊠ *$295, $245 after 11 am, $195 after 1:30 pm* ⚐ *18 holes, 7250 yards, par 72.*

★ Mauna Lani Golf Courses

GOLF | Black lava flows, lush green turf, white sand, and the Pacific's many blue hues define the 36 holes at Mauna Lani. The **South Course** includes the par-3 15th across a turquoise bay, one of Hawaii's most photographed holes. It shares "signature hole" honors with the seventh, a long par 3, which plays downhill over convoluted patches of black lava, with the Pacific immediately to the left and a dune to the right. The **North Course** plays a couple of shots tougher. Its most distinctive hole is the 17th, a par 3 with the green set in a lava pit 50 feet deep. The shot from an elevated tee must carry a pillar of lava that rises from the pit and partially blocks a view of the green. ⊠ *68-1310 Mauna Lani Dr., Waimea (Hawaii County)* ☎ *808/885–6655* ⊕ *aubergeresorts.com/ maunalani* ⊠ *From $247, but dynamic pricing means greens fee fluctuates* ⚐ *South Course: 18 holes, 6025 yards, par 72. North Course: 18 holes, 6057 yards, par 72.*

★ Waikoloa Beach Resort

GOLF | Robert Trent Jones Jr. built the Beach Course at Waikoloa (1981) on an old flow of crinkly *aa* lava, which he used to create holes that are as artful as they are challenging. The par-5 12th hole is one of Hawaii's most picturesque and plays through a chute of black lava to a seaside green. At the Kings' Course (1990), Tom Weiskopf and Jay Morrish built a links-esque track. It turns out lava's natural humps and declivities replicate the contours of seaside Scotland. There are a few island twists—such as seven lakes. This is "option golf," as Weiskopf and Morrish provide different risk-reward

tactics on each hole. Resort guests receive a lower rate. ⊠ *600 Waikoloa Beach Dr., Waikoloa* ☎ *808/886–7888* ⊕ *www.waikoloabeachgolf.com* ⊠ *From $150* ⚐ *Beach Course: 18 holes, 6566 yards, par 70. Kings' Course: 18 holes, 7074 yards, par 72.*

Volcano Golf Course

GOLF | Just outside Hawaii Volcanoes National Park—and barely a stone's throw from Halemaumau Crater—this is by far Hawaii's highest course. At 4,200 feet elevation, shots tend to fly a bit farther than at sea level, even in the often cool, misty air. Because of the elevation and climate, this Hawaii course features Bermuda and seashore paspalum grass putting greens. The course is mostly flat, and holes play through stands of ohia lehua (flowering evergreen trees) and multitrunk hau trees. The uphill par-4 15th doglegs through a tangle of hau. At this writing, regular carts are not available, but golfers can rent pushcarts. ⊠ *99-1621 Pii Mauna Dr., off Hwy. 11, Volcano* ☎ *808/319–4745* ⊕ *www.volcanogc.com* ⊠ *From $56* ⚐ *18 holes, 6106 yards, par 72.*

Hiking

Ecologically diverse, Hawaii Island has four of the five major climate zones and eight of 13 subclimate zones—a lot of variation for one island—and you can experience almost all of them on foot. The ancient Hawaiians cut trails across the lava plains, through the rain forests, and up along the mountain heights. Many of these paths are still in use today. Part of the King's Trail at Anaehoomalu winds through a field of lava rock covered with ancient petroglyphs. Many other trails—historic and modern—crisscross the huge Hawaii Volcanoes National Park and other parts of the island. Plus, the serenity of certain remote beaches is accessible only to hikers. Check the statewide trail system website (⊕ *hawaiitrails.*

Hawaii Volcanoes National Park's 155 miles of trails offer easy to moderately difficult day hikes.

ehawaii.gov) for up-to-date information on hiking trails.

Department of Land and Natural Resources, State Parks Division

HIKING & WALKING | The division provides information on all the Big Island's state parks and jurisdictions. Check online for the latest additions, information, and advisories. ⊠ *75 Aupuni St., Hilo* 🕾 *808/961–9544* ⊕ *dlnr.hawaii.gov/dsp.*

BEST SPOTS

Hawaii Volcanoes National Park. Perhaps the Big Island's premier area for hikers, the park has more than 155 miles of trails providing close-up, often jaw-dropping views of fern and rain forest environments, cinder cones, craters, steam vents, lava fields, rugged coastline, and current eruption activity. Day hikes range from easy to moderately difficult, and from one or two hours to a full day. For a bigger challenge, consider an overnight or multiday backcountry hike with a stay in a park cabin (available en route to the remote coast, in a lush forest, or atop frigid Mauna Loa). To do

so, you must first obtain a permit ($10) at the Backcountry Office, off Chain of Craters Road. Daily guided hikes are led by knowledgeable, friendly park rangers. The bulletin boards outside Kilauea Visitor Center have the day's schedule of guided hikes. ⊠ *Hwy. 11, 30 miles south of Hilo, Hawaii Volcanoes National Park* 🕾 *808/985–6000* ⊕ *www.nps.gov/ havo.*

Kekaha Kai State Park. A 1.8-mile unimproved road leads to Mahaiula Bay, a gorgeous little piece of paradise, while on the opposite side is lovely Kua Bay. Connecting the two is the 4½-mile Ala Kahakai historic coastal trail. Midway between the two white-sand beaches, you can hike to the summit of Puu Kuili, a 342-foot-high cinder cone with an excellent view of the coastline. Mahaiula has picnic tables and vault toilets but no other amenities. It's dry and hot, with no drinking water, so pack sunblock, hats, and extra water. Park gates close at 7 pm sharp. ⊠ *Trailhead on Hwy. 19, about*

2 miles north of Kona airport, Kailua-Kona ⊕ *dlnr.hawaii.gov/dsp.*

Muliwai Trail. On the western side of mystical Waipio Valley on the Hamakua Coast, this trail leads to the back of the valley, then switchbacks up through a series of gulches and finally emerges at Waimanu Valley. Only very experienced hikers should attempt the entirety of this remote 18-mile trail, the hike of a lifetime. It can take two to three days of backpacking and camping, which requires camping permits from the Division of Forestry and Wildlife in Hilo. ✉ *Trailhead at end of Hwy. 240, Honokaa* ☎ *808/974–4221* ⊕ *hawaiitrails. ehawaii.gov.*

Onomea Bay Trail. This short but beautiful trail is packed with stunning views of the cliffs, bays, and gulches of the Hamakua Coast, on the east side of the island. The trail is just under a mile and fairly easy, with access down to the shore if you want to dip your feet in; we don't recommend swimming in the rough waters. Unless you pay the entry fee to the nearby Hawaii Tropical Bioreserve & Garden, entering its gates (even by accident) will send one of the guards running after you to point you back to the trail. ✉ *Trailhead on Old Hawaiian Belt Rd., just before botanical garden* ⊕ *hawaiitrails.ehawaii. gov.*

GUIDES

To get to some of the best trails and hiking spots (some of which are on private property), it's worth going with a skilled, professional guide, many of whom are certified national park guides. Costs range from about $100 to more than $250, and some hikes include transportation, full meals, and refreshments and gear such as binoculars, ponchos, parkas, and walking sticks. The outfitters mentioned here also offer customized adventure tours.

★ Hawaii Forest and Trail

WALKING TOURS | Since 1993, this locally owned and operated outfit has built a reputation for outstanding nature tours and eco-adventures. Sustainability, cultural sensitivity, and forging island connections are company missions. They have access to thousands of acres of restricted or private lands and employ expert, certified guides who are entertaining and informative. Choose one of the bird-watching tours, a journey that takes you deep into the Hakalau Forest National Wildlife Refuge with local bird experts at the helm. Other tours include treks to Kilauea Volcano in Hawaii Volcanoes National Park, a Kohala waterfall trip, or the Hidden Craters Tour, which takes you through private land to explore the slopes of Hualalai Volcano. They can also design custom private tours. ✉ *73-5593A Olowalu St., Kailua-Kona* ☎ *808/331–8505, 800/464–1993* ⊕ *www. hawaii-forest.com* 🖼 *From $160.*

★ KapohoKine Adventures

WALKING TOURS | **FAMILY** | One of the best-loved outfitters on the island, locally owned KapohoKine Adventures offers a number of excellent hiking tours that depart from both Hilo and Kona. The epic full-day Elite Volcano Hike (departs from both Kona and Hilo) hits all the great spots, including now-quiet areas in Puna impacted by the 2018 eruption. Hikers will encounter a 40-foot wall of lava and follow it to the sea and an enormous black-sand beach. Also included are Kalapana, the Kaumana Caves, the Steaming Bluffs, and a tour of Hawaii Volcanoes National Park. All tours are led by a national park–certified guide. Enjoy a final stop at Volcano House for views from the enormous picture windows overlooking the crater. A hearty dinner is included, as well as lunch and snacks. ✉ *Grand Nanioloa Hotel Hilo, 93 Banyan Dr., Hilo* ☎ *808/964–1000* ⊕ *www.kapohokine. com* 🖼 *From $269.*

Horseback Riding

With its *paniolo* (cowboy) heritage and the ranches it spawned, the Big Island is a great place for equestrians. Riders can gallop through upcountry green pastures or saunter through lush valleys for a taste of old Hawaii.

TOURS

Paniolo Adventures

HORSEBACK RIDING | The company offers an open-range horseback ride on a working Kohala Mountain cattle ranch, spectacular views of three volcanoes and the coastline, and an authentic *paniolo* (cowboy) experience from 3,000 feet up. You don't ride nose-to-tail and can spread out and trot or canter if you wish: this is an 11,000-acre ranch, so there's room to roam. The company caters to beginning and experienced riders and offers special private rides as well. ⊠ *Kohala Mountain Rd. (Hwy. 250) at mile marker 13.2, Waimea (Hawaii County)* ☎ *808/889–5354* ⊕ *www.panioloadventures.com* ⊠ *From $69.*

Kayaking

The leeward (west coast) areas of the Big Island are protected for the most part from the northeast trade winds, making for ideal near-shore kayaking conditions. Miles and miles of uncrowded Kona and Kohala coastline present close-up views of stark, raw, lava-rock shores and cliffs; lava-tube sea caves; pristine, secluded coves; and deserted beaches.

Ocean kayakers can get close to shore—places the commercial snorkel and dive cruise boats can't reach. This opens up all sorts of possibilities for adventure, such as near-shore snorkeling among the expansive coral reefs and lava-rock formations that teem with colorful tropical fish and Hawaiian green sea turtles. You can pull ashore at a quiet cove for a picnic and a plunge into turquoise waters.

With a good coastal map and some advice from the kayak vendor, you might paddle past ancient battlegrounds, burial sites, bathing ponds for Hawaiian royalty, or old villages.

Kayaking can be enjoyed via a guided tour or on a self-guided paddling excursion. Either way, the kayak outfitter can brief you on recommended routes, safety, and how to help preserve and protect Hawaii's ocean resources and coral reef system.

Whether you're a beginning or experienced kayaker, choose appropriate location, distance, and conditions for your excursion.

■ Ask the outfitter about local conditions and hazards, such as tides, currents, and advisories, but also judge conditions for yourself and *never* launch in rough weather.

■ Beginners should practice getting into and out of the kayak and capsizing (called a *huli*, the Hawaiian word for "flip") in shallow water.

■ Before departing, secure the kayak's hatches to prevent water intake.

■ Use a line to attach the paddle to the kayak to avoid losing it.

■ Always use a life vest or jacket, and wear a rash guard and hat; apply plenty of reef-safe sunblock.

■ Carry appropriate amounts of water and food.

■ Don't kayak alone. Create a float plan; tell someone where you're going and when you will return.

BEST SPOTS

Hilo Bay. This is a favorite kayak spot. The best place to put in is at Reeds Bay Beach Park. Parking is plentiful and free at the bayfront. Most afternoons you'll share the bay with local paddling clubs. Stay inside the breakwater unless the ocean is calm (or you're feeling unusually adventurous). Conditions range from extremely calm to quite choppy. ✉ *Banyan Way and Banyan Dr., 1 mile from downtown Hilo.*

Hookena Beach Park. Located in South Kona, this lovely little bay is perfect for kayaking. A concessionaire offers both double and single kayaks for rent by the hour. ✉ *86-4322 Mamalahoa Hwy, Captain Cook.*

Kailua Bay and Kamakahonu Beach. The small sandy beach that fronts the Courtyard King Kamehameha's Kona Beach Hotel is a nice place to rent or launch kayaks. You can unload in the cul-de-sac and park in nearby free or paid lots. The water here is especially calm, and the surroundings are historical and scenic. ✉ *Alii Dr., next to Kailua Pier, Kailua-Kona.*

Kealakekua Bay State Historical Park. The excellent snorkeling and likelihood of seeing dolphins (morning is best) make Kealakekua Bay one of the most popular kayaking spots on the Big Island. An ocean conservation district, the bay is usually calm and tranquil. (Use caution and common sense during surf advisories.) Tall coral pinnacles and clear visibility surrounding the Captain James Cook Monument also make for stupendous snorkeling. Regulations permit only a few operators to lead kayak tours in the park. ✉ *Napoopoo Rd. and Manini Beach Rd., Captain Cook* ⊕ *dlnr.hawaii.gov/dsp.*

Oneo Bay. Right in downtown Kailua, this is usually a placid place to kayak. It's fairly easy to access. If you can't find parking along the road, there's a free lot across the street from the library and farmers' market. ✉ *Alii Dr., Kailua-Kona.*

EQUIPMENT, LESSONS, AND TOURS

There are several rental outfitters on Highway 11 between Kainaliu and Captain Cook, but only a few are permitted to lead kayak trips in Kealakekua Bay.

Aloha Kayak Co.

KAYAKING | The outfitter is one of the few permitted to guide kayaking tours to the stunningly beautiful Kealakekua Bay, leaving from Napoopoo, including about 1½ hours at the Captain Cook Monument. The 3½-hour morning and afternoon tours include snacks and drinks, while the five-hour tour includes lunch. Local guides discuss the area's cultural, historical, and natural significance. You may see spinner dolphins, but you will observe them from a distance only, as this is a protected marine reserve and dolphins are protected by federal law. Keauhou Bay tours are also available, including a two-hour evening manta ray tour. Advance reservations are highly recommended. ✉ *82-5674 Kahau Pl., Captain Cook* ☎ *808/322–2868* ⊕ *www.alohakayak.com* ✉ *Tours from $105 (price includes mandatory wharf fee).*

★ **Kona Boys**

KAYAKING | On the highway above Kealakekua Bay, this full-service, environmentally conscious outfitter handles kayaks, bodyboards, surfboards, stand-up paddleboards, and snorkeling gear. Single-seat and double kayaks are offered. Surfing and stand-up paddleboarding lessons are available for private or group instruction. One of the few companies permitted to lead tours in Kealakekua Bay, Kona Boys offer their Morning Magic and Midday Meander tours, two half-day guided kayaking and snorkeling trips with gear, lunch, snacks, and beverages. They also run a beach shack fronting the Courtyard King Kamehameha's Kona Beach Hotel, with everything for the beachgoer such as rentals of beach mats, chairs, and other gear. ■TIP➔ **The Kailua-Kona location offers Hawaiian outrigger canoe rides and SUP lessons.** ✉ *79-7539 Mamalahoa Hwy., Kealakekua* ☎ *808/328–1234 Kealakekua location, 808/329–2345 Kailua-Kona location* ⊕ *www.konaboys.com* ✉ *Tours from $199.*

Ocean Safari's Kayak Adventures

KAYAKING | On the guided, 3½-hour morning sea-cave tour that begins in Keauhou Bay, you can visit lava-tube sea caves along the coast, then swim ashore for a snack. The kayaks are already on the water, so you won't have the hassle of transporting them. The company also offers stand-up paddleboard rentals and lessons. Book online for best availability. ✉ 78-7128 Kaleiopapa St., Kailua-Kona ☎ 808/326–4699 ⊕ www.oceansafa-riskayaks.com ✍ From $89.

Sailing

For old salts and novice sailors alike, there's nothing like a cruise on the Kona or Kohala Coast. Calm waters, serene shores, and the superb scenery of Maunakea, Mauna Loa, and Hualalai, the Big Island's primary volcanic peaks, make for a great sailing adventure. You can drop a line over the side and try your luck at catching dinner, or grab some snorkel gear and explore when the boat drops anchor in one of the quiet coves and bays. A cruise may well be the most relaxing and adventurous part of a Big Island visit.

Honu Sail Charters

SAILING | The fully equipped, 32-foot cutter-rigged sloop Honu (Hawaiian for sea turtle) carries up to six passengers on full-day, half-day, and sunset sailing excursions along the scenic Kona Coast, including time to snorkel in clear waters over coral reefs during the day tours and heavy pupus (appetizers) for the sunset excursion. This friendly outfitter allows passengers to get some hands-on sailing experience or to kick back and relax, and there are plenty of cushions and lots of shade. Private charters are an option. ✉ Honokohau Harbor, Kailua-Kona ☎ 808/896–4668 ⊕ www.sailkona.com ✍ Tours from $250/hr.

Paradise Sailing Hawaii

SAILING | Married Captains Eric and Yumi Wakely spent 20 years running charters in West Hawaii and decided to open their own charter company. Kolea, a comfortable, sleek, 36-foot Kurt Hughes catamaran, provides plenty of shade, ample seating, tables, restrooms, and a shower. Take a private morning, afternoon, or sunset sail along the Kona Coast. ✉ Honokohau Marina, 74-380 Kealakehe Pkwy., #J24, Kailua-Kona ☎ 808/883–0399 ⊕ paradisesailinghawaii.com ✍ From $995 for maximum of 8 people.

Scuba Diving

The Big Island's underwater world is the setting for a dramatic diving experience. With generally warm and calm waters, vibrant coral reefs and rock formations, and plunging underwater drop-offs, the Kona and Kohala Coasts offer premier scuba diving. There are some good dive locations in East Hawaii, not far from the Hilo area, but the best spots are all on the west coast. Divers find much to occupy their time, including marine reserves teeming with tropical reef fish, Hawaiian green sea turtles, an occasional and critically endangered Hawaiian monk seal, and some playful spinner dolphins. On special night dives to see manta rays, divers descend with underwater lights that attract plankton, which in turn attract these otherworldly creatures.

BEST SPOTS

Garden Eel Cove. Accessible only by boat, this is a great place to see manta rays somersaulting overhead as they feast on a plankton supper. It's also home to hundreds of tiny garden eels darting out from their sandy homes. There's a steep drop-off and lots of marine life. ✉ Rte. 19, near the Kona Airport, Kailua-Kona.

Manta Village. Booking with a night-dive operator is required for the short boat ride to this area, one of Kona's best night-dive spots. If you're a diving or snorkeling

The Kona Coast's relatively calm waters and colorful coral reefs are excellent for scuba diving.

fanatic, it's well worth it to experience manta rays drawn by the lights of the hotel. ■ TIP➔ **If night swimming isn't your cup of tea, you can catch a glimpse of the majestic creatures from the Outrigger's viewing areas. No water access is allowed from the hotel's property.** ⊠ *78-128 Ehukai St., off Outrigger Kona Resort and Spa at Keauhou Bay, Kailua-Kona.*

Pawai Bay Marine Preserve. Clear waters, abundant reef life, and interesting coral formations make this protected preserve ideal for diving. Explore sea caves, arches, and lava-rock formations and dive into lava tubes. An easy, boat-only dive spot is ½ mile north of Old Airport Park. (No shoreline access to protected Pawai Bay is available due to its cultural and environmental significance.) ⊠ *Kuakini Hwy., north of Old Kona Airport Park, Kailua-Kona.*

Puako. Just south of Hapuna Beach State Recreation Area, beautiful Puako (a small oceanfront neighborhood) offers easy entry to some fine reef diving. Deep chasms, sea caves, and rock arches abound with marine life. Trade winds pick up in the afternoons. ⊠ *Puako Rd., off Hwy. 19, Kailua-Kona.*

EQUIPMENT, LESSONS, AND TOURS

There are quite a few good dive shops along the Kona Coast. Most are happy to take on all customers, but a few focus on specific types of trips. Trip prices vary, depending on whether you're already certified and whether you're diving from a boat or from shore. Instruction with PADI, SDI, or TDI certification in three to five days costs $600 to $850. Most instructors rent dive equipment and snorkel gear, as well as underwater cameras. Most organize otherworldly manta ray dives at night and whale-watching cruises in season.

Big Island Divers

SCUBA DIVING | This company offers several levels of certification as well as numerous excursions, including night dives, two-tank charters, and in-season whale-watching. ⊠ *74-5467 Kaiwi St.,*

Kailua-Kona ☎ *808/329–6068* ⊕ *bigisland-divers.com* ⤢ *From $179.*

Jack's Diving Locker

SCUBA DIVING | Good for novice and intermediate divers, Jack's has trained and certified tens of thousands of divers since 1981, with classrooms and a dive pool for instruction. Four boats that accommodate up to 18 divers and six snorkelers visit more than 80 established dive sites along the Kona Coast, yielding sightings of turtles, manta rays, garden eels, and schools of barracuda. They even take you lava tube diving. Snorkelers can accompany their friends on the dive boats or take guided morning trips and manta night trips, and dolphin-watch and reef snorkels. Combined sunset/night manta ray dives are offered as well. ■ TIP➜ **Kona's best deal for scuba newbies is Jack's pool and shore dive combo.** ✉ *75-5813 Alii Dr., Kailua-Kona* ☎ *808/329–7585, 800/345–4807* ⊕ *www.jacksdivinglocker.com* ⤢ *Tours from $199 certified divers, $300 intro divers.*

★ Kohala Divers

SCUBA DIVING | The Kohala Coast's gorgeous underwater topography of lava tubes, caves, vibrant coral reefs, and interesting sea life makes it a great diving destination. This full-service PADI dive shop has been certifying divers since 1984. A one-day intro dive course has you in the ocean the same day. A four-day, full-certification course is offered, too. The company rents any equipment needed for boat or shore excursions and takes divers to the best diving spots on their fully outfitted, comfortable, 46-foot Newton dive boat. The retail shop is packed with everything needed for diving, snorkeling, and the beach. ✉ *Kawaihae Harbor Shopping Center, Hwy. 270, Kawaihae* ☎ *808/882–7774* ⊕ *www.kohaladivers.com* ⤢ *Two-tank dive $179; open-water certification from $699.*

Snorkeling

A favorite pastime on the Big Island, snorkeling is perhaps one of the easiest and most enjoyable water activities for visitors. By floating on the surface, peering through your mask, and breathing through your snorkel, you can see lava-rock formations, sea arches, sea caves, and coral reefs teeming with colorful tropical fish. While the Kona and Kohala Coasts boast more beaches, bays, and quiet coves to snorkel, the east side around Hilo is also a great place to get in the water.

If you don't bring your own equipment, you can easily rent all the gear needed from a beach activities vendor, who will happily provide directions to the best sites for snorkeling in the area. For access to deeper water and assistance from an experienced crew (to say nothing of typically great food and drink), you can opt for a snorkel cruise. Excursions generally range from two to five hours; be sure to ask what equipment and food is included. ■ TIP➜ **Use a few drops of baby shampoo on your mask for a perfect, cheap, and easy-on-the-eyes defogger.**

BEST SPOTS

Carlsmith Beach Park. This calm group of lagoons near Hilo is a great place to bring kids. Freshwater springs might cloud your mask and keep the water cool, but you'll see lots of turtles and tropical fish here. There are showers, a lifeguard, and picnic tables. ✉ *1815 Kalanianaole Ave., 10 min. east of Hilo on Hwy. 137.*

Puako Tide Pools. The large shelf of extensive reef and tide pools at this sleepy beach town along the Kohala Coast makes for fantastic snorkeling as long as conditions are calm. ✉ *South end of Puako Beach Rd., Puako, off Hwy. 11.*

Kahaluu Beach Park. Since ancient times, the waters around Kahaluu Beach have provided traditional throw net–fishing grounds. With super-easy access, the bay offers good swimming and outstanding snorkeling, revealing turtles, angelfish, parrotfish, needlefish, puffer fish, and many types of tangs. ■TIP→ **Stay inside the breakwater and don't stray too far, as dangerous and unpredictable currents swirl outside the bay.** ✉ *Alii Dr., Kailua-Kona.*

Kealakekua Bay State Historical Park. This protected Marine Life Conservation District is hands-down one of the best snorkeling spots on the island, thanks to clear visibility, fabulous coral reefs, and generally calm waters. Pods of dolphins can be abundant, but they're protected under federal law and may not be disturbed or approached. Access to the area is restricted, but a few companies are permitted to escort tours to the bay. ■TIP→ **Overland access is difficult, so opt for one of the guided snorkel cruises permitted to moor here.** ✉ *Napoopoo, at end of Beach Rd. and Hwy. 160, Captain Cook.*

Magic Sands Beach Park. Also known as White Sands or Disappearing Sands Beach Park, this is a great place for beginning and intermediate snorkelers. In winter, it's also a prime spot to watch for whales. ✉ *Alii Dr., Kailua-Kona.*

EQUIPMENT, LESSONS, AND TOURS
Body Glove Cruises
SNORKELING | FAMILY | A good choice for families, this operator has a waterslide and high-dive platform that kids love. On the daily Snorkel and BBQ Adventure, the 65-foot catamaran sets off from Kailua-Kona pier for stunning Red Hill in uncrowded South Kona. The morning snorkel cruise includes breakfast and a barbecue burger lunch, with vegetarian options. A three-hour historical dinner cruise to Kealakekua Bay is a great way to relax, watch the sunset, and learn about Kona's history. It includes an excellent Hawaiian-style meal, complimentary cocktail, and live music. Seasonal

whale-watch cruises and all dolphin snorkel cruises guarantee you will see the featured mammals or you can go again for free. The company follows a NOAA-approved Dolphin SMART policy, encouraging responsible viewing, on all their cruises. Children under five are always free. ✉ *75-5629 Kuakini Hwy., Kailua-Kona* ☎ *808/326–7122, 800/551–8911* ⊕ *www.bodyglovehawaii.com* ⚓ *From $158.*

★ *Fair Wind* Cruises
SNORKELING | FAMILY | In business since 1971, Fair Wind offers morning and afternoon snorkel trips into breathtaking Kealakekua Bay. Great for families with small kids, the custom-built, 60-foot catamaran *Fair Wind* has two 15-foot waterslides, freshwater showers, and a staircase descending directly into the water for easy access. Snorkel gear is included, along with flotation equipment and prescription masks. The 4½-hour cruise is known for its delicious meals; 3½-hour snack cruises are offered, too. For ages seven and older, the company also operates the *Hula Kai* snorkel cruise, on a 55-foot luxury hydrofoil catamaran that takes guests to several remote South Kona locations. Their five-hour morning snorkel cruise includes a gourmet breakfast and barbecue lunch. ✉ *Keauhou Bay, 78-7130 Kaleiopapa St., Kailua-Kona* ☎ *808/322–2788, 800/677–9461* ⊕ *www.fair-wind.com* ⚓ *From $159.*

Sea Quest
SNORKELING | Careful stewardship of the Kona Coast and its sea life is a major priority for this company, which offers catamaran charters and other snorkeling excursions. Trips leave from Keauhou Bay and head to Captain Cook Monument and other points south. ■TIP→ **Book five days in advance for $10 off.** ✉ *78-7138 Kaleiopapa St., Kailua-Kona* ☎ *808/329–7238* ⊕ *www.seaquesthawaii.com* ⚓ *From $98.*

Passengers aboard the *Atlantis X* submarine visit the aquatic world without getting wet. They may even see a scuba diver in action.

Stand-Up Paddling

Stand-up paddleboarding (or stand-up paddling; SUP for short), a sport with roots in the Hawaiian Islands, has grown popular worldwide in recent years. It's available for all skill levels and ages, and even novice stand-up paddleboarders can get up, stay up, and have a great time paddling around a protected bay or exploring the gorgeous coastline. All you need to get started is a large body of calm water, a board, and a paddle. The workout tests your core strength as well as your balance and offers an unusual vantage point from which to enjoy the beauty of island and ocean.

BEST SPOTS

Anaehoomalu Bay Beach. In this well-protected bay, it's usually fairly calm even when surf is rough on the rest of the island, though trade winds pick up heartily in the afternoon. Boards are available for rent at the north end, and the safe area for stand-up paddling is marked by buoys. ⊠ *Off Waikoloa Beach Dr., south of Waikoloa Beach Marriott, Kohala Coast.*

Hilo Bay. The bay is calm most days, as well as shallow, so it's a great place for novices to try stand-up paddling. The beach is about 3,000 feet long, one of the longest in Hawaii, so there's lots of room on the beach and in the water. Free parking is abundant fronting the bay off Bayfront Highway, so you won't usually have to schlep your board and paddle too far from your car. ⊠ *Bayfront Hwy., downtown Hilo.*

Kailua Bay and Kamakahonu Beach. The small, sandy beach that fronts the Courtyard King Kamehameha's Kona Beach Hotel is great for kids; the water here is especially calm and gentle. If you're more daring, you can easily paddle out of the bay and along the coast for some great exploring. ⊠ *Alii Dr., next to Kailua Pier, Kailua-Kona.*

EQUIPMENT AND LESSONS
Alii Adventure Shack
STAND UP PADDLEBOARDING | This small company specializes in paddleboard rentals and can give you some great tips about where to go in Kailua-Kona for the best experience. ☒ 75-5663 Palani Rd., Kailua-Kona ☎ 808/657-4606 ⊕ aliiadventureshack.com ☜ From $20/hr.

★ Hypr Nalu Hawaii
STAND UP PADDLEBOARDING | FAMILY | Veteran waterman and fitness enthusiast Ian Foo and his wife, Lauren, run this top-of-the-line board shop at the beach fronting the Waikoloa Beach Marriott Resort. From stand-up paddleboards to surfboards to lessons, accessories, clothing, and gear, they do it all with passion and expertise. More impressively, they make the elegant stand-up boards—arguably the most beautiful paddleboards in the world—themselves and will ship worldwide. So if you take a lesson, fall in love with the sport, and want one sent home, this is the place to go. ☒ 69-275 Waikoloa Beach Dr., Waikoloa ☎ 808/960–4667 ⊕ www.hyprnalu.com.

Submarine Tours

Atlantis Submarines
BOATING | FAMILY | Want to stay dry while exploring the tropical undersea world? Climb aboard the 48-passenger Atlantis X submarine, anchored off Kailua Pier, across from Courtyard King Kamehameha's Kona Beach Hotel. A large glass dome in the bow and 13 viewing ports on each side allow clear views of the aquatic world more than 100 feet down. They take you to a pristine, 25-acre coral garden brimming with sea creatures of all kinds. This is a great trip for kids and nonswimmers. ■ TIP➔ Book online for discounts and specials. ☒ 75-5669 Alii Dr., Kailua-Kona ☎ 808/326–7939, 800/381–0237 ⊕ www.atlantisadventures.com ☜ $134.

Surfing

The Big Island does not have the variety of great surfing spots found on Oahu or Maui, but it does have decent waves and a thriving surf culture. Local kids and avid surfers frequent a number of places up and down the Kona and Kohala Coasts of West Hawaii; some have become famous surf champions. Expect high surf in winter and much calmer activity during summer. The surf scene is much more active on the Kona side.

BEST SPOTS
Honolii Cove. North of Hilo, this is the best surfing spot on the eastern side of the island. It hosts many exciting surf contests. ☒ Off Hwy. 19, near mile marker 4, Hilo.

Kahaluu Beach Park. Slightly north of this beach park and just past the calm lagoon filled with snorkelers, beginning and intermediate surfers can have a go at some nice waves. ☒ Alii Dr., Kailua-Kona.

Kohanaiki. Also known as Pine Trees, this community beach park is among the best places to catch waves. Keep in mind that it's a very popular local surf spot on an island where there aren't all that many surf spots, and be respectful. ☒ Off Hwy. 11, Kohanaiki entrance gate, about 2 miles south of Kona airport, Kailua-Kona.

Old Kona Airport Park. The park is a good place for catching wave action. A couple of the island's outfitters conduct surf lessons here, as the break is far from potentially dangerous rocks and reefs. ☒ Kuakini Rd., Kailua-Kona.

EQUIPMENT AND LESSONS
★ Hawaii Lifeguard Surf Instructors
SURFING | This family-owned, lifeguard-certified school helps novices become wave riders at Kahaluu Beach Park in Kailua-Kona and offers lessons for more experienced riders at Kona's top surf spots. A two-hour introductory lesson has one instructor per two to four

Humpback whales are visible off the coast of the Big Island between December and April.

students and is gentle and reassuring. Private instruction is available as well. If the waves are on the smaller side, the school converts to stand-up paddle-board lessons for the same prices as surfing. ⊠ *75-5909 Alii Dr., Kailua-Kona* ☎ *808/324–0442, 808/936–7873* ⊕ *www.surflessonshawaii.com* ✉ *From $95.*

Ocean Eco Tours Surf School

SURFING | Family owned and operated, Kona's oldest surf school emphasizes the basics and specializes in beginners. It's one of a handful of operators permitted to conduct business in Kaloko-Honoko-hau National Historical Park, which gets waves even when other spots on the west side are flat. All lessons are taught by certified instructors, and the school guarantees that you will surf. There's an authentic soul surfer's vibe to this operation, and they are equally die-hard about teaching you about the ocean and having you standing up riding waves on your first day. Group, private, and semi-private lessons are available. ⊠ *Courtyard King Kamehameha's Kona Beach Hotel,* *75-5660 Palani Rd., Suite 304, Kailua-Kona* ☎ *808/324–7873* ⊕ *www.oceanecotours.com* ✉ *From $119.*

Whale-Watching

One of the most highly anticipated Hawaii experiences for visitors and residents alike from December through May is the annual migration of the North Pacific humpback whales. They travel about 3,200 miles from Alaska's icy waters to the Hawaiian Islands in as few as 40 days, swimming 24 hours a day. As early as October, mother whales with nursing calves arrive first, followed by mothers with yearlings. These moms have taught the migration to their offspring and then begin to wean them. Adult males arrive next, followed by adult females, and finally by pregnant mothers who maximize their feeding in Alaska before making the journey and giving birth. Once here, they do not feed. The population of migrating humpbacks in Hawaiian waters is now estimated at about 12,000 individuals.

Behaviors that you might witness include pectoral slapping, spy-hops, tail slapping, and the most spectacular of all—leaping barrel rolls. Toward the end of the season, you may see mothers nurturing newborn calves. Humpbacks tend to stick close to shore, so you will often witness them from many accessible locations, especially along the Kohala Coast.

Eighteen species of dolphins live here year-round, including spotted, spinner, rough-toothed, and bottlenose. Be sure to choose excursions that respect the natural boundaries of dolphins and that don't disturb or impact their resting states, as they are all protected by federal law. ■ TIP➜ **If you take a morning cruise, you're more likely to see dolphins.**

In addition to the outfitters listed below, see the Snorkeling section for more outfitters that offer whale- and dolphin-watching cruises.

TOURS

Captain Dan McSweeney's Whale Watch Learning Adventures

WILDLIFE-WATCHING | Captain Dan McSweeney, self-described whale researcher and conservationist, offers three-hour trips on his double-decker, 40-foot cruise boat. In addition to humpbacks (in winter), he'll try to show you dolphins and some of the six other whale species that live off the Kona Coast throughout the year. McSweeney guarantees you'll see whales or he'll take you out again for free. ⊠ *Honokohau Harbor, 74-381 Kealakehe Pkwy., Kailua-Kona* ☎ *808/322–0028, 888/942–5376* ⊕ *www.ilovewhales.com* ⌨ *$120.*

Hawaii Nautical

WILDLIFE-WATCHING | A NOAA-designated Dolphin SMART operator, this company practices strict guidelines for viewing protected marine animals, including dolphins and whales. You can be assured that you'll enjoy a wonderful ocean tour, see plenty of animals, and not be a part of harming or impacting the animals' activities or habitats. Excursions include affordable powerboat cruises, catamaran snorkel sails, and even a pampering yacht adventure that takes a maximum of six guests to Pawai Bay or Makalawena. Private charters are also available. ⊠ *74-425 Kealakehe Pkwy., Slip I-10, Kailua-Kona* ☎ *808/234–7245* ⊕ *www.hawaiinautical.com* ⌨ *From $79.*

Zip Line Tours

Kohala Zipline

ZIP-LINING | Located in the canopy of the Halawa Gulch in North Kohala, this tour features nine zips and five suspension bridges for a thrilling, within-the-canopy adventure in the forest. You'll bounce up to the site in a six-wheel-drive, military-style vehicle. Two certified guides accompany each small group. Designed for all ability levels, the Kohala Zipline focuses on fun and safety, offering a dual line for efficient, confident braking. You'll soar more than 100 feet above the ground and feel like a pro by the last platform. A quickie lesson in rappelling is included. Zip and Dip tours (combining zip line, nature walk, lunch, snacks, and waterfall swim) are also available. ⊠ *54-3676 Akoni Pule Hwy., Kapaau* ☎ *808/331–8505* ⊕ *www.kohalazipline.com* ⌨ *From $205.*

Chapter 6

KAUAI

Updated by Joan Conrow,
Cheryl Crabtree, and
Mary F. Williamson

⊙ Sights	🍴 Restaurants	🛏 Hotels	🛍 Shopping	🍸 Nightlife
★★★★★	★★★☆☆	★★★☆☆	★★★☆☆	★★☆☆☆

WELCOME TO KAUAI

TOP REASONS TO GO

★ **Beaches:** Pristine strips of sand and palm-fringed shores make vacation dreams real.

★ **Napali Coast:** Its towering cliffs astonish all who see them from land, sea, or air.

★ **Outdoor fun:** Kauai offers great surfing and snorkeling, plus top-notch golf and hiking.

★ **Charming towns:** Artsy Hanapepe, colorful Hanalei, historic Koloa, and more invite lingering.

★ **Kayaking:** Paddling on a river is a tranquil way to discover the island's allure.

★ **Scenic drives:** Cruise the North Shore's Route 560 or the West Side's Waimea Canyon Drive.

1 **North Shore.** Dreamy beaches, verdant mountains, breathtaking scenery, and abundant rain, waterfalls, and rainbows characterize the North Shore, which includes Kilauea, Princeville, Hanalei, and Haena.

2 **East Side.** This is Kauai's commercial and residential hub, dominated by the island's largest town, Kapaa. The airport, main harbor, and government offices are found in the county seat of Lihue. It can be a convenient base for travelers, too.

3 **South Shore.** Peaceful landscapes, sunny weather, and beaches that rank among the best in the world make the South Shore the resort capital of Kauai. The Poipu resort area is here, along with the main towns of Koloa and Lawai.

4 **West Side.** Dry, sunny, and sleepy, the West Side includes the historic towns of Hanapepe, Waimea, and Kekaha. The area is ideal for outdoor adventurers because it's both the entryway to Waimea Canyon and Kokee State Park and the departure point for most Napali Coast boat trips.

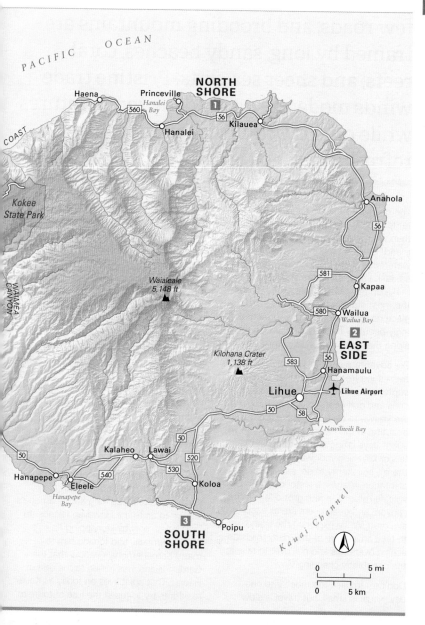

PACIFIC OCEAN

Haena
Princeville
NORTH SHORE [1]
560
Hanalei Bay
COAST
Hanalei
56
Kilauea

Kokee State Park

Anahola
56

WAIMEA CANYON

Waialeale
5,148 ft ▲

581

Kapaa

580 Wailua
Wailua Bay

Kilohana Crater
1,138 ft ▲

583

[2] **EAST SIDE**

56

Hanamaulu

Lihue ✈ Lihue Airport

50
58

Nawiliwili Bay

50

Kalaheo Lawai
50
520

540
530

Hanapepe
Eleele
Koloa

Hanapepe Bay

[3]
SOUTH SHORE
Poipu

Kauai Channel

0 — 5 mi
0 — 5 km

Even a nickname like "the Garden Island" fails to do justice to Kauai's beauty. Verdant trees grow canopies over the few roads, and brooding mountains are framed by long, sandy beaches, coral reefs, and sheer sea cliffs. Pristine trade winds moderate warm daily temperatures while offering comfort for deep, refreshing sleep through gentle nights.

The main road tracing Kauai's perimeter takes you past much more scenery than would seem possible on one small island. Chiseled mountains, thundering waterfalls, misty hillsides, dreamy beaches, lush vegetation, and small towns make up the physical landscape. Perhaps the most stunning piece of scenery is a place no road will take you—breathtakingly beautiful Napali Coast, which runs along the northwest side of the island.

For adventure seekers, Kauai offers everything from difficult hikes to helicopter tours. The island has top-notch spas and golf courses, and its beaches are known to be some of the most beautiful in the world. Even after you've spent days lazing around drinking mai tais or kayaking your way down a river, there's still plenty to do, as well as see: plantation villages, a historic lighthouse, wildlife refuges, a fern grotto, a colorful canyon, and deep rivers are all easily explored. While exploring the island, try to take advantage of the many roadside scenic overlooks and pull over to take in the constantly changing view.

Don't try to pack too much into one day. Kauai is small, but travel is slow.

The island's sights are divided into four geographic areas, in clockwise order: the North Shore, the East Side, the South Shore, and the West Side.

Kauai is the oldest and northernmost of the main Hawaiian Islands. Five million years of wind and rain have worked their magic, sculpting fluted sea cliffs and whittling away at the cinder cones and caldera that prove its volcanic origin. Foremost among these is Waialeale, one of the wettest spots on Earth. Its approximate 450-inch annual rainfall feeds the mighty Wailua River, the only navigable waterway in Hawaii. The vast Alakai Swamp soaks up rain like a sponge, releasing it slowly into the watershed that gives Kauai its emerald sheen.

Kauai's residents have had a reputation for independence since ancient times. Called "the Separate Kingdom," Kauai alone resisted King Kamehameha's charge to unite the Hawaiian Islands. In fact, it was only by kidnapping Kauai's king, Kaumualii, and forcing him to marry Kamehameha's widow that the Garden Island was joined to the rest of Hawaii. That spirit lives on today as Kauai residents try to resist the lure of tourism dollars captivating the rest of the Islands. Local building tradition maintains that no structure be taller than a coconut tree, and Kauai's capital, Lihue, is still more small town than city.

Although all of the islands have a few stories about the Menehune—magical, tiny people who accomplished great feats—Kauai is believed to be their home base. The Menehune Fishpond, above Nawilwili Harbor, is a prime example of their work. The story goes that the large pond (initially 25 miles in diameter) was built in one night by thousands of Menehune passing stones from hand to hand. A spy disrupted their work in the middle of the night, leaving two gaps that are still visible today (drive to the pond on Hulemalu Road, or kayak up Huleia Stream).

Planning

Getting Here and Around

AIR

On Kauai, visitors fly into Lihue Airport (LIH), on the East Side of the island. Visitor information booths are outside each baggage-claim area. Visitors will also find a newsstand, flower shop, Starbucks, bar, restaurant, and gift shop in the terminal.

For most domestic and international flights, however, Honolulu International Airport (HNL) is the main stopover. From Honolulu, interisland flights to Kauai depart regularly from early morning until evening. In addition, some carriers offer nonstop service directly from the U.S. mainland to Lihue Airport.

To travel interisland from Honolulu on Hawaiian Air, you will depart from the connected interisland terminal (Terminal 1). Southwest Airlines flies out of Terminal 2. A free bus service, the Wiki Wiki Shuttle, operates between terminals.

BUS

On Kauai, the County Transportation Agency operates the Kauai Bus, which provides service between Hanalei and Kekaha. It also provides limited service to the airport and to Koloa and Poipu. The fare is $2 for adults, and frequent-rider passes are available. The new North Shore Shuttle now operates to Kee Beach from either Waipa or Princeville, depending on road construction. Updates about fares, routes, and a hop-on, hop-off option are posted at ⊕ gohaena.com. The website ⊕ getaroundkauai.com has information about resources for sustainable transportation choices.

CAR

The independent way to experience all of Kauai's stunning beauty is to get in a car and explore. The 15-mile stretch of Napali Coast, with its breathtaking, verdant-green sheer cliffs, is the only outer part of the island that's not accessible by car. Otherwise, one main road can get you from Barking Sands Beach on the West Side to Haena on the North Shore.

While driving on Kauai, you will come across several one-lane bridges. If you are the first to approach a bridge, the car on the other side will wait while you cross. If a car on the other side is closer to the bridge, then you should wait while the driver crosses. If you're enjoying the island's dramatic views, pull over to the shoulder so you don't block traffic.

Only recently has Kauai instituted parking fees for nonresidents at a few popular tourist areas, and these fees are collected for upkeep. Under consideration at the time of writing is a daily fee of $10 for nonresidents to park at high-use county beach parks. There is a $10 fee for nonresidents to park at Kee Beach, and a $10 fee for nonresidents covers the four fantastic lookouts over Waimea Canyon and in Kokee. Otherwise, there are parking meters at only a couple of state office buildings but no pay-to-park garages, tags, or lots. If there's room on the side

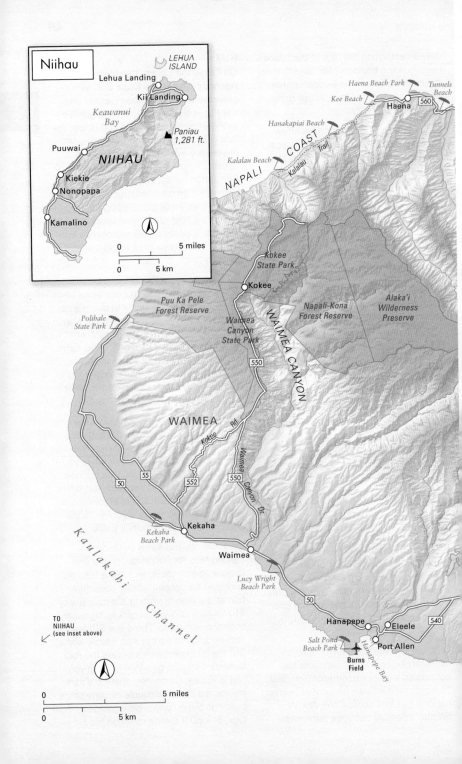

Niihau

LEHUA ISLAND

Lehua Landing

Kii Landing

Keawanui Bay

Puuwai

NIIHAU

▲ *Paniau 1,281 ft.*

Kiekie

Nonopapa

Kamalino

0   5 miles
0   5 km

Haena Beach Park

Kee Beach

Tunnels Beach

Haena

560

Hanakapiai Beach

NAPALI COAST

Kalalau Beach

Kalalau Trail

Kokee State Park

Kokee

Napali-Kona Forest Reserve

Alaka'i Wilderness Preserve

Puu Ka Pele Forest Reserve

Waimea Canyon State Park

WAIMEA CANYON

Polihale State Park

550

WAIMEA

Kokee Rd.

Waimea Canyon Dr.

50

55

552

550

Kekaha

Kekaha Beach Park

Waimea

Lucy Wright Beach Park

50

TO NIIHAU (see inset above)

Kaulakahi Channel

Hanapepe

Eleele

540

Salt Pond Beach Park

Port Allen

Burns Field

Hanapepe Bay

0   5 miles
0   5 km

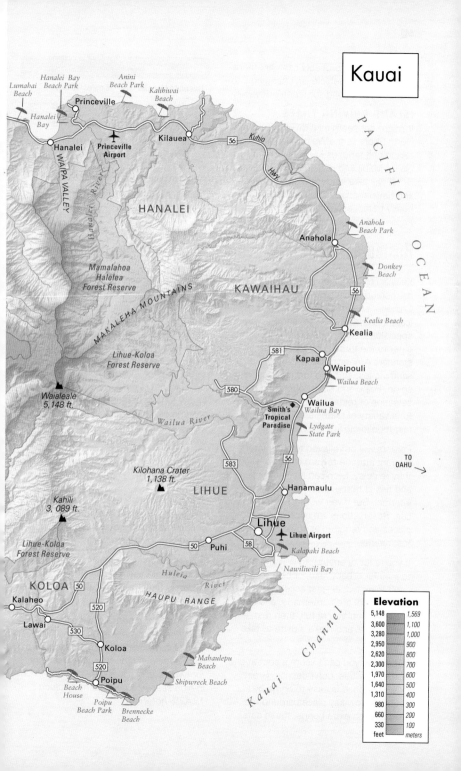

of the road, you probably can park there as long as your vehicle isn't hanging into the road or blocking someone's driveway.

ISLAND DRIVING TIMES

It might not seem as if driving from the North Shore to the West Side, say, would take much time, as Kauai is smaller than Oahu, Maui, and certainly the Big Island. But it will take longer than you'd expect, and Kauai roads are subject to some heavy traffic, especially going through Kapaa and Lihue.

Restaurants

Kauai's cultural diversity is apparent in its restaurants, which offer authentic Chinese, Korean, Japanese, Thai, Mexican, Italian, Vietnamese, and Hawaiian specialties. Less specialized restaurants cater to the tourist crowd, serving standard American fare—burgers, pizza, sandwiches, surf-and-turf combos, and so on. Poipu and Kapaa offers the best selection of restaurants, with options for a variety of tastes and budgets; most fast-food joints are in Lihue.

Parents will be relieved to encounter a tolerant attitude toward children, even if they're noisy. Men can leave their jackets and ties at home; attire tends toward informal. But if you want to dress up, you can. Reservations are accepted in most places and required at some of the top restaurants.

If you're lucky enough to win an invitation to a potluck, baby luau, or beach party, don't think twice—just accept. The best grinds (food) are homemade, and so you'll eat until you're full, then rest, eat some more, and make a plate to take home, too.

But even if you can't score a spot at one of these parties, don't despair. Great local-style food is easy to come by at countless low-key places around the island. As an extra bonus, these eats

Driving Times

Haena to Hanalei	8 miles/15 mins
Hanalei to Princeville	4 miles/10 mins
Princeville to Kilauea	5 miles/10 mins
Kilauea to Anahola	8 miles/12 mins
Anahola to Kapaa	5 miles/15 mins
Kapaa to Lihue	10 miles/25 mins
Lihue to Poipu	13 miles/25 mins
Poipu to Kalaheo	8 miles/15 mins
Kalaheo to Hanapepe	4 miles/10 mins
Hanapepe to Waimea	7 miles/15 mins

are often inexpensive, and portions are generous. Expect plenty of meat—usually deep-fried or marinated in a teriyaki sauce and grilled *pulehu*-style (over an open fire)—and starches. Rice is standard, even for breakfast, and it's often served alongside potato–macaroni salad, another island specialty. Another local favorite is *poke,* made from chunks of raw tuna or octopus seasoned with sesame oil, soy sauce, onions, and pickled seaweed. It's a great *pupu* (appetizer) when paired with a cold beer.

Hotels

There are several top-notch resorts on Kauai, as well as a wide variety of condos, vacation rentals, and bed-and-breakfasts to choose from.

■ TIP➔ **Reserve your room far in advance. Be sure to ask about discounts and special packages (hotel websites often have online-only deals).**

Restaurant and hotel reviews have been shortened. For more information, visit Fodors.com. Restaurant prices are for a main course at dinner. Hotel prices are for two people in a standard double room in high season. Prices do not include 13.42% hotel tax.

Where to Stay in Kauai

Neighborhood	Local Vibe	Pros	Cons
The North Shore	Properties here have the "wow" factor with ocean and mountain beauty; laid-back Hanalei and Princeville set the high-end pace.	When the weather is good, this area has it all. Epic winter surf, gorgeous waterfalls, and verdant vistas create some of the best scenery in Hawaii.	Frequent winter rain (being green has a cost) means you may have to travel south to find the sun; expensive restaurants and shopping offer few deals.
The East Side	The most reasonably priced area to stay for the practical traveler; lacks the pizzazz of expensive resorts on North and South Shores; more traditional beach hotels.	The best travel deals show up here; more direct access to the local population; plenty of decent restaurants with good variety, along with delis in food stores.	Beaches aren't the greatest (rocky, reefy) at many of the lodging spots; congested traffic at times; some crime issues in parks.
The South Shore	Resort central; plenty of choices where the consistent sunshine is perfect for those who want to do nothing but play golf or tennis and read a book by the pool.	Beautiful in its own right; many enchanted evenings with stellar sunsets; summer surf a bit easier for beginners to handle.	Though resorts are lush, surrounding landscape is desert-like with scrub brush; travel time to North Shore sights is long.
The West Side	There are few options for lodging in this mostly untouristed setting, with contrasts such as the extreme heat of an August day in Waimea to a frozen winter night up in Kokee.	A gateway area for exploration into the wilds of Kokee or for boating trips on Napali Coast; main hub for boat and helicopter trips; outstanding sunsets.	Least convenient side for most visitors; daytime is languid and dry; river runoff can ruin ocean's clarity.

What It Costs in U.S. Dollars

$	$$	$$$	$$$$
RESTAURANTS			
Under $18	$18–$26	$27–$35	Over $35
HOTELS			
Under $180	$180–$260	$261–$340	Over $340

Tours

Guided tours are convenient; you don't have to worry about finding a parking spot or getting admission tickets. Certified tour guides have taken special classes in Hawaiian history and lore. On the other hand, you won't have the freedom to proceed at your own pace, nor will you have the ability to take a detour trip if something else catches your attention.

Roberts Hawaii Tours

BUS TOURS | The Round-the-Island Tour, sometimes called the Waimea Canyon–Fern Grotto Tour, gives a good overview of half the island, including Fort Elizabeth and Opaekaa Falls. Guests are transported in air-conditioned, 25-passenger minibuses. The trip includes a boat ride up the Wailua River to the Fern Grotto and a visit to the lookouts above Waimea Canyon. Roberts also offers a Kauai Movie Tour. ⊠ 3–4567 Kuhio Hwy., Hanamaulu ☎ 808/245–9101, 800/831–5541 ⊕ www.robertshawaii.com/kauai ⊠ From $98.

Waimea Historic Tour

DRIVING TOURS | **FAMILY** | Tuesday through Thursday, the West Kauai Heritage Center offers private, car-based tours of historic Waimea Town by reservation, led by a local kupuna (elder). You can also get their map and take a self-guided walking tour. ⊠ 9565 Kaumualii Hwy., Waimea (Kauai County) ☎ 808/338–1332 ⊕ www.wsmmuseum.org ⊠ Suggested tour donation $10.

Visitor Information

Before you go, check the Kauai Visitors Bureau website (⊕ www.gohawaii.com/islands/kauai) for a free travel planner with information on accommodations, transportation, sports and activities, dining, arts and entertainment, and culture. You can also take a virtual tour of the island that includes great photos and helpful planning information. The Hawaii Tourism Authority's website (⊕ www.hawaiitourismauthority.org) offers tips on everything from packing to flying around the state.

The Hawaii Department of Land and Natural Resources site (⊕ dlnr.hawaii.gov) has information on hiking, fishing, and camping permits and licenses; state parks; hiking safety and mountain and ocean preservation; and details on volunteer programs.

Go Haena (⊕ gohaena.com) has details about the reservations and fees required to visit the popular park, beaches, and trails at the end of the road on Kauai's North Shore; there's also info about shuttle service.

Keep your beach time safe by checking out Hawaiian Beach Safety (⊕ hawaiibeachsafety.com) online before you head out.

The North Shore

The North Shore of Kauai includes the environs of Kilauea, Princeville, Hanalei, and Haena, as well as the world-famous Napali Coast. Heading north on Route 56 from the airport in Lihue, the coastal highway crosses the Wailua River and the busy towns of Wailua and Kapaa before emerging into a decidedly rural and scenic landscape, with expansive views of the island's rugged interior mountains. As the two-lane highway turns west and narrows, it winds through

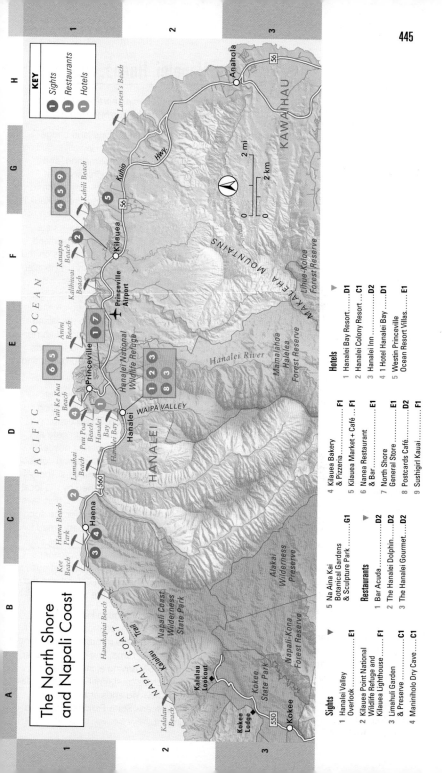

The North Shore and Napali Coast

KEY
- ● Sights
- ● Restaurants
- ● Hotels

Sights ▶

1 Hanalei Valley
Overlook **E1**
2 Kilauea Point National
Wildlife Refuge and
Kilauea Lighthouse **F1**
3 Limahuli Garden
& Preserve **C1**
4 Maniniholo Dry Cave **C1**

5 Na Aina Kai
Botanical Gardens
& Sculpture Park **G1**

Restaurants ▶

1 Bar Acuda **D2**
2 The Hanalei Dolphin **D2**
3 The Hanalei Gourmet **D2**

4 Kilauea Bakery
& Pizzeria **F1**
5 Kilauea Market + Café ... **F1**
6 Nanea Restaurant
& Bar **E1**
7 North Shore
General Store **E1**
8 Postcards Café **D2**
9 Sushigirl Kauai **F1**

Hotels ▶

1 Hanalei Bay Resort **D1**
2 Hanalei Colony Resort ... **C1**
3 Hanalei Inn **D2**
4 Hotel Hanalei Bay **D1**
5 Westin Princeville
Ocean Resort Villas **E1**

spectacular scenery and passes the posh resort community of Princeville before dropping down into Hanalei Valley. Here it narrows further and becomes a federally recognized scenic roadway, replete with one-lane bridges (the local etiquette is for five to seven cars to cross at a time, before yielding to those on the other side), hairpin turns, and heart-stopping coastal vistas. The road ends at Haena State Park and Kee Beach, where the ethereal rain forests and fluted sea cliffs of Napali Coast Wilderness State Park begin. Seeing Napali Coast by boat, on foot, or by helicopter is a highlight of any trip to Kauai. Floods in 2018 caused major physical changes to the North Shore, including landslide areas and general infrastructure chaos. One result is a permitting system for visitors to Haena State Park, which begins with a check-in system at the park. Rules limit vehicles to 900 per day, compared with the previous average of 2,000 per day. The result is a less crowded and calmer atmosphere at Kee Beach.

From Kee Beach, you can hike 2 miles to Hanakapiai Beach on Napali Coast, and as long as you've come this far, you might as well take the 2-mile hike into Hanakapiai Valley to a towering 300-foot waterfall. Along the way you'll see mind-blowing scenes of coastal beauty. In winter, Kauai's North Shore receives more rainfall than other areas of the island. Don't let this deter you from visiting. The clouds drift over mountains, including Namolokama, creating a mysterious mood, and then, in a blink, disappear, rewarding you with mountains laced with a dozen waterfalls or more. The views of the mountain—as well as the sunsets over the ocean—from Hanalei Bay and Kee Beach are fantastic. The North Shore attracts all kinds—from celebrities to surfers. In fact, the late Andy Irons, three-time world surfing champion, along with his brother Bruce and legend Laird Hamilton, grew up riding waves along the North Shore.

Hanalei, Haena, and West

Hanalei is 32 miles northwest of Lihue; Haena is 5 miles northwest of Hanalei.

Crossing the historic one-lane bridge into Hanalei reveals old Hawaii, including working taro farms, poi making, and evenings of throwing horseshoes at Black Pot Beach Park—the latter found unmarked (as many places are on Kauai) at the east end of Hanalei Bay Beach Park. Although the current real-estate boom on Kauai has attracted mainland millionaires to build estate homes on the few remaining parcels of land in Hanalei, there's still plenty to see and do. It's *the* gathering place on the North Shore. Restaurants, shops, and people-watching here are among the best on the island, and you won't find a single brand-name, chain, or big-box store around—unless you count surf brands like Quiksilver and Billabong.

The beach and river at Hanalei offer swimming, snorkeling, bodyboarding, surfing, and kayaking. Those hanging around at sunset often congregate at the Hanalei Pavilion, where a husband-and-wife slack-key-guitar–playing combo makes impromptu appearances. There's an old rumor, since quashed by the local newspaper, the *Garden Island,* that says Hanalei was the inspiration for the song "Puff, the Magic Dragon," performed by the 1960s singing sensation Peter, Paul, and Mary. Even with the newspaper's clarification, some tours still point out the shape of the dragon carved into the mountains encircling the town.

Once you pass through Hanalei Town, the road shrinks even more as you skirt the coast and pass through Haena. Blind corners, quick turns, and one-lane bridges force slow driving along this scenic stretch across the Lumahai and Wainiha Valleys. The road ends at Kee Beach and the Haena State Park entrance and parking lot.

⊙ Sights

★ Hanalei Valley Overlook

VIEWPOINT | Dramatic mountains and a patchwork of neat taro farms bisected by the wide Hanalei River make this one of Hawaii's loveliest views, even with the flood damage it sustained in 2018. The fertile Hanalei Valley has been planted with taro since perhaps AD 700, save for an 80-year-long foray into rice that ended in 1960. (The historic Haraguchi Rice Mill is all that remains of that era.) Many taro farmers lease land within the 900-acre Hanalei National Wildlife Refuge, helping to provide wetland habitat for four species of endangered Hawaiian waterbirds. ⊠ *Rte. 56, across from Foodland, Princeville.*

★ Limahuli Garden & Preserve

GARDEN | **FAMILY** | Narrow Limahuli Valley, with its fluted mountain peaks and ancient stone taro terraces, creates an unparalleled setting for this botanical garden and nature preserve, one of the most gorgeous spots on Kauai and the crown jewel of the National Tropical Botanical Garden. Dedicated to protecting native plants and unusual varieties of taro, it represents the principles of conservation and stewardship held by its founder, Juliet Rice Wichman. Limahuli's primordial beauty and strong *mana* (spiritual power) eclipse the extensive botanical collection. Call ahead to check if guided tours are being offered, or tour on your own. A reservation is required to park here, though North Shore Shuttle riders are exempt. ■ **TIP➜ Check out the quality gift shop and revolutionary compost toilet, and be prepared to walk a somewhat steep hillside.** ⊠ *5–8291 Kuhio Hwy., Hanalei* ☎ *808/826–1053* ⊕ *www.ntbg. org* ⊠ *Self-guided tour $25, guided tour $100 (when available).*

Maniniholo Dry Cave

CAVE | Across the highway from Haena Beach Park is Maniniholo Dry Cave, a place steeped in legends. You can walk for a few minutes through a 30-yard-long cave, which darkens and becomes more claustrophobic as you glide across its sandy floor, hearing the drips down the walls and wondering at its past. Legend has it that Maniniholo was the head fisherman of the Menehune—Kauai's quasi-mythical first inhabitants. After gathering too much food to carry, Maniniholo's men stored the excess under a cliff overnight. When he returned in the morning, the food had vanished, and he blamed the imps living in the cliff's cracks. He and his men dug into the cliff to find and destroy the imps, leaving behind the dry cave. ⊠ *Rte. 560, Haena* ⊠ *Free.*

ⓣ Beaches

★ Haena Beach Park

BEACH | This drive-up beach park favored by campers year-round has a wide bay named Makua bordered by two large reef systems, creating favorable waves for skilled surfers during peak winter conditions. Entering the water can be dangerous in winter when the big swells roll in. In July and August, waters at this same beach are usually as calm as a lake, and throughout summer this is a premier snorkeling site. It's not unusual to find a food vendor parked here, selling sandwiches and drinks out of a converted bread van. Adjacent to this beach is Tunnels Beach.

Parking is extremely limited (the lot typically fills up by 8:30 am), and all vehicles illegally parked outside of designated parking zones are subject to fees and towing. You can also park your car in the shuttle parking lot in Waipa, west of Hanalei Town, and board the North Shore Shuttle for a ride to the beach park ($35 round-trip with seven stops); see ⊕ *gohaena.com* for details and reservations. **Amenities:** food and drink; lifeguards; parking (free); showers; toilets. **Best for:** snorkeling; surfing; walking. ⊠ *Near*

end of Rte. 560, Haena ⊹ *Across from Maniniholo Dry Cave* 🖃 *Free.*

★ Hanalei Bay

BEACH | FAMILY | This 2-mile crescent beach cradles a wide bay in a setting that is quintessential Hawaii: the sea is on one side, and behind you are the mountains, often ribboned with waterfalls and changing color in the shifting light. In winter, Hanalei Bay boasts some of the biggest onshore surf breaks in the state, attracting world-class surfers, and the beach is plenty wide enough for sunbathing and strolling. In summer, the bay is transformed—calm waters lap the beach, sailboats moor in the bay, and outrigger-canoe paddlers ply the sea. Pack the cooler, haul out the beach umbrellas, and don't forget the beach toys because Hanalei Bay is worth scheduling for an entire day, maybe two. Several county beach parks, some with pavilions, can be found along the bay: Waioli, Black Pot, and Hanalei Pavilion (with ample facilities). **Amenities:** lifeguards; parking (free); showers; toilets. **Best for:** sunset; surfing; swimming; walking. ⊠ *Weke Rd., Hanalei* 🖃 *Free.*

★ Kee Beach

BEACH | Highway 560 on the North Shore literally dead-ends at this beach, pronounced "*kay*-eh," which is also the start of the challenging, permit-required 11-mile Kalalau Trail on Napali Coast and a culturally significant area to Native Hawaiians, who still use an ancient *heiau* (a stone platform used as a place of worship) dedicated to hula. (It's not appropriate to hang out on the platform or leave offerings there; stay at a respectful distance.) The setting is gorgeous, with Makana (a prominent peak that Hollywood dubbed "Bali Hai" in the blockbuster musical *South Pacific*) imposing itself on the lovely coastline and lots of lush tropical vegetation.

The small beach is protected by a reef—except during high surf—creating a small, sandy-bottom lagoon that's a popular snorkeling spot. There can be a strong current in winter. A mandatory permit system limits guests and prevents overcrowding. Unless you are a Hawaii resident with identification, you must reserve a spot online (reservations open 30 days prior); the prized spaces sell out weeks in advance. See ⊕ gohaena.com for reservations. Passes are valid during specified time periods. The parking area is ⅓ mile from the beach on a path partially on a boardwalk, so be prepared to lug your beach gear. Kee Beach is a great place to watch the sunset lighting up Napali Coast. **Amenities:** lifeguards; parking (fee); showers; toilets. **Best for:** snorkeling; sunset; swimming; walking. ⊠ *Haena State Park, end of Rte. 560* ⊹ *7 miles west of Hanalei* ⊕ *dlnr.hawaii.gov/dsp* 🖃 *$5 per person nonresident entry fee, plus $10 for nonresident vehicle parking.*

Lumahai Beach

BEACH | Famous as the beach where Nurse Nellie washed that man right out of her hair in *South Pacific*, Lumahai is picturesque, with a river and ironwood grove on the western end and stands of hala (pandanus) trees and black lava rock on the eastern side. In between is a long stretch of olivine-flecked sand that can be wide or narrow, depending on the surf. The beach can be accessed in two places from the highway; one involves a steep hike from the road. Avoid swimming and water activities here—the ocean can be dangerous, with a snapping shore break year-round and monster swells in the winter; in addition, the current can be strong near the river. Parking is very limited, along the road or in a rough dirt lot near the river. **Amenities:** none. **Best for:** solitude; sunset; walking. ⊠ *Hanalei* ⊹ *On winding section of Rte. 560, near mile marker 5* 🖃 *Free.*

Best Beaches by Activity

He says "to-*mah*-toe," and she says "to-*may*-toe." When it comes to beaches on Kauai, the meaning behind that axiom holds true: people are different. What thrills one person may leave another cold. Here are some suggestions for choosing a beach that's right for you.

Best for Families

Lydgate State Park, East Side. The kid-designed playground, the protected swimming pools, and Kamalani Bridge guarantee you will not hear these words from your child: "Mom, I'm bored."

Poipu Beach Park, South Shore. The *keiki* (children's) pool and lifeguards make this a safe spot for kids. The near-perpetual sun isn't so bad, either.

Best Stand-Up Paddling

Anini Beach Park, North Shore. The reef and long stretch of beach give beginners a calm place to try stand-up paddling. You won't get pummeled by waves here.

Wailua Beach, East Side. The Wailua River bisects the beach and heads inland 2 miles, providing stand-up paddlers with a long and scenic stretch of water before they have to figure out how to turn around.

Best Surfing

Hanalei Bay, North Shore. In winter, Hanalei Bay offers a range of breaks, from beginner to advanced. Surfing legends Laird Hamilton and the Irons brothers grew up surfing the waters of Hanalei.

Waiohai Beach, South Shore. Surf instructors flock to this spot with their students for its gentle, near-shore break. Then, as students advance, they can paddle out a little farther to an intermediate break—if they're ready.

Best Sunsets

Kee Beach, North Shore. Even in winter, when the sun sets in the south and out of view, you won't be disappointed here because "golden hour," as photographers call the time around sunset, paints Napali Coast with a warm, gold light. Plan ahead, as reservations are required and visitor numbers are limited: ⊕ *gohaena.com.*

Polihale State Park, West Side. This due-west-facing beach may be tricky to get to, but it does offer the most unobstructed sunset views on the island. The fact that it's so remote means you won't have strangers in your photos, but you will have the island of Niihau in view. Do plan to depart right after sunset or risk getting spooked in the dark.

Best for Celeb Spotting

Haena Beach Park, North Shore. Behind those gated driveways and heavily foliaged yards that line this beach live—at least, part time—some of the world's most celebrated music and movie moguls. Plan ahead and reserve at ⊕ *gohaena.com.*

Hanalei Bay, North Shore. We know we tout this beach often, but it deserves the praise. It's a mecca for everyone—regular Joes, surfers, fishers, young people, older folks, locals, visitors, and, especially, the famous. You may also recognize Hanalei Bay from the 2011 movie *The Descendants.*

🍴 Restaurants

★ Bar Acuda

$$$$ | TAPAS | Hip and pricey, this tapas bar is a top place in Hanalei in terms of flavor and creativity, with food that's often organic and consistently remarkable. The dining room is super-casual but chic, with a welcoming bar and a nice porch for outdoor dining. **Known for:** short, often-changing menu with innovative specials; interesting wine list; sophisticated, eclectic cuisine. $ *Average main: $40* ✉ *Hanalei Center, 5–5161 Kuhio Hwy., Hanalei* ☎ *808/826–7081* ⊕ *www.cudahanalei.com* ⊙ *No lunch. Closed Sun. and Mon.*

★ The Hanalei Dolphin

$$$ | SEAFOOD | Fresh fish caught in local waters by local fishers take star billing at this upscale, tropical-theme restaurant and sushi lounge on the banks of the Hanalei River. There are also many land-based dishes on the menu, including Hawaiian and *haole* (white-person) chicken, beef tenderloin, and steaks. **Known for:** fresh local ingredients; on-site fish market also carries cheeses and steaks; extensive wine and sake list. $ *Average main: $28* ✉ *5–5016 Kuhio Hwy., Hanalei* ☎ *808/826–6113* ⊕ *www.hanaleidolphin.com* ⊙ *No lunch Mon.–Sat.*

The Hanalei Gourmet

$$ | AMERICAN | Hanalei's restored old schoolhouse holds an airy restaurant offering dolphin-safe tuna, low-sodium meats, fresh-baked breads, and house-made desserts, as well as a casual atmosphere where both families and the sports-watching crowd can feel equally comfortable. Lunch and dinner menus feature sandwiches, burgers, hearty salads, a variety of *pupus* (appetizers), and nightly specials of fresh local fish. **Known for:** consistently good food; fish taco nights; friendly bar. $ *Average main: $26* ✉ *Hanalei Center, 5–5161 Kuhio Hwy., Hanalei* ☎ *808/826–2524* ⊕ *www.hanaleigourmet.com.*

Postcards Café

$$$$ | AMERICAN | This plantation-cottage restaurant has a menu full of seafood but also offers additive-free vegetarian and vegan options. Top menu picks include crispy leek salad with buckwheat noodles, miso-chocolate beef short ribs, and grilled yucca. **Known for:** cozy dining room in historic setting; desserts with no refined sugar; meat-free options, local-market fish. $ *Average main: $38* ✉ *5–5075A Kuhio Hwy., Hanalei* ☎ *808/826–1191* ⊕ *postcardscafe.com* ⊙ *No lunch. Closed Sun. and Mon.*

🛏 Hotels

Hanalei Colony Resort

$$$$ | RESORT | The only true beachfront resort on Kauai's North Shore, Hanalei Colony is a laid-back, go-barefoot kind of resort sandwiched between towering mountains and the sea. **Pros:** kitchens in units; private, quiet property; well-maintained units with Hawaiian-style furnishings. **Cons:** damp in winter; no TVs, room phones, or air-conditioning (rooms have ceiling fans); weak cell-phone reception. $ *Rooms from: $475* ✉ *5–7130 Kuhio Hwy., Haena* ☎ *808/826–6235, 800/628–3004* ⊕ *www.hcr.com* ⥅ *48 units* ⦿ *No Meals.*

Hanalei Inn

$ | APARTMENT | If you're looking for lodgings that won't break the bank and put you just a block from gorgeous Hanalei Bay, look no further, as this is literally the only choice among the town's pricey vacation rentals. **Pros:** quick walk to beach, bus stop, and shops; full kitchen; coin-operated laundry on-site. **Cons:** daytime traffic noise; older property; strict cancellation policy. $ *Rooms from: $179* ✉ *5–5468 Kuhio Hwy., Hanalei* ☎ *808/826–9333, 877/769–5484* ⊕ *www.hanaleiinn.net* ⥅ *4 studios* ⦿ *No Meals.*

Nightlife

The Hanalei Gourmet Bar

BARS | The sleepy North Shore stays awake—until 10:30, that is—each evening in this small, convivial deli and bar inside Hanalei's restored old school building. There's local live Hawaiian, jazz, rock, and folk music on Saturday and Sunday evenings. ⊠ *Hanalei Center, 5–5161 Kuhio Hwy., Hanalei* ☎ *808/826–2524* ⊕ *www.hanaleigourmet.com.*

Tahiti Nui

BARS | This venerable and funky institution in sleepy Hanalei still offers its famous luau at 5 on Tuesday and Wednesday evenings, although the bar is the big attraction. The spirits of locals and visitors alike are always high at this popular hangout, which features live nightly entertainment and Hawaiian music on Friday evening. It's open until 1 am on weekends. ⊠ *5–5134 Kuhio Hwy., Hanalei* ☎ *808/826–6277* ⊕ *www.thenui. com.*

Performing Arts

Hanalei Slack Key Concerts

CONCERTS | Relax to the instrumental music form created by Hawaiian *paniolo* (cowboys) in the early 1800s. Shows are Wednesday in Kapaa at All Saints' Church and Tuesday at the Princeville Community Center. If you're looking for a scenic setting, though, head to Hale Halawai Ohana O Hanalei on Friday and Sunday; it's *mauka* (toward the mountains) down a dirt access road across from St. William Catholic Church (Malolo Road) and then left down another dirt road. ⊠ *5–5299 Kuhio Hwy., Hanalei* ☎ *808/826–1469* ⊕ *www.hawaiianslackkeyguitar.com* ⊗ *From $10.*

Shopping

Ching Young Village

SHOPPING CENTER | This popular, family-run shopping center has its roots in the Chinese immigrants who came to Hawaii in the early 19th century. Hanalei's only full-service grocery store is here, along with other shops useful to locals and visitors, such as a music shop selling ukuleles and CDs, jewelry stores, art galleries, a surf shop, a variety store, and several smallish restaurants. ⊠ *5–5190 Kuhio Hwy., near mile marker 2, Hanalei* ☎ *808/826–7222* ⊕ *chingyoungvillage. com.*

Crystal & Gems Gallery

JEWELRY & WATCHES | Sparkling crystals of every shape, size, type, and color, as well as locally made jewelry and paintings, are sold in this amply stocked boutique. The knowledgeable staff can help you choose crystals for specific healing purposes. ⊠ *4489 Aku Rd., Hanalei* ☎ *808/826–9304* ⊕ *www.crystals-gems.com.*

Hanalei Center

SHOPPING CENTER | Once an old Hanalei schoolhouse, the Hanalei Center now houses a bevy of boutiques and restaurants. You can dig through '40s and '50s vintage memorabilia, find Polynesian artifacts, or search for that unusual gift, including fine jewelry and paper art jewelry. Buy beach gear as well as island wear and women's clothing. A full-service salon and a yoga studio are in the two-story modern addition to the center. ⊠ *5–5161 Kuhio Hwy., near mile marker 2, Hanalei* ☎ *808/826–7677.*

Princeville, Kilauea, and Around

Princeville is 4 miles northeast of Hanalei; Kilauea is 5 miles east of Princeville.

Built on a bluff offering gorgeous sea and mountain vistas, including Hanalei Bay, Princeville is the creation of a 1970s resort development. A few large hotels, world-class golf courses, and lots of condos and time-shares anchor the area.

Kilauea Lighthouse is located in the Kilauea Point National Wildlife Refuge, a sanctuary for seabirds.

Five miles east down Route 56, Kilauea, a former sugar plantation town, maintains its rural flavor in the midst of unrelenting gentrification encroaching on all sides. Especially noteworthy are its historic lava-rock buildings, including Christ Memorial Episcopal Church on Kolo Road and, on Keneke Street at Kilauea Road (commonly known as Lighthouse Road), the former Kong Lung Company, which is now an expensive shop.

GETTING HERE AND AROUND

There is only one main road, Route 56, through the Princeville resort area, so maneuvering a car here can be a nightmare. If you're trying to find a smaller lodging unit, get specific driving directions. Parking is available at the Princeville Shopping Center at the entrance to the resort. Kilauea, about 5 miles east on Route 56, has a public parking lot in the town center as well as parking at the end of Kilauea Road for access to the lighthouse.

Sights

★ Kilauea Point National Wildlife Refuge and Kilauea Lighthouse

WILDLIFE REFUGE | FAMILY | A beacon for sea traffic since it was dedicated in 1913, this National Historic Landmark has the world's largest clamshell lens in a lighthouse and stands within a wildlife refuge where thousands of seabirds soar on the trade winds and nest on the steep ocean cliffs. It's well worth the site's modest entry fee to see nene geese (the state bird, a threatened species), white- and red-tailed tropicbirds, and more (identifiable by educational signboards), as well as native plants, dolphins, humpback whales (in season), huge winter surf, and gorgeous North Shore views. The gift shop has a great selection of books about the island's natural history and an array of unique merchandise, with all proceeds benefiting education and preservation efforts. Advance reservations are required via ⊕ *recreation.gov.* ✉ *Kilauea Lighthouse Rd., Kilauea* ☎ *808/828–0384* ⊕ *www.fws.gov/kilaueapoint, www.*

kilaueapoint.org ✉ *$10, kids under 16 free* ⏱ *Closed Sun.–Wed.; reservations required via recreation.gov.*

★ Na Aina Kai Botanical Gardens & Sculpture Park

GARDEN | Joyce and Ed Doty's love for plants and art spans the 240 acres here and includes many different gardens, a hardwood plantation, an *ahupuaa* (a Hawaiian land division), a re-created Navajo compound, an Athabascan village, a Japanese teahouse, a hedge maze, a waterfall, and access to a sandy beach. Throughout the grounds are more than 200 bronze sculptures, one of the nation's largest collections. One popular feature is a children's garden with a 16-foot-tall Jack and the Beanstalk bronze sculpture, gecko maze, tree house, kid-size train, and, of course, a tropical jungle. Located in a residential neighborhood and hoping to maintain good neighborly relations, the nonprofit organization limits tours (guided only). Tour lengths vary from 1½ to 5 hours. Reservations are required. ✉ *4101 Wailapa Rd., Kilauea* ☎ *808/828–0525* ⊕ *www.naainakai.org* ✉ *Tours from $40.*

 Beaches

Anini Beach Park

BEACH | **FAMILY** | A great family park, Anini features one of the longest and widest fringing reefs in all Hawaii, creating a shallow lagoon that is good for snorkeling and kids splashing about, even though there are no lifeguards. It is safe except when surf is raging outside the reef and strong currents are created. A rip current exists between the two reefs where the boats enter and exit the beach ramp, so avoid swimming there. The entire reef follows the shoreline for some 2 miles and extends 1,600 feet offshore at its widest point. There's a narrow ribbon of sandy beach, with lots of grass and shade, as well as a county campground at the western end and a small boat ramp. **Amenities:** parking (free); showers;

toilets. **Best for:** sunrise; swimming; walking. ✉ *Anini Rd., off Rte. 56, Princeville* ✉ *Free.*

Kalihiwai Beach

BEACH | A winding road leads down a cliff face to picture-perfect Kalihiwai Beach, which fronts a bay of the same name. It's another one of those drive-up beaches, so it's very accessible. Most people park under the grove of ironwood trees, near the stream, where young kids like to splash and older kids like to bodyboard. ⚠ **The stream carries leptospirosis, a potentially lethal bacteria that can enter through open cuts. In winter months, beware of a treacherous shore break. Summer is the only truly safe time to swim.** The local-favorite winter surf spot off the eastern edge of the beach is for advanced surfers only. Toilets here are the portable kind, and there are no showers. **Amenities:** parking (free); toilets. **Best for:** solitude; surfing; swimming; walking. ✉ *Kalihiwai Rd., on Kilauea side of Kalihiwai Bridge, Kilauea* ✉ *Free.*

Kauapea Beach (*Secret Beach*)

BEACH | This beach was relatively unknown—except by local fishers, of course—for a long time, hence the common reference to it as "Secret Beach." You'll understand why once you stand on the coarse white sands of Kauapea and see the solid wall of rock that runs the length of the beach, making it fairly inaccessible. For the hardy, there is a steep hike down the western end. From there, you can walk for a long way in either direction in summer. During winter, big swells cut off access to sections of the beach. You may witness dolphins just offshore, and it's a great place to see seabirds, as Kilauea Point National Wildlife Refuge and its historic lighthouse lie at the eastern end. Nudity is not uncommon, though it is illegal in Hawaii. A consistent onshore break makes swimming here typically very dangerous. On big-surf days, don't go near the shoreline. **Amenities:** parking (free). **Best**

for: solitude; sunrise; walking. ⊠ *Kalihiwai Rd., just past turnoff for Kilauea, Kilauea* 🖼 *Free.*

Restaurants

Kilauea Bakery & Pizzeria
$$ | AMERICAN | FAMILY | Open from 6:30 am, the bakery serves coffee drinks, delicious fresh pastries, bagels, and breads in the morning, but late risers should beware: breads and pastries sell out quickly. Pizza (including a gluten-free dough option), soup, and salads can be ordered for lunch or dinner. **Known for:** specialty pizzas topped with eclectic ingredients; fresh chocolate chip cookies made in-house daily; its starter of Hawaiian sourdough made with guava. 🟢 *Average main: $20* ⊠ *Kong Lung Center, 2484 Keneke St., Kilauea* ☎ *808/828–2020* ⊕ *www.kilaueabakery.com.*

Kilauea Market + Café
$$ | HAWAIIAN | Order freshly prepared Hawaiian and American meals—breakfast, lunch, and dinner—snacks, beer, and wine at the counter at this casual, contemporary restaurant, coffee bar, and beer and wine bar in an upscale grocery store. The extensive and eclectic menus include something for everyone, from *loco moco* (white rice topped with a hamburger patty, brown gravy, and fried egg), plate lunches, and fresh-catch fish-and-chips to pizzas, burgers, salads, and sandwiches. **Known for:** daily specials; indoor and outdoor seating; convenient stop on the way to and from lighthouse and beaches. 🟢 *Average main: $19* ⊠ *2555 Ala Namahana Pkwy., Kilauea* ☎ *808/828–2837* ⊕ *www.kilaueamarket.com.*

Nanea Restaurant & Bar
$$$ | HAWAIIAN | FAMILY | The signature restaurant of the Westin Princeville Ocean Resort Villas has casual, open-air seating that perfectly complements an island-style menu sure to please a wide range of diners. Grilled rib eye is served with bacon and sour cream mashed potatoes, while the chicken—smoked kalua style—is accompanied by Molokai sweet potatoes. **Known for:** inventive cocktails; local ingredients; kids eat free. 🟢 *Average main: $35* ⊠ *Westin Princeville Ocean Resort Villas, 3838 Wyllie Rd., Princeville* ☎ *808/827–8808* ⊕ *www.marriott.com.*

North Shore General Store
$ | AMERICAN | Attached to a gas station and small-items store, this classic hole-in-the-wall has the best deals for a take-out breakfast or lunch on the North Shore. Darron's local-beef burgers have a loyal following, and you may have to get in line for his lunchtime favorite, chili-pepper chicken. **Known for:** closes at 6:30 pm; food truck at Anini Beach on weekdays; espresso bar and homestyle breakfast and lunch plates. 🟢 *Average main: $10* ⊠ *Princeville Shopping Center, 5–4280 Kuhio Hwy., Princeville* ☎ *808/826–1122* ⊕ *pizzakauai.com* 🕓 *No dinner.*

Sushigirl Kauai
$ | SUSHI | Pick up some of Kauai's tastiest made-to-order rolls, sushi burritos, and poke bowls with ahi, smoked salmon, and (sometimes) ono at this modest trailer. Dine in the adjacent courtyard (snag a table with an umbrella) or picnic at the beach. **Known for:** entire menu is gluten-free; fresh, local, organic ingredients; veggie and vegan options. 🟢 *Average main: $13* ⊠ *Kong Lung Center, 2484 Keneke St., Kilauea* ☎ *808/320–8646* ⊕ *www.sushigirlkauai.com.*

Hotels

Hanalei Bay Resort
$$$$ | RESORT | FAMILY | The nicest feature of this three-story condominium resort overlooking Hanalei Bay is its upper-level pool with authentic lava-rock waterfalls, an open-air hot tub, and a kid-friendly sand beach. **Pros:** beautiful views; pool, tennis courts, and fitness center on property; lively lounge. **Cons:** some units far from main building and restaurant;

long walk to beach; steep walkways. [$] *Rooms from: $422* ✉ *5380 Honoi-ki Rd., Princeville* ☎ *808/826–6522, 877/344–0688* ⊕ *www.hanaleibayresort.com* ⤳ *134 units* ❑ *No Meals.*

1 Hotel Hanalei Bay

$$$$ | RESORT | FAMILY | Set to open in late 2022 and not available for final viewing at the time of this writing, this swanky wellness resort—the newly renovated former St. Regis Princeville—offers expansive views of the sea and mountains, including Makana, the landmark peak immortalized as mysterious Bali Hai in the film *South Pacific*. **Pros:** state-of-the-art spa; attractive lobby area; numerous dining options. **Cons:** beach not ideal for swimming; expensive even for the area; minimal grounds. [$] *Rooms from: $1900* ✉ *5520 Ka Haku Rd., Princeville* ☎ *808/826–9644, 833/623–2111* ⊕ *www.1hotels.com* ⤳ *252 rooms* ❑ *No Meals.*

★ Westin Princeville Ocean Resort Villas

$$$$ | RESORT | FAMILY | Spread out over 18½ acres on a bluff above Anini Beach, this Westin property marries the comforts of spacious condominium living with the top-notch service and amenities of a luxurious hotel resort. **Pros:** on-site minimarket; ocean views; kids' program. **Cons:** whirlpool tub is small; units can be far from parking; path to the nearby beach is a steep six- to seven-minute walk. [$] *Rooms from: $356* ✉ *3838 Wyllie Rd., Princeville* ☎ *808/827–8700* ⊕ *www.marriott.com* ⤳ *366 units* ❑ *No Meals.*

Nightlife

★ Happy Talk Lounge

BARS | You can sip an umbrella cocktail while you gaze at the original Bali Hai from this lounge, open on two sides and offering breezy views across Hanalei Bay to plush emerald mountains. If you think the scene looks familiar, maybe you've seen the classic movie *South Pacific*, filmed here. The Hollywood version of Bali Hai is actually Kauai's Mt. Makana. Order a tropical cocktail and *pupu* (Hawaiian hors d'oeuvres) and enjoy a truly enchanted evening as the sun sets over the sparkling waters. Local musicians entertain guests Thursday through Monday. ■**TIP➔ Nearby Tunnels Beach (aka Haena Beach and Makua) is often called Nurses' Beach, where Mitzi Gaynor sang about washing that man right outta her hair; Hanalei Bay is where Bloody Mary sang "Bali Hai."** ✉ *Hanalei Bay Resort, 5380 Honoiki Rd., Princeville* ☎ *808/431–4084* ⊕ *www.happytalklounge.com.*

Shopping

Kong Lung Trading

SOUVENIRS | Sometimes called the Gump's of Kauai, this store sells elegant clothing, glassware, books, gifts, and artwork—all very lovely and expensive. The shop is housed in a beautiful 1892 stone building in the heart of Kilauea. It's the showpiece of the pretty little Kong Lung Center, where everything from handmade soaps to hammocks can be found. A great bakery and pizza joint (Kilauea Bakery & Pizzeria) rounds out the center's offerings, along with an exhibit of historical photos. ✉ *Kong Lung Center, 2484 Keneke St., Kilauea* ☎ *808/828–1822* ⊕ *www.konglungkauai.com.*

Princeville Shopping Center

SHOPPING CENTER | The big draws at this small center are a full-service grocery store and a hardware store, but there's also the North Shore General Store (famed for its burgers and other food to go), a fun toy store, a bar, a mailing service, a nice sandal boutique, women's clothing, and an ice cream shop. This is also the last stop for gas and banking when you're heading west along the North Shore. ✉ *5–4280 Kuhio Hwy., near mile marker 28, Princeville* ☎ *808/826–9497* ⊕ *www.princevillecenter.com.*

Continued on page 466

NAPALI COAST: EMERALD QUEEN OF KAUAI

If you're coming to
Kauai, Napali ("the cliffs"
in Hawaiian) is a major must see.
More than 5 million years old, these
sea cliffs rise thousands of feet above the
Pacific, and every shade of green is represented in the vegetation that blankets their
lush peaks and folds. At their base, there are
caves, secluded beaches, and waterfalls to explore.

The big question is how to explore this gorgeous
stretch of coastline. You can't drive to it, through it, or
around it. You can't see Napali from a scenic lookout.
You can't even take a mule ride to it. The only way to
experience its magic is from the sky, the ocean, or the trail.

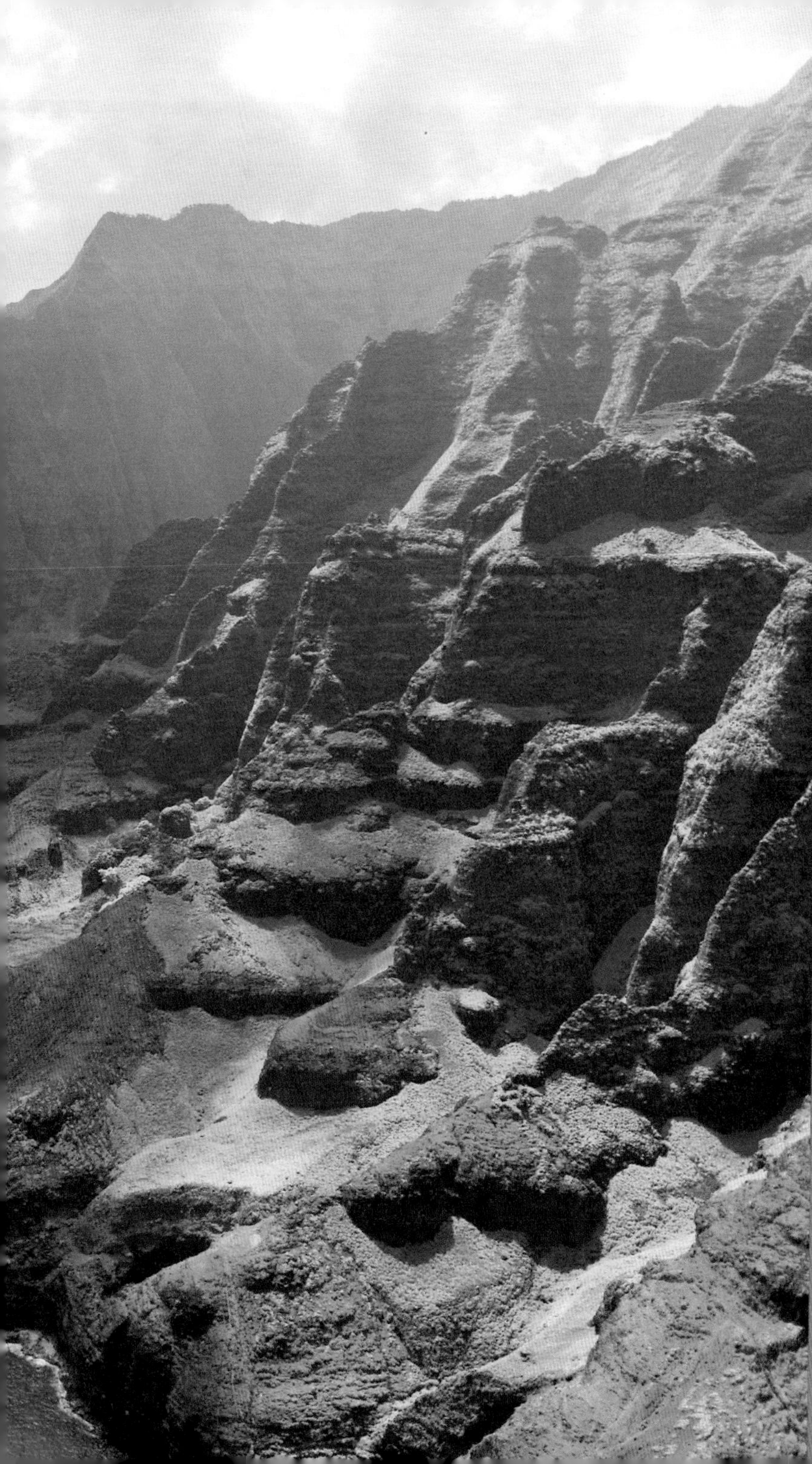

FROM THE SKY

If you've booked a helicopter tour of Napali, you might start wondering what you've gotten yourself into on the way to the airport. Will it feel like being on a small airplane? Will there be turbulence? Will it be worth all the money you just plunked down?

Your concerns will be assuaged on the helipad, once you see the faces of those who have just returned from their journey: Everyone looks totally blissed out. And now it's your turn.

Climb on board, strap on your headphones, and the next thing you know the helicopter gently lifts up, hovers for a moment, and floats away like a spider on the wind—no roaring engines, no rumbling down a runway. If you've chosen a flight with music, you'll feel as if you're inside your very own IMAX movie.

Pinch yourself if you must, because this is the real thing. Your pilot shares history, legend, and lore. If you miss something, speak up: pilots love to show off their island knowledge. You may snap a few pictures (not too many or you'll miss the eyes-on experience!), nudge a friend or spouse, and point at a whale breeching in the ocean, but mostly you stare, mouth agape. There is simply no other way to take in the immensity and greatness of Napali but from the air.

(left) The Napali Coast is a breathtaking stretch of Kauai coastline lined by sea cliffs rising thousands of feet into the sky. (bottom) Helicopter tours over Napali Coast

GOOD TO KNOW

Helicopter companies depart from the north, east, and west sides of the island. Most are based in Lihue, near the airport.

If you want more adventure—and air—choose one of the helicopter companies that flies with the doors off.

Some companies offer flights without music. Know the experience you want ahead of time. Some even sell a video of your flight, so you don't have to worry about taking pictures.

Wintertime rain grounds some flights; plan your trip early in your stay in case the flight gets rescheduled.

IS THIS FOR ME?

Taking a helicopter trip is the most expensive way to see Napali—as much as $340 for an hour-long tour.

Claustrophobic? Choose a boat tour or hike. It's a tight squeeze in the helicopter, especially in one of the middle seats.

Short on time? Taking a helicopter tour is a great way to see the island.

WHAT YOU MIGHT SEE

■ Nualolo Kai (an ancient Hawaiian fishing village) with its fringed reef

■ The 300-foot Hanakapiai Falls

■ A massive sea arch formed in the rock by erosion

■ The 11-mile Kalalau Trail threading its way along the coast

■ The amazing striations of *aa* and *pahoehoe* lava flows that helped push Kauai above the sea

FROM THE OCEAN

Napali from the ocean is two treats in one: spend a good part of the day on (or in) the water, and gaze up at majestic green sea cliffs rising thousands of feet above your head.

There are three ways to see it: a mellow pleasure-cruise catamaran allows you to kick back and sip a mai tai; an adventurous raft (Zodiac) tour will take you inside sea caves under waterfalls, and give you the option of snorkeling; and a daylong outing in a kayak is possible in the summer.

Any way you travel, you'll breathe ocean air, feel spray on your face, and see pods of spinner dolphins, green sea turtles, flying fish, and, if you're lucky, a rare Hawaiian monk seal.

Napali stretches from Kee Beach in the north to Polihale beach on the West Side. You'll be heading towards the lush Hanakapiai Valley, where within a few minutes, you'll see caves and waterfalls galore. About halfway down the coast just after the Kalalau Trail ends, you'll come to an immense arch—formed where the sea eroded the less dense basaltic rock—and a thundering 50-foot waterfall. And as the island curves near Nualolo State Park, you'll begin to notice less vegetation and more rocky outcroppings.

(Left and top right) Kayaking on Napali Coast
(Bottom right) Dolphins off Napali Coast

GOOD TO KNOW

If you want to snorkel, choose a morning rather than an afternoon tour—preferably during a summer visit—when seas are calmer.

If you're on a budget, choose a non-snorkeling tour.

If you want to see whales, take any tour, but be sure to plan your vacation for December through March.

You can only embark from the North Shore in summer. If you're staying on the South Shore, it might not be worth your time to drive to the north, so head to the West Side.

IS THIS FOR ME?

Boat tours are several hours long, so if you have only a short time on Kauai, a helicopter tour is a better alternative.

Even on a small boat, you won't get the individual attention and exclusivity of a helicopter tour.

Prone to seasickness? A large boat can be surprisingly rocky, so be prepared. Afternoon trips are rougher because the winds pick up.

WHAT YOU MIGHT SEE

■ Hawaii's state fish—the humuhumunukunukuapuaa— otherwise known as the reef triggerfish

■ Waiahuakua Sea Cave, with a waterfall coming through its roof

■ Tons of marine life, including dolphins, green sea turtles, flying fish, and humpback whales, especially in February and March

■ Waterfalls—especially if your trip is after a heavy rain

FROM THE TRAIL

If you want to be one with Napali—feeling the soft red earth beneath your feet, picnicking on the beaches, and touching the lush vegetation—hiking the Kalalau Trail is the way to do it.

Most people hike only the first 2 miles of the 11-mile trail and turn around at Hanakapiai. This 4-mile round-trip hike takes three to four hours. It starts at sea level and doesn't waste any time gaining elevation. (Take heart—the uphill lasts only a mile and tops out at 400 feet; then it's downhill all the way.) At the half-mile point, the trail curves west and the folds of Napali Coast unfurl.

Along the way you might share the trail with feral goats and wild pigs. Some of the vegetation is native; much is introduced.

After the 1-mile mark the trail begins its drop into Hanakapiai. You'll pass a couple of streams of water trickling across the trail, and maybe some banana, ginger, the native uluhe fern, and the Hawaiian ti plant. Finally the trail swings around the eastern ridge of Hanakapiai for your first glimpse of the valley and then switchbacks down the mountain. You'll have to boulder-hop across the stream to reach the beach. If you like, you can take a 4-mile, round-trip fairly strenuous side trip from this point to the gorgeous Hanakapiai Falls.

(Left) View along Napali Coast
(Top right) Feral goats in Kalalau Valley
(Bottom right) Napali Coast

GOOD TO KNOW

Wear comfortable, amphibious shoes. Unless your feet require extra support, wear a self-bailing sort of shoe (for stream crossings) that doesn't mind mud.

During winter the trail is often muddy, so be extra careful; sometimes it's completely inaccessible.

Don't hike after heavy rain—flash floods are common.

If you plan to hike the entire 11-mile trail (most people do the shorter hike described at left) you'll need a permit to go past Hanakapiai.

Hikers must carry out all their trash.

IS THIS FOR ME?

Of all the ways to see Napali (with the exception of kayaking the coast), this is the most active. You need to be in decent shape to hit the trail.

If you're vacationing in winter, this hike might not be an option due to flooding—whereas you can take a helicopter year-round.

WHAT YOU MIGHT SEE

■ Big dramatic surf right below your feet

■ Amazing vistas of the cool blue Pacific

■ The spectacular Hanakapiai Falls; if you have a permit don't miss Hanakoa Falls, less than ½ mile off the trail

■ Wildlife, including goats and pigs

■ Zany-looking hala trees, with aerial roots and long, skinny serrated leaves known as lauhala. Early Hawaiians used them to make mats, baskets, and canoe sails.

Napali Coast

Napali Coast is considered the jewel of Kauai, and for all its greenery, it would surely be an emerald. After seeing the coast, many are at a loss for words because its beauty is so overwhelming. Others resort to poetry. Pulitzer Prize–winning poet W. S. Merwin wrote a novel-in-verse, *The Folding Cliffs,* based on a true story set in Napali. *Napali* means "the cliffs," and while that sounds like a simple name, it's quite an apt description. The coastline is cut by a series of small valleys, like fault lines, running to the interior, with the resulting cliffs seeming to bend back on themselves like an accordion-folded fan made of green velvet. More than 5 million years old, these sea cliffs rise as high as 4,000 feet above the Pacific, and every shade of green is represented in the vegetation that blankets their lush peaks and folds. At the base of the cliffs there are caves, secluded beaches, and waterfalls to explore.

Let's put this in perspective: even if you had only one day on Kauai, we'd still recommend heading to Napali Coast on Kauai's northwest side. Once you're there, you'll understand why no road traverses this series of folding-fan cliffs. That leaves three ways to experience the coastline—by air, by water, or on foot. We recommend all three, in that order—each one gets progressively more sensory. *(See the Napali Coast feature in this chapter.)* A helicopter tour is your best bet if you're strapped for time; we recommend Jack Harter Helicopters (*see Aerial Tours in the Activities and Tours chapter for more information*). Boat tours are great for family fun and a day on the water; hiking, of course, is the most budget-friendly option, though it's physically challenging.

Whatever way you choose to visit Napali, you might want to keep this awe-inspiring fact in mind: at one time, thousands of Hawaiians lived self-sufficiently in these valleys.

GETTING HERE AND AROUND

Napali Coast runs 15 miles from Kee Beach (one of Kauai's more popular snorkeling spots) on the island's North Shore to Polihale State Park (the longest stretch of beach in the state) on the West Side of the island. How do you explore this gorgeous stretch of coastline? You can't drive to it, through it, or around it. You can't see Napali from a scenic lookout. You can't even take a mule ride to it. The only way to experience its magic is from the sky, the ocean, or the trail. The Kalalau Trail can be hiked from the "end of the road" at Kee Beach, where the trailhead begins in Haena State Park at the northwest end of Kuhio Highway (this part is Route 560). There's no need to hike the trail's entire, challenging 11 miles (one-way) to get a full experience. Doing that requires a camping permit, which you can apply for up to 90 days in advance of your planned trip (*see ⊕ dlnr. hawaii.gov/dsp*).

An option for seeing Napali Coast on foot is to hike the first 2 miles into **Hanakapiai Beach** and then another 2 miles up that valley; that is allowed without a permit. The beach is accessed from a trailhead in the parking lot at Kee Beach; check ⊕ *gohaena.com* before you travel for information about reservations and shuttle service. The beach is a small jewel, but swimming and other water activities are not recommended because there are no lifeguards; the shore break is often dangerous. It's more for sunning and relaxing.

For information on permitted Napali Coast tour operators, see the Aerial Tours and Boat Tours sections in the Activities and Tours chapter. Also see the Hiking section of the Activities and Tours chapter for information on the Kalalau Trail.

🏖 Beaches

⭐ Kalalau Beach

BEACH | Located at the end of the trail with the same name, Kalalau is a remote beach in spectacular Napali Coast State Wilderness Park, and reaching it requires an arduous 11-mile hike along sea cliff faces (permit required), through steaming tropical valleys, and across sometimes-raging streams. The trail has no to limited cell phone service and is recommended for experienced hikers only. Another option is to paddle a kayak to the beach—summer only, though, or else the surf is way too big. All boat and kayak tours must be through a permitted, guided company. The beach is anchored by a *heiau* (a stone platform used as a place of worship) on one end and a waterfall on the other.

The safest time to come is summer, when the trail is dry and the beach is wide, cupped by low, vegetated sand dunes and a large walk-in cave on the western edge. Day hikes into the valley offer waterfalls, freshwater swimming pools, and wild, tropical fruits. Though state camping permits are required, the valley often has a significant illegal crowd, which has strained park facilities and degraded much of its former peaceful solitude. Helicopter overflights are near-constant in good weather. **Amenities:** none. **Best for:** sunset; walking; solitude. ✉ *Napali Coast State Wilderness Park* ⛢ *Trailhead starts at end of Rte. 560, 7 miles west of Hanalei* ⊕ *www.hawaiistateparks.org.*

The East Side

The East Side encompasses Kapaa, Wailua, and Lihue. It's also known as the Royal Coconut Coast for the coconut plantation where today's aptly named Coconut Marketplace is located and the small coconut groves that still sit on each side of Kuhio Highway. It's a convenient place for the practical traveler, as all the necessities are nearby and the coast is beautiful.

From much of the East Side you can enjoy a clear view of the eternally Sleeping Giant mountain behind you. On the *makai* (ocean) side of the highway, a short walk takes you to a semi-rocky shoreline.

Kapaa Town was Kauai's commercial hub during the sugar and pineapple eras. Many descendants still live on the land they inherited from their Hawaiian, Japanese, and Portuguese ancestors who worked the fields as immigrants a hundred years ago. The past few decades have seen Kapaa's residential areas expand as newcomers lead demand for more housing. The island population has grown steadily in recent years to reach its present-day 73,298. For the visitor, Kapaa is a small town with jewelry and dress boutiques, smaller restaurants, tourist emporiums, food trucks, and shops. It's a good area to meet local people who work at the smaller establishments.

Kapaa connects with Wailua by means of the ill-defined Waipouli area. Here you'll find restaurants, bike shops, a chiropractor, a bikini shop, and a general assortment of small businesses. The Wailua area, now marked with the shell of the former Coco Palms Hotel across from Wailua Beach, was the traditional home of Kauai's famous *alii*, rulers of the commoners. Much of Kauai's Hawaiian history can be traced to the Wailua River area. More recently, Sinatra and Presley graced the coast while filming movies and enjoying the laid-back scene of old Kauai.

Lihue is the county seat, and the whole East Side is the island's center of commerce, so early-morning and late-afternoon drive times (or rush hours) can get very congested in what's known locally as Kapaa Krawl. If you're driving, take advantage of the Kapaa bypass, which

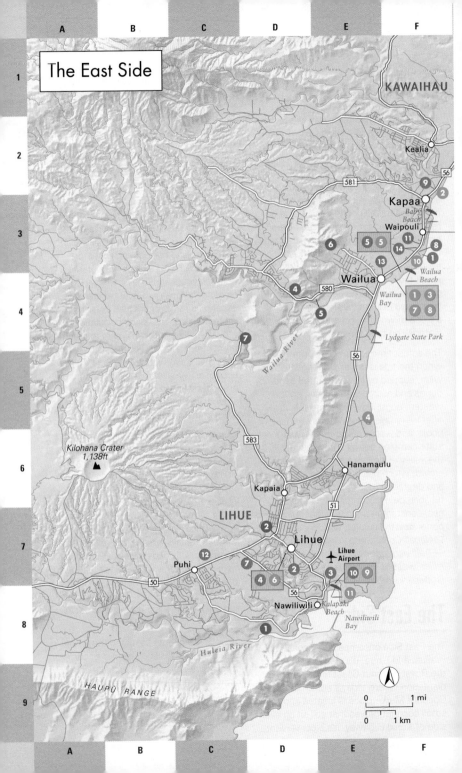

The East Side

KAWAIHAU

G　　H　　I

56

Kealia Beach

3

PACIFIC OCEAN

KEY

1 *Sights*
1 *Restaurants*
1 *Hotels*

G　　H　　I

can take you from northern Kapaa Town all the way past Wailua, avoiding most of the traffic.

Kapaa and Wailua

Kapaa is 16 miles southeast of Kilauea; Wailua is 3 miles southwest of Kapaa.

Old Town Kapaa was once a sugar and pineapple plantation town, which is no surprise—most of the larger towns on Kauai once were. It's where you'll find the best selection of shops in the area, most of them tucked into a quaint collection of wooden-front shops, some built by plantation workers and still run by their progeny today. Kapaa houses two grocery stories: a large Safeway and locally owned Big Save. It also offers plenty of dining options and easy access to the ocean and a walking-biking trail that runs along the coast. If the timing is right, plan to cruise the town on the first Saturday evening of each month, when the bands are playing and the town's wares are on display. To the south, Wailua comprises a few restaurants, shops, and resorts along the coastline, as well as Lydgate State Park, with its wonderful playground and safe swimming areas.

◉ Sights

★ Ke Ala Hele Makalae

TRAIL | Running from the southern end of Lydgate Park north to Donkey Beach, between Kealia and Anahola, this 8-mile seaside path is a favorite of visitors and locals alike. Sea breezes, gorgeous ocean views, smooth pavement, and friendly smiles from everyone as they bike, walk, skate, and run add to the pleasures of the trail. The path has many entry points, and you'll have your choice of bike shops just off the trail. ⊠ *1121 Moanakai Rd., Kapaa* ⊕ *www.kauaipath. org/kauaicoastalpath.*

Opaekaa Falls

WATERFALL | FAMILY | The mighty Wailua River produces many dramatic waterfalls, and Opaekaa (pronounced "oh-pie-kah-ah") is one of the best, plunging hundreds of feet to the pool below. It can be easily viewed from a scenic overlook with ample parking. Opaekaa means "rolling shrimp," which refers to tasty native crustaceans that were once so abundant they could be seen tumbling in the falls. Do not attempt to hike down to the pool. ■ TIP→ **Just before reaching the parking area for the waterfall, turn left into a scenic pullout for great views of the Wailua River and its march through the valley to the sea.** ⊠ *Kuamoo Rd., Wailua (Kauai County)* ⊕ *From Rte. 56, turn mauka (toward the mountains) onto Kuamoo Rd. and drive 1½ miles.*

★ Poliahu Heiau

RELIGIOUS BUILDING | Storyboards near this ancient *heiau* (sacred site) recount the significance of the many sacred structures found along the Wailua River. It's unknown exactly how the ancient Hawaiians used Poliahu Heiau—one of the largest pre-Christian temples on the island—but legend says it was created by the Menehune, the legendary race of little people who were quick builders, because of the unusual stonework found in its walled enclosures. From this site, drive downhill toward the ocean to *pohaku hanau*, a two-piece birthing stone said to confer special blessings on all children born there, and *pohaku piko*, whose crevices were a repository for umbilical cords left by parents seeking a clue to their child's destiny, which reportedly was foretold by how the cord fared in the rock. ■ TIP→ **Some Hawaiians feel these sacred stones shouldn't be viewed as tourist attractions, so always treat them with respect. Never stand or sit on the rocks or leave any offerings.** ⊠ *5558–5568 Kuamoo Rd., Wailua (Kauai County)* ▨ *Free.*

Sleeping Giant

MOUNTAIN | Although its true name is Nounou, this landmark mountain ridge is more commonly known as the Sleeping Giant because of its resemblance to a very large man sleeping on his back. Legends differ on whether the giant is Puni, who was accidentally killed by rocks launched at invading canoes by the Menehune, or Nunui, a gentle creature who has not yet awakened from the nap he took centuries ago after building a massive temple and enjoying a big feast. The ridge can be experienced up close via one of several trails that traverse the giant's body (*see Hiking in the Activities and Tours chapter*). ⊠ *Rte. 56, Kapaa* ✛ *About 1 mile north of Wailua River.*

★ Wailua Falls

WATERFALL | **FAMILY** | Kauai has plenty of noteworthy waterfalls, but this one is especially gorgeous, easy to find, and easy to photograph. You may recognize the impressive cascade from the opening sequences of the *Fantasy Island* television series. To reach it, drive north from Lihue following Maalo Road in Hanamaulu, then travel uphill for 3 miles. ⊠ *Maalo Rd., off Rte. 580, Lihue.*

Beaches

Baby Beach

BEACH | **FAMILY** | There aren't many safe swimming beaches on Kauai's East Side; however, this one usually ranks highly with parents because there's a narrow, lagoonlike area between the beach and the near-shore reef perfect for small children. In winter, watch for east and northeast swells that would make this not such a safe option. There are minimal beach facilities—and no lifeguards—so watch your babies. There is an old-time shower spigot (cold water only) along the roadside available to rinse off the salt water. **Amenities:** parking (free); showers. **Best for:** sunrise; swimming. ⊠ *Moanakai Rd., Kapaa* 🖼 *Free.*

Kealia Beach

BEACH | Adjacent to the highway heading north out of Kapaa, ½-mile-long Kealia Beach attracts bodyboarders and surfers year-round. It's a favorite with locals and visitors alike. Kealia is not generally a great beach for swimming, but it's a place to sunbathe and enjoy the beach scene. The safest area to swim is at the far north end of the beach, protected by a lava rock sea wall. The waters are often rough and the waves crumbly due to an onshore break (no protecting reef) and northeasterly trade winds. A scenic lookout on the southern end, accessed off the highway, is a superb location for saluting the morning sunrise or spotting whales during winter. A level, paved section of the Ke Ala Hele Makalae bike path, with small, covered pavilions, runs along the coastline here and is popular for walking and biking. **Amenities:** lifeguard; parking (free); showers; toilets. **Best for:** sunrise; surfing; swimming; walking. ⊠ *Rte. 56, at mile marker 10, Kealia* 🖼 *Free.*

Lydgate State Park

BEACH | **FAMILY** | This is by far the best family beach park on Kauai: the waters off the beach are protected by a hand-built breakwater, creating two boulder-enclosed saltwater pools for safe swimming and snorkeling most of the year. Heavy rains upriver do occasionally deposit driftwood, clogging the pools. The smaller of the two pools is perfect for *keiki* (children). Behind the beach is Kamalani Playground; children of all ages—that includes you—enjoy the swings, lava-tube slides, tree house, and open field. Picnic tables abound in the park, and pavilions for day use and overnight camping are available by permit. The Kamalani Kai Bridge is a second playground, south of the original. (The two are united by the Ke Ala Hele Makalae bike and pedestrian coastal path.) Note that at this writing, plans were under way to institute a $10 parking fee for nonresidents. ■ **TIP→ This park system is perennially popular; the quietest times to visit are early mornings and weekdays.** **Amenities:** lifeguards; parking (free); showers; toilets. **Best for:** partiers; sunrise; swimming; walking. ✉ *Leho Dr., Wailua (Kauai County)* ✥ *Just south of Wailua River* 🎫 *Free.*

🍴 Restaurants

Bull Shed

$$$ | **STEAKHOUSE** | The A-frame structure makes this popular restaurant look distinctly rustic from the outside, but inside, light colors and a full wall of glass highlight an ocean view that is one of the best on Kauai. The food is simple, but they know how to do surf and turf well, including prime rib and Australian rack of lamb. **Known for:** combo dinner platters; quiet bar; views of surf crashing on the rocks. [$] *Average main: $35* ✉ *796 Kuhio Hwy., Kapaa* ☎ *808/822–3791* 🌐 *www.bullshedrestaurant.com* 🕓 *No lunch.*

★ Hukilau Lanai

$$$ | **AMERICAN** | Relying heavily on super fresh island fish and local meats and produce, this restaurant offers creatively prepared food that is a great choice for value and consistent quality on the East Side. The nightly fish specials—served grilled, steamed, or sautéed with succulent sauces—shine here. **Known for:** gluten-free options; delicious desserts; ahi poke nachos. [$] *Average main: $28* ✉ *Kauai Coast Resort, Coconut Marketplace, 520 Aleka Loop, Wailua (Kauai County)* ☎ *808/822–0600* 🌐 *www.hukilaukauai.com* 🕓 *Closed Mon. No lunch.*

★ JO2 Restaurant

$$$ | **FUSION** | This creation of Jean-Marie Josselin, the renowned chef who brought Hawaii Regional Cuisine to Kauai in 1990, reflects his culinary growth. The food is imaginative, with its French, Japanese, and Islands influences, and it's served with flair in a chic yet casual dining room that's tucked away in a nondescript strip mall. **Known for:** daily-changing menu; excellent service; the $35 prix-fixe 5–6 pm. [$] *Average main: $35* ✉ *4–971 Kuhio Hwy., Kapaa* ☎ *808/212–1627* 🌐 *www.jotwo.com* 🕓 *Closed Sun. and Mon. No lunch.*

Kenji Burger

$$ | **FUSION** | The humble hamburger gets an Asian twist at Kenji's, a small, casual, friendly eatery that uses 100% grass-fed Kauai beef and also has plenty of nonbeef offerings. Choose the teriyaki, veggie, truffle, or hapa burger, each topped with goodies like caramelized onions, Japanese mushrooms, and tomato jam. **Known for:** lychee soda; french fries with Japanese seasoning; sushi burritos filled with seafood. [$] *Average main: $19* ✉ *4–788 Kuhio Hwy., Kapaa* ☎ *808/320–3558* 🌐 *www.kenjiburger.com* 🕓 *No lunch.*

Kountry Kitchen

$ | **AMERICAN** | **FAMILY** | If you like a hearty breakfast, try this family-friendly restaurant with its cozy, greasy-spoon atmosphere and friendly service; it's a great spot for omelets, banana pancakes, waffles, and eggs Benedict in two sizes. Lunch selections include sandwiches, burgers, and *loco moco* (a popular local rice, beef, gravy, and eggs concoction). **Known for:** takeout options; hearty portions; all-day breakfast. [$] *Average main: $14* ✉ *1485 Kuhio Hwy., Kapaa* ☎ *808/822–3511* 🌐 *www.kountrystyle-kitchen.com* 🕓 *Closed Tues. and Wed. No dinner.*

Lemongrass Grill

$$ | **ASIAN FUSION** | The decor of this restaurant known for its eclectic, Asian-influenced menu may remind you of a Pacific Rim–theme rustic tavern, with its stained-wood interior and numerous paintings and carvings. There's something for everyone here: salads, poultry, steaks and ribs, vegetarian fare, and, of course, a wide selection of seafood, all with an island flair. **Known for:** lively bar; fresh fish; curries and satays. [$] *Average*

main: $25 ✉ 4–871 Kuhio Hwy., Kapaa ☎ 808/821–2888 ⏲ Closed Thurs. No lunch.

Russell's by Eat Healthy Kauai
$$ | **VEGETARIAN** | A restored plantation cottage surrounded by tropical foliage is the casual setting for this island café. The vegan menu offers a limited but tasty array of plant-based options, including hummus wraps, Beyond Beef burgers, and tofu-based entrées. **Known for:** evening music; small-bites menu in afternoon; alfresco dining in leafy garden. [$] *Average main: $22 ✉ 4–369 Kuhio Hwy., Wailua (Kauai County) ☎ 808/822–7990 🌐 eathealthykauai.com ⏲ Closed Sun. and Mon. No dinner Tues. and Wed.*

Shivalik Indian Cuisine
$$ | **INDIAN** | This eatery provides a refreshing alternative to the typical surf and turf offerings at most of Kauai's restaurants. Offering a variety of Indian regional styles, this hideaway in a small plaza turns out biryani and tandoori dishes, light and flavorful naan, and many vegetarian items, as well as curries and chicken and lamb dishes. **Known for:** tandoor oven; extensive menu; Friday dinner buffet. [$] *Average main: $19 ✉ 4–771 Kuhio Hwy., Wailua (Kauai County) ☎ 808/821–2333 🌐 www.shivalikindian-cuisines.com ⏲ Closed Tues.*

Tiki Tacos
$ | **MEXICAN** | Not surprisingly, tacos take center stage here, though there are tamales and a quesadilla. The tacos are made from quality ingredients, many of which are organic and locally sourced, and you can mix and match. **Known for:** house-made corn tortillas; vegetarian options; large portions. [$] *Average main: $8 ✉ 4–971 Kuhio Hwy., Kapaa ☎ 808/823–8226.*

Hotels

Aston Islander on the Beach
$$$ | **HOTEL** | A low-rise, Hawaii-plantation-style design gives this 6-acre beachfront property a pleasant, relaxed feeling; the guest rooms are spread over eight three-story buildings, each with a lanai that looks out on lovely green lawns. **Pros:** convenient location near shops and restaurants; coin-operated laundries; online rate deals. **Cons:** no restaurant on the property; no resort amenities but still charges fee; smallish pool. [$] *Rooms from: $339 ✉ 440 Aleka Pl., Wailua (Kauai County) ☎ 808/822–7417, 866/774–2924 🌐 www.aquaaston.com 🛏 200 rooms 🍴 No Meals.*

Hotel Coral Reef
$$ | **HOTEL** | **FAMILY** | In business since 1956, this small, three-story hotel is something of a Kauai beachfront landmark, with clean, comfortable rooms, some with great ocean views, and a large pool that overlooks the water; expect great sunrises. **Pros:** free parking; oceanfront setting; convenient location near restaurants and shops. **Cons:** ocean swimming is marginal; traffic noise; located in a busy section of Kapaa. [$] *Rooms from: $238 ✉ 4–1516 Kuhio Hwy., Kapaa ☎ 808/822–4481, 800/843–4659 🌐 www.hotelcoralreefresort.com 🛏 27 rooms 🍴 Free Breakfast.*

Kapaa Sands
$$ | **APARTMENT** | An old rock etched with *kanji* (Japanese characters) reminds you that the site of this condominium gem was once occupied by a Shinto temple. **Pros:** discounts for extended stays; walking distance to shops, restaurants, and beach; turtle and monk seal sightings common. **Cons:** small bathrooms; traffic noise in rear units; no-frills lodging. [$] *Rooms from: $189 ✉ 380 Papaloa Rd., Wailua (Kauai County) ☎ 808/822–4901, 800/222–4901 🌐 www.kapaasands.com 🛏 24 units 🍴 No Meals.*

★ Kauai Coast Resort at the Beachboy
$$$$ | **TIMESHARE** | **FAMILY** | Fronting an uncrowded stretch of beach, this three-story, primarily timeshare condo resort is convenient and a bit more upscale than nearby properties.

Pros: central location; nice sunrises; attractive pool. **Cons:** ocean not ideal for swimming; daily housekeeping fee; beach is narrow. $ *Rooms from: $379* ✉ *520 Aleka Loop, Wailua (Kauai County)* ☎ *808/822–3441, 866/729–7182* 🌐 *www.shellhospitality.com* 🛏 *108 units* 🍴 *No Meals.*

Kauai Shores Hotel
$$ | **HOTEL** | Once an oceanfront inn and now an affordable boutique hotel, this property remains no-frills lodging, but rooms have a refrigerator and are comfortable, bright, and clean. **Pros:** near walking path, shops, and dining; free Wi-Fi; great sunrises. **Cons:** minimal amenities; daily hospitality fee; coral reef makes ocean swimming marginal. $ *Rooms from: $254* ✉ *420 Papaloa Rd., Wailua (Kauai County)* ☎ *808/822–4951, 800/560–5553* 🌐 *www.kauaishoreshotel.com* 🛏 *202 rooms* 🍴 *No Meals.*

Lae Nani Resort Kauai by Outrigger
$$$$ | **APARTMENT** | Ruling Hawaiian chiefs once returned from ocean voyages to this spot, now host to comfortable condominiums, and Outrigger has created attractive plant, water, and rock features. **Pros:** nice beach; walking distance to playground; attractively furnished (though units differ due to individual ownership). **Cons:** no Wi-Fi; cleaning fee; third floor is walk-up. $ *Rooms from: $356* ✉ *410 Papaloa Rd., Wailua (Kauai County)* ☎ *808/823–1401, 866/994–1588* 🌐 *www.outrigger.com/hotels-resorts* 🛏 *84 units* 🍴 *No Meals.*

Sheraton Kauai Coconut Beach Resort
$$$ | **RESORT** | One of the few true oceanfront properties on Kauai, this popular hotel sits on a ribbon of sand in Kapaa and has bright, spacious rooms that face the ocean or pool. **Pros:** access to coastal path; near shops and restaurants; pleasant grounds. **Cons:** small pool; high daily parking fee; coastline not conducive to swimming. $ *Rooms from: $269* ✉ *650 Aleka Loop, Wailua (Kauai County)* ☎ *808/822–3455, 800/760–8555* 🌐 *www.marriott.com* 🛏 *311 rooms* 🍴 *No Meals.*

Nightlife

★ Hukilau Lanai Bar
BARS | Trade winds waft through this modest little open-air bar, which looks out onto a coconut grove. The bar and restaurant is on the property of the Kauai Coast Resort but operates independently. If the mood takes you, go on a short walk to the sea, or recline in big, comfortable chairs in Wally's Bar in the lobby while listening to Hawaiian slack key guitar. Live music plays from Wednesday through Saturday evenings. Poolside happy hour runs from 3 to 5. Try one of the freshly infused tropical martinis or Kauai-made mead, or choose from a good selection of wines by the glass. ✉ *520 Aleka Loop, Wailua (Kauai County)* ☎ *808/822–0600* 🌐 *www.hukilaukauai.com.*

Performing Arts

★ Smith Family Garden Luau
CULTURAL FESTIVALS | A 30-acre tropical garden on the Wailua River provides the lovely setting for this popular luau, which begins with the traditional blowing of the conch shell and *imu* (pig roast) ceremony, followed by cocktails, an island feast, great music, hula, and an international show in the amphitheater overlooking a torch-lighted lagoon. Presented Monday and Wednesday through Friday, it's fairly authentic and the oldest commercial luau on Kauai. ✉ *Smith's Tropical Paradise, 174 Wailua Rd., Kapaa* ☎ *808/821–6895* 🌐 *www.smithskauai.com* 🎟 *$125; kids 7–13 $35, kids 3–6 $25.*

Shopping

Deja Vu Surf Hawaii: Kapaa
MIXED CLOTHING | This family operation has a great assortment of branded surf wear and clothes for outdoors fanatics, including tank tops, caps, swimwear, and Kauai-style T-shirts. They also carry bodyboards and water-sports accessories. Good deals can be found at sidewalk

sales. ⊠ 4–1419 Kuhio Hwy., Kapaa
☎ 808/320–7108 ⊕ www.dejavusurf.com.

Jim Saylor Jewelers
JEWELRY & WATCHES | Jim Saylor and his
team of jewelers have been designing
beautiful keepsakes on Kauai since 1976.
Gems from around the world, including black pearls, diamonds, and more,
appear in his unusual settings, and he
welcomes custom orders. ⊠ 4–1318
Kuhio Hwy., Kapaa ☎ 808/822–3591
⊕ www.jimsaylorjewelers.com.

Kauai Village Shopping Center
SHOPPING CENTER | The buildings of this
Kapaa shopping village are in the style
of a 19th-century plantation town. ABC
Discount Store sells sundries; Safeway
carries groceries and alcoholic beverages; Papaya's has health foods and a
minimalist café. Also here are a small
bakery, a bar, Ross Dress for Less, a UPS
store, a Chinese restaurant, GNC, and
Starbucks. ⊠ 4–831 Kuhio Hwy., Kapaa
☎ 808/822–3777.

Kela's Glass Gallery
ART GALLERIES | The colorful vases, bowls,
and other fragile items sold in this distinctive gallery are definitely worth viewing if you appreciate quality handmade
glass art. It's expensive, but if something
catches your eye, they'll happily pack it
for safe transport home. The gallery also
ships worldwide. ⊠ 4–1400 Kuhio Hwy.,
Kapaa ☎ 808/822–4527 ⊕ www.glass-art.
com.

Kinipopo Shopping Village
SHOPPING CENTER | At this tiny center on
Kuhio Highway, Korean BBQ Restaurant
fronts the highway, as does Goldsmiths
Kauai, a gallery selling handcrafted
Hawaiian-style gold jewelry. A bakery,
a real estate company, and Avalon Gas-
tropub round out the businesses here.
⊠ 4–356 Kuhio Hwy., Kapaa ⊕ www.
kinipopovillage.com.

Vicky's Fabric Shop
FABRICS | Tropical and Hawaiian prints,
silks, slinky rayons, soft cottons, quilting

kits, and other fine fabrics fill this small
store. A variety of sewing patterns and
notions are featured as well, making it a
must-stop for any sewing enthusiast and
a great place to buy unique island-made
gifts. Check out the one-of-a-kind selection of purses, aloha wear, and other
quality hand-sewn items. ⊠ 4–1326 Kuhio
Hwy., Kapaa ☎ 808/822–1746 ⊕ www.
vickysfabrics.com.

Lihue

7 miles southwest of Wailua.

The commercial and political center of
Kauai County, which includes the islands
of Kauai and Niihau, Lihue is home to
the island's major airport, harbor, and
hospital. This is where you can find the
state and county offices that issue camping and hiking permits and the same
fast-food eateries and big-box stores
that blight the mainland. The county has
revived the downtown by sprucing up
Rice Street, but there's still little reason
to linger in lackluster Lihue.

◉ Sights

★ Alekoko (Menehune) Fishpond
HISTORIC SIGHT | No one knows just
who built this large, intricate, almost
1,000-year-old aquaculture structure in
the Huleia River, but legend attributes it
to the Menehune, a mythical—or real,
depending on who you ask—ancient
race of people known for their small
stature, industrious nature, and superb
stone-working skills. Volcanic rock was
cut and skillfully fit together into massive
walls four feet thick and five feet high,
forming a centuries-old enclosure for
raising mullet and other freshwater fish.
Volunteers removed invasive mangroves
and restored the pond to its original condition. You can view it from an overlook
about 4 miles from downtown Lihue.
⊠ End of Hulemalu Rd., Niumalu.

★ Kauai Museum

HISTORY MUSEUM | Maintaining a stately presence on Rice Street, the historical museum building is easy to find and features a permanent display, "The Story of Kauai," that provides a competent overview of the Garden Island and Niihau. The exhibit traces the Islands' geology, mythology, and cultural history. Local artists are represented in changing exhibits in the second-floor Mezzanine Gallery. **■ TIP→ The gift shop alone is worth a visit, with a fine collection of authentic Niihau shell lei, feather hatband lei, hand-turned wooden bowls, reference books, and other quality arts, crafts, and gifts—many of them locally made.** ✉ *4428 Rice St., Lihue* ☎ *808/245–6931* 🌐 *www.kauaimuseum.org* 🎟 *$15* 🕒 *Closed Fri.–Sun.*

Roadside Vendors

Lei. Tropical flowers. Fresh fish. Rambutan. Avocados. Grilled *huli huli* chicken. Kalua pork. It's not uncommon to run across individuals selling flowers, produce, and food on the side of the road. Some are local farmers trying to make a living; others are people fundraising for the local canoe club. Don't be afraid to stop and buy. The prices are usually good, and most vendors are friendly and enjoy chatting.

Beaches

Kalapaki Beach

BEACH | **FAMILY** | Five minutes south of the airport in Lihue, you'll find this wide beach and sandy-bottom bay fronting the Kauai Marriott. It's almost always safe from rip currents and undertows because it's around the back side of a peninsula, in its own cove. Tons of activities take place here, including all the usual water sports—beginning and intermediate surfing, bodyboarding, bodysurfing, and swimming. In addition, two outrigger canoe clubs paddle in the bay, and the Nawiliwili Yacht Club's boats sail around the harbor. Kalapaki is the only place on Kauai where double-hulled canoes are available for rent (at Kauai Beach Boys, which fronts the beach next to Duke's Kauai restaurant). Visitors can also rent snorkel gear, surfboards, bodyboards, and kayaks from Kauai Beach Boys, as well as sign up for surf lessons and sunset boat tours. A volleyball court on the beach is often used by a loosely organized group of local players; visitors are always welcome. **■ TIP→ Avoid the stream on the south side of the beach; it often has high bacteria counts.** Duke's Kauai is one of only a couple of restaurants on the island actually on a beach. The restaurant's lower level is casual—even welcoming beach attire and sandy feet—making it perfect for lunch or an afternoon cocktail. **Amenities:** food and drink; lifeguards; parking (free); showers; toilets; water sports. **Best for:** surfing; swimming; walking. ✉ *Off Rice St., Lihue* 🌐 *kauaibeachboys.com* 🎟 *Free.*

Restaurants

Dani's Restaurant

$ | **HAWAIIAN** | **FAMILY** | Kauai residents frequent this no-frills eatery near the Lihue Fire Station for hearty, local-style food at breakfast and lunch. It's a good place to try Hawaiian food, such as *laulau* (pork and taro leaves wrapped in ti leaves and steamed) or kalua pig, slow roasted in an underground oven. **Known for:** Hawaiian comfort food at low prices; rice served with everything; Japanese options like teriyaki beef. [$] *Average main: $9* ✉ *4201 Rice St., Lihue* ☎ *808/245–4991* 🕒 *Closed Sun. No dinner.*

Duke's Kauai

$$$ | **SEAFOOD** | Surfing legend Duke Kahanamoku (1890–1968) is immortalized at this casual bi-level restaurant and bar

Did You Know?

According to legend, the mythical Menehune built the Alekoko Fishpond more than 1,000 years ago, in just one night.

on Kalapaki Beach where surfboards, photos, and other memorabilia marking Duke's long tenure as a waterman adorn the walls. Downstairs, you'll find simple, less expensive fare from fish tacos to stir-fried cashew chicken to hamburgers, served 11 am to 10:30 pm; upstairs, at dinner, fresh fish prepared in a variety of styles is the best choice, though the prime rib is a favorite among locals. **Known for:** lively bar; hula pie ice-cream dessert; downstairs level good for lunch at the beach. $ *Average main: $35* ✉ *Royal Sonesta Kauai Resort Lihue, 3610 Rice St., Kalapaki Beach, Lihue* ☎ *808/246–9599* ⊕ *www.dukeskauai. com.*

Hamura Saimin

$ | **ASIAN** | Folks just love this cash-only, old plantation-style diner, though the very simple food doesn't quite live up to the buzz. Locals and tourists still stream in and out all day long: the famous *saimin* noodle soup is the big draw, and each day the Hiraoka family dishes up about 1,000 bowls of the steaming broth and house-made noodles topped with a variety of garnishes. **Known for:** grilled chicken and beef sticks; open late for Lihue; counter-style dining. $ *Average main: $9* ✉ *2956 Kress St., Lihue* ☎ *808/245–3271* ▭ *No credit cards.*

Kalapaki Joe's

$$ | **AMERICAN** | Both locations—in Lihue's Kukui Grove and in Poipu—appeal to sports fans who like a rip-roaring happy hour. The appetizer menu is extensive, and you can also choose from burgers, salads, sandwiches, tacos, fresh fish, and local favorites like kalua pork and cabbage. **Known for:** boisterous bar; affordable, casual dining; plenty of TVs. $ *Average main: $20* ✉ *3–2600 Kaumualii Hwy., Lihue* ☎ *808/245–6366* ⊕ *www. kalapakijoes.com* ☿ *Closed Sun. in Lihue.*

Kukui's on Kalapaki Beach

$$ | **ECLECTIC** | **FAMILY** | The meals at Kukui's feature Hawaiian, Asian, and contemporary American influences, and

the open-air setting with a view of the ocean makes it a pleasant place to dine. It's spacious, making it well suited to families and those who want a relaxed setting. **Known for:** quiet atmosphere; evening entertainment; garden setting. $ *Average main: $25* ✉ *Royal Sonesta Kauai Resort Lihue, 3610 Rice St., Kalapaki Beach, Lihue* ☎ *808/245–5050* ⊕ *www.sonesta.com.*

The Plantation House by Gaylord's

$$$$ | **ECLECTIC** | Located in what was once Kauai's most expensive plantation estate, Gaylord's pays tribute to the elegant dining rooms of 1930s high society—candlelit tables sit on a cobblestone courtyard that surrounds a fountain and overlooks a wide lawn. The menu is eclectic, offering cioppino, sake short ribs, duck two ways, lamb shank, fresh fish, and a few vegan and vegetarian options. **Known for:** quiet dining; delightful outdoor seating; lavish Sunday brunch buffet. $ *Average main: $39* ✉ *Kilohana Plantation, 3–2087 Kaumualii Hwy., Lihue* ☎ *808/245–9593* ⊕ *www.kilohanakauai. com.*

 # Hotels

Kauai Beach Resort & Spa

$$$ | **RESORT** | This plantation-style hotel provides a relaxing, upscale oceanfront experience close to the airport, but without the noise. **Pros:** four pools with fun features; lawn games; resort amenities. **Cons:** beach not good for swimming; no nearby restaurants or resorts; high parking fee. $ *Rooms from: $269* ✉ *4331 Kauai Beach Dr., Hanamaulu* ☎ *808/246–5576* ⊕ *www.kauaibeachresortandspa. com* ⇥ *350 rooms* ⦿| *No Meals.*

Kauai Palms Hotel

$ | **HOTEL** | Not only is this low-cost alternative close to the airport, but it's also a great base for day trips to all sides of the island. **Pros:** friendly staff; decent value for the money; centrally located. **Cons:** smallish rooms (ask about studios and cottages); traffic noise; bare-bones amenities. $ *Rooms from: $154* ✉ *2931 Kalena St., Lihue* ☎ *808/246–0908* ⊕ *www.kauaipalmshotel.com* ↘ *38 rooms* ¡○¡ *No Meals.*

Royal Sonesta Kauai Resort Lihue
$$$$ | RESORT | FAMILY | The former Marriott has changed hands, and its new owner, Sonesta, is conducting a $50 million refurbishment of guest rooms and common areas while the resort remains open. **Pros:** oceanfront setting; plenty of resort amenities; convenient location near shops and restaurants. **Cons:** ocean water quality can be poor at times; located near an industrial area; airport noise. $ *Rooms from: $352* ✉ *3610 Rice St., Kalapaki Beach, Lihue* ☎ *808/245–5050, 800/220–2925* ⊕ *www.sonesta.com* ↘ *367 rooms* ¡○¡ *No Meals.*

Timbers Kauai Ocean Club & Residences
$$$$ | HOUSE | With an enviable spot along the Lihue coastline, 450 acres of land-scaped grounds, and a choice of elegant homes and townhomes, Timbers Kauai is an excellent choice for those who are seeking a self-contained resort experience with an air of exclusivity. **Pros:** luxurious amenities in lodgings and at resort; ocean and mountain views; private and quiet. **Cons:** extremely expensive; somewhat isolated; three-night minimum stay. $ *Rooms from: $2,900* ✉ *3770 Alaoli Way, Lihue* ☎ *855/420–9225* ⊕ *www. timberskauai.com* ↘ *47 residences* ¡○¡ *No Meals.*

 ## Nightlife

Duke's Barefoot Bar
BARS | One of the liveliest bars in Nawiliwili is this beachside bar and restaurant at Kalapaki Beach. Contemporary Hawaiian music is performed daily from 3:30 to 8 pm and from 9:30 to 11:30 am during Sunday brunch. ✉ *Royal Sonesta Kauai Resort Lihue, 3610 Rice St., Kalapaki Beach, Lihue* ☎ *808/246–9599* ⊕ *www. dukeskauai.com.*

Rob's Good Times Grill
BARS | Let loose at this popular restaurant and sports bar, which has live music Wednesday through Saturday nights. Thursday is trivia night, and sports are broadcast all weekend and Monday night. It offers local microbrews and a full menu of pub fare. ✉ *4303 Rice St., Lihue* ☎ *808/246–0311* ⊕ *www.kauaisports-barandgrill.com.*

 ## Performing Arts

Kauai Concert Association
CONCERTS | This group offers a program of well-known classical musicians, including soloists and small ensembles, at a range of venues around the island, from hotel ballrooms to private rooms. ✉ *Lihue* ☎ *808/652–5210* ⊕ *www.kauai-concert. org* ✉ *Tickets from $40.*

Luau Kalamaku
CULTURAL FESTIVALS | Set on the grounds of a historic sugar plantation, this luau bills itself as the only "theatrical" luau on Kauai. The luau feast is served buffet style, there's an open bar, and the performers aim to both entertain and educate about Hawaiian culture. Guests sit at tables around a circular stage; tables farther from the stage are elevated, providing unobstructed views. Additional packages offer visitors the opportunity to watch the show only, tour the 35-acre plantation via train, or enjoy special romantic perks like a lei greeting and champagne. ■TIP➔ **Check the website for days and times; the luau is not offered daily.** ✉ *Kilohana Plantation, 3–2087 Kaumualii St., Lihue* ☎ *877/622–1780* ⊕ *www. luaukalamaku.com* ✉ *$146, kids 13–17 $98, kids 3–12 $56.*

 ## Shopping

Hilo Hattie, The Store of Hawaii
MIXED CLOTHING | This is the big name in aloha wear for tourists throughout the Islands, and Hilo Hattie has only one store on Kauai, located a mile from Lihue

Kauai: Undercover Movie Star

Though Kauai has played itself in the movies, starring in *The Descendants* (2011), for example, much of its screen time has been as a stunt double for a number of tropical paradises. The island's remote valleys portrayed Venezuelan jungle in Kevin Costner's *Dragonfly* (2002) and a Costa Rican dinosaur preserve in Steven Spielberg's *Jurassic Park* (1993). Spielberg was no stranger to Kauai, having filmed Harrison Ford's escape via seaplane from Menehune Fishpond in *Raiders of the Lost Ark* (1981). Recently, the island stood in for parts of South America in Disney's *Jungle Cruise* (2021).

The fluted cliffs and gorges of Kauai's rugged Napali Coast play the misunderstood beast's island home in *King Kong* (1976), and a jungle dweller of another sort, in *George of the Jungle* (1997), also frolicked on Kauai. Harrison Ford returned to the island for 10 weeks during the filming of *Six Days, Seven Nights* (1998), a romantic adventure set in French Polynesia. Part-time Kauai resident Ben Stiller used the island as a stand-in for the jungles of Vietnam in *Tropic Thunder* (2008), and Johnny Depp came here to film some of *Pirates of the Caribbean: On Stranger Tides* (2011). But these are all relatively contemporary movies. What's truly remarkable is that Hollywood discovered Kauai in 1933 with the making of *White Heat*, which was set on a sugar plantation and—like *South Pacific* (also filmed on Kauai)— dealt with an interracial love story.

Then it was off to the races, as Kauai saw no fewer than a dozen movies filmed on the island in the 1950s,

though not all of them were Oscar contenders. Among them were *She Gods of Shark Reef* (1956) and *Miss Sadie Thompson* (1953), which starred Rita Hayworth.

The movie that is still immortalized on the island in the names of restaurants, real estate offices, a hotel, and even a sushi item is *South Pacific* (1957). (You guessed it, right?) That mythical place called Bali Hai is never far away on Kauai.

In the 1960s, Elvis Presley filmed *Blue Hawaii* (1961) and *Girls! Girls! Girls!* (1962) on the island. All in all, Kauai has welcomed plenty of Hollywood's A-list: John Wayne in *Donovan's Reef* (1963); Jack Lemmon in *The Wackiest Ship in the Army* (1960); Richard Chamberlain in *The Thorn Birds* (1983); Gene Hackman in *Uncommon Valor* (1983); Danny DeVito and Billy Crystal in *Throw Momma from the Train* (1987); and Dustin Hoffman, Morgan Freeman, Rene Russo, and Cuba Gooding Jr. in *Outbreak* (1995).

Kauai has also appeared on a long list of TV shows and made-for-TV movies, including *Gilligan's Island, Fantasy Island, Starsky & Hutch, Baywatch Hawaii*—even reality TV shows *The Bachelor* and *The Amazing Race 3*.

For the record, just because a movie did some filming here doesn't mean the entire movie was filmed on Kauai. *Honeymoon in Vegas* (1992) filmed just one scene here; the murder mystery *A Perfect Getaway* (2009) was set on the famous Kalalau Trail and featured beautiful Kauai backdrops, but was shot mostly in Puerto Rico.

Airport. Come here for cool, comfortable muumuu and aloha shirts for men, women, and children in bright floral prints, as well as other souvenirs. Also, be sure to check out the line of Hawaii-inspired home furnishings. ⊠ *3252 Kuhio Hwy., Lihue* ☎ *808/245–3404* ⊕ *www.hilohattie. com.*

★ Kapaia Stitchery

SOUVENIRS | Hawaiian quilts made by hand and machine, a beautiful selection of fabrics, quilting kits, handmade aloha shirts, and unique fabric arts fill a cute, small, red plantation-style building a mile outside Lihue. There are also many locally made gifts and quilts for sale in this locally owned store. The staff is friendly and helpful, even though a steady stream of customers keeps them busy. ⊠ *3–3551 Kuhio Hwy., Lihue* ☎ *808/245–2281* ⊕ *kapaiastitchery.com* ⊗ *Closed Sun.*

★ Kauai Community Market

MARKET | FAMILY | This is the biggest and best farmers' market on Kauai, sponsored by the Kauai Farm Bureau and Kauai Community College and held 9:30 am to 1 pm Saturday in the college's parking lot in Lihue. You'll find fresh produce and flowers, as well as packaged products like breads, goat cheese, pasta, honey, coffee, soaps, lotions, and more, all made locally. The market also offers educational displays and cooking tips. Seating areas are convenient if you want to grab a tasty snack or lunch from the food booths and lunch wagons that set up here. ⊠ *3–1901 Kaumualii Hwy., Lihue* ☎ *808/855–5429* ⊕ *www.kauaicommunitymarket.com.*

Kauai Fruit & Flower Company (*The Pineapple Store*)

At this shop near Lihue and five minutes away from the airport, you can buy fresh Hawaii Gold pineapples, sugarcane, ginger, tropical flowers, coconuts, and local jams, jellies, and honey, plus papayas, bananas, and mangoes from Kauai. ■ **TIP→ Note that some of the fruit sold here cannot be shipped out of state.** ⊠ *3–4684 Kuhio Hwy., Lihue* ☎ *808/320–8870* ⊕ *www.kauaifruit.com* ⊗ *Closed Sat. afternoon and Sun.*

★ Kauai Museum Shop

CRAFTS | The gift shop at the museum sells some fascinating books, maps, and prints, as well as lovely authentic Niihau shell jewelry, handwoven lauhala hats, and koa wood bowls. Also featured at the Kauai Museum are tapa cloth, authentic hand-carved tiki figurines, as well as other good-quality local crafts and books at reasonable prices. ⊠ *4428 Rice St., Lihue* ☎ *808/245–6931* ⊕ *www.kauaimuseum. org* ⊗ *Closed Fri.–Sun.*

Kilohana Plantation Shops

SHOPPING CENTER | With shops and art galleries tucked into the 16,000-square-foot Tudor mansion and restored outbuildings, Kilohana Plantation offers quality clothing, jewelry, candy, handmade pottery, Hawaiian collectibles, and train memorabilia. The grounds are home to Koloa Rum Company, Luau Kalamaku, and a restaurant, while the historic mansion is filled with antiques from the previous owner. Train rides on a restored railroad are available, with knowledgeable guides recounting the history of sugar on Kauai. ⊠ *3–2087 Kaumualii Hwy., Lihue* ☎ *808/245–5608* ⊕ *www.kilohanakauai. com.*

Kukui Grove Center

SHOPPING CENTER | This is Kauai's only true mall. Anchor tenants are Longs Drugs, Macy's, Ross, Kukui Grove Cinemas, and Times Supermarket. The mall's stores offer women's clothing, surf wear, art, toys, athletic shoes, jewelry, a hair salon, and locally made crafts. Restaurants range from fast food and sandwiches to sushi and Korean, with a popular Starbucks and Jamba Juice. The center stage often has entertainment, especially on Friday night, and there is a farmers' market on Monday afternoon. ⊠ *3–2600 Kaumualii Hwy., Lihue* ☎ *808/245–7784* ⊕ *www.kukuigrovecenter.com.*

Two Frogs Hugging

HOUSEWARES | On display here are lots of interesting housewares, accessories, knickknacks, and hand-carved collectibles, as well as baskets and furniture from Indonesia, the Philippines, and China. Antiques and reproductions for the home and outdoors are available. The shop occupies expansive quarters in the Lihue Industrial Park. ⊠ *3094 Aukele St., Lihue* ☎ *808/246–8777* ⊕ *www.twofrogshugging.com.*

The South Shore

As you follow the main road south from Lihue, the landscape becomes lush and densely vegetated before giving way to drier conditions that characterize Poipu, the South Side's major resort area. Poipu owes its popularity to a steady supply of sunshine and a string of sandy beaches, although the beaches are smaller and more covelike than those on the island's West Side. With its extensive selection of accommodations, services, shopping, and activities, the South Shore attracts more visitors than any other area of Kauai. It has also attracted developers with big plans for the onetime sugarcane fields that are nestled in this region and enveloped by mountains. There are few roads in and out, and local residents are concerned about increased traffic as well as construction. If you're planning to stay on the South Side, ask if your hotel, condo, or vacation rental will be affected by development during your visit. Both Poipu and nearby Koloa, the latter the site of Kauai's first sugar mill, can be reached via Route 520 (Maluhia Road) from the Lihue area. Route 520 is also known as Tree Tunnel Road because of the graceful eucalyptus trees planted here on both sides of the road at the turn of the 20th century. The canopy of trees was destroyed two times by hurricanes in the 20th century, but the trees have grown back, their branches arching

overhead to create an impressive tunnel and a perfect photo op. It's a distinctive way to announce, "You are now on vacation," and there's a definite feel of leisure in the air here. There's still plenty to do—snorkel, bike, walk, horseback ride, take an ATV tour, surf, scuba dive, shop, and dine—everything you'd want on a tropical vacation. From the west, Route 530 (Koloa Road) starts in Lawai—a good stop for a coffee, quick bite, or handmade gifts—and then slips into downtown Koloa, a row of fun shops and eateries in historical plantation buildings well worth exploring, at an intersection with the only gas station on the South Shore.

Koloa

11 miles southwest of Lihue.

Hawaii's lucrative foray into sugar was born in this sleepy town, where the first cane was milled in 1836. You still can see the mill's old stone smokestack, though little else remains, save for the vintage plantation-style buildings that have kept Koloa from becoming a tacky tourist trap for Poipu-bound visitors. The original small-town character has been preserved by converting historic structures along the main street into boutiques, restaurants, and outlets for edible gifts. Placards describe the original tenants and life in the old mill town. Places to look for include Koloa Fish Market (now at 3390 Poipu Road), Crazy Shirts, and Billabong surf shop.

 Sights

★ Old Koloa Town

TOWN | Koloa's first sugar plantation opened in 1835, ushering in an era of sugar production throughout the islands, with more than 100 plantations established by 1885. Many of the workers came from the Philippines, Japan, China,

Continued on page 488

HAWAII'S PLANTS 101

Tropical Hibiscus

Hawaii is a bounty of rainbow-colored flowers and plants. The evening air is scented with their fragrance. Just look at the front yard of almost any home, travel any road, or visit any local park and you'll see a spectacular array of colored blossoms and leaves. What most visitors don't know is that many of the plants they are seeing are not native to Hawaii; rather, they were introduced during the last two centuries as ornamental plants, or for timber, shade, or fruit.

Hawaii boasts nearly every climate on the planet, excluding the two most extreme: arctic tundra and arid desert. The Islands have wine-growing regions, cactus-speckled ranchlands, icy mountaintops, and the rainiest forests on earth.

Plants introduced from around the world thrive here. The lush lowland valleys along the windward coasts are predominantly populated by non-native trees including yellow- and red-fruited **guava**, silvery-leafed **kukui**, and orange-flowered **tulip trees**.

The colorful **plumeria flower**, very fragrant and commonly used in lei making, and the giant multicolored **hibiscus flower** are both used by many women as hair adornments, and are two of the most common plants found around homes and hotels. The umbrella-like **monkeypod tree** from Central America provides shade in many of Hawaii's parks including Kapiolani Park in Honolulu. Hawaii's largest tree, found in Lahaina, Maui, is a giant **banyan tree**. Its canopy and massive support roots cover about two-thirds of an acre. The native **ohia tree**, with its brilliant red brush-like flowers, and the **hapuu**, a giant tree fern, are common in Hawaii's forests and are also used ornamentally in gardens.

Naupaka, Limahuli Garden

Bougainvillea

Guava

Monkeypod

Banyan

Ohia Lehua*

Tulip Tree

Plumeria

Pandanus

Hibiscus

Anthurium

Kukui

Hapuu

*endemic to Hawaii

DID YOU KNOW?

More than 2,200 plant species are found in the Hawaiian Islands, but only about 1,000 are native. Of these, 320 are so rare, they are endangered. Hawaii's endemic plants evolved from ancestral seeds arriving in the Islands over thousands of years as baggage with birds, floating on ocean currents, or drifting on winds from continents thousands of miles away. Once here, these plants evolved in isolation, creating many new species known nowhere else in the world.

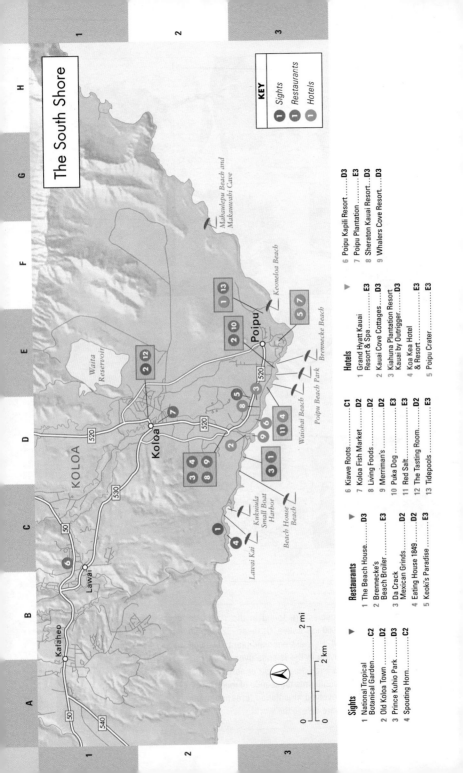

The South Shore

KEY
- 1 Sights
- 1 Restaurants
- 1 Hotels

Sights
1 National Tropical Botanical Garden..........**C2**
2 Old Koloa Town..........**D2**
3 Prince Kuhio Park..........**D3**
4 Spouting Horn..........**C2**

Restaurants
1 The Beach House..........**D3**
2 Brennecke's Beach Broiler..........**E3**
3 Da Crack Mexican Grinds..........**D2**
4 Eating House 1849..........**D2**
5 Keoki's Paradise..........**E3**
6 Kiawe Roots..........**C1**
7 Koloa Fish Market..........**D2**
8 Living Foods..........**D2**
9 Merriman's..........**E3**
10 Puka Dog..........**E3**
11 Red Salt..........**E3**
12 The Tasting Room..........**D2**
13 Tidepools..........**E3**

Hotels
1 Grand Hyatt Kauai Resort & Spa..........**E3**
2 Kauai Cove Cottages..........**D3**
3 Kiahuna Plantation Resort Kauai by Outrigger..........**D3**
4 Koa Kea Hotel & Resort..........**E3**
5 Poipu Crater..........**E3**
6 Poipu Kapili Resort..........**D3**
7 Poipu Plantation..........**E3**
8 Sheraton Kauai Resort..........**D3**
9 Whalers Cove Resort..........**D3**

Mahaulepu Beach and Makauwahi Cave

Keoneloa Beach

Brennecke Beach

Poipu

Waita Reservoir

KOLOA

Koloa

Poipu Beach Park

Waiohai Beach

Lawai Kai

Kukuiula Small Boat Harbor

Beach House Beach

Lawai

Kalaheo

0   2 mi
0   2 km

540
50
530
520

Korea, and Portugal, creating Hawaii's multiethnic mélange. Today, many of Koloa's historic buildings, beneath the shade of stately old monkeypod trees, have been converted into fun shops, galleries, and places to eat. Even the newer developments mimic quaint plantation camp architecture. You'll just want to stroll and take it all in. Try a sweet treat from The Fresh Shave, Kauai Gourmet Nuts, or Koloa Mill Ice Cream after a food truck lunch taken to nearby Knudsen Park. **■ TIP→ Be sure to approach Old Koloa Town via the Tree Tunnel, a romantic canopy of eucalyptus trees planted more than a century ago along a stretch of Maluhia Road.** ✉ *Koloa Rd., Koloa* 🌐 *www.oldkoloa.com.*

Restaurants

Koloa Fish Market
$ | **SEAFOOD** | Having outgrown its tiny shop by the post office, Koloa Fish Market now offers tasty take-out poke, plate lunches, fresh fish, and party platters at a location along the road to Poipu. **Known for:** long lines at lunchtime; family-owned deli; plantation-style storefront. [$] *Average main: $14* ✉ *3390 Poipu Rd., Koloa* ☎ *808/742–6199* 🕒 *Closed Sun. No dinner.*

★ **The Tasting Room**
$$ | **AMERICAN** | Popular for a predinner gathering or a full evening out, this trendy wine bar on Koloa's main street has great flights and small bites, and has added a few larger entrées. A venture run by the daughters of the owner of the wine shop next door, it offers knowledgeable, nonsnooty service and an extensive list of wines, beers, and spirits. **Known for:** charcuterie and small plates; friendly neighborhood vibe; farmhouse decor. [$] *Average main: $26* ✉ *5476 Koloa Rd., Koloa* ☎ *808/431–4311* 🌐 *www.tastingroomkauai.com* 🕒 *Closed Sun. and Mon. No lunch.*

Shopping

★ **The Wine Shop**
WINE/SPIRITS | As you browse shelves stocked with international wines, gourmet nibbles, local rum, and etched glassware, you may notice romance in the air. The Wine Shop is where couples can obtain a state marriage license, gather charcuterie supplies for a honeymoon beach picnic, or order a gift basket for a milestone anniversary. Want a particular vintage for an upcoming family trip? They will bring in special orders and hold them for your arrival. ✉ *5470 Koloa Rd., Koloa* ✣ *Across from Koloa Post Office* ☎ *808/742–7305* 🌐 *www.thewineshopkauai.com.*

Poipu

2 miles southeast of Koloa.

Thanks to its generally sunny weather and a string of golden-sand beaches dotted with oceanfront lodgings, Poipu is a top choice for many visitors. Beaches are user-friendly, with protected waters for *keiki* (children) and novice snorkelers, lifeguards, restrooms, covered pavilions, and a sweet coastal promenade ideal for leisurely strolls. Some experts have even ranked Poipu Beach Park number one in the nation. It depends on your preferences, of course, though it certainly does warrant high accolades.

GETTING HERE AND AROUND

Poipu is the one area on Kauai where you could get by without a car, though that might mean an expensive taxi ride from the airport and limited access to other parts of the island. To reach Poipu by car, follow Poipu Road south from Koloa. After the traffic circle, the roads curve to follow the coast, leading to some of the popular South Shore beaches.

The Kauai Marathon

Heading into its second decade, the Kauai Marathon (⊕ *thekauaimara-thon.com*) and its larger, concurrent Half Marathon attract runners and walkers from all over the world in September. Conch shells are blown to signal the start, and participants set off from the heart of Poipu, then turn up the Koloa Bypass Road as the sun rises behind the old sugar mill. Even the most competitive will stop for a selfie in the Tree Tunnel before continuing west along the highway (lanes closed for the occasion) and down through Omao, where neighbors cheer from front porches. Full marathoners then turn right for a long loop into the tough hills of Lawai and Kalaheo; "halfers" turn left to head back to the waterfront. Hula dancers and Japanese *taiko* drummers pepper the route. The large free Health & Wellness Expo is open to the public, as are many marathon-related events at nearby shopping centers and sponsor hotels.

◉ Sights

★ National Tropical Botanical Garden (*NTBG*)

GARDEN | FAMILY | Tucked away in Lawai Valley, this collection of gardens includes lands and a cottage once used by Hawaii's Queen Emma (1836–85) for a summer retreat. Trams depart frequently to transport people from the visitor center to the gardens. The rambling 252-acre McBryde Garden has exhibits and easy trails to help visitors learn about biodiversity and plants collected throughout the tropics, including a Canoe Garden that features plants introduced to Hawaii by early Polynesian voyagers. ■ **TIP→ The biodiversity path in McBryde is accessible for people with mobility issues.** The 100-acre Allerton Garden, which can be visited only on a guided tour, artfully displays statues and water features originally developed as part of a private estate. A famous scene in *Jurassic Park* was filmed here.

Reservations and closed-toe shoes are required for all tours. The visitor center has a high-quality gift shop and grab-and-go refreshments. Besides propagating rare and endangered plants from Hawaii and elsewhere, NTBG functions as a scientific research and education center. The organization also operates gardens in Limahuli, on Kauai's North Shore; in Hana, on Maui's east shore; and in Florida. ⊠ *4425 Lawai Rd., Poipu* ☎ *808/742–2623* ⊕ *www.ntbg.org* ◿ *McBryde self-guided tour $30, Allerton guided tour $60.*

Prince Kuhio Park

CITY PARK | A field next to Prince Kuhio Condominiums honors the birthplace of Kauai's beloved Prince Jonah Kuhio Kalanianaole. Known for his kind nature and tireless work on behalf of the Hawaiian people, he lost his chance at the throne when Americans staged an illegal overthrow of Queen Liliuokalani in 1893 and toppled Hawaii's constitutional monarchy. He served as a delegate to the U.S. Congress for 19 years after Hawaii became a territory in 1900. An annual commemoration is held around his March birthday, a state holiday. This is a great place to watch wave riders surfing a popular break known as PKs, or to see the sun sink into the Pacific. ⊠ *Lawai Rd., Poipu.*

★ Spouting Horn

NATURE SIGHT | When conditions are right, a natural blowhole in the rocky shoreline behaves like Old Faithful, shooting salt water high into the air and making a

Did You Know?

Spouting Horn on Kauai's South Shore is a blowhole that shoots water through a lava tube up to 50 feet in the air. This impressive natural feature is a great photo op.

Seal-Spotting on the South Shore

When strolling on one of Kauai's lovely beaches, don't be surprised if you find yourself in the rare company of a Hawaiian monk seal. These seals are among the most endangered of all marine mammals, with perhaps fewer than 1,400 remaining. They primarily inhabit the Northwestern Hawaiian Islands, although more are showing their sweet faces on the main Hawaiian Islands, especially Kauai. They're fond of hauling out on the beach for a long snooze in the sun, particularly after a night of gorging on fish. They need this time to rest and digest, safe from predators.

Female seals regularly birth their young on the beaches around Kauai, where they stay to nurse their pups for upward of six weeks. It seems the seals enjoy particular beaches for the same reasons we do: the shallow, protected waters.

If you're lucky enough to see a monk seal, keep your distance and let it be. Although they may haul out near people, they still want and need their space. Stay several hundred feet away, and forget photos unless you have a zoom lens. It's illegal to do anything that causes a monk seal to change its behavior, with penalties that include big fines and even jail time. In the water, seals may appear to want to play. It's their curious nature. Don't try to play with them. They are wild animals—mammals, in fact, with teeth.

If you have concerns about the health or safety of a seal, or just want more information, contact the **Hawaiian Monk Seal Conservation Hui** (☎ *808/651–7668*).

hollow, echoing sound. It's most dramatic during big summer swells, which jam large quantities of water through an ancient lava tube with great force. Most sidewalk vendors hawk inexpensive souvenirs, but a few carry locally set South Sea pearls or rare Niihau-shell creations, with prices ranging from affordable to several thousand dollars. Look for green sea turtles bobbing in the adjacent cove. ⊠ *End of Lawai Rd., Poipu* ⊕ *www. gohawaii.com.*

🅣 Beaches

Brennecke's Beach

BEACH | FAMILY | This beach is synonymous on Kauai with board surfing and bodysurfing, thanks to its shallow sandbar and reliable shore break. Because the beach is small and often congested, surfboards are prohibited near shore.

The water on the rocky eastern edge of the beach is a good place to see the endangered green sea turtles noshing on plants growing on the rocks. Monk seals sometimes haul out here; please allow them to rest. Playground equipment is available here, and there's free street parking. **Amenities:** food and drink. **Best for:** sunset; surfing. ⊠ *Hoone Rd., off Poipu Rd., Poipu* 🅟 *Free.*

Keoneloa Beach (*Shipwreck Beach*)

BEACH | The Hawaiian name for this stretch of beach, Keoneloa, means "long sand," but many refer to this beach fronting the Grand Hyatt Kauai Resort & Spa as Shipwreck Beach. Both make sense. It is a long stretch of crescent beach punctuated by stunning sea cliffs on both ends, and, yes, a ship once wrecked here. With its rough onshore break, the waters off "Shippies" are best for bodyboarding and bodysurfing experts;

South Shore beaches have good surf breaks. Head to Poipu Beach for board rentals or lessons.

however, the beach itself is plenty big for sunbathing, sandcastle building, Frisbee throwing, and other beach-related fun. The eastern edge of the beach is the start of an interpretive cliff and dune walk (complimentary) held by the hotel staff; check with the concierge for days and times, and keep an eye out for snoozing monk seals below. Parking is limited. **Amenities:** food and drink; parking (free); showers; toilets. **Best for:** walking, photography, surfing. ✉ *Ainako Rd., Poipu* ✛ *Continue on Poipu Rd. past Grand Hyatt Kauai, turn makai (toward the ocean) on Ainako Rd.* 🚗 *Free.*

Lawai Kai

BEACH | One of the most spectacular beaches on the South Shore is inaccessible by land unless you tour the National Tropical Botanical Garden's Allerton Garden, which we highly recommend. On the tour, you'll see the beach, but you won't step on the sand. The only way to legally access the beach on your own is by paddling a kayak 1 mile from Kukuiula Harbor. However, you have to rent the kayaks elsewhere and haul them on top of your car to the harbor. Also, the wind and waves usually run westward, making the in-trip a breeze but the return trip a workout against Mother Nature. ■ **TIP ➜ Do not attempt this beach in any manner during a south swell; do not trespass. Amenities:** none. **Best for:** solitude; sunset. ✉ *4425 Lawai Rd., off Poipu Rd.* ☎ *808/742–2623 for tour information at the National Tropical Botanical Garden* ⊕ *www.ntbg.org* 🚗 *NTBG tour $60.*

★ Mahaulepu Beach and Makauwahi Cave

BEACH | This 2-mile stretch of coast, with its sand dunes, limestone hills, sinkholes, and the Makauwahi Cave, is unlike any other on Kauai. Remains of a large, ancient settlement, evidence of great battles, and the discovery of a now-underwater petroglyph field indicate that Hawaiians lived in this area as early as AD 700. Mahaulepu's coastline is unprotected and rocky, which makes venturing into the ocean hazardous. There are three beach areas with bits of sandy-bottom swimming; however, the best way to experience Mahaulepu is simply to roam, on foot or horseback, along the sand or trails. Pack water and sun protection. **TIP→ Access to this beach is via private property. Before driving or hiking here, check current gate hours and conditions as the unpaved road can be closed due to weather, grading, or movie filming. Access is during daylight hours only, so be sure to depart before sunset or risk getting locked in for the night.** **Amenities:** parking (free). **Best for:** solitude; sunrise; walking. ✉ *Poipu Rd., Poipu* ✣ *Past Grand Hyatt Kauai and CJM Stables* 🌐 *www.cavereserve.org* 🎟 *Free.*

★ Poipu Beach Park
BEACH | FAMILY | At the most popular beach on the South Shore, the snorkeling and swimming are good during calm seas, and when the surf's up, the bodyboarding and surfing are good, too. Frequent sunshine, grassy lawns, play equipment, and easy access add to the appeal, especially with families. The beach is frequently crowded and great for people-watching. Even the endangered Hawaiian monk seal often makes an appearance. Take a walk west on a path fronting numerous resorts. Note that at time of writing, this beach is one of a few on Kauai that may institute a parking fee for nonresidents. **Amenities:** food and drink; lifeguards; parking (free); showers; toilets. **Best for:** partiers; snorkeling; sunbathing; swimming. ✉ *Hoone Rd., off Poipu Rd., Poipu* ☎ *808/742–7444* 🎟 *Free.*

Waiohai Beach
BEACH | FAMILY | The first hotel built in Poipu in 1962 overlooked this beach, adjacent to Poipu Beach Park. Actually, there's little to distinguish where this one ends and the other begins, other than a crescent reef at the eastern end of Waiohai Beach. That crescent, however, is important. It creates a small, protected bay—good for snorkeling and beginning surfers. However, when a summer swell kicks up, the near-shore conditions become dangerous; offshore, there's a splendid surf break for experienced surfers. The beach itself is narrow and, like its neighbor, gets very crowded in summer. **Amenities:** parking (free). **Best for:** snorkeling; sunset; surfing; swimming. ✉ *Hoone Rd., off Poipu Rd., Poipu* 🎟 *Free.*

🍴 Restaurants

The Beach House
$$$$ | MODERN HAWAIIAN | This busy restaurant has a dreamy ocean view, making it one of the best settings on Kauai for a special dinner or a cocktail and appetizer while the sun sinks into the glassy blue Pacific and surfers slice the waves. The prices have gone up, but you can still find satisfaction in the pork potsticker appetizer or fresh catch of the day served with *lilikoi* (passion fruit) lemongrass beurre blanc. **Known for:** small bar with a big view; indoor-outdoor dining; gluten-free and vegan entrées. [$] *Average main: $45* ✉ *5022 Lawai Rd., Poipu* ☎ *808/742–1424* 🌐 *www.the-beach-house.com* 🕓 *No lunch.*

Brennecke's Beach Broiler
$$$ | AMERICAN | FAMILY | Casual and fun, with a busy mai tai bar and windows overlooking the beach, Brennecke's specializes in big portions in a wide range of offerings including rib-eye steak, burgers, fish tacos, pasta, and shrimp. You can create your own combination meal if you can't pick only one. **Known for:** fresh catch of the day; take-out deli with shave ice; good-value happy hours. [$] *Average main: $27* ✉ *2100 Hoone Rd., Poipu* ☎ *808/742–7588* 🌐 *www.brenneckes.com.*

Da Crack Mexican Grinds
$ | MEXICAN | FAMILY | Fresh, fast, and affordable, Da Crack is everything you could ask for when refueling between outdoor activities. Fill your burrito, bowl, or taco with locally caught fish, traditional beans, house-made salsa,

and local avocado guacamole—or many other choices made from scratch—then head back out to eat and explore more of the island. **Known for:** vegan friendly; children's menu; no MSG or trans fat oils. [$] *Average main: $13* ✉ *2827 Poipu Rd., by Kukuiula Market, Poipu* ☎ *808/742–9505* 🌐 *www.dacrackkauai.com.*

★ Eating House 1849

$$$ | **ASIAN FUSION** | Hawaii's culinary superstar, Roy Yamaguchi, runs his signature Hawaiian-fusion-cuisine restaurant on Kauai's South Shore in a shopping village that suits the name and creative fare. Though billed as "plantation cuisine," the hot pot rice bowl, spicy ramen, and burger that's half wild boar are about the only items that might have their roots in the days when sugar was king; otherwise, the menu is classic Asian fusion. **Known for:** use of local ingredients; lively atmosphere; molten chocolate soufflé. [$] *Average main: $35* ✉ *Shops at Kukuiula, 2829 Ala Kalanikaumaka Rd., No. A-201, Poipu* ☎ *808/742–5000* 🌐 *www.eatinghouse1849.com* 🕒 *Closed Mon. and Tues. No lunch.*

Keoki's Paradise

$$$ | **ASIAN FUSION** | **FAMILY** | Built to resemble a dockside boathouse, this active, semi-outdoor place fills up quickly for dinner thanks to a busy lounge and frequent live music. The day's fresh catch is available in various styles and sauces, and other favorites include coconut shrimp, seafood risotto, and roasted pork ribs that are cooked in a traditional Hawaiian *imu* (an underground oven). **Known for:** children's menu; Hawaiian atmosphere, with hula; weekend brunch and theme nights. [$] *Average main: $35* ✉ *Poipu Shopping Village, 2360 Kiahuna Plantation Dr., Poipu* ☎ *808/742–7534* 🌐 *www.keokisparadise.com* 🕒 *No lunch weekends. No brunch weekdays.*

Living Foods

$$ | **AMERICAN** | **FAMILY** | A range of light fare is served from lunchtime through evening on the covered lanai attached to Living Foods general store at The Shops at Kukuiula. Locally sourced starters, sandwiches, fish preparations, entrée salads, and desserts can be ordered via the café's website, which speeds up table service. **Known for:** all-day menu; weekend breakfast, with cocktails; grab-and-go bakery. [$] *Average main: $17* ✉ *The Shops at Kukuiula, 2829 Ala Kalanikaumaka St., Suite D124, Poipu* ☎ *808/320–7642* 🌐 *www.livingfoodshawaii.com.*

Merriman's

$$$$ | **MODERN HAWAIIAN** | The Hawaii Regional Cuisine served up at chef Peter Merriman's namesake restaurant is enhanced by a sophisticated setting and lovely views from a pretty second-floor dining veranda. Start at the bar, where fine wines are offered by the glass, and then continue to the dinner menu, which states the origins of the fish, shrimp, lamb, beef, chicken, and veggies: 90% is locally grown or caught. **Known for:** sunset views; upscale, plantation-home atmosphere; partnerships with local fishers and farmers. [$] *Average main: $46* ✉ *2829 Ala Kalanikaumaka St., G-149, Poipu* ☎ *808/742–8385* 🌐 *www.merrimanshawaii.com.*

Puka Dog

$ | **AMERICAN** | **FAMILY** | It takes four steps to customize a Hawaiian-style hot dog here, so your crew may want to study the menu in advance. Choose a Polish sausage or veggie dog, top it with a house-made sauce and one of six intriguing tropical fruit relishes, then add mustard (*lilikoi*—passion fruit —is best.) All this deliciousness won't fall out on your bathing suit because the bun is baked with a *puka*, a hole, rather than sliced. **Known for:** Hawaiian sweet bread bun; Kauai Special with mango relish; secret garlic lemon sauce with four heat levels. [$] *Average main: $10* ✉ *Poipu Beach Park, 2100 Hoone Rd., below Brennecke's restaurant, Poipu* ☎ *808/742–6044* 🌐 *www.pukadog.com* 🕒 *No dinner.*

★ Red Salt

$$$$ | ECLECTIC | Smart, sophisticated decor, attentive and skilled service, and an exceptional menu that highlights Hawaiian seafood make Red Salt a great choice for leisurely fine dining. A daily breakfast also is served, featuring lobster Benedict and lemon-pineapple soufflé pancakes. **Known for:** perfectly grilled meats; sushi and sake; dramatic presentation. $ *Average main: $51* ⊠ *Koa Kea Resort, 2251 Poipu Rd., Poipu* ☎ *808/742–4200* ⊕ *meritagecollection. com/koa-kea* ⊗ *No dinner Sun. and Mon. No lunch.*

Tidepools

$$$$ | SEAFOOD | Of the Grand Hyatt's restaurants, this is definitely the most tropical and campy, with grass-thatch huts that seem to float on a koi-filled pond beneath starry skies while torches flicker in the lushly landscaped grounds nearby. The equally distinctive food has an island flavor that comes from the chef's advocacy of Hawaii Regional Cuisine and extensive use of island-grown products, including fresh herbs from the resort's organic garden. **Known for:** macadamia nut–crusted mahimahi; excellent service; reservations needed weeks in advance. $ *Average main: $50* ⊠ *Grand Hyatt Kauai Resort and Spa, 1571 Poipu Rd., Poipu* ☎ *808/742–1234* ⊕ *grandhyattkauai. com* ⊗ *No lunch.*

 Hotels

★ Grand Hyatt Kauai Resort & Spa

$$$$ | RESORT | FAMILY | Dramatically handsome, Kauai's best megaresort is this classic Hawaiian low-rise built into the cliffs overlooking an unspoiled coastline; it boasts mouthwatering restaurants and also has taken great strides to reduce its carbon footprint. **Pros:** fabulous pool and spa; cultural activities; elegant Hawaiian ambience. **Cons:** small balconies; the large size may not appeal to all tastes; dangerous swimming beach during summer swells. $ *Rooms from: $424*

⊠ *1571 Poipu Rd., Poipu* ☎ *808/742–1234* ⊕ *www.grandhyattkauai.com* ⤴ *604 rooms* ⦿ *No Meals.*

Kauai Cove Cottages

$$ | APARTMENT | Located in a residential neighborhood, this vacation rental includes quaint studio units near the mouth of Waikomo Stream, about two blocks from a nice snorkeling cove, and the Pool Cottage in central Poipu. **Pros:** walk to shops and restaurants; great snorkeling nearby; quiet neighborhood. **Cons:** $105–$125 cleaning fee upon departure; better for couples than families; not on beach. $ *Rooms from: $180* ⊠ *2672 Puuholo Rd., Poipu* ☎ *808/631– 9313* ⊕ *www.kauaicove.com* ⤴ *3 units* ⦿ *No Meals.*

Kiahuna Plantation Resort Kauai by Outrigger

$$$ | APARTMENT | FAMILY | This longtime Kauai condo project consists of 42 plantation-style, low-rise buildings with individually owned one- and two-bedroom units set on grassy fields leading to a lovely beach. **Pros:** great sunset and ocean views are bonuses in some units; convenient to restaurants, shops, athletic club; swimmable beach and lawn for picnics and games. **Cons:** be prepared for stairs; housekeeping is extra; no air-conditioning. $ *Rooms from: $289* ⊠ *2253 Poipu Rd., Poipu* ☎ *808/742– 6411, 866/994–1588 reservations* ⊕ *www.outrigger.com* ⤴ *100 units* ⦿ *No Meals* ☞ *Additional units managed by Castle Resorts.*

★ Koa Kea Hotel & Resort

$$$$ | RESORT | This boutique property offers a stylish, high-end experience without the bustle of many larger resorts, making it a great place to forget it all while relaxing at the spa or lounging by the pool on a honeymoon or babymoon. **Pros:** incredibly comfortable beds; friendly service; perfect romantic getaway. **Cons:** all parking is valet; very busy area; not much for children. $ *Rooms from: $599* ⊠ *2251 Poipu Rd., Poipu* ☎ *808/742–4200* *general information, 808/742–4271 reservations* 🌐 *www.koakea.com* 🛏 *121 rooms* 🍴 *No Meals.*

Poipu Crater

$$ | **APARTMENT** | **FAMILY** | Set down within an extinct volcanic crater known as Piha ke Akua, or "Place of the Gods," these two-bedroom condominium units in South Pacific–style townhomes are fairly spacious, with large windows, high ceilings, and full kitchens. **Pros:** attractive and generally well-kept; jungle-in-crater setting; family-friendly, with table tennis, pool, and clubhouse. **Cons:** few resort amenities; individually owned units means upkeep and decor vary; beach isn't good for swimming. [$] *Rooms from: $249* ✉ *2330 Hoohu Rd., Poipu* ☎ *808/742–7260* 🌐 *VRBO.com, Suite-Paradise.com, Parrish.Kauai.com* 🛏 *30 units* 🍴 *No Meals.*

Poipu Kapili Resort

$$$ | **APARTMENT** | **FAMILY** | White-frame exteriors and double-pitched roofs complement the tropical landscaping at this resort, which offers spacious one- and two-bedroom condo units—with full kitchens, bedroom air-conditioning, entertainment centers, and garden or ocean views—that are minutes from Poipu's restaurants and across the street from a nice beach. **Pros:** units are well-spaced; parking is close to the unit; tennis and pickleball on-site. **Cons:** three-night minimum stay; minimal amenities; units are ocean-view but not oceanfront. [$] *Rooms from: $325* ✉ *2221 Kapili Rd., Poipu* ☎ *808/742–6449, 800/443–7714* 🌐 *www.poipukapili.com* 🛏 *60 units* 🍴 *No Meals.*

Poipu Plantation

$ | **APARTMENT** | Plumeria, ti, and other tropical foliage create a lush landscape for this resort, which rents a four-bedroom/four-bath plantation home and nine one- and two-bedroom cottage apartments. **Pros:** attractively furnished; air-conditioning; free Wi-Fi and parking. **Cons:** not on the ocean; no resort amenities; three-night minimum. [$] *Rooms from: $165* ✉ *1792 Pee Rd., Poipu* ☎ *808/742–6757, 800/634–0263* 🌐 *www.poipubeach.com* 🛏 *13 units* 🍴 *No Meals.*

★ Sheraton Kauai Resort

$$$ | **RESORT** | The Sheraton is a sprawling resort with rooms that offer views of the ocean and lovely landscaped gardens; it's worth splurging on the ocean-wing accommodations, which are so close to the water you can practically feel the spray of the surf as it hits the rocks below. **Pros:** ocean-view pool; restaurant with spectacular sunset views; good facilities for meetings, events, reunions. **Cons:** renovated rooms but some dated infrastructure; basic gym and no spa; parking can be a ways from the room. [$] *Rooms from: $340* ✉ *2440 Hoonani Rd., Poipu Beach, Koloa* ☎ *808/742–1661, 888/627–8113* 🌐 *www.sheraton-kauai.com* 🛏 *188 rooms* 🍴 *No Meals.*

Whalers Cove Resort

$$$$ | **APARTMENT** | Perched about as close to the water's edge as they can get, these one-, two-, and three-bedroom condos are the most luxurious on the South Shore. **Pros:** on-site staff and housekeeping; outstanding setting; spacious, with full kitchens. **Cons:** no air-conditioning; resort fee, but few amenities (curb-free parking, enhanced Wi-Fi); rocky beach not ideal for swimming. [$] *Rooms from: $430* ✉ *2640 Puuholo Rd., Poipu* ☎ *808/742–7571, 800/225–2683* 🌐 *www.whalerscoveresort.com* 🛏 *24 units* 🍴 *No Meals.*

Nightlife

Grand Hyatt Kauai Luau

CULTURAL FESTIVALS | **FAMILY** | Excellent unlimited buffet food, an open bar, and exciting music and dance performances characterize this traditional luau, held twice weekly (Wednesday and Saturday) in a garden setting near majestic Keoneloa Bay. ✉ *Grand Hyatt Kauai Resort and Spa, 1571 Poipu Rd., Poipu*

☎ *808/742–1234* 🌐 *www.grandhyattkauai-luau.com* 🎟 *From $175.*

Keoki's Paradise Bar

COCKTAIL LOUNGES | A young, energetic crowd makes this a lively spot on Friday and Saturday evenings. When the dining room clears out, there's a bit of a scene in the tropical lounge. Live music, Taco Tuesday, and Burger & Beer Wednesday keep the Bamboo Bar a happening place. Try the Poipu Piña to sip from a pineapple. ✉ *Poipu Shopping Village, 2360 Kiahuna Plantation Dr., Poipu* ☎ *808/742–7534* 🌐 *www.keokisparadise.com.*

🛍 Shopping

Halelea Gallery

ART GALLERIES | In addition to offering original works by Hawaii artists, this stylish gallery in The Shops at Kukuiula doubles as a boutique that sells a unique sampling of clothing, jewelry, bags, and gifts by local designers. Its other location, The Black Pearl, focuses on fine art and fine jewelry. ✉ *2829 Kalanikaumaka Rd., Suite K, Poipu* ☎ *808/742–9525* 🌐 *www.haleleagallery.com.*

Poipu Shopping Village

SHOPPING CENTER | FAMILY | Convenient to hotels and condos along the shore, the two dozen shops at Poipu Shopping Village sell resort wear, gifts, souvenirs, jewelry, and art. This complex also has a number of food choices, from casual Thai and pizza sit-down restaurants to a gelato stand and Starbucks. Hula shows and farmers' markets in the open-air courtyard add to the ambience. ✉ *2360 Kiahuna Plantation Dr., Poipu* ☎ *808/742–2831* 🌐 *www.poipushoppingvillage.com.*

★ **The Shops at Kukuiula**

SHOPPING CENTER | The South Shore's upscale shopping center has boutiques, exclusive galleries, several great restaurants, a gourmet grocer, a large drugstore, and Kauai-made Lappert's Ice Cream. The flagship of the Malie Organics bath line, used by many top hotels and spas, is here. Check out the Kauai Culinary Market on Wednesday afternoon to see cooking demonstrations, listen to live music, and shop from local vendors. This attractive open-air, plantation-style center gets busy on Friday night. It's at the roundabout as you enter Poipu. ✉ *2829 Kalanikaumaka St., Poipu* ☎ *808/742–9545* 🌐 *www.theshopsatkukuiula.com.*

Lawai

4½ miles west of Poipu, 11 miles west of Lihue.

Lawai is becoming a trendy hub for artists' studios, food trucks, and independent shops. It's worth a stop, especially if you want a snack, when passing through between the West Side and South Shore. The terraced hills of the Lawai and Kalaheo Valleys once supplied golden pineapples to the Lawai Cannery. After closing in 1964, the cannery was ravaged by two hurricanes and eventually demolished.

🍴 Restaurants

★ **Kiawe Roots**

$$ | MODERN HAWAIIAN | FAMILY | This place is back, with both dine-in and takeout, at a cozy storefront where family recipes bring a mix of local cultures to the table. Meats are grilled over *kiawe*, Hawaiian mesquite. **Known for:** tropical BBQ flavors; gluten-free choices; comfort food with a local twist. [$] *Average main: $22* ✉ *2-3687 Kaumualii Hwy., Lawai* ✥ *Next to Lawai post office* ☎ *808/855–5055* 🌐 *www.eatatkiawe.com* 🕒 *Closed Sun. and Mon.*

🛍 Shopping

Monkeypod Jam

FOOD | The storefront café has closed, but Monkeypod's award-winning preserves made from tropical fruits can be found at its "provisions cottage" tucked away

Sunshine Markets

If you want to rub elbows with the locals and purchase fresh produce and flowers at (somewhat) reasonable prices, head for Sunshine Markets, also known as Kauai's farmers' markets. These busy markets are held throughout the week, usually in the afternoon, at locations around the island—just ask any local person. They're good fun, and they support neighborhood farmers and vendors. Arrive a little early, bring dollar bills to speed up transactions and your own shopping bags to carry your produce, and be prepared for some pushy shoppers. Farmers are usually happy to educate visitors about unfamiliar fruits and veggies, especially when the crowd thins.

The pandemic affected the markets and their schedules: for current information on the Sunshine Markets, see Kauai's government website at ⊕ *www.kauai.gov.* Here are a couple in operation at this writing.

East Side Sunshine Market. ✉ *Kapaa Beach Park, Kapaa. Wednesday 3 pm.*

West Side Sunshine Market. ✉ *Hana-pepe Park, Hanapepe. Thursday 3 pm.*

in Lawai. In winery fashion, you can sign up for a tasting ($10; deducted from purchase) and then buy jars. At weekly classes, people cook jelly, jam, curd, chutney, salsa, or pickles, depending on what's in season. Or you can learn to make local favorites like Spam musubi, poke bowls, and coconut mochi. A six-week produce plan is perfect for folks staying on the Garden Island for a longer winter escape. At this writing, weekly tastings, shopping, and classes are by appointment, though this could change. ✉ *3540 Koloa Rd., Lawai* ✛ *Exact location provided after booking a tasting or class* ☎ *808/378–4208* ⊕ *www.monkeypod-jam.com.*

Warehouse 3540

OTHER SPECIALTY STORE | An old warehouse has new life as a marketplace for a dozen creative entrepreneurs and as a hub for food trucks. Hand-printed clothing, authentic lauhala hats, boho chic jewelry, letterpressed cards, specialty food products, and locally crafted soaps are offered at the oft-changing microshops. On Second Saturday evenings each month, craft vendors, farmers, take-out food cooks, and musicians join the shops. Locals and visitors mingle at picnic tables outside. ✉ *3540 Koloa Rd., Lawai* ⊕ *www.ware-house3540.com.*

The West Side

Exploring the West Side is akin to visiting an entirely different world. The landscape is dramatic and colorful—a patchwork of green, blue, black, and orange. The weather is hot and dry, the beaches long, and the sand dark. Niihau, a private island and the last remaining place in Hawaii where Hawaiian is spoken exclusively, can be glimpsed offshore. This is rural Kauai, where sugar made its last stand and taro is still cultivated in the fertile river valleys. The lifestyle is slow, easy, and traditional, with many folks fishing and hunting to supplement their diets. Here and there modern industry has intruded into this pastoral scene: huge generators turn oil into electricity at Port Allen; seed companies cultivate experimental crops of genetically engineered plants in Kekaha and Waimea; the Navy launches rockets at Mana to test the "Star Wars" missile defense system; and NASA has a tracking station in the wilds of Kokee.

It's a region of contrasts that simply shouldn't be missed. Heading west from Lihue or Poipu, you pass through a string of tiny towns, plantation camps, and historic sites, each with a story to tell of centuries past. There's Kalaheo, with its ranching roots; Hanapepe, whose coastal salt ponds have been harvested since ancient times; Kaumakani and Makaweli, picturesque former sugar camps; and Waimea, where Captain Cook made his first landing in the Islands, forever changing the face of Hawaii. From Waimea Town you can head up into the mountains, skirting the rim of magnificent Waimea Canyon and climbing higher still until you reach the cool, often-misty forests of Kokee State Park. From vantage points at the top of this gemlike island, 3,200 to 4,200 feet above sea level, you can gaze into the deep, verdant valleys of the North Shore and Napali Coast. This is where the "real" Kauai can still be found: the native plants, insects, and birds that are located nowhere else on Earth.

Kalaheo

6½ miles northwest of Poipu, 13 miles southwest of Lihue.

Cool, upcountry Kalaheo—"the proud day" in Hawaiian—offers worthy stops for visitors. The world-famous Kauai Coffee Company, the largest producer of export-quality Hawaiian coffee, is based here, along with the headquarters of the National Tropical Botanical Garden, which has operations throughout Hawaii and Florida. The hilltop Kukuiolono Park offers a friendly nine-hole golf course, minigolf, walking paths, and special gardens. You'll also find a gas station, notable eateries, and services that welcome visitors, like a yoga studio and nail salon. Kalaheo was never a plantation town; instead, Portuguese homesteaders and ranchers settled the area.

While many communities go crazy for their sports teams, Kauai fans feel

Rainbow Capital of the World

While folks in Western Europe and North America may catch a rainbow only a dozen times a year, these beautiful optical effects make a daily showing in Hawaii thanks to sunny days and frequent light, passing showers. Look for them in the afternoon, with the sun behind you. Also keep an eye out for double rainbows, which make a lovely photograph. Rainbows even appear on state license plates and University of Hawaii logo wear.

intense pride in their Kalaheo-based hula *halau* (school)—a troupe of powerful, precise, elegant women that in 2022 swept the prestigious Merrie Monarch Festival competition on the Big Island of Hawaii. They perpetuate not only traditional dance but also the very soul of Hawaiian culture.

◉ Sights

★ Kauai Coffee Estate Visitor Center
FARM/RANCH | FAMILY | Two restored camp houses, dating from the days when sugar was the main agricultural crop on the Islands, have been converted into a museum, visitor center, snack bar, and gift shop. About 3,100 acres of McBryde sugar land have become Hawaii's largest coffee plantation, with its 4 million trees producing more than half of the state's beans. You can walk among the trees, view old grinders and roasters, watch a video to learn how coffee is harvested and processed, sample various estate roasts, and check out the gift store.

The center offers free self-guided tours through a small coffee grove (about 20 minutes) and a personalized, one-hour "coffee on the brain" tour for a fee. From

Kalaheo, take Route 50 in the direction of Waimea Canyon (west) and veer left onto Route 540. It's 2½ miles from the Route 50 turnoff. ✉ *870 Halewili Rd., Kalaheo* ✥ *Between Kalaheo and Eleele on Rte. 540* ☎ *808/335–0813* 🌐 *www.kauaicoffee.com* 🎟 *Free; guided tour $25, $20 kids 8–16.*

🍴 Restaurants

Kalaheo Café & Coffee Company
$$ | AMERICAN | FAMILY | Folks love this roadside café—especially at breakfast and lunch, though it's good for dinner, too—for its casual neighborhood feel and lengthy menu with omelets, sandwiches, burgers, and plenty more. Lots of Kauai products are used here, including Anahola Granola, fruit for smoothies, fresh-caught fish, and coffee, which you can also buy by the pound. **Known for:** often busy, especially weekend mornings; hearty portions, like the Kahili Breakfast; fresh-baked pastries and bread. [$] *Average main: $22* ✉ *2–2560 Kaumualii Hwy. (Rte. 50), Kalaheo* ☎ *808/332–5858* 🌐 *www.kalaheo.com* ⏲ *No dinner Sun. and Mon.*

🛏 Hotels

Kalaheo Inn
$ | B&B/INN | FAMILY | It isn't easy to find good budget lodgings on the southwest side of the island, but this old-fashioned neighborhood inn with studios and one-, two-, and three-bedroom suites does an adequate job in cooler upcountry Kalaheo Town. **Pros:** free Wi-Fi; walking distance to café and takeout; coin-operated laundry on-site. **Cons:** no air-conditioning; dated furnishings; three-night minimum stay. [$] *Rooms from: $83* ✉ *4444 Papalina Rd., Kalaheo* ☎ *808/332–6023, 888/332–6023* 🌐 *www.kalaheoinn.com* 🛏 *15 units* 🍴 *No Meals.*

🛍 Shopping

Kauai Coffee Estate Visitor Center Shop
FOOD | Kauai produces more coffee than any other Island, and this is the largest coffee farm in the United States. The 100% local product can be purchased from grocery stores or here at the plantation, where you can sample nearly two dozen coffees before or after a self-guided tour. Be sure to try some of the exclusive estate-roasted varieties. Coffee is available online, too. Fun fact: The factory, quaint old camp houses, and visitor center are located in a settlement called Numila, which is a Hawaiian way to say "new mill." ✉ *870 Halewili Rd., off Rte. 50, Kalaheo* ☎ *808/335–0813* 🌐 *www.kauaicoffee.com.*

Hanapepe

6 miles west of Kalaheo, 15 miles west of Poipu.

Kauai's "biggest little town" is now an art colony with galleries, craft studios, cafés, a bookshop, and a lively street fair on Friday night. The main street has a new vibrancy enhanced by the restoration of several historic buildings where entrepreneurs have set up shop.

Once a bustling "free town" not tied to a plantation, Hanapepe was the center of West Side commerce, home to pool halls, a movie theater, and multiple brothels. By the 1980s, though, it was fast becoming a ghost town, its farm-based economy mirroring the decline of agriculture on the island. The emergence of Kauai coffee as a major West Side crop, a housing boom, and expanded activities at Port Allen—now the main departure point for tour boats—have given the town's economy a boost.

GETTING HERE AND AROUND

Hanapepe is just past the Eleele Shopping Center on the main highway (Route 50) as you head west. A sign leads you

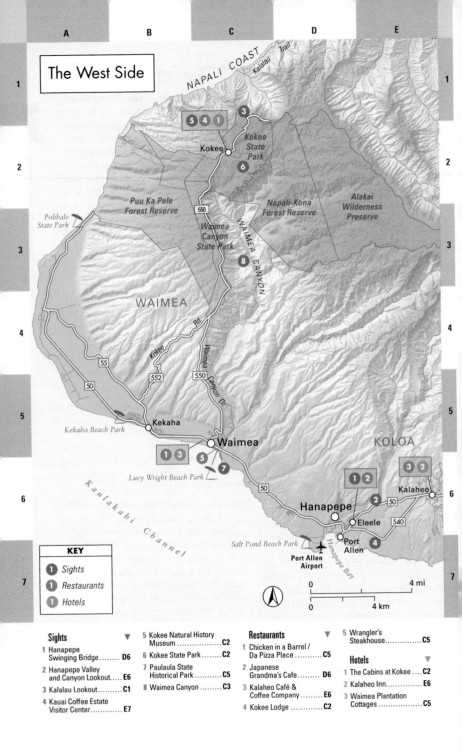

The West Side

NAPALI COAST

Kalalau Trail

⑤ ④ ①

Kokee

③

Kokee State Park

⑥

Puu Ka Pele Forest Reserve

Napali-Kona Forest Reserve

Alakai Wilderness Preserve

Polihale State Park

550

Waimea Canyon State Park

⑧

WAIMEA CANYON

WAIMEA

Kokee Rd

55

552

550

Waimea Canyon Dr

50

Kekaha Beach Park

Kekaha

① ③

⑤

Waimea

⑦

Lucy Wright Beach Park

KOLOA

③ ②

Kalaheo

② 50

Hanapepe

① ②

50

Eleele

540

② 50

Salt Pond Beach Park

Hanapepe Bay

Port Allen

④

Port Allen Airport

Kaulakahi Channel

KEY
- ① Sights
- ① Restaurants
- ① Hotels

0   4 mi
0   4 km

Sights ▼
1 Hanapepe Swinging Bridge **D6**
2 Hanapepe Valley and Canyon Lookout..... **E6**
3 Kalalau Lookout........ **C1**
4 Kauai Coffee Estate Visitor Center............. **E7**
5 Kokee Natural History Museum **C2**
6 Kokee State Park **C2**
7 Paulaula State Historical Park **C5**
8 Waimea Canyon **C3**

Restaurants ▼
1 Chicken in a Barrel / Da Pizza Place **C5**
2 Japanese Grandma's Cafe **D6**
3 Kalaheo Café & Coffee Company **E6**
4 Kokee Lodge **C2**
5 Wrangler's Steakhouse............... **C5**

Hotels ▼
1 The Cabins at Kokee **C2**
2 Kalaheo Inn............... **E6**
3 Waimea Plantation Cottages **C5**

to the town center, where street parking is easy and there's an enjoyable walking tour. Don't miss the swinging bridge.

 Sights

Hanapepe Swinging Bridge

BRIDGE | FAMILY | This narrow, pedestrian-only bridge may not be the biggest adventure on Kauai, but it's enough to make your heart hop. What is interesting is that it's not just for show; it actually provides the only access to taro fields across the Hanapepe River. Considered a historic suspension bridge even though it was rebuilt in 1996 after the early 1900s original was destroyed—like so much of the island—by Hurricane Iniki, the bridge was also repaired following flood damage in 2019. If you're in the neighborhood, it's worth a stroll. ⊠ *Off Hanapepe Rd., next to Banana Patch Studios parking lot, Hanapepe.*

Hanapepe Valley and Canyon Lookout

VIEWPOINT | From the roadside lookout, you can take in the farms on the valley floor with the majestic mountains and misty valley as a backdrop. This dramatic divide and fertile river valley once housed a thriving Hawaiian community of taro farmers, with some of the ancient fields still in cultivation. ⊠ *Rte. 50, Hanapepe.*

 Beaches

Salt Pond Beach Park

BEACH | FAMILY | A great family spot, Salt Pond Beach Park features a naturally made, shallow swimming pond behind a curling finger of rock where *keiki* (children) splash and snorkel. This pool is generally safe except during a large south summer swell. The center and western edge of the beach are popular with bodyboarders and bodysurfers. The beach is also an easy spot to see stilts, tattlers, shearwaters, and other seabirds. Pavilions with picnic tables offer shade, and there's a campground that tends to attract a rowdy bunch at the eastern end.

On a cultural note, the mudflat behind the beach is the last spot in Hawaii where salt is harvested in the dry heat of summer, using pans passed down within families. The park is popular with locals, and it can get crowded on weekends and holidays. **Amenities:** lifeguard; parking (free); showers; toilets. **Best for:** sunset; swimming; walking. ⊠ *Lolokai Rd., off Rte. 50, Hanapepe* 🅿 *Free.*

🍴 Restaurants

★ Japanese Grandma's Cafe

$$ | JAPANESE | Traditional methods for sushi, tempura, bento, and bowls meet fresh local ingredients to create delicious food in this intimate modern café at the center of old Hanapepe. One of the few sit-down dinner options in the area, Grandma's also brings in chefs for monthly tasting menus. **Known for:** trendy atmosphere; ume-tini (plum wine martini); build-your-own bento bowl. 🅢 *Average main: $22* ⊠ *3871 Hanapepe Rd., Hanapepe* 🕾 *808/855–5016* ⊕ *www.japanesegrandma.com* 🕙 *Closed Tues.*

👜 Shopping

Eleele Shopping Center

SHOPPING CENTER | Kauai's West Side has a scattering of stores, including those at this no-frills strip mall. It has a post office, several banks, a hardware store around back, a pharmacy, a laundromat, and a hair salon, and you'll rub elbows with local folks at the Big Save grocery store. Also here are a McDonald's, a Subway, and a few little local eateries. ⊠ *4469 Waialo Rd., Eleele* 🕾 *808/245–7238* ⊕ *www.eleeleshoppingcenter.com.*

★ Kauai Chocolate Company

CHOCOLATE | The signature treat here, the chocolate opihi, is made with a dash of culinary humor: layers of crispy cookie, gooey caramel, crunchy macadamia nut, and chocolate shell form a little cone … a lot like the shape and texture of limpets found clinging to shoreline rocks and also considered a delicacy. Fear not: no seafood is involved in this decadent candy. Fudge, bars, and chocolate-covered pretzels make good gifts, and the gelato is *ono* (delicious). ⊠ *4353 Waialo Rd., Suite 1B, Eleele ⊹ In Port Allen Marina* ☎ *808/335–0448* ⊕ *kauaichocolate.com.*

Talk Story Bookstore

BOOKS | Located in a historic building in quiet Hanapepe Town, this is the only bookstore on Kauai, with some 25,000 titles and a resident cat named Celeste. When Friday Art Nights are on, local authors sign their books while live music and food trucks entertain meandering crowds outside. New, used, rare, and out-of-print books are sold here, as well as vinyl records, comics, vintage video games, and Celeste's own cute sticker line. ⊠ *3785 Hanapepe Rd., Hanapepe* ☎ *808/335–6469* ⊕ *www.talkstorybookstore.com.*

Waimea and Waimea Canyon

Waimea is 7 miles northwest of Hanapepe; Waimea Canyon is approximately 10 miles northeast of Waimea.

An ideal place for a refreshment break while sightseeing on the West Side, Waimea is a serene, pretty town that has the look of the Old West and the feel of old Hawaii, with a lifestyle that's decidedly laid-back. The town has played a major role in Hawaiian history since 1778, when Captain James Cook became the first European to set foot on the Hawaiian Islands. Waimea was also the place where Kauai's King Kaumualii acquiesced to King Kamehameha's island unification drive in 1810, averting a bloody war. The town hosted the first Christian missionaries, who hauled in massive timbers and coral-stone blocks to build the sturdy Waimea Foreign Church in 1846. It's one of many lovely historic buildings preserved by residents who take great pride

in their heritage and history. The Historic Waimea Theater, which opened in 1938 with the first electric marquee lights on the island, still shows movies.

North of Waimea town, via Route 550, you'll find vast, gorgeous Waimea Canyon, also known as the Grand Canyon of the Pacific. The spectacular vistas from the lookouts along the road culminate in two overviews of Kalalau Valley, and various hiking trails lead to the inner heart of Kauai. A camera is a necessity in this region.

GETTING HERE AND AROUND

Route 50 continues northwest to Waimea and Kekaha from Hanapepe. You can reach Waimea Canyon and Kokee State Park from either town—the way is clearly marked. Some pull-off areas on Route 550 are fine for a quick view of the canyon, but the designated lookouts have bathrooms and parking.

Sights

Kalalau Lookout

VIEWPOINT | At the end of the road, high above Waimea Canyon, the Kalalau Lookout marks the start of a 1-mile (one-way) walk along the road to the Puu o Kila Lookout. On a clear day at either spot, you can see a dreamy landscape of gaping valleys, sawtooth ridges, waterfalls, and turquoise seas, where whales can be seen spouting and breaching during the winter months. If clouds block the view, don't despair—they tend to blow through fast, giving you time to snap that photo of a lifetime. You may spot wild goats clambering on the sheer rocky cliffs and white-tailed tropicbirds. If it's very clear to the northwest, drink in the shining sands of Kalalau Beach, gleaming like golden threads against the deep blue of the Pacific. ⊠ *Kokee State Park, Waimea Canyon Dr. ⊹ 4 miles beyond Kokee Museum* ⊕ *dlnr.hawaii.gov/dsp/parks* ☞ *$10 parking and $5 per person admission fee for nonresidents.*

Birds of Kauai

Kauai offers some of the best birding in the state, due in part to the absence of the mongoose. Many nene (the endangered Hawaiian state bird) reared in captivity have been successfully released here, along with an endangered forest bird called the puaiohi. The island is also home to multiple species of migratory nesting seabirds and has three refuges protecting endangered Hawaiian waterbirds and seabirds. The Kokee

Natural History Museum and Kilauea Lighthouse have informative displays.

Kauai's most noticeable fowl, however, is the wild chicken. A cross between jungle fowl (*moa*) brought by the Polynesians and domestic chickens and fighting cocks that escaped during the last two hurricanes, they are everywhere, and the roosters crow when they feel like it, not only at dawn. Consider yourself warned.

Kokee Natural History Museum

SCIENCE MUSEUM | FAMILY | A great place to start your visit in Kokee State Park, the museum has friendly staff who are knowledgeable about trail conditions and weather, as well as informative displays and a good selection of books about the area's unique native flora and fauna and social history. You may also find that special memento or gift you've been looking for. ■ TIP→ Note that the park has no cell service, but a pay phone is outside the museum. ⊠ *Rte. 550, Kokee* ⊹ *In Kanaloahuluhulu Meadow, after mile marker 15 mile* ☎ *808/335–9975* ⊕ *kokee.org* 🎫 *Donations welcome.*

Kokee State Park

STATE/PROVINCIAL PARK | FAMILY | This 4,345-acre wilderness park is 4,000 feet above sea level, an elevation that affords you breathtaking views and a cooler, wetter climate that's in marked contrast to the beach. You can gain a deeper appreciation of the island's rugged terrain and dramatic beauty from this vantage point. Large tracts of native ohia and koa forest cover much of the land, along with many varieties of exotic plants. Hikers can follow a 45-mile network of trails through diverse landscapes that feel wonderfully remote—until the tour helicopters pass overhead. The small nonprofit museum

provides park information, and the lodge offers hearty lunches. ■ TIP→ Note that there's no cell phone service in the park. ⊠ *Rte. 550, Kekaha* ⊹ *15 miles north of Kekaha* ⊕ *kokee.org, dlnr.hawaii.gov/dsp* 🎫 *$10 parking and $5 per person fee for nonresidents.*

Paulaula State Historical Park (*Russian Fort Elizabeth*)

RUINS | The ruins of this stone fort, built in 1816 by an agent of the imperial Russian government named Georg Anton Schäffer, are a reminder of the days when he tried to conquer the island for his homeland, or so one story goes. Another claims that Schäffer's allegiance lay with King Kaumualii, who was attempting to keep leadership of his island nation from the grasp of Kamehameha the Great. The crumbling walls of the fort, a National Historic Landmark, are not particularly interesting, but the signs loaded with historical information are. A bronze statue of King Kaumualii was installed in 2021, marking 200 years since the king was kidnapped to Oahu aboard the ship *Haaheo o Hawaii* in July 1821, during a reception aboard. ⊠ *Rte. 50, Waimea (Kauai County)* ⊹ *Just above Waimea River bridge* ⊕ *dlnr.hawaii.gov/dsp, www.kauaikingkaumualii.org* 🎫 *Free.*

★ Waimea Canyon

CANYON | Carved over countless centuries by the Waimea River and the forces of wind and rain, Waimea Canyon is a dramatic gorge nicknamed the "Grand Canyon of the Pacific"—but not by Mark Twain, as many people mistakenly think. Hiking and hunting trails wind through the canyon, which is more than 3,600 feet deep, 1 mile wide, and about 14 miles long. The cliff sides have been sharply eroded, exposing swatches of colorful soil. The deep red, brown, and green hues are constantly changing in the sun, and frequent rainbows and waterfalls enhance the natural beauty. This is one of Kauai's prettiest spots, and it's worth stopping at both the Puu ka Pele and Puu Hinahina lookouts within the state park.

Clean public restrooms and parking are at both lookouts, and the main lookout has ramps for strollers and wheelchairs. If you stop at small pullouts, park completely off the highway and be alert to cyclists. ✉ *Waimea Canyon State Park, Rte. 550 (Kokee Rd.), Waimea (Kauai County)* ☎ *808/274–3444* ⊕ *dlnr.hawaii. gov/dsp* ☁ *$10 parking and $5 per person daily fee for nonresidents at main park lookouts.*

Beaches

Kekaha Beach Park

BEACH | This is one of the premier spots on Kauai for sunset walks and the start of the state's longest beach. We don't recommend much water activity here without first talking to a lifeguard. The beach is exposed to open ocean and has an onshore break that can be hazardous any time of year. However, there are some excellent surf breaks for experienced surfers. If you'd like to run or stroll on a beach, this is the one—the hard-packed sand goes on for miles, all the way to Napali Coast, but you won't get past the Pacific Missile Range Facility and its access restrictions. Another bonus for this beach is its relatively dry weather year-round. If it's raining where you are, try Kekaha Beach Park. Toilets at the west MacArthur Park section are the portable kind. **Amenities:** lifeguards; parking (free); showers; toilets. **Best for:** sunset; surfing; walking. ✉ *Rte. 50, near mile marker 27, Kekaha* ☁ *Free.*

★ Polihale State Park

BEACH | The longest stretch of beach in Hawaii starts in Kekaha and ends west about 15 miles away at the start of Napali Coast. On the far west end is the 5-mile-long, 140-acre Polihale State Park, a remote beach accessed via a rough, rutted, potholed, 5-mile road at the end of Route 50 in Mana. (Four-wheel drive is recommended, and rental car companies may prohibit use of their vehicles here.) In addition to being long, this beach is 300 feet wide in places and backed by sand dunes 50 to 100 feet tall. Cultural sites, including burials, are located within the sensitive dune system. It is frequently very hot, with almost no shade and scorching sand. Start the day with a full tank of gas and a cooler filled with food and drink. ⚠ **Though it's a popular beach, the ocean here has dangerous currents and is not recommended for recreation.** No driving is allowed on the beach. The U.S. Navy's Pacific Missile Range Facility is adjacent, so access to the coastline in front of the base is monitored and restricted. Note that the park is open for day use only; camping permits are required when overnight use is allowed. **Amenities:** parking (free); showers; toilets. **Best for:** solitude; sunset; walking. ✉ *Dirt road at end of Rte. 50, Kekaha* ☎ *808/587–0300* ⊕ *dlnr.hawaii.gov/dsp.*

Restaurants

Chicken in a Barrel / Da Pizza Place

$ | AMERICAN | FAMILY | Located in the laid-back Waimea Plantation Cottages hotel, this equally casual eatery has a veranda that's a great place to sit with a beer and watch the sunset while the kids run around on the lawn. The fare is simple and hearty: barrel-smoked barbecue chicken, pork, brisket, or ribs; plus salads, tacos, burgers, and pizza. **Known for:** good breakfast options; great selection of sides; large portions. S *Average main: $15* ✉ *9400 Kaumualii Hwy., Waimea (Kauai County)* ☎ *808/320–8379* ⊕ *www. chickeninabarrel.com.*

Kokee Lodge

$ | AMERICAN | Talk about "farm to table"—Kokee Lodge grows much of its own produce, and the tables are handmade from local lumber. Makaweli beef is used for *loco mocos* (white rice topped with a hamburger patty, brown gravy, and fried egg) and burgers, which can be served on fresh greens with house-made dressings; a veggie strata or a kalua pork plate, with Kokee plum barbecue sauce, is a perfect hot lunch on chilly days. **Known for:** Portuguese bean soup; pie and specialty coffee; live music on weekends. S *Average main: $12* ✉ *Kokee State Park, 3600 Kokee Rd., mile marker 15, Kokee* ☎ *808/335–6061* ⊕ *kokeelodge.com* ⊙ *No dinner.*

Wrangler's Steakhouse

$$$ | STEAKHOUSE | FAMILY | Steaks are grilled over kiawe wood and ribs are succulent here, although Wrangler's could be called "Anglers" instead, as they do a nice job with fresh fish, too; a trip to a small salad bar, soup, and sides are included with entrées. Local folks love the *kaukau* tin special: rice, chicken teriyaki, and vegetable tempura with kimchi served in a three-tier *kaukau* tin, a lunch pail just like the ones sugar-plantation workers once carried. **Known for:** local, grass-fed beef; sushi nights (reservations required); Western decor. S *Average main: $32* ✉ *9852 Kaumualii Hwy., Waimea (Kauai County)* ☎ *808/338–1218* ⊙ *Closed Sun. and Mon. No lunch.*

Hotels

The Cabins at Kokee

$ | HOUSE | If you're an outdoors enthusiast, you can appreciate Kauai's mountain wilderness from the dozen rustic cabins—of varying age and quality—that make up this lodge. **Pros:** outstanding setting; more refined than camping; cooking facilities. **Cons:** no Wi-Fi or cell service; $45 cleaning fee; wood-burning stove is the only heat. S *Rooms from: $89* ✉ *Kokee State Park, 3600 Kokee Rd., at mile marker 15, Kokee* ☎ *808/652–6852* ⊕ *www.westkauailodging.com* ⤳ *12 cabins* ○| *No Meals.*

★ Waimea Plantation Cottages

$$ | RESORT | Originally built in the early 1900s, these relocated and refurbished one- to five-bedroom sugar-plantation workers' cottages are tucked in a coconut grove along a lovely, walkable stretch of beach on the sunny West Side. **Pros:** unique lodging experience; quiet and low-key; lovely grounds. **Cons:** rooms are simple; cottages can be hot in summer; not a good swimming beach. S *Rooms from: $250* ✉ *9400 Kaumualii Hwy., Waimea (Kauai County)* ☎ *808/338–1923, 800/716–6199* ⊕ *www.coasthotels.com* ⤳ *56 cottages* ○| *No Meals.*

● Shopping

Menehune Food Mart

CONVENIENCE STORE | Besides the grocery stores in Waimea Town two miles away, this locally owned minimart in Kekaha is the last stop for snacks, beverages, ice, sunscreen, and limited grocery items before folks head up to Waimea Canyon or out to Polihale Beach. ✉ *8171 Kekaha Rd., at Rte. 50, Kekaha* ☎ *808/337–1335.*

Activities and Tours

Kauai's outdoor recreation options extend well beyond the sand and surf, with plenty of activities to keep you busy on the ground and even in the air. You can hike the island's many trails, or consider taking your vacation into flight with a treetop zip line. You can have a backcountry adventure in a four-wheel drive, or relax in an inner tube floating down old cane-field irrigation canals.

Before booking tours, check with your concierge to find out what the forecast is for water and weather conditions. If you check online weather sources, be sure you search for Kauai-specific weather. There's plenty of variation around the Islands. If you happen to arrive during a lull in the North Shore surf, you'll want to plan to be on the ocean in a kayak or snorkeling on the reef. If it's raining, ATV tours are the activity of choice.

Golfers should be aware that Kauai's spectacular courses are rated among the most scenic, as well as the most technical, in the country. Princeville Makai Golf Course has garnered accolades from numerous national publications, and Poipu Bay Golf Course hosted the prestigious season-end PGA Grand Slam of Golf for 13 years.

One of the most popular, though pricey, Kauai experiences is to tour the island from the air. In an hour or so, you can see waterfalls, craters, and other places that are inaccessible even by hiking trails (some say that 70% or more of the island is inaccessible). The majority of flights depart from the Lihue airport and follow a clockwise pattern around the island. Be prepared to relive your flight in dreams for the rest of your life. The most popular flight is 60 minutes long. ■ TIP→ If you plan to take an aerial tour, it's a good idea to fly when you first arrive, rather than saving it for the end of your trip. It will help you visualize what's where on the island, and it may help you decide what you want to see from a closer vantage point during your stay.

Ancient Hawaiians were water-sports fanatics—they invented surfing, after all—and that propensity hasn't strayed far from today's mindset. Even if you're not into water sports or sports in general, there's only a slim chance that you'll leave this island without getting out on the ocean, because Kauai's top attraction—Napali Coast—is not to be missed.

For those who can't pack enough snorkeling, fishing, bodyboarding, or surfing time into a vacation, Kauai has it all—everything except parasailing, that is, as it's illegal to do it here (though not on Maui, the Big Island, or Oahu). If you need to rent gear for any of these activities, you'll find plenty of places with large selections at reasonable prices. And no matter what part of the island you're staying on, you'll have several options for choice spots to enjoy playing in the water.

One thing to note, and we can't say this enough—the waters off the coast of Kauai have strong currents and can be unpredictable, so always err on the side of caution and know your limits. Follow the tagline repeated by the island's lifeguards—"When in doubt, don't go out."

Aerial Tours

If you only drive around Kauai in your rental car, you will not see *all* of Kauai. There is truly only one way to see it all, and that's by air. Helicopter tours are the favorite way to get a bird's-eye view of Kauai—they fly at lower altitudes, hover above waterfalls, and wiggle their way into areas that a fixed-wing aircraft cannot. That said, if you've already tried the helitour, how about flying in the open cockpit of a biplane, à la the Red Baron?

Air Tour Kauai

AIR EXCURSIONS | This company can hold up to six people in its Cessna 206 plane, where every seat has a big window. The flights take off from less crowded Port Allen Airport on the West Side and last 65 to 70 minutes. ⊠ *Port Allen Airport, 3441 Kuiloko Rd., Hanapepe* ☎ *808/335–5859* ⊕ *www.airtourkauai.com* 🖳 *$99.*

Blue Hawaiian Helicopters

AIR EXCURSIONS | This multi-island operator flies the latest in helicopter technology, the spacious Eco-Star. It boasts 23% more interior space for its six passengers, as well as unparalleled viewing and a few extra safety features. As the name implies, the helicopter is also a bit more environmentally friendly, with a 50% noise-reduction rate. A DVD of your tour is available for an additional $25. Charters can be arranged. ⊠ *3651 Ahukini Rd., Heliport 8, Lihue* ☎ *808/245–5800, 800/745–2583* ⊕ *www.bluehawaiian.com* 🖳 *$339.*

★ Jack Harter Helicopters

AIR EXCURSIONS | The first company to offer helicopter tours on Kauai flies the six-passenger ASTAR helicopter with floor-to-ceiling windows, as well as the four-person Hughes 500, which is flown with no doors. The exciting doorless ride can get windy, but it's the best bet for taking reflection-free photos. Pilots provide information on the Garden Island's history and geography through two-way intercoms. The company flies out of Lihue. Tours are longer than the average at 60 to 65 minutes and 90 to 95 minutes. ⊠ *4231 Ahukini Rd., Lihue* ☎ *808/245–3774, 888/245–2001* ⊕ *www. helicopters-kauai.com* 🖳 *From $339.*

Sunshine Helicopters

AIR EXCURSIONS | If the name of this company sounds familiar, it may be because its pilots fly on all the main Hawaiian Islands except Oahu. On Kauai, Sunshine Helicopters flies the six-passenger FX STAR or the super-roomy six-passenger WhisperSTAR birds. Flights are from Lihue and last 50 to 55 minutes. ■ TIP→ **Discounts can be substantial by booking online and taking**

advantage of the "early bird" seating during off-hours. ⊠ *3730 Ahukini Rd., #2, Lihue* ☎ *808/270–3999, 866/501–7738* ⊕ *www. sunshinehelicopters.com* 🖳 *From $230.*

ATV Tours

Although all the beaches on the island are public, much of the low-elevation interior land—once sugar and pineapple plantations—is privately owned. This is really a shame, because the valleys and mountains that make up the vast interior of the island easily rival the beaches in sheer beauty. The good news: some tour operators have agreements with landowners that make exploration possible, albeit a bit bumpy—and unless you have back troubles, that's half the fun. ■ TIP→ **If it looks like rain, book an ATV tour ASAP. That's the thing about these tours: the muddier, the better.**

★ Kauai ATV

FOUR-WHEELING | This is *the* thing to do when it rains on Kauai—if you're into an extreme mud bath. Kauai ATV in Koloa is the originator of the island's all-terrain-vehicle tours and has upgraded with a brand-new fleet of UTVs (utility task vehicles). The three-hour Koloa tour takes you on 18 miles of trails through a private sugar plantation and historic haul-cane tunnel. It includes visits to movie filming sites and Waita Reservoir for catch-and-release fishing. You must be 18 or older to operate your own vehicle, but Kauai ATV also offers its four-passenger "Ohana Bug" and two-passenger "Mud Bugs" to accommodate families with kids ages 5 and older. You must be 25 or older to drive minors under age 18. ⊠ *3477A Weliweli Rd., Koloa* ☎ *808/742–2734* ⊕ *www.kauaiatv.com* 🖳 *From $253 for 2 people.*

Kipu Ranch Adventures

FOUR-WHEELING | This 3,000-acre property extends from the Huleia River to the top of Mt. Haupu. *Jurassic Park* and *Indiana Jones* were filmed here, and you'll see the locations for them on either of the three-hour tours. The Ranch Tour covers a lot of territory so you'll see a range of landscapes, from pastures to rain forest. The Waterfall Tour includes waterfall views and a swim. Once a sugar plantation, Kipu Ranch today is a working cattle ranch, so you'll be in the company of bovines as well as pheasants, wild boars, and peacocks. If you're not an experienced ATV driver, they also offer guide-driven tour options. ⊠ *235 Kipu Rd., off Hwy. 50, Lihue* ☎ *808/246–9288* ⊕ *www.kiputours.com* ☎ *From $187.*

Biking

Kauai is a labyrinth of cane-haul roads, which are fun for exploring on two wheels. The challenge is finding roads where biking is allowed and then not getting lost in the maze. Maybe that explains why Kauai is not a hub for the sport—yet. Still, there are some epic rides for those who are interested, both the adrenaline-rush and the mellower beach-cruiser kind. If you want to grind out some mileage, you could take the main highway that skirts the coastal area, but be careful: there are only a few designated bike lanes, the shoulders are often crowded with invasive guinea grass, and the terrain is hilly. You may find that keeping your eyes on the road rather than the scenery is your biggest challenge. "Cruisers" should head to Kapaa, where Ke Ala Hele Makalae, a pedestrian and bicycle trail, runs along the East Side of Kauai for miles.

You can rent bikes (with helmets) from the activities desks of certain hotels, but these are not the best quality. You're better off renting from Hele On Kauai in Kapaa, Outfitters Kauai in Poipu, or Pedal 'n' Paddle in Hanalei. Ask for the "Go Green Kauai" map for a full description of Kauai biking options.

BEST SPOTS
★ Ke Ala Hele Makalae

BIKING | FAMILY | This county beach park multi-use path follows the coastline on Kauai's East Side and is perfect for cruisers. Eventually, the path is projected to run some 20 miles, but an existing 8-mile-long stretch already offers scenic views, picnic pavilions, and restroom facilities along the way—all in compliance with the Americans with Disabilities Act. The path runs from Lydgate Beach Park north to secluded Kuna Bay (aka Donkey Beach).

An easy way to access the longest completed section of the path is from Kealia Beach. Park here and head north into rural lands with spectacular coastline vistas, or head south into Kapaa for a more immersive experience. ⊠ *Kealia Beach, Kapaa* ✛ *Trailhead: 1 mile north of Kapaa; park at north end of Kealia Beach* ⊕ *www.kauaipath.org.*

Kokee Road

BIKING | Those wanting a challenging workout can climb this road, also known as Route 550. After a 3,000-foot climb, Kokee Road levels out somewhat and continues for several miles past the Kokee Natural History Museum, ending at the spectacular Kalalau Lookout. It's uphill 100% and curvy, and the ride down can be a bit wild. Cyclists should exercise extreme caution on this road. Though it is paved the entire way, expect potholes and consistent vehicular traffic, including tour buses. Some cyclists use Waimea Canyon Road for the ascent, but it is steeper and narrower, with more potholes and an extremely precarious descent. ■ **TIP→ There's not much of a shoulder on either road—sometimes none—so be extra careful.** Both roads get busier as the day wears on, so you may want to consider a sunrise ride.

Bicycles aren't allowed on the hiking trails in and around Waimea Canyon and Kokee State Park, but there are miles of wonderful four-wheel-drive roads perfect

Bikers who prefer a leisurely cruise can pedal along the Ke Ala Hele Makalae trail, an 8-mile, multiuse path in Kapaa.

for mountain biking. Check at the Kokee Museum for a map and conditions. ⊠ *Off Rte. 50, near grocery store, Waimea (Kauai County).*

Moalepe Trail

BIKING | Intermediate to advanced trail-bike riders can tackle this trail on the East Side. The first 2 miles of the 5-mile narrow dirt road wind through pastureland, but the real challenge begins when you reach the steep and rutted switchbacks. A rainy spell can make the mud slick and hazardous. Moalepe intersects the Kuilau Trail, which you can follow to its end at the Keahua Arboretum stream, though the riding is more challenging on this section. ⊠ *Wailua (Kauai County)* ⊕ *From Kuhio Hwy. in Kapaa drive mauka (toward mountains) on Kuamoo Rd. for 3 miles and turn right on Kamalu Rd., which dead-ends at Olohena Rd. Turn left and follow until road veers sharply right.*

Powerline Trail

BIKING | Even advanced riders are challenged by this trail, which is actually an abandoned electric-company service road that splits the island. It's 13 miles long; the first 5 miles go from 620 feet in elevation to almost 2,000. The remaining 8 miles descend gradually over a variety of terrain, some technical. You'll have to carry your bike through some sections, but the views will stay with you forever. It offers little shade, so be prepared for the heat. ■**TIP**➔ **When it's wet—in summer or winter—this trail is a mess. Check with a knowledgeable bike shop for trail conditions first and be prepared to improvise.** ⊠ *Powerline Rd., Kilauea* ⊕ *The trailhead is mauka (toward the mountains), just past stream crossing at Keahua Arboretum, or at end of Powerline Rd. in Princeville, past Princeville Ranch Stables.*

Spalding Monument

BIKING | A good option for the novice rider, this ride offers a workout and a summit ocean view that's not overly strenuous to reach. If you pick up a bike at Kauai Cycle in Kapaa, you can pedal a mile up Ke Ala Hele Makalae to reach the start of the ride. From near the end of Kealia Beach, ride up a gradual incline 2 miles through horse pastures to Spalding Monument, named for a former plantation owner. Palms circle the lava-rock wall, where you can picnic while enjoying a 180-degree ocean view. Behind you is the glorious mountain backdrop of Kalalea. Coasting back down the road offers an almost continual ocean view along with a peek into rural Kauai most visitors miss. ⊠ *Kealia* ✛ *The loop begins at the end of Kealia Beach, past mile marker 10 on mauka (mountain) side of road.*

Wailua Forest Management Road

BIKING | For the novice mountain biker, this is an easy ride, and it's also easy to find. From Route 56 in Wailua, turn *mauka* (toward the mountains) on Kuamoo Road and continue 6 miles to the picnic area known as Keahua Arboretum; park here. After crossing the stream on a bridge, you'll be biking along a potholed four-wheel-drive road through lush vegetation—stay away during heavy rains because the streams flood—that continues for 2 miles to a T-stop, where you should turn right. Stay on the road for about 3 miles until you reach a gate; this is the spot where the gates in the movie *Jurassic Park* were filmed, though it looks nothing like the movie. Go around the gate and down the road for another mile to a confluence of streams at the base of Mt. Waialeale. Be sure to bring your camera. ⊠ *Kuamoo Rd., Kapaa.*

EQUIPMENT AND TOURS
Hele On Kauai

BIKING | In a location offering easy access to the Ke Ala Hele Makalae bike trail, this shop has a range of rental options, including beach cruisers, hybrids, mountain bikes, road bikes, and even electric bikes, by the hour and day. They also service bikes and sell bikes and riding gear. You can even arrange to have bikes delivered to a riding location for a fee. Rental hours are 11 am to 2 pm, Tuesday through Sunday. ⊠ *4–1302 Kuhio Hwy., Kapaa* ☎ *808/822–4628* ⊕ *www. kauaibeachbikerentals.com* 🚲 *Rentals from $15 per hr.*

Kauai Cycle

BIKING | This reliable, full-service bike shop sells and repairs bikes and has a wide range of cycling gear. The Ke Ala Hele Makalae coastal path is right out the back door. ⊠ *4–934 Kuhio Hwy., Kapaa* ✛ *Across from Taco Bell* ☎ *808/821–2115* ⊕ *www.kauaicycle.com.*

Pedal 'n' Paddle

BIKING | Located in the heart of Hanalei, this company rents old-fashioned, single-speed beach cruisers. This is a great way to cruise the town. It's not recommended to venture out of town because there are no bike lanes on the twisting-and-turning road. ⊠ *Ching Young Village, 5–5190 Kuhio Hwy., Hanalei* ☎ *808/826–9069* ⊕ *www.pedalnpaddle. com* 🚲 *Rentals from $15 per day and $60 per wk.*

Boat Tours

Deciding to see Napali Coast by boat is an easy decision, but choosing the outfitter to go with is not. There are numerous boat-tour operators to choose from, and, quite frankly, they all do a good job. Before you even start thinking about whom to go out with, answer these three questions: What kind of boat do I prefer? Where am I staying? Do I want to go in the morning or afternoon? Once you settle on these three, you can easily zero in on the tour outfitter.

First, the boat. The most important thing is to match your personality and that of your group with the personality of the boat. If you like thrills and adventure, the rubber inflatable rafts—often Zodiacs, which Jacques Cousteau made famous and which the U.S. Coast Guard uses—will entice you. They're fast, likely to leave you drenched and windswept, and quite bouncy. If you prefer a smoother, more leisurely ride, then the large catamarans are the way to go.

The next boat choice is size. Both the rafts and catamarans come in small and large. Again—think smaller, more adventurous, and a rougher ride or larger, more leisurely, and comfortable. ■TIP➡ **Do not choose a smaller boat simply because you think there will be fewer people. There might be fewer people, but you'll be jammed together sitting close to strangers.** If you prefer privacy over socializing, go with a larger boat, so you'll have more room to spread out. The smaller boats will take you along the coast at a higher rate of speed, making photo opportunities a bit more challenging. One advantage to smaller boats, however, is that—depending on ocean conditions—some may slip into a sea cave or two. If that sounds interesting to you, call the outfitter and ask their policy on entering sea caves. Some won't, no matter the conditions, because they consider such actions inappropriate or because they don't want to cause any environmental damage.

Boats leave from three points around the island (Hanalei, Port Allen, and Waimea), and all head to the same spot: Napali Coast. If you're staying on the North Shore, choose to depart out of the North Shore, except in wintertime when the boats sometimes can't navigate the big surf. If you're staying anywhere else, depart out of the West Side. It's that easy. Sure, the North Shore is closer to Napali Coast; however, you'll pay more for less overall time. The West Side boat operators may spend more time getting to Napali Coast, but they'll spend about the same amount of time along Napali, plus you'll pay less.

Finally, you'll also have to decide whether you want to go on a morning tour, which includes a deli lunch and a stop for snorkeling, or an afternoon tour, which does not always stop to snorkel but does include a sunset over the ocean. The morning tours with snorkeling are more popular with families and those who love dolphins, as the animals enjoy the "waves" created by the front of the catamarans and might just escort you down the coast. Hawaiian spinner dolphins are so plentiful in the mornings that some tour companies guarantee you'll see them, though you won't get in the water and swim with them. The winter months will also be a good chance to spot some whales breaching, though surf is much rougher along Napali. You don't have to be an expert snorkeler or even have any prior experience, but if it is your first time, note that although there will be some snorkeling instruction, there might not be much and you'll be in deep water in the open ocean. The afternoon tours are more popular with nonsnorkelers—obviously—and photographers interested in capturing the setting sunlight on the coast. Another factor to consider is that the winds often pick up in the afternoons, making the water rougher. ■TIP➡ **No matter which tour you select, book it online whenever possible to ensure a spot.**

CATAMARAN TOURS
★ Blue Dolphin Charters

BOATING | Offering the largest selection of tours, Blue Dolphin operates 65-foot sailing (rarely raised and always motoring) catamarans designed with three decks of spacious seating with great visibility, as well as motorized rafts. ■TIP➡ **The lower deck is best for shade seekers.** The most popular is a daylong tour of Napali Coast, which includes snorkeling and diving. Morning snorkel tours of Napali include a deli lunch. Sunset sightseeing tours include a Hawaiian-style buffet. North Shore and South Shore rafting tours are also available, as are daily sportfishing charters of four to eight hours for no more than six guests. Blue Dolphin promises dolphin sightings and the best mai tais "off the island." Book online in at least ten days advance for a $10 discount. ✉ *4353 Waialo Rd., #7B, Eleele* ☎ *808/335–5553* ⊕ *www.kauaiboats.com* ✆ *From $180; 2-hr whale-watching/sunset tours, winter only, $110.*

Boat Tour Weather Cancellations

If it's raining where you're staying, that doesn't mean it's raining over the water, so don't shy away from a boat tour. Besides, it's not the rain that should concern you—it's the wind and waves. Especially from due north and south, wind creates surface chop and makes for rough riding. Larger craft are designed to handle winter's ocean swells, however, so unless monster waves are out there, your tour should depart without a hitch. If the water is too rough, your boat captain may reroute to calmer waters. It's a tough call to make, but your comfort and safety are always the foremost factor.

In winter months, North Shore departures are cancelled much more often than those departing the West Side. This is because the waves are often too big for the boats to leave Hanalei Bay, and as a result, some operators only work the summer season. If you want the closest thing to a guarantee of seeing Napali Coast in winter, choose a West Side outfitter. Oh, and even if your tour boat says it cruises the "entire Napali," keep in mind that "ocean conditions permitting" is always implied.

★ **Capt. Andy's Sailing Adventures**
BOATING | FAMILY | Departing from Port Allen on the West Side and running 55- and 60-foot sailing catamarans, as well as 24-foot inflatables out of Kikiaola Harbor in Kekaha, Capt. Andy's offers something for every taste, from raft expeditions to yachting. They have several lunch and snorkeling packages and four-hour sunset tours along Napali Coast. The Zodiac rafts have hydrophones to hear whales and other underwater sounds. The longtime Kauai company also operates a snorkel barbecue sail and a dinner sunset sail aboard its *Southern Star* yacht, originally built for private charters, for an upgraded feel. ■TIP➔ **If the winds and swells are up on the North Shore, this company is usually a good choice—especially if you're prone to seasickness.** ⊠ *4353 Waiola Rd., Suite 1A–2A, Eleele* ☎ *808/335–6833* ⊕ *www.napali.com* ⌲ *From $99.*

Catamaran Kahanu
BOATING | Hawaiian-owned and-operated, Catamaran Kahanu has been in business since 1985 and runs a 40-foot power catamaran with 18-passenger seating. It offers seasonal whale-watching and snorkeling

cruises, ranging from two to five hours, and departs from Port Allen. The five-hour, year-round Napali Coast tour includes snorkeling at Nualolo Kai, plus a deli lunch and soft drinks. No alcohol is allowed. Check-in is at 7 am, and the boat returns at approximately 1 pm. The tour feels more personal than some operations, with a laid-back, *ohana* (family) style, and information is shared about Hawaiian culture and the natural environment. The two-hour whale-watching tour is available from late December through March and begins at 1 and 3:30 pm. ⊠ *4353 Waialo Rd., near Port Allen Marina Center, Eleele* ☎ *808/645–6176* ⊕ *www.catamarankahanu.com* ⌲ *From $90.*

Holo Holo Charters
BOATING | Choose between the 50-foot catamaran called *Leila* for a morning snorkel sail to Napali Coast or the 65-foot *Holo Holo* for a seven-hour catamaran trip to the "forbidden island" of Niihau. Both boats have large cabins and little outside seating. Holo Holo also offers a four-hour seasonal voyage along Napali from Hanalei Bay on its rigid-hull inflatable rafts, specifically for diving and snorkeling. Originators of the Niihau tour,

If you choose to sail by yourself in Kauai, be prepared for strong currents and know your limits.

Holo Holo Charters built their 65-foot powered catamaran with a wide beam to reduce side-to-side motion and twin 425 HP turbo diesel engines specifically for the 17-mile channel crossing to Niihau. It's the only outfitter running daily Niihau tours. The *Holo Holo* also embarks on a daily sunset and sightseeing tour of Napali Coast. *Leila* can hold 37 passengers, while her big sister can take a maximum of 47. Check-in is at Port Allen Marina Center. ✉ *4353 Waialo Rd., Suite 5A, Eleele* ☎ *808/335-0815* ⊕ *www.holoholocharters.com* ⌨ *From $159.*

Kauai Sea Tours

BOATING | Sailing from Port Allen, this company operates the *Lucky Lady,* a 60-foot sailing catamaran with spacious seating, and the sleeker, faster *Imiloa,* a 40-foot express catamaran. Snorkeling tours anchor near Makole (based on the captain's discretion). If snorkeling isn't your thing, try the two-hour, seasonal whale-watching cruise or the four-hour sunset tour with beer, wine, mai tais, *pupu* (appetizers), and a hot buffet dinner.

Tours of Napali, one with a beach landing in a remote valley, are offered on inflatable rafts. ✉ *4353 Waialo Rd., 2B–3B, Eleele* ☎ *808/335-5309, 800/733-7997* ⊕ *www.kauaiseatours.com* ⌨ *From $125.*

Liko Kauai Cruises

BOATING | There are many things to like about Liko Kauai Cruises, including the choice of a 49-foot smooth-riding powered catamaran that carries a maximum of 32 passengers or the 32-foot custom-built lightning catamaran that accommodates 12. Sometimes, Captain Liko himself—a Native Hawaiian—still takes the helm. The larger vessel, with its 360-degree walk-around, is perfect for photography. Both boats have a freshwater shower on board and offer five-hour morning and afternoon tours of Napali that include snorkeling, food, and soft drinks. Trips usually depart out of Kikiaola Harbor in Waimea, a bit closer to Napali Coast than those leaving from Port Allen. ✉ *4516 Alawai Rd., Waimea (Kauai County)* ☎ *808/338-0333* ⊕ *www.liko-kauai.com* ⌨ *From $169.*

RAFT TOURS

Blue Ocean Adventure Tours

BOATING | This West Side–based company focuses on Napali Coast tours using either rafts or a super-fast and comfortable 48-foot catamaran. The five-hour morning and afternoon tours cover the entire 17-mile coast, with snorkeling, snacks, and photography stops. A six-hour tour option also includes landing at Nualolo Kai for a Hawaiian-style buffet picnic on the beach and 30-minute nature walk. The tours are lively and informative. Private adventures can be arranged. ✉ *Kikiaola Small Boat Harbor, 8932 Kekaha Rd., Kekaha* ☎ *800/451–6133* ⊕ *goblueadventure.com* ✆ *From $169.*

Kauai Sea Tours

BOATING | The company holds a special permit from the state to land at Nualolo Kai along Napali Coast, ocean conditions permitting. Here, you'll enjoy a picnic lunch, as well as an archaeological tour of an ancient Hawaiian fishing village, ocean conditions permitting. Kauai Sea Tours operates four 24-foot inflatable rafts—maximum occupancy 14. These are small enough for checking out the insides of sea caves and the undersides of waterfalls. Four different tours are available, with morning and afternoon departures. ✉ *Port Allen Marina Center, 4353 Waialo Rd., 2B–3B, Eleele* ☎ *808/335–5309, 800/733–7997* ⊕ *www.kauaiseatours. com* ✆ *From $180.*

Na Pali Riders

BOATING | This tour-boat outfitter distinguishes itself by cruising the entire 17-mile Napali Coast, clear to Kee Beach and back. It's a no-frills tour—no lunch provided, just beverages and snacks. The company runs morning and afternoon four-hour snorkeling, sightseeing, and whale-watching trips out of Kikiaola Harbor in Waimea on a 30-foot inflatable raft with a 28-passenger maximum, which can feel a bit cramped. ✉ *9600 Kaumualii Hwy., Waimea (Kauai County)* ☎ *808/742–6331* ⊕ *www.napaliriders.com* ✆ *$169.*

Z-Tourz

BOATING | FAMILY | What we like about Z-Tourz is that it's a boat company that makes safety and snorkeling its priority. Its two- and three-hour guided tours focus solely on the South Shore's abundant offshore reefs. If you're new to snorkeling, or want someone to actually identify the tropical reef fish you're seeing, this is your company. Turtle sightings are pretty much guaranteed. The craft is a 26-foot rigid-hull inflatable (think Zodiac) with a maximum of 16 passengers. Rates include snacks and snorkel gear. Snorkeling tours that depart from the shore (no boats) are also available. ✉ *3417 Poipu Rd., #105, Poipu* ☎ *808/742–7422* ⊕ *www.kauaiztours.com* ✆ *From $125.*

RIVERBOAT TOURS TO FERN GROTTO

Smith's Motor Boat Service

BOATING | The 2-mile trip up the lush and lovely Wailua River, the only navigable waterway in Hawaii, culminates at the Fern Grotto, a yawning lava tube that is covered with fishtail ferns. During the boat ride, guitar and ukulele players serenade you with Hawaiian melodies and tell the history of the river. It's a kitschy, but fun, bit of Hawaiiana, and the river scenery is beautiful. Flat-bottom, 150-passenger riverboats (they rarely fill up) depart from Wailua Marina at the mouth of the Wailua River. ■ TIP→ It's extremely rare, but occasionally after heavy rains the tour doesn't disembark at the grotto; if you're traveling in winter, ask beforehand. Round-trip excursions take 1½ hours, including time to walk around the grotto and environs; check the website for times and days. ✉ *5971 Kuhio Hwy., Kapaa* ☎ *808/821–6895* ⊕ *www.smithskauai. com/fern-grotto* ✆ *$30.*

Bodyboarding and Bodysurfing

The most natural form of wave riding is bodysurfing, a popular sport on Kauai because there are many shore breaks around the island. Wave riders of this style stand waist deep in the water, facing shore, and swim madly as a wave picks them up and breaks. It's great fun and requires no special skills and absolutely no equipment other than a swimsuit. The next step up is bodyboarding, also called boogie boarding. In this case, wave riders lie with their upper body on a foam board about half the length of a traditional surfboard and kick as the wave propels them toward shore. Again, this is easy to pick up, and there are many places around Kauai to practice.

The locals wear short-finned flippers to help them catch waves, which is a good idea to enhance safety in the water. It's worth spending a few minutes watching these experts as they spin, twirl, and flip—that's right—while they slip down the face of the wave. ■TIP➔ **Of course, all beach-safety precautions apply, and just because you see wave riders of any kind in the water doesn't mean the water is safe for everyone. Be especially cautious when there's a strong shore break.** Most snorkeling-gear outfitters also rent bodyboards.

Some of our favorite bodysurfing and bodyboarding beaches are **Brennecke's, Wailua, Kealia, Kalihiwai,** and **Hanalei Bay**.

Deep-Sea Fishing

Simply step aboard and cast your line for mahimahi, ahi, ono, and marlin. That's about how quickly the fishing—mostly trolling with lures—begins on Kauai. The water gets deep quickly here, so there's less cruising time to fishing grounds, which is nice, since Hawaii's seas are notoriously rough. Of course, your captain may elect to cruise to a hot location where they've had good luck lately.

There are oodles of charter fishers around; most depart from Nawiliwili Harbor in Lihue, and most use lures instead of live bait. Inquire about each boat's "fish policy"; that is, what happens to the fish if any are caught. Some boats keep all; others will give you enough for a meal or two, even doing the cleaning themselves. On shared charters, ask about the maximum passenger count and about the fishing rotation. You'll want to make sure everyone gets a fair shot at reeling in the big one. Another option is to book a private charter. Shared and private charters run four, six, and eight hours in length.

BOATS AND CHARTERS
Captain Don's Sportfishing

FISHING | Captain Don is very flexible and treats everyone like family—he'll stop to snorkel or whale-watch if that's what the group (four to six) wants. Saltwater fly fishers (bring your own gear) are welcome. He'll even fish for bait and let you keep part of whatever you catch, as long as the fish is less than 25 pounds. On a shared trip, everyone gets part of the catch. His *Happy Ryder,* a 39-foot Hatteras boat, sails out of Nawiliwili, near Lihue. ✉ *Nawiliwili Small Boat Harbor, 2494 Niumalu Rd., Nawiliwili* ☎ *808/639–3012* ⊕ *www.captaindonsfishing.com* ✆ *From $175 (shared); from $750 (private).*

Kai Bear

FISHING | What's particularly nice about this company is its roomy, 38-foot Bertram, *Kai Bear.* It docks in Nawiliwili Small Boat Harbor near Lihue, which is convenient for those staying on the East Side. The prices are reasonable ($180 per person for the four-hour shared charter or $1,375 for the eight-hour private charter), and they share the catch. ✉ *Nawiliwili*

Small Boat Harbor, 2900 Nawiliwili Rd., Nawiliwili ☎ *808/652–4556* ⊕ *www.kaibear.com* 🏷 *From $180; private charters from $900.*

Golf

For golfers, the Garden Isle might as well be known as the Robert Trent Jones Jr. Isle. Four of the island's eight courses, including Poipu Bay—onetime home of the PGA Grand Slam of Golf—are the work of Jones, who previously lived at Princeville. Combine these four courses with those from Jack Nicklaus, Robin Nelson, and local legend Toyo Shirai, and you'll see that golf sets Kauai apart from the other Islands as much as the Pacific Ocean does. ■TIP→ **Afternoon tee times at most courses can save you big bucks.**

Anaina Hou Community Park

MINIATURE GOLF | FAMILY | The island's first miniature-golf course comes with a small botanical garden and a 300-seat theater/arts center. The 18-hole course was designed to be challenging, beautiful, and family-friendly. Replacing the typical clown's nose and spinning wheels are some water features and tropical tunnels. Surrounding each hole is plant life that walks players through different eras of Hawaiian history.

The Porter Pavilion hosts concerts, plays, private parties, and community meetings. A children's playground made from recycled materials is also on-site, and a gift shop with local products and a concessions counter make this place a fun activity for any time of day. On Saturday morning, a farmers' market adjacent to the course sells fresh Kauai produce and local goods. ⊠ *5–273 Kuhio Hwy., Kilauea* ☎ *808/828–2118* ⊕ *www.anainahou. org* 🏷 *$19, $15 kids 4–12* ☉ *Closed Mon.–Wed.*

Kiahuna Golf Club

GOLF | A meandering creek, lava outcrops, and thickets of trees give Kiahuna its character. Robert Trent Jones Jr. was given a smallish piece of land just inland at Poipu, and defends par with smaller targets, awkward stances, and optical illusions. In 2003 a group of homeowners bought the club and brought Jones back to renovate the course (it was originally built in 1983), adding tees and revamping bunkers. The pro here boasts his course has the best putting greens on the island. This is the only course on Kauai with a complete set of tee boxes for juniors. ⊠ *2545 Kiahuna Plantation Dr., Koloa* ☎ *808/742–9595* ⊕ *www.kiahunagolf. com* 🏷 *$115, including cart* 🏌 *18 holes, 6787 yards, par 70.*

The Ocean Course at Hokuala

GOLF | The Jack Nicklaus–designed Ocean Course at Hokuala offers a beautiful and distinctly Hawaiian golf experience. With an assortment of plants and tropical birds adding to the atmosphere, this course winds through dark ravines and over picturesque landscape. The fifth hole is particularly striking, as it requires a drive over a valley populated by mango and guava trees. The final holes feature unmatched views of Nawiliwili Bay, including the harbor, a lighthouse, and secluded beaches. This course also offers footgolf, played with a soccer ball, on a nine-hole loop. ■TIP→ **Get the lowest rates by booking online.** ⊠ *3351 Hoolaulea Way, Lihue* ☎ *808/241–6000* ⊕ *www. golfhokuala.com* 🏷 *From $260* 🏌 *18 holes, 7156 yards, par 72.*

Poipu Bay Golf Course

GOLF | Poipu Bay on the South Shore has been called the Pebble Beach of Hawaii, and the comparison is apt. Like Pebble Beach, Poipu is a links course built on headlands, not true links land. There's wildlife galore. It's not unusual for golfers to see monk seals sunning on the beach below, sea turtles bobbing outside the

The Makai course at Princeville Makai Golf Club has consistently been ranked a top course in the United States.

shore break, and humpback whales leaping offshore. From 1994 to 2006, the course (designed by Robert Trent Jones Jr.) hosted the annual PGA Grand Slam of Golf. Tiger Woods was a frequent winner here. Prices are slightly higher in the winter high season. The course is adjacent to the Grand Hyatt Kauai Resort & Spa. ⊠ *2250 Ainako St., Koloa* 🖀 *808/742–8711* ⊕ *www.poipubaygolf.com* ✉ *$219 before noon, $195 after noon* ⚐ *18 holes, 6127 yards, par 72.*

★ Princeville Makai Golf Club

GOLF | The 27-hole Princeville Makai Golf Club on the North Shore was named for its five ocean-hugging front holes. Designed by golf-course architect Robert Trent Jones Jr. in 1971, the 18-hole championship Makai Course has consistently been ranked a top golf course in the United States. ■**TIP→ Check the website for varying rates as well as other nongolf activities at the facility, including disc golf or the Sunset Golf Cart Tour, where you ride the course, sans clubs, and take in the spectacular ocean views.** ⊠ *4080 Lei*

O Papa Rd., Princeville 🖀 *808/826–1912* ⊕ *www.makaigolf.com* ✉ *$315* ⚐ *Makai Course: 18 holes, 7223 yards, par 72; Woods Course: 9 holes, 3445 yards, par 36.*

Wailua Municipal Golf Course

GOLF | Considered by many to be one of Hawaii's best public golf courses, this seaside course provides an affordable game with minimal water hazards, but it is challenging enough to have been chosen to host three USGA Amateur Public Links Championships. It was first built as a nine-holer in the 1930s, and the second nine holes were added in 1961. Course designer Toyo Shirai created a course that is fun but not punishing. The trade winds blow steadily on the East Side of the island, adding a challenge to play. An ocean view and affordability make this one of the most popular courses on the island with locals and visitors alike. Tee times are accepted up to seven days in advance and can be paid in cash and some credit cards. ⊠ *3–5350 Kuhio Hwy., Lihue* 🖀 *808/241–6666* ⊕ *www.kauai.*

gov/golf 🖂 *$48 weekdays, $60 weekends; cart rental $20* 🏌 *. 18 holes, 6585 yards, par 72.*

Hiking

The best way to experience the *aina*—the land—on Kauai is to step off the beach and hike in the hills and valleys of the island's interior. You'll find waterfalls so tall you'll strain your neck looking, pools of crystal-clear water for swimming, tropical forests teeming with plant life, and ocean vistas that will make you wish you could stay forever.

All hiking trails on Kauai are free. Hikers are reminded to leave no trace and pay attention to weather conditions, especially flash flood warnings, that could leave them stranded. Backcountry hikers anywhere in Hawaii should also clean their shoes, gear, and clothing thoroughly before and after a hike to prevent the spread of ohia rust, a deadly fungal disease that is killing the beautiful ohia trees that dominate Hawaii forests. ■TIP➔ **For your safety, wear sturdy shoes, preferably water-resistant ones.**

BEST SPOTS
★ Kalalau Trail

HIKING & WALKING | Of all the hikes on Kauai, the Kalalau Trail (11 miles one-way; permit and reservation required) is by far the most famous and the most strenuous, and one to be undertaken only by well-prepared hikers. A moderate hiker can handle the 2-mile trek to Hanakapiai Beach. This steep, often muddy trail is best approached with a walking stick. If there has been any steady rain, wait for drier days for a more enjoyable trek. A hardy outdoorsperson may wish to hike an additional 2 miles up to the falls. But be prepared to rock-hop along a creek and ford waters that can get waist high and dangerous during the rain. Round-trip to Hanakapiai Falls is 8 miles.

The narrow Kalalau Trail delivers one startling ocean view after another along a path that is alternately shady and sunny. Wear hiking shoes or water sandals, and bring drinking water since natural sources are not potable. Plenty of food is always encouraged on a strenuous hike such as this one. You must make a reservation at ⊕ *gohaena.com* to get into Haena State Park, where you'll find the trailhead, and hike to Hanakapiai.

If you plan to hike beyond Hanakapiai Valley or stay overnight, you must acquire a camping permit, either online or at the State Building in Lihue, for $35 per person per night. Hikers with camping permits do not need a reservation to enter Haena State Park. Trail and campground capacity beyond Hanakapiai is limited to 60 hikers/campers, and permits, issued 90 days out, are snapped up quickly. Hikers and campers may want to make reservations to catch the Go Haena shuttle at Waipa, just west of Hanalei. ⊕ *Drive north past Hanalei to end of road. Trailhead is directly across from Kee Beach* ⊕ *dlnr.hawaii.gov/dsp/hiking/kauai* 🖂 *$35 per person per night for camping permit.*

Mahaulepu Heritage Trail

HIKING & WALKING | This trail offers the novice hiker an accessible way to appreciate the rugged southern coast of Kauai. A 2-mile trail wends its way along the water, high above the ocean, through a lava field, and past a sacred *heiau* (stone structure). Walk north to Mahaulepu for a two-hour, 4-mile round-trip. If conditions and the season are right, you should be able to see dolphins, *honu* (green sea turtles), and whales. ⊕ *Drive north on Poipu Rd., turn right at Poipu Bay Golf Course sign. The street name is Ainako, but sign is hard to see. Drive down to beach and park in lot.*

Okolehao Trail

HIKING & WALKING | *Okolehao* basically translates to "moonshine" in Hawaiian: this steep, challenging, and often muddy

Requiring a permit, the very strenuous 11-mile (one-way) Kalalau Trail will lead you from Kee Beach to Kalalau Beach on Napali Coast.

trail follows the Hihimanu Ridge and was established in the days of Prohibition, when this backyard liquor was distilled from the roots of ti plants. The 2-mile hike climbs 1,200 feet and offers a 360-degree view of Hanalei Bay and Waioli Valley. Your ascent begins at the China Ditch off the Hanalei River. Follow the trail through a lightly forested grove and then climb up a steep embankment. From here the trail is well marked. Most of the climb is lined with hala, ti, wild orchid, and eucalyptus. You'll get your first of many ocean views at mile marker 1. ⊠ *Hanalei* ⊹ *Follow Ohiki Rd. (north of Hanalei Bridge) 5 miles to U.S. Fish and Wildlife Service parking area. Directly across street is small bridge that marks trailhead.*

Sleeping Giant (Nounou Mountain) Trail
HIKING & WALKING | An easily accessible trail practically in the heart of Kapaa, the moderately strenuous Sleeping Giant Trail—or simply Sleeping Giant—gains 1,000 feet over 2 miles for a 4-mile round trip. We prefer an early-morning—say,

sunrise—hike up from the East Side trailhead, with sparkling blue-water vistas, but there are other backside approaches. At the top is a grassy plot with a picnic table. The trail is a local favorite, with many East Siders meeting here to exercise. ⊠ *Haleilio Rd., off Rte. 56, Wailua (Kauai County).*

Waimea Canyon and Kokee State Park
HIKING & WALKING | This park contains a 50-mile network of hiking trails of varying difficulty that take you through acres of native forests, across the highest-elevation swamp in the world, to the river at the base of the canyon, and onto pinnacles of land sticking out over Napali Coast. All hikers are encouraged to register at the Kokee Natural History Museum, which has trail maps, current trail information, and specific directions. Camping permits ($30 per night per campsite) can be obtained 90 days ahead of the date.

The steep **Kukui Trail** descends 2,200 feet over 2½ miles into Waimea Canyon to the edge of the Waimea River. The **Awaawapuhi Trail**, with 1,600 feet of elevation gains and losses over 3¼ miles, feels more gentle than the Kukui Trail, but it offers its own huffing-and-puffing sections in its descent along a spiny ridge to a perch overlooking the ocean.

The 3½-mile **Alakai Swamp Trail** is accessed via the **Pihea Trail** or a four-wheel-drive road. There's one strenuous valley section, but otherwise it's a pretty level trail—once you access it. This trail is a bird-watcher's delight and includes a painterly view of Wainiha and Hanalei Valleys at the trail's end. The trail traverses the purported highest-elevation swamp in the world via a boardwalk so as not to disturb the fragile plant and wildlife. It is typically the coolest of the hikes due to the tree canopy, elevation, and cloud coverage.

The **Canyon Trail** offers much in its short trek: spectacular vistas of the canyon and its only dependable waterfall. This easy 2-mile hike is especially lovely when the late-afternoon sun sets the canyon walls ablaze in color. (All distances are one-way.) ✉ *Kokee Natural History Museum, 3600 Kokee Rd., Kekaha* ☎ *808/335–9975 for trail conditions* ⊕ *dlnr.hawaii.gov/dsp/parks/kauai* 🎫 *$5 entrance fee for nonresidents; $10 parking fee for nonresidents.*

EQUIPMENT AND TOURS
★ **Kauai Nature Tours**
SPECIAL-INTEREST TOURS | Scientist Chuck Blay started this hiking tour business and continues to lead informative excursions to coastal and mountain localities, such as the Kokee State Park area, Mahaulepu, and other areas upon request, aside from the Kalalau Trail. His emphasis is on exploring and discussing the natural history of each place, including its geology, botany, fauna, and cultural aspects. While he will lead small groups, personal tours are encouraged so he can tailor the location and duration of hikes to the interests and physical condition of participants. ■TIP➔ **If you have a desire to see a specific location, just ask. He will do custom hikes to spots he doesn't normally hit if there is interest.** Hikes range from easy to strenuous. ✉ *5162 Lawai Rd., Koloa* ☎ *888/233–8365* ⊕ *www.kauainaturetours.com* 🎫 *From $175 per participant.*

Horseback Riding

Most of the horseback-riding tours on Kauai are primarily walking tours with little trotting and no cantering or galloping, so no experience is required. Zip. Zilch. Nada. If you're interested, most of the stables offer private lessons. The most popular tours are the ones including a picnic lunch by the water. Your only dilemma may be deciding what kind of water you want—waterfalls or ocean. You may want to make your decision based on where you're staying. The "waterfall picnic" tours are on the wetter North Shore, and the "beach picnic" tours take place on the South Shore.

Princeville Ranch
HORSEBACK RIDING | A longtime *kamaaina* (resident) family operates Princeville Ranch, and their tour focuses on culture, history, and the local flora and fauna while also offering guidance on horsemanship. The two-hour rides are limited to four to six people, and they'll take out as few as two riders. The tour offers some splendid views of the mountains and the sea. They also offer riding lessons in their arena. ✉ *Kuhio Hwy., off Kapaka Rd., between mile markers 27 and 28, Princeville* ☎ *808/855–0064* ⊕ *www.princevilleranch.com* 🎫 *$199; private tours from $189.*

Kayaking

Kauai is the only Hawaiian island with navigable rivers. As the oldest inhabited island in the chain, Kauai has had more time for wind and water erosion to

Wailua River, Hanalei River, and Huleia River are Kauai's most scenic spots to river kayak.

deepen and widen cracks into streams and streams into rivers. Because this is a small island, the rivers aren't long, and there are no rapids, which makes them generally safe for kayakers of all levels, even beginners, except when rivers are flowing fast from heavy rains.

For more advanced paddlers, there aren't many places in the world more beautiful for sea kayaking than Napali Coast. If this is your draw to Kauai, plan your vacation for the summer months, when the seas are at their calmest. ■ TIP➔ **Tour and kayak-rental reservations are recommended at least two weeks in advance during peak summer and holiday seasons.**

In general, tours and rentals are available year-round, Monday through Saturday. Pack a swimsuit, sunscreen, a hat, rash guard, bug repellent, water shoes (sport sandals, aqua socks, old tennis shoes), and water and motion sickness medication (take in advance) if you're planning on sea kayaking.

RIVER KAYAKING

Tour outfitters operate on the Huleia, Wailua, and Hanalei Rivers with guided tours that combine kayaking with hiking to waterfalls, in the case of the first two rivers, and snorkeling, in the case of the third. Another option is renting kayaks and heading out on your own. Each river has its advantages and disadvantages, but it boils down as follows.

If you want to swim at the base of a remote, 100-foot-tall waterfall, sign up for a five-hour kayak (4-mile round-trip) and hiking (2-mile round-trip) tour of the **Wailua River.** It includes a dramatic waterfall that is best accessed with the aid of a guide, so you don't get lost. ■ TIP➔ **Remember—it's dangerous to swim under waterfalls no matter how good a water massage may sound. Rocks and logs are known to plunge down, especially after heavy rains.**

If you want to kayak on your own, choose the **Hanalei River.** It's most scenic from the kayak itself; there are no trails to hike to hidden waterfalls. And better yet, a rental company is right on the river—no hauling kayaks on top of your car.

If you're not sure of your kayaking abilities, head to the **Huleia River**; a 3½-hour tour includes easy paddling upriver, a nature walk through a rain forest with a cascading waterfall, a rope swing for playing Tarzan and Jane, and a ride back downriver—into the wind—on a motorized, double-hull canoe.

As for the kayaks themselves, most companies use the two-person sit-on-top style that is quite buoyant—no Eskimo rolls required. The only possible danger comes in the form of communication. The kayaks seat two people, which means you'll share the work with a guide (good), or with your spouse, child, parent, or friend (the potentially dangerous part). On the river, the two-person kayaks are jokingly known as "divorce boats," so be patient with your partner. Counseling is not included in the tour price.

SEA KAYAKING

Kayaking Napali Coast has long been a thrill-seeker's dream, ranking right up there with rafting the Colorado River through the Grand Canyon. It's the adventure of a lifetime in one day, involving eight hours of paddling beneath the tropical sun or overnight camping in remote valleys. Although it's good to have some kayaking experience, feel comfortable on the water, and be reasonably fit, it doesn't require the preparation, stamina, or fortitude of, say, climbing Mt. Everest. Tours run May through September, ocean conditions permitting. In the winter months, sea-kayaking tours operate on the South Shore—a beautiful area, though not as dramatic as Napali.

EQUIPMENT AND TOURS

Kayak Kauai

KAYAKING | The company that pioneered kayaking on Kauai offers guided tours on the Wailua River and sea kayak tours departing out of Hanalei Bay, Haena, and Polihale. Adventure seekers can take

multiday escorted summer sea kayak tours and camping trips on Napali Coast. From its convenient location in the Wailua Marina, Kayak Kauai can launch kayaks right into the Wailua River for its five-hour Secret Falls hike-paddle tour and three-hour paddle to a swimming hole. Sea-kayak whale-watching tours round out the aquatic repertoire. The company will shuttle kayakers as needed, and, for rentals, it provides the hauling gear necessary for your rental car. Snorkel gear, bodyboards, and stand-up paddleboards also can be rented, but note that it is closed weekends. ☒ *Wailua Marina, 3–5971 Kuhio Hwy., Wailua (Kauai County)* ☎ *808/826–9844, 888/596–3853* ⊕ *www.kayakkauai.com* ☐ *From $85 (river tours) and $240 (sea tours); kayak rentals from $110 per day.*

Kayak Wailua

KAYAKING | We can't quite figure out how this family-run business offers pretty much the same Wailua River kayaking tour as everyone else—except for lunch and beverages, which are BYO—for the lowest price, but it does. They say it's because they don't discount and don't offer commissions to activities and concierge desks. Their trip, a 4½-hour kayak, hike, and waterfall swim, is offered six times a day, with the last at 1 pm. With the number of kayaks going out, large groups can be accommodated. No tours are allowed on the Wailua River on Sunday. ☒ *4565 Haleilio Rd., Kapaa* ⊹ *Behind old Coco Palms hotel* ☎ *808/822–3388* ⊕ *www.kayakwailua.com* ☐ *$75.*

★ Napali Kayak

KAYAKING | A couple of longtime guides ventured out on their own to create this company, which focuses solely on sea-kayaking paddles and multiday camping voyages along Napali Coast. These guys are highly experienced and still highly enthusiastic about their livelihood. They operate from April to October, offering full-day Napali Coast tours departing from Haena and five-hour tours out of Polihale; both tours stop for a lunch break at Milolii. They also rent river and ocean kayaks, camping equipment, and first-aid kits. Reservations well in advance are suggested. ⊠ *5–5075 Kuhio Hwy., next to Postcards Café, Hanalei* 🕾 *808/826–6900* ⊕ *www.napalikayak. com* 🖳 *From $235.*

Outfitters Kauai

KAYAKING | FAMILY | This well-established tour outfitter operates year-round river-kayak tours that go through some lovely scenery on the Huleia and Wailua rivers. Their specialty (though they have other tours) is the Kipu Safari, an all-day adventure that starts with an easy paddle up the Huleia River and includes swinging on a rope over a swimming hole, a wagon ride through a working cattle ranch, a picnic lunch by a private waterfall, hiking, and two "zips" across the rain-forest canopy (strap on a harness, clip into a cable, and zip over a quarter of a mile). They then offer a one-of-a-kind Waterzip Zip Line at their mountain stream–fed blue pool. The day ends with a leisurely ride on a motorized double-hull canoe. It's a great tour for the family, because no one ever gets bored. ⊠ *230 Kipu Rd., Lihue* 🕾 *808/742–9667, 888/742–9887* ⊕ *www.outfitterskauai. com* 🖳 *Kipu Safari $219, $179 kids under 15.*

Wailua Kayak & Canoe

KAYAKING | This purveyor of kayak rentals is right on the Wailua River, which means no hauling your kayak on top of your car (a definite plus). Morning and afternoon five-hour guided kayak tours are also offered, with a short hike to a waterfall and refreshments. The company is closed on weekends. ⊠ *162 Wailua Rd., Kapaa* 🕾 *808/821–1188* ⊕ *www.wailuariverkayaking.com* 🖳 *$65 per day for a single kayak, $125 per day for a double; guided tours from $115.*

Mountain Tubing

Hawaii's sugarcane plantations have steadily closed one by one. In 2009, Gay & Robinson announced the closure of Kauai's last plantation; in 2016, HC&S ended the last operation in the state, on Maui. However, the sugarcane irrigation ditches remain, striating these Islands like spokes in a wheel. Inspired by the Hawaiian *auwai*, which diverted water from streams to taro fields, these engineering feats also diverted streams, often from many miles away. One ingenious tour company on Kauai has figured out a way to make exploring them an adventure: float inflatable tubes down the route.

Kauai Backcountry Adventures

LOCAL SPORTS | FAMILY | Both zip-lining and tubing tours are offered by this company. Popular with all ages, the tubing adventure can book up two weeks in advance in busy summer months. Here's how it works: you recline in an inner tube and float down fern-lined irrigation ditches that were built more than a century ago—the engineering is impressive—to divert water from Mt. Waialeale to sugar and pineapple fields around the island. You are even given a headlamp so you can see as you float through five covered tunnels. The scenery from the island's interior at the base of Mt. Waialeale on Lihue Plantation land is superb. Ages five and up are welcome. The tour takes about three hours and includes a picnic lunch and a dip in a swimming hole. ■**TIP→ You'll definitely want to pack water-friendly shoes (or rent some from the outfitter), sunscreen, a hat, bug repellent, and a beach towel.** Thirteen tours are offered daily on the half hour. ⊠ *3–4131 Kuhio Hwy., across from gas station, Hanamaulu* 🕾 *808/245–2506, 855/846–0092* ⊕ *www.kauaibackcountry. com* 🖳 *$136.*

Scuba Diving

The majority of scuba diving on Kauai occurs on the South Shore. Boat and shore dives are available, although boat sites surpass the shore sites for a couple of reasons. First, they're deeper and exhibit the complete symbiotic relationship of a reef system, and second, the visibility is better a little farther offshore. You'll also visit more than one site on a boat dive.

The dive operators on Kauai offer a full range of services, including certification dives, referral dives, boat dives, shore dives, night dives, and drift dives. Be sure to inquire about a company's safety record and precautions if you are new to the activity. ■TIP➔ **As for certification, we recommend completing your confined-water training and classroom testing before arriving on the island.** That way, you'll spend less time training and more time diving.

BEST SPOTS

The closest and safest scuba-diving sites are accessed by boat on the South Shore of the island, right off the shores of Poipu. The captain selects the actual site based on ocean conditions of the day. Beginners may prefer shore dives, which are best at **Koloa Landing** on the South Shore year-round.

For the advanced and adventuresome diver, the island of **Niihau**—across an open ocean channel in deep and crystal-clear waters—beckons and rewards, usually with some big fish. Seasport Divers, Fathom Five, and Bubbles Below venture the 17 miles across the channel in summer when the crossing is smoothest. Divers can expect deep dives, walls, and strong currents at Niihau, where conditions can change rapidly. To make the long journey worthwhile, three dives and Nitrox are included.

EQUIPMENT, LESSONS, AND TOURS

Bubbles Below

SCUBA DIVING | Marine ecology is the emphasis here aboard the 36-foot, eight-passenger *Kai Manu*. This longtime Kauai company discovered some pristine and adventuresome dive sites on the West Side of the island where white-tip reef sharks are common—and other divers are not. Thanks to the addition of a 32-foot powered catamaran—the six-passenger *Dive Rocket*—the group also runs Niihau, Napali, and North Shore dives year-round (depending on ocean conditions, of course). They're also known for their South Side trips, including a shore dive. A bonus on these tours is the wide variety of food served between dives. Open-water certification dives, check-out dives, and intro shore dives are available upon request. ✉ *Port Allen Small Boat Harbor, 4353 Waialo Rd., Eleele* ☎ *808/332–7333* ⊕ *www.bubblesbelowkauai.com* ✍ *$160 for 2-tank boat dive; Niihau charter $400.*

Dive Kauai

SCUBA DIVING | This company offers boat dives but specializes in shore diving for beginners, typically at Koloa Landing (year-round) on the South Shore. They're not only geared toward beginning divers and those who haven't been diving in a while—for whom they provide a gentle introductory/refresher dive—but they also offer scooter (think James Bond) dives for certified divers. Their main emphasis is a detailed review of marine biology, such as pointing out rare dragon eels and harlequin shrimp tucked away in pockets of coral. ■TIP➔ **Hands down, we recommend Dive Kauai for beginners, certification (all levels), and refresher dives.** One reason is that their instructor-to-student ratio does not exceed 1:4 for beginners; for certified divers the ratio can be 1:6. All dive gear is included. ✉ *Sheraton Kauai Resort, 2440 Hoonani Rd., Koloa* ☎ *808/321–9900* ⊕ *divekauai.*

com ✉ $156 for a 2-tank certified shore dive; $196 for a 2-tank boat dive.

★ Fathom Five

SCUBA DIVING | This operator offers it all: boat dives, shore dives, night dives, Niihau-Lehua dives, certification dives. They pretty much do what everyone else does with a few twists. First, they offer a three-tank premium charter for those really serious about diving. Second, they operate a Nitrox continuous-flow mixing system, so you can decide the mix rate. Third, they add on a twilight dive to the standard, one-tank night dive, making the outing worth the effort. Fourth, their shore diving isn't an afterthought. Fifth, they don't mix advanced and rusty divers on their fleet of six-passenger boats. Finally, we think their dive masters are pretty darn good, too. Book well in advance. ✉ 3450 Poipu Rd., Koloa ☎ 808/742–6991, 800/972–3078 ⊕ www. fathomfive.com ✉ From $210 for boat dives; from $153 for shore dives; $65 for gear rental, if needed.

Seasport Divers

SCUBA DIVING | Rated highly by readers of *Scuba Diving* magazine, Seasport Divers' 48-foot *Anela Kai* tops the chart for dive-boat luxury, including hot water showers. But owner Marvin Otsuji didn't stop with that. A second boat—the 32-foot cata-maran *Ahuhea*—is outfitted for diving, but we like it as an all-around charter. The company does brisk business, which means it won't cancel at the last minute because of a lack of reservations. They limit passengers to 12 on the three-tank, 12-hour Niihau trips (available in summer) but may book up to 18 people per boat on South Shore dives. ■TIP→ **There are slightly more challenging trips in the morning; mellower dive sites are in the afternoon. Night dives are offered, too.** The company runs a good-size dive shop for purchases and rentals, as well as a classroom for certification. ✉ 2827 Poipu Rd., Poipu ⊕ Look for yellow submarine

in parking lot ☎ 808/742–9303 ⊕ www. seasportdivers.com ✉ From $165 for certified divers; $125 1-tank shore dive, plus $40 gear charge.

Snorkeling

BEST SPOTS

Generally speaking, the calmest water and best snorkeling can be found on Kauai's North Shore in summer and South Shore in winter. The East Side, known as the windward side, has year-round, prevalent northeast trade winds that make snorkeling unpredictable, although there are some good pockets. The best snorkeling on the West Side is accessible only by boat.

A word on feeding fish: don't. As Captain Ted with Holo Holo Charters says, fish have survived and populated reefs for much longer than we have been donning goggles and staring at them. They will continue to do so without our interven-tion. Besides, fish food messes up the reef and—one thing always leads to another—can eliminate a once-pristine reef environment.

As for gear, if you're snorkeling with one of the Napali boat-tour outfitters, they'll provide it; however, depending on the company, it might not be the latest or greatest. If you have your own, bring it. On the other hand, if you're going out with Z-Tourz, the gear is top-notch. If you need to rent or want to buy, hit one of the "snorkel-and-surf" shops, such as Snorkel Bob's in Koloa and Kapaa, Nuku-moi Surf Co. in Poipu, or Seasport Divers in Poipu. ■TIP→ **If you wear glasses, you can rent prescription masks at some rental shops—just don't expect them to match your prescription exactly.**

Spas

THE NORTH SHORE
Hanalei Day Spa

SPAS | The single-lane bridges may be one reason life slows down as you travel past tony Princeville; another is this boutique day spa on the grounds of the Hanalei Colony Resort in Haena, with in-spa and beachside spa services. Owner Darci Frankel is an Ayurveda practitioner with three decades of experience. Spa treatments include body wraps, scrubs, and packages for individuals and couples. Its specialty is massage: lomilomi (a traditional Hawaiian-style massage), deep tissue, relaxation, and a special four-hand massage. ⊠ *Hanalei Colony Resort, 5–7132 Kuhio Hwy., Haena* ⊹ *6 miles past Hanalei* ☎ *808/826–6621* ⊕ *www.hanaleidayspa.com* ✉ *Massages from $228.*

THE EAST SIDE
Alexander Day Spa & Salon at the Royal Sonesta Kauai Resort Lihue

SPAS | This sunny, pleasant spa focuses on body care rather than exercise, so don't expect any fitness equipment or exercise classes, just pampering and beauty treatments. Massages are available in treatment rooms, your room, and on the beach, although the beach locale isn't as private as you might imagine. Wedding-day and custom spa packages can be arranged. ⊠ *Royal Sonesta Kauai Resort Lihue, 3610 Rice St., Suite 9A, Lihue* ☎ *808/246–4918* ⊕ *www.alexanderspa.com* ✉ *Massages from $145.*

THE SOUTH SHORE
Anara Spa

SPAS | The luxurious Anara Spa has all the equipment and services you expect from a top resort spa, along with a pleasant, professional staff. Best of all, it has indoor and outdoor areas that capitalize on the tropical locale and balmy weather, further distinguishing it from other hotel spas. Its 46,500 square feet of space includes the lovely Garden Treatment Village, an open-air courtyard with private thatched-roof huts, each featuring a relaxation area, misters, and an open-air shower in a tropical setting. Ancient Hawaiian remedies and local ingredients are featured in many treatments, such as a pineapple-papaya body hydration, a coffee body polish, and a traditional lomilomi massage. The open-air lava-rock showers are wonderful, introducing many guests to the delightful island practice of showering outdoors. The spa, which includes a full-service salon, adjoins the Grand Hyatt's legendary swimming pool. ⊠ *Grand Hyatt Kauai Resort and Spa, 1571 Poipu Rd., Poipu* ☎ *808/742–1234* ⊕ *www.anaraspa.com* ✉ *Massages from $180.*

Try a Lomilomi Massage

Life in ancient Hawaii wasn't about sunbathing and lounging at the beach. Growing taro was hard work, and building canoes, fishing for dinner, and pounding tapa cloth for clothing, sails, and blankets were hard too. Enter lomilomi—a Hawaiian-style massage. It's often described as being more vigorous, more rhythmic, and faster than Swedish massage, and it incorporates more elbow and forearm work. It might even involve chanting, music, and four hands (in other words, two people).

Stand-Up Paddling

This is an increasingly popular sport that even a novice can pick up—*and* have fun doing. Beginners start with a heftier surfboard and a longer-than-normal canoe paddle. And, just as the name implies, stand-up paddlers stand on their surfboards and paddle out from the beach,

Winter brings big surf to Kauai's North Shore. You can see some of the sport's biggest celebrities catching waves at Haena and Hanalei Bay.

which requires calm water, especially for beginners. The perfect place to learn is a river or bay (think **Hanalei** or **Kalapaki**) or a calm lagoon (try **Anini**). But this sport isn't just for beginners. Tried-and-true surfers turn to it when the waves are not quite right for their preferred sport because it gives them another reason to be on the water. Stand-up paddlers catch waves earlier and ride them longer than longboard surfers. Professional stand-up paddling competitions have popped up, and surf shops and instructors have adapted to the sport's quick rise in popularity.

EQUIPMENT

Not all surf instructors teach stand-up paddling, but more and more are, like Titus Kinimaka's Hawaiian School of Surfing (*see the Surfing section*).

Back Door Surf Shop

WATER SPORTS | Along with its sister store across the street—Hanalei Surf Company—Back Door provides just about all the rentals necessary for a fun day at Hanalei Bay, along with clothing and new boards.

✉ *Ching Young Village, 5–5190 Kuhio Hwy., Hanalei* ☎ *808/826–9000* ⊕ *www. hanaleisurf.com/our-sister-stores.*

Hawaiian Surfing Adventures

WATER SPORTS | This Hanalei location has the largest variety of surfboards and stand-up boards and paddles for rent by the hour or day. Check in at the storefront and then head down to the beach, where your gear will be waiting. The 90-minute private and group lessons start on the scenic Hanalei River and then move to Hanalei Bay if the students are ready and conditions are right. This Native Hawaiian–owned company also offers surfboard and kayak rentals and surfing lessons. It is closed Sunday. ✉ *5134 Kuhio Hwy., Hanalei* ☎ *808/482–0749* ⊕ *www.hawaiiansurfingadventures. com* ✍ *Paddleboard rental from $30; surfboard rentals from $20; group lessons from $65.*

Kauai Beach Boys

WATER SPORTS | There's no hauling your gear on your car with this outfitter, which is right on the beach at Kalapaki. The

90-minute classes are offered four times daily. In addition to stand-up paddle lessons, they offer surfing lessons and a chance to paddle a traditional outrigger canoe. ✉ *3610 Rice St., Lihue* ☎ *808/246–6333* ⊕ *www.kauaibeachboys.com* ✉ *$89 for 90-min surf or SUP lesson.*

Surfing

Good ol' stand-up surfing remains extremely popular on Kauai, especially in winter's high-surf season on the North Shore. If you're new to the sport, we highly recommend taking a lesson. Not only will this ensure you're up and riding waves in no time, but instructors will also provide the right board for your experience and size, help you time a wave, and give you a push to get your momentum going. You don't need to be in top physical shape to take a lesson. Because your instructor helps push you into the wave, you won't wear yourself out paddling.

If you're experienced and want to hit the waves on your own, most surf shops rent boards for all levels, from beginners to advanced. ■ TIP➜ **Just be aware that surfing on Kauai is often more challenging than elsewhere.**

BEST SPOTS
Perennial-favorite beginning surf spots include **Poipu Beach Park** (the area fronting the Marriott Waiohai Beach Club), **Hanalei Bay** near the pier, and the stream end of **Kalapaki Beach.** More advanced surfers move down the beach in Hanalei to an area fronting a grove of pines known as **Pine Trees,** or paddle out past the pier. When the trade winds die, the north ends of **Wailua** and **Kealia** beaches are teeming with surfers. Breaks off **Poipu** and **Beach House/Lawai Beach** attract intermediates year-round. During high surf, the break on the cliff side of **Kalihiwai** is for experts only. Advanced riders will head to **Polihale** to face the heavy West Side waves when conditions are right.

EQUIPMENT AND LESSONS
Hanalei Surf Company
SURFING | You can rent short- and longboards here and shop for rash guards, wet suits, and some hip surf-inspired apparel. ✉ *Hanalei Center, 5–5161 Kuhio Hwy., Hanalei* ☎ *808/826–9000* ⊕ *www.hanaleisurf.com.*

Nukumoi Surf Co.
SURFING | Owned by the same folks who own Brennecke's restaurant, this shop arranges surfing lessons and provides board (surfing, body, and stand-up paddle), snorkel, and beach-gear rental, as well as casual clothing. Their primary surf spot is the beach fronting the Sheraton. ✉ *2080 Hoone Rd., Koloa* ☎ *808/742–8019* ⊕ *www.nukumoi.com* ✉ *$75 for groups for 90 min; $250 for private sessions.*

Progressive Expressions
SURFING | This full-service shop has a choice of rental boards and a whole lotta shopping for clothes, swimsuits, and casual beach wear. ✉ *5428 Koloa Rd., Koloa* ☎ *808/742–6041* ⊕ *www.progressiveexpressions.com.*

Tamba Surf Company
SURFING | Kauai's homegrown surf shop is your best East Side bet for surfboard, stand-up paddle, and snorkel gear rentals. It also sells new boards and offers surfing lessons. Tamba is a big name in local surf apparel. ✉ *4–1543 Kuhio Hwy., Kapaa* ☎ *808/823–6942* ⊕ *www.tamba.com* ✉ *$75 group lesson.*

Titus Kinimaka's Hawaiian School of Surfing
SURFING | Famed as a pioneer of big-wave surfing, this Hawaiian believes in giving back to his sport. Beginning and intermediate lessons are offered on the half hour eight times a day at Hanalei, with a maximum of three students. If you want to learn to surf from a living legend, this is the man. Advanced surfers can also take an extreme tow-in lesson

Humpback whales arrive near Kauai in November and stick around until early April. You can see these majestic creatures breach and spout from shore, or take a boat tour

with a Jet Ski. ■TIP→ He employs other instructors, so if you want Titus, be sure to ask for him. (And good luck, because if the waves are going off, he'll be surfing, not teaching.) Customers are able to use the board for a while after the lesson is complete. ⊠ *Quicksilver, 5–5088 Kuhio Hwy., Hanalei* 🕾 *808/652–1116* ⊕ *www. hawaiianschoolofsurfing.com* 🖅 *$75, 90-min group lesson; $250 Jet Ski surf; $130, 90-min stand-up paddle lesson.*

Whale-Watching

Every winter North Pacific humpback whales swim some 3,000 miles over 30 days, give or take a few, from Alaska to Hawaii. Whales arrive as early as November and sometimes stay through April, though they seem to be most populous in February and March. They come to Hawaii to breed, calve, and nurse their young.

TOURS

Nothing beats the thrill of seeing a whale up close. During the season, any boat on the water is looking for whales; they're hard to avoid, whether the tour is labeled "whale-watching" or not. Consider the whales a benefit to any boating event that may interest you. If whales are definitely your thing, though, you can narrow down your tour-boat decision by asking a few whale-related questions, like whether there's a hydrophone on board, how long the captain has been running tours in Hawaii, and if anyone on the crew is a marine biologist or trained naturalist.

Several boat operators will add two-hour afternoon whale-watching tours during the season that run on the South Shore (not Napali). Operators include Blue Dolphin, Catamaran Kahanu, and Holo Holo Charters (*see the Boat Tours section*). Trying one of these excursions is a good option for those who have no interest in snorkeling or sightseeing along Napali Coast, although keep in mind, the longer you're on the water, the more likely you'll be to see the humpbacks.

One of the more unique ways to (possibly) see some whales is atop a kayak. For such an encounter, try Outfitters Kauai's South Shore kayak trip (*see the Kayaking section*).

A few lookout spots around the island have good land-based viewing: Kilauea Lighthouse on the North Shore, the Kapaa Scenic Overlook just north of Kapaa Town on the East Side, and the cliffs to the east of Keoniloa (Shipwreck) Beach on the South Shore.

Zip Line Tours

Whether you call this popular, relatively new adventure on Kauai "zipping" or "zip-lining," chances are you'll scream like a rock star while trying it. Strap on a harness, clip onto a cable running from one side of a river or valley to the other, and "zip" across. The step off is the scariest part. ■ TIP → **Pack knee-length shorts or pants, athletic shoes, and courage for this adventure.**

Outfitters Kauai

ZIP-LINING | This outfitter offers four zip line adventures, including the state's longest and biggest lines. Adventures range from a 2-mile zip to a shorter version that has you flying in a head-first position at speeds up to 50 mph. Tandem lines spare you from going it alone. The most popular adventure is the Kipu Zipline Safari Tour, which features an 1,800-foot tandem zip, a paddle on the Wailua River, and a hike. Outfitters Kauai emphasizes safety, and a zipper must be at least seven years old. ✉ *230 Kipu Rd., Poipu* ☎ *808/742–9667, 888/742–9887* ⊕ *www.outfitterskauai.com* 🖃 *From $50.*

Chapter 7

MOLOKAI

7

Updated by
Laurie Lyons-Makaimoku

 Sights
★★★★★

 Restaurants
★★★★☆

 Hotels
★★★☆☆

 Shopping
★★★★☆

 Nightlife
★☆☆☆☆

WELCOME TO MOLOKAI

TOP REASONS TO GO

★ **Kalaupapa Peninsula:** Hike or take a mule ride down the world's tallest sea cliffs, or take a plane to a fascinating historic community that still houses a few former Hansen's disease patients and learn more about the people who have been hidden away from the world.

★ **A waterfall hike in Halawa:** A fascinating guided (intermediate) hike through private property takes you past ancient ruins, restored taro patches, and a sparkling cascade.

★ **Deep-sea fishing:** Sport fish are plentiful in these waters, as are gorgeous views of several islands. Fishing is one of the Island's great adventures.

★ **Closeness to nature:** Deep valleys, sheer cliffs, endless rainbows, and the untamed ocean are the main attractions on Molokai.

★ **Papohaku Beach:** This 3-mile stretch of golden sand is one of the most sensational beaches in all of Hawaii. Sunsets and barbecues are perfect here.

Molokai is about 10 miles wide on average and four times that long. It comprises east, west, and central regions, plus the Kalaupapa Peninsula and the Kalaupapa National Historic Park. The north shore thrusts up from the sea to form the tallest sea cliffs on Earth, while the south shore slides almost flat into the water, then fans out to form the largest shallow-water reef system in the United States. Kaunakakai, the island's main town, has most of the stores and restaurants. Surprisingly, the highest point on Molokai rises to only 4,970 feet.

1 West Molokai. The most arid part of the island, known as the west end, has two inhabited areas: the coastal stretch includes a few condos and luxury homes, along with the largest beaches on the island; nearby is the fading hilltop hamlet of Maunaloa, a former plantation town, whose backdrop is the dormant volcano that shares its name. Papohaku Beach, one of the remote beaches found here, is the Hawaiian Islands' second-longest white-sand beach.

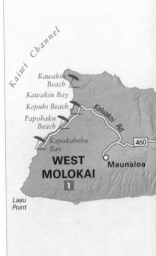

2 Central Molokai. The island's only true town, Kaunakakai, with its mile-long wharf, is here. Nearly all the island's eateries and stores are in or close to Kaunakakai. Highway 470 crosses the center of the island, rising to the top of the sea cliffs and the Kalaupapa overlook. At the base of the cliffs is Kalaupapa National Historical Park, a top attraction.

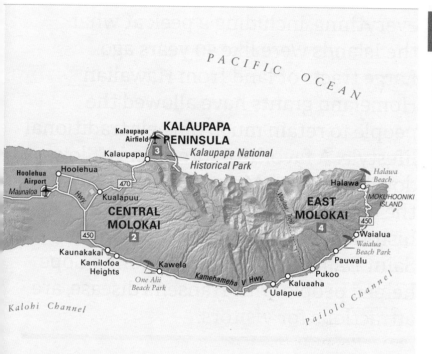

3 Kalaupapa Peninsula. One of the most remote areas in the entire Hawaiian Islands is currently accessible only by air. It is typically accessible by foot or on a mule, but as of late 2019 the path is closed indefinitely due to a landslide. It's a place of stunning beauty with a tragic history.

4 East Molokai. The scenic drive on Route 450 around this undeveloped area, also called the east end, passes through the green pastures of Puu O Hoku Ranch and climaxes with a descent into Halawa Valley. As you continue east, the road becomes increasingly narrow and the island ever more lush.

With sandy beaches to the west, sheer sea cliffs to the north, and a rainy, lush eastern coast, Molokai offers a bit of everything, including a peek at what the Islands were like 50 years ago. Large tracts of land from Hawaiian Homeland grants have allowed the people to retain much of their traditional lifestyle. A favorite expression is "Slow down, you're on Molokai." Exploring the great outdoors and visiting the historic Kalaupapa Peninsula, where Saint Damien and Saint Marianne Cope helped people with Hansen's disease, are attractions for visitors.

Molokai is generally thought of as the last bit of "real" Hawaii. Tourism has been held at bay by the Island's unique history and the pride of its predominantly Native Hawaiian population. Only 38 miles long and 10 miles wide at its widest point, Molokai is the fifth-largest island in the Hawaiian archipelago. Eight thousand residents call Molokai home, nearly 60% of whom are Hawaiian.

Molokai is a great place to be outdoors. There are no tall buildings, no traffic lights, no streetlights, no stores bearing the names of national chains, and nothing at all like a resort. You will, however, find 15 parks and more than 100 miles of shoreline to play on. At night the whole

Island grows dark, creating a velvety blackness and a wonderful rare silence.

The first thing to do on Molokai is to drive everywhere. It's a feat you can accomplish comfortably in two days. Depending on where you stay, spend a day exploring the west end and another exploring the east end. Basically, you have one 40-mile west–east highway (two lanes, no stoplights) with three side trips: the nearly deserted little west-end town of Maunaloa; the Highway 470 drive (just a few miles) to the top of the north shore and the overlook of Kalaupapa Peninsula; and the short stretch of shops in Kaunakakai town. After you learn the general lay of the land, you can return to the places that interest you most. Directions on the

Island—as throughout Hawaii—are often given as *mauka* (toward the mountains) and *makai* (toward the ocean).

■ **TIP→ Most Molokai establishments cater to the needs of locals, not tourists, so you may need to prepare a bit more than if you were going to a more popular destination. Pick up a disposable cooler in Kaunakakai town, and then buy supplies in local markets. Don't forget to carry some water, and bring sunscreen and mosquito repellent to the Island with you.**

GEOGRAPHY

Molokai was created when two large volcanoes—Kamakou in the east and Maunaloa in the west—broke the surface of the Pacific Ocean to create an island. Afterward, a third section of the Island emerged when a much smaller caldera, Kauhako, popped up to form the Kalaupapa Peninsula. But it wasn't until an enormous landslide sent much of Kauhako Mountain into the sea that the island was blessed with the sheer sea cliffs—the world's tallest—that make Molokai's north shore so spectacularly beautiful.

HISTORY

Molokai is named in chants as the child of the moon goddess Hina. For centuries the Island was occupied by native people, who took advantage of the reef fishing and ideal conditions for growing taro.

When leprosy broke out in the Hawaiian Islands in the 1840s, the Kalaupapa Peninsula, surrounded on three sides by the Pacific and accessible only by a steep trail, was selected as the place to exile people suffering from the disease. The first patients were thrown into the sea to swim ashore as best they could, and left with no facilities, shelter, or supplies. In 1873, a missionary named Father Damien arrived and began to serve the peninsula's suffering inhabitants. He died in 1889 from leprosy and was canonized as a saint by the Catholic Church in 2009. In 1888, a nun named Mother Marianne

Cope moved to Kalaupapa to care for the dying Father Damien and continue his vital work. Mother Marianne stayed at Kalaupapa until her death in 1918; she was canonized in 2012.

Although leprosy, known now as Hansen's disease, is no longer contagious and can be remitted, the buildings and infrastructure created by those who were exiled here still exist, and some longtime residents have chosen to stay in their homes. Today the area is Kalaupapa National Historical Park. Visitors are typically welcome with a tour group, but the Kalaupapa Trail and Kalaupapa Trail are currently closed to protect the residents from the pandemic.

THE BIRTHPLACE OF HULA

Tradition has it that, centuries ago, Lailai came to Molokai and lived on Puu Nana at Kaana. She brought the art of hula and taught it to the people, who kept it secret for her descendants, making sure the sacred dances were performed only at Kaana. Five generations later, Laka was born into the family and learned hula from an older sister. She chose to share the art and traveled throughout the Islands teaching the dance, although she did so without her family's consent. The yearly Ka Hula Piko Festival, held on Molokai in May, celebrates the birth of hula at Kaana.

Planning

When to Go

If you're keen to explore Molokai's beaches, coral beds, or fishponds, summer is your best bet for nonstop calm seas and sunny skies. The weather mimics that of the other Islands: low to mid-80s year-round, slightly rainier in winter. As you travel up the mountainside, the weather changes with bursts of downpours. The strongest storms occur in winter when winds and rain shift to come in from the south.

For a taste of Hawaiian culture, plan your visit around a festival. In January, Islanders and visitors compete in ancient Hawaiian games at the Ka Molokai Makahiki Festival. The Molokai Ka Hula Piko, an annual daylong event in May, draws premier hula troupes, musicians, and storytellers. Long-distance canoe races from Molokai to Oahu are in late September and early October. Although never crowded, the Island is busier during these events—book accommodations and transportation six months in advance.

Note: Some events have been modified due to the COVID-19 pandemic and are slow to return.

Getting Here and Around

AIR
If you're flying in from the mainland United States, you must first make a stop in Honolulu, Oahu or Kahului, Maui. From either of those, Molokai is just a short hop away. Molokai's transportation hub is Molokai Airport (MKK), a tiny airstrip 8 miles west of Kaunakakai and about 18 miles east of Maunaloa. An even smaller airstrip serves the little community of Kalaupapa on the north shore.

From Molokai Airport (sometimes called Hoolehua Airport), it takes about 10 minutes to reach Kaunakakai and 25 minutes to reach the west end of the Island by car. There's no public bus. A taxi costs about $27 from the airport to Kaunakakai with Hele Mai Taxi. Keep in mind, however, that it's difficult to visit the Island without a rental car.

AIRPORT CONTACTS Molokai Airport (MKK). ⊠ *3980 Airport Loop, Hoolehua* ☎ *808/567–9660* ⊕ *airports.hawaii.gov/mkk.*

TAXI CONTACTS Hele Mai Taxi. ⊠ *Kaunakakai* ☎ *808/336–0967* ⊕ *molokaitaxi.com.*

CAR
If you want to explore Molokai from one end to the other, you must rent a car. With just a few main roads to choose from, it's a snap to drive around here. The gas stations are in Kaunakakai. Ask your rental agent for a free *Molokai Drive Guide.*

Alamo maintains a counter at Molokai Airport. Make arrangements in advance, because the number of rental cars on Molokai is limited. Be sure to check that the vehicle's four-wheel drive is working before you depart from the agency. Off-road driving is not allowed; beware of fees for returning the car dirty. If Alamo is fully booked, check out Molokai Car Rental.

CONTACTS Alamo Rent a Car. ⊠ *3980 Airport Loop, Building 2, Hoolehua* ☎ *808/567–6381* ⊕ *www.alamo.com.* **Mobettah Car Rentals.** ⊠ *3980 Airport Loop, Hoolehua* ☎ *808/308–9566* ⊕ *www.mobettahcarrentals.com.*

Beaches

Molokai's unique geography gives the Island plenty of drama and spectacle along the shorelines but not so many places for seaside basking and bathing. The long north shore consists mostly of towering cliffs that plunge directly into the sea and is inaccessible except by boat, and even then only in summer. Much of the south shore is enclosed by a huge reef, which stands as far as a mile offshore and blunts the action of the waves. Within this reef you can find a thin strip of sand, but the water here is flat, shallow, and at times clouded with silt. This reef area is best suited to wading, pole fishing, kayaking, and paddleboarding.

The big, fat, sandy beaches lie along the west end. The largest of these—the second largest in the Islands—is Papohaku Beach, which fronts a grassy park shaded by a grove of *kiawe* (mesquite) trees. These stretches of west-end sand are generally unpopulated. At the east end, where the road hugs the sinuous shoreline, you encounter a number of pocket-size beaches in rocky coves, good for snorkeling. Don't venture too far out, however, or you can find yourself caught in dangerous currents. The Island's east-end road ends at Halawa Valley with its unique double bay, which is not recommended for swimming.

■TIP→ **To rent kayaks, SUPs, and snorkel gear, check out Molokai Outdoors at molokai-outdoors.com.**

Hotels

Molokai appeals most to travelers who appreciate genuine Hawaiian ambience rather than swanky digs. Most hotel and condominium properties range from adequate to funky, but the prices are significantly lower than hotels on the other Islands. Visitors who want to lollygag on the beach should choose one of the condos or home rentals in West Molokai. Travelers who want to immerse themselves in the spirit of the Island should seek out a condo or cottage, the closer to East Molokai the better. Hotel Molokai in Kaunakakai is the closest thing you'll find to a resort.

■TIP→ **Maui County has regulations concerning vacation rentals; to avoid disappointment, always contact the property manager or the owner and ask if the accommodations have the proper permits and are in compliance with local ordinances.**

The coastline along Molokai's west end has ocean-view condominium units and luxury homes available as vacation rentals. Central Molokai offers seaside condominiums. The only lodgings on the

east end are some guest cottages in magical settings and the cottages and ranch lodge at Puu O Hoku. Note that room rates do not include the 13.42% sales tax.

Hotel reviews have been shortened. For full information, visit Fodors.com. Hotel prices are the lowest cost of a standard double room in high season. Condo price categories reflect studio and one-bedroom rates.

WHAT IT COSTS in U.S. Dollars

$	$$	$$$	$$$$
HOTELS			
under $181	$181–$260	$261–$340	over $340

Molokai Vacation Rentals

HOTEL | FAMILY | Vacasa Vacation Rentals handles condo rentals across the Island. There is a two-night minimum on all properties. Contactless check-in is available at most properties. ⊠ *130 Kamehameha V Hwy., Kaunakakai* ☎ *808/460–4421* ⊕ *www.molokaivacationrental.com.*

Restaurants

Dining on Molokai, for the most part, is simply a matter of eating—there are no fancy restaurants, just pleasant low-key places to dine. Paddlers Restaurant and Bar and Hiro's Ohana Grill currently have the best dinner and ambience offerings. Other options include burgers, plate lunches, pizza, coffee shop-style sandwiches, and make-it-yourself fixings.

During a week's stay, you might easily hit all the dining spots worth a visit and then return to your favorites for a second round. The dining scene is fun because it's a microcosm of Hawaii's diverse cultures. You can find locally grown vegetarian foods, spicy Filipino cuisine, or Hawaiian fish with a Japanese influence—such as tuna, mullet, and moonfish that's grilled, sautéed, or mixed with seaweed to make poke (salted and seasoned raw fish).

Most eating establishments are on Ala Malama Street in Kaunakakai. If you're heading to West Molokai for the day, be sure to stock up on provisions, as there is no place to eat there. If you are on the east end, stop by **Manae Goods & Grindz** (☎ *808/558–8186*) near mile marker 16 for good local seafood plates, burgers, and ice cream.

Restaurant reviews have been short-ened. For full information, visit Fodors. com. Restaurant prices are the average cost of a main course at dinner or, if dinner is not served, at lunch.

WHAT IT COSTS in U.S. Dollars

$	$$	$$$	$$$$
RESTAURANTS			
under $18	$18–$26	$27–$35	over $35

Nightlife

Local nightlife consists mainly of gathering with friends and family, sipping a few cold ones, strumming ukuleles and guitars, singing old songs, and talking story. Still, there are a few ways to kick up your heels. Pick up a copy of the weekly *Molokai Dispatch* and see if there's a concert, church supper, or dance. Paddlers Restaurant is a great option for live music and a full bar most nights of the week.

Shopping

Molokai has one main commercial area: Ala Malama Street in Kaunakakai. There are no department stores or shopping malls, and the clothing is typical island wear. A small number of family-run businesses defines the main drag of

Maunaloa, a rural former plantation town, and there are a couple of general stores and other random stores throughout the Island. Most stores in Kaunakakai are open Monday–Saturday 10 am–6 pm, but posted hours are sometimes just a suggestion. If you find that a store isn't open at the posted time, grab a coffee, shop at a couple of other spots, then circle back around. Almost everything shuts down on Sundays, so be sure to plan ahead.

Visitor Information

CONTACTS Destination Molokai Visitors Bureau. ✉ *3980 Airport Loop, Hoolehua* ☎ *808/553–5221* ⊕ *gohawaii.com/molokai.*

West Molokai

Papohaku Beach is 17 miles west of the airport; Maunaloa is 10 miles west of the airport.

The remote beaches and rolling pastures on Molokai's west end are presided over by Maunaloa, a dormant volcano, and a sleepy little former plantation town of the same name. Papohaku Beach, the Hawaiian Islands' second-longest white-sand beach, is one of the area's biggest draws.

GETTING HERE AND AROUND

The sometimes winding paved road through West Molokai begins at Highway 460 and ends at Kapukahehu Bay. The drive from Kaunakakai to Maunaloa is about 30 minutes.

Sights

Kaluakoi

TOWN | Although the mid-1970s Kaluakoi Hotel and Golf Club is closed and forlorn, some nice condos and a gift shop are operating nearby. Kepuhi Beach, the white-sand beach along the coast, is worth a visit. ✉ *Kaluakoi Rd., Maunaloa.*

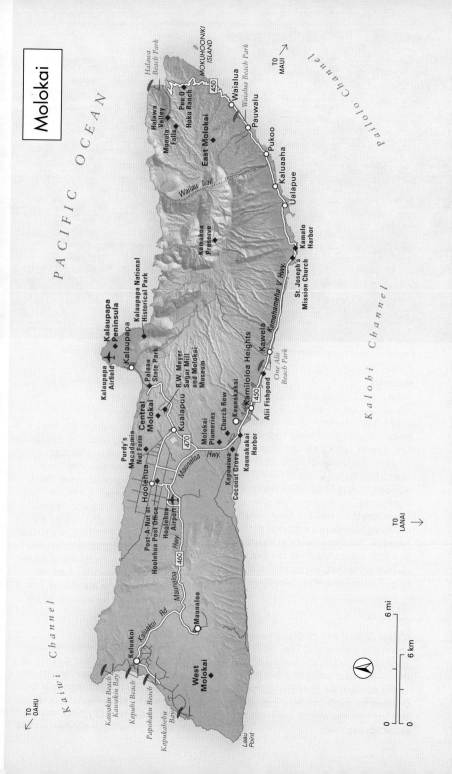

Molokai

Lava ridges make Kepuhi Beach beautiful, but swimming here is difficult unless the water is calm.

Maunaloa

TOWN | Built in 1923, this quiet community at the western end of the highway once housed workers for the Island's pineapple plantation. Many businesses have closed, but it's the last place you can buy supplies when exploring the nearby beaches. If you're in the neighborhood, stop at Maunaloa's Big Wind Kite Factory. You'll want to talk with Uncle Jonathan, who has been making and flying kites here for more than three decades. There's not much in Maunaloa anymore, but it's not every day that you can see something this close to a ghost town. ⊠ *Maunaloa Hwy., Maunaloa.*

Beaches

Molokai's west end looks across a wide channel to the island of Oahu. This crescent-shape cup of coastline holds the island's best sandy beaches as well as the sunniest weather. Remember: all beaches are public property, even those that front developments, and most have public access roads.

Beaches in this section are listed from north to south.

Kawakiu Beach

BEACH | Seclusion is yours at this remote, beautiful, white-sand beach, accessible by four-wheel-drive vehicle (through a gate that is sometimes locked) or a 45-minute walk (wear close-toed shoes as you may find yourself in a thorny situation). To get here, drive to Paniolo Hale off Kaluakoi Road and look for a dirt road off to the right. Park here and hike in or, with a four-wheel-drive vehicle, drive along the dirt road to the beach. ⚠ **Rocks and undertow make swimming extremely dangerous at times, so use caution. Amenities:** none. **Best for:** solitude. ⊠ *Off Kaluakoi Rd., Maunaloa.*

Kepuhi Beach

BEACH | The Kaluakoi Hotel is closed, but its half mile of ivory sand is still accessible. The beach shines against the turquoise sea, black outcroppings of lava, and magenta bougainvillea blossoms. When the sea is perfectly calm, lava ridges in the water make good snorkeling spots. With any surf at all, however, the water around these rocky places churns and foams, wiping out visibility and making it difficult to avoid being slammed into the jagged rocks. Stick to the northern part of the beach to avoid as many of the rocks as possible. If the surf is too big for snorkeling, there's a nice bench up the path that lets you relax and take it all in. **Amenities:** none. **Best for:** snorkeling; walking. ⊠ *Kaluakoi Rd., Maunaloa.*

★ Papohaku Beach

BEACH | One of the most sensational beaches in Hawaii, Papohaku is a three-mile-long strip of white sand, the longest of its kind on the Island. There's so much sand here that Honolulu once purchased bargeloads of the stuff to replenish Waikiki Beach. A shady beach park just inland is the site of the Ka Hula Piko Festival, held each year in May. The park is also a great sunset-facing spot for a rustic afternoon barbecue. A park ranger patrols the area periodically. ⚠ **Swimming is not recommended, except on exceptionally calm summer days, as there's a dangerous undertow. Amenities:** showers; toilets. **Best for:** sunset; walking. ⊠ *Kaluakoi Rd., Maunaloa* ⊕ *2 miles south of the former Kaluakoi Hotel.*

Hotels

If you want to stay in West Molokai so you'll have access to unspoiled beaches, you can choose from condos or vacation homes. Note that units fronting the abandoned Kaluakoi golf course present a bit of a dismal view.

Ke Nani Kai

$ | **APARTMENT** | These pleasant, spacious one- and two-bedroom condos near the beach—each with a washer, dryer, and a fully equipped kitchen—have ocean views and nicely maintained tropical landscaping. **Pros:** on island's secluded west end; uncrowded pool; beach across the road. **Cons:** far from commercial center; some units overlook abandoned golf

Beach Safety

Unlike protected shorelines like Kaanapali on Maui, the coasts of Molokai are exposed to rough sea channels and dangerous rip currents. The ocean tends to be calmer in the morning and in summer. No matter what the time, however, always study the sea before entering. Unless the water is placid and the wave action minimal, it's best to stay on shore, even though locals may be in the water. Don't underestimate the power of the ocean. Protect yourself with sunblock; cool breezes make it easy to underestimate the power of the sun as well.

course; amenities vary from unit to unit. $ *Rooms from: $162* ⊠ *50 Kepuhi Pl., Maunaloa* 🕾 *808/460–4421* ⊕ *molokai-vacation-rental.net* ⊐ *120 units* ⦿ *No Meals.*

★ Paniolo Hale

$ | **APARTMENT** | Perched high on a ridge overlooking a favorite local surfing spot, this is Molokai's best condominium property and boasts mature tropical landscaping and a private serene setting. **Pros:** close to beach; quiet surroundings; perfect if you are an expert surfer. **Cons:** far from shopping; golf course units front abandoned course; amenities vary. $ *Rooms from: $167* ⊠ *100 Lio Pl., Maunaloa* 🕾 *808/460-4221* ⊕ *molokai-vacation-rental.net* ⊐ *77 units* ⦿ *No Meals.*

Shopping

ARTS AND CRAFTS
★ Big Wind Kite Factory

CRAFTS | The factory has custom-made kites you can fly or display. Designs range from Hawaiian flags to Hawaiian animals like *pueo* (owls) with a little bit of mermaid fun in between. Also in stock are paper kites, mini kites, and wind socks. The adjacent gallery carries an eclectic collection of merchandise, including locally made crafts, Hawaiian books and CDs, jewelry, and other souvenirs. ⊠ *120 Maunaloa Hwy., Maunaloa* ☎ *808/552–2364* ⊕ *bigwindkites.com.*

FOOD

Maunaloa General Store

FOOD | Stocking meat, produce, beverages, and dry goods, this shop is a convenient stop if you're planning a picnic at one of the west-end beaches. Stop for other treats as well—they've got ice cream, beer, and plenty of tasty snacks. ⊠ *200 Maunaloa Hwy., Maunaloa* ☎ *808/552–2346.*

Kalaupapa Peninsula

One of the more remote areas in the Hawaiian Islands is a place of stunning natural beauty coupled with a tragic past. It's here that residents of Hawaii who displayed symptoms of Hansen's disease were permanently exiled beginning in 1866. Today, the peninsula is still isolated. But a day spent here is, without a doubt, a profound, once-in-a-lifetime experience.

GETTING HERE AND AROUND

Unless you fly (through Makani Kai Air on-island or Mokulele Airlines off-island), the only way into Kalaupapa National Historical Park is to travel down a dizzying switchback trail, either on foot or by mule. Going down on foot takes at least an hour, but you must allow 90 minutes for the return; going down by mule is even slower, taking two hours down, and the same to travel back up. The switchbacks are numbered—26 in all—and descend 1,700 feet to sea level in just under 3 miles. The steep trail is more of a staircase, and most of the trail is shaded. However, the footing is uneven, and there is little to keep you from pitching over the side. If you don't mind heights, you can stare straight down to the ocean

for most of the way. It's strenuous regardless of which method you choose.

The Kalaupapa Trail and Peninsula are all part of Kalaupapa National Historical Park (☎ *808/567–6802*), which is open every day but Sunday for tours only. Keep in mind there are no public facilities (except an occasional restroom) anywhere in the park. Pack your own food and water, as well as light rain gear, sunscreen, and bug repellent. ■ **TIP→ To learn more about this unique place be sure to visit the Molokai Museum and view the community from the Kaulapapa Overlook.**

TOURS

★ Kalaupapa Guided Mule Tour

SCENIC DRIVE | Mount a friendly, well-trained mule and wind along a thrilling 3-mile, 26-switchback trail to reach the town of Kalaupapa, which was once home to patients with leprosy who were exiled to this remote spot. The path was built in 1886 as a supply route for the settlement below. Once in Kalaupapa, you take a guided tour of the town and enjoy a light picnic lunch. The trail traverses some of the highest sea cliffs in the world, and views are spectacular.

Only those in good shape should attempt the ride, as two hours each way on a mule can take its toll. You must be at least 16 years old and weigh no more than 250 pounds; pregnant women are not allowed. The entire event takes seven hours. The same outfit can arrange for you to hike down or fly in. No one is allowed in the park or on the trail without booking a tour. ⚠ **Currently closed in order to protect residents from exposure to COVID-19. Call** ☎ *808/567-6088* **for updates.** ✉ *100 Kalae Hwy., Kualapuu* ☎ *808/567–6088, 800/567–7550* ⊕ *www.muleride.com* ✉ *$209.*

Mokulele Airlines

AIR EXCURSIONS | To fly into Kalaupapa from another island your only option is Mokulele Airlines (they'll make a layover at the Molokai Airport). As with other ways of traveling into the area, you'll need to arrange a tour so that they can secure permits for you—all visitors must have a sponsor and may not roam around Kalaupapa freely; your tour company serves as your sponsor. Mokulele will require sponsor information before booking. Mokulele Airlines is now part of Southern Airways. ✉ *Kalaupapa* ☎ *866/260–7070 Reservations only.*

⊙ Sights

Kalaupapa National Historical Park

NATIONAL PARK | For 100 years, this remote strip of land was "the loneliest place on Earth," a beautiful yet feared place of exile for those suffering from leprosy (now known as Hansen's disease). Today, visitors to Molokai's Kalaupapa Peninsula, open every day but Sunday, can admire the tall sea cliffs, rain-chiseled valleys, and tiny islets along the coast. The park tells a poignant human story, as the Kalaupapa Peninsula was once a community of about 1,000 people who were banished from their homes in Hawaii. It also recounts the wonderful work of Father Damien, a Belgian missionary who arrived in 1873

Hawaii's First Saint

A long-revered figure on Molokai and in Hawaii, Father Damien, who cared for the desperate patients at Kalaupapa, was elevated to sainthood in 2009. Visitors who cannot visit Kalaupapa can find information on Saint Damien at St. Damien Church in Kaunakakai and may worship at Our Lady of Seven Sorrows (just west of Kaunakakai), St. Damien Church, or at St. Vincent Ferrer in Maunaloa.

to work with the patients. He died in 1889 from leprosy and was canonized as a saint by the Catholic Church in 2009. Mother Marianne Cope, who continued St. Damien's work after his death, was canonized in 2012.

Today there are about eight patients still living in Kalaupapa—now by choice, as the disease is treatable. Out of respect to these people, visitors must be at least 16 years old, cannot stay overnight, and must be on a guided tour or invited by a resident. Photographing patients without their permission is forbidden. There are no public facilities (except an occasional restroom) anywhere in the park. Pack your own food and water, as well as light rain gear, sunscreen, and bug repellent. ✉ *Hwy. 470, Kualapuu* ☎ *808/567–6802* ⊕ *www.nps.gov/kala.*

Central Molokai

Kaunakakai is 8 miles southeast of the airport.

Most residents live centrally, near the Island's one and only true town, Kaunakakai. It's just about the only place on the Island to get food and supplies—it

The Truth About Hansen's Disease

- A cure for leprosy has been available since 1941. Multi-drug therapy, a rapid cure, has been available since 1981.

- With treatment, none of the disabilities traditionally associated with leprosy need occur.

- Most people have a natural immunity to leprosy. Only 5% of the world's population is even susceptible to the disease.

- There are still more than 200,000 new cases of leprosy each year; the majority are in India.

- All new cases of leprosy are treated on an outpatient basis.

- The term "leper" is offensive and should not be used. It is appropriate to say "a person is affected by leprosy" or "by Hansen's disease."

is Molokai. Go into the shops along and around Ala Malama Street to shop and talk with the locals. Take your time, and you'll really enjoy being a visitor. On the north side is Coffees of Hawaii, a 500-acre coffee plantation, and the Kalaupapa National Historical Park, one of the Island's most notable sights.

GETTING HERE AND AROUND

Central Molokai is the hub of the Island's road system, and Kaunakakai is the commercial center. Enjoy the slow pace, and watch for kids, dogs, and people crossing the street downtown.

 Sights

Church Row

CHURCH | Standing together along the highway are seven houses of worship with primarily native-Hawaiian congregations. Notice the unadorned, boxlike architecture so similar to missionary homes. ⊠ *Rte. 460, Kaunakakai* ✛ *5½ miles south of airport.*

Kapuaiwa Coconut Grove

HISTORIC SIGHT | From far away this spot looks like a sea of coconut trees. Closer up you can see that the tall stately palms are planted in long rows leading down to the sea. This is a remnant of one of

the last surviving royal groves planted for Prince Lot, who ruled Hawaii as King Kamehameha V from 1863 until his death in 1872. The grove is planted on private property—visitors should observe from outside of the perimeter fence. ⊠ *30 Mauna Loa Hwy., Kaunakakai.*

Kaunakakai Harbor

MARINA/PIER | Once bustling with barges exporting pineapples, these docks now host visiting boats and the regular barge from Oahu. The wharf, the longest in the state, is also the starting point for fishing, sailing, snorkeling, whale-watching, and scuba-diving excursions. It's a nice place at sunset to watch fish rippling the water. To get here, take Kaunakakai Place, which dead-ends at the wharf. ⊠ *Rte. 450, at Ala Malama St., Kaunakakai* ⊕ *kaunakakaiharbor.com.*

Kaunakakai

TOWN | Central Molokai's main town looks like a classic 1940s movie set. Along the short main drag is a cultural grab bag of restaurants and shops, and many people are friendly and willing to supply directions or just "talk story." Preferred dress is shorts and a tank top, and no one wears anything fancier than a cotton skirt or aloha shirt. ⊠ *Rte. 460, 3 blocks north of Kaunakakai Wharf, Kaunakakai.*

Kapuaiwa Coconut Grove in Central Molokai is a survivor of royal plantings from the 19th century.

Molokai Plumerias

GARDEN | The sweet smell of plumeria surrounds you at this 10-acre orchard containing thousands of these fragrant trees. Purchase a lei to go, or for $25 owner Dick Wheeler will give you a basket, set you free to pick your own blossoms, then teach you how to string your own lei. Whether purchasing a lei or making your own, it's best to call first for an appointment or to order your lei in advance. ⊠ *1342 Maunaloa Hwy., Kaunakakai* ☎ *808/553–3391* ⊕ *molokaiplumerias.com.*

★ Palaau State Park

FOREST | **FAMILY** | One of the Island's few formal recreation areas, this 233-acre retreat sits at a 1,000-foot elevation. A short path through an ironwood forest leads to Kalaupapa Lookout, a magnificent overlook with views of the town of Kalaupapa and the 1,664-foot-high sea cliffs protecting it. Informative plaques have facts about leprosy, Saint Damien, and the colony. The park is also the site of Kaule O Nanahoa (Phallus of Nanahoa), where women in old Hawaii would come to the rock to enhance their fertility; it is said some still do. Because the rock is a sacred site, be respectful and don't deface the boulders. The park is well maintained, with trails, camping facilities, restrooms, and picnic tables. ⊠ *Rte. 470, Kualapuu* ✛ *Take Hwy. 460 west from Kaunakakai and then head mauka (toward the mountains) on Hwy. 470, which ends at the park* ☎ *808/567–6923* ⊕ *dlnr. hawaii.gov/dsp/parks/molokai/palaau-state-park* ⊠ *Free.*

Post-A-Nut at Hoolehua Post Office

GOVERNMENT BUILDING | At this small, rural post office you can mail a coconut anywhere in the world. Postmaster Gary Lam provides the coconuts and colored markers. You decorate and address your coconut, and Gary affixes eye-catching stamps on it from his extensive collection. Costs vary according to destination, but for domestic addresses they start around $10. ⊠ *69-2 Puupeelua Ave., Hoolehua* ☎ *808/553–5112* ⊕ *postanut. com* ☉ *Closed weekends.*

Kaule O Nanahoa at Palaau State Park

Purdy's Macadamia Nut Farm

FARM/RANCH | Molokai's only working macadamia nut farm is open for educational tours hosted by the knowledgeable and entertaining owners. A family business in Hoolehua, the farm takes up 1½ acres with a flourishing grove of 50 original trees that are more than 90 years old, as well as several hundred younger trees. The nuts taste delicious right out of the shell, home roasted, or dipped in macadamia-blossom honey. Look for Purdy's sign behind Molokai High School. ⊠ *Lihi Pali Ave., Hoolehua* ☎ *808/567–6601* ⊕ *molokai-aloha.com/macnuts* 🖅 *Free* 🕙 *Sun. and holidays by appointment only.*

★ R. W. Meyer Sugar Mill and Molokai Museum

HISTORY MUSEUM | Built in 1877, the fully restored, three-room sugar mill has been reconstructed as a testament to Molokai's agricultural history. It is located next to the Molokai Museum and is usually included in the museum tour. Several interesting machines from the past are on display, including a mule-driven cane crusher and a steam engine. The museum contains changing exhibits on the Island's early history and has a gift shop. Currently (and for the foreseeable future) the museum is home to an incredible photography exhibit that showcases the people of and life in Kalaupapa; attending the exhibit and speaking with docents is a great way to learn more about the community if you aren't able to visit. Be sure to step into the gift shop for some unique, locally made items. ⊠ *Rte. 470, Kualapuu* ✛ *2 miles southwest of Palaau State Park* ☎ *808/567–6436* 🖅 *$5 (cash only)* 🕙 *Closed Sun.*

🔱 Beaches

The south shore is mostly a huge, reef-walled expanse of flat saltwater edged with a thin strip of gritty sand and stones, mangrove swamps, and the amazing system of fishponds constructed by the chiefs of ancient Molokai. From this shore you can look out across glassy water to see people standing on top of the sea—actually, way out on top of the reef—casting fishing lines into the distant waves. This is not a great area for swimming beaches, but it is a good place to snorkel or wade in the shallows.

One Alii Beach Park

BEACH | Clear, close views of Maui and Lanai across the Pailolo Channel dominate One Alii Beach Park (*One* is pronounced "o-nay," not "won"), the only well-maintained beach park on the Island's south-central shore. Molokai folks gather here for family reunions and community celebrations; the park's tightly trimmed expanse of lawn could almost accommodate the entire Island's population. Swimming within the reef is perfectly safe, but don't expect to catch any waves. Nearby is the restored One Alii fishpond (it is appropriate only for Native Hawaiians to fish here). **Amenities:** playground, showers; toilets. **Best for:** parties; swimming. ✉ *Rte. 450, Kaunakakai* ✣ *east of Hotel Molokai.*

Molokai Vibes

Molokai is one of the last places in Hawaii where most of the residents are living an authentic rural lifestyle and wish to retain it. Many oppose developing the Island for visitors or outsiders, so you won't find much to cater to your needs; but if you take time and talk to the locals, you will find them hospitable and friendly. Some may even invite you home with them. It's a safe place, but don't interrupt private parties on the beach or trespass on private property. Consider yourself a guest in someone's house, rather than a customer.

🍴 Restaurants

★ Hiro's Ohana Grill

$$$ | **MODERN HAWAIIAN** | Located in Hotel Molokai, the Island's only oceanfront restaurant is also its fanciest and best place to grab a drink or watch the game on TV. Enjoy pasta, steak, shrimp, or fish while watching the sunset and listening to live music, and don't be surprised if the couple you saw hiking is seated at the table right next to you. **Known for:** live music and hula; whale-watching from your table in winter; shrimp pesto over linguini. [$] *Average main: $31* ✉ *Hotel Molokai, 1300 Kamehameha V Hwy., Kaunakakai* ☎ *808/660–3400* 🌐 *hirosohanagrill.com* ☞ *Breakfast available on Sundays.*

Kamoi Snack-n-Go

$ | **AMERICAN** | **FAMILY** | The old school interior at this "Molokai rest stop" feels a bit like a time warp, making it the perfect place to try one (or two) of the 30 or more flavors of Dave's Hawaiian Ice Cream; it's the only place that serves it on the Island. Sit in the refreshing breeze on one of the benches outside to enjoy your cone and pick up snacks, crack seed, water, and cold drinks. **Known for:** Icees; grab-n-go snacks and drinks; unique, tropical flavors of Dave's Hawaiian Ice Cream. [$] *Average main: $6* ✉ *28 Kamoi St., Kaunakakai* ☎ *808/553–3742* 🌐 *facebook.com/kamoisnack.*

★ Kanemitsu's Bakery and Coffee Shop

$ | **CAFÉ** | Stop at this James Beard–nominated Molokai institution for morning coffee, a *loco moco* (white rice, burger patty, fried egg, and brown sauce), and some Molokai bread—a sweet, pan-style white loaf that makes excellent cinnamon toast. Prices are nice and portions are large; breakfast can easily carry you through lunch. **Known for:** taro pancakes; poi donuts; fast and friendly service. [$] *Average main: $9* ✉ *79 Ala Malama St., Kaunakakai* ☎ *808/553–5855* ⏲ *Closed Tues.*

Kualapuu Cookhouse

$ | **AMERICAN** | Across the street from Kualapuu Market, this laid-back diner is a local favorite set in a classic, refurbished, green-and-white plantation house that's decorated with local photography and artwork and accented with a shady lanai. Typical fare at Kualapuu's only restaurant is a plate of chicken, pork, or hamburger steak served with rice, but there's also the more expensive spicy crusted *ahi* (yellowfin tuna) at dinner and daily specials. **Known for:** BYOB; Thursday night prime rib; chicken katsu. $ *Average main: $13* ⊠ *102 Farrington Ave., one block west of Rte. 470, Kualapuu* 📞 *808/567–9655* ▭ *No credit cards* ⊙ *Closed for dinner Sun. and Mon.*

Manae Goods & Grindz

$ | **HAWAIIAN** | The best place to grab a snack or picnic supplies is this store, 16 miles east of Kaunakakai. It's the only place on the east end where you can find essentials such as ice and bread, and not-so-essentials such as seafood plate lunches, bentos, burgers, shakes, and refreshing smoothies. **Known for:** hurricane chips with seaweed and spicy mayo; loco moco (white rice and a burger patty topped with a fried egg and gravy) and plate lunches; famous macaroni salad. $ *Average main: $9* ⊠ *8615 Kamehameha V Hwy., Kaunakakai* 📞 *808/558–8498* ⊙ *Lunch counter closed Wed.; no dinner.*

Molokai Burger

$ | **BURGER** | Clean and cheery, Molokai Burger offers both drive-through and eat-in options. Often compared to In-n-Out, this is the Island's version of fast food, and the tasty burger buns and super crispy fries (including enormous waffle fries as an option) help to elevate this past a typical experience. **Known for:** twofer Tuesdays; air-conditioning and Wi-Fi; affordable burgers. $ *Average main: $9* ⊠ *20 W. Kamehameha V Hwy., Kaunakakai* 📞 *808/553–3533* ⊕ *facebook. com/molokaiburgerHI* ⊙ *Closed Sun.*

Molokai Pizza Cafe

$ | **AMERICAN** | **FAMILY** | This is a popular gathering spot for local families and a good place to pick up food for a picnic.

Pizza, sandwiches, burgers, salads, pasta, and chicken are simply prepared and served without fuss. **Known for:** linguine alfredo; open Sundays; vegetarian options. $ *Average main: $15* ⊠ *15 Kaunakakai Pl., at Wharf Rd., Kaunakakai* 📞 *808/553–3288.*

★ Paddlers Restaurant and Bar

$$ | **AMERICAN** | New owners breathed new life—and a new menu—into this popular Molokai standout, and the result is a laid-back setting and a fusion of gourmet cuisine that stays true to the Island's roots, highlighted by excellent burgers, garlic shrimp, and nightly specials. The bar has the Island's only draft beer, there's live music and dancing most nights, and produce is locally sourced when available—especially with daily fish specials. **Known for:** tomato jam burger; live music at night; an umami explosion in the Paddler Fries. $ *Average main: $18* ⊠ *10 S. Mohala St., Kaunakakai* 📞 *808/553–3300* ⊕ *paddlersrestaurant. com* ⊙ *Closed Sun.*

Sundown Deli

$ | **SANDWICHES** | A Molokai staple for more than 20 years, this small deli focuses on freshly made takeout food. Sandwiches come on a half dozen types of bread, and the homemade soups are outstanding. **Known for:** homemade soups; small but lovely breakfast menu; super friendly owner. $ *Average main: $9* ⊠ *145 Puali Pl., Kaunakakai* 📞 *808/553–3713* ⊕ *sundowndeli.com* ⊙ *Closed weekends. No dinner.*

Hotels

Hotel Molokai is the closest thing to a resort that can be found on the Island, with a pool, on-site dining, activities desk, and more. In addition, there are two condo properties in this area, one close to shopping and dining in Kaunakakai, and the other on the way to the east end.

★ Hotel Molokai

$$ | HOTEL | FAMILY | At this local favorite, Polynesian-style bungalows are scattered around the nicely landscaped property, many overlooking the reef and distant Lanai. **Pros:** five minutes to town; some units have kitchenettes; authentic Hawaiian entertainment. **Cons:** lower-priced rooms are small and plain; walls can feel thin; Wi-Fi can be somewhat spotty. $ Rooms from: $217 ✉ 1300 Kamehameha V Hwy., Kaunakakai ☎ 808/660–3408, 877/553–5347 Reservations only ⊕ hotel-molokai.com ⇆ 40 rooms ❏ No Meals.

Molokai Shores

$ | APARTMENT | Many of the units in this three-story condominium complex have a view of the ocean and Lanai in the distance, and there's a chance to see whales in season. **Pros:** convenient location; some units upgraded; near water. **Cons:** units close to highway can be noisy; beach is narrow and water is too shallow for swimming; Internet can be spotty in this area. $ Rooms from: $175 ✉ 1000 Kamehameha V Hwy., Kaunakakai ☎ 808/460-4421 ⊕ molokai-vacation-rental.net ⇆ 100 units ❏ No Meals.

Wavecrest

$ | APARTMENT | This 5-acre oceanfront condominium complex is convenient if you want to explore the east side of the Island—it's 13 miles east of Kaunakakai, with access to a beautiful reef, excellent snorkeling, and kayaking. **Pros:** friendly staff; good value; nicely maintained grounds. **Cons:** far from shopping; area sometimes gets windy; cell and Internet service can be spotty. $ Rooms from: $150 ✉ 7148 Kamehameha V Hwy., near mile marker 13, Kaunakakai ☎ 808/460-4421 ⊕ molokai-vacation-rental.net ⇆ 126 units ❏ No Meals.

▶ Nightlife

Nightlife on Molokai may not be exactly what you think of for a typical night on the town, but that's what makes it special. It's easy to get to know locals and other travelers when you're singing karaoke, tasting Island-brewed beers, or enjoying the sounds of the ukulele at sunset.

Hiro's Ohana Grill

LIVE MUSIC | The bar at Hiro's Ohana Grill at Hotel Molokai is always a good place to enjoy a drink and beautiful views, with a rotating lineup of local musicians adding ambience to stunning sunset views. ✉ 1300 Kamehameha V Hwy., Kaunakakai ☎ 808/660–3400 ⊕ hirosohanagrill.com.

★ Paddlers Restaurant and Bar

BARS | Paddlers Restaurant and Bar offers the most diverse nightlife on the Island, with music and dancing most nights of the week. Start off with happy hour from 2 to 5 pm Monday through Saturday, then stick around for the fun. If you're looking for a football game or UFC fight, this is the place for it. ✉ 10 Mohala St., Kaunakakai ☎ 808/553–3300 ⊕ paddlers-restaurant.com ⊗ Closed Sun. and Mon.

Shopping

GIFTS

Imports Gift Shop

MIXED CLOTHING | You'll find soaps and lotions, a small collection of 14-karat-gold chains, rings, earrings, and bracelets, and a jumble of Hawaiian quilts, pillows, souvenirs, books, and postcards at this local favorite. T-shirts, aloha wear, beach clothes, and muu muu are all available if you're clothes shopping. ✉ 82 Ala Malama St., Kaunakakai ☎ 808/553–5734 ⊕ molokaiimports.com.

ARTS AND CRAFTS

Molokai Art from the Heart

CRAFTS | A small downtown shop, this arts and crafts co-op has locally made folk art like dolls, clay flowers, silk sarongs, and children's items. The shop also carries rotating original art by more than 100 Molokai artists and Giclée prints, jewelry, locally produced music, and Saint Damien keepsakes. ✉ *64 Ala Malama St., Kaunakakai* ☎ *808/553–8018* ⊕ *molokaigallery.com* ☉ *Closed Sun.*

CLOTHING AND SHOES

★ All Things Molokai

MIXED CLOTHING | This vibrant shop on the Ala Malama strip sells quirky souvenirs like funny T-shirts, jewelry, and local products. They have a café counter offering sandwiches, smoothies, and salads. The owners act as informal area guides, helping visitors find their way around and arrange services that they may need. ✉ *61 Ala Malama Ave., Unit 3, Kaunakakai* ☎ *808/553–3299* ⊕ *allthingsmolokai.com* ☉ *Closed Sun.*

★ Hawaii's Finest

MIXED CLOTHING | **FAMILY** | One of Hawaii's better-known clothing lines for contemporary aloha apparel, Hawaii's Finest sells just that, and at fair prices. This shop on the Ala Malama shopping strip fits in with the Hawaiian pride that permeates Molokai's culture. Their modern designs and bold colors adorn light cotton fabrics and accessories, and the apparel comes in a variety of sizes. This is your best option if you're looking for matching family wear. ✉ *75B Ala Malama Ave., Kaunakakai* ☎ *808/553–5403* ⊕ *hifinest. com* ☉ *Closed Sun.*

FOOD

Friendly Market Center

FOOD | The best-stocked supermarket on the Island has a slogan ("Your family store on Molokai") that is truly credible. Sun-and-surf essentials keep company with fresh produce, meat, groceries, and liquor. Locals say the food is fresher here than at the other major supermarket. ✉ *90 Ala Malama St., Kaunakakai* ☎ *808/553–5595* ⊕ *friendlymkt.com* ☉ *Closed Sun.*

Kualapuu Market

FOOD | This small market that's been open since 1938 has a little bit of everything and is a good stop for provisions, drinks,

and other goodies before visiting the western or northern part of the Island. This multigenerational mom-and-pop store is run by the same family as Molokai Wines and Spirits. ✉ *311 Farrington Hwy., Kualapuu* ☎ *808/567–6223* ⊕ *kualapuumarket.wixsite.com/kmltd* ☉ *Closed Sun.*

★ Molokai Wines and Spirits

WINE/SPIRITS | Don't let the name fool you; along with a surprisingly good selection of fine wines and liquors, the store also carries cheeses and snacks for a nice wine and cheese at sunset experience. ✉ *77 Ala Malama St., Kaunakakai* ☎ *808/553–5009* ⊕ *kualapuumarket. wixsite.com/kmltd* ☉ *Closed Sun.*

SPORTING GOODS

★ Molokai Fish & Dive

SPORTING GOODS | This is the source for your sporting needs, from snorkels to free and friendly advice. Other island essentials like high-quality sunglasses and wide-brimmed hats are also for sale. This is also a good place to pick up original-design Molokai T-shirts, water sandals, books, and gifts. ✉ *53 Ala Malama St., Kaunakakai* ☎ *808/553–5926* ⊕ *molokaifishanddive.com.*

East Molokai

Halawa Valley is 36 miles northeast of the airport.

On the beautifully undeveloped east end of Molokai you can find ancient fishponds, a magnificent coastline, splendid ocean views, and a fertile valley that's been inhabited for 14 centuries. The eastern uplands are flanked by Mt. Kamakou, the Island's highest point at 4,970 feet and home to the Nature Conservancy's Kamakou Preserve. Mist hangs over waterfall-filled valleys, and ancient lava cliffs jut out into the sea.

Halawa Valley is an iconic site in East Molokai.

GETTING HERE AND AROUND

Driving the east end is a scenic adventure, but the road narrows and becomes curvy after the 20-mile marker. Take your time, especially in the seaside lane, and watch for oncoming traffic. Driving at night is not recommended.

Sights

★ Alii Fishpond

RUINS | With its narrow rock walls arching out from the shoreline, Alii is typical of the numerous fishponds that define southern Molokai. Many were built around the 13th century under the direction of powerful *alii* (chiefs), who were typically the only ones allowed to eat the harvest from the ponds. This early type of aquaculture, particular to Hawaii, exemplifies the ingenuity of Native Hawaiians. One or more openings were left in the wall, where gates called *makaha* were installed. These gates allowed seawater and tiny fish to enter the enclosed pond but kept larger predators

out. The tiny fish would then grow too big to get out. At one time there were 62 fishponds around Molokai's coast. Visits are available via guided tours with Ka Honua Momona International with a recommended donation of $25 per person. ✉ *Kamehameha V Hwy., Kaunakakai* ✛ *1/4 mile past Hotel Molokai* ⊕ *kahonuamomona.org* ✉ *$25 per adult* ⌨ *Reserve online.*

★ Halawa Valley

RUINS | The Solatorio *ohana* (family) leads hikes through the valley, the oldest recorded habitation on Molokai. It is home to two sacrificial temples and many historic sites. Inhabitants grew taro and fished from 650 until the 1960s when an enormous flood wiped out the taro patches and forced old-timers to abandon their traditional lifestyle. Now, a new generation of Hawaiians has begun the challenging task of restoring the taro fields. Much of this work involves rerouting streams to flow through carefully engineered level ponds called *loi*. Taro plants, with their big, dancing leaves, grow in the submerged mud of the *loi,* where the water is always cool and flowing. Hawaiians believe that the taro plant is their ancestor and revere it both as sustenance and as a spiritual necessity. The 3.4-mile round-trip valley hike, which goes to Moaula Falls, a 250-foot cascade, is rated intermediate to advanced and includes two moderate river crossings (so your feet will get wet). A $70 fee per adult supports restoration efforts. ⊠ *Eastern end of Rte. 450* ☎ *808/542–1855* ⊕ *halawavalleymolokai.com* ⊑ *$70.*

Kamalo Harbor

VIEWPOINT | A natural harbor used by small cargo ships during the 19th century and a favorite fishing spot for locals, Kamalo Harbor is a quick stop worth making to take in the quiet calm and hang out with shore birds; look for the "Drive Slow" signs just before the highway bends. This area is also the location of St. Joseph's Church, a tiny white church built by Saint Damien of the Kalaupapa colony in the 1880s. ⊠ *Rte. 450, Kaunakakai* ✛ *11 miles east of Kaunakakai.*

Puu O Hoku Ranch

FARM/RANCH | A 14,000-acre private ranch in the highlands of East Molokai, Puu O Hoku was developed in the 1930s by wealthy industrialist Paul Fagan. Route 450 ambles right through this rural treasure with its pastures and grazing horses and cattle. As you drive slowly along, enjoy the splendid views of Maui and Lanai. The small Island off the coast is Mokuhooniki, a favorite spot among visiting humpback whales and nesting seabirds. The ranch is also a retreat center and organic farm, and it offers limited accommodations. ⊠ *Rte. 450, mile marker 25, Kaunakakai* ✛ *25 miles east of Kaunakakai* ☎ *808/558–8109* ⊕ *puuohoku.com.*

St. Joseph's Mission Church

CHURCH | At this small, white church, a quick stop off the highway, you can learn more about Father Damien and his work. It's a state historic site and place of pilgrimage. The door is often open; if it is, slip inside, sign the guest book, and make a donation. The congregation keeps the church in beautiful condition. ⊠ *Kamehameha V Hwy., Kaunakakai* ☎ *808/558–0109* ⊕ *damienchurchmolokai. org.*

Beaches

The east end unfolds as a coastal drive with turnouts for tiny cove beaches—good places for snorkeling, shore fishing, or scuba exploring. Rocky little Mokuhooniki Island marks the eastern point of the Island and serves as a nursery for humpback whales in winter, nesting seabirds in spring, and hammerhead sharks in the fall. The road loops around the east end, then descends and ends at Halawa Valley.

Halawa Beach Park

BEACH | The vigorous water that gouged the steep, spectacular Halawa Valley also carved out two adjacent bays. Accumulations of coarse sand and river rock have created some protected pools that are good for wading or floating around. You might see surfers, but it's not wise to entrust your safety to the turbulent open ocean along this coast. Most people come here to hang out and absorb the beauty of Halawa Valley. The valley itself is private property, so do not wander without a guide. **Amenities:** toilets. **Best for:** solitude. ⊠ *End of Rte. 450, Kaunakakai.*

Waialua Beach Park

BEACH | Also known as Twenty Mile Beach, this arched stretch of sand leads to one of the most popular snorkeling spots on the Island. The water here, protected by the flanks of the little bay, is often so clear and shallow that even from land you can watch fish swimming among the coral heads. Watch out for

St. Joseph's Church is one of Molokai's most historic sites.

traffic when you enter the highway. ■ **TIP→ This is a pleasant place to stop on the drive around the east end. Amenities:** none. **Best for:** snorkeling; swimming. ✉ *Rte. 450 near mile marker 20.*

Hotels

Two unique lodging options await on the remote, far east end of the Island. Dunbar Beachfront Cottages, which lives up to its name as it's just steps from the sand, is great for families. Puu O Hoku Ranch, an active ranch and retreat facility, offers on-site ocean and waterfall views.

★ Dunbar Beachfront Cottages

$$ | **HOUSE** | **FAMILY** | Perfect for a comfortable base in the country, think of these two oceanfront, plantation-style cottages as your own private beach home on Molokai's east end; each has a full kitchen, washer and dryer, and ocean-facing lanai. **Pros:** complete privacy; well-stocked kitchens; convenient location to east end beaches. **Cons:** very popular, so bookings can be hard to come by; additional cleaning fee; isolated and far from town. [$] *Rooms from: $240* ✉ *9750 Kamehameha V Hwy., Kaunakakai* ✥ *Just past mile marker 18* ☎ *808/336–0761* 🌐 *www.molokaibeachfrontcottages.com* 🛏 *2 cottages* 🍴 *No Meals.*

Puu O Hoku Ranch

$$$$ | **B&B/INN** | At the east end of Molokai, these ocean-view accommodations are on 14,000 isolated acres of pasture and forest—a remote and serene location for people who want to get away from it all or meet in a retreat atmosphere. **Pros:** on-site store with unique gifts and treats; authentic working ranch; great hiking. **Cons:** road to property is narrow and winding; very high cleaning fee; on remote east end of island. [$] *Rooms from: $445* ✉ *Rte. 450 near mile marker 25, Kaunakakai* ☎ *808/558–8109* 🌐 *puuohoku.com* 🛏 *2-room cottage, 11-room lodge* 🍴 *No Meals.*

Activities and Tours

Molokai's shoreline topography limits opportunities for water sports. Sea cliffs dominate the north shore; the south shore is largely encased by a huge, taming reef.

⚠ **Open-sea access at west-end and east-end beaches should be used only by experienced ocean swimmers, and even then with caution as seas are rough, especially in winter.**

Generally speaking, there's no one around—certainly not lifeguards—if you are in need of assistance. For this reason alone, guided excursions are recommended. At the very least, be sure to ask for advice from outfitters or residents. Two kinds of water activities predominate: kayaking within the reef area and open-sea excursions on charter boats, most of which tie up at Kaunakakai Wharf.

Activity vendors in Kaunakakai are a good source of information on outdoor adventures on Molokai. For a mellow round of golf, head to the island's only golf course, Ironwood Hills, where you'll likely share the greens with local residents. Molokai's steep and uncultivated terrain offers excellent hikes and some stellar views. Although the island is largely wild, most land is privately owned, so get permission before hiking.

Biking

Cyclists who like to eat up the miles love Molokai, because its few roads are long, straight, and extremely rural. You can really go for it—there are no traffic lights and (most of the time) no traffic.

Molokai Bicycle

BIKING | You can rent a bike here for the day; prices depend on the model, with reductions for additional days or weeklong rentals. Bike trailers (for your drinks cooler, perhaps), including doubles for the kids, are also available. Hours are limited due to the owner's teaching schedule, but drop-offs and pickups are available for free at certain locations and for $25 at the airport. ✉ *80 Mohala St., Kaunakakai* ☎ *808/553–5740* ⊕ *maui-molokaibicycle.com* 🚲 *Bikes from $25 per day, bike trailers from $15 per day.*

Deep-Sea Fishing

For Molokai people, as in days of yore, the ocean is more of a larder than a playground. It's common to see residents fishing along the shoreline or atop South Shore Reef, using poles or lines. Deep-sea fishing by charter boat is a great Molokai adventure. The sea channels here, though often rough and windy, provide gorgeous views of several islands. Big fish are plentiful in these waters, especially *mahimahi* (dolphinfish), marlin, and various kinds of tuna. Generally speaking, boat captains will customize the outing to your interests, share a lot of information about the island, and let you keep some or all of your catch.

EQUIPMENT
Molokai Fish & Dive

FISHING | If you'd like to try your hand at fishing, you can rent or buy equipment, book a trip, and ask for advice from the friendly staff here. They also host snorkel, scuba, and whale-watching tours. ✉ *53 Ala Malama St., Kaunakakai* ☎ *808/553–5926* ⊕ *molokaifishanddive.com.*

BOATS AND CHARTERS
Alyce C.

FISHING | This 31-foot cruiser runs excellent sportfishing excursions in the capable hands of Captain Joe. Full-day, half-day, ¾-day, and full around-the-island trips are available upon the six-passenger boat; gear is provided. It's a rare day when you don't snag at least one memorable fish. Whale-watching trips are also available. ✉ *Kaunakakai Wharf, Kaunakakai Pl., Kaunakakai* ☎ *808/558–8377* ⊕ *www.alycecsportfishing.com* 🖅 *From $450.*

Fun Hogs Sportfishing

FISHING | Trim and speedy, the 27-foot flybridge boat named *Ahi* offers four-hour, six-hour, and eight-hour sportfishing excursions, either near-shore or deepsea. Skipper Mike Holmes also provides sunset cruises, scuba and snorkeling excursions, and whale-watching trips in winter. ✉ *Kaunakakai Wharf, Kaunakakai Pl., Kaunakakai* ☎ *808/336–0047* ⊕ *www.molokaifishing.com* 🖅 *From $450.*

Molokai Action Adventures

FISHING | Walter Naki has traveled (and fished) all over the globe. He will create customized fishing expeditions and gladly share his wealth of experience. He will also take you to remote beaches for a day of swimming. If you want to explore the north side under the great sea cliffs, this is the way to go. His 21-foot Boston Whaler is usually seen in the east end at the mouth of Halawa Valley. ✉ *Kaunakakai* ☎ *808/558–8184* 🖅 *From $300.*

Golf

Molokai is not a prime golf destination, but the sole nine-hole course makes for a pleasant afternoon.

Ironwood Hills Golf Course

GOLF | Like other nine-hole plantation-era courses, Ironwood Hills is in a prime spot, with basic fairways and not always manicured greens. It helps if you like to play laid-back golf with locals and can handle occasionally rugged conditions. On the plus side, most holes offer views of the ocean, as well as those of peaks of Oahu and Molokai's sea cliffs. Fairways are *kukuya* grass and run through pine, ironwood, and eucalyptus trees. Clubs are rented on the honor system; there's not always someone there to assist you

and you should bring your own water. Access is via a bumpy, unpaved road. ✉ *Kalae Hwy., Kualapuu* ☎ *808/567–6000* 🖅 *$20 for 9 holes* 🏌 *9 holes, 3088 yards, par 34.*

Hiking

Rural and rugged, Molokai is an excellent place for hiking. Roads and developments are few. The island is steep, so hikes often combine spectacular views with hearty physical exertion. Because the island is small, you can come away with the feeling of really knowing the place. And you won't see many other people around. Much of what may look like deserted land is private property, so be careful not to trespass—seek permission or use an authorized guide.

BEST SPOTS

Kalaupapa Trail

HIKING & WALKING | You can hike down to the Kalaupapa Peninsula and back via this 3-mile, 26-switchback route. The trail is often nearly vertical, traversing the face of the high sea cliffs. You can reach Kalaupapa Trail off Highway 470 near Kalaupapa Overlook. Only those in excellent shape should attempt it. You must have made prior arrangements with Kekaula (Mule Ride) Tours in order to access Kalaupapa via this trail. ✉ *Off Hwy. 470, Kualapuu* ☎ *808/567–6088 Kekaula Tours* ⊕ *nps.gov/kala.*

GUIDES

★ Halawa Valley Falls Cultural Hike

HIKING & WALKING | This gorgeous, steepwalled valley was carved by two rivers and is rich in history. Site of the earliest Polynesian settlement on Molokai, Halawa is a sustained island culture with its ingeniously designed *loi*, or taro fields. Because of a tsunami in 1948 and changing cultural conditions in the 1960s, the valley was largely abandoned. The Solatorio *ohana* (family) is restoring the loi and taking visitors on guided hikes through the valley, which includes two of Molokai's *luakini heiau* (sacred temples), many historic sites, and the trail to Moaula Falls, a 250-foot cascade. Bring water, food, a *hookupu* (small gift or offering), insect repellent, and wear sturdy shoes that can get wet. The 3½-mile round-trip hike is rated intermediate to advanced and includes two moderate river crossings. ⊠ *14777 Kamehameha V Hwy., Kaunakakai* ✛ *Guide will meet you at the Halawa Beach Park pavilion* ☎ *808/542–1855* ⊕ *halawavalleymolokai. com* ⊠ *$70.*

Kayaking

Molokai's south shore is enclosed by the largest reef system in the United States—an area of shallow, protected sea that stretches over 30 miles. This reef gives inexperienced paddlers an unusually safe, calm environment for shoreline exploring.

⚠ **Outside the reef, Molokai waters are often rough, and strong winds can blow you out to sea. Kayakers out here should be strong, experienced, and cautious.**

BEST SPOTS
South Shore Reef
KAYAKING | This reef's area is superb for flat-water kayaking any day of the year. Get out in the morning before the wind picks up and paddle east, exploring the ancient Hawaiian fishponds. When you turn around, the wind will usually give you a push home. ■ **TIP→ For a kayak or paddleboard lessons, check out Molokai Outdoors at molokai-outdoors.com.** ⊠ *Kaunakakai.*

EQUIPMENT, LESSONS, AND TOURS
★ Molokai Outdoors
KAYAKING | For guided kayak and paddleboard tours, this longtime Molokai activity company offers guided downwind runs along Molokai's southern coast, options for sunset and sunrise tours, as well as kayak and paddleboards for those looking to go solo. ⊠ *1529 Kamehameha V Hwy, Kaunakakai* ✛ *inside Hotel Molokai* ☎ *808/633–8700, 855/208–0811* ⊕ *molokai-outdoors.com* ⊠ *From $99 per person.*

Scuba Diving

Molokai Fish & Dive is the only PADI-certified dive company on Molokai and offers opportunities for beginner through advanced divers. Shoreline access for divers is extremely limited, even nonexistent in winter. Boat diving is the way to go. Without guidance, visiting divers can easily find themselves in risky situations with wicked currents. Proper guidance, however, opens an undersea world rarely seen.

Snorkeling

Snorkeling is particularly nice in Molokai with its beautiful fringed reef that hasn't been decimated by sunscreen and global warming. During the times when swimming is safe—mainly in summer—just about every beach on Molokai offers good snorkeling along the lava outcroppings in the Island's clean and pristine waters. Although rough in winter, Kepuhi Beach is a prime spot in summer. Certain spots inside the South Shore Reef are also worth checking out.

BEST SPOTS
During the summer, **Kepuhi Beach** on Molokai's west end offers excellent snorkeling opportunities. The ½-mile-long stretch has plenty of rocky nooks that swirl with sea life. Take Kaluakoi Road all the way to the west end, park at the now-closed Kaluakoi Resort, and walk to the beach. Avoid Kepuhi Beach in winter, as the sea is rough here.

At **Waialua Beach Park,** on Molokai's east end, you'll find a thin curve of sand that rims a sheltered little bay loaded with

Did You Know?

A hike through the Kamakou Preserve in East Molokai, on the slopes of the island's highest peak, reveals a lush rain forest with bogs and native wildlife. Sign up well in advance for a monthly guided hike with the Nature Conservancy, it's the only access available.

coral heads and aquatic life. The water here is shallow—sometimes so shallow that you bump into the underwater landscape—and it's crystal clear. Pull off the road near mile marker 20.

EQUIPMENT AND TOURS

All the charter boats carry snorkel gear and include dive stops.

Fun Hogs Sportfishing

SNORKELING | Mike Holmes, captain of the 27-foot *Ahi,* knows the island waters intimately, likes to have fun, and is willing to arrange any type of excursion—for example, one dedicated entirely to snorkeling. His two-hour snorkel trips leave early in the morning and explore rarely seen fish and turtle sites outside the reef. ⊠ *Kaunakakai Wharf, Kaunakakai Pl., Kaunakakai* ☎ *808/336–0047* ⊕ *molokaifishing.com* ✒ *From $75 per person.*

Spas

Molokai Acupuncture & Massage

SPAS | This relaxing retreat offers acupuncture, massage, herbal remedies, and wellness treatments by appointment only. The wellness center also offers a regular Vinyasa Flow class; call for prices and location. ⊠ *40 Ala Malama St., Suite 206, Kaunakakai* ☎ *808/553–3930* ⊕ *www.molokai-wellness.com.*

Molokai Lomi Massage

SPAS | Allana Noury of Molokai Lomi Massage has studied natural medicine for nearly 40 years and is a licensed massage therapist, master herbalist, and master iridologist. She will come to your hotel or condo by appointment. ⊠ *Kaunakakai* ☎ *808/553–8034* ⊕ *molokaimassage.com.*

Whale-Watching

Although Maui gets all the credit for the local wintering humpback whale population, the big cetaceans also visit Molokai December–April. Mokuhooniki Island at the east end serves as a whale nursery and courting ground, and the whales pass back and forth along the south shore. This being Molokai, whale-watching here will never involve floating amid a group of boats all ogling the same whale.

BOATS AND CHARTERS

Alyce C.

WILDLIFE-WATCHING | Although this six-passenger sportfishing boat is usually busy hooking *mahimahi* (dolphinfish) and marlin, the captain will gladly take you on an excursion to admire the humpback whales or other points of interest around the Island. ■TIP→ **The price is based on the length of the trip: ½ day, ¾ day, full day, or round-island trips.** ⊠ *Kaunakakai Wharf, Kaunakakai Pl., Kaunakakai* ☎ *808/558–8377* ⊕ *alycecsportfishing.com.*

Ama Lua and Coral Queen

WILDLIFE-WATCHING | Molokai Fish & Dive offers two boats for whale-watching. The *Ama Lua* is a 31-foot dive boat that holds up to 12 passengers, while the *Coral Queen* is a 38-footer that holds up to 25 passengers. On both boats, the crew is respectful of the whales and the laws that protect them. A two-hour whale-watching trip departs from Kaunakakai Wharf at 7 am daily (as long as minimum passenger requirements are met), from December to April. ⊠ *Molokai Fish & Dive, 53 Ala Malama St., Kaunakakai* ☎ *808/553–5926* ⊕ *molokaifishanddive.com* ✒ *From $99 per adult.*

Fun Hogs Sportfishing

WILDLIFE-WATCHING | The *Ahi,* a flybridge sportfishing boat, takes you on two-hour whale-watching trips in the morning, December to April. ■TIP→ **No food or drink is provided.** ⊠ *Kaunakakai Wharf, Kaunakakai Pl., Kaunakakai* ☎ *808/336–0047* ⊕ *molokaifishing.com* ✒ *From $75 per person.*

LANAI

8

Updated by
Laurie Lyons-Makaimoku

👁 Sights	🍴 Restaurants	🛏 Hotels	🛍 Shopping	🍸 Nightlife
★★★★★	★★★☆☆	★★★☆☆	★★★☆☆	★☆☆☆☆

WELCOME TO LANAI

TOP REASONS TO GO

★ **Seclusion and serenity:** Lanai is small; local motion is slow motion. Get into the spirit, and go home rested.

★ **Keahiakawelo (Garden of the Gods):** Walk amid the eerie red-rock spires at this Hawaiian sacred spot. The ocean views are magnificent, too; sunset is a good time to visit.

★ **Diving at Cathedrals:** Explore underwater pinnacle formations and mysterious caverns illuminated by shimmering rays of light.

★ **Dole Park:** Hang out in the shade of the Cook pines in Lanai City, and talk story with the locals for a taste of old-time Hawaii.

★ **Hulopoe Beach:** This beach may have it all—good swimming, a shady park for perfect picnicking, great reefs for snorkeling, and—if you're lucky—schools of spinner dolphins.

1 Lanai City. Quaint and quiet, this historic plantation town is home to most of the Island's residents, restaurants, shops, and businesses. Dole Park, with its stately Cook pines and picnic benches, sits in the middle of the action.

2 Manele Bay. Rest and relaxation characterize this coastal area, home to Manele Harbor, Four Seasons Resort Lanai, iconic Puu Pehe, and the golden sands of Hulopoe Beach.

3 Windward Lanai. This area is the long white-sand beach at the base of Lanaihale. Now uninhabited, it was once occupied by thriving Hawaiian fishing villages and a sugarcane plantation.

Polihua Beach

Keahiakawelo (Garden of the Gods)

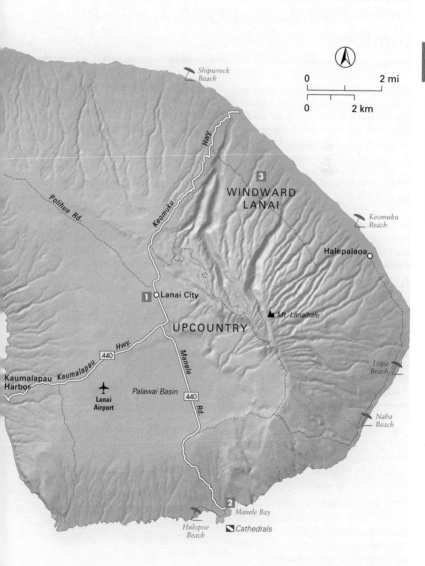

0   2 mi

0   2 km

Shipwreck
Beach

Polihue Rd.

Keomuku Hwy.

WINDWARD
LANAI

3

Keomuku
Beach

Halepalaoa

Lanai City

1

▲ Mt. Lanaihale

UPCOUNTRY

440 Hwy.

Kaumalapau

Manele Rd.

Kaumalapau
Harbor

Lanai
Airport

Palawai Basin

440

Lopa
Beach

Naha
Beach

Manele Bay

2

Hulopoe
Beach

◥ Cathedrals

Mostly privately owned, Lanai is the smallest inhabited island in Hawaii and is a true getaway for slowing down and enjoying serenity amid world-class comforts.

With no traffic or traffic lights and miles of open space, Lanai seems suspended in time, and that can be a good thing. Small (141 square miles) and sparsely populated, it has just over 3,000 residents, most of them living Upcountry in Lanai City. An afternoon strolling around Dole Park in historic Lanai City offers shopping, dining, and the opportunity to mingle with locals. Though it may seem a world away, Lanai is only separated from Maui and Molokai by two narrow channels and is easily accessed by commercial ferry from Maui.

FLORA AND FAUNA

Lanai bucks the "tropical" trend of the other Hawaiian Islands with African *kiawe* (mesquite) trees, Cook pines, and eucalyptus in place of palm trees, and deep blue sea where you might expect shallow turquoise bays. Abandoned pineapple fields are overgrown with drought-resistant grasses, Christmas berry, and lantana; native plants *aalii* and *i lima* are found in uncultivated areas. Axis deer from India dominate the ridges, and wild turkeys lumber around the resorts. Whales can be seen November–May, and a family of resident spinner dolphins rests and fishes regularly in Hulopoe Bay.

ON LANAI TODAY

Despite its fancy resorts, Lanai still has that languid Hawaii feel. The island is 98% owned by billionaire Larry Ellison, who is in the process of revitalizing Lanai. Old-time residents are a mix of just about everything: Hawaiian, Chinese, German, Portuguese, Filipino, Japanese, French, Puerto Rican, English, Norwegian—you name it. When Dole owned the island in the early 20th century and grew pineapples, the plantation was divided into ethnic camps, which helped retain cultural cuisines. Potluck dinners feature sashimi, Portuguese bean soup, *laulau* (morsels of pork, chicken, butterfish, or other ingredients steamed in ti leaves), potato salad, teriyaki steak, chicken *hekka* (a gingery Japanese chicken stir-fry), and Jell-O. The local language is Pidgin English, a mix of words as complicated and rich as the food. Newly arrived residents have added to the cultural mix.

THE GHOSTS OF LANAI

Lanai has a reputation for being haunted (at one time by "cannibal spirits") and evidence abounds: a mysterious purple *lehua* (a native tree that normally produces red flowers) at Keahialoa; the crying of a ghost chicken at Kamoa; Pohaku O, a rock that calls at twilight; and remote spots where cars mysteriously stall, and lights are seen at night. Tradition has it that Puu Pehe (an offshore sea stack) was a child who spoke from the womb, demanding *awa* root. A later story claims it is the grave of a woman drowned in a cave at the nearby cliffs. Hawaiians believe that places have *mana* (spiritual power), and Lanai is no exception.

MAJOR REGIONS

Lanai City, Windward Lanai, and Manele Bay.
Cool and serene, Upcountry is graced by Lanai City, towering Cook pine trees, and misty mountain vistas. The historic plantation village of Lanai City is inching into the modern world. Locals hold conversations in front of Dole Park shops and from their pickups on the road, and kids ride bikes in colorful impromptu parades. Six miles north of Lanai City, Keahiakawelo (nicknamed "Garden of the Gods") is a stunning rocky plateau. The more developed beach side of the island, Manele Bay is where it's happening: swimming, picnicking, off-island excursions, and boating are all concentrated in this accessible area. Windward Lanai is the long white-sand beach at the base of Lanaihale. Now uninhabited, it was once occupied by thriving Hawaiian fishing villages and a sugarcane plantation

Planning

When to Go

Lanai has an ideal climate year-round, hot and sunny at the sea and a few delicious degrees cooler Upcountry. In Lanai City and Upcountry, the nights and mornings can be almost chilly when fog or harsh trade winds settle in. Winter months are known for *slightly* rougher weather— periodic rain showers, occasional storms, and higher surf.

Because higher mountains on Maui capture the trade-wind clouds, Lanai receives little rainfall and has a near-desert ecology. Consider the wind direction when planning your day. If it's blowing a gale on the windward beaches, head for the beach at Hulopoe or check out Keahiakawelo (Garden of the Gods). Overcast days, when the wind stops or comes lightly from the southwest, are common in whale season. At that time,

try a whale-watching trip or the windward beaches.

Whales are seen off Lanai's shores November–May (peak season January–March). A Pineapple Festival on the July 4 Saturday in Dole Park features traditional entertainment, a pineapple-eating contest, and fireworks. Buddhists hold their annual outdoor Obon Festival, honoring departed ancestors with joyous dancing, local food, and drumming, in early July. During hunting-season weekends, mid-February–mid-May and mid-July–mid-October, watch out for hunters on dirt roads even though there are designated safety zones. On Sundays, many shops and restaurants have limited hours or are closed altogether.

Getting Here and Around

AIR

Mokulele Airlines is the only commercial airline routinely serving Lanai City. Direct flights are available from Oahu; if you're flying to Lanai from any other Hawaiian Island, you'll make a stop in Kahului. Guests of the Four Seasons Resort Lanai can arrange private charters on Lanai Air.

If you're staying at the Four Seasons Resort Lanai you'll be met at the airport or ferry dock by a bus that shuttles between the resort and Lanai City.

AIRLINE CONTACTS Mokulele Airlines.
✉ *Lanai Ave., Lanai City* ☎ *866/260–7070 toll free, 808/495-4188* ⊕ *mokuleleairlines.com.*

AIRPORT CONTACTS Lanai Airport (LNY).
✉ *Lanai Ave., Lanai City* ☎ *808/565–7942* ⊕ *airports.hawaii.gov/lny.*

CAR

It's always good to carry a cell phone. Lanai has only 30 miles of paved roads; its main road, Highway 440, refers to both Kaumalapau Highway and Manele Road. Keomuku Highway starts just past Sensei Lanai and runs northeast to the dirt road that goes to Kaiolohia (aka Ship wreck Beach) and Lopa Beach. Manele Road (Highway 440) runs south down to Manele Bay, the Four Seasons Resort Lanai, and Hulopoe Beach. Kaumalapau Highway (also Highway 440) heads west to Kaumalapau Harbor. The rest of your driving takes place on bumpy dusty roads that are unpaved and unmarked. Driving in thick mud is not recommended, and the rental agency will charge a stiff cleaning fee. Watch out for blind curves on narrow roads. Take a map, be sure you have a full tank, and bring a snack and plenty of water (including water to rinse off at the beaches, as many of the remote beaches have no showers or other facilities).

Renting a four-wheel-drive vehicle is expensive but almost essential if you'd like to explore beyond the resorts and Lanai City. Make reservations far in advance of your trip, because Lanai's fleet of vehicles is limited. Ask the rental agency or your hotel's concierge about road conditions before you set out.

Stop from time to time to find landmarks and gauge your progress. Never drive or walk to the edge of lava cliffs, as rock can give way under you. Directions on the island are often given as *mauka* (toward the mountains) and *makai* (toward the ocean).

If you're visiting for the day, Rabaca's Limousine Service or Lanai Taxi will take you wherever you want to go. Advance reservations are required.

CONTACT Rabaca's Limousine Service. ✉ *552 Alapa St., Lanai City* ☎ *808/559–0230.* **Lanai Taxi.** ✉ *Lanai City* ☎ *808/649–8330* ⊕ *facebook.com/lanaitaxi.*

FERRY
Ferries operated by Expeditions cross the channel four times daily between Lahaina on Maui to Manele Small Boat Harbor on Lanai. The crossing takes 45 minutes and costs $30 (discounts for children). Be warned: passage can be rough, especially in winter.

CONTACT Expeditions. ✉ *658 Front St., Lahaina* ☎ *808/661–3756, 800/695–2624* ⊕ *go-lanai.com.*

SHUTTLE
The high-end resorts provide free ground transportation for their guests to/from the harbor or the airport in a luxury shuttle.

Beaches

Lanai offers miles of secluded white-sand beaches on its windward side, plus the moderately developed Hulopoe Beach, which is adjacent to the Four Seasons Resort Lanai. Hulopoe is accessible by car or hotel shuttle bus; to reach the windward beaches you need a four-wheel-drive vehicle. Reef, rocks, and coral make swimming on the windward side problematic, but it's fun to splash around in the shallow water. Expect debris on the windward beaches due to the Pacific convergence of ocean currents. Driving on the beach itself is illegal and can be dangerous.

Biking

Many of the same red-dirt roads that invite hikers are excellent for biking, offering easy, flat terrain and long clear views.

A favorite biking route is along the fairly flat red-dirt road northward from Lanai City through the old pineapple fields to Keahiakawelo (Garden of the Gods). Start your trip on Keomuku Highway in town. Take a left just before Sensei Lanai's tennis courts, and then a right where the road ends at the fenced pasture, and continue on to the north end and the start of Polihua and Awalua dirt roads. If you're really hardy, you could bike down to Polihua Beach and back, but it would be a serious all-day trip. In wet weather these roads turn to mud and are not advisable. Go in the early morning or late afternoon, because the sun gets hot in the middle of the day. Take plenty of water, spare parts, and snacks.

For the exceptionally fit, it's possible to bike from town down the Keomuku Highway to the windward beaches and back. Experienced bikers also travel up and down the Manele Highway from Manele Bay to town.

Hotels

The good news is that you're sure to escape the crowds on this quaint island. The bad news is that Lanai has limited accommodation options, including the pricey Four Seasons Resort Lanai, or the (relatively speaking) affordable Hotel Lanai.

Hotel and dining reviews have been shortened. For full information, visit Fodors.com.

HOTEL AND RESTAURANT PRICES

Restaurant prices are the average cost of a main course at dinner or, if dinner is not served, at lunch. Hotel prices are the lowest cost of a standard double room in high season. Condo price categories reflect studio and one-bedroom rates.

WHAT IT COSTS in U.S. Dollars			
$	$$	$$$	$$$$
RESTAURANTS			
under $18	$18–$26	$27–$35	over $35
HOTELS			
under $181	$181–$260	$261–$340	over $340

Restaurants

Lanai has a wide range of choices for dining, from simple plate-lunch local eateries to gourmet resort restaurants.

Lanai's own version of Hawaii regional cuisine draws on the fresh bounty provided by local farmers and fishermen, combined with the skills of well-regarded chefs. The upscale menus at the Four Seasons Resort Lanai encompass European- and Asian-inspired cuisine as well as innovative preparations of international favorites and vegetarian delights. All Four Seasons Resort restaurants offer children's menus. Lanai City's eclectic ethnic fare runs from construction-worker-size local plate lunches to *poke* (raw fish), pizza, and pasta.

TIP→ Lanai "City" is really a small town; restaurants sometimes close their kitchens early, and only a few are open on Sunday.

Lanai City

Lanai City is 3 miles northeast of the airport.

A tidy plantation town, built in 1924 by Jim Dole to accommodate workers for his pineapple business, Lanai City is home to old-time residents, resort workers, and second-home owners. With its charming plantation-era shops and restaurants kept up-to-date with new paint jobs and landscaping, Lanai City is worthy of whiling away a lazy afternoon.

You can easily explore Lanai City on foot. In its center, Dole Park is surrounded by small shops and restaurants and is a great spot for sitting, strolling, and talking story. Try a picnic lunch in the park and visit the Lanai Culture & Heritage Center in the Old Dole Administration Building to glimpse this island's rich past, purchase historical publications and maps, and get directions to anywhere on the island.

GETTING HERE AND AROUND

Lanai City serves as the island's hub, with roads leading to Manele Bay, Kaumalapau Harbor, and windward Lanai. Keahiakawelo (Garden of the Gods) is usually possible to visit by car, but

Ocean views provide a backdrop to the eroded rocks at Keahiakawelo (aka Garden of the Gods).

beyond that you will need four-wheel drive.

 Sights

Kanepuu Preserve

NATURE PRESERVE | Hawaiian sandalwood, olive, and ebony trees characterize Hawaii's largest example of a rare native dryland forest. Thanks to the efforts of volunteers at the Nature Conservancy and a native Hawaiian land trust, the 590-acre remnant forest is protected from the axis deer and mouflon sheep that graze on the land beyond its fence. More than 45 native plant species can be seen here. A short, self-guided loop trail, with eight signs illustrated by local artist Wendell Kahoohalahala, reveals this ecosystem's beauty and the challenges it faces. The reserve is adjacent to the sacred hill, Kane Puu, dedicated to the Hawaiian god of water and vegetation. ⊠ *Polihua Tr., Lanai City* ✛ *4.8 miles north of Lanai City.*

★ Keahiakawelo (Garden of the Gods)

NATURE SIGHT | This preternatural plateau is scattered with boulders of different sizes, shapes, and colors, the products of a million years of wind erosion. Time your visit for sunset, when the rocks begin to glow—from rich red to purple—and the fiery globe sinks to the horizon. Magnificent views of the Pacific Ocean, Molokai, and, on clear days, Oahu, provide the perfect backdrop for photographs.

The ancient Hawaiians shunned Lanai for hundreds of years, believing the island was the inviolable home of spirits. Standing beside the oxide-red rock spires of this strange raw landscape, you might be tempted to believe the same. This lunar savanna still has a decidedly eerie edge, but the shadows disappearing on the horizon are those of mouflon sheep and axis deer, not the fearsome spirits of lore. According to tradition, Kawelo, a Hawaiian priest, kept a perpetual fire burning on an altar here, in sight of the Island of Molokai. As long as the fire burned, prosperity was assured for the

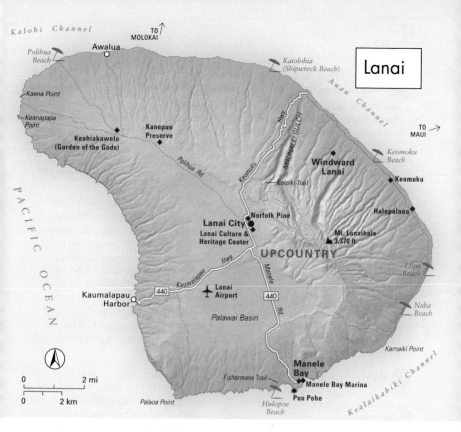

people of Lanai. Kawelo was killed by a rival priest on Molokai, and the fire went out. The Hawaiian name for this area is Keahiakawelo, meaning the "fire of Kawelo." ⊠ *Off Polihua Rd., Lanai City* ✛ *6 miles north of Lanai City.*

★ Lanai Culture & Heritage Center

HISTORY MUSEUM | Small and carefully arranged, this historical museum features artifacts and photographs from Lanai's varied and rich history. Plantation-era clothing and tools, ranch memorabilia, old maps, precious feather lei, poi pounders, and family portraits combine to give you a good idea of the history of the island and its people. Postcards, maps, books, and pamphlets are for sale. The friendly staff can orient you to the island's historical sites and provide directions, making this the best place to start your explorations. ■ TIP→ **The Heritage Center's**

Lanai Guide app is a trove of information—both practical and historical—on the island's sites. ⊠ *730 Lanai Ave., Lanai City* ☎ *808/565–7177* ⊕ *lanaichc.org* ✉ *Free* ☉ *Closed weekends.*

Norfolk Pine

NATURE SIGHT | Considered the "mother" of all the pines on the island, this 160-foot-tall tree was planted here, at the former site of the ranch manager's house, in 1875. Almost 30 years later, George Munro, the manager, observed how, in foggy weather, water collected on its foliage, dripping off rain. This led Munro to supervise the planting of Cook pines along the ridge of Lanaihale and throughout the town in order to add to the island's water supply. This majestic tree is just in front of Sensei Lanai. ⊠ *Sensei Lanai, 1 Keomuku Hwy., Lanai City.*

The Story of Lanai

Rumored to be haunted by hungry ghosts, Lanai was sparsely inhabited for many centuries. Most of the earliest settlers lived along the shore and made their living from fishing the nearby waters. Others lived in the Upcountry near seasonal water sources and traded their produce for seafood. The high chiefs sold off the land bit by bit to foreign settlers, and by 1910 the island was owned by the Gay family.

When the Hawaiian Pineapple Company purchased Lanai for $1.1 million in 1922, it built the town of Lanai City, opened the commercial harbor, and laid out the pineapple fields. Field workers came from overseas to toil in what quickly became the world's largest pineapple plantation. Exotic animals and birds were imported for hunting. Cook pines were planted to catch the rain, and eucalyptus windbreaks anchored the blowing soil.

Everything was stable for 70 years, until the plantation closed in 1992. When the resorts opened their doors, newcomers arrived, homes were built, and other ways of life set in. Today, most of the island is owned by billionaire Larry Ellison, and vast areas remain untouched and great views abound. Although the ghosts may be long gone, Lanai still retains its ancient mysterious presence.

Restaurants

In Lanai City you can enjoy everything from local-style plate lunches to upscale gourmet meals. For a small area, there are a number of good places to eat and drink, but remember that Lanai City mostly closes down on Sunday.

Blue Ginger Café

$ | ECLECTIC | This cheery Lanai City institution offers simply prepared, consistent, tasty food. Local paintings and photos line the walls inside, while townspeople parade by the outdoor tables. **Known for:** comfort food; fresh-baked bread and pastries; authentic local cuisine. $ *Average main: $12 ⊠ 409 7th St., Lanai City ☎ 808/565–6363 ⊕ bluegingercafelanai. com ⊟ No credit cards.*

Coffee Works

$ | AMERICAN | A block from Dole Park, this Northern California–style café offers an umbrella-covered deck where you can sip cappuccinos and get in tune with the slow pace of life. Bagels with lox, deli sandwiches, and pastries are served, while blended espresso shakes and gourmet ice cream complete the coffeehouse vibe. **Known for:** hearty breakfast burritos; varied drink selection; great place to vibe with locals. $ *Average main: $12 ⊠ 604 Ilima St., Lanai City ☎ 808/565–6962 ⊕ coffeeworkshawaii.com ⊗ Closed Sat. and Sun.*

No Ka Oi Grindz Lanai

$ | HAWAIIAN | FAMILY | A local favorite, this lunchroom-style café has picnic tables in the landscaped front yard where diners can watch the town drive by, plus a few more tables in the no-frills interior. The menu includes local favorites like kimchi fried rice and massive plate lunches, plus daily specials. **Known for:** large portions; reasonable prices; local comfort food. $ *Average main: $10 ⊠ 335 9th St., Lanai City ☎ 808/565–9413.*

Pele's Other Garden

$$ | ITALIAN | Small and colorful, Pele's is a deli and bistro all in one. For lunch, sandwiches or daily hot specials satisfy hearty appetites; at night, it's transformed into a busy bistro, with an intimate back-room

bar where entertainers often drop in for impromptu jam sessions. **Known for:** quaint atmosphere; good beer and wine selection; tasty thin-crust pizzas. [$] *Average main: $22* ✉ *811 Houston St., Lanai City* ☎ *808/565–9628* 🌐 *pelesothergarden.com* 🕒 *Closed Sat. and Sun.*

Hotels

Hotel Lanai

$$$$ | HOTEL | Built in 1923 to house visiting pineapple executives, this historic inn is like new following a massive renovation. **Pros:** porches attached to several rooms; walking distance to town; bathrooms include Toto bidet toilets. **Cons:** can be very noisy; small rooms; far from beach. [$] *Rooms from: $389* ✉ *828 Lanai Ave., Lanai City* ☎ *800/795–7211 toll free, 808/565–7211* 🌐 *hotellanai.com* 🛏 *10 rooms, 1 cottage* 🍴 *Free Breakfast.*

★ Sensei Lanai, a Four Seasons Resort

$$$$ | RESORT | This exclusive wellness retreat is the pinnacle of Hawaii luxury. **Pros:** walking distance to Lanai City; onsen outdoor baths; unique private spa hales. **Cons:** activity registration can sometimes be problematic; guests must be aged 16+; not in the price range of the average traveler. [$] *Rooms from: $880* ✉ *1 Keomoku Hwy., Lanai City* ☎ *800/819–5053 toll free, 808/565–2000* 🌐 *fourseasons.com/sensei* 🛏 *96 rooms* 🍴 *No Meals.*

Shopping

A cluster of Cook pines in the center of Lanai City surrounded by small shops and restaurants, Dole Park is the closest thing to a mall on Lanai. Except for high-end resort boutiques and pro shops, it's the island's only shopping option. A morning or afternoon stroll around the park offers an eclectic selection of gifts and clothing, plus a chance to chat with friendly shopkeepers. Well-stocked general stores are reminiscent of the 1920s, and galleries and a boutique have original art and fashions for everyone.

CLOTHING

★ The Local Gentry

MIXED CLOTHING | Spacious and classy, this store has clothing for every need, from casual men's and women's beachwear to evening resort wear, shoes, jewelry, home decor, accessories, and hats. There are fancy fashions for tots and a selection of original Lanai-themed clothing and accessories as well. Proprietor Jenna Gentry Majkus will mail your purchases. ✉ *363 7th St., Lanai City* ☎ *808/565–9130* 🌐 *facebook.com/thelocalgentrylanai.*

FOOD

Pine Isle Market

GENERAL STORE | One of Lanai City's two all-purpose markets, Pine Isle stocks everything from beach toys and electronics to meats and vegetables. The staff is friendly, and it's the best place around to buy fresh fish. ✉ *356 8th St., Lanai City* ☎ *808/565–6488.*

Richard's Market

FOOD | Richard's is the best spot to find quality meats, fine wines, and imported gourmet items. There's also a deli, poke bar, bakery, and fresh fish selections, as well as produce from Lanai's Sensei Farms. ✉ *434 8th St., Lanai City* ☎ *808/565–3780* 🌐 *facebook.com/LanaiRichardsMarket.*

GALLERIES

Lanai Art Center

ART GALLERIES | Local artists display their work at this dynamic center staffed by volunteers (hours are a bit flexible because of this). Workshops in pottery, photography, woodworking, and painting welcome visitors. The gift shop sells Lanai handicrafts and special offerings, the sale of which underwrites children's art classes. The gathering spot also hosts occasional special events for the community. ✉ *339 7th St., Lanai City* ☎ *808/565–7503* 🌐 *lanaiart.org* 🕒 *Closed Sun.*

★ Mike Carroll Gallery

ART GALLERIES | The dreamy, soft-focus oil paintings of award-winning painter Mike Carroll are inspired by island scenes. His work is showcased along with those of other local artists and visiting plein air painters. You can also find handcrafted jewelry, functional art, and other accessories. ⊠ *443 7th St., Lanai City* ☎ *808/565–7122* ⊕ *mikecarrollgallery. com.*

GENERAL STORES

Lanai City Service

FOOD | Lanai's only gas station is a convenient stop to fill your belly, too. The on-site Plantation Deli is famous for its massive sandwiches packed with quality ingredients, as well as other delicious items. Snacks, beer, and souvenirs and friendly faces round out the selection. ⊠ *1036 Lanai Ave., Lanai City* ☎ *808/565–7227.*

🏃 Activities

HIKING

Only 30 miles of Lanai's roads are paved, but red-dirt roads and trails, ideal for hiking, will take you to sweeping overlooks, isolated beaches, and shady forests. Take a self-guided walk through Kane Puu Preserve, Hawaii's largest native dryland forest. You can also explore the Munro Trail over Lanaihale with views of plunging canyons (currently closed for repairs), hike along an old coastal fisherman trail, or head out across Koloiki Ridge. Wear hiking shoes, a hat, and sunscreen, and carry a windbreaker, cell phone, and plenty of water.

Koloiki Ridge

HIKING & WALKING | This marked trail starts behind Sensei Lanai and takes you along the cool and shady Munro Trail to overlook the windward side, with impressive views of Maui, Molokai, Maunalei Valley, and Naio Gulch. The average time for the 4.2-mile round trip is two hours. Bring snacks, water, and a windbreaker; wear good shoes; and take your time. *Moderate.* ⊠ *Lanai City.*

ZIP-LINING

★ Lanai Adventure Park

ZIP-LINING | FAMILY | For an afternoon of adventure this park features on-site and off-site activities for the whole family. Options include zip-lining over Kaiholena Valley, a kid-friendly two-story aerial adventure, guided e-bike tours (location determined by skill of everyone in your party), and a guided hike of Koloiki Ridge Trail. Excursions offer plenty of cultural and historical information, giving guests the opportunity to learn more about Lanai. ⊠ *1 Keomoku Hwy., Lanai City* ☎ *808/563–0096* ⊕ *lanaiadventurepark. com* ✉ *$50–$120 depending on activity.*

Manele Bay

Manele Bay is 9 miles southeast of Lanai City and 10 miles south of the airport.

Manele Bay is an ocean lover's dream: Hulopoe Beach offers top-notch snorkeling, swimming, picnicking, tide pools, and sometimes spinner dolphins. Off-island ocean excursions depart from nearby Manele Small Boat Harbor. Take the short but rugged hike to the Puu Pehe (Sweetheart Rock) overlook, and you'll enjoy a bird's-eye view of this iconic Lanai landmark.

GETTING HERE AND AROUND

You don't really need a car to get around Manele Bay as the resorts provide shuttle service from the airport and to other areas, but having a car would be useful for exploring other areas of the island.

Sights

Manele Bay Marina

MARINA/PIER | Ferries from Maui dock four times a day, and visiting yachts pull in here, as it's the island's only small boat harbor. Public restrooms, grassy lawns, and picnic tables make it a busy pit

One of the pools at Four Seasons Resort Lanai

stop—you can watch the boating activity as you rest. ⊠ *12 Manele Rd., Lanai City.*

Puu Pehe

NATURE SIGHT | Often called Sweetheart Rock, this isolated 80-foot-high islet is steeped in romantic Hawaiian lore. The rock is said to be named after Pehe, a woman so beautiful that her husband kept her hidden in a sea cave. One day, the surf surged into the cave, and she drowned. Her grief-stricken husband buried her on this rock and jumped to his death. It is also believed that the enclosure on the summit is a shrine to birds, built by bird-catchers. Protected shearwaters nest in the nearby sea cliffs July–November. ⊠ *Hwy. 440, Manele, Lanai City.*

Beaches

★ Hulopoe Beach

BEACH | **FAMILY** | A short stroll from the Four Seasons Resort Lanai, Hulopoe is one of the best beaches in Hawaii. The sparkling crescent of this Marine Life Conservation District beckons with calm waters safe for swimming almost year-round, great snorkeling reefs, tide pools, and sometimes spinner dolphins. A shady, grassy beach park is perfect for picnics. If the shore break is pounding, or if you see surfers riding big waves, stay out of the water. In the afternoon, watch Lanai High School students heave outrigger canoes down the steep shore break and race one another just offshore. To get here, take Highway 440 south to the bottom of the hill and turn right. The road dead-ends at the beach's parking lot. **Amenities:** parking (no fee); showers; toilets. **Best for:** snorkeling; surfing; swimming. ⊠ *Off Hwy. 440, Lanai City.*

Hotels

★ Four Seasons Resort Lanai

$$$$ | **RESORT** | **FAMILY** | With stunning views of Hulopoe Bay and the astonishing rocky coastline, this sublime retreat offers beachside urban chic decor with meticulously curated artwork from across Polynesia, Micronesia, and Hawaii and manicured grounds that feature an array of native Hawaiian plants and species. **Pros:** nearby beach; outstanding restaurants and high-tech amenities; rental vehicles available on property. **Cons:** need a car to explore the area; not all guest rooms have coast views; 20 minutes from town. $ *Rooms from: $2005* ✉ *1 Manele Bay Rd., Manele, Lanai City* ☎ *808/565–2000, 800/819–5053* 🌐 *fourseasons.com/lanai* 🛏 *213 rooms* 🍴 *No Meals.*

Restaurants

Dining at Manele Bay is reliant on the range of options provided by the Four Seasons Resort Lanai, from informal poolside meals to relaxed eclectic dining.

★ Nobu Lanai

$$$$ | **JAPANESE** | Chef Nobuyuki "Nobu" Matsuhisa offers his signature new-style Japanese cuisine in this open-air, relaxed luxury venue that features a lounge, outdoor tables, and a sushi bar overlooking Holopoe Bay. This is fine dining without the stress, as black-clad waiters present dish after dish of beautifully seasoned, raw and lightly cooked seafood from local waters, or flown in directly from Alaska and Japan. **Known for:** Nobu's famous miso cod; exceptional levels of service; 15-course Teppanyaki experience. $ *Average main: $40* ✉ *Four Seasons Resort Lanai, 1 Manele Bay Rd., Lanai City* ☎ *808/565–2832* 🌐 *noburestaurants.com/lanai* 🕑 *No breakfast, lunch.*

ONE FORTY

$$$$ | **AMERICAN** | Named after the island's 140 square miles, this ocean-view restaurant serves prime cuts of beef and the freshest local fish in airy comfort on a terrace that overlooks the wide sweep of Hulopoe Bay. Retractable awnings provide shade on sunny days, and comfy rattan chairs, potted palms, and tropical decor create an inviting setting. **Known for:** decadent and delicious seafood tower; poke prepared tableside; tasty upscale breakfasts. $ *Average main: $55* ✉ *Four Seasons Resort Lanai, 1 Manele Bay Rd., Lanai City* ☎ *808/565–2000* 🌐 *fourseasons.com/lanai* 🕑 *No lunch.*

VIEWS at Manele Golf

$$ | **AMERICAN** | A stunning view of the legendary Puu Pehe rock only enhances the imaginative fare of this open-air restaurant, which also has great views of frolicking dolphins from its terrace. Tuck into a Hulopoe Bay prawn BLT, the crispy battered fish-and-chips with Meyer lemon tartar sauce, or any one of the tempting salad options. **Known for:** superb service; house-made ice cream sandwiches; fabulous cocktails. $ *Average main: $26* ✉ *Four Seasons Resort Lanai, 1 Manele Bay Rd., Manele, Lanai City* ☎ *808/565–2230* 🌐 *fourseasons.com/lanai* 🕑 *No dinner; closed Mon.*

Activities

GOLF

Manele Golf

GOLF | You'll need to be a Four Seasons Resort Lanai guest to play at this renowned course. Designed by Jack Nicklaus in 1993, the course sits right over the water of Hulopoe Bay. Built on lava outcroppings, the five-tee course is on every good golfer's bucket list due to its challenging nature and beauty. Three holes are positioned on cliffs, utilizing the Pacific Ocean as a natural water hazard, while other shots must navigate challenging gorges and ravines to get to the hole. Unspoiled natural terrain provides a stunning backdrop, and every hole offers ocean views. Early-morning tee times are recommended to avoid the midday heat. ✉ *Four Seasons Resort Lanai, Challenge Dr., Manele, Lanai City* ☎ *808/565–4000* 🌐 *fourseasons.com/lanai* 🎟 *$385 for resort guests* ⛳ *18 holes, 7039 yards, par 72.*

Some holes at Manele Golf use the Pacific Ocean as a water hazard.

HIKING

Fisherman's Trail

HIKING & WALKING | Local anglers still use this trail to get to their favorite fishing spots. The trail takes about 1½ hours (4.4 miles round trip) and follows the rocky shoreline below the Four Seasons Resort Lanai. The marked trail entrance begins at the west end of Hulopoe Beach. Keep your eyes open for spinner dolphins cavorting offshore and the silvery flash of fish feeding in the pools below. The condition of the trail varies with weather and frequency of maintenance; it can be slippery and rocky. Take your time, wear a hat and enclosed shoes, and carry water. *Moderate.* ⊠ *Manele, Lanai City.*

Puu Pehe Trail

HIKING & WALKING | Beginning to the left of Hulopoe Beach, this trail travels a short distance around the coastline and then climbs up a sharp rocky rise. At the top, you're level with the offshore stack of Puu Pehe and can overlook miles of coastline in both directions. The trail is not difficult, but it's hot and steep. Be aware of nesting seabirds and don't approach their nests.

⚠ **Stay away from the edge, as the cliff can easily give way.**

The hiking is best in the early morning or late afternoon, and it's a perfect place to look for whales in season (November–May, peak season January–March) and to catch a stunning sunset. Wear a hat and enclosed shoes, and take water so you can spend some time at the top admiring the view. *Moderate.* ⊠ *Manele, Lanai City.*

SCUBA DIVING

When you have a dive site such as Cathedrals—with eerie pinnacle formations and luminous caverns—it's no wonder that scuba-diving buffs consider exploring the waters off Lanai akin to a religious experience.

★ Cathedrals

SCUBA DIVING | Just outside Hulopoe Bay, Cathedrals is the best cavern dive site in Lanai. Shimmering light makes the many openings resemble stained-glass windows. A current generally keeps the water crystal clear, even if it's turbid outside. In these unearthly chambers, large *ulua* (giant trevally) and small reef sharks add to the adventure. Tiger sharks may appear in certain seasons. ⊠ *Manele, Lanai City.*

SNORKELING

Snorkeling is the easiest ocean sport available on the island, requiring nothing but a snorkel, mask, fins, and good sense. Borrow equipment from your hotel or purchase some in Lanai City if you didn't bring your own. Wait to enter the water until you are sure no big sets of waves are coming, and observe the activity of locals on the beach. If little kids are playing in the shore break, it's usually safe to enter.

■TIP➜ **To get into the water safely, always swim in past the breakers, and in the comparative calm put on your fins, then mask and snorkel.**

The best snorkeling on Lanai is at **Hulopoe Beach** and **Manele Small Boat Harbor.** Hulopoe, which is an exceptional snorkeling destination, has schools of manini that feed on the coral and coat the rocks with flashing silver. You can also easily view *kala* (unicorn fish), *uhu* (parrot fish), and *papio* (small trevally) in all their rainbow colors. Beware of rocks and surging waves. At Manele Harbor, there's a wade-in snorkel spot beyond the break wall. Enter over the rocks, just past the boat ramp.

⚠ **Do not enter if the waves are breaking.**

SPAS

Hawanawana Spa

SPAS | No two experiences are alike at Hawanawana Spa, where every treatment is tailored to your individual desires. Spa and salon services—like the Ocean Potions Ritual or Lanai Tai Signature Scrub—feature locally inspired ingredients and techniques. Massages are also available in couples' suites and poolside. The spa also offers a wide range of yoga (including aerial yoga), fitness, and meditation classes. ⊠ *Four Seasons Resort Lanai, 1 Manele Bay Rd., Manele, Lanai City* ☎ *808/565–2088* ⊕ *fourseasons.com/lanai* ✉ *$240 for 60 minute massage, Ocean Ritual $460 per person for two hours.*

SURFING

Surfing on Lanai can be truly enjoyable. Quality, not quantity, characterizes this isle's few breaks. Be considerate of the locals, and they will be considerate of you—surfing takes the place of megaplex theaters and pool halls here, serving as one of the island's few recreational luxuries.

★ Lanai Surf School & Safari

SURFING | Nick Palumbo offers the only surf instruction on the island. The Lanai native is a former Hawaii State Surfing Champion, so you're in good hands—he and his staff are highly experienced and are great with beginners. Stand-up paddleboard lessons and rentals are also available. Experienced riders can rent surfboards overnight, and kids can enjoy the surf with boogie boards, also available to rent. ⊠ *Hulopoe Beach Park, Lanai City* ☎ *808/649–0739* ⊕ *lanaisurfsafari.com* ✉ *Lessons from $200.*

Windward Lanai

Windward Lanai is 9 miles northeast of Lanai City; 17 miles northeast of the airport.

The eastern shore of Lanai is mostly deserted. A few inaccessible *heiau,* or temples, rock walls and boulders marking old shrines, and a restored church at Keomuku reveal traces of human habitation. Four-wheel-drive vehicles are a must to explore this side of the isle. Pack a picnic lunch, a hat and sunscreen, and plenty of drinking water. A mobile phone is also a good idea.

GETTING HERE AND AROUND

Once you leave paved Keomuku Highway and turn left toward Kaiolohia (Shipwreck Beach) or right to Naha Beach, the roads are dirt and sand; conditions vary with the seasons. Mileage doesn't matter much here, but figure on 20 minutes from the end of the paved road to Shipwreck Beach, and about 45 minutes to Lopa Beach. A four-wheel-drive vehicle is necessary to visit these remote areas.

Sights

Halepalaoa

BEACH | Named for the whales that once washed ashore here, Halepalaoa, or the "House of Whale Ivory," was the site of the wharf used by the short-lived Maunalei Sugar Company in 1899. Some say the endeavor failed because the sacred stones of nearby Kahea Heiau were used for the construction of the cane railroad. The brackish well water turned too salty, forcing the sugar company to close in 1901, after just two years. The remains of the *heiau*, once an important place of worship for the people of Lanai, are now difficult to find through the *kiawe* (mesquite) overgrowth. This is a nice place for sunbathing and whale-watching, but it's not easy to get to—a 4WD vehicle is definitely required. Take Highway 440 (Keomuku Highway) to its eastern terminus, then turn right on the dirt road and continue south for 5½ miles. ⊠ *On dirt road off Hwy. 440, Lanai City.*

Keomuku

RUINS | There's a peaceful beauty about the former fishing village of Keomuku. During the late 19th century, this small Lanai community served as the headquarters of the Maunalei Sugar Company. After the company failed, the land was abandoned. Although there are no other signs of previous habitation, its church, Ka Lanakila O Ka Malamalama, built in 1903, has been restored by volunteers. Visitors often leave some small token, a shell or lei, as an offering. Take Highway

440 to its eastern terminus, then turn right onto a dirt road and continue south for 5 miles. The church is on your right in the coconut trees. ⊠ *On dirt road off Hwy. 440.*

 Beaches

Kaiolohia (Shipwreck Beach)

BEACH | The rusting World War II tanker abandoned off this 8-mile stretch of sand adds just the right touch to an already photogenic beach. Strong trade winds have propelled vessels onto the reef since at least 1824, when the first shipwreck was recorded. Beachcombers come to this fairly accessible beach for shells and washed-up treasures, and photographers take great shots of Molokai, just across the Kalohi Channel. A deserted plantation-era fishing settlement adds to the charm. It's still possible to find glass-ball fishing floats as you wander along. Kaiolohia, its Hawaiian name, is a favorite local diving spot. Beyond the beach, about 200 yards up a trail past the Shipwreck Beach sign, are the Kukui Point petroglyphs, marked by reddish-brown boulders.

■ TIP→ **An offshore reef and rocks in the water mean that it's not for swimmers, though you can play in the shallow water on the shoreline.**

To get here, take Highway 440 to its eastern terminus, then turn left onto a dirt road and continue to the end. **Amenities:** none. **Best for:** solitude; windsurfing. ⊠ *Off Hwy. 440, Lanai City.*

Lopa Beach

BEACH | A difficult surfing spot that tests the mettle of experienced locals, Lopa is also an ancient fishpond. With majestic views of West Maui and Kahoolawe, this remote white-sand beach is a great place for a picnic.

⚠ **Don't let the sight of surfers fool you: the channel's currents are too strong for swimming.**

Take Highway 440 to its eastern terminus, turn right onto a dirt road, and continue south for 7 miles. **Amenities:** none. **Best for:** solitude; sunrise; walking. ⊠ *On dirt road off Hwy. 440.*

Naha Beach

BEACH | An ancient rock-walled fishpond—visible at low tide—lies where the sandy shore ends and the cliffs begin their rise along the island's shores. Accessible by four-wheel-drive vehicle, the beach is a frequent dive spot for local fishermen.

⚠ **Treacherous currents make this a dangerous place for swimming.**

Take Highway 440 to its eastern terminus, then turn right onto a sandy dirt road and continue south for 11 miles. The shoreline dirt road ends here. **Amenities:** none. **Best for:** fishing; walking. ⊠ *On dirt road off Hwy. 440, Lanai City.*

Polihua Beach

BEACH | This often-deserted beach features long wide stretches of white sand and unobstructed views of Molokai. The northern end of the beach ends at a rocky lava cliff with some interesting tide pools and sea turtles that lay their eggs in the sand. (Do not drive on the beach and endanger their nests.) However, the dirt road leading here has deep sandy places that are difficult in dry weather and impassable when it rains. In addition, strong currents and a sudden drop in the ocean floor make swimming dangerous, and strong trade winds can make walking uncomfortable. Thirsty wild bees sometimes gather around your car. To get rid of them, put out water some distance away and wait. The beach is in windward Lanai, 11 miles north of Lanai City. To get here, turn right onto the marked dirt road past Keahiakawelo (Garden of the Gods). **Amenities:** none. **Best for:** solitude; sunrise; walking. ⊠ *East end of Polihua Rd., Lanai City.*

The Coastal Road

Road conditions can change overnight and become impassable due to rain in the Upcountry. Your car-rental agency will give you an update before you hit the road. Some of the spur roads leading to the windward beaches from the coastal dirt road cross private property and are closed off by chains. Look for open spur roads with recent tire marks (a fairly good sign that they are safe to drive on). It's best to park on firm ground and walk in to avoid getting your car mired in the sand.

🏃 Activities

SCUBA

Sergeant Major Reef

SCUBA DIVING | Off Kamaiki Point, Sergeant Major Reef is named for big schools of yellow- and black-striped *manini* (sergeant major fish) that turn the rocks silvery as they feed. There are three parallel lava ridges separated by rippled sand valleys, a cave, and an archway. Depths range 15–50 feet. Depending on conditions, the water may be clear or cloudy. ⊠ *Lanai City.*

Photo Credits

Front Cover: H. Mark Weidman Photography / Alamy Stock Photo [Description: View from Canyon Lookout, Waimea Canyon State Park, Kauai, Hawaii, USA]. **Back cover, from left to right:** Carmengabrielafilip/Dreamstime. Maridav/iStockphoto. MNStudio/Shutterstock. **Spine:** EpicStockMedia/iStockphoto. **Interior, from left to right:** ShaneMyersPhoto/iStockphoto (1). Alex Schmitt/Shutterstock (2-3). Sergiyn/Dreamstime (5). **Chapter 1: Experience Hawaii:** ImagineGolf/iStockphoto (6-7). Nataliya Hora/Dreamstime (8-9). Swaengpic/ Dreamstime (9). Michael DeFreitas North America/Alamy (9). Tor Johnson/Hawaii Tourism Authority (10). Bonita Cheshier/Dreamstime (10). EQRoy/Shutterstock (10). Shane Myers Photography/Shutterstock (10). Gardendreamer/Dreamstime (11). Idreamphotos/Dreamstime (12). Dave/Flickr (12). Courtesy of Luau Kalamaku (13). Follow2find/Shutterstock (14). Courtesy of Dave Sansom (14). John Elk III/Alamy (14). Dejjf82/Dreamstime (14). MNStudio/Dreamstime (15). Nalukai/Dreamstime (15). Esusek/Dreamstime (16). Picturist21/Dreamstime (16). Reinhard Dirscherl / Alamy Stock Photo (17). Vacclav/Dreamstime (18). Hawaii Tourism Authority (HTA)/Dana Edmunds (18). Jewhyte/ Dreamstime (18). Johnbronk/Dreamstime (18). Jeff Whyte/Shutterstock (19). O'ahu Visitor's Bureau (19). Thediver123/Dreamstime (20). Kelly Headrick/Shutterstock (20). Kyrien/Dreamstime (20). Flyingwolf/Dreamstime (20). 7maru/ iStockphoto (21). Galina Barskaya/Dreamstime (22). James Wright/Dreamstime (22). MNStudio/Dreamstime (22). BorislavaR/iStockphoto (22). Robert Randall/Dreamstime (23). Hawaii Magazine/Iao Valley Hawaii (23). Brent Hofacker/Shutterstock (28). Hawaii Tourism (28). Dana Edmunds (28). Magdanatka/Shutterstock (29). Big Island Visitors Bureau (BIVB) / Kirk Lee Aeder (29). Alla Machutt/iStockphoto (30). Lost Mountain Studio/Shutterstock (30). Hawaii Tourism Authority (HTA) / Brooke Dombroski (30). Temanu/Shutterstock (30). Mongkolchon Akesin/Shutterstock (30). Hawaii Tourism Authority (HTA) / Heather Goodman (31). Olgakr/ iStockphoto (31). Hawaii Tourism Authority (HTA) / Dana Edmunds (31). Hawaii Tourism Authority (31). Hawaii Tourism Authority (HTA) / Heather Goodman (31). Marilyn Gould/ Dreamstime (32). Douglas Peebles Photography / Alamy Stock Photo (32). Ancha Chiangmai/ Shutterstock (32). Pr2is/Dreamstime (32). Vfbjohn/Dreamstime (32). Eddygaleotti/ Dreamstime (33). Koondon/ Shutterstock (33). Caner CIFTCI/Dreamstime (33). Elmar Langle/iStockphoto (33). Big Island Visitors Bureau (BIVB) / Kirk Lee Aeder (33). Cathy Locklear/Dreamstime (39). HVCB_photo01a (40). Thinkstock LLC (41). Linda Ching/HVCB (43). Sri Maiava Rusden/HVCB (43). Leis of Hawaii/ leisofhawaii.com (44). Kelly Alexander Photography (44). Leis of Hawaii/leisofhawaii.com (44). Leis of Hawaii/leisofhawaii.com (44). Leis of Hawaii/ leisofhawaii.com (44). Kelly Alexander Photography (44). Tim Wilson [CC BY 2.0]/ Flickr (45). Douglas Peebles Photography / Alamy Stock Photo (46). Douglas Peebles Photography / Alamy Stock Photo (46). Dana Edmunds/ Polynesian Cultural Center's Alii Luau (46). Douglas Peebles Photography / Alamy Stock Photo (46). Purcell Team / Alamy Stock Photo (46). Hawaii Visitors and Convention Bureau (47). Hawaii Visitors and Convention Bureau (47). Hawaii Visitors and Convention Bureau (47). Oahu Visitors Bureau (47). **Chapter 3: Oahu:** Izabela23/ Shutterstock (77). HelioSanMiguel_DiamondHead (89). 7maru/iStockphoto (99). Library of Congress (113). Rebecca Adams/Dreamstime (115). NPS/ USS Arizona Memorial Photo Collection (115). USS Missouri Memorial Association (116). Army Signal Corps Collection in the U.S. National Archives (116). USS Bowfin Submarine Museum & Park (117). 7maru/Shutterstock (121). Rico Leffanta/Dreamstime (129). 7maru/ Shutterstock.com (135). MH Anderson Photography/ Shutterstock (136). Harry Beugelink/Shutterstock (147). Dudarev Mikhail/Shutterstock (149). Mkojot/ Dreamstime (152). MNStudio/Shutterstock (157). Phillip B. Espinasse/Shutterstock (163). Eddygaleotti/Dreamstime (164). Damien VERRIER/Shutterstock (166). Ppictures/ Shutterstock (171). Blue Hawaiian Helicopters (174). Life//iStockphoto (181). Malgorzata litkowska/Alamy (184). Photo Resource Hawaii / Alamy Stock Photo (188). Karen Wilson (192). **Chapter 4: Maui:** NIntellectual/iStockphoto (195). Joe West/Shutterstock (209). CJ Anderson/Flickr, [CC BY-ND 2.0] (218). Mike7777777/Dreamstime (227). Igokapil/Dreamstime (232). EQRoy/Shutterstock (237). Derek Robertson/Shutterstock (241). Vlue/Dreamstime (253). 7Michael/iStockphoto (256). Laroach/Dreamstime (257). Estivillml/Dreamstime (258). Diane39/iStockphoto (260). Tracy Immordino/Shutterstock (263). Shane Myers Photo/ iStockphoto (270). Dejetley/Shutterstock (272). Peter Rimkus/Dreamstime (285). Ron Dahlquist/HVCB (293). Shane Myers Photography/ Shutterstock (294). Orxy/ Shutterstock (296). Gert Vrey/Dreamstime (296). Shane Myers Photography/Shutterstock (297). Manuel Balesteri/ Shutterstock (302). Featurecars/Dreamstime (305). **Chapter 5: The Big Island of Hawaii:** Atommy/Shutterstock (307). Mariusz S. Jurgielewicz/Shutterstock (319). Alexander Demyanenko/ Shutterstock (331). Maria Luisa Lopez Estivill/Dreamstime (332). Hawaii Tourism Authority (HTA) / Heather Goodman (337). Mhgstan/Shutterstock (344). Instacruising/ Shutterstock (356). Georgeburba/Dreamstime (361). Estivillml/Shutterstock (370). Russ Bishop / Alamy (374). JMP Traveler/iStockphoto (377). Risaacman/Dreamstime.com (385). Dirkr/ Dreamstime.com (398). Dmitri Kotchetov / iStockphoto (399). Janice Wei/iStock (401). Theartist312/ iStockphoto (402). Blagov58/Dreamstime (403). MNStudio/Dreamstime (412). Cameron Nelson (415). Russ Bishop / Alamy Stock Photo (421). MNStudio/Dreamstime (423). Andre Seale / Alamy (428). David Fleetham / Alamy (431). Yaroslav Williams/Shutterstock (433). **Chapter 6: Kauai:** Kumakuma1216/iStockphoto (435). Nickolay Stanev/Shutterstock (448-449). STLJB/Shutterstock (454). Sergiyn/Dreamstime (458-459). Sergiyn/Dreamstime (460-461). Estivillml/iStock (461). Aerial View NalCoast (461). Design Pics Inc / Alamy Stock Photo (462-463). Photo Resource Hawaii / Alamy (463). Ventu Photo/Shutterstock (463). IndustryAndTravel/ Shutterstock (464-465). Photo Resource Hawaii / Alamy (465). Alexander Demyanenko/Shutterstock (465). Juergen Wallstabe/Shutterstock (473). Sara Bowen of Mālama Hulēʻia (478-479). Cphoto/Dreamstime (485). Kauai Visitors Bureau (486). Jack Jeffrey (487). Adam Springer/ iStockphoto (491). Tor Johnson/Hawaii Tourism Authority (HTA) (493). MNStudio/Shutterstock (506-507). Tor Johnson/Hawaii Tourism Authority (HTA) (513). Americanspirit/ Dreamstime (517). Courtesy of St. Regis Princeville Golf (521). Galyna Andrushko/Shutterstock (523). Bob Pool/Shutterstock (525). Jarvis gray/Shutterstock (531). Chase Clausen/Shutterstock (533). **Chapter 7: Molokai:** Kridsada Kamsombat/ iStockphoto (535). Michael Brake/iShutterstock (544). Ralf Broskvar/Shutterstock (549). Ralf Broskvar/ Dreamstime (550). Reimar/Shutterstock (555). Norinori303/Shutterstock (557). Greg Vaughn / Alamy (561). **Chapter 8: Lanai:** Islandleigh/Dreamstime (563). Aleksei Potov/ Shutterstock (570). Courtesy of Four Seasons/Resort Lanai (575). Golf Club/Hawaii Tourism Japan (HTJ) (577). **About Our Writers:** All photos are courtesy of the writers except for the following: Courtesy of Karen Anderson (590). Courtesy of Kristina Anderson (590). Sweet Rain Media (590). Andréa Cimini Photography 2014 (590). Matt Tuohy Photography (591).

*Every effort has been made to trace the copyright holders, and we apologize in advance for any accidental errors. We would be happy to supply the corrections in the following edition of this publication.

Fodor's ESSENTIAL HAWAII

Publisher: Stephen Horowitz, *General Manager*

Editorial: Douglas Stallings, *Editorial Director*; Jill Fergus, Amanda Sadlowski, *Senior Editors;* Kayla Becker, Brian Eschrich, Alexis Kelly, *Editors;* Angelique Kennedy-Chavannes, *Assistant Editor*

Design: Tina Malaney, *Director of Design and Production;* Jessica Gonzalez, *Senior Designer;* Erin Caceres, *Graphic Design Associate*

Production: Jennifer DePrima, *Editorial Production Manager*, Elyse Rozelle, *Senior Production Editor;* Monica White, *Production Editor*

Maps: Rebecca Baer, *Senior Map Editor*, David Lindroth, Mark Stroud (Moon Street Cartography), *Cartographers*

Photography: Viviane Teles, *Senior Photo Editor;* Namrata Aggarwal, Neha Gupta, Payal Gupta, Ashok Kumar, *Photo Editors;* Eddie Aldrete, *Photo Production Intern;* Kadeem McPherson, *Photo Production Associate Intern*

Business and Operations: Chuck Hoover, *Chief Marketing Officer*, Robert Ames, *Group General Manager*, Devin Duckworth, *Director of Print Publishing*

Public Relations and Marketing: Joe Ewaskiw, *Senior Director of Communications and Public Relations*

Fodors.com: Jeremy Tarr, *Editorial Director;* Rachael Levitt, *Managing Editor*

Technology: Jon Atkinson, *Director of Technology;* Rudresh Teotia, *Lead Developer*

Writers: Karen Anderson, Kristina Anderson, Powell Berger, Marla Cimini, Joan Conrow, Cheryl Crabtree, Tiffany Hill, Laurie Lyons-Makaimoko, Syndi Halualani Texeira, Anna Weaver, Mary F. Williamson

Editor: Amanda Sadlowski

Production Editor: Monica White

4th Edition

ISBN 978-1-64097-547-7

ISSN 2471-9048

PRINTED IN THE UNITED STATES OF AMERICA

10 9 8 7 6 5 4 3 2

About Our Writers

Karen Anderson resides in Kona, Hawaii, and works as a freelance journalist, managing editor, and professional photographer. For 13 consecutive years, she has been the managing editor of *At Home, Living with Style in West Hawaii*. She also writes for a variety of publications including *West Hawaii Today; Hawaii Island Midweek; Hawaii Luxury Magazine; Ke Ola Magazine; Hawaii Drive Magazine; Edible Hawaiian Islands Magazine;* and *USA Today Travel Tips*. Karen is the author of *The Hawaii Home Book: Practical Tips for Tropical Living,* which reached #1 on the *Honolulu Advertiser*'s nonfiction bestseller list and received the Award of Excellence from the Hawaii Book Publishers Association. Her monthly humor column is known throughout the Big Island. She also writes the weekly "Onolicious Dining Guide" for *West Hawaii Today,* as well as feature articles for local real estate publications. She is the longtime advertising/marketing chairperson for the annual King Kamehameha Day Celebration Parade in Kailua-Kona. Karen contributed to the Travel Smart chapter and updated the Hilo, Hawaii Volcanoes National Park, Puna, and Kau sections on Big Island.

Kristina Anderson has been writing professionally for more than 30 years. After working as an advertising copywriter and creative director in Southern California for more than a decade, she moved to Hawaii in 1992 and began working as a senior copywriter and broadcast producer for Hawaii agencies and client direct. Since 2006, she has also written for national and regional publications, most notably for *At Home in West Hawaii* magazine, which profiled a variety of homes—from coffee shacks to resort mansions—and for *Hawaii Island Midweek* magazine. When there's time, she runs, paddles outrigger canoes competitively, and plays tennis very noncompetitively. Her brightest accomplishment of all, however, is raising twin sons as a single mom. For this book, Kristina updated the Kailua-Kona and the Kona Coast, the Kohala Coast and Waimea, the Hamakua Coast with Maunakea, and Activities and Tours sections of Big Island.

Powell Berger lives in the heart of Honolulu's Kakaako neighborhood, where she's ever in search of the best poke bowl. Her wanderlust has taken her to more than 50 countries around the world, and her writing appears in numerous state and regional publications, AAA magazines, *The Atlantic,* and various websites, in addition to Fodor's. Powell updated the Activities and Tours section of Oahu for this edition.

Marla Cimini (⊕ *www. marlacimini.com*) is an award-winning writer with a passion for travel, beaches, music, and culinary adventures. As an avid globetrotter and frequent Oahu visitor, she has covered topics such as Hawaii's luxury hotels, fascinating and fun surf culture, and the innovative restaurant scene on the islands. She appreciates Oahu's unique dichotomy, and enjoys the bustling Waikiki neighborhood as much as exploring the island's quieter beaches. And she's always up for surfing or an outrigger canoe ride in Waikiki! Marla's articles have appeared in numerous publications worldwide, including *USA Today* and many others. Marla updated the Waikiki section of the Oahu chapter.

Joan Conrow is a longtime journalist and editor who has written extensively about Hawaii politics, culture, environment, travel, and lifestyles for many regional and national publications. Joan lived on Kauai for nearly 30 years before relocating to the high desert of New Mexico. She helped write the original Fodor's guide to Kauai and updated the East Side and Activities and Tours sections of Kauai for this edition.

 Cheryl Crabtree first visited Hawaii as a kindergartner, a trip that sparked a life-long passion for the islands and led to frequent visits. She spends months at a time in residence on Oahu's North Shore. Cheryl has also contributed to *Fodor's California* for nearly two decades and is a regular updater for *Fodor's National Parks of the West*. She also contributes to numerous regional and national publications. For this edition, Cheryl updated the North Shore and the West (Leeward) and Central Oahu sections of Oahu as well as the North Shore section of Kauai.

 Tiffany Hill, who contributed to the Travel Smart chapter, grew up on Oahu and has lived on both the Leeward and Windward sides, but today she calls Portland, Oregon, home. She specializes in travel, culture, and business. Her work is regularly published in regional and national publications, as well as online. When she's not on assignment, you can find her playing roller derby.

 Laurie Lyons-Makaimoku began travel writing in 2014, soon after receiving her master's degree in New Media Journalism. She started by sharing the secrets of some of Austin's best food, festivals, celebrities, entertainment, events, and locales, eventually as the editor of Austin.com. Eventually, after moving to Hawaii Island in 2016, she had the opportunity to start writing about the special place that she now called home in publications like Fodor's, The Matador Network, and Local Getaways. After marrying into a Hawaiian family Laurie developed a deep passion for ethical, sustainable travel, especially how it affects the quality of life and land in the Islands. Family travel, as well as food and beverage, are also some of her favorite things to write about. When she's not island-hopping to take in all she can throughout Hawaii's diverse landscapes, Laurie spends most of her weekends exploring tidepools and the dynamic shoreline of East Hawaii, chasing sunshine on the west side of the Island, and constantly growing her knowledge of and palate for the eclectic cuisines that make up Hawaii's ever-evolving food scene. She shares her home with her husband, two children, and a menagerie of rescue animals. She updated the West Maui, South Shore, North Shore, Road to Hana, and East Maui sections of Maui along with the Molokoi and Lanai chapters.

About Our Writers

 Syndi Halualani Texeira is a native Hawaiian, small-town girl who was born and raised on Hawaii Island. Though she has traveled the world, including living in California, Washington, D.C., New York, Paris, and Monaco, her heart always belongs to Hawaii. After working with two of the most prominent media firms in the nation, Syndi has made her way back home to Hawaii, focusing her professional efforts on helping visitors embrace culturally sensitive and regenerative travel to Hawaii. Syndi enjoys time with her ohana, and her pets, traveling, reading, and advocating for indigenous rights. She also serves as Executive Director of a Hawaii Island nonprofit animal rescue organization. She contributed to the Travel Smart chapter and updated the Central Maui, Upcountry, and Activities and Tours sections of Maui.

 Writer and multimedia journalist **Anna Weaver** is a sixth-generation *kamaaina*, born and raised in Kailua, Oahu. She can never get enough of Spam *musubi, malasadas*, or the gorgeous Koolau mountains in her home state. Anna has written for *Slate, Simplemost,* and such Hawaii publications as the *Honolulu Advertiser* (now the *Star-Advertiser*), *Honolulu Magazine,* and *Pacific Business News.* In this guide, she updated all but Waikiki in the Honolulu and Pearl Harbor section, the East (Leeward) Oahu section, and the feature on Hawaiian cultural traditions.

 Mary F. Williamson grew up in Honolulu and lives on Kauai, where her husband's family moved in the late 1800s. A former nonprofit director, she now organizes bicycle races and helps small businesses and organizations with public communication and events. She contributed to the Travel Smart chapter and updated the South Shore and West Side sections of the Kauai chapter.